Symbol	Definition
$i_{foreign}$	The foreign short-term nominal rate of interest
$i(1)$, $i(2)$, $i(3)$	The one-year, two-year, and three-year nominal rates of interest
i (long term)	The long-term nominal rate of interest
$i_{foreign}$ (long term)	The foreign long-term nominal rate of interest
I	Investment purchases by businesses (gross private domestic investment)
I_0	The autonomous part of investment demand
I_1	The marginal propensity to invest (MPI) from an investment function
I^D	Purchases of domestically produced investment goods
I^F	Purchases of investment goods produced overseas
I_p	Planned investment
I_R	Replacement investment
I_u	Unplanned investment
IM	Imports of goods and services
IM_0	The autonomous part of import demand
IM_1	The marginal propensity to import (MPM)
IS	The schedule giving combinations of income and the cost of funds where the goods market is in equilibrium
K	The capital input to production
K^d	Desired capital stock
k	The coefficient of income in the money demand equation
$L(.)$	The demand for money function
LM	Schedule giving combinations of income and the short-term nominal rate of interest where the money market is in equilibrium
M	The nominal stock of money
M1	The narrowest definition of money; currency held by the public and demand deposits
M2	A broader definition of money than M1. It includes time deposits.
M3	A broader definition of money than M2. It includes many liquid assets.
M^d/P	The real demand for money
M^s/P	The real supply of money
MB	Monetary base
MM	Money multiplier
M/P	The real stock of money
MPC	The marginal propensity to consume
MPI	The marginal propensity to invest
MPT	The marginal propensity to tax
N	The labor input to production (employment or hours worked)
$N*$	The augmented labor input to production
N^d	The demand for labor
N^s	The supply of labor

(continued inside back cover)

Thank you for your interest in **Macroeconomics, Financial Markets, and the International Sector**, Second Edition, by Martin Neil Baily and Philip Friedman.

Input from instructors like you has been the key to the successful revision of this text. Our goal was to take the solid foundation of the first edition and make it even more accessible for you. So we put the question out there: how could we revise the text so it would work best in today's macro classrooms? The specific results of our research appears in the chapters of the text. In brief, however, the second edition reflects some deletion, some clarification, some streamlining, and an overall reorganization of material.

This new organization allows the second edition to maintain the popular applications-oriented approach while making better use of three major themes which run through it

- Long-Term Growth and Productivity
- The Financial Sector in the Macro-Economy
- The Importance of the International Sector

John Knudsen (of the University of Idaho) certainly concurs: ''The tone of the text on competitiveness and industrial dynamism in a growing economy is excellent. I like the extensive coverage of the financial aspects of fluctuations and policy. The increased emphasis on the long term and on inflation problems certainly is welcome.'' These three themes are more vital than ever before, given today's typical intermediate macro classroom, which is filled with business majors and future entrepreneurs. A detailed discussion of each of these themes appears on the pages that follow. You'll also find a visual discussion of key pedagogical tools employed in *Macroeconomics, Financial Markets, and the International Sector*, Second Edition.

Please be sure to note the reviewer feedback which we have included in this walkthrough. Publishers are always prepared (and thrilled) to tell their potential adopters all about the wonderful features of their books, but we at Irwin recognize that you may place a higher value on what your colleagues have to say. That's why when Barry Bosworth applauds Baily and Friedman's discussion of aggregate supply and demand, or when Alan Blinder says this text breaks new pedagogical ground, we think you should know about it. Comments like these have been used throughout this frontpiece to point to topics, ideas, and/or tools which the reviewers themselves told us may affect *their* choice of a text, and which Baily and Friedman handle particularly well. Use them as you see fit.

We encourage you to contact your Irwin sales representative or the editors directly if you have any questions or comments about this **Macroeconomics, Financial Markets, and the International Sector**. Irwin's toll-free number is 1-800/634-3963.

Thank you again for your interest in this text.

Martin Neil Baily was educated at Cambridge University, England, and at the Massachusetts Institute of Technology, where he completed a Ph.D. in economics in 1972. After teaching at MIT and Yale he became a Senior Fellow at the Brookings Institution in 1979 and Professor of Economics at the University of Maryland in 1989. He is currently a Fellow of the McKinsey Global Institute. His fields of interest are productivity and technology, the relation between productivity growth and employment, macroeconomic policy, and applied microeconomics. He has served as academic adviser to the Congressional Budget Office and the Federal Reserve Board, and is a research associate of the National Bureau of Economic Research.

During his stay at the McKinsey Global Institute, Martin Baily helped direct the Institute's project of manufacturing productivity in the United States, Germany, and Japan that was released in October 1993. He is now working on a project examining determinants of employment, with special emphasis on the slow growth of employment in Europe.

In 1987 Martin Baily co-founded the Microeconomics issue of the Brookings Papers on Economic Activity, and is now its co-editor. He is the author of many professional articles and the editor or co-author of four books.

Philip Friedman is the Vice President for Academic Affairs and Provost and Professor of Economics at Bentley College in Waltham, Massachusetts. He has published books on macroeconometrics, economic theory, and joint corporate ventures, and has written numerous articles on economic issues and corporate policy. Prior to joining Bentley, he was the Dean of the Joseph M. Bryan School of Business and Economics at the University of North Carolina/Greensboro. He has also formerly directed the MBA program and headed the department of Finance and Economics at Boston University. He received his Ph.D. in economics from Massachusetts Institute of Technology and earned his B.B.A. from the City College of New York Baruch School of Business and Public Administration.

LONG-TERM GROWTH AND PRODUCTIVITY

Macroeconomics used to be only about income determination and the business cycle. Now, concerns about productivity and growth appropriately deserve more course time. Recently, there has been heightened attention paid to growth issues by both academics and policymakers. In response, Baily and Friedman have shifted much of their discussion of these growth topics prominently to the very beginning of the text. Long-term considerations are, of course, evaluated whenever appropriate throughout the text, but you'll find the most detailed discussions as follows:

"It's a good idea to get the long-run concerns into the heads of the students early in the course."
Robert B. Archibald
College of William and Mary

Chapter 1 Introduction of Long-Term Growth, Productivity and Competitiveness
Slowdown in Productivity Growth

Chapter 2 Short-Term Variations in Output
Long-Term Trends in Output
Introduction of Key Concepts like *Technology, New Growth Theories, and Human Capital*
Policy Implications

Chapter 15 Importance of Technology and Growth

Chapter 16 Labor Market and Growth

Chapter 17 Role of Aggregate Supply in Growth
Impact of New Growth Theory
Technology and Growth

THE FINANCIAL SECTOR IN THE MACRO-ECONOMY

"Baily & Friedman have incorporated various issues relating to the financial market throughout their book. That's commendable. Most of my students have a business background, so they understand and appreciate the intricate working of the financial market and its impact on the macroeconomy."
Abdur Chowdhury
Marquette University

In the actual economy, the financial sector is a critical element. This text describes how the financial sector provides the link that explicitly connects shifts in monetary conditions to changes in real investment demand. It discusses the term structure of interest rates and the importance of real rates of interest, and shows how business investment decisions are influenced by the real costs of funds.

The text also defines the interest-rate gap as the difference between the cost of funds that affects investment and the short-term nominal rate of interest determined in the money market and shows how expectations about inflation and future Federal Reserve policy can alter this gap. The interest-rate gap then allows them to analyze several current policy issues, including the problems with nominal interest rate targeting in an inflationary environment and the need for policy credibility.

It's not surprising that first-edition users grabbed hold of this theme as one of the most important innovations of the text. Students find it interesting as well as motivational.

"Financial markets and the role of expectations are emphasized as in no other text."
Cihan Bilingsoy
University of Utah

THE INTERNATIONAL SECTOR

Baily and Friedman have completely incorporated the international sector into the second edition. The importance of this facet of the economy is emphasized throughout the text. While students will find the international sector in the form of examples throughout the text, the most in-depth treatment can be found in the following chapters as indicated:

Chapter 1   Global Economy
Chapter 2   International Competitiveness
Chapter 5   The Budget Deficit and the Trade Deficit
Chapter 7   Exchange Rate, Trade Deficit, and the Role of Monetary and Fiscal Policy
Chapter 11 New Policies (Managed Trade) and Older Issues (Protectionism & Intervention)

The pedagogical framework of the book also serves to highlight this international theme. One example—boxes which offer business, policy, or heuristic explanations are an important text feature. A logo has been developed to call out the international boxes from the more applications-oriented boxes.

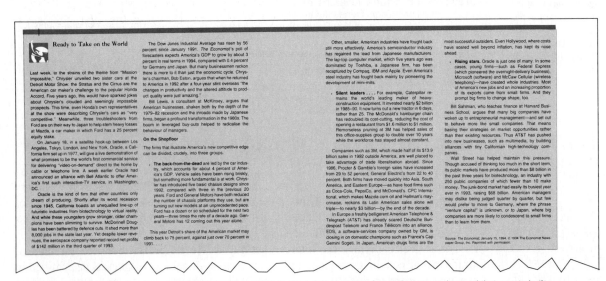

"The international sector has been incorporated quite well into the text. It is important for students to understand that events in the global economy do affect the US. That is done very well in this text."
John Mukum Mbaku
Weber State University

WORKED EXAMPLES

Baily and Friedman use Worked Examples throughout their text, particularly in the more mathematical chapters. In fact, all the math-oriented chapters contain at least two of them. In these Worked Examples, the authors lead students and instructors alike through a ''word problem'' that describes not only the situation at hand, but also takes them step-by-step to the solution. It's a great way for students to check their understanding as they read, and many instructors build their lesson plans around them. Additionally, much of the problem material in Baily and Friedman calls on students to pull from the logic and skills they've obtained in the Worked Examples.

Our current adopters agree: Worked Examples are excellent teaching and learning tools. Still, we realize that an instructor may not have enough time to teach each and every one of them. So, to make the text more adaptable to your teaching needs, the authors have moved all Worked Examples to immediately before the end-of-the-chapter summary in this second edition. In each case, a detailed reference, which is called out in the second color, directs students and instructors to the end of the chapter to find the Worked Example:

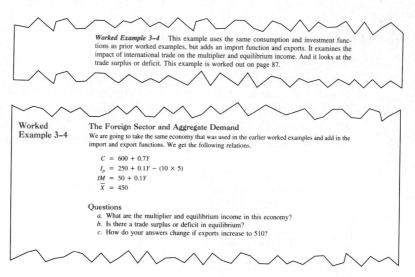

Worked Example 3–4 This example uses the same consumption and investment functions as prior worked examples, but adds an import function and exports. It examines the impact of international trade on the multiplier and equilibrium income. And it looks at the trade surplus or deficit. This example is worked out on page 87.

Worked Example 3–4

The Foreign Sector and Aggregate Demand
We are going to take the same economy that was used in the earlier worked examples and add in the import and export functions. We get the following relations.

$$C = 600 + 0.7Y$$
$$I_p = 250 + 0.1Y - (10 \times 5)$$
$$IM = 50 + 0.1Y$$
$$\overline{X} = 450$$

Questions
a. What are the multiplier and equilibrium income in this economy?
b. Is there a trade surplus or deficit in equilibrium?
c. How do your answers change if exports increase to 510?

KEY TERMS

Key terms are introduced in boldfaced type, defined in a Marginal Glossary, and collected in a list at the end of each chapter. Many books fail to recognize this important learning and review tool.

BOXED MATERIAL

Boxed Material appears in every chapter. These boxes serve two key purposes: to provide the student with additional background or explanations on various economic issues and to spotlight current events and thought. Articles from *The Wall Street Journal* and other periodical sources are commonplace and underscore the real-world focus of the text. We showed you an international box earlier in this Note from the Publisher. The application boxes are also marked with a distinctive logo, and demonstrate alternate viewpoints or help students to apply skills revealed within the chapter text:

DISCUSSION QUESTIONS AND PROBLEMS

Each chapter also contains Discussion Questions and Problems which reinforce the concepts learned and give students the opportunity to test themselves so they can be sure they are able to *apply* these concepts to the world around them. In many cases the problem material mimics the Worked Examples in the chapter. Reviewers characterize the end-of-chapter problems as "excellent," "challenging," "well-balanced," and "varying in degree of difficulty." A few sample questions follow:

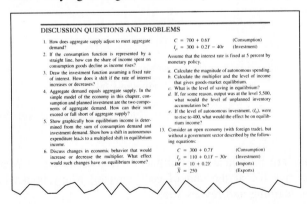

WHAT PEOPLE ARE SAYING ABOUT THE NEW CHAPTERS

"Chapters 1 and 2 give a thorough understanding of the present and past macroeconomics of the U.S. economy. It is an innovative approach to introducing macroeconomics to undergraduate students."
G. S. Laumas
Southern Illinois University

"The discussion of expectations in Chapter 6 is excellent, perhaps the best I've ever seen on this level."
Herbert M. Bernstein
Drexel University

"This text provides a detailed discussion of the various schools of thought in economics, and goes beyond the usual Classical background and Keynesian-Monetarist debate."
Margaret Landman
Bridgewater State

PART 1
CORE MACROECONOMICS   1

CHAPTER 1
The Issues of Macroeconomics   2

CHAPTER 2
Long-Term Growth and Competitiveness   32

CHAPTER 3
Aggregate Supply and Demand and Income Determination   60

CHAPTER 4
Interest Rates, Goods, and Money-Market Equilibrium   91

CHAPTER 5
Fiscal Policy, Budgets, and Equilibrium Income   114

CHAPTER 6
Monetary Policy and Inflation   141

CHAPTER 7
The Exchange Rate, Macroeconomic Policy in an Open Economy and the Trade Deficit   178

CHAPTER 8
Aggregate Demand, Inflation, Financial Risks, and Policymaking   220

PART 2
ADVANCED TOPICS   261

CHAPTER 9
Consumption, Capital Investment, and Economic Fluctuations   263

CHAPTER 10
The Federal Reserve Banking System and Financial Crunches   298

CHAPTER 11
External Balances and International Economic Policy   332

CHAPTER 12
Supply-Shock Inflation and Economic Policy   373

CHAPTER 13
Forecasting, Stabilization Policy, and the Variability of the Economy   402

CHAPTER 14
Monetarism: Classical Roots and Contemporary Implications   433

CHAPTER 15
Controversy in Macroeconomics: Equilibrium Models and the Neo-Keynesian Response   462

CHAPTER 16
Employment Creation, Unemployment, and Earnings Distribution   502

CHAPTER 17
Aggregate Supply, Long-Term Growth, and Productivity   532

"The current structure of the . . . text lends itself well to multiple class structures. The non-core chapters (and a few of the core chapters) can stand alone allowing for nonsequential study of those chapters."
Terry Truitt
Mississippi State University

FOR THE INSTRUCTOR

Instructor's Manual to accompany Macroeconomics, Financial Markets, and the International Sector, Second Edition, Book Number 94747100.
The authors have prepared a traditional Instructor's Manual to accompany their text. In addition to teaching tips and solutions to end-of-chapter problems, the authors have developed a system that will enable instructors to support a variety of syllabi—syllabi that depend in large part on student preparation and the instructor's areas of interests.

Test Bank to accompany Macroeconomics, Financial Markets, and the International Sector, Second Edition, Book Number 96006600.
Terry Truitt of Mississippi State University has prepared a test bank which includes multiple-choice questions, analytical problems, and essays. The questions are graded by level of difficulty and employ graphs and data when appropriate. A computerized version test generator (which allows instructors to add and edit questions as well as save tests) is also available to adopters. (Refer to book number 93748100.)

FOR THE STUDENT

Readings, Cases, and Problems for use with Macroeconomics, Financial Markets, and the International Sector, Second Edition, Book Number 93746300.
This "study guide" has been prepared by David Ring of SUNY Oneonta. The Ring Workbook follows a philosophy that students gain a much better understanding of a model when they either have practice working with numerical examples of the model or use the model to analyze macroeconomic data. To that end, Ring takes traditional study guide self-test tools and then takes it several steps beyond. He uses features like analytical essay questions and worked problems similar to the Worked Examples in the main text. Also, each chapter contains a case or reading that either applies the material presented in the corresponding chapter in the Baily and Friedman text to a particular historical event in the U.S. economy or further discusses the economics of the text chapter. It's truly a hands-on student workbook that reinforces key concepts and adds to the overall learning process.

Macroeconomics,
Financial Markets, *and the*
International Sector

THE IRWIN SERIES IN ECONOMICS

Appleyard and Field
International Economics
second edition

Appleyard and Field
International Trade
second edition

Appleyard and Field
International Monetary Theory
second edition

Baily and Friedman
Macroeconomics, Financial Markets, and the International Sector
second edition

Barron and Lynch
Economics
third edition

Baye and Beil
Managerial Economics and Business Strategy

Blair
Urban and Regional Economics

Bornstein
Comparative Economic Systems: Models and Cases
sixth edition

Brown and Moore
Readings, Issues, and Problems in Public Finance
fourth edition

Colander
Economics
second edition

Colander
Microeconomics
second edition

Colander
Macroeconomics
second edition

Denzau
Microeconomic Analysis: Markets & Dynamics

Fisher
State and Local Public Finance

Hadjimichalakis and Hadjimichalak
Contemporary Money, Banking, and Financial Markets

Hyman
Economics
third edition

Hyman
Microeconomics
third edition

Hyman
Macroeconomics
third edition

Hyman
Modern Microeconomics: Analysis and Applications
third edition

Katz and Rosen
Microeconomics
second edition

Lehmann
Real World Economic Applications: The Wall Street Journal Workbook
fourth edition

Lindert
International Economics
ninth edition

Maurice and Phillips
Economic Analysis: Theory and Application
sixth edition

Maurice and Thomas
Managerial Economics: Applied Microeconomics for Decision Making
fifth edition

Nadler and Hansen
Microcomputer Macroeconomics with IBM Disk

O'Sullivan
Urban Economics
second edition

O'Sullivan
Essentials of Urban Economics

Peterson
Principles of Economics: Micro
eighth edition

Peterson
Principles of Economics: Macro
eighth edition

Prager
Applied Microeconomics: An Intermediate Approach

Rima
Development of Economic Analysis
fifth edition

Roger and Daniel
Principles of Economics Software Simulation

Rosen
Public Finance
fourth edition

Schwarz and Van Dyken
Manager: Managerial Economics Software

Seo
Managerial Economics: Text, Short Cases
seventh edition

Sharp, Register, and Leftwich
Economics of Social Issues
eleventh edition

Shepherd
Public Policies Toward Business
eighth edition

Shugart
The Organization of Industry

Slavin
Introduction to Economics
fourth edition

Streifford
Economic Perspective

Walton and Wykoff
Understanding Economics Today
fourth edition

Macroeconomics,
Financial Markets, and the
International Sector
Second Edition

Martin Neil Baily
Professor of Economics and Public Policy
University of Maryland and the McKinsey Global Institute

Philip Friedman
Provost, Vice President for Academic Affairs and Professor of Economics
Bentley College

IRWIN

Chicago • Bogotá • Boston • Buenos Aires • Caracas
London • Madrid • Mexico City   Sydney • Toronto

IRWIN
Concerned About Our Environment

In recognition of the fact that our company is a large end-user of fragile yet replenishable resources, we at IRWIN can assure you that every effort is made to meet or exceed Environmental Protection Agency (EPA) recommendations and requirements for a "greener" workplace.

To preserve these natural assets, a number of environmental policies, both companywide and department-specific, have been implemented. From the use of 50% recycled paper in our textbooks to the printing of promotional materials with recycled stock and soy inks to our office paper recycling program, we are committed to reducing waste and replacing environmentally unsafe products with safer alternatives.

Senior sponsoring editor: *Gary Nelson*
Developmental editor: *Ellen Cleary*
Senior marketing manager: *Ron Bloecher*
Project editor: *Jean Lou Hess*
Production manager: *Ann Cassady*
Cover designer: *Josh Carr*
Cover illustrator: *David Shannon*
Art coordinator: *Heather Burbridge*
Compositor: *Better Graphics*
Typeface: *10/12 Times Roman*
Printer: *R. R. Donnelley & Sons Company*

Library of Congress Cataloging-in-Publication Data

Baily, Martin Neil.
   Macroeconomics, financial markets, and the international sector / Martin Neil Baily, Philip Friedman. — 2nd ed.
     p. cm. — (The Irwin series in economics)
   Includes bibliographical references and index.
   ISBN 0-256-12552-X
   1. Macroeconomics.   2. International finance.   3. International trade.   I. Friedman, Philip.   II. Title.   III. Series.
HB172.5.B339 1995
339—dc20   94–27884

Printed in the United States of America
1 2 3 4 5 6 7 8 9 0 DO 1 0 9 8 7 6 5 4

To Vickie Baily and Sue Friedman with love for the partnership we have with them; and to the friendship we have together.

"This is an exciting but challenging time to teach macroeconomics. Macroeconomics issues are being debated widely and the newspapers are full of stories about the exchange rate, recession fears, concerns about rising inflation, and interest rates."

That was our introduction to the first edition and the last few years since then have proved to be even more challenging. Although the fear of recession is absent from the current concerns in the United States, the economy continues to dominate the national and world scene. This has been especially true in the relationship between the global economy and financial markets—a centerpiece of this text. President Clinton talks publicly about the difference between short-term and long-term interest rates. The Federal Reserve Board is under fire for raising interest rates. Trade relations between the United States and Japan are under strain. G-7 finance ministers work to stabilize world markets. A strange economic recovery is in place—one that was very sluggish to begin with, but that has suddenly built up steam. Debates about economic policy have turned more pointedly toward issues of long-term growth and productivity, and inflationary expectations are driving markets even as current inflation rates hit all time lows.

We have worked to recast this text in the light of recent events and new insights into the workings of the economy.

TEACHING MACROECONOMICS

Given our experience in teaching macroeconomics (to economics majors, MBA students, undergraduate business majors, master's students in public policy, and liberal arts and science majors with a general interest in economic policy), we have found that they *all* want nearly the same thing—a course that will help them understand what is going on in the economic world around them, as well as prepare them for later courses.

Part of the difficulty that faculty face in macro courses is that within the economics profession there is disagreement about the basic approach to the subject, making it hard to give a coherent perspective to students. It is important to provide a fair and rigorous discussion of macroeconomic controversy so that economics majors or graduate students are prepared for advanced courses. At the same time, it is perhaps more important to satisfy the need of all students for a course that is relevant and interesting and that fits with what they observe about ongoing economic events as well as actual business and household behavior.

The standard *IS-LM* model is clearly unrealistic in several respects, notably its depiction of a single rate of interest linking the real and monetary, the domestic and global sectors of the economy, and short-run aggregate demand with long-run aggregate supply. Though we recognize the many limitations of the standard *IS-LM* model, we are convinced that it remains the best framework for laying out the core of a course on macroeconomics. Even within the core section, we extend this framework by introducing growth, financial markets, and the international sector. We also stress the importance of expectations. Once we move beyond the core material, we also look at alternatives to the *IS-LM* framework.

This text develops its ideas using only simple algebra (and not much of that), plus figures, and a series of numerical Worked Examples that we urge you to go over in class. They are designed to present new material in a way that makes it accessible to as many students as possible.

WHY WE WROTE THE SECOND EDITION IN THE WAY WE DID

In the first edition of this text, we attempted a grand synthesis of money, financial, and real markets using the term structure of interest rates to couple the money market [*LM*] with real aggregate goods markets. To that end, we invoked an alternative to the standard *IS-LM* model. The feedback we received from users to this was very positive, with many telling us that ours was the first text to provide a model for students that matched with what they read about the economy.

Unfortunately, many prospective users of the text judged that the extended three chapter development of financial markets was too long and complex for their students. In response, we have tried to preserve the realism and originality of the first edition, but in a shorter and simpler form. The benefits we derived from extending the old model were significant in terms of relevance to current economic issues; these benefits remain. Students are given a richer description of the economy than that which is found in competing texts. This description is just as accessible, if not more so.

As in the first edition, we have tried to bring the best aspects of the new economics to bear on a standard framework in order to give a workable and exciting presentation of the complexity of modern macroeconomics.

Thanks to the input from first-edition adopters, reviewers, and other intermediate macro instructors, a major change can be seen in the splitting of the text into two parts: Part 1, "Core Macroeconomics," covers the essential material of the subject, including one chapter on long-term growth and competitiveness; and Part 2, "Advanced Topics," introduces new issues and deals with others in greater depth. The core analysis of the book is presented in the first eight chapters and then a series of individual chapters on, what we term, advanced topics gives the instructor considerable flexibility in designing a course to meet differing needs and interests of his or her students. The overall structure of the book is as follows:

Part 1: Core Macroeconomics
Chapter 1: The Issues of Macroeconomics
Chapter 2: Long-Term Growth and Competitiveness
Chapter 3: Aggregate Supply and Demand and Income Determination
Chapter 4: Interest Rates, Goods, and Money-Market Equilibrium
Chapter 5: Fiscal Policy, Budgets and Equilibrium Income
Chapter 6: Monetary Policy and Inflation

Chapter 7:   The Exchange Rate, Macroeconomic Policy in an Open Economy and the Trade Deficit

Chapter 8:   Aggregate Demand, Inflation, Financial Risks, and Policymaking

Part 2: Advanced Topics

Chapter 9:   Consumption, Capital Investment, and Economic Fluctuations

Chapter 10: The Federal Reserve Banking System and Financial Crunches

Chapter 11: External Balances and International Economic Policy

Chapter 12: Supply-Shock Inflation and Economic Policy

Chapter 13: Forecasting, Stabilization Policy and the Variability of the Economy

Chapter 14: Monetarism: Classical Roots and Contemporary Implications

Chapter 15: Controversy in Macroeconomics: Equilibrium Models and the Neo-Keynesian Response

Chapter 16: Employment Creation, Unemployment, and Earnings Distribution

Chapter 17: Aggregate Supply, Long-Term Growth, and Productivity

Several central themes emerged clearly from this new organization.

Long-Term Growth and Productivity

In this edition, we decided to introduce long-term growth in Chapter 2. This change reflects the heightened attention being paid to growth issues by both academics and policymakers. The early section focuses on the contrast between short-term variations in output, driven by fluctuations in aggregate demand, and long-term trends in output, driven by outward shifts in aggregate supply. Macroeconomics used to be only about income determination and the business cycle. Now, concerns about productivity growth appropriately deserve more course time. We describe the role of aggregate supply in growth, the importance of technology, and human capital investment, and the impact of the new growth theory. We also discuss the slowdown in productivity growth over the past twenty years.

The Financial Sector in the Macro Economy

In the actual economy, the financial sector is a critical element. We describe how the financial sector provides the link that explicitly connects shifts in monetary conditions to changes in real investment demand. We discuss the term structure of interest rates and the importance of real rates of interest, and we show how business investment decisions are influenced by the real cost of funds. We define the interest-rate gap as the difference between the cost of funds that affects investment and the short-term nominal rate of interest determined in the money market. We show how expectations about inflation and future Federal Reserve policy can alter this gap. The interest-rate gap then allows us to analyze several current policy issues, including the problems with nominal interest-rate targeting in an inflationary environment and the need for policy credibility.

The Importance of the International Sector

Extensive coverage of the international sector is absolutely essential in a modern macro course. To that end, the global economy is introduced in the very first chapter of our text. International competitiveness is introduced in the second chapter along with long-term growth. And the relationship between the budget deficit and the trade deficit (the new crowding out) is covered in Chapter 5.

There are also two extensive separate chapters dealing with the international sector. Chapter 7 covers the exchange rate and the trade deficit and the role played by monetary and fiscal policy in an open economy. This chapter also covers interest-rate differentials and expected exchange rate changes. Chapter 11 looks at the new policies of managed trade and the older issues of protectionism and intervention.

Alternative Approaches to Macro-economics

In the core section of the text, we do not include any extended discussion of the alternative approaches to macroeconomics. But instructors who judge that this material is essential to a solid introduction to the subject can have students read ahead to the chapters that cover this material. The Monetarist model and the more recent developments of classical thinking including the equilibrium business-cycle models are presented in the advanced topics portion of the text. We also discuss the issue of price flexibility and stickiness and contributions of the neo-Keynesian analyses in this section.

ALTERNATIVE WAYS TO USE THE TEXT

This text has been designed for students who have had at least one previous course in macroeconomics at the introductory level. The entire book can be presented easily in a two-course sequence. Or, by moving rapidly, the entire text can also be covered in a one-semester course if the students have had more exposure to economics than the typical introductory sequence of micro and macroeconomics. For well-prepared students, much of Chapters 1–6 can be covered quickly. Even so, for most curricula there is more material in the text than can be effectively covered in one semester or quarter.

In many departments, a one-semester course will cover only the core material. The advanced topics will then serve as the reading for a more advanced macro course for majors or other students who wish to go further. In other departments, the instructor will move more rapidly through the core material, and include a selection of advanced topics depending on individual choices. Now, a one-semester course using this book can be taught in several different ways by combining and/or omitting various chapters, and we expect that this is typically the way the book will be used. The particular combinations of chapters covered will depend upon the interests and preparation of students, the program of study in which the course is being offered, and the preferences of the instructor.

By selecting certain chapters, the text can support a variety of syllabi. Following are examples of different approaches to a one-semester course. In each, the amount of time you'll want to spend on the early chapters will depend largely upon the preparation of your students.

If you want to concentrate on:	**We suggest you teach these chapters:**
Basic Macroeconomics and Policy	Chapters 1–8, 9*, 10, 12, 13 and 16*
International Macroeconomics	Chapters 1–7 and 11
Macroeconomics and the Financial Sector	Chapters 1–8, 10, and 14
Long-Term Growth and the Macroeconomy	Chapters 1–7, 9, 14, and 17
Macroeconomic Fluctuations	Chapters 1–8, 9, 10, 12, 13–16
	* optional

THE APPROACH TO PEDAGOGY

Explanations in the text rely heavily on descriptions of simple, but relevant, economic scenarios. The microeconomic basis of macroeconomics is imbedded in these descriptions. We've worked hard to keep the writing accessible and direct, and to make sure that references to the behavior of individuals in the economy are not confused with references to economic models. For example, we might say that a change in the behavior of consumers can be represented by a shift in the consumption function, rather than saying that consumers shifted up the consumption function. As before, this text develops its ideas using only simple algebra. Students will not require a knowledge of calculus, although some material will allow students who do have previous exposure to it to use that knowledge.

There are several specific learning features:

Key statements are highlighted to aid understanding. *Boxes* that offer business, policy, or heuristic explanations are an important text feature. Logos have been developed to differentiate ''international'' boxes from the more ''applications''-oriented boxes. Additionally, most chapters have numerical *Worked Examples*. In the first edition, these Worked Examples appeared within the main text of each chapter; this time, however, we moved them to the end of each chapter in order to improve flow and readability. Notations (called out in the second color) direct students and instructors alike to the appropriate Worked Example for the concept(s) just encountered. *Key terms* are defined in a *Marginal Glossary* where they first occur and are then collected in a list at the end of each chapter. Of course, bulleted-list *Summaries* appear at the end of every chapter. Each chapter also contains *Discussion Questions and Problems* which reinforce the concepts learned and give students the opportunity to test themselves.

ACKNOWLEDGMENTS

We have many debts to those who have helped us in the task of writing this book. We both learned macro as fellow graduate students at MIT and have been learning since then from many students and colleagues, especially those at The Brookings Institution, the University of Maryland, McKinsey and Company, Boston University, the University of North Carolina at Greensboro, and at Bentley College who have provided help and support.

Many of our colleagues have given us invaluable advice and criticism at each stage of development and revision. We extend to each of them our sincere thanks for their hard work.

Robert Archibald	College of William and Mary
Francis W. Ahking	University of Connecticut
Shaghil Ahmed	Pennsylvania State University
Christine Amsler	Michigan State University
Philip F. Bartholomew	University of Michigan/Dearborn
Harry Bernstein	Drexel University
Cihan Bilginsoy	University of Utah
Scott Bloom	North Dakota State University

Noel Brodsky	University of Eastern Illinois
James H. Breece	University of Maine
Margaret Chapman	Illinois Wesleyan
Abdur R. Chowdhury	Marquette University
Richard Clarida	Columbia University
Gary Dymski	University of Southern California
Charles Engel	University of Washington
Roger T. Kaufman	Smith College
Michael Klein	Tufts University
John Knudson	University of Idaho
Margaret Landman	Bridgewater State University
John Laitner	University of Michigan
Gurcharan Laumas	Southern Illinois University/Carbondale
William J. Leonard	St. Joseph's University
John Mukum Mbaku	Weber State University
Doug McMillin	Louisiana State University
Joe Peek	Boston College
David Ring	SUNY Oneonta
Richard Schiming	Mankato State University
William E. Spellman	Coe College
David E. Spencer	Brigham Young University
Scott Sumner	Bentley College
Terry Truitt	Mississippi State University

We repeat our sentiments from the first edition in giving special thanks to Alan Blinder and Barry Bosworth who read the whole manuscript of the first edition prior to the last round of revisions and made important suggestions for improvement. Thanks also to Martin Feldstein, who first asked us to tackle this book.

The second edition has extended our relationship with Richard D. Irwin, Inc. Thanks go to Gary Nelson, who has been with the project for over seven years and who has given much help and encouragement, and to Ellen Cleary who has brought fresh insights and energy to the difficult task of redesign and rewriting. Other people at Irwin deserve our recognition and thanks as well: Ron Bloecher, Ann Cassady, Jean Lou Hess, Elois Mason, and Branka Rnich.

For continuing to support our commitment to this multiyear project, we thank our strongest supporters: Vickie Baily and Sue Friedman. Our children, Ethan, Nick, Damon, Katie, Chris, Sharin, and Lizzie have encouraged and motivated us.

Martin Neil Baily
Philip Friedman

BRIEF CONTENTS

PART 1

CORE MACROECONOMICS   1

CHAPTER 1

The Issues of Macroeconomics   2

CHAPTER 2

Long-Term Growth and
Competitiveness   32

CHAPTER 3

Aggregate Supply and Demand and
Income Determination   60

CHAPTER 4

Interest Rates, Goods, and Money-
Market Equilibrium   91

CHAPTER 5

Fiscal Policy, Budgets, and
Equilibrium Income   114

CHAPTER 6

Monetary Policy and Inflation   141

CHAPTER 7

The Exchange Rate,
Macroeconomic Policy in an Open
Economy and the Trade Deficit   178

CHAPTER 8

Aggregate Demand, Inflation,
Financial Risks, and Policymaking   220

PART 2

ADVANCED TOPICS   261

CHAPTER 9

Consumption, Capital Investment,
and Economic Fluctuations   263

CHAPTER 10

The Federal Reserve Banking
System and Financial Crunches   298

CHAPTER 11

External Balances and
International Economic Policy   332

CHAPTER 12

Supply-Shock Inflation and
Economic Policy   373

CHAPTER 13

Forecasting, Stabilization Policy,
and the Variability of the Economy   402

CHAPTER 14

Monetarism: *Classical Roots and
Contemporary Implications*   433

CHAPTER 15

Controversy in Macroeconomics:
*Equilibrium Models and the Neo-
Keynesian Response*   462

CHAPTER 16

Employment Creation,
Unemployment, and Earnings
Distribution   502

CHAPTER 17

Aggregate Supply, Long-Term
Growth, and Productivity   532

CONTENTS

PART 1

CORE MACROECONOMICS 1

CHAPTER 1

The Issues of Macroeconomics 2

Introduction 2
Long-Term Growth, Productivity, and
Competitiveness 3
   GDP per Capita and Living Standards 4
   Productivity and the Growth Slowdown 6
   Competitiveness 6
Long-Run Trends and Short-Term Fluctuations 10
Recessions and the Business Cycle 11
   Business Cycles 12
   Potential Output: Benchmarking the Cycle 13
   The Output Ratio 13
Employment and Unemployment 15
   Total Employment 15
   Unemployment 15
   Full Employment 17
The Price Level, Inflation, and Interest Rates 17
   The Price Level 18
   The Rate of Inflation 18
   Interest Rates 20
The Budget Deficit 21
The Three Critical Issues of Macroeconomics 22
Summary 23
Key Terms and Concepts 24
Discussion Questions and Problems 24
Appendix 1A Measuring National Income
Accounting 25
   Gross Domestic Product 25
   Exclusions from Aggregate Measures of
Production 27
   National Income and Product Accounts 28

   Overview of Expenditure Categories 29
   GDP and National Income 30

CHAPTER 2

Long-Term Growth and Competitiveness 32

Introduction 32
The Aggregate Production Function 34
   Diminishing Returns to a Single Factor and Returns
to Scale 35
Capital Accumulation and Labor Force Growth 37
   Allocating Growth to Capital and Technology 38
   Economic Growth with Technological Change 38
Postwar Economic Growth in the U.S. Economy 42
The Slowdown in Productivity Growth 43
   Reasons for Slow Productivity Growth 43
   Conclusions on the Productivity Growth
Slowdown 46
The Competitiveness of U.S. Manufacturing 46
   Productivity in U.S. Manufacturing 47
   The Performance of Manufacturing in the
International Economy 48
   Why Does U.S. Manufacturing Have so Much
Trouble with Trade? 49
Policies for Long-Term Growth and
Competitiveness 51
   Increasing National Saving 52
   Increasing National Investment 53
   Maintaining Competitive Markets 54
   Training 55
   Technology Policy 55
   Conclusions 57
   From Long-Term Growth to the Business Cycle 57
Summary 58
Key Terms and Concepts 59
Discussion Questions and Problems 59

CHAPTER 3

Aggregate Supply and Demand and Income Determination   60

Introduction 60

Aggregate Supply and Demand and Price Stickiness 61

   The Aggregate-Supply Schedule 61

   Aggregate Demand and Output Changes in the Short Run 62

Aggregate Supply and Demand and Quantity Adjustment 64

   Planned and Unplanned Expenditures 65

   Consumption Demand and the Consumption Function 67

   The Average and Marginal Propensities to Consume 67

   Investment Demand and the Investment Function 68

Goods-Market Equilibrium 72

   Equilibrium with a Given Interest Rate 72

   Adjustment to Equilibrium 73

   Changes in Equilibrium Income and the Multiplier 74

   The Multiplier and a Change in Investment Demand 75

Goods-Market Equilibrium, Interest Rates, Investment, and Saving 76

   Interest Rates and Aggregate Demand 77

   Equilibrium Income and the Interest Rate: The *IS* Schedule 78

   Investment and Saving 79

   Saving—Investment Coordination 80

The Foreign Sector: A First Look 81

   Import Demand, Income, and the Trade Balance 81

   Goods—Market Equilibrium with Foreign Trade 82

   Changes in Equilibrium Income and the Trade Balance 84

Worked Examples 84

Summary 89

Key Terms and Concepts 89

Discussion Questions and Problems 90

CHAPTER 4

Interest Rates, Goods, and Money-Market Equilibrium   91

Introduction 91

The Nature of Money 92

Transactions and the Medium of Exchange 92

   Unit of Account 93

Financial Assets and Money 93

   The Messy Problem of Defining Money 94

The Market for Money 95

   The Demand for Money 95

   Transactions and the Demand for Money 95

   Financial-Asset Holding and the Demand for Money 96

   The Supply of Money 99

   Money-Market Equilibrium 100

   Income and Interest Rates in Money Markets: The *LM* Schedule 102

Goods Markets and Money Markets Together: The *IS-LM* Framework 105

   Equilibrium Income and the Interest Rate 105

   The Effect of a Change in Autonomous Expenditure 106

Worked Examples 108

Summary 111

Key Terms and Concepts 111

Discussion Questions and Problems 112

CHAPTER 5

Fiscal Policy, Budgets, and Equilibrium Income   114

Introduction 114

Government Purchases and Government Expenditures 115

What Is the Government Buying and Why? 116

   Public Goods, Income Distribution, and Merit Goods 116

Taxes, Transfers, and the Tax Function 118

   Gross and Net Tax Revenues 118

   Transfer Payments 119

   Taxes and Income 119

   The Tax Function 119

   Disposable Income 120

Goods-Market Equilibrium with Taxes and Government Spending 120

   Equilibrium with an Unchanged Interest Rate 121

   The Tax-Rate Multiplier 124

Fiscal Policy and Money-Market Conditions 125

   Fiscal Policy and Interest-Rate Effects 125

   Money Demand and Fiscal-Policy Effectiveness 127

   Crowding Out 128

Government Finance and the Budget Balance 129
    The Budget Deficit 130
    Government Borrowing 130
    The Effect of the Budget Balance on Saving 131
    Short-Term versus Chronic Deficits 132
    The Budget Deficit over the Business Cycle 132
    The Structural Deficit 133
    Cyclical Deficits and the Automatic Stabilizers 134
    Structural Deficits 135
    Conclusions about Fiscal Policy 135
Worked Examples 135
Summary 138
Key Terms and Concepts 138
Discussion Questions and Problems 139

CHAPTER 6

Monetary Policy and Inflation   141

Introduction 141
Changing the Money Supply: Monetary Policy 142
    Coordinated Monetary and Fiscal Policies 142
    Independent Monetary Policy 143
    The Responsiveness of Investment to the Interest Rate and Credit Conditions 144
    The Interest-Rate Responsiveness of Money Demand 146
The Trade-Off between Output and Inflation 147
    Shifts in Aggregate Supply and Demand and the Price Level 148
The Output–Inflation Trade-Off 150
    The Trade-Off with Competitive Markets 150
    The Trade-Off with Sticky Prices 153
    Potential Output and the NAIRU 154
    The Short-Run Output–Inflation Trade-Off 155
    Shifts of the Output–Inflation Trade-Off 156
Inflation, Output, and Expectations 157
    Expectations Formed by the Past History of Inflation 158
    Past Inflation and Shifts in the Trade-Off 159
    The Vertical Long-Run Trade-Off 159
    Expectations Formed by Rational Forecasts of Inflation 162
Inflation, Monetary Policy, and Aggregate Equilibrium 162
    Inflation and the Real Supply of Money 163
    Current and Expected Rates of Inflation 163
    Benchmarking Monetary Policy in an Inflationary Economy 164
    The Trade-Off and the *IS-LM* Framework Combined 165
    The Trade-Off and Monetary Policy 167
    Fighting Inflation with Monetary Policy 167
    Conclusions on Monetary Policy and Inflation 171
Worked Examples 171
Summary 176
Key Terms and Concepts 177
Discussion Questions and Problems 177

CHAPTER 7

The Exchange Rate, Macroeconomic Policy in an Open Economy, and the Trade Deficit   178

Introduction 178
International Trade and Foreign Exchange 179
    The Exchange Rate 180
    Changes in the Exchange Rate and the Flow of Trade 180
    The Trade-Weighted Real Exchange Rate 181
    The Trade Balance and the Exchange Rate 183
The Balance of Payments on Current Account 185
    The Balance of Trade 185
    Trade in Services 187
    Income Earned on Foreign Assets and Transfers 187
    The Current-Account Deficit 187
International Financial Assets and the Exchange Rate 189
    International Interest Rates and Expectations 190
    The Interest Parity Condition and Capital Flows 190
Supply and Demand in the Foreign-Exchange Market 192
    Equilibrium in the Foreign-Exchange Market 192
    Changes in the Exchange Rate 194
    The Exchange Rate and Income 194
    The Exchange Rate and Capital Flows 195
Macroeconomic Policy in an Open Economy 198
    Aggregate Demand in an International Economy 198
    Increased Export Demand 202
    A Rise in Foreign Interest Rates 203
    Domestic Macroeconomic Policies in an Open Economy 205

Comparing Policy Tools in an International Environment 209

The Budget Deficit, Trade Deficit, and Crowding Out 209

Sustaining Income in the Deep Recession of the Early 1980s 210

The Twin Deficits in the 1980s Recovery 211

The Recession of 1990–91 213

Conclusions and Prognosis for the Future 213

Worked Examples 214

Summary 217

Key Terms and Concepts 218

Discussion Questions and Problems 218

CHAPTER 8·

Aggregate Demand, Inflation, Financial Risks, and Policymaking   220

Introduction 220

Investment Demand and the Cost of Funds 221

Financing Investment 222

Opportunity Cost View of the Cost of Funds 223

Discounted Cash Flow View of the Cost of Funds 224

The Real Rate of Interest 226

Inflation and the Cost of Funds 227

Risk and the Cost of Funds 228

Credit Rationing and the Cost of Funds 228

The Cost of Funds: A Summary 229

The Money Market and the Short-Term Nominal Rate of Interest 230

The Effect of Inflation on T Bills and Money 230

The Demand for Money and the Short-Term Nominal Rate of Interest 231

Short-Term and Long-Term Interest Rates 232

Expected Future Interest Rates 232

Interest-Rate Risk 233

Risk and Term to Maturity 234

The Term Structure and the Yield Curve 235

Expectations and the Slope of the Yield Curve 235

The Interest-Rate Gap and Equilibrium Income 235

IS and *LM* with Different Rates of Interest 236

The Interest-Rate Gap 236

Expected Inflation and a Contractionary Monetary Policy 240

Monetary Expansion and the Interest-Rate Gap 241

Interest Rates and Contractionary Monetary Policy: A Case Study of 1979–83 242

Variations in Monetary Policy, 1979–82 243

The T-Bill Rate and the Yield Curve 243

Changes in the Risk Premium and Credit Availability 246

Changes in Expected Inflation, 1979–83 248

A Summary of the Effect of Monetary Contraction on Interest Rates 248

Pushing on a String: Monetary Policy, 1990–93 249

Interest Rates and the Slow Recovery, 1991–92 251

Conclusion 251

Worked Examples 251

Summary 257

Key Terms and Concepts 258

Discussion Questions and Problems 258

PART   2

ADVANCED TOPICS

CHAPTER 9

Consumption, Capital Investment, and Economic Fluctuations   263

Introduction 263

The Consumption Standard of Living 264

Consumption Smoothing 264

The Permanent-Income Hypothesis 266

The Life-Cycle Hypothesis 269

The Constraints on Consumption Smoothing 272

Capital Investment and Economic Fluctuations 274

The Variability of Total Capital Investment 274

The Accelerator and the Desired Stock of Capital 275

The Flexible Accelerator and Capital Investment 277

The Multiplier–Accelerator Interaction 278

Inventory Investment and the Inventory Cycle 280

Expectations, Interest Rates, and Investment Demand 282

Expectations and Variability in Investment Demand 282

The Interest Rate and the Accelerator 284

The Capital Stock, Expectations, and *IS–LM* Equilibrium 285

Investment Fluctuations and the Cycle, a Case Study, 1987–93 286

Worked Examples 291

Summary 295

Key Terms and Concepts 296

Discussion Questions and Problems 296

CHAPTER 10

The Federal Reserve Banking System and Financial Crunches 298

Introduction 298

The Banking System and Money Creation 299

Money Creation, Loans, and Reserves 301

Deposits, Reserves, and Loans 302

The Reserve Ratio 302

The Banking System Creates Money 303

The Money Supply and the Amount of Reserves 304

Changes in the Money Supply: Controlling the Monetary Base 307

T-Bill Prices and the Short-Term Rate of Interest 307

The Federal Reserve System 309

Open-Market Operations 310

Open-Market Purchases: Increasing the Monetary Base 311

Open-Market Sales: Decreasing the Monetary Base 312

Borrowed Reserves 312

The Discount Rate 313

Changing the Required Reserve Ratio 313

The Usefulness of the Concept of the Money Supply 314

Fed Targets: Money Supply and Interest Rates 314

Financial Crunches 315

Financial-Market Aspects of a Loss of Business Confidence 316

Financial Crises and the Supply of Credit 317

Fears of a Future Financial Crisis 320

Corporate Debt, Leveraged Buyouts, and Junk Bonds 321

Assessing Excessive Indebtedness 322

Banking Sector Credit or Capital Crunch in the Early 1990s 327

Conclusion 328

Worked Example 328

Summary 330

Key Terms and Concepts 330

Discussion Questions and Problems 331

CHAPTER 11

External Balances and International Economic Policy 332

Introduction 332

What Is the Problem with an External Imbalance? 334

Loss of Jobs 334

Loss of Wealth 335

Crisis of Confidence 336

What Is The Problem with Fluctuating Exchange Rates? 336

Why Do Exchange-Rate Changes Fail to Bring About External Balance? 337

Trade Adjustment Lags and the J-Curve 339

The Trade Balance and the J-Curve 340

Income Changes and the Trade Balance in the Early 1990s 342

Summary of the Effects of Exchange Rates and Income 343

The Iron Law of the External Imbalance 344

Using Trade Policies to Achieve External Balance 345

The Theory of Comparative Advantage 345

Trade Policies 346

Dynamic Arguments for and against Trade Restrictions 349

The Evidence That Trade Improves Productivity 350

Example: The Effect of Competition on the U.S. Auto Industry 352

Do Learning Curves Make a Case for Trade Restrictions? 353

Example: U.S. Trade Policy and the DRAM Market 354

Trade Restrictions to Protect Jobs in Specific
Industries 355

Conclusions on Trade Restrictions 357

Economic Policies toward the Foreign-Exchange
Market 358

  The Sustained Swings in Exchange Rates 358

  Short-Term Exchange-Rate Swings and Foreign-
  Currency Speculation 360

  Destabilizing Speculation 362

  A Fixed–Exchange-Rate System 366

  Fixed– and Flexible–Exchange-Rate Policies 365

  A Fixed–Exchange-Rate System 366

  Policy Intervention with Flexible Exchange
  Rates 368

  Conclusion on Exchange-Rate Policies 370

Summary 371

Key Terms and Concepts 372

Discussion Questions and Problems 372

CHAPTER 12

Supply-Shock Inflation and Economic Policy   373

Introduction 373

Supply Shocks as a Cause of Inflation 374

  Adverse Supply Shocks in the 1970s 376

  Supply Shocks and the Price Level 379

  Supply Shocks, the Cost of Living, and Wages 382

Supply Shocks and the Shifting Trade-Off 387

  The Transition from Supply Shocks to Chronic
  Inflation 388

Supply-Shock Inflation and Economic Policy 391

  Targeting a Return toward Potential Output 391

  Reducing Inflation to Preshock Levels 393

Keeping Inflation under Control in the 1980s and
90s 394

  Favorable Supply Shocks, 1981–1988 395

  Adverse Oil Shocks in the 1990s? 396

Worked Examples 397

Summary 400

Key Terms and Concepts 401

Discussion Questions and Problems 401

CHAPTER 13

Forecasting, Stabilization Policy, and the Variability of the Economy   402

Introduction 402

Forecasting the Macro Economy 403

  Surveys of Business Managers and Consumers 404

  Survey of Forecasts 404

  Leading Indicators 405

  Econometric Forecasting Models 408

  The Statistical Analysis of Leading Indicators 411

  Forecasting, and Lessons for Stabilization
  Policy 413

Stabilization Policy 413

  Hitting a Moving Target When Visibility Is
  Bad 414

Creating a Policy Regime for Stability 418

  The Policy Regime 419

  Permanent and Temporary Fiscal Policies 424

Has the Economy Become More Stable? 426

  Conclusions on Stabilization Policy 430

Summary 431

Key Terms and Concepts 432

Discussion Questions and Problems 432

CHAPTER 14

Monetarism: *Classical Roots and Contemporary Implications*   433

Introduction 433

The Classical Underpinnings of Monetarist Theory 434

  The Demand for Labor 435

  The Supply of Labor 438

  Equilibrium Output and the Labor Market 439

  The Classical Basis for the Quantity Equation 441

Aggregate Supply and Demand in the Classical
Model 443

  The Role of Aggregate Demand and the Price
  Level 443

Monetarism, Aggregate Demand, and Inflation 444

  The Basic Monetarist Framework 445

Monetarist Monetary Policy 451

Assessing the Monetarist Model 455

Monetarist Criticisms of the Income–Expenditure
Model 459

Summary 460

Key Terms and Concepts 461

Discussion Questions and Problems 461

CHAPTER 15

Controversy in Macroeconomics:
*Equilibrium Models and the Neo-
Keynesian Response* 462

Introduction 462

Inflationary Expectations 464

The Output–Inflation Trade-Off with Rational
Expectations 465

Combining Rational Expectations with Market
Clearing 467

Equilibrium Business Cycles 467

The Rationalist Critique of Stabilization Policy 476

The Policy-Ineffectiveness Theorem 476

The Critique of Econometric-Policy Evaluation 479

Real–Business-Cycle Models 480

Technology Shocks 481

Assessing Equilibrium–Business-Cycle and
Real–Business-Cycle Models 483

Support from Efficient Markets and Arbitrage 483

Doubts about Rational Expectations 484

Doubts about Price and Wage Flexibility 487

Criticisms of the Real–Business-Cycle Model 489

Conclusions on Equilibrium–Business-Cycle and
Real–Business-Cycle Models 492

Neo-Keynesian Analysis of Price Stickiness 492

Wage Contracts 493

Price Stickiness 495

Coordination Failure and Real and Nominal
Stickiness 497

Assessing the Neo-Keynesian Analysis 498

Summary 499

Key Terms and Concepts 500

Discussion Questions and Problems 500

CHAPTER 16

Employment Creation,
Unemployment, and Earnings
Distribution 502

Introduction 502

Employment Growth Patterns 503

Explaining the Patterns of Employment Growth 508

Unemployment 510

The Phillips Curve 510

The NAIRU and Okun's Law 511

Job Search Unemployment 514

Structural Unemployment 516

How Earnings Are Distributed 521

Causes of Increased Earnings Inequality 522

Immigration 525

Policies to Foster Flexibility and Productivity in the
Labor Market 525

Conclusions 530

Summary 530

Key Terms and Concepts 531

Discussion Questions and Problems 531

CHAPTER 17

Aggregate Supply, Long-Term
Growth, and Productivity 532

Introduction 532

A Review of the Aggregate Production Function 533

Average Labor Productivity 533

Capital per Worker and Economic Growth 534

The Solow Long-Term Growth Model 536

Capital Adequacy in the Growth Model 538

Steady-State Growth 541

Long-Term Growth with Technological Change 546

The Contribution of Technology to Productivity
Growth 546

The Solow Long-Term Growth Model Where
Technology Augments Labor 547

The Accumulation of Knowledge to Improve
Technology 551

Growth Accounting and Econometric Estimates 553

Using Business Knowledge to Explain Productivity Differences 554

Conclusions on Growth and Productivity in Theory and Practice 561

Worked Examples 562

Summary 563

Key Terms and Concepts 564

Discussion Questions and Problems 564

Index   **566**

CORE MACROECONOMICS

1   The Issues of Macroeconomics

2   Long-Term Growth and Competitiveness

3   Aggregate Supply and Demand and Income Determination

4   Interest Rates, Goods, and Money-Market Equilibrium

5   Fiscal Policy, Budgets, and Equilibrium Income

6   Monetary Policy and Inflation

7   The Exchange Rate, Macroeconomic Policy in an Open Economy, and the Trade Deficit

8   Aggregate Demand, Inflation, Financial Risks, and Policymaking

Among the key questions of macroeconomics, such as long-term growth, business cycles, and unemployment, we pay special attention to the questions of what determines the level of output and the rate of inflation. The first eight chapters of the text include the material that gives the basic answers to these questions, including a look at how the answers depend upon the fact that the United States trades with the rest of the world. Chapter 1 gives the concepts used in the rest of the book and reviews the performance of the U.S. and other economies.

Over the long term, the level of output depends upon the amounts of labor and capital used in production and the technology that determines its productivity. We address this issue in Chapter 2. Over the short term, output and the rate of inflation are determined by the level of aggregate demand in the economy. Over the long term, the growth of the money supply sets the rate of inflation. These points are developed in Chapters 3 through 8, with Chapter 7 developing the impact of trade and foreign capital movements, and Chapter 8 developing the role of capital markets and the movements of different rates of interest.

THE ISSUES OF MACROECONOMICS

INTRODUCTION

Economic issues have been at the center of events worldwide. The challenge of economic reform in Eastern Europe, the former Soviet Union, and China is immense. Money and production facilities now move from country to country, as do imports and exports of goods and services. Trade relations between the United States and its neighbors in Canada and Mexico are edging closer.

Over much objection and in the face of the fear of heightened competitive pressure, President William Clinton prevailed in the passage of NAFTA (North American Free Trade Agreement). The major trading arrangement among industrial economies—GATT (the General Agreement on Trade and Tariffs)—barely survived a seven-year process of renegotiation. In Europe, following the collapse of the Soviet empire, the transformation of the new independent states into market economies has been a painful and dangerous process. Old conflicts and new challenges combine to shape the economic and political environment.

New markets mean opportunities for many, but tough challenges for some. Farmers in Japan and Europe protest imports from the United States, while factory workers in the United States protest imports from Japan and Southeast Asia.

Concerns about the economy have been uppermost in the minds of Americans in the 1990s. President George Bush lost his bid for reelection largely because of the persistent recession that started in 1990 and continued through the election of 1992. President Bush was not the only president in recent U.S. history to lose an election because of the economy: Gerald Ford in 1976 and Jimmy Carter in 1980 lost their bids for reelection partly or wholly because of concerns about the economy. American voters expect the president to adopt policies that promote economic prosperity. If the voters do not see concrete results, they will look for a new president.

Despite the fact that the economy is of prime importance to voters, many of those voting report they do not understand the economic issues very well.

In this book we will examine the main issues of macroeconomics: long-term economic growth and competitiveness, recessions and business cycles, and unemployment and inflation. We will show that economic policies made by the president, the Congress, the central bank, members of groups in the private sector, and individuals exert a large collective influence on the performance of the U.S. economy.

In this first chapter we describe the main macroeconomics issues, and we present data to illustrate each issue. For example, we will show how inflation is measured, how it has varied over the past 40 years, and when and why inflation has been a serious problem. By the end of the chapter, you should have a good sense of the performance of the U.S. economy and of its strengths and weaknesses.

Another purpose of this chapter is to lay the groundwork for the analysis of the economy in subsequent chapters. Most students reading this text will have already taken an introductory course in macroeconomics, but it is easy to forget the basics of national income accounting. Since we focus much attention on income determination, we will review basic concepts.

LONG-TERM GROWTH, PRODUCTIVITY, AND COMPETITIVENESS

Gross Domestic Product (GDP)
The total amount of goods and services produced within a national economy in a given year.

An important measure of overall economic performance is the total amount of goods and services produced within a national economy in a given year, called the **Gross Domestic Product (GDP).** Gross Domestic Product (GDP) is used here instead of an older and perhaps more familiar measure, Gross National Product (GNP). U.S. GDP measures the production of goods and services by factories and offices located in the United States. GNP includes the income of U.S. owned assets located overseas and excludes the income of foreign owned assets in the United States. When the external portion of overall production was small, this distinction was unimportant; but since the 1980s, the growth of multinational companies and their associated investments overseas has led to a measurable difference between income received by households in the United States and production generated by U.S. firms. Since we want a measure that reflects the production of goods and services associated with the income we receive from *domestic* production, we need a measure of economic performance that measures *domestic* output. Thus, the replacement of GDP for GNP.

The GDP of the U.S. economy has grown substantially over the long term. The sources of this growth include increases in the size and quality of the labor force employed (with quality rising mostly as a result of education and training), increases in productive capital (machines, factories, and offices), and the many new technolo-

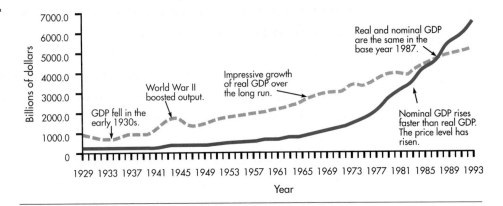

gies of production available. Figure 1–1 shows the GDP over the period 1929–1993. Two different measures of GDP, nominal and real, are presented in the figure.

nominal GDP

Sum of the total dollar value of all goods and services produced in the economy in a given year.

real GDP

The dollar value of all goods and services produced in the economy in a given year, using prices that prevailed in some fixed, base year.

Nominal GDP is the total dollar value of all goods and services produced in the economy in a given year. Nominal GDP changes over time, both because there are changes in the quantity of goods and services produced and because the prices of these goods and services change. We need to separate these two components, price and quantity, to use the growth in GDP to assess the overall growth of economic activity. **Real GDP** measures the dollar value of the output of all the goods and services produced in the economy in a given year, *using prices that prevailed in some fixed, base year.* The base year in use as this is written is 1987, so here the real GDP refers to the GDP in "1987 dollars." Thus, by holding the prices of goods and services constant, real GDP expresses the growth of total goods and services that is attributable to increased production.

Nominal GDP rose by 5.6 percent from 1992 to 1993; but when the outputs of the two years are evaluated, using the base year (1987 prices), the increase in real GDP was only 2.9 percent. The difference is attributable to inflation, which accounted for about 50 percent of the rise in nominal GDP. The gain in real GDP was at a pretty strong rate as the economy was recovering from a lingering recession. From this point on, when we refer to GDP in this textbook, that means real GDP unless we specifically refer to nominal GDP.

Figure 1–1 shows that GDP rose over 260 percent for the period 1959–1993, a huge increase in the size of the economy and its productive capacity. Nominal GDP increased over 1,200 percent for the same period. This indicates that prices have risen by close to 500 percent in that period.

GDP per Capita and Living Standards

We have established that GDP has grown over the long run. What does this increase mean to the average citizen? One way to assess this is to find the average level of output per person. We do this by dividing GDP by the number of persons living in the United States. This measure is called **real GDP per capita;** it measures overall economic output produced per person. The increase in GDP per capita over time gives an indication of how average living standards have risen in the United States. A comparison of GDP per capita for different countries shows how the U.S. average

FIGURE 1–2
Comparison of
GDP per Capita—
Selected Countries,
1870–1992

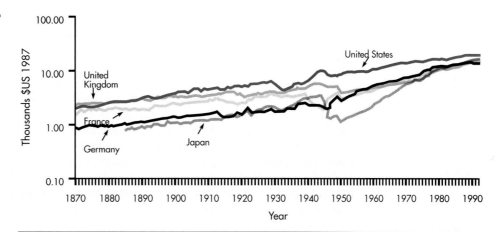

real GDP per capita
Average level of output
per person found by
dividing real GDP by the
number of persons living
in the United States.

living standard compares internationally. Figure 1–2 shows this information, including our best estimates of GDP per capita going as far back as 1870.

We see the growth of the U.S. economy has far outpaced the growth in the number
of people residing in the United States. This increase in output per person has allowed
average living standards to become much higher today than they were in the 19th
century. We also see the United States is a very high-output economy, with per capita
GDP well over that of the other industrialized countries.

The success of the U.S. economy in increasing real GDP per capita is perhaps the
most important fact about the U.S. economy, and the prospects for continuing this
trend is the source of great interest both if you're an optimist and if you're a pessimist
about our future circumstances. Growth in real GDP per capita meant that on average[1]
each generation of Americans could look forward with confidence to improvements in
their standard of living. Investments in hard work would pay off, putting capital at risk
would pay off, taking on the challenge of immigration to the United States would pay
off. The real potential for long-term success was and still is an essential part of the
uniqueness of the American experience. The fact that the long-term growth of real
GDP per capita generated one of the highest average levels of real income among
industrial economies added to the special character of the U.S. economy. For many
nations, macroeconomics often focuses on questions concerning the source of growth,
the prospects for its continuation, and the roles that national policy can and cannot
play in fostering growth.

The success of the U.S. economy may be surprising, because much attention in
recent years has focused on concerns about its performance. We will examine some of
these problems in this book; however, we should not let economic problems obscure
the fact that output and income per person in the U.S. economy have continued to

---

[1] Real GDP per capita is an average measure that does not reflect the large range of differences in living
   standards among individuals and groups. For the U.S. economy, these differences are important, since
   poverty and wealth are serious concerns. However, the U.S. economy does have a broad middle class,
   which allows us to generalize about economic performance by looking at overall averages, in contrast to
   economies where a very small portion of the population garners a very high share of all output, making
   averages less meaningful as measures of typical living standards in the economy.

grow over time and are still higher than that of other major industrialized countries and may well continue to be higher through the end of the century.

Productivity and the Growth Slowdown

productivity
Measures the output produced in relation to the resources used in production.

average labor productivity
The output of the business sector divided by the hours of labor used in production.

Why is there a concern about U.S. economic performance when the economy and living standards have grown mightily over the long term. The answer lies in a slowdown of that growth. The growth of U.S. productivity has been much slower in the past 20 years than it was for a number of years after the end of World War II. **Productivity** measures the output produced in relation to the resources used in production. The higher is productivity, the larger is the available output relative to how much capital or labor it took to produce the output. The simplest overall measure of productivity is to take the output of the business sector and divide this by the hours of labor used in production. This is called **average labor productivity,** and the average annual growth rate of labor productivity for selected years is shown in Figure 1–3.

Because productivity growth is an increase in the rate at which output outstrips work, productivity growth is the most important source of increase in per capita GDP and, hence, of living standards. The decline in the rate of productivity increase indicates a decline in the *growth* of living standards. In recent years, Americans on average are finding it harder to improve their economic conditions.

Competitiveness

competitiveness
The ability to produce and market a product or service profitably at a price which sells to customers.

The slowdown in U.S. productivity has occurred along with a decline in a related but separate characteristic—international **competitiveness.** For the individual economic unit, being competitive means being able to produce and market a product or service profitably at a price that attracts customers. This is not necessarily the same as being productive—for instance, a competitive building contractor could offer an attractive house at a market price because of superior production and fabrication technologies (high productivity) or because of large quantities of low-wage employees (low productivity). In terms of international comparisons between the United States and the rest of the world, competitiveness and productivity are related. If an entire economy is noncompetitive, it means that, on average, the combination of wages, prices, exchange

**FIGURE 1–3
Annual Growth
Rate of Labor
Productivity,
1948–1993**

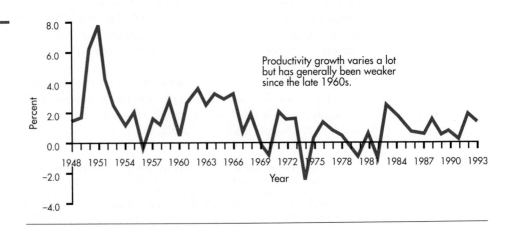

Productivity growth varies a lot but has generally been weaker since the late 1960s.

rates and productivity are out of line so that companies cannot sell profitably overseas (wages and prices could be too high in relation to the exchange rate; or productivity could be too low; or some combination of them). For years the United States exported competitively priced goods and services while simultaneously generating high wages and incomes. That combination of price competitiveness and highly paid labor can only be accomplished through high productivity. Today, there are many developing countries that compete internationally even though their productivity is low because they have very low wages. There are different ways to be competitive.

In every year from 1946 until 1970, the United States sold more goods overseas than it bought. In every year from 1971 to 1992, the opposite has been the case, with a merchandise trade deficit that hit a record $160 billion in 1987. This change in trading patterns is reflected in changes in the international value of currencies. In 1973, it took 292 Japanese yen to buy one U.S. dollar. In 1993, the exchange rate was approximately 111 yen to the dollar. Figures 1–4a and 1–4b show these trends in the U.S. trade balance and the dollar–yen exchange rate.

FIGURE 1–4a
U.S. Merchandise
Trade Balance,
1946–1993

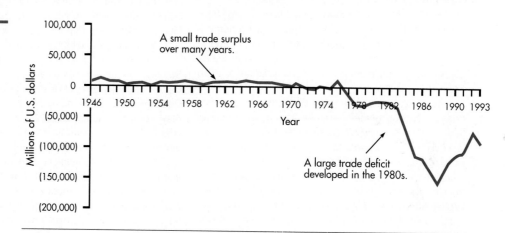

FIGURE 1–4b
The Exchange
Rate between the
Yen and the
Dollar, 1973–1993

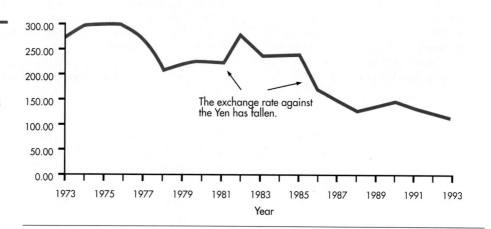

The U.S. Economy May Dominate for Years

By virtually any measure, the U.S. economy outshines those of Japan and Germany.

While the U.S. jobless rate fell last month to a three-year low of 6.4 percent, Germany's climbed to 8.1 percent. The U.S. economy probably expanded at better than a 4.5 percent pace in the fourth quarter. Japan's probably shrank during the period. With some reason, Treasury Secretary Lloyd Bentsen boasted last week that the United States is "the world's economic leader, the engine of growth."

Can this last, once Germany and Japan emerge from recession? After all the hand-wringing over America's deficit, inadequate investment, shortsighted corporations, and social ills, is it conceivable the United States will be the economic envy of the industrialized world five years from now? Yes.

Like a once-flabby athlete, the United States has been working out at the health club for the past couple of years. And it has paid off. Germany and Japan have just finished a big lunch and are only now signing up at the local economic gym.

In the United States, a banking system that seemed so troubled just a couple of years back is flush with profit and capital. Interest rates are at the lowest level in decades, the product of deficit-reduction and an improved inflation outlook. Corporate dinosaurs are showing surprising willingness to change. Both because of productivity gains and slow wage growth, U.S. manufacturers have an edge. Morgan Stanley figures U.S. workers cost $16.70 an hour at current exchange rates; Japanese labor costs $19.30 and German $25.50. The gap will narrow, but the U.S. advantage is likely to persist.

Japan's predicament is startling because the country was seen as an economic superstar. . . . Japan's experience suggests a country can invest too much. Its dependence on exports has run into increasingly tough political challenge from the United States and economic competition from the rest of Asia, forcing wrenching change at Japanese manufacturing giants. What's more, Japan's political system—which holds sway over the economy—has cracked, and renovations have only just begun.

Japan also is discovering, much as the United States did, that it's hard to stimulate an economy with lower interest rates when banks don't much want to lend and businesses don't much want to borrow. Cutting taxes to stimulate consumer demand is one option, though an unappetizing one to the conservative Ministry of Finance. Signs are that the tax cut will be too little, too late, prolonging the economic torpor.

"The Germans are a much bigger question," says Stanley Fischer, former chief economist for the World Bank. "Their social welfare state has gotten out of hand. Dealing with East Germany is a much bigger deal than they—or we—had any idea." As a result, Germany faces years of discomfort as its government cuts its budget deficit and its companies restructure. Sound familiar?

Germany is "overweight and overpaid," says MIT economist Rudiger Dornbusch. The unpleasant prescription: German workers must work harder, earn less, and pay more taxes. Not the kind of change that comes easily. In contrast to Japan, where corporations are slow to lay off workers but quick to shift them around internally, German workers have been brought up to believe they deserve a specific job at a specific plant forever—with six weeks vacation and the highest wages in the industrialized world.

Changes in the world economy also play to U.S. strengths. If the 1980s was the decade of VCRs and

---

The manufacturing sector of the economy is the sector most affected by foreign trade and foreign competition, so the record trade deficits of the 1980s were accompanied by large dislocations among manufacturing companies and firms. Thousands of workers in the auto, steel, apparel, consumer electronics, and other industries were laid off, while new jobs for young people were not available in manufacturing industries as they had once been.

personal computers, the 1990s is the decade of video-cassettes and software. In the first game, Japan was tough. But the U.S. lead in software, be it movies or spreadsheets, is unquestioned.

The United States is also much farther along in the inevitable and often-unpleasant shift of workers from manufacturing to services than Japan and, especially, Germany, where factories employ nearly three times as many workers proportionally as in the United States.

It is folly to be too confident about any forecast of the economy five years out. Mr. Fischer says that the United States likely will do better in the next 10 years than it did in the previous 15 years—and that Japan and Germany likely will do worse. "But I suspect that four years from now, we'll be growing a little slower per capita than they,"

he says. So does economist Walter Cadette, who predicts that Japan and Germany will bounce back from recession with vigor just as the U.S. did in 1982.

The United States will have plenty of chances to stumble. The stock market could crash. The Federal Reserve could prematurely choke off the expansion. Congress and the president could enact a health-care plan that backfires. The productivity boomlet could prove temporary. That said, given the current horizon the prospects for the United States are better than they have been in years, and far better than those facing its main rivals.

Source: Reprinted by permission of *The Wall Street Journal,* © 1994 Dow Jones and Company, Inc. All Rights Reserved Worldwide.

THE UNITED STATES EDGE

Unit labor costs in manufacturing 1980=100; based on maket exchange rates.

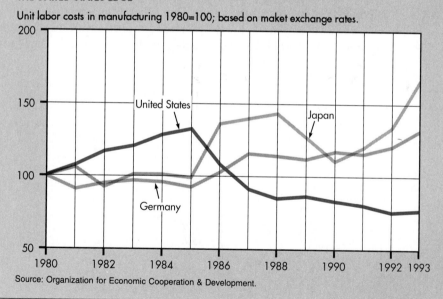

Source: Organization for Economic Cooperation & Development.

In the late 1980s and early 1990s, a combination of chronic trade deficits and a fall in the availability of manufacturing jobs raised concerns about the competitiveness of the U.S. economy. Many people feared that the United States would become a low-skill, low-wage nation of hamburger flippers. As *The Wall Street Journal* noted recently, however, (see box) the competitiveness of the U.S. economy looks much better.

LONG-RUN TRENDS AND SHORT-TERM FLUCTUATIONS

Because productivity drives living standards, and because over the long term the performance of the economy depends on the growth of its productive capacity (its capacity to supply more goods and services), the study of macroeconomics is concerned with long-term growth trends over years and decades. However, a focus on the long term only would ignore important questions about the here and now. The economy does not grow in a smooth and regular fashion. Economic performance is jagged, with lots of ups (booms) and downs (slumps). Week to week, month to month, and quarter to quarter fluctuations of output, employment, income, and prices have great effects on economic circumstances. Households and business managers are often much more concerned with any near-term changes in revenues and expenditures than with the long-term future of the economy. Further, short-term fluctuations may generate a level of economic performance that is very different from the economic circumstances realized over a longer time period.

Figure 1–5 describes two hypothetical paths for real GDP per capita. First, notice that the economy has had a particular history, where GDP has grown and varied in the past culminating with the current level of output at point A. Macroeconomics focuses on how a given level of income or output comes about and, when we describe income determination, we are explaining the forces that bring about a current level of output, such as shown at point A. Since the future performance of the economy is unknown, we show two alternative paths, a high-growth track (I) and a low-growth track (II).

FIGURE 1–5

Hypothetical Long-Run Trends and Short-Run Fluctuations: *Alternative Future Paths for Real GDP per Capita*

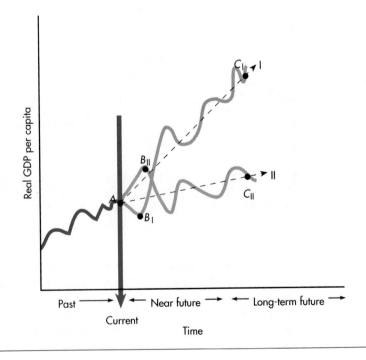

While the high-growth track is clearly preferable in the long run (the level of real GDP per capita is much higher at point C_I than at point C_{II}) the superiority of the high-growth trend may not be obvious in the short run. In the figure, the short-run experience on the high-growth track (point A to point B_I) has the economy going into a slump, with real GDP per capita declining. In contrast, the low-growth alternative future shows a short-run boom (point A to point B_{II}), with a growth in economic performance coming before a downturn. The study of the fluctuations around these trends is an important aspect of macroeconomics, along with the study of the forces that determine which trend in productive capacity, high or low growth, will describe the long-term growth of the economy. Policymakers are concerned with both long-run and short-run economic performance and with the consequences of policy actions on both the immediate and longer-term trends as well as the trade-offs that arise when short-term goals are in conflict with long-term aspirations.

RECESSIONS AND THE BUSINESS CYCLE

Because of the dislocation, loss, and discomfort associated with a stall in growth—or worse, an economic decline—we focus more attention on slumps than on booms. When the slump is an actual decline of real GDP for at least two quarters (six months) we name it a *recession*. Extremely long and deep recessions are called *depressions*. A clear example of a slump occurred in the 1930s, during the Great Depression. In 1933, about 25 percent of the people who wanted to work in the U.S. economy were unable to find work. Worldwide, factories and offices were idle because the businesses that owned them could not find customers for their products. In the United States, GDP fell by about 30 percent between 1929 and 1933.

While fortunately there has not been another depression in the U.S. economy since the 1930s, the problem of fluctuations in the economy has not gone away. Figure 1–6 shows the growth of the economy between 1947 and 1993 has been far from even. In recent years, the year-to-year percentage changes in GDP have varied from an increase of 6 percent in 1984 to a decline of greater than 2 percent in 1982. The 1992 presidential election provides evidence of the impact of such fluctuations. The voters in the 1992 presidential election were most concerned by a persistent recession, with its ongoing weakness in real GDP, in incomes, and in jobs.

Economic downturns are costly not only because there is a decline in average income but also because they disrupt people's lives. Workers are laid off, and those who still have jobs fear they may be next. Bankruptcies rise sharply during downturns, and even healthy companies find their profits declining. Moreover, recessions trigger painful changes that are actually the result of longer-term economic forces. Companies that need to restructure put off the task until a recession hits, and then they are forced to make large layoffs.

The recession that started in 1990 lasted only until 1991; however, unlike past recoveries where GDP grew back at around 6 percent per year after the downturn, the recovery that began in late 1991 evidenced only about a 1 percent growth rate. That growth was so slow that the unemployment rate (the percent of those looking for work who are unemployed), which normally falls in a recovery, remained stuck at 7 percent.

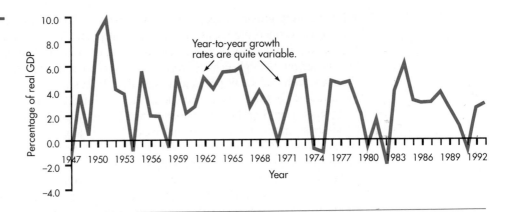

FIGURE 1-6
The Growth Rate of Real GDP, 1947–1993

The recovery was only strong enough to create jobs at the rate at which the work force grew, but not enough to reduce unemployment rates. It was not until late 1993 and 1994 that a more robust recovery began.

While short-lived recession may be healthy in bringing about changes that are needed for future productivity gains, severe or prolonged recessions are very costly. In deep recessions, people are laid off who do not find work again for many months or even years. Students unlucky enough to graduate during a recession find job opportunities limited; and, even if it does not adversely affect their lifetime careers, it is certainly disturbing and costly to students and parents alike.

The intent of macroeconomics policy is to reduce the range of fluctuations. Policies are adopted to prevent the very deepest and most long-lasting recessions and to avoid the inflationary pressures associated with an economy where demand is too strong. To understand these policies, we need to examine the business cycle.

Business Cycles

business cycle
The business cycle is a recurring fluctuation of aggregate output in the economy. Each cycle consists of a peak, a recession or contraction, a trough, and a recovery or expansion.

A **business cycle** is a recurring fluctuation of real GDP. Each cycle consists of a **peak** (the highest level of output and employment reached before a sustained decline in output), a **recession** or **contraction** (where output is falling for at least two quarters), a **trough** (the low point for output), and a **recovery** or **expansion** (where output is rising).

The business cycle gets its name from the notion that the major cause of economic fluctuation comes from changes in the investment, production, and hiring decisions of businesses. But business behavior is not the only source of economywide variations—changes in government policies and international trade and finance and shifts in expectations about the future can also contribute to the cycle. Nevertheless, the term *business cycle* is used to describe the short-term fluctuations around long-term economic trends.

Output fluctuates in business cycles, with production sometimes falling below the economy's capacity to produce and employment falling below full employment. And production sometimes goes above the level that can be produced with normal levels of utilization of the economy's resources. There has been no great regularity to business-cycle fluctuations in the U.S. economy. Some cycles have lasted only a couple of years and some have lasted many years. Since World War II, business expansions have been much longer than contractions.[2]

Business cycles consist of fluctuations in GDP around a benchmark level that reflects the long-term–growth trend in the productive capacity of the economy. The level of GDP that is used as a benchmark is called *potential output.* In our study of business-cycle fluctuations, we will be asking why real GDP is sometimes below potential output and sometimes above it.

Potential Output: Benchmarking the Cycle

potential output
The level of output that is produced when the resources of the economy are fully utilized in a sustainable manner.

Potential output or **potential GDP** is defined as the level of output that can be produced in a given year when the available capital and labor resources of the economy are fully utilized but not at so high a rate that it cannot be sustained. Potential output is not maximum output. The maximum possible output would be generated if everyone worked 24 hours a day, seven days a week, and ran all our machinery at full throttle with no time taken for maintenance and no provisions for replacement. This is not a meaningful number. We certainly could not sustain this level of effort for any length of time. Rather, potential output measures the *sustainable* productive capacity of the economy. And since potential output is not the maximum possible level of output, there will be years when output exceeds potential output (i.e., when capital and labor are utilized more intensively than the benchmark levels).

Potential output must be estimated. This is usually done using information on unemployment (a measure of the degree of utilization of the labor force) and business reports of how close firms are to full capacity (a measure of capital utilization). When Arthur Okun first introduced the concept of potential output, he said that output was equal to potential output when there was 4 percent unemployment.[3] That benchmark has been adjusted—today potential output corresponds to somewhere between 5.5 and 6.5 percent unemployment.

Over the course of the business cycle, actual output can be either higher or lower than its potential or capacity. If actual output is less than capacity, the standard of living that is achieved is worse than it could have been—the economy is suffering unemployment of labor and underutilization of capital. That gap between what was produced and the potential to produce reflects a waste of opportunities for improving the economic lives of our citizens. Real GDP can also be greater than potential output for a time with very low unemployment and factories running overtime or extra shifts. The problem in this case is that inflation will accelerate.

The Output Ratio

A measure of economic performance that compares actual output to potential output is the **output ratio.**

---

[2] Robert J. Gordon, ed., *The American Business Cycle: Continuity and Change* (Chicago: University of Chicago Press, 1986).

[3] Arthur M. Okun, "Potential GNP: Its Measurement and Significance," in *Proceedings of the Business and Economic Statistics Section of the American Statistical Association,* 1962, pp. 98–104.

FIGURE 1–7

Ratio of Actual
GDP to Potential
GDP, 1950–1992

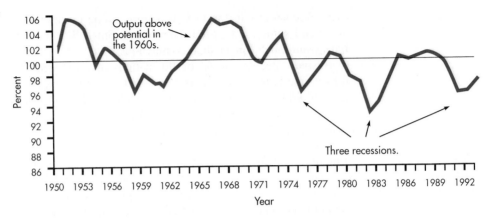

Source: U.S. Department of Commerce, Bureau of Economic Analysis. Potential GDP estimated by the authors.

output ratio

The ratio of actual
output to potential
output, usually given in
percent terms.

$$\text{Output ratio} = \frac{\text{Output}}{\text{Potential output}} \times 100$$

Since real GDP is our main measure of output, the output ratio is usually defined as the ratio of real GDP to potential real GDP, and the ratio is multiplied by 100 to express it as an index number. Figure 1–7 shows the output ratio for the U.S. economy over the period 1950–92. It shows that there have been persistent business-cycle fluctuations, such as 1975–77 and 1982–84 when the economy operated well below potential output (i.e., when the output ratio was well below 100 percent). And there was a long period in the 1960s when output was well above potential output (when the ratio was above 100 percent).

Sometimes, instead of talking about the output ratio, a concept called the *output gap* is used, especially when the output ratio is less than 100 percent. The output gap is simply the amount by which output falls below potential output. If the output ratio were 97 percent, the output gap would be 3 percent.

The Relation between the Cycle and Long-Term Growth Trends   The concept of potential output helps us understand the relation between long-term trends and short-term fluctuations. Long-term economic performance, as in the trend of real GDP per capita (sketched as the trend lines I and II in Figure 1–5, in contrast with the fluctuations around those trend lines from point A to B_I and B_{II}), is determined by long-run supply conditions measured by the growth of the productive capacity of the economy; that is to say, it depends on the growth over several years of potential output, not actual output in any particular month or year. The business cycle describes the fluctuations of actual output around potential output that occur over the short run, from quarter to quarter and year to year. The path of potential output over long periods describes long-term growth trends.

In studying long-term growth, we will look at time periods long enough so that the ups and downs of the business cycle have averaged out. In studying the business cycle, we will often assume that potential output is constant and focus solely on variations in current or actual output.

One reason we look at the two issues separately is that most economists believe the business cycle results from fluctuations in the aggregate demand for goods and services in the economy, while long-term growth depends on shifts in aggregate supply. In the short run, actual output may be below potential output, because of shortfalls in consumption demand by households, investment demand by businesses, and other sources of demand for goods and services.

Separating long-term growth from the cycle does have its drawbacks. Business investment not only is a source of aggregate demand but also is how companies add to their stocks of productive capital. Weakness in investment can lead not only to recessions but also problems with long-term growth. Alternatively, recessions may induce companies to restructure their activities to provide a better basis of their long-term growth. While sometimes we refer to the connection between growth and the cycle, for the most part we will separate long-term supply issues from short-run demand issues.

EMPLOYMENT AND UNEMPLOYMENT

So far we have discussed long-term growth and the business cycle only in terms of output and income. But an important part of macroeconomics is the study of employment and unemployment. For most people, earned income from a job is the most important, if not the only, source of their economic well-being.

Because employment is so important both economically and politically (an economy with high unemployment will likely generate political turnover and upheaval as the citizenry presses on government to ''do something''), much of economic policy is directed at employment. Employment policies work either indirectly, through policies intended to moderate large swings in prices, interest rates, and exchange rates, thereby building a stable business environment, which hopefully leads to job creation, or directly through government created jobs, government direct expenditures, and unemployment insurance.

Total Employment

Figure 1–8 shows there has been an increase in the fraction of the adult population that is employed in the United States since the 1960s. By this measure, the economy has done well in creating employment opportunities.

Over the past two or three decades, much of the increase in employment has come from the increased labor force participation of women—a change with several implications. As opportunities developed in previously male-dominated occupations, many women have chosen to enter the labor market to develop careers and economic independence. However, some families have all the adults work outside the home from economic necessity, even though they might prefer to have one member remain at home.

Unemployment

There has been a tremendous growth in employment in the U.S. economy; but there have also been periods when large numbers of people looking for work could not find it.

FIGURE 1–8

Labor Force Participation Rate and Employment to Population Ratio, 1948–1993

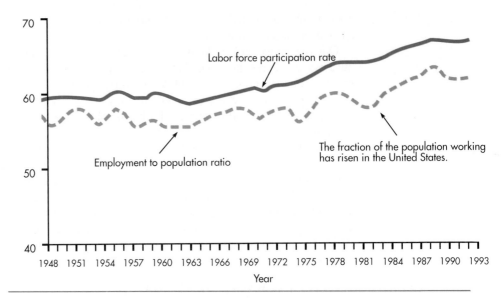

Source: Economic Report of the President, February 1994.

Every month surveyors from the Census Bureau, a federal government agency, interview a sample of U.S. residents about their employment status. They ask someone in each family surveyed to say whether the family members have jobs, are actively looking for jobs, are on temporary layoff from a job, do not want to take paid employment, or are sick or unable to work. The unemployed are those people over 16 years of age who are able to work and are looking for work who do not have a job or who are on layoff. The number of people in the economy who either have jobs (are employed) or are unemployed is the total **labor force.** The **unemployment rate** is the percentage of the labor force that is unemployed, and this provides a measure of the economy's unused labor resources.

Figure 1–9 shows the unemployment rate for the U.S. economy from 1929 to 1993. The Great Depression in the 1930s is the period of the worst sustained unemployment in U.S. history. The unemployment rate averaged 19 percent over the 10 years of 1931–40. Although the situation improved after 1933, the economy did not reach low unemployment rates until 1942. Very low unemployment rates were sustained throughout World War II, and the rate generally stayed low after the war until 1974. There were two deep recessions in 1975 and 1980–82 and a generally higher average rate of unemployment in the 1970s and 80s, although by 1989 the recovery had brought the rate close to 5 percent. In 1990, the economy slipped into a recession and unemployment moved over 7 percent in 1992, before stronger growth resumed in 1993 and 1994.

Some unemployment is inevitable in the normal operation of the economy, but in a recession unemployment exceeds this normal or natural level. There is no question that the public considers excessive unemployment a problem. Productive employment is vital to people's immediate well-being (both economic and psychological), and it is the source of experience and skill building that enhances future well-being.

labor force

The total number of people in the economy who are either employed or unemployed.

unemployment rate

The percentage of the labor force that is unemployed. The unemployed are those people over 16 years old who are able to work and are looking for work who do not have a job or who are on layoff.

FIGURE 1–9
Civilian Unemployment Rate,
1929–1993

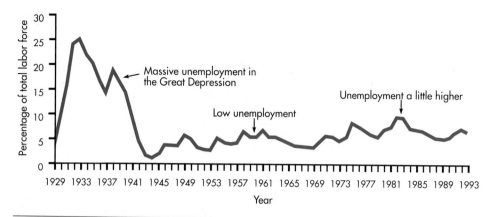

Source: Economic Report of the President, February 1994.

Full Employment

Even when the economy is producing a level of output equal to potential output, there is a substantial amount of unemployment. Imagine a factory in the Midwest whose workers have been laid off and are looking for work, while there are jobs without qualified applicants in an insurance company on the West Coast. Even when the labor market is operating normally, workers can be separated from jobs by location and training. They will have to search for the right job; they may have to relocate; and they may have to wait for a new job to open up or wait for their old job to reopen.

Since some level of unemployment is normal, full employment in the economy is a misleading term. It doesn't mean that everyone is employed. Full employment is often used to describe the economy when it is operating with output equal to potential output and the unemployment rate is equal to a concept called the **NAIRU** (the *Non-Accelerating Inflation Rate of Unemployment*). We will explain this concept more later in the book, but the basic idea is that when unemployment goes below the NAIRU, inflation starts to increase. During the late 1980s potential output was reached when the NAIRU stood between 5 and 6 percent.

NAIRU

ment that occurs when output equals potential output. Unemployment below the NAIRU leads to inflationary pressure.

THE PRICE LEVEL, INFLATION, AND INTEREST RATES

The level of real income and the number of jobs provide important measures of the performance of the economy, but prices, inflation, and interest rates are also important. When inflation is very high, people become concerned about the stability of the economy and the value of their savings.

High and variable rates of inflation generate uncertainty about prices and values, so employers do not know whether their prices are in line with costs and households do not know whether their wages are increasing or decreasing. Inflation inflicts a cost on the economy through an increase in the general level of uncertainty.

Increased uncertainty discourages investment and makes it hard for people to plan for retirement. Inflation is costly to the economy, because an unexpected burst of inflation surprises people and ends up changing the effective terms of arrangements or contracts that have been agreed to. If you sell goods or services, or if you offer labor or rent capital, you expect to be compensated. Unexpected inflation can lower the real value of amounts received under the terms of a contract, because the money received for goods and services rendered buys less when prices rise.

The Price Level

price level
A price index is set equal to unity (or 100) in the base year. Changes in the price level over time reflect the average change of all prices.

The **price level** is an index number that reflects the prices of all the goods and services produced and sold in a particular year. Changes in the price level from year to year are measured as an average of the price changes in all the goods and services produced and sold. The bigger the amount spent on the product, the more important on average is its price increase.[4] If the economy produced only two goods, food and clothing, and if we spent three-quarters of our incomes on food and one-quarter on clothing, and if food prices rose by 10 percent in a year and clothing prices rose by 2 percent, then the price level would have risen by 8 percent $[(0.75 \times 10\%) + (0.25 \times 2\%)]$.

Nominal GDP is the measure we get when we simply add up the dollar values of aggregate demand. The price level is related to nominal GDP and real GDP in the following way:

Nominal GDP = Real GDP × Price level

or alternatively

Real GDP = Nominal GDP/Price level

For example, Real GDP grew from $2.47 trillion in 1965 to $5.13 trillion in 1993. The value in 1965 dollars of all the goods and services produced in the economy in 1965 was $703 billion; that is, nominal GDP was $703 billion. In standard data sources the price level is expressed as an index number, 28.4 in 1965 or 124.2 in 1993, which relates the price level in any given year to the price level in a particular period or base year. The base year now being used is 1987. Real GDP is reported as ''1989 GDP in 1987 dollars'' or ''1965 GDP in 1987 dollars.'' The price level in 1987 is set equal to 100 and then the price level in 1965 is the ratio of the price index in 1965 to the price index in 1987. So, the price level in 1965 was 0.284 of the price level in 1987 and 1965's real GDP in 1987 dollars is then $703 billion ÷ 0.284, which equals $2.47 trillion.

Similarly, the nominal GDP in 1993 was $6.37 trillion. The price level in 1993 was 1.242 (124.2 ÷ 100), so that 1993's real GDP in 1987 dollars is then $6.37 trillion ÷ 1.242, which equals $5.13 trillion.

Nominal GDP in 1993 was much greater than nominal GDP in 1965, but much of the increase in nominal GDP was the result of an increase in the level of prices. Real GDP increased between 1965 and 1993 but by roughly two times (5.13 ÷ 2.47) rather than the more than nine times (6.37 ÷ 0.703) indicated by comparing nominal values.

The Rate of Inflation

Inflation is an increase in the overall level of prices. Throughout the history of world economies there have been periods when inflation was a serious problem. In modern times, the price level has risen continuously in the United States since the mid-1950s,

---

4 The average used is a weighted average. See the discussion of price indexes and inflation below.

inflation
The rate of increase of the price level.

but the problem of high rates of inflation emerged in the United States and in most other economies in the mid-1960s. The rate of inflation is defined as the proportional or percent increase in the price level from one year to the next.

Rate of inflation = [Price level (given year) − Price level (prior year)]
÷ Price level (prior year)

Rate of inflation (in percent) = Percent rate of growth of the price level

In the U.S. economy, there have been periods when the price level has fallen. This happened in the 1930s, for example. A falling price level is called *deflation* and the rate of deflation is simply the negative of the rate of inflation.

Although the price level has sometimes fallen, this has not been the normal case for the U.S. economy since the 1950s. As we noted earlier, the price level in 1992 was between four and five times as high as it was in 1959. From 1965 to 1993, the rate of inflation has ranged mostly between 3 and 6 percent with short bursts of higher inflation. Inflation has averaged nearly 5 percent a year over this period. In 1993 and 1994 the economy has been able to sustain strong economic growth with moderate inflation, a welcome change from the problems of the 1970s and 80s.

implicit price deflator
The price level for all GDP. The deflator is computed as the ratio of nominal GDP to real GDP.

The price level as we are using it here is an index number that is based on all of the goods and services that are part of GDP. This price index is known as the **implicit price deflator for GDP.** It provides a measure of overall inflation, but it can give a misleading picture if there are changes over time in the kinds of goods produced in the economy.

consumer price index
An index that tracks the prices of the purchases made by typical households in a particular year relative to the prices for the same collection of goods and services in a base year.

An alternative price index, one whose changes capture inflation as it affects consumers, is the consumer price index. The **consumer price index** (CPI) is constructed by looking at changes in the prices of the things that typical households buy. Figure 1–10 shows the rate of inflation (annual percent change in the CPI) measured by this important price index. The CPI tracks the average annual rate of increase in the prices consumers pay for a representative group or "basket" of purchases.

There are thousands of different items purchased by consumers, but the U.S. Department of Labor's Bureau of Labor Statistics, the federal government agency that

FIGURE 1–10
Percent Change in the Consumer Price Index, 1951–1993

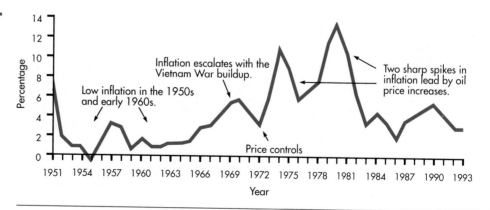

Source: U.S. Department of Labor, Bureau of Labor Statistics.

weighted average
Each item is counted (weighted) for relatively more or less in arriving at the average. The weight of an item reflects the relative importance of that item.

prepares the CPI, looks at a sample of these and then forms a **weighted average** of their rates of increase. Each price in the survey is given a relative importance in the average, depending on how large a fraction of the consumer dollar is spent on this type of good or service.

People dislike inflation intensely; but economists, who are used to evaluating economic conditions in real terms, after inflation adjustment, would argue that the intensity of dislike for inflation may be excessive and may stem partly from misunderstanding. Inflation is seen as reducing existing income even though real income may be unaffected.

Interest Rates

From 1933 until 1965, the interest rate on short-term borrowing by the federal government never went over 4 percent. In the early 1960s, the interest rate on new home mortgages was below 6 percent. In 1981, the short-term interest rate averaged over 14 percent, and, in 1982, the mortgage interest rate averaged over 15 percent. In the early 1990s, the interest rate on short-term borrowing had dipped below 3 percent, and the mortgage interest rate was between 7 and 9 percent. Figure 1–11 shows how interest rates have moved over the postwar period. One reason interest rates were higher in the 1970s and 80s is that inflation was more of a problem. Savers demanded higher interest rates to compensate them for the loss of value of their funds resulting from inflation.

Interest rates have been volatile in recent years, making it harder to finance long-term investments, to conduct monetary policy, and to generate sustainable profits for banks and other financial institutions. To compete for funds, banks have had to offer much higher interest rates to depositors, and then, to earn enough to cover the interest they were paying to depositors, they had to use these funds to make loans that were very risky. Many of the loans soured and the banks lost large amounts of money and became insolvent. Few banks failed between 1945 and 1981; but, after 1981, a huge banking crisis developed (due in part to a combination of financial market competition

FIGURE 1–11
Selected Interest Rates, 1970–1993

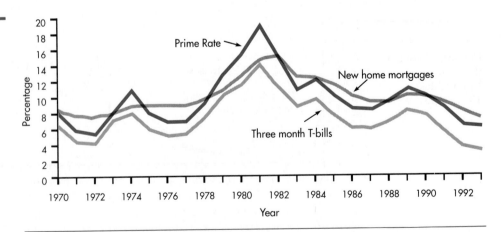

Source: Economic Report of the President, 1994.

The Macroeconomic Scorecard: How Are We Doing?

We can assess macroeconomic performance in historical terms: How are we doing relative to our own past performance? We can also assess performance relative to other countries. The grades are mixed on both counts. We start with the long view and compare the postwar period from 1948 to the present, relative to economic performance over the period before World War II.*

- The post–World War II period, 1948–1992, is one of greatly increased stability in real GDP compared to earlier periods. The *business cycle has been reduced in severity.* In particular there has been no depression comparable to the Great Depression of the 1930s.
- There has been a large deficit in the budget of the federal government.

The bad news is that performance has deteriorated in recent years. The macroeconomy is still doing well, but not as well as it did in the 1950s and 1960s. How does this performance look, compared to that of other countries?

- In recent years, inflation has been higher in Europe than in the United States. Japan has had very little inflation.
- Unemployment has been much higher on average in Europe than in the United States in recent years. It has stayed persistently high, rather than showing

a cyclical pattern as U.S. unemployment has done. Japan has had very little unemployment.

- The level of productivity and the level of real GDP per person remain higher in the United States than in Europe and Japan. The growth rates of productivity have been higher overseas than here but it does not look as if our productivity lead will be eliminated any time soon. Real GDP and employment have grown slowly in Europe.
- Japan and Germany are running large trade surpluses, in contrast to our large trade deficit.

Even though U.S. economic performance has deteriorated, it compares reasonably well with the other main industrial countries' economies. In fact, given all the gloom and doom that one hears about the economy, the relative U.S. performance looks surprisingly good. One reason for the gloom and doom is that people are always comparing the United States to Japan, particularly in terms of the two countries' performances in international trade. Japan's economy has done outstandingly well by a variety of measures, and Japanese exports have taken some of our industries by storm. Keep in mind, however, that Japan's success has been somewhat selective. Many of its industries perform poorly. And Japan's success has come as part of a process of catch-up, so living standards in Japan are still well below those in the United States.

* Historical data can be found in U.S. Department of Commerce, *Historical Statistics of the United States.*

and high interest rates), with noticeable failures of savings and loans and commercial banks. Because bank deposits are ultimately guaranteed by insurance provided by the federal government, taxpayers have had to foot much of the bill for the bank failures.

THE BUDGET DEFICIT

In the fiscal year 1992, the federal government ran a budget deficit of close to $300 billion, pushing the total federal indebtedness to over $4 trillion. In 1973, the federal debt was equal to about one-third of GDP; but by 1992, this ratio was about two-thirds, and the interest payments on the debt were nearly $200 billion dollars. Running up huge budget deficits in the 1980s and into the 1990s had the United States facing a fiscal crisis. Figure 1–12 shows the total federal debt as a percent of GDP over the past 20 years.

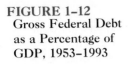

FIGURE 1–12
Gross Federal Debt
as a Percentage of
GDP, 1953–1993

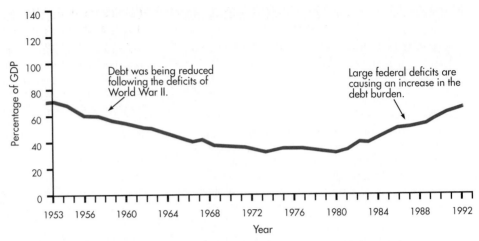

Federal budget deficits are not always inadvisable. A budget deficit for a year or two can help sustain aggregate demand during periods when private investment is weak. However, large chronic deficits are very costly to the economy and should be avoided. A budget deficit when the economy is at full employment diverts private saving, raises interest rates, and reduces the funds available for investment and long-term growth. Budget deficits also distort foreign exchange markets. The large U.S. federal budget deficit in the 1980s drove up interest rates and the value of the dollar, and it precipitated the U.S. trade deficit.

THE THREE CRITICAL ISSUES OF MACROECONOMICS

There are many puzzles and controversies in macroeconomics: Why are interest rates so high or so low? Why does unemployment vary or why does it exist at all? How should the supply of money be controlled, and does it matter? Is the budget deficit a problem? We will be examining these and other puzzles in detail in this text. But these questions and similar ones should be answered within the context of the three critical issues of macroeconomics.

1. *Inflation and short-run fluctuations in output.* In a given year, the economic well-being of an economy depends critically on the state of the business cycle. If GDP is too low relative to the economy's capacity to produce (if output is less than potential output) then there are slack resources, people are out of work, and factories and offices underutilized. If GDP is too high relative to potential output, then inflation will accelerate. We will be developing concepts that point to variations in the aggregate demand for goods and services as the principal source of the recessions and booms that make up the business cycle. These are models that tell us about the role of policy as either a cause of fluctuations or a partial cure for them.

2. *Long-run growth and productivity.* The trend of growth in GDP, and the economic standard of living that follow from this, depends most importantly on the increase in the productive capacity of an economy and on growth in productivity. Recessions come and go, so over periods of a decade or more, economic well-being is more dependent on the ability of the economy to supply goods and services than on the impact of demand and the business cycle. We will be working with models in which long-run growth is determined by investment in machinery, factories, and offices and from improvements in technology. These models suggest which economic policies may be conducive to long-term growth.

3. *International trade and competitiveness.* Given the links between the United States and other countries, it is important to look at the business cycle in an international context. Demand and hence employment in the U.S. economy depend on changes in the world economy, and policy actions to stimulate demand here at home affect the volume of imports. As people buy more goods, they will buy more from overseas. But trade has also become a longer-term issue. The United States has had a trade deficit for much of the 1980s and 1990s. In the past, U.S. companies could hire U.S. workers, pay good wages, and still make money selling overseas. There is a concern whether this can still be done. We will be looking at how policies can affect both the short-run trade position and the long-run competitiveness of the economy.

In the next chapter, we introduce the issues surrounding long-term growth, international competitiveness, and policies to sustain them. Chapter 3 begins a development of aggregate demand models. Business cycle issues will take more of our attention than long-term growth, partly because recession and inflation are areas where macroeconomic policies are so important. By contrast, while there are growth-promoting policies and there are certainly policies that can harm productivity, long-term growth depends primarily on how well the private sector itself performs. Short-term stability may be one of the most important ways in which policy can make a difference in promoting long-term growth.

SUMMARY

- There have been fluctuations in the growth rate of real GDP, reflecting the recurrent changes in output that make up the business cycle. The phases of the cycle are the peak, recession, trough, and recovery. Since 1948 the trend rate of growth of real GDP and the trend rate of productivity growth have been historically high. Living standards for most Americans have increased enormously.

- Inflation has been a persistent problem, especially since the mid-1960s. The average rate of inflation has been higher since 1948. In earlier periods, prices would rise substantially—but they would also fall. The persistence of inflation is a phenomenon of the postwar economy.

- Generating an adequate level of employment growth is an important part of economics performance. Unemployment was very high in the Great Depression and has been much lower since, although there have been serious recessions since 1970. The unemployment rate averaged 4.7 percent from 1948 to 1969. From 1970 to 1993, unemployment averaged 6.7 percent, a full two percentage points higher.

- Productivity growth occurs when output grows faster than the inputs into production. Productivity growth has slowed in recent years. The rate of increase of productivity has been much slower since the late 1960s than it was earlier. The rate of growth of real GDP has also slowed, but by less than productivity, because there has been a large increase in employment as the baby-boom generation entered the work force and the fraction of women in paid employment increased.

- The United States has run a large trade deficit since the early 1980s. This has come down in the early 1990s but remains a problem.

KEY TERMS AND CONCEPTS

average labor productivity, p. 6

business cycle, p. 12

competitiveness, p. 6

consumer price index, p. 19

Gross Domestic Product (GDP), p. 3

implicit price deflator, p. 19

inflation, p. 18

labor force, p. 16

NAIRU, p. 17

nominal GDP, p. 4

output ratio, p. 13

potential output, p. 13

price level, p. 18

productivity, p. 6

real GDP, p. 4

real GDP per capita, p. 4

unemployment rate, p. 16

weighted average, p. 20

DISCUSSION QUESTIONS AND PROBLEMS

1. Review the performance of the U.S. aggregate economy. Rank income, productivity, employment, and price stability as goals for national policy.

2. Review the role of inventory accumulation as a balancing item in the National Income and Product Accounts.

3. In the short run, policies that reduce unemployment may worsen inflation. Do you think it likely that tolerating a high rate of inflation would allow us to maintain low unemployment in the long run?

4. Which of the following contribute to GDP? Indicate whether all or part of the transaction is a contribution.
   Someone sells 50 shares of stock to someone else.
   A couple hires a housekeeper to look after their children.
   IBM imports components, assembles them, and sells the computers to business customers.

5. Consider the following figures for the components of GDP in 1990 in billions of 1987 dollars:

Personal consumption expenditures	3,272.6
Gross private domestic investment	746.8
Net exports of goods and services	−54.7
Government purchases of goods and services	932.6

Use these numbers to calculate GDP.

6. Use the following data on prices:

Year	GDP Price Deflator (1987 = 100)		
1988	103.9	1991	117.7
1989	108.5	1992	121.1
1990	113.3	1993	124.2

Calculate the rates of inflation for 1989, 1990, 1991, 1992 and 1993.

APPENDIX 1A
MEASURING OUTPUT AND NATIONAL INCOME ACCOUNTING

Gross Domestic Product

The standard measure of national output is Gross Domestic Product (GDP). This measure is defined as the current market value of all final goods and services produced by the domestic economy during a specific period (normally one year). GDP measures the market value of all goods and services sold and the value of goods added to business inventories during one year. While the definition of GDP seems straightforward, its composition reveals several potential problems; namely, how do we measure the market value of goods and services, and what types of activities does GDP exclude?

Measurement   GDP is measured in practice by the value of *sales to final users* of all goods and services. But this is also equal to the *value added* in each stage of production.

An example of how value added equals final sales can be illustrated with a loaf of bread. Our loaf of bread has four stages of production, performed by the farmer, miller, baker, and grocer. The consumer buys the bread from the grocer as a final good. Since the wheat is transformed into flour and baked as bread, each stage of production has a sales price. The value added for a stage of production expresses the additional value or additional price in the sales price resulting from that production stage. In our example, the miller receives a unit of wheat from the farmer for 30¢, the miller then mills the wheat and sells flour for 55¢ per unit. The miller's value added during this production stage is 25¢ (see Table 1A).

The amount of GDP contained in our loaf of bread is $1. To obtain $1 we add the value added for each stage of production. We do not add the sales price at each stage of production because this method counts the values of intermediate goods twice. Notice in Table 1A that, by adding the sales price for each stage of production, we overestimate GDP by $1.75 = $2.75 − $1.00. When we add the value added for each stage of production we calculate the correct GDP value of $1.

Note that the value added for each stage of production is a net contribution. If the miller is inefficient and wastes wheat in the mill, this is reflected in a lower value added for the miller's production.

TABLE 1A–1
Value Added for a Loaf of Bread

Stages of Production	Sales Price/ Unit	Value Added/ Stage of Production
Farmer → Miller	30¢	30¢
Miller → Baker	55¢	25¢
Baker → Grocer	90¢	35¢
Grocer → Consumer	**$1.00**	10¢
	$2.75	**$1.00**

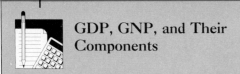

GDP, GNP, and Their Components

GDP is the total value of all goods and services produced in the economy over a given period. The U.S. Department of Commerce collects the information required to estimate GDP, and, in the process, the agency divides the goods and services into components, based on who bought the item. Consumption consists of all of the goods and services (except for new residential housing) bought by private households. Investment consists of all business purchases of durable goods, such as machine tools, computers, and factories. New construction of residential housing—apartment buildings and single-family houses—is also included in investment. Government purchases of goods and services includes all of the products and services that federal, state, and local governments buy from the private sector, such as desks, paper, aircraft, and fire trucks. The salaries paid to government employees are also included in government purchases of goods and services. GDP also includes the net purchases of goods and services by foreigners. Exports are an addition to U.S. GDP, but imports are a subtraction. Figure 1A–1 illustrates the breakdown of GDP into its components.

Figure 1A–1 also shows the relation between GDP and the Gross National Product, GNP. U.S. companies own assets overseas, such as the operations of Ford, GM, or IBM in Europe and other countries, and these assets earn income for their U.S. parents. Similarly, foreign companies now own factories and offices in the United States. For example, the Rockefeller Center is now owned by Japanese investors, while Shell Oil is affiliated with Royal Dutch/Shell, the multinational oil company based in Holland and the United Kingdom (UK); these assets earn income for their overseas parents. The net flow of income from foreign assets is called "net factor income," and this amount is added to GDP (or subtracted from it, if the net flow is negative) to give the GNP. GDP gives the income and production derived from workers and assets based in the United States. GNP includes the net income derived from the **ownership** of assets, regardless of where the assets are located. GDP has become the international standard measure of aggregate economic activity for any particular country because it is linked most directly to jobs and profits created in the domestic economy.

In the United States, the estimates of GDP and its components are presented as part of the National Income and Products Accounts published by the U.S. Department of Commerce. A basic understanding of national income accounting is important to an understanding of macroeconomics. The business cycle is caused by fluctuations in aggregate demand, which is equal to the sum of demand from consumers, investors, government, and net foreign demand. We assume that most readers are familiar with the basics of national income accounting. If that is not the case, we strongly recommend that you read the appendix to this chapter.

FIGURE 1A–1 GDP, GNP, and Their Components, 1993 (measured in billions of 1987 dollars and percent)

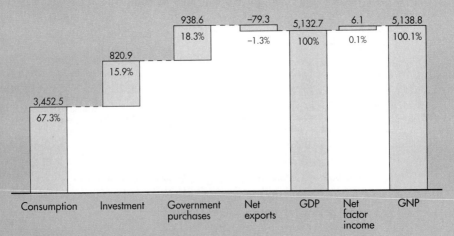

Relation to GNP   A different measure of aggregate economic activity called *Gross National Product (GNP)* used to be cited frequently. This measure is similar to GDP except for the accounting of net foreign factor payments. When a U.S. company owns a profit-making factory outside the United States, this income is included in GNP but is **not** included in GDP. Likewise, when a foreign company owns a factory in the United States, the income generated for the foreign firm is included in GDP but is not included in GNP. Thus, GDP more accurately measures the outputs produced by factors of production residing in the United States regardless of their ownership.

GNP = GDP + (Domestic income from foreign operations
        − Foreign income from domestic operations)

The calculation for 1993 is:

Gross Domestic Product	=	$5,132.7 billion
Plus: Net income from foreign operations	=	6.1 billion
Equals: Gross National Product	=	$5,138.8 billion

Net factor payments for the United States traditionally has been positive; that is, U.S. firms earned more from foreign operations than foreign firms earned from their U.S. operations.

Exclusions from Aggregate Measures of Production

Used Goods and Transfers   GDP measures *aggregate production,* and thus does not include the value of such used goods as used cars or homes that are sold during the year. These items were included in production measures when they were new, it would be a form of double counting to include them a second time. However, the value added by realtors or used-car dealers is added to this year's GDP. Also excluded from our aggregate measure are transfers from one owner to another.

Nonmarket Production   Some portions of aggregate production are not tracked in the market and do not have a market price. For example, if you rent an apartment, the rental payment is counted in GDP as the value of the service you receive in living in the apartment. If your building was converted to condominiums and you buy the apartment, the measure of GDP remains the same because an allowance is made for imputing the rental value of the apartment that you still occupy. You are counted as renting from yourself. A value for the imputed rent of owner-occupied houses and condominiums is estimated by the U.S. Department of Commerce and is added to GDP.

Many nonmarket sources of goods and services are provided in our society, such as services produced inside the family structure and benefits offered to employees ''in kind.'' These are not counted in GDP. Whether or not a nonmarket activity should be imputed into GDP is based on the size of the nonmarket activity, its variation from year to year, and the availability of market comparisons.

The largest source of nonmarket contributions to GDP is the government. Government itself produces services, such as the national defense and those whose administer federal, state, and local social programs. These services are given a value in GDP equal to the amount of wages paid to government employees. This typically under-values the contribution of government to production, because there is no test of market value applied to government output and there is no estimated value of government capital.

Can you think of other sectors in the economy where it is difficult to impute a market value? Consider the service sector.

The Underground Economy   Some market production is missed by the usual methods of data collection, because people do not want the government to know about it. People who wish to avoid taxes may insist on cash payments. Others may overstate expenses, thereby understating the value of their production. Still other economic activity may be illegal. Production and distribution of illegal drugs reportedly generates billions of dollars in revenues, yet none is reported to the government.

Some economists suggest that the underground economy is very large and has become much larger in recent years. They argue that GDP is being understated by increasing amounts. While there is no way to verify this argument, the U.S. Department of Commerce includes in GDP an estimate of the under-reporting of income and the over-statement of expenses for tax purposes.

National Income and Product Accounts

Over the past 50 years the U.S. Department of Commerce has developed and maintained an accounting system intended to provide a record of the domestic economy over time. These accounting systems were designed to facilitate policy decisions and provide a basis for understanding economic fluctuations. In a sense, the National Income and Product Accounts (NIPA) are similar to those accounts used by businesses to make decisions and track performance.

The basis of these accounts is the aggregate equality of production, expenditure, and income. By definition, total production equals the value of all expenditures made on goods and services; it also equals the value of all income payments received by those who produced the goods and services. We, therefore, can examine the inflow to GDP (production) and the outflow of GDP (income).

Consider a simple economy with business firms and households (see Figure 1A–2). Households purchase goods and services from firms; thus, goods flow from firms to households and payment of these goods flows from households to firms. Households may also provide factors of production for business firms. Typically we think of households providing labor services to firms; and so, as labor flows from households to firms, income or wages flows from the firm to the households. From this simple circular flow diagram we understand that income must equal the payment of goods and services, which in turn is equal to the value of goods and services received by the households. This shows the aggregate equality of production, expenditure, and income.

Production in the aggregate economy equals expenditure. The total value of production, Y, equals the total value of expenditure, GDP.

GDP = Total production = Total expenditure ≡ Y

The total amount of expenditure in the economy for a given time period is assigned to one of four categories: consumption (C), investment (I), government (G), and net exports $(X - IM)$. Hence,

$$GDP \equiv Y = C + I + G + (X - IM)$$

The breakdown of GDP into its categories was shown in Figure 1A–1, which also includes net foreign income and GNP.

Overview of Expenditure Categories

Consumption (C)   Consumption includes the value of all final goods and services that households and nonprofit institutions purchase, including food, clothing (nondurable), durable goods, such as automobiles and furniture, and consumption services. At times it is difficult to distinguish consumption from investment or intermediate goods. For example, construction materials are intermediate goods if used in the construction industry; they are consumption goods if households buy them for do-it-yourself projects.

Durable consumption goods pose our first accounting problem. Durable goods are those that provide value for more than one period. So in a sense, durable goods provide a value stream over the lifetime use of the good. An automobile, for example, provides benefit for several years. Yet, the accounts treat the automobile as only providing service during the period in which it was purchased. The only exception to this rule is consumer housing.

Investment (I)   Investment in the NIPA is called gross private domestic investment. The Department of Commerce classifies the following as investment:

- All business expenditures on structures and equipment.
- All expenditures on new residential structures.
- All changes in inventories by business.

The change in inventories is an important balancing item. The inclusion of inventory accumulation ensures that production and expenditure are equal. Goods produced and not sold to an outside customer are kept by the producer as part of inventory. When firms produce more than they sell, the unsold goods are added to inventories.

FIGURE 1A–2
Circular Flow Diagram of a Simple Economy

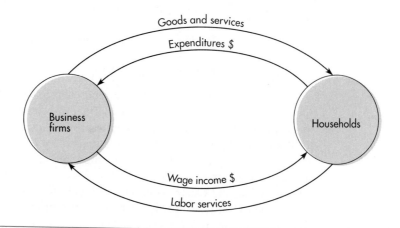

Those inventories are included in investment and valued in GDP at the same market prices as comparable items that have been sold during the period.

Government Purchases (G)   This category includes purchases of goods and services by all levels of government (national, state, local). These purchases include such items as aircraft, computers, educational supplies, and the wages and salaries of government employees. Certain transfer payments, such as Social Security payments or unemployment compensation, are not included. Transfers are considered a transfer of ownership of already produced income (similar to the transfer of already produced assets); therefore, including them would double-count their value. Typically transfer payments are given to households.

Exports and Imports (X − IM)   When consumers purchase goods and services from abroad, the amount of expenditure is considered an import. The production of these items is not in the United States and should not be added to domestic product (the value of goods produced in the country). Furthermore, a product produced in the United States but purchased overseas is considered an export. Even though it is used overseas, the product or service was produced domestically. In short, those items produced domestically should be included in GDP, or total production; items not produced domestically are not to be counted as domestic production.

GDP and National Income

In the aggregate economy, production equals income; but in the NIPA, there is a difference between GDP and national income (NI). The main differences between GDP and NI are depreciation and indirect taxes.

GDP	
less:	Capital consumption allowance
------	
equals:	Net domestic product (NDP)

NDP	
less:	Indirect business taxes
less:	Business transfers
less:	Business payments to government enterprises
------	
equals:	National income (NI)

National income also equals the income received by those who contributed to production within the country. It is defined as compensation of employees, proprietors' income, rental income, corporate profits, and net interest.

The factories, office buildings, and machinery (capital goods) purchased by businesses during a year are part of production and are included in GDP. But GDP does not account for the fact that capital goods wear out over time. The **capital stock** consists of all the capital goods still in use, including those purchased in previous years. The extent to which the capital stock wears out is called "depreciation." Our GDP measure of output doesn't account for depreciation of our capital stock.

While GDP is a good measure of total production, it can be misleading as an income measure. A business makes a profit and other forms of business income, but uses up part of its capital stock. It subtracts from profit an allowance for the reduction of its existing capital. Business income net of depreciation is included in national income. In national income accounting, depreciation is a **capital consumption allowance** and measures the capital consumed or used up in the production process. We do not have good information on depreciation, because the accounting rules for depreciation that businesses actually use are not connected to the true wearing out of the capital. These rules are creatures of our tax laws. Nevertheless, the Department of Commerce estimates as best it can a measure of depreciation. GDP less depreciation is **net domestic product (NDP).**

When $100 is paid for a good, not all of the money is kept by the business firm. Some of it goes to the government. These payments to the government are called ''indirect taxes.'' They include state sales taxes and business property taxes, as well as various state and federal excise taxes. The value of these taxes is included in GDP but not in NI.

The other subtractions performed on GDP to obtain NI are business transfer payments, net payments to government enterprises, and statistical discrepancies. Business transfers are the largest of these other items and include gifts that corporations make to individuals, universities, public television, and so on. These payments are included in GDP but not in NI.

C H A P T E R   2

LONG-TERM GROWTH AND COMPETITIVENESS

INTRODUCTION

Competition forces firms, employees, and entire nations to become more productive. Closing off competition, either nationally or internationally, discourages innovation and takes away the incentive for change and improvement. Competition is the life blood of productive market economics.

In this chapter we will look at the forces that either contribute to or hinder an economy's ability to combine national and international competitiveness with long-term growth: growth of productivity, growth of potential output, and growth of standards of living. We will conclude the chapter by taking our first look at the economic policies that can contribute to growth. Much of the remainder of the text will be devoted to understanding how the economy operates and how policies influence that operation. We will continually remind ourselves how a well-functioning economy, with policies directed toward long-term growth, can foster significant improvements in living standards for its citizens.

The status of average living standards can be seen by looking at real GDP per capita. Real GDP per capita in the U.S. economy has increased by a factor of 6 during this century. Almost all of this increase in output per person consisted of an increase in our ability to supply goods and services—growth in the size of potential output, (Y^p), relative to the population. While fluctuations in aggregate demand were important in recessions and recoveries, their effects balanced out over the long run, leaving the growth of potential output the primary cause of long-term growth in real GDP per capita.

The period 1929–1990 is a good one to look to assess long-term growth. Data prior to this are not good and this period starts before the downturn of the 1930s and ends before the early 90s recession. Real income per capita grew by approximately 1.8 percent per year from 1929 to

1990, but there is nothing preordained about a 1.8 percent long-term per capita rate of growth. Many preindustrial economies experience near zero per capita growth, and rapidly developing economies, such as China in the 1990s, can sustain double-digit growth rates. Good economic policies can make a difference to long-term growth. Paul Samuelson, the first American winner of the Nobel prize in economics, pointed out that "if economic rationality can improve policies so that GNP grows by 0.5 percent more per year, then economics is worth the effort." The reason that seemingly small differences in growth have such dramatic effects comes from the impact of compounding growth rates over long periods.

If over that 1929–90 period, real per capita income growth had averaged one-half of a percent per year higher (2.3 percent) or lower (1.3 percent) than realized, then the level of per capita GNP in 1990 would have been 35 percent higher or lower than was actually obtained. Had growth occurred at a hypothetical 2.3 percent, rather than the actual 1.8 percent rate, the typical family would have had better health insurance, a larger apartment or house, some vacation, a newer car, and perhaps a heightened sense of confidence in the U.S. economy. Conversely, had the growth path been 0.5 percent worse than actual, median household income would have been a third lower and many more families would have been below the poverty level! Over time, small differences in the growth rates of economic performance make a very large difference. If we look forward 60 years, the effect of rates of growth that differ by one-half of 1 percent are just as dramatic in terms of the future of our standard of living.

GDP per capita depends on the amount of work done by the population and the productivity of that work. Additional hours of work generate more income, but at a cost in reduced leisure. Simply earning more because of more hours worked would not be a clear gain in living standard. A 70–90-hour work week, such as was the norm in the 19th century, generates more income than a 35-hour week, but leaves little time or energy for enjoying the gains in income. Fortunately, the modern trend in industrialized economies has been a decline in the number of hours worked per week, declining to below 40 hours in the United States.

While the United States has experienced a long-term decline in hours worked per employee, there has been a long-term rise in the fraction of the population that is working. There has been some decline in male labor force participation, but a much larger rise in female labor force participation.

The other element that generates growth in per capita income is productivity. As we said in Chapter 1, the simplest measure of productivity is average labor productivity and we will look at this in terms of *output per full-time worker*. However, because of the changes in hours worked per full-time employee, we will at times also look at output per hour of work.

THE AGGREGATE PRODUCTION FUNCTION

Looking at trends in output per worker will only tell us the history of growth. We need to look at how output is produced—what goes into the process of production—to understand which factors bring about higher or lower rates of growth.

Most goods and services are supplied by businesses employing labor, capital, land, technology, and management to produce and sell output (products and services). Each business has a different capacity to produce output, depending on the resources under their control and how well they use technology and management to organize production. Since each business enterprise is somewhat unique, with a large number of different arrangements for bringing about production, we need a way to describe how the productive capacity of the economy is determined without having to focus on the particulars of each business. We do this by collapsing many different sources of contribution to production into just a few broad categories, the simplest being capital and labor. Using capital and labor to generate output, we can then describe three ways to increase output: more labor (more workers or everybody working more), more capital (increasing the amount of physical capital), and perhaps most importantly, by getting more output without increasing the quantity of labor or capital (i.e., by improving the techniques used to generate production, by better technology. Economists employ a shorthand description of this simplified description of the production process for the economy as a whole: the aggregate **production function.**

production function
A way to describe how the productive capacity of the economy is determined by capital, labor, and technology. $Y^p = F(K, N, T_{ECH})$

This function relates how much can be produced: potential output (Y^p) to **labor input** (N), **capital input** (K), and **technology** (T_{ECH}). Labor input is either the number of employees or the number of hours worked. Capital input is an estimate of the services provided by the available stock of machinery, factories, and offices. The state of technology describes the cumulative effects of scientific advances and applied research and development. Changes in technology also incorporate improvements in management methods and ways of organizing production that raise the productive capacity of factories and offices. In the United States, the growth in labor, capital, and technology has contributed to the economy's substantial growth in potential output.

labor input
Labor input, N, is either the number of employees or the number of hours worked.

The aggregate production function is shown in Equation 2–1.

$$Y^p = F(K, N, T_{ECH}) \tag{2-1}$$

capital input
Capital input, K, is an estimate of the services provided by the available stock of machinery, factories, and offices.

Potential output depends on the labor and capital inputs used in production and on the technology in which they are used. Our description of production has separate effects for technology and inputs. Growth can come from increasing either capital or labor, or both, even if there is no change in technology. Similarly, improvements in technology with no changes in capital or labor will also increase potential output. When increases in technological improvements are combined with increases in the amount of capital and/or labor, potential output goes up by more than the increase in technology or inputs alone. This makes sense. We can certainly produce more with more inputs working the same way as before and we can produce even more with the more inputs working smarter than before.

technology
The state of technology, T_{ECH}, describes the cumulative effects of improved methods of production.

Diminishing Returns to a Single Factor and Returns to Scale

diminishing returns
To a single factor of production means that successive incremental increases in a *single* input result in smaller and smaller increments to output.

constant returns to scale
Constant returns to scale occur when a given percentage increase in all of the inputs to production results in an equal percentage increase in output.

Increases in capital, labor, and technology will raise potential output, but by how much and for how long? Many economic models of growth argue that, because of **diminishing returns,** increases in either capital or labor *alone* will not be able to generate sustained growth. If capital alone is increased, workers eventually reach the point where extra tools and machinery fail to make a productive difference, because there aren't enough people or hours available to use the new equipment. The gains in potential output garnered from adding capital begin to slow down.

Successive incremental increases in employment with no increase in capital or change in technology will generate successively smaller and smaller incremental increases in output. The same is true for increments to capital with no change in the labor input or in technology.

At the same time, traditional models have usually assumed that increases in the size or scale of production (keeping capital and labor in the same proportions) will result in a proportional increase in output. Suppose a factory is constructed of a given size with a given set of machines inside it, and the factory is staffed by a work force of a given size. Then suppose that an identical factory is built next to it. We can make a presumption about production. The two identical factories will produce twice the output of one of the factories alone. Holding technology constant, output will go up proportionally, and the economy is said to have **constant returns to scale.** If there are constant returns to scale, a 10 percent increase or decrease in *both capital and labor together* will result in a 10 percent increase or decrease in output. The change in output will result from the change in inputs, not because labor productivity changed but because more labor capital was applied to the task. Output per unit of labor input will remain the same.

Returns to scale are assessed by considering the impact of increases in capital and labor with technology taken as given. Of course, in any practical situation, technology will change as the amount of capital and labor change, so statistical methods have to be used to decide whether there are constant returns to scale. For example, we can see how the output from small and large plants differs when they have similar technologies. Such studies have indicated that constant returns to scale is a reasonable generalization of production conditions in U.S. factories and offices.

However, in the last few years it has been suggested that a comparison of plants or companies of different sizes does not tell the full story about returns to scale. Firms in the same industry tend to congregate in certain areas, such as auto companies in Detroit or high-tech companies in Silicon Valley. This suggests there are synergies among companies that are close together, that grow together, and that foster productivity growth. These synergies, it is argued, lead to *increasing returns to scale,* where doubling of capital and labor inputs leads to more than a doubling of output. Putting two identical factories together more than doubles output. We explore this idea in the box on Worldwide Growth Experiences. In the main part of our analysis, we will assume constant returns to scale (CRS). Working with a model of production that exhibits CRS is a useful simplification of the complex reality of the actual economy. Assuming CRS allows us to convert from the aggregate production to the *intensive*

FIGURE 2–1
The Intensive Pro-
duction Function:
Diminishing
Returns

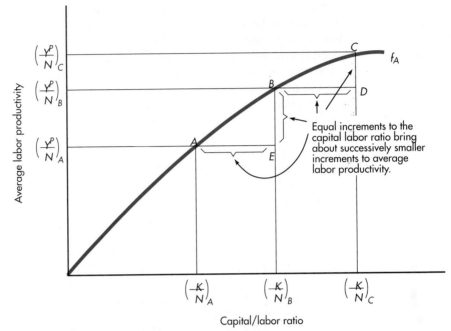

As the capital/labor ratio increases, there are diminishing returns.

production function, which describes productivity as depending on only two charac-teristics of the economy—the amount of capital available for each worker and the level of technology employed in production.

Provided there are constant returns to scale, average labor productivity is deter-mined only by the two elements of capital per worker (K/N) and technology (T_{ECH}). The production function from Equation 2–1 is transformed in Equation 2–2 into the **intensive production function.**

intensive production function
The relationship between capital per worker, *K/N* and output per worker.

$$Y_P/N = f(K/N, T_{ECH}) \tag{2-2}$$

Figure 2–1 illustrates diminishing returns to capital along an intensive production function. As the amount of capital increases relative to the amount of labor, capital intensity (K/N) rises. By providing more capital per worker, output goes up, but at a diminishing rate of increase. Successive increases in capital intensity [$(K/N)_A$ to $(K/N)_B$ to $(K/N)_C$] along a particular production function [f_A], also brings about increases in average labor productivity, once again at a diminishing rate of increase. Successive increases in capital intensity [$(K/N)_B$ to $(K/N)_C$] along a particular produc-tion function [f_A], also brings about increases in average labor productivity, once again at a diminishing rate of increase.

The constraint created by diminishing returns to increasing capital intensity can be overcome if there is an improvement in technology, which accompanies the increases in capital per worker. In Figure 2–2, we describe several intensive production

FIGURE 2–2

The Intensive
Production
Function: Shifts in
Technology

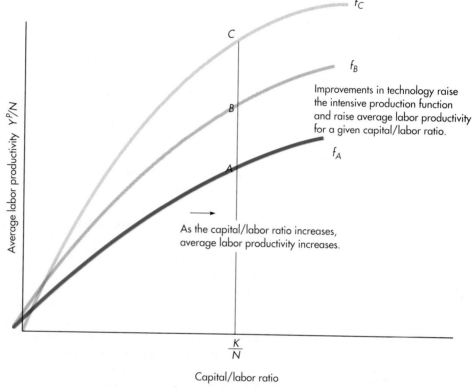

Average labor productivity depends on the capital/labor ratio and technology.

functions (f_A, f_B, and f_C), where the function is shifted up from A to B to C with improvements in technology. Even with an unchanged capital/labor ratio, improvements in the state of technology raise productivity.

CAPITAL ACCUMULATION AND LABOR FORCE GROWTH

The relationship along the intensive production function between capital intensity and productivity formed the basis of the neo-classical model of growth, initially developed by Robert M. Solow.[1] The intensive production shown in Equation 2–2 describes how the average labor productivity grows at a diminishing rate as the amount of capital per

---

[1] Robert M. Solow, "A Contribution to the Theory of Economic Growth," *Quarterly Journal of Economics,* February 1956.

In this chapter we simply introduce the basic concepts of the neo-classical growth model. This model provides the major framework for the study of growth and is so named because, akin to classical economics (see Chapter 14), it posits labor and capital markets without necessary shortages or surpluses, but rather flexibility in the proportions of each. In Chapter 17 we describe the model more completely along with a further analysis of the causes of growth.

worker rises (K/N). In a growing economy, capital intensity will rise when the rate of growth of capital exceeds the rate of growth of the labor force.

So, in a growing economy, increasing labor productivity will come about if there is an accumulation of capital relative to the growth of the labor force. But remember, the capacity for bringing about productivity gains via capital accumulation alone is limited because of diminishing returns. Solow developed a key result in his model of growth: in the absence of improvements in technology, the growth of productivity would slow down and stall. Economies that saved and invested larger fractions of their income in capital goods would reach a higher *level* of productivity than those that saved less. But eventually productivity *growth* would stall no matter how high the saving rate.

Solow's model pointed to the crucial role for technology in maintaining productivity growth and in maintaining the profitability of capital.

Allocating Growth to Capital and Technology

The neo-classical growth model illustrates the limits to what capital alone can achieve over the very long run, and this points to technological change as a key to productivity growth in the long run. How relevant is this conclusion for growth in practice? Solow estimated how much the intensive production function had moved up over time (see Figure 2–2). Solow estimated that 87 percent of the increase in average labor productivity had come from technological change (the upward shift in the function) and only 13 percent from the increase in capital per worker at the same level of technology (the movement along the function). Other researchers using different methods came up with somewhat different results: but *there was a general and surprising consensus that in the 20th century technological change rather than capital accumulation, was the key factor in the long-term growth of productivity.*

Economic Growth with Technological Change

Solow found that is was vital to incorporate technological change into a growth model, and he did this in a very specific way. The model assumes that technology has the effect of "augmenting" the labor input. Technology is used to make people more productive. With this key assumption, the model provides an analysis of long-term growth in an economy with both capital accumulation and technological change. If the rate of growth of the work force and the fraction of income devoted to saving are constant, then the model makes the following predictions about long-term growth:

> Potential output will grow over the long term at a steady rate, and the capital input will grow at the same rate.
>
> Over the long term, labor productivity will grow at a rate equal to the rate of technological change. Wages will grow at the same rate as labor productivity.
>
> Over the long term, the capital input will grow faster than the labor input, but the profitability of capital will not decline.
>
> Over the long term, the rate of productivity *growth* does *not* depend on the fraction of income that is devoted to saving and investment.
>
> Over the long term, the *level* of productivity is high for economies with high-saving propensities and low for economies with high rates of labor force growth.

· For economies that have not yet reached their long-run path of stable growth, saving and investing a larger fraction of their incomes will increase their rates of productivity growth.

The neo-classical growth model states technological change allows the economy to achieve steady growth, and productivity can increase indefinitely. Improvements in technology also help to sustain the profitability of capital. The amount of capital per worker can increase over the long run without running into the effect of diminishing returns, as long as there are improvements in technology. Technological change, to a degree, can offset the effect of diminishing returns to capital.

On the other hand, even in the model with technological change, there are limits to what capital can do for productivity growth. If an economy saves so much that its rate of capital accumulation gets ahead of what can be accommodated by increases in the work force and improvements in technology, then diminishing returns to capital sets in, the profitability of investment declines, and the growth rate of productivity will gradually slow down.

These lessons from the growth model carry implications about policies to increase growth. They suggest a balanced approach is needed, in which new technology is accompanied by additions to the capital stock. If there is not enough technological change, the profitability of investment will start to decline. If there is not enough investment, the economy will not be taking advantage of the potential for growth created by its improved technology (including improved management methods as part of technological change).

The neo-classical growth model provides an adequate broad-brush picture consistent with the long-term history of the United States, except for business cycles. The Solow model also provides an important framework for thinking about growth and examining the impact of increases in capital per worker and improvements in technology; but the predictions it makes about steady growth depend on the assumptions there are steady increases in technology and in the work force. The actual economy is much more complicated than the simple model. Solow's original work was done in the 1950s and 60s, and, while his neo-classical model correctly pointed to the critical role for technology enhancement, it did not describe the economic forces that bring about technology gains. Recent work on productivity has placed attention on the sources of technological change. This new literature has described technological change as a form of capital accumulation itself, namely the accumulation of **knowledge capital:** investments in education, R&D, and new ways of making production more efficient.

As part of this new interest in growth there has also been an increased interest in why so many countries in the world have been unable to develop. It has been pointed out that the Solow model also does not really explain why some countries have succeeded in growing rapidly and others have not. We will look more closely at the historical experience of U.S. growth and productivity as we make comparisons and analyses of how several nations experienced growth over time.

In the next section, we will take our own look at U.S. economic growth over the period since World War II. We will use the lessons of the growth model to help us understand actual growth, and we will see why there is not an exact match between the model's predictions and the actual historical experience of U.S. economic growth.

knowledge capital

The accumulation of ideas, skills, research and education that contribute to productivity.

Worldwide Growth Experiences

The first country to industrialize was Great Britain while Australia had the highest per capita income at the end of the 19th century because of its abundance of natural resources and small population. U.S. production per person overtook those in Britain and Australia around the turn of the century and has remained at the top of the international ladder since then. Over this same period, some countries have moved up in the rankings of per capita GDP, and others have moved down. Japan, Korea, and Taiwan are good examples of some very poor countries that have grown rapidly. Other countries have fallen behind, such as Britain, Argentina, and Australia.

In recent years new economic research has examined patterns of economic growth over the long term and tried to understand why some countries have achieved sustained economic development and others have not. This new research has provided support for the standard ways of looking at growth, notably the neo-classical growth model, but it has also challenged old ideas, specifically the idea of constant returns to scale. Many economists now believe that, as economies grow richer, they achieve certain advantages that help them to keep growing rapidly.

The new debate over the way to achieve economic growth has centered first on the issue of "convergence." Is there a natural tendency for countries that have low per capita GDP to grow faster than countries with high per capita GDP and hence to catch up to the rich countries? Will economies converge to the same level of per capita income? William Baumol and Edward Wolff developed the idea of economic convergence among the main industrial countries. As we showed in Figure 1–2, the main industrial countries have converged to much closer levels of GDP per capita in the 1990s than was the case a century ago.

Baumol and Wolff suggest a number of reasons why countries grow faster if they are below the most productive and richest country. These ideas build on the findings of the neo-classical growth model, particularly in

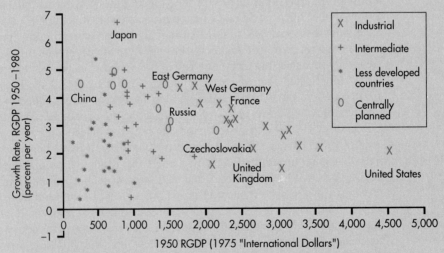

Growth rates of real gross domestic product (RGDP), 1950–1980, versus 1950 RGDP, for 72 countries classified by 1960 RGDP (in 1975 "international dollars").

seeing technological change and capital accumulation as the main sources of growth. Countries that have less capital per worker than the most developed countries will have opportunities for profitable investment. They can exploit these with saving and investment generated internally or they can encourage businesses in the rich countries to invest in their country. Technology can also be borrowed. The U.S. imported steam locomotives, internal combustion engines, chemicals, and textiles in the 19th and early 20th centuries. As the U.S. became the technology leader during this century, Europe as well as Japan took advantage of its technology. In practice, technology and capital accumulation often go together, because machinery and equipment embody the latest technological developments.

Baumol and Wolff's data and reasoning are very compelling. Almost certainly, there is some validity to the idea of convergence; but the story of convergence, is more complicated than it looks initially. The sample of countries in Figure 1–2 is very small. If the countries of Africa, Latin America, and Asia are added to the sample, the picture changes dramatically.

If there is a tendency for convergence, the lower initial level of GDP per capita, the faster will be the subsequent growth of GDP per capita. The convergence hypothesis argues that starting out below the frontier of technology allows countries to borrow technology and grow more rapidly. The figure in the box illustrates that most countries have not closed the gap with the group of richest countries. There is no tendency for the countries that were poor in 1960 to grow more rapidly after 1960. Critics argue that the supporting data was simply selected from the group of countries that had converged and did not provide a valid test of whether there is convergence.

The pattern of growth in many countries suggests to some economists an *increasing returns to scale,* which occurs when an increase in all of the inputs to production of a given percentage result in a larger percentage increase in output. The *new growth theory,* led by economist Paul Romer, argues that capital accumulation is the basic source of long-term growth, once the definition of capital is broadened to include "knowledge capital" and

"human capital." The neo-classical growth model assumes that increasing capital alone will result in diminishing returns. The *new growth theory* assumes instead that an increase in capital *by itself* of, say, 10 percent will also increase output by 10 percent. An increase in both capital and labor will then increase output by a larger percentage than the percentage increase in the two inputs to production. Increasing returns to scale is one explanation of why richer countries continue to grow more rapidly than poorer countries.

When the definition of capital accumulation includes knowledge and human capital, the new growth theory does not look so inconsistent with the old Solow growth model. The new models simply include technological change as part of a broader concept of capital accumulation.

The new theory stresses that changing the technology or adding to the skills of the work force require resources. The new theorists argue technological change does not arrive "exogenously" at a rate that is fixed and independent of economic decisions within the economy. Technology should be modeled as part of the process of economic growth.

The new theorists may be trying to do the impossible, however, in trying to explain *fully* the origin of technological change. New scientific ideas come with a good deal of serendipity, and the same is true for new technologies. In practice, attempts to accumulate knowledge capital by stepping up R&D funds run into diminishing returns. For any given country, especially small countries, the pace of technological change may be partly or even primarily exogenous, depending on scientific and technological progress around the world.

Over time, the best ideas of the Solow neo-classical model are being combined with the best ideas of the new analysis to give us a better understanding of the sources of long-term economic growth. When we look at policies to increase growth, we will take lessons from both approaches to the theory of growth.

For a more detailed review of the new growth theory see the Winter 1994 issue of the *Journal of Economic Perspectives.* Paul Romer, Robert Solow and others discuss these ideas.

POSTWAR ECONOMIC GROWTH IN THE U.S. ECONOMY

Figure 2–3 shows output in the business sector of the U.S. economy grew at well over 3 percent a year from 1948 until 1968 but has slowed somewhat since then. The capital input grew between 3 and 4 percent a year except for a brief period, 1968–73. Capital grew slower than output before 1968 (the ratio of output to capital was falling) but grew faster than output after 1968 (this ratio was rising).

The growth rate of labor input (hours of work in Figure 2–3) has been quite variable, reflecting many different factors, such as immigration, changing birth rates, changing participation of women, early retirement, and reductions in hours worked per employee. Labor input growth has always been less than output growth, so average labor productivity has risen. The growth of average labor productivity has declined, being 2.65 percent a year over the period 1948–68 but much less than that in the 1970s and 80s.

Figure 2–3 also shows the rate of technological change calculated by using a method developed by Solow. The picture that emerges is a rapid rate rate of technological change fueled the growth of productivity prior to 1968 but has declined as productivity growth has declined since 1968 and especially since 1973. From this perspective, the U.S. economy did not experience smooth and steady growth. This is not surprising since the labor force, the capital stock, and the improvements in technology have not grown steadily. More problematic has been the trend toward a substantial reduction or slowdown in the rate of productivity growth.

In summary, these figures indicate that the U.S. economy has not converged to a steady rate of growth. The main reasons for this are that the rate of growth of the labor input and the rate of technological change have not been constant. This has resulted in a substantial slowdown in the rate of productivity growth. Though this slowdown has shown signs of turnaround since 1992, it's still too soon to tell if a 20-year downtrend has been permanently reversed.

FIGURE 2–3   Rates of Growth for Output, Average Labor Productivity, Capital, and Technology—U.S. Nonfarm Business Sector, 1948–1990 (percent per year)

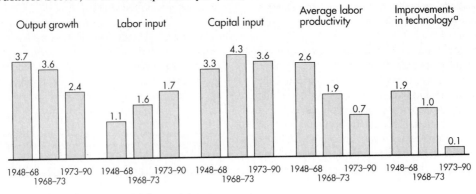

ªCalculated as the growth in multifactor productivity.

Source: Calculated by the authors from data provided by the Bureau of Labor Statistics.

THE SLOWDOWN IN PRODUCTIVITY GROWTH

The slowdown in productivity growth has had major consequences for the economy. The neo-classical growth model suggests there is a close link between productivity growth and wage growth. For real wages (adjusted for inflation) to rise each year, workers have to generate the extra output necessary to bring in additional revenues needed to pay the higher wages. Were wage increases to continue in the absence of productivity growth, labor costs would quickly grow to exceed all revenues; and not only would firms fail to have enough income to pay for capital, rents, materials, and so on, they would not be able to generate enough revenue to cover labor costs and production would cease. Therefore, in the long run, the growth of wages that are highly related to standards of living are linked to the growth of productivity. A productivity slowdown, if unreversed and continued for a long time will force a similar decline in the growth of real wages. Figure 2–4 shows the historical patterns of productivity and wage growth. Both trend lines show a slowdown in rates of growth in the 1970s. Productivity is measured by output per hour of work, and wages are measured by the hourly compensation of employees.

The slowing of technology improvements can push down the profits of businesses. Slow productivity growth is bad news for workers and bad news for the owners of businesses. What has caused the problem?

Reasons for Slow Productivity Growth

Although political rhetoric often suggests that every problem has a single identifiable cause, economic research reveals reality to be complex—there is no single factor that has been identified as the cause of the productivity growth slowdown. There is, however, a well-researched list of likely suspects.

FIGURE 2–4
Output per Hour and Real Compensation: 1947–1990 (1973 = 100)

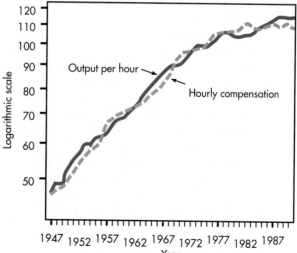

Note: Output per hour and real hourly compensation in the U.S. business sector.

Quality of the Work Force   The level of skill and experience of the work force has declined, or has grown less rapidly than it once did. As the baby boom generation left school in the 1970s and started to work, this created a younger and less experienced work force. The increased numbers of women finding jobs also meant that the average experience level of the employed population declined in the 70s and 80s. This problem contributed somewhat to slower productivity growth in the United States over those decades, although it is now solving itself, because the new labor force entrants of the 70s and 80s become the experienced workers in the 1990s.

As the problem of inexperience has abated, however, there has been a new concern about the capability of the new work force—a decline in the quality of education for most students and the adverse effects of this on productivity. Standardized tests of general academic achievement rose rapidly after World War II but have stagnated since then or even fallen. There is a particular problem with high school students who do not go on to college. They see little to be gained from studying, and, too often, they miss out on the literacy and numeracy skills that are increasingly important even on semiskilled jobs. Employers complain they have trouble introducing new technologies that require careful recordkeeping or an understanding of written instructions.

Capital per Worker   Output per worker increases with the amount of capital per worker, and there has been some decline in the productivity boost from capital accumulation. The United States is a low-saving economy, and, in fact, the national saving rate has declined dangerously. This has been offset in part, but only in part, by foreign borrowing. The rate of capital accumulation has been declining in the past few years. Moreover, there have been major structural changes in the economy. Many factories and offices that were productive in one line of business have been closed, because that business has been lost to foreign competition or to the effect of changing patterns of demand at home. As a result of these structural changes, more of our investment has had to be used to replace old capital.

infrastructure
The network of systems that are in the public sector, such as interstate highways, roads, and sewers.

There has also been a decline in investment in public capital, the so-called **infrastructure.** The building of the interstate highway system in the 1950s and 60s, and other similar projects, increased the productivity of the private sector. The ending of those projects, with no comparable new ones being added, contributed to the slowing of productivity growth.

Measurement Error   One piece of good news is that the severity of the slowdown has been exaggerated, because of the way in which productivity is measured. The slowdown is not quite as severe in reality as it looks in official data series. Productivity in practice is measured relatively well in manufacturing and in some parts of the service sector; but it is measured very poorly, or not at all, in some other parts of the service sector. Productivity as it is measured in manufacturing has done well in the 1980s and early 90s, achieving a growth rate equal to its increase after World War II. Some service industries have also done well over this same period, such as telecommunications and wholesale and retail trade. The weakest industries for productivity growth have been in finance, insurance, real estate, and construction where productivity measurement is very weak.

It is not possible to explain away all of the slowdown in productivity growth as simply a measurement error. But part of the slowdown can be explained that way.

Government Regulation   Government regulation of the economy has increased, and we have paid a productivity price for that. Some of the regulations were necessary, such as control of toxic waste, but some of them were not worthwhile or were badly designed to meet a specific goal. Regardless of the value of the regulations, such industries as electricity generation, mining, and chemicals have had to invest in pollution abatement equipment and other measures to meet environmental or worker safety regulations. This prevented using these resources for productivity improvements. When regulations were influenced by political considerations (e.g., requiring power plants to use smokestack scrubbers, rather than low-sulfur coal), the productivity price of these regulations was higher than necessary.

Some Slowdown May Have Been Inevitable   There was an unusual period after World War II when new technologies were waiting to be exploited, and businesses were eager to invest to serve the demands of consumers who had been unable to buy many products during the war. Part of the slowdown of the 70s and 80s was a return to more normal rates of productivity growth after the unusual 1950s and 60s.

Technological Depletion   Perhaps the rate of technological change has declined because the opportunities for pushing out the frontier of technology have been depleted. Electric power, the internal combustion engine, the introduction of mass production methods, the development of plastics, the tremendous gains achieved from building huge steel mills and power plants, the introduction of the supermarket, magnetic encoding of checks, and many other developments over the last century fueled very large increases in productivity. Further changes of this magnitude may not be possible in some industries. R&D has become much more complex and expensive. The easy ways to improve things have been tried already. There has been an exhaustion of technological opportunities in some areas, and a failure to open up enough new ones.

There is one puzzle, though, before we accept this as one of the reasons for the slowdown. There has been an explosion of technology in one area, namely computers and electronics. Why has this not led to the kind of productivity advances that followed from earlier technologies? One answer is that businesses are still learning how to benefit from information technology. This could mean future productivity increases will be better. Let's hope so.

Management Problems   Management strategies that led to success in the 1950s and 60s were no longer appropriate to the changed economic environment of the 70s and beyond. Starting in the 1970s, U.S. managers had to cope with bouts of severe inflation and recession, increased foreign competition, an energy crisis, new health and safety regulations, and other changes. These may have diverted their time away from managing the changes needed to increase productivity.

The growth of scientific management may have actually made things worse. A new generation of business school trained managers demanded the benefits from every innovation or investment be quantified, and they often concluded that the costs of change were not worth the benefits. Their calculations may have missed the full effects of innovation, including the options for further change that are created by innovation. It is easy to miss vague and uncertain future benefits, even though these may be important in practice. Scientific management can be an important tool for raising productivity by finding sources of inefficiency and through redesign of production processes; but when misapplied, it can lead to missed opportunities and underinvestment.

Conclusions on the Productivity Growth Slowdown

The problem of slow productivity growth has been of concern for over 20 years. There is no shortage of economists and noneconomists who are convinced they know exactly what has caused the problem, including many who believe the slowdown is not real but simply an illusion created by faulty measurement. In our judgment, the evidence does not justify such certainty. Most likely, the slowdown is real but not as severe as standard data suggest, and there are several causes of slower growth, not just one.

The slow growth of productivity in the U.S. economy is linked in many people's minds with an apparent decline of the ability of U.S. manufacturers to compete internationally. The United States seems to have a competitiveness problem.

THE COMPETITIVENESS OF U.S. MANUFACTURING

The manufacturing sector of our economy is vital to overall economic health. Manufacturing output comprises 20 percent of total GDP, and manufacturing employment is about the same share of total employment. The manufacturing sector performs most of the R&D in the economy, and the manufacturing sector accounts for the largest share of U.S. exports and the competitiveness of U.S. goods. This makes manufacturing the prime determinant of the terms under which we trade in the world economy.

Recently Economist Paul Krugman has strongly attacked the concept of competitiveness, calling it a dangerous national obsession. Krugman makes some good points. Only a modest fraction of GDP is directly involved in international trade. U.S. living standards depend more on services than manufacturing. Still, competitiveness is an important concept. It points to competition, and competition against international best practice. Increasingly, multinational companies in service industries are competing against each other worldwide just as manufacturers compete. Facing the competition against the best in the world is a key to productivity improvement.

In this section, we look at the performance of U.S. manufacturing, focusing on its productivity and its international competitiveness. There are legitimate concerns about the performance of this sector. In particular, workers in American manufacturing have had a very tough time over the past 20 years. Many companies have closed plants or closed down altogether in the face of fierce competition from overseas. Another concern is the erosion of the lead in technology that the United States once enjoyed.

On the other hand, the picture of U.S. manufacturing is not all bleak. The manufacturing sector of the U.S. economy has done much better in terms of productivity growth than the rest of the economy. The United States still retains a lead in technology in many areas and has been gaining ground in semiconductors where it seemed the U.S. industry had fallen behind. Some of the things that are held up as problems of manufacturing should be seen as necessary parts of a dynamic industry. A successful manufacturing sector should have high and growing productivity and will experience a lot of turnover with frequent plant closings. If manufacturing is participating as it should be in international trade, then production and jobs will be moved around. Many jobs will be lost, although others will be gained.

Productivity in U.S. Manufacturing

We have seen that productivity growth has slowed in the U.S. economy as a whole since the late 1960s, but, somewhat surprisingly, the manufacturing sector is an exception to this general rule. Figure 2–5 shows labor productivity growth over three periods since 1948, and it is growing strongly except for the spell from 1973–81.[2]

Productivity growth in U.S. manufacturing has been doing pretty well in relation to the recent past, but perhaps we have been overtaken by other countries. Figure 2–6 shows the levels of productivity in the United States, Germany, the United Kingdom, and Japan for manufacturing over the period 1973–89. In the figure, the level of productivity is set equal to 100 for the United States in 1973 simply for illustrative purposes. It shows the U.S. manufacturing sector still has a lead in productivity over the other countries. To the extent the time series comparisons are valid, the figure shows very little catch-up of productivity. In fact, Germany appears to have closed the productivity gap in the late 70s and then fallen back. The U.K. data are notable for showing a "Mrs. Thatcher effect," with productivity flat until 1981 and then rising rapidly. As well as looking good relative to the past, U.S. manufacturing productivity looks surprisingly good, relative to its main international competitors.

FIGURE 2–5
Productivity Growth in U.S. Manufacturing (various periods)

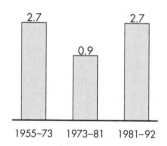

Source: Bureau of Labor Statistics.

---

[2] The data shown in Figure 2–5 have recently been brought into question. Computers are playing a large role in the result shown, too large because of the way in which the index numbers were constructed. In the future, output is measured in units of a base year (1982); and when there are very rapid changes in the prices of major classes of goods, then the index of overall output can be distorted. If real output is measured in 1987 dollars, productivity growth is much slower. However the Department of Commerce has been experimenting with using several base years linked together—a much better approach. And when they do this, they find that the estimates we have shown in Figure 2–5 look pretty good.

FIGURE 2–6
Relative
Productivity:
1973–93, Germany,
Japan, United
Kingdom, and
United States
of America

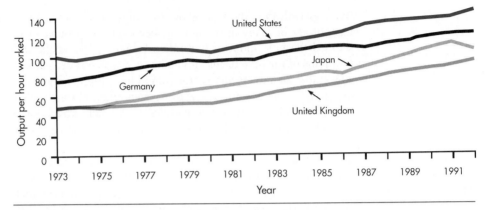

Sources: Bureau of Labor Statistics; Bart van Ark, University of Groningen.

The Performance of Manufacturing in the International Economy

In its trade with the rest of the world, U.S. manufacturing is not what it once was. The most frequently cited sign of this is there has been a trade deficit in manufactured goods for about a decade. For an extended period after World War II, the United States ran a substantial trade surplus in manufactured goods, and there was actually a small manufacturing surplus until 1982–83. After that, manufacturing trade fell into a large deficit, peaking in 1987. By 1991, the deficit in manufactured goods had come down, but it was still $47.3 billion, and this figure has risen since 1991.

The overall trade balance conceals substantial differences in our trade on a product-by-product basis. Figure 2–7 shows how the trade deficit in certain manufactured goods has developed over time, showing the product areas of strength and the areas where there have been serious deficits. Clearly, performance in trade has been a mixed bag for U.S. manufacturing. While there are strong positive balances in some areas, notably in capital goods, commercial aircraft, and chemicals, there are some high-tech products, such as computers, computer accessories, and semiconductors, where we might have expected solid surpluses but have in fact had declining surpluses or even small deficits at times. The large deficits have been in apparel, other consumer goods, and, perhaps most importantly, in autos. (See Figures 2–7a and 2–7b.)

In Chapter 7, we will look at the causes of the overall U.S. trade deficit, and we will argue the overall trade deficit is driven by the balance between domestic saving and domestic investment. Saving is the part of our income we set aside as a nation by refraining from consumption. Investment is the amount businesses buy of new equipment and offices plus the amount households put into new housing. The large deficit in the budget of the federal government is a subtraction from national saving. To oversimplify somewhat, the reason for the U.S. trade deficit is we are consuming more than we are producing, and so we import the difference.

But even though the trade deficit is attributable to the imbalance in the macroeconomy and even though U.S. manufacturing continues to outperform its Japanese and German counterparts in productivity, a concern remains about U.S. international competitiveness. If the value of the dollar were high in foreign exchange markets, then we would say U.S. manufacturing is certainly competitive but is being hamstrung by the fact foreign borrowing has led to a high dollar; but in fact, the dollar is not high.

FIGURE 2–7a
Trade Surpluses in Major Manufactured Goods

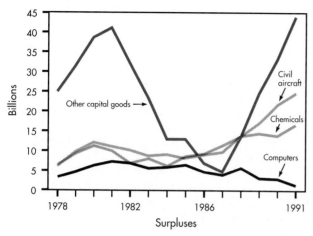

Surpluses

FIGURE 2–7b
Trade Deficits in Major Manufactured Goods

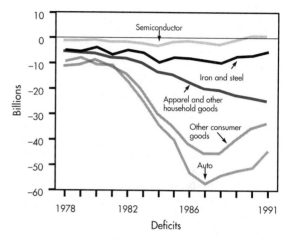

Deficits

Source: USDOC, Bureau of Economic Analysis.

Since 1988, the United States has had both a trade deficit and a low exchange rate, one that makes U.S. wages and other costs look low, compared to our main competitors. It seems our manufacturing industries need a tremendous assist from the exchange rate to be able to sell competitively. This is the fundamental or long-term puzzle of U.S. competitiveness.

Why Does U.S. Manufacturing Have so Much Trouble with Trade?

There are two somewhat related explanations of the U.S. competitiveness puzzle. The first is not all of our industries have a productivity advantage, and the second is we have lost our lead in technology and product quality in some areas.

Studies of productivity for individual industries reveal Japan has a productivity lead in machinery and autos, while the United States has a huge lead in such industries as food processing and textiles. The United States is a fairly open economy that allows Japan to sell here those goods where it has a cost advantage, but Japan does not buy the U.S. goods for which we have an advantage. Japan has an unusually low level of imports from all countries, and this is because of various formal and informal trade restraints. These restraints include the workings of the Japanese kairetsu system, in which Japanese companies join together and buy from each other and not from outsiders.[3]

---

[3] Considerations such as these have motivated the pressure to open Japanese markets or close ours, but keep in mind that, without progress on saving and investment, such policies will *only rearrange the deficit.* We could follow policies that reduced our deficit with Japan, but then find that our deficit with other countries had risen. What this discussion does help to explain is why such a large part of our deficit is with Japan, which has followed an export lead growth strategy with the U.S. market targeted specifically.

Ready to Take on the World

Last week, to the strains of the theme from "Mission Impossible," Chrysler unveiled two sister cars at the Detroit Motor Show: the Stratus and the Cirrus are the American car maker's challenge to the popular Honda Accord. Five years ago, this would have sparked jokes about Chrysler's clouded and seemingly impossible prospects. This time, even Honda's own representatives at the show were describing Chrysler's cars as "very competitive." Meanwhile, three troubleshooters from Ford are on their way to Japan to help stem heavy losses at Mazda, a car maker in which Ford has a 25 percent equity stake.

On January 18, in a satellite hook-up between Los Angeles, Tokyo, London, and New York, Oracle, a California firm set up in 1977, will give a live demonstration of what promises to be the world's first commercial service for delivering "video-on-demand" direct to the home by cable or telephone line. A week earlier Oracle had announced an alliance with Bell Atlantic to offer America's first such interactive-TV service, in Washington, DC.

Oracle is the kind of firm that other countries only dream of producing. Shortly after its worst recession since 1945, California boasts an unequalled line-up of futuristic industries from biotechnology to virtual reality. And while these youngsters grow stronger, older champions have been slimming to survive. McDonnell Douglas has been battered by defence cuts. It shed more than 8,000 jobs in the state last year. Yet despite lower revenues, the aerospace company reported record net profits of $142 million in the third quarter of 1993.

The Dow Jones Industrial Average has risen by 56 percent since January 1991. *The Economist*'s poll of forecasters expects America's GDP to grow by about 3 percent in real terms in 1994, compared with 0.4 percent for Germany and Japan. But many businessmen reckon there is more to it than just the economic cycle. Chrysler's chairman, Bob Eaton, argues that when he returned to America in 1992 after a four-year stint overseas "the changes in productivity and the altered attitude to product quality were just amazing."

Bill Lewis, a consultant at McKinsey, argues that American businesses, shaken both by the depth of the 1979–82 recession and the inroads made by Japanese firms, began a profound transformation in the 1980s. The boom in leveraged buy-outs helped to radicalise the behaviour of managers.

On the Shopfloor

The firms that illustrate America's new competitive edge can be divided, crudely, into three groups.

- **The back-from-the-dead** are led by the car industry, which accounts for about 4 percent of America's GDP. Vehicle sales have been rising briskly, but something more fundamental is at work. Chrysler has introduced five basic chassis designs since 1992, compared with three in the previous 20 years. Ford and General Motors have both reduced the number of chassis platforms they use, but are turning out new models at an unprecedented pace. Ford has a dozen or so scheduled for the next two years—three times the rate of a decade ago. General Motors has 12 coming out this year alone.

This year Detroit's share of the American market may climb back to 75 percent, against just over 70 percent in 1991. . . .

There has been some good news and some bad news about the long-term growth and competitiveness of the U.S. economy. The United States remains a very productive economy, and the manufacturing sector has achieved solid productivity growth (see box above); however, productivity growth outside of manufacturing has been weak, and the manufacturing sector may have lost its lead in some technologies. It has proven hard to compete internationally, except by means of a low and declining dollar. What policies can improve long-term growth and competitiveness?

Other, smaller, American industries have fought back still more effectively. America's semiconductor industry has regained the lead from Japanese manufacturers. The lap-top computer market, which five years ago was dominated by Toshiba, a Japanese firm, has been recaptured by Compaq, IBM and Apple. Even America's steel industry has fought back mainly by pioneering the development of mini-mills.

- **Silent leaders** . . . . For example, Caterpillar remains the world's leading maker of heavy-construction equipment. It invested nearly $2 billion in 1985–90. It now turns out a new tractor in 6 days, rather than 25. The McDonald's hamburger chain has redoubled its cost-cutting, reducing the cost of opening a restaurant from $1.6 million to $1 million. Remorseless pruning at 3M has helped sales of this office-supplies group to double over 10 years while the workforce has stayed almost constant.

Companies such as 3M, which made half of its $13.9 billion sales in 1992 outside America, are well placed to take advantage of trade liberalisation abroad. Since 1986, Procter & Gamble's foreign sales have increased from 29 to 52 percent; General Electric's from 22 to 40 percent. Both firms have moved quickly into Asia, South America, and Eastern Europe—as have food firms such as Coca-Cola, PepsiCo, and McDonald's. CPC International, which makes Mazola corn oil and Hellman's mayonnaise, reckons its Latin American sales alone will triple—to nearly $3 billion—by the end of the decade.

In Europe a freshly belligerent American Telephone & Telegraph (AT&T) has already scared Deutsche Bundespost Telekom and France Télécom into an alliance. EDS, a software-services company owned by GM, is closing in on domestic champions such as France's Cap Gemini Sogeti. In Japan, American drugs firms are the most successful outsiders. Even Hollywood, where costs have soared well beyond inflation, has kept its nose ahead.

- **Rising stars.** Oracle is just one of many. In some cases, young firms—such as Federal Express (which pioneered the overnight-delivery business), Microsoft (software) and McCaw Cellular (wireless telephony)—have created whole industries. Most of America's new jobs and an increasing proportion of its exports come from small firms. And they prompt big firms to change shape, too.

Bill Sahlman, who teaches finance at Harvard Business School, argues that many big companies have woken up to entrepreneurial management—and set out to behave more like small companies. That means basing their strategies on market opportunities rather than their existing resources. Thus AT&T has pushed into new businesses, such as multimedia, by building alliances with tiny Californian high-technology companies.

Wall Street has helped maintain this pressure. Though accused of thinking too much in the short term, its public markets have produced more than $8 billion in the past three years for biotechnology, an industry with 250 public companies of which fewer than 10 make money. The junk-bond market had easily its busiest year ever in 1993, raising $68 billion. American managers may dislike being judged quarter by quarter, but few would prefer to move to Germany, where the phrase "venture capital" is unknown, or to Japan, where big companies are more likely to condescend to small firms than to learn from them.

Source: *The Economist*, January 15, 1994. © 1994 The Economist Newspaper Group, Inc. Reprinted with permission.

POLICIES FOR LONG-TERM GROWTH AND COMPETITIVENESS

The private sector is the key to innovation, to capital investment, and to productive management and workers. Many of the best policies for long-term growth and competitiveness are those that let the private sector do as well as it can without interference from the government. Growth also provides flexibility for an economy where structural changes can have painful effects. There are always some industries that are declining relative to others. There are some regions of the country doing worse than the average, and some groups of workers or consumers that are being adversely affected by structural changes. In an economy without growth, every allocation toward one sector, region, or group comes at the expense of another sector, region, or group. The economy becomes what is called a "zero sum game," where one person's losses are another person's gains. In such an economy there are often political pressures to protect the incomes of groups that are being hurt. And the result can be policies that adversely effect efficiency. In a growing economy, structural changes will leave fewer people actually worse off, so adjustments are easier. There are many ways for the government to get in the way of growth and competitiveness, including misguided policies that are intended to help, but in fact hurt.

With that caution stated, however, some active growth and competitiveness policies can be justified on sound economic principles. Markets provide the best overall basis for the allocation of resources, but markets do not always work perfectly. Companies that are allowed to collude often fail to innovate or to improve productivity. Companies that spend on R&D may find others are imitating their ideas, reverse-engineering their products, or copying their processes. Education and training are vital to growth, and these are often the province of government. Productivity in the United States has improved since 1992 and, compared with industrial competitors in Europe and Asia, U.S. business is strong. Much of this strength can be traced to an improved economic environment, both private and public in origin.

Policies should be explored on their merits, whether a particular policy involves reduced government intervention or additional government actions. The following suggestions reflect our views of appropriate policies for long-term growth and competitiveness. We think they are policies that enhance the working of the market, rather than distorting it. Do you agree or disagree?

Increasing National Saving

There are three main ways in which income generated in the United States is set aside for the future: personal saving by households, corporate saving in the form of retained earnings, and government saving or dissaving.

Households may set aside part of their incomes as personal saving; and for many people, the main forms of saving are company pension plans and repayment of mortgages. On top of this, some households build up savings accounts, buy stocks, or hold mutual funds. Companies will also save by retaining part of their earnings. Not all of the cash flow of the company is paid out as dividends or interest; some is set aside to sustain or expand the capital assets of the company. Companies decide how much to pay out and how much to retain, but the resulting company saving is made on behalf of the owners of the companies. It is really a part of the saving made by the household sector, even though the individual stockholders of the company do not make the saving decisions themselves. Personal saving and corporate saving are often added together to make private saving.[4]

---

[4] Each year, part of the existing stock of capital wears out. This is called "depreciation." If saving includes the amounts set aside for depreciation, then it is called "gross saving," corresponding to the concept of Gross Domestic Product, which also includes depreciation. If depreciation is subtracted off, then saving becomes "net saving," the amount available to increase the stock of capital.

If the government sector (including the federal government and states and localities) takes in more in tax revenue than it spends, then there is government saving on top of private saving. Unfortunately, this is all too rare. In the past several years, there has been a large deficit from the government sector, coming primarily from a budget deficit of the federal government. A government deficit is a subtraction from saving; it is a form of dissaving. Adding private saving and government saving together gives national saving. With a budget deficit, national saving is less than private saving.

During the 1980s private saving fell as a percent of income, while, at the same time, the government sector has been running a large budget deficit. This has meant that *national saving in the U.S. economy has fallen sharply as a percent of income.*[5]

We will see in later chapters that sometimes there can be too much saving in the economy, leading to weak aggregate demand and recession, but this is a short-run problem. Over the long run, saving is vital as a way of freeing the resources needed for investment. If saving is inadequate, this drives up interest rates and discourages businesses from investing. Moreover, since not a large enough flow of saving is being generated here at home, American businesses borrow from overseas. The government also borrows from overseas to finance its own deficit. The United States has eroded its national wealth by accumulating huge foreign debts.

The most important policy to solve this problem is to reduce the federal budget deficit. Government deficits have been the most important source of the problem, and getting the government to reverse this policy is the best way to solve the problem. Achieving this will require some cuts in government spending and some increases in taxes. Politicians often claim that they refuse to burden taxpayers with higher taxes, but running chronic deficits is not a way of avoiding the true tax burden. These politicians are passing on a larger and larger national debt to our children and grandchildren who will be forced to pay the taxes today's citizens are not paying.

Increasing National Investment

If there is success in increasing national saving, this should lead to a lowering of long-term interest rates and provide more incentive for investment in machinery, equipment, factories, and offices. There is a direct link from increased saving to increased investment even without any specific policy to encourage investment. We believe that there is an economic case for going beyond the incentive provided by the market and using specific policies to stimulate business investment, especially investment in machinery and equipment.

There is evidence countries that invest heavily in equipment achieve rapid productivity growth, with the impact of equipment investment on growth being greater than would be predicted from standard growth models.[6] At this point, it is not certain this finding applies directly to the U.S. economy, but it is plausible that this type of investment is particularly important for growth. In the simple growth model, technological change and capital investment were considered separately. But in practice, new

---

[5] The actual percentage depends whether or not depreciation is included. Gross saving in 1992 was 12.0 percent of GDP. Net savings in the same year was 1.3 percent of NDP. The corresponding figures for 1979 are 18.8 percent and 8.8 percent.

[6] J. Bradford DeLong and Lawrence Summers, "Equipment Investment and Economic Growth," *Quarterly Journal of Economics*, May 1991.

capital goods embody new technologies; investment is the transmission belt on which many kinds of technology enter the factory or the office. Moreover, when new equipment is introduced, this will require new skills to be acquired, so investment can stimulate the acquisition of human capital.

One policy that can be used to stimulate equipment investment is an investment tax credit, in which companies can receive a tax credit equal to, say, 10 percent of the cost of the investment. There was such a credit in place in the United States over many years in the 1960s and 70s, and the evidence suggested it was an effective incentive for increased investment.[7] An alternative to the investment tax credit is to allow favorable tax depreciation rules for equipment investment, or possibly for equipment and structures, if the goal is to provide a broader incentive for all types of investment. Some countries allow investment to be expensed in the year it is made.

Maintaining Competitive Markets

We have seen the U.S. economy has a very high level of productivity, compared to other countries. An important reason for this is that we encourage competition in all of our industries, not just in certain export industries. There are trade restrictions in the United States, but they are less binding than the barriers to trade set up by most other countries.

Within the service sector, where international competition is less important, we have encouraged competition through deregulation. A recent study of service sector productivity compared airlines, banking, retailing, and telecommunications in the United States with comparable industries in Europe and Japan.[8] The study concluded greater competition and less state ownership, compared to Europe and Japan, had forced the U.S. companies to achieve higher service sector productivity.

Some policymakers have argued there should be reregulation of service industries and there should be trade barriers erected to protect our industries from foreign competition. We believe such proposals are mistaken. There can be a period of disruption in an industry following deregulation, as has been the case in airlines, but, over the long term, competition forces companies to become more efficient. The response to any loss of competitiveness in the manufacturing sector should be for companies to push harder in the areas where the United States has an advantage, but not for the government to try to resolve economic losses already decided in the marketplace. In some industries, consumer electronics, for example, it may be better simply to let foreign companies take over the industry. We are better off overall to concentrate on industries where we are more productive.

Policies to maintain competition, including deregulation, minimal restrictions on trade, and a clear antitrust policy to discourage monopolies, are a vital part of an overall strategy for competitiveness and long-term growth. Such policies consist largely of avoiding unwarranted government intervention in the economy.

---

7   Robert E. Hall and Dale T. Jorgenson, "Application of the Theory of Optimum Capital Accumulation," in Gary Fromm, ed., *Tax Incentives and Capital Spending* (Washington D.C.: The Brookings Institution, 1971).

8   McKinsey Global Institute, *Service Sector Productivity* (Washington, D.C.: McKinsey and Company, 1992); Martin Neil Baily, "Competition Regulation and Efficiency in Service Industries," *Brookings Papers on Economic Activity, Microeconomics 2:1993.*

Training

A competitive economy can be tough on workers. Someone who has worked hard and well for 30 years in a particular job may suddenly find he or she is out of work with little marketable skills because of a cutback or a plant closing. Unemployment insurance provides one immediate source of support for workers that are displaced. This program in the United States pays a weekly benefit to workers who lose their jobs, usually for up to six months. The U.S. system is less generous than similar programs in Europe, and many workers eligible for benefits in Europe would not be eligible here.

There is a danger in providing too much income support to laid-off workers, however, or providing it in the wrong way. This can discourage reemployment. The long-term answer to job displacement is to encourage workers to retrain and take new jobs. The incidence of long-term unemployment in Europe is much higher than in the United States, partly because workers there are unwilling to take a new job unless it pays more than their unemployment insurance benefits, benefits that can last for years even for people who have never worked.

In a market economy, skills that have provided someone a good income for many years may become obsolete, and new skills must then be acquired. Workers are often reluctant to accept that reality; they keep hoping to get their old jobs back. Firms can be reluctant to provide job skills to new workers when these workers may quit and take their skills to another company. The overall efficiency of the labor market could be enhanced by increasing the opportunities and incentives for training or retraining. This is done most effectively by employers that have jobs to be filled.

Technology Policy

For the most part, the development of new commercial technology should be left to the private sector. New products and processes generally do not involve major changes in the basic science. They reflect the application of established science and engineering in new ways. Knowledge of the market is vital to successful commercial innovation. When the government intervenes too heavily in technology development, the results can be disastrous.

Many policy initiatives in the United States have fallen into the trap of trying to displace the market. In their book *The Technology Pork Barrel,* Linda Cohen and Roger Noll and their coauthors assess the synfuels project, the SST project, the photovoltaics project, the breeder reactor, the communications satellite initiative, and the space shuttle.[9] Their judgments are not kind. The NASA initiative on communications satellites achieved its technical objectives but was killed because the existing communications industry viewed the new technology as a threat to its own position and lobbied hard to remove government funding. The photovoltaics project made technical progress, also, but was scaled back because political support died once energy prices fell. The SST project was scrapped because of doubts about the cost and feasibility of the project and because of environmental concerns. The Clinch River Breeder reactor was sustained for a long time because of the resources it was bringing to Tennessee, but it was eventually killed when the costs became too high, technical

---

[9] Linda R. Cohen and Roger Noll, with Jeffrey S. Banks, Susan A. Edelman, and William M. Pegman, *The Technology Pork Barrel* (Washington, D.C.: Brookings Institution, 1991).

problems were not solved, and the price of energy fell. Little of value was learned from this project. The space shuttle remains an ongoing project, but its goals have been scaled back greatly. The shuttle suffered from well-known safety problems and has been subject to substantial competition from conventional launch vehicles. The synfuels project did make technical progress, developing the combined cycle coal–gas project (cool water), but billions of dollars were spent on pilot and demonstration projects that failed before the program was killed.

Despite the fact that Cohen and Noll have documented serious problems with some past projects, we believe there is still a case for an active government policy to support technology development. When a single company uses its funds for an R&D project, it hopes to develop a new product or process that will generate profits for the company. But if it is successful, its competitors will be able to reverse engineer the new product or learn about the technology of the new process.[10] The R&D done by one company is borrowed by other companies. As several different companies enter the market with the new technology, this means competition will drive prices down, giving more of the benefits of the new technology to consumers. This process has advantages in allowing all of us to share in the benefits of technological change, but it means the incentives companies have to spend on the development of new technology are less than is optimal for the society as a whole. Having government policy support technology can, in principle, make the market work better.

Moreover, offsetting the mixed or negative record Cohen and Noll describe are examples where direct government support of technology development has been very successful, particularly when the project is specifically **precommercial.** The goal of this kind of R&D is to develop a promising new direction of technology, rather than to develop a specific new product or process. The incentive for private companies to do such research on their own is very weak indeed.

In his book *Creating the Computer,* Kenneth Flamm looks at the main elements of the computer and how each was developed, at least in its early stages.[11] He finds the Department of Defense, and the Defense Advanced Research Projects Agency (DARPA) in particular, was behind the main developments in semiconductors and computers. A similar story of federal government involvement can be told for commercial jet aircraft and telecommunications.[12] It is impressive that our leading high-technology industries today were driven in their early evolution by government support of technology. There is no question federal funds can play a vital role in building U.S. industries that then have a global competitive advantage. U.S. competitiveness today is stronger because of the computer, telecommunications, and aerospace industries.

The key policy question, then, is how to support technology without getting into the problems of the technology pork barrel. Cohen and Noll actually offer some sugges-

precommercial
The goal of this kind of research and development is to develop a promising new direction of technology, rather than to develop a specific new product or process.

---

[10] Patents provide only limited protection for what is called "intellectual property."
[11] Kenneth Flamm, *Creating the Computer* (New York: Brookings, 1990).
[12] Richard R. Nelson, "U.S. Technological Leadership: Where Did It Come From and Where Did It Go?" in F.M. Scherer and Mark Perlman, eds., *Entrepreneurship, Technological Innovation, and Economic Growth* (Ann Arbor: University of Michigan, 1992), pp. 25–50.

tions on this point, based on the problems that they found. First, the ideas for the projects to be supported should come from the private sector, mainly corporations and small businesses, but also universities with strong technological capabilities and other nonprofits. This would ensure the projects are not being dreamed up by federal agencies or politicians having no clear knowledge of the ultimate commercial usefulness of the results. Further, participating private companies should partially fund the projects from their own resources. This is particularly important if funded projects go beyond early technology exploration and commit to pilot plants. Second, the emphasis should be on a wide diversity of projects directed toward the same general goal, each of which receives modest funding. This serves a dual purpose. It allows the exploration of many options, rather than encouraging commitment too early to a particular technology strategy,[13] and it reduces the dangers of pork barrel because no single project generates enough jobs to be a focus of state or local lobbying efforts. Third, congressional oversight should not lead to meddling into exactly which projects should be funded and how the research should proceed. Congress should determine the rules of the game and not call the plays on fourth and one. Fourth, it is vital that congress have a long time-horizon. There is much talk of the short time horizon problem for U.S. companies, but this problem may be even worse for political decisions than for business decisions.

Conclusions

We have introduced some ideas on policies to improve the long-term growth and competitiveness of the U.S. economy. These ideas are intended to stimulate discussion, and many economists would disagree with our suggestions. There is a basic agreement, though, on how such policies should be evaluated. The test is whether a policy helps make an inefficient market more efficient. Intervention is appropriate only if the private market is not working efficiently. An efficient market should be left to work on its own.

From Long-Term Growth to the Business Cycle

Over the long run, living standards depend most importantly on long-term growth driven by the productive capacity of the economy—the ability to supply goods and services; but increases in the rate of long-term growth of the economy come about quite slowly and policy is not very effective in changing long-run growth. Even if all of the proposals we suggested were adopted, the long-term rate of growth of the U.S. economy would not increase by very much.

In the short run, economic well-being depends on whether the economy is in a recession or a boom and whether inflation is high or low. Here policy plays a major role in the short-run determination of well-being and short run conditions are driven more by shifts in aggregate demand than by movements in aggregate supply. For this reason, we will spend much of the remainder of this book analyzing the determinants

---

[13] In the shuttle project, there was not adequate consideration given to radically different designs for the shuttle. The initial project evaluation ignored the possibility of improvements that could be made in unmanned launch vehicles. In the breeder project, only very high conversion targets were considered —targets that turned out to be costly and difficult to meet. In the synfuels project, the focus was on using eastern coal, even though western coal is much easier to convert into gas or liquid fuel.

of the aggregate demand for goods and services. For better or worse, that is something we know policy can change. Government policies can cause inflations and recessions, or they can ameliorate them. We are not done with the issues of long-term growth and competitiveness, however. We will come back to them in Chapter 17.

SUMMARY

- Aggregate demand fluctuations are the focus of short-run economic policies and concerns.
- Aggregate supply trends are the focus of short-run economic policies and concerns.
- Long-run growth in aggregate supply is necessary for long-run growth in the standard of living. This can only be sustained if there is growth in the capacity to produce goods and services—growth in potential output.
- The long-run growth of productivity—output per unit of input—is the primary cause of growth in real GDP per capita.
- Productivity growth allows for competitiveness—goods and services produced at competitive prices—to be maintained without having to suffer reductions in real wages and income.
- If population is growing, then living standards will increase in the long run only if potential output is growing faster than population. And the impact of the growth in potential output compounds in the long run. After several years, large differences in economic performance are the result of small differences in growth rates.
- The economy's productive capacity (potential output) depends on how much capital and labor are available for production and the technology that is used. If more capital and labor are used in production, more output can be produced.
- With a given technology, increasing labor input to produce more output will depress average labor productivity and living standards for those employed unless the amount of capital rises by enough to prevent the effects of diminishing returns from lowering labor productivity.
- In an economy where production is subject to constant returns to scale, average labor productivity does not depend on the size of the economy. Rather, it depends on the capital/labor ratio—the capital intensity of the economy.
- An increase in capital intensity is a disproportional increase of capital relative to labor. More capital per worker raises the level of average labor productivity, but there are diminishing returns to capital as capital intensity increases.
- Saving is a source of the resources that are set aside for investment, and investment is the amount that is added to the capital stock.
- More saving generates more capital accumulation, which can raise labor productivity. But, in the absence of technology improvements, only at a decreasing rate, because of diminishing returns to capital.
- It has been found that technological change, rather than capital accumulation, has been the main source of increased productivity and living standards.
- Somewhere between 1968 and 1973, the rate of technological change seems to have slowed down sharply and thrown the U.S. economy below its former post-1945 high growth path.
- The slowdown appears to have been a worldwide phenomenon and U.S. productivity is still high compared to the rest of the world.
- The reason for the slowdown cannot be found in a single source or event, but rather a combination of factors, including: Work force quality and education, capital infrastructure, regulation, management problems, technological depletion.
- Policies to support long-run growth and competitiveness are not directly connected to short-run macroeconomic policies.

KEY TERMS AND CONCEPTS

capital input, p. 34
diminishing returns, p. 35
constant returns to scale, p. 35
infrastructure, p. 44

intensive production function,
  p. 36
labor input, p. 34
knowledge capital, p. 39

precommercial, p. 56
production function, p. 34
technology, p. 34

DISCUSSION QUESTIONS AND PROBLEMS

1. Can the standard of living be improved without productivity growth? If so, how and is the improvement sustainable?

2. "The post-1973 productivity slowdown in the United States was inevitable. Our high rate of productivity growth was only a result of being the dominant economy in the world. As soon as Western European and Asian industrialized economies began to catch up, the U.S. lead was bound to evaporate." Comment.

3. "The productivity decline is easily explained—people stopped working hard and they stopped saving." Comment.

4. "The productivity slowdown is a mirage. First of all, most of what we now produce are services, and pro-ductivity gains in services can't be measured. Second, the huge investment we've made in computer technology is going to pay off in the 1990s. Economists simply like to worry." Comment.

5. Macroeconomic policies for long-run growth require stimulating aggregate supply. How can government policies contribute to private-sector productivity?

6. How does the new growth theory differ from the neoclassical model developed by Solow?

7. How is the word *competitiveness* used in the debate about the U.S. economy? Is it being misused?

AGGREGATE SUPPLY AND DEMAND AND INCOME DETERMINATION

INTRODUCTION

We now set up a model of a very simple economy and then show how aggregate demand and supply interact to determine income and output within it and how changes in aggregate demand bring about short-run changes in income and output. This is a basic and stripped down model of the economy that has no government sector, so there are no taxes and no government expenditures.

Even though this model is sparse, with few elements, it serves a useful purpose as the basis for understanding how supply and demand work at the aggregate level. The simple model also demonstrates the interaction between income and output in the economy. The level of aggregate demand in the model economy determines the level of production; but production generates income, which then feeds back into demand. The model shows how equilibrium is determined, given this interdependence among income, demand, and production. We are also able to use this model to describe the connections between saving and capital investment. We then extend the model to take a first look at the effect of imports and exports. We find that foreign trade can affect the levels of production and employment. A trade deficit reduces the level of aggregate demand in the economy.

AGGREGATE SUPPLY AND DEMAND AND PRICE STICKINESS

aggregate demand
The amount that households, businesses, and the government decide to purchase, plus net foreign demand.

aggregate supply
The amount of goods and services that businesses offer for sale.

The level of output in the economy is determined by the interaction of aggregate supply and aggregate demand. In an economy with government and foreign sectors, **aggregate demand** is the amount that households, businesses, and the government decide to purchase, plus net foreign demand. In the simple economy we are studying now, the government and foreign sectors are excluded, so aggregate demand includes only household demand and business investment demand.

Aggregate supply is the amount of goods and services that businesses offer for sale. It depends on the productive capacity of the factories and offices in the economy and the prices businesses expect to receive. Since this is an analysis of short-run economic movements, we are taking the productive capacity of the economy—the technology and the amount of capital—as given, giving us an aggregate-supply schedule that relates the output produced in the economy to the price level.

The Aggregate-Supply Schedule

Figure 3–1 depicts an upward-sloping aggregate-supply schedule, indicating that as production costs rise firms are only willing to supply higher levels of output at higher prices. It shows that an increase in aggregate supply (from Y_A to Y_B) will be associated with an increase in the price level (from P_A to P_B). However, the figure says that, for most levels of output, excluding the extremely high levels on the right-hand side of the aggregate-supply schedule, *large changes in the level of output are associated with small changes in the price level.*

FIGURE 3–1
The Aggregate-Supply Schedule

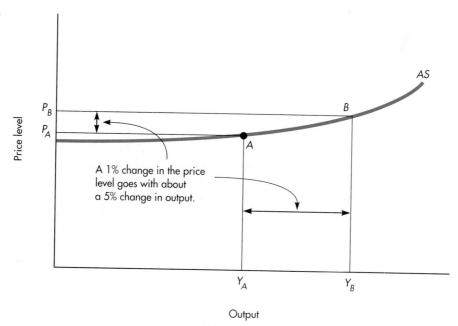

The aggregate-supply schedule is rather flat. A large change in output induces only a small change in the price level in the same year.

As is marked in Figure 3–1, a change in output equal to about 5 percent of GDP will lead to a change in the price level of only about 1 percent *in the same year.*[1] That elasticity of about five corresponds to a fairly flat supply curve. An increase or decrease of real GDP by 5 percentage points—equal to about $300 billion and about 6 million workers employed—is a dramatic change in economic conditions. A one–percentage-point change in the price level is much less significant. Moreover, when GDP changes by 5 percent, there are much bigger changes in the outputs of such cyclically sensitive parts of the economy as auto, appliance, and machine-tool production. And yet the changes in the prices of these goods may be even less than the change in the overall price level.

In general, when there is a change in supply or demand in any market, the response to the change will involve adjustments of both price and quantity. Why is it that, in the overall economy, the response of prices to changes is fairly small compared to the larger changes in output? An important part of the answer lies with timing. Prices adjust to changes in supply and demand, *but they adjust slowly—prices are sticky.*

There are some perfectly competitive markets in the economy where prices for such standard commodities as wheat or soybeans vary according to shifts in supply and demand. And prices in these markets are quite volatile. But the price level in a modern economy is determined largely by companies that set their prices based on what they see as their best long-run competitive strategy. One cannot expect the prices of complex products sold by large firms, such as aircraft or banking services, to have prices that vary as quickly and easily as do the prices of agricultural products. The forces of supply and demand assert themselves over time in all markets, but these market forces work slowly in changing prices.

Aggregate Demand and Output Changes in the Short Run

The aggregate-demand schedule represents the way in which the demand from the business and household sectors varies with changes in the price level. In Figure 3–2, an aggregate-demand schedule, *AD,* is shown intersecting with an aggregate-supply schedule, *AS,* at a level of output Y_A and price level P_0.

The aggregate-demand schedule is shown as downward-sloping in Figure 3–2 and the reason for this is that, when the price level is lower and the amount of money in the economy is fixed, then interest rates will fall and this will encourage spending. This is not the usual intuitive way one thinks about downward-sloping demand schedules. In microeconomic models a demand schedule slopes downward because people will shift from buying one good to buying another when their *relative* prices change. But in macroeconomics, at the aggregate level, a general change in the price level that involves no change in people's real incomes will not change aggregate spending by any similar mechanism. We will look at the relation between the price level and aggregate demand in a later chapter.

---

[1] The slope of the aggregate-supply curve can be inferred from inflation studies such as George L. Perry, ''Inflation in Theory and Practice,'' *Brookings Papers on Economic Activity* 1 (1980), pp. 207–41; and Robert J. Gordon, ''Inflation, Exchange Rates and the Natural Rate of Unemployment,'' in *Workers Jobs and Inflation,* Martin Neil Baily, ed. (Washington, D.C.: Brookings Institution, 1982).

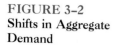

FIGURE 3–2
**Shifts in Aggregate
Demand**

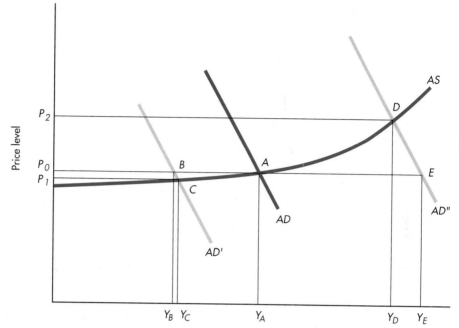

By neglecting the effect of changes in the price level on the aggregate demand, we make an error. To the
left of *A*, the error is small.

Changes in the economy other than changes in the price level can lead to shifts in
the aggregate-demand schedule. We show the effect of leftward and rightward shifts
in the aggregate-demand schedule in Figure 3–2. For example, a decline in income
would lead to a shift such as that from *AD* to *AD'*. And an increase in income will lead
to a shift such as the one from *AD* to *AD"*.

As we study the short-run fluctuations of output in these early chapters we will
concentrate on the impact of shifts in the aggregate-demand schedule, particularly
those resulting from changes in income, rather than on the movements along the
aggregate-demand schedule associated with changes in the price level. This is an
oversimplification but is not too serious a problem, provided we focus on recessions or
situations where there are slack resources in the economy. Figure 3–2 illustrates the
error we are making by neglecting the effects of changes in the price level on
aggregate demand.

If aggregate demand falls to *AD'*, output will fall to Y_C and the price level will fall
to P_1. By neglecting the effect of the price-level change, we would erroneously
conclude that output falls to Y_B, rather than Y_C. Since the price-level effects would
result in a serious overstatement of the resulting increase in output.

*The analysis of the next few chapters is geared to the study of the short-run changes
in an economy where there are slack resources, an economy where increases or
decreases in aggregate demand primarily affect output and have only a minor effect
on the price level.*

The Vertical Aggregate-Supply Schedule: A Very Different Perspective

Some economists argue that the aggregate-supply schedule is not flat at all; it is actually very steep, or even vertical. A vertical supply schedule means that, when aggregate demand increases, this will cause prices and wages to rise, rather than real output and employment. This is illustrated below.

The Effect of an Increase in Aggregate Demand with a Vertical Aggregate-Supply Schedule

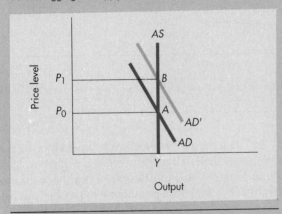

With a vertical aggregate-supply schedule, the shift in the aggregate-demand schedule from *AD* to *AD'* will increase the price level from P_0 to P_1 with no change in the level of income.

The idea of a vertical aggregate-supply schedule is based on models of the economy in which markets are competitive and all wages and prices adjust quickly to eliminate any imbalance between supply and demand. With perfect markets, an increase in aggregate demand will increase individual prices and wages without changing relative prices or the real wage (the wage in relation to the price level). This means that no firm has an incentive to produce more and no worker has an incentive to work more, so output remains unchanged.

The real issue here in assessing the slope of the aggregate-supply schedule is timing. Most economists, including ourselves, agree that the aggregate-supply schedule is vertical in the long run. Prices and wages adjust to ensure equilibrium in the long run. But when we observe business-cycle fluctuations in the economy, we see imperfect markets with sticky wages and prices. We also see that changes in aggregate demand fall mainly on output in the short run. This is why we assume a rather flat aggregate-supply schedule for the analysis of short-run income changes.

The different assumptions about the slope of the supply schedule have important implications for the role of policy. We are developing a framework in which economic policy can affect aggregate demand and hence income and output. If there is a vertical aggregate-supply schedule, these aggregate-demand policies will have no effect on output. In Chapters 14 and 15 we present the alternative view of the economy in which prices adjust very quickly, and policies that change aggregate demand are to be avoided.

AGGREGATE SUPPLY AND DEMAND AND QUANTITY ADJUSTMENT

In Chapter 1, we said that GDP is equal to the sum of consumption expenditure, investment expenditure, government expenditure, and net exports. In the economy we are studying now, there is no government and no foreign trade, so GDP *(Y)* is defined as the sum of consumption *(C)* and investment *(I):*

$$Y \equiv C + I \tag{3-1}$$

identity

An equation that is true by definition for all values of the variables in the equation.

Equation 3–1 is an **identity** because Y is defined as total output and then each good or service that is part of total output is defined either as part of consumption or as part of investment. In particular, total investment includes the buildings and machines that businesses order from other businesses, but investment as measured in the national income accounts also includes any goods that are produced but not sold. Unsold goods become part of inventory accumulation and are included in total investment in the accounts. This means that the fact that Equation 3–1 is always satisfied does not tell us very much at all about how GDP is determined. It does not tell us whether aggregate demand is less than, equal to, or greater than aggregate supply.

The economy is in equilibrium when producers do not wish to change the level of output they are producing. In this model, the economy is assumed to be in equilibrium only if there are no unintended changes in inventories. Only if the unsold goods held in inventory were intended to be part of inventory will the economy be in equilibrium.

In addition, we will assume that the way in which the economy adjusts when it is not in equilibrium also depends on what is happening to inventories. We will assume that businesses decide to increase or decrease their level of production, depending on whether inventories are piling up or are being depleted. If businesses in general are producing more than the amount they are selling plus the amount they planned to add to or subtract from inventories, they will reduce production. If businesses are producing less than the amount they are selling plus the amount that they planned to add to inventory, then they will expand production.

Studies of businesses have found that in practice they respond quickly to any unplanned piling up or running down of inventories. If sales are less than expected and inventories start to pile up, businesses cut back on production and start laying off workers within a month or two. If inventories are being depleted, companies start to use overtime and then increase hiring to expand production. The idea that there are quantity (output and employment) adjustments in the economy in response to gaps between supply and demand is one that matches well with observed business behavior.[2]

Planned and Unplanned Expenditures

The level of investment that is planned by businesses (I_p) includes only their expected or intended change in inventory. However, firms can wind up with larger or smaller inventories than they wanted as they react to customers' orders. This unanticipated or unplanned change in inventory is part of businesses' expenditure on investment, regardless of the fact that it was unplanned or unwanted. Total investment (I) is the sum of the planned and unplanned (I_U) components:

$$I \equiv I_p + I_U \tag{3–2}$$

[2] The behavior of inventories is shown in Alan S. Blinder and Douglas Holtz-Eakin, "Inventory Fluctuations in the United States since 1929," in *The American Business Cycle: Continuity and Change*, Robert J. Gordon, ed. (Chicago: University of Chicago Press for National Bureau of Economics Research, 1986), pp. 183–236.

Do Inventory Adjustments Take Place in the Service Sector?

We have talked about how businesses adjust their production in response to a piling up or running down of inventories. And we described equilibrium as "goods-market equilibrium." But we know that the majority of employment in our economy is now in services. Aren't we ignoring the service sector?

Yes, we have shortchanged the service sector in this discussion. One reason is that cyclical fluctuations in the economy are very heavily concentrated in the goods-producing sector of the economy. In a recession, it is construction, autos, machine tools, and other similar industries that take the biggest declines in output and employment. In fact, the service sector often continues to increase employment right through a recession. Still, some specific service industries decline in recessions, so let's look at how they adjust.

Service industries can almost never hold inventories. There is no way to hold an inventory of haircuts when there are too many barbers for the number of customers. In the electricity-generation service industry, it is possible to store electricity rather than run a power plant, but the storage is so expensive that it is rarely done. In general, there are no inventories of service outputs.

Excess supply in a service industry will show up as excess capacity or as "inventory" of underutilized employees. There will be too many barbers for the number of customers; too many lawyers and not enough clients; too much generating capacity for the demand for electricity. The response of service firms to this excess capacity will be similar to the response of goods producers to unplanned additions to inventory. Service firms will slowly lay off workers and reduce capacity.

Excess demand in a service firm will mean that customers may be turned away or will have to wait some time before being able to buy the service. In this situation, service firms will respond just like goods producers with inventories running down. They will increase hiring and expand production.

The adjustment of supply to variations in demand in service industries is similar to the adjustment in goods industries, even though there are no inventories of services. Unplanned excess capacity or unplanned shortages of capacity are similar to unplanned inventory changes. When we talk about goods-market equilibrium, you should think of this as equilibrium for both goods and services.

Unplanned investment (I_U) will be positive if inventories are piling up, or negative if they are being run down.[3] Expressing investment in this way gives us the condition for equilibrium in the goods market in terms of investment. *There is goods-market equilibrium when there is no unplanned investment* ($I_U = 0$), *so planned investment and actual or realized investment are equal* ($I = I_p$).

Since unplanned investment refers to unplanned changes in inventories, equilibrium between the quantity of goods produced and aggregate demand takes place when unplanned inventories are zero. The national income identity becomes an equilibrium condition when $I_U = 0$. The identity is given in Equation 3–3.

$$Y \equiv C + I_p + I_U \tag{3–3}$$

And then the equilibrium condition in Equation 3–4.

$$Y = \text{Aggregate production or aggregate supply } (AS) \tag{3–4}$$
$$C + I_p = \text{Aggregate demand } (AD)$$

---

[3] Typically businesses will have some planned changes in inventory, so that, strictly speaking, I_U refers to the gap between actual inventory adjustments and planned inventory adjustments.

When

Aggregate supply = Aggregate demand
$$Y_e = C + I_p$$

The economy is in goods-market equilibrium when output equals consumption plus planned investment.[4] The left-hand side of the equation is aggregate output; that is, aggregate supply. The right-hand side of the equation is consumption demand plus investment demand. Investment demand includes all the purchases of factories and equipment that businesses wanted to make and excludes the unintended changes in inventories.

Having specified the condition for goods-market equilibrium, the task now is to determine how this equilibrium comes about: At what level of output, Y, will there be equality between supply and demand? Since we have argued that production will adjust to meet aggregate demand through inventory changes, we will answer this question by seeing how the components of aggregate demand are determined.

Consumption Demand and the Consumption Function

consumption function
The relationship between consumption and those economic variables that determine the decision to consume.

Demand originating in the household sector is called "consumption demand." We describe the relationship between consumption and those economic variables that determine the decision to consume by a **consumption function.** In general, households spend more on consumption goods when they have higher incomes. As a result, the sum of consumption by all households increases as aggregate income increases. Households buy more when income rises. We describe the relation between income and consumption by using a simple straight-line consumption function where C is consumption demand:

$$C = C_0 + C_1 Y \tag{3-5}$$

Earlier we used the term Y to denote output, but, as we saw in Chapter 1, output and income are equal, so Y also denotes income. C_0 is a positive constant and C_1 is the coefficient of income, also called the "marginal propensity to consume."[5]

The Average and Marginal Propensities to Consume

marginal propensity to consume (MPC)
The amount of increased consumption (ΔC) that results from an amount of increased income (ΔY) expressed as ($\Delta C/\Delta Y$).

Figure 3–3 shows the consumption function, with the slope of the line DAB reflecting the *change* in consumption resulting from a given *change* in income (the slope is $\Delta C/\Delta Y$). This slope is C_1, from the consumption function, and is called the **marginal propensity to consume,** or MPC.

---

[4] Notice that, in this equilibrium condition, the regular equal sign has replaced the identity sign, $\equiv$, and we have written Y_e instead of Y to emphasize that this is the level of income where there is goods-market equilibrium.

[5] In general, terms such as C_0 and C_1 are called the *parameters* or *coefficients* of a function. When the values of consumption and income change, the relationship between income and consumption will not change as long as the coefficients of the consumption function are constant.

In empirical studies of the actual economy, the coefficients of equations are estimated using *econometric analysis.* Econometrics combines statistics with economic theory to subject data to statistical tests. For example, the shape of the consumption function and, thus, the interpretation of saving behavior associated with income would change if the coefficients were different. Whether the value of C_0 was zero or positive and whether the value of C_1 was constant or changed with income can be ascertained by using data on consumption and income.

The MPC does not change for different levels of income. Our consumption function assumes that the *change* in consumption resulting from a given *change* in income does not vary with the level of income. (See Figure 3–3.)

We have described a consumption function that emphasizes the impact of current income on people's buying decisions, but there are other factors that could be included. In particular the amount of wealth owned by households and the amount of their debts will be important and so will people's expectations about their future income. In Chapter 9 we look in more detail at some of these other determinants of consumption, but for now we will assume that any changes in the economy (other than changes in income) that affect consumption will be reflected in possible shifts in C_0; that is, shifts in the consumption function.

average propensity to consume (APC)
The fraction of income that households spend on consumption, expressed as a ratio, C/Y.

Investment Demand and the Investment Function

We describe the relationship between investment and those economic variables that determine the decision to invest by an **investment function.** Investment demand follows consumption as the main source of aggregate demand coming from the private sector of the economy. In addition to being important to aggregate demand, invest-

FIGURE 3–3
The Consumption Function, the MPC, and the APC

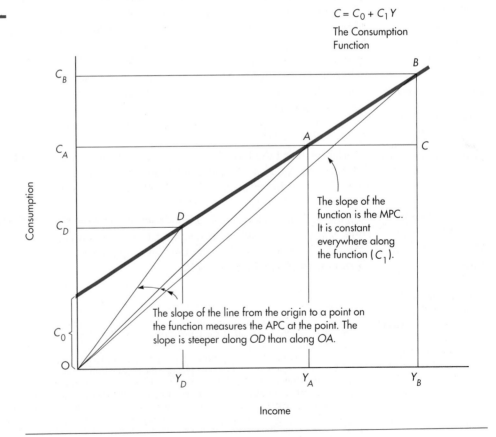

$$C = C_0 + C_1 Y$$

The Consumption Function

The slope of the function is the MPC. It is constant everywhere along the function (C_1).

The slope of the line from the origin to a point on the function measures the APC at the point. The slope is steeper along *OD* than along *OA*.

Income

investment function
The relationship be-
tween investment
demand and those
economic variables
that determine the
decision by firms to
purchase capital goods.

ment is also important because of the role it plays in maintaining and increasing the productive capacity of the economy.

The main components of investment are business structures (new office buildings and factories), business equipment (machine tools, computers, and office furniture), and new residential structures (apartment buildings and single-family houses). The decisions to purchase these investment or capital goods are made primarily by the people that manage businesses in the economy. When households decide to buy houses or condominiums, rather than renting, they are making business-investment decisions, also. Household demand for residential structures is included in investment demand.

planned investment
The amount businesses
want to spend on capital
goods, including the
amount they want to
add to their inventories.

Planned Investment   **Planned investment** is the amount businesses would like to spend on capital goods plus the amount they want to add to their inventories. The reason businesses decide to buy capital goods is that they foresee profits accruing to them from using these capital goods. A firm will add capacity if it sees the potential for increased production and sales, or if it can lower the costs of producing to meet its current level of sales. A real estate company will build an office building or an apartment block based upon the anticipated rents it will receive.

We will identify two variables that affect the level of investment demand: the level of income or output in the economy, Y, and the interest rate in the economy, denoted by r. We specify an investment-demand function incorporating these two variables:

$$I_p = I_0 + I_1 Y - I_2 r \tag{3-6}$$

The most important influence on investment demand has been found to be the level of income and output in the economy. If income is depressed and the economy is in a recession, then businesses do not expect to be able to use new equipment and factories profitably. Instead, they anticipate slow sales, unused production capacity, and reduced profitability from any additions to their equipment or factories. A high level of income means that firms will anticipate strong demand from consumers and from other businesses, so adding capacity makes sense.

**marginal propensity to
invest (MPI)**
The amount of increased
investment (ΔI_p) that
results from an amount
of increased income
(ΔY) expressed as
($\Delta I_p / \Delta Y$).

The responsiveness of investment demand to income (I_1) is called the **marginal propensity to invest** (MPI). Figure 3–4 shows the investment function. When income rises (Y_A to Y_B), the level of investment expenditures rises by the MPI times the increase in income (investment demand rises from I_A to I_B). The function is shown for some particular value (r_1) of the interest rate, so the intercept ($I_0 - I_2 r_1$) is the level of investment expenditure that is not related to the level of income.

Investment Demand and the Interest Rate   The interest rate affects the decision to invest directly when businesses borrow to buy capital goods. If the bank charges interest on money it is lending, or if a company must issue a corporate bond to finance the investment, then the interest will be a cost to the company that must be subtracted from the profits earned by the investment. Even if investment is financed by a company out of its retained earnings, the interest rate is still important. The company could pay out the earnings as dividends and allow shareholders to earn interest by

FIGURE 3–4
The Investment
Function

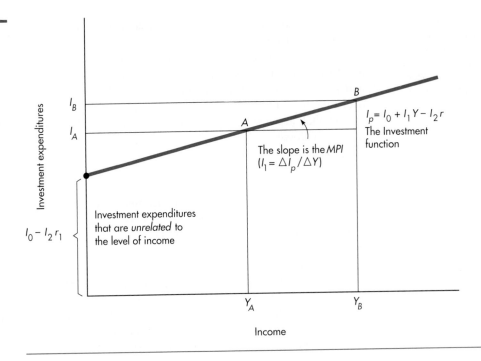

buying bonds with the money. Or the company could use the earnings to repay past debts that it has incurred and thereby reduce its interest burden.

Household investment in new houses is very sensitive to the interest rate, because most new houses are financed by mortgages. The most visible impact of interest rates on investment in the U.S. economy occurs in the housing sector. High interest rates have played an important role in initiating recessions. There were sharp declines in residential construction that began with high mortgage interest rates in the 1974–75 recession and again in the 1982–83 and 1990–91 recessions.

The responsiveness of investment to the interest rate is reflected in the interest parameter in the investment function (I_2) in Equation 3–6. The negative sign of the interest parameter indicates that the higher the interest rate, the lower is investment demand.

Figure 3–5 shows how the investment function shifts as the interest rate changes. At a given level of income (Y_A), the higher the interest rate, the lower is investment demand. As shown, investment demand is lower at point D than at point A.

With a given rate of interest, investment demand rises with income. When income increases from Y_A to Y_B, investment demand rises from I_A to I_B as shown in Figure 3–5 (point A to point B when $r = r_1$). If at point B the rate of interest rose (r_1 to r_2), then investment expenditures would drop from I_B to I_C (point B to point C when there is no change in income).

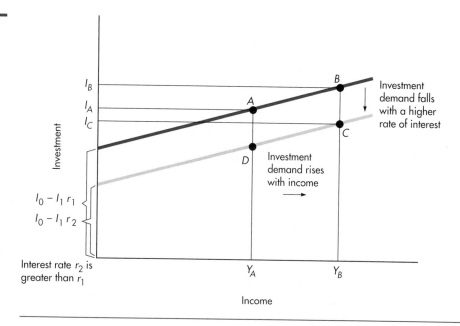

FIGURE 3-5
Investment Demand Varies with Both Income and the Rate of Interest

In the actual economy, income and the interest rate both change and their changes are often interrelated. In fact, a rise in income often accompanies a rise in the interest rate. We are describing here the *separate* effects on investment demand, first of income changes and then of interest-rate changes. In any practical case we would look at the *combined* effect of changes in both income and the interest rate.

Variability of Investment   We have pointed to income and the interest rate as two important influences on the level of investment demand. But in practice there are many factors influencing investment demand, making it a part of demand that is very variable and hard to predict. *The variability of investment demand is a major source of instability in aggregate demand.*[6]

We have described how income and the interest rate determine consumption and investment. We will now examine how these separate demands of households and businesses combine and how income and the interest rate move toward a goods-market equilibrium.

---

[6] One view of investment demand is that it depends on not only the level of production in the current period but also the level of production in the previous period. The accelerator model of investment says that investment demand depends on the change in income and production. When income rises, businesses will need more machines than they needed in the previous period. Investment will be high. When income falls, businesses will have more than enough machines and will not buy new ones. We look at the accelerator model in Chapter 9, where we see how the accelerator model predicts large swings in investment demand.

GOODS-MARKET EQUILIBRIUM

The condition that insures goods-market equilibrium in this simple economy was given in Equation 3–4:

$$Y_e = C + I_p$$

In this expression, Y_e denotes the equilibrium level of income and output. Since we have developed functions that show how consumption demand and planned-investment demand are determined, we can substitute these into the equilibrium condition to give:

$$Y_e = C_0 + C_1 Y_e + I_0 + I_1 Y_e - I_2 r \tag{3–7}$$

If we know the values of the parameters in the consumption and investment functions and the rate of interest, we can solve Equation 3–7 for the level of income where there is no unplanned investment; that is, where aggregate supply equals aggregate demand. We will have used our knowledge of the components of aggregate demand to determine equilibrium income, the level of income for which aggregate supply equals aggregate demand.

Solving for Y_e in Equation 3–7, we get an expression that describes equilibrium in the goods market:

$$Y_e = \frac{1}{1 - (C_1 + I_1)} \times (C_0 + I_0 - I_2 r) \tag{3–8}$$

Equation 3–8 determines the level of aggregate demand where the value of income equals the value of output with no unintended increases or decreases in inventories. This is the expression of equilibrium of aggregate demand and supply that we have been working toward. At this level of income, businesses will not increase or decrease supply. Thus, this level of aggregate demand, which is equal to aggregate supply, represents goods-market equilibrium for the economy.

Equilibrium with a Given Interest Rate

For the time being, we are going to study the determination of equilibrium income with the rate of interest taken as given. For example, we could suppose that the interest rate was fixed by monetary policy. This is a useful simplifying assumption that we later will change to see how the interest rate affects goods-market equilibrium. We write r as $\bar{r}$ to denote that we are fixing the interest rate.

In this equilibrium solution, C_0, I_0, and $I_2 \bar{r}$ represent the *autonomous* parts of expenditure. These components of expenditure include the intercept terms in the consumption and investment schedules plus the part of investment demand that varies with the interest rate, $I_2 \bar{r}$. This last term is included at this stage of our analysis in what we have called ''autonomous'' expenditure, because here we are assuming a fixed interest rate.

multiplier
In the simple income determination model, the level of equilibrium income is proportional to autonomous expenditure. The factor of proportionality is called the "multiplier."

Equilibrium income is proportional to total autonomous expenditure. The factor of proportionality is given a special name: the **multiplier.**

Equilibrium income =   Multiplier $\times$ Autonomous expenditure

$$Y_e \qquad = \frac{1}{1 - (C_1 + I_1)} \times \qquad (C_0 + I_0 - I_2 \bar{r}) \qquad (3-9)$$

In this simple model of the economy, the multiplier is equal to $1 \div [1 - (C_1 + I_1)]$ and it depends on the marginal propensities to spend in the model: the marginal propensity to consume (MPC) and the marginal propensity to invest (MPI). As we develop the simple model of the economy later, the exact expression for the multiplier will change. But the concept will continue to be important. *Equilibrium in the goods market occurs where the levels of income and output are equal to aggregate demand—the autonomous parts of expenditure (the ones that do not vary with income) times the multiplier.*

> *Worked Example 3–1*   This worked example gives a numerical consumption function and a numerical investment function and then shows how to determine the equilibrium level of income with a given rate of interest. The magnitude of the multiplier is derived and the effect of an increase in the MPC is explored. The example is worked out on p. 84.

The determination of equilibrium income is shown in Figure 3–6. The dark red line $[(C + I_p)_0]$ through point E is the aggregate-demand line. It shows the investment function added to (sitting on top of) the consumption function. Consumption and planned investment are added vertically to give total expenditures $(C + I_p)$. In the figure, the points all along the 45-degree line are where the vertical and horizontal distances are equal. The point where the aggregate-demand line intersects with the 45-degree line (point E) is the point where the vertical distance (aggregate demand) equals the horizontal distance (output or aggregate supply).

Adjustment to Equilibrium

If the economy is not at a point of equilibrium income, aggregate supply and demand will adjust so that the economy reaches equilibrium. Suppose aggregate production or supply exceeds the total of consumption demand and planned-investment demand $(Y_A > Y_e$ at point A in Figure 3–6; point A' along the aggregate demand line is below point A along the 45-degree line). This would mean that inventories are piling up and that there is unintended inventory accumulation. Producers respond to this by cutting back production (a drop in aggregate supply) and *this means a fall in income, because income is generated by production.* The fall in income shows up most obviously in layoffs of workers and a decline in the wage income that they earn. When income falls, this causes a fall in consumption demand and in planned-investment demand (a drop in aggregate demand), because both depend on income. So if the economy starts from a point where supply exceeds planned demand (point A), then, as firms cut production to close the gap, they end up causing a further reduction in demand,

FIGURE 3–6
The Determination of Goods-Market Equilibrium

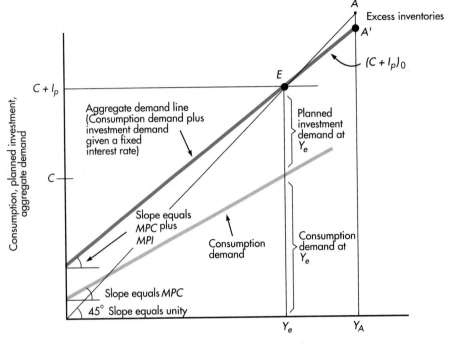

The aggregate demand line crosses the 45-degree line at point *E*.

meaning that the gap may not be closed until there are further reductions in income (point *A* to point *E*).[7]

Changes in Equilibrium Income and the Multiplier

The relationships between income and the interest rate and the demand for consumption and investment expenditures can change. Households may become more optimistic about future income; firms may find that they would rather invest more even at the current income and interest rate. We capture these changes in demand by allowing for a shift in the consumption or the investment functions,[8] or both. This increase or decrease in the autonomous part of consumption, C_0 or of investment I_0, initially increases aggregate demand, which eventually leads to a change in equilibrium income that is a multiple of the initial change in expenditures. Small shifts in the consumption-demand or investment-demand schedules will lead to much larger

---

7 We have neglected one aspect of the adjustment process. When excess inventories pile up, not only will firms cut production to match demand, they will go beyond this to work off the excess inventories. In practice this can give rise to overshooting of equilibrium, a phenomenon known as an inventory cycle.

8 Changes in the demand for consumption or investment expenditures, or both, can also be due to increases or decreases in the marginal propensities to spend (MPC and MPI). These changes would be shown as twists or changes of slope in the straight-line consumption and investment functions used in graphical analysis of an adjustment to equilibrium.

changes in income and output. The reason is that, when businesses or customers step up their expenditures, demand rises, and then producers respond by increasing output. The boost in output then raises employment and income. And the increase in income then induces a further increase in demand until a new equilibrium is reached. There is a similar chain-reaction process working to reduce equilibrium output when the demand schedules shift down.

The effect of shifts in the demand schedules on equilibrium income can be analyzed algebraically, using the multiplier in Equation 3–10. The multiplier gives the factor of proportionality between equilibrium income and autonomous expenditure, and it also indicates that a change in autonomous expenditure results in a change in income.

The Multiplier and a Change in Investment Demand

Suppose there is increased optimism among businesses about future sales. At any level of income and interest rate, there would be a higher level of expenditure on investment goods. The change in planned investment would be represented by an increase in autonomous investment ($\Delta I_0 > 0$). The new level of planned investment is:

$$I_p = I_0 + \Delta I_0 + I_1 Y - I_1 \bar{r} \tag{3–10}$$

This shift in investment demand leads to a shift in equilibrium income. Before the increase in autonomous investment demand, the equilibrium condition was:

$$Y_e \times [1 - (C_1 + I_1)] = (C_0 + I_0 - I_1 \bar{r}) \tag{3–11}$$

After the increase in autonomous investment expenditure, the equilibrium condition becomes:

$$(Y_e + \Delta Y_e) \times [1 - (C + I_1)] = (C_0 + I_0 + \Delta I_0 - I_1) \tag{3–12}$$

Subtracting 3–11 from 3–12 and dividing by $[1 - (C_1 + I_1)]$ gives the expression that describes the change in equilibrium income:

$$\Delta Y_e = \frac{1}{1 - (C_1 + I_1)} \times \Delta I_0 \tag{3–13}$$

The change in equilibrium income and output is equal to the multiplier times the change in the autonomous portion of planned investment.

The multiplier formula shows that the final increase in equilibrium income is larger than the initial increase in autonomous expenditure, provided the multiplier is greater than unity.

For example, if planned investment increases by $1 billion and the sum of the MPC and MPI is 0.75, then output increases by $4 billion. In this example, an investment-demand increase of $1 billion adds $1 billion directly to aggregate demand and stimulates an extra $3 billion of subsequent production. The $3 billion of subsequent production comes about in the adjustment process leading to the new equilibrium level of income.

The $1 billion increase of income resulting from a $1 billion increase in investment demand is the initial or first-round effect. The second-round effect of the rise in investment expenditure includes two elements that then follow from the increase in income. Consumers spend a fraction (C_1) of that extra billion dollars of income. And then the same rise of income of $1 billion also triggers a change in planned investment over and above the initial change in autonomous planned investment. Investment expenditure increases when firms spend a fraction (I_1) of the extra billion dollars of income. The second-round effect, therefore, is the total of the marginal propensities ($C_1 + I_1$). If ($C_1 + I_1$) equals 0.75, then the second-round effect on income and expenditure is $750 million.

The $750 million of production and expenditure from the second round also generates extra income. In our example, the third round of expenditure and income is 0.75 of $750 million, which is $562.5 million. In general, the third-round effect is ($C_1 + I_1$) × ($C_1 + I_1$) or ($C_1 + I_1$)^2.

This process continues until the initial increase in demand of $1 billion leads to a much larger final effect on output and income because of the chain reaction it induces.[9]

Although we have looked at the multiplier effect in terms of a change in investment demand, the same analysis applies to a change in autonomous consumption. If consumers become more optimistic and decide that a recession any time soon is unlikely, they will spend more now and save less. Or perhaps the consumption of automobiles increases with no offsetting reduction in other purchases because gasoline prices have fallen, financing arrangements are improved, or new car models are more attractive. Regardless, if consumption shifts up, sales revenues go up, automakers and other producers will respond with higher production, and the chain reaction works itself out in the same manner as described for investment demand.

Worked Example 3–2   This worked example uses the same consumption and investment functions that were used in Worked Example 3–1 and asks what happens if there is a change in autonomous expenditure. The example is worked through on p. 86.

GOODS-MARKET EQUILIBRIUM, INTEREST RATES, INVESTMENT, AND SAVING

We have looked at how equilibrium income is determined by aggregate supply and demand in the goods market. Equilibrium income was determined *assuming a fixed interest rate.* That was a useful simplification and gave us insights into the real economy, about how changes in production feed back into changes in demand. However, interest rates change and those changes affect the level of equilibrium income. The interest rate is determined in part by financial markets and in part by the supply and demand for real goods and services. The interest rate is the link between

---

[9] Those of you familiar with the algebra of series will realize the final change in income and output that results from the initial investment stimulus can be described by the relation:

$$\Delta Y = \Delta I_0 \times [1 + (C + I_1) + (C_1 + I_1)^2 + (C_1 + I_1)^3 + \ldots]$$

Each term in parentheses represents a successive round of the chain reaction—unity on the first round; ($C_1 + I$) on the second round; ($C_1 + I$)^2 on the third round; ($C_1 + I$)^3 on the fourth round; and so on. The sum of this series is just equal to $1 \div [1 - (C_1 + I_1)]$, the multiplier. Looking at the sum of an infinite series gives us exactly the same answer as we found before.

the money and financial markets and the goods market. We have to see how the interest rate affects goods-market equilibrium and vice versa.

We will make one important change in this part of the chapter to simplify the exposition. *From now on in the algebraic discussion we will refer only to points of goods-market equilibrium. Total investment (I) and planned investment (I_p) will always be the same, and we will refer only to investment (I). Unless specifically noted, income (Y) will be equilibrium income ($Y = Y_e$).* When we talk about changing Y, from now on, we are talking about changes in the level of income for which the goods market is in equilibrium.

Interest Rates and Aggregate Demand

The interest rate affects aggregate demand through investment demand. An increase in the interest rate leads to a fall in investment demand, and a decrease in the interest rate leads to a rise in investment. Figure 3–7 shows how equilibrium income is determined at two rates of interest, r_1 and r_2, where r_2 is lower than r_1. At interest rate r_1, equilibrium income is at Y_1. At the lower rate of interest, r_2, the investment-demand function shifts up, the aggregate-demand line moves up ($[C + I]_1$ to $[C + I]_2$), and the equilibrium point shifts out (E_1 to E_2). The result of the drop in the interest rate is much the same as the result of an increase in autonomous expenditure; it causes investment demand to rise. The multiplier effects of that initial increase in investment expenditure drive up equilibrium income (Y_1 to Y_2).

FIGURE 3–7
The Effect of a Fall in the Rate of Interest on Goods-Market Equilibrium

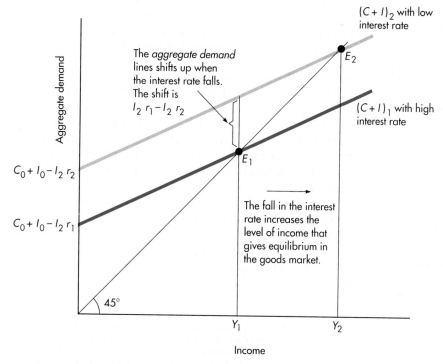

The *aggregate demand* lines shifts up when the interest rate falls. The shift is $I_2 r_1 - I_2 r_2$

$(C + I)_2$ with low interest rate

$(C + I)_1$ with high interest rate

E_2

E_1

The fall in the interest rate increases the level of income that gives equilibrium in the goods market.

$C_0 + I_0 - I_2 r_2$

$C_0 + I_0 - I_2 r_1$

Aggregate demand

45°

Y_1 Y_2

Income

Algebraically, the upward shift in the investment function is given as follows:

Investment demand at $r_1 = I_0 + I_1Y - I_2r_1$
Investment demand at $r_2 = I_0 + I_1Y - I_2r_2$
Shift in investment demand $= I_2r_1 - I_2r_2$

The effect of this shift in the investment-demand function on equilibrium income then follows from the multiplier analysis:

$$\Delta Y = \frac{1}{1 - (C_1 + I_1)} \times (I_2r_1 - I_2r_2)$$
$$= Y_2 - Y_1 \qquad (3-14)$$

A decline in the rate of interest is like a shift in the autonomous component of investment. It produces a multiplied response, an increase in income.

Suppose that the economy has been in a recession for a while, and then the rate of interest falls (perhaps because of a policy change by the Federal Reserve Board). This fall in the rate of interest increases the demand for investment goods, particularly new houses and other construction. This increase in investment demand has an initial, or first-round, effect on income and output. Then the initial rise in income generates second-round effects on both consumption demand and investment as the multiplier process works its way through the economy. The final result of the fall in the interest rate is an increase in equilibrium income.

The process also works in reverse. If the rate of interest rises, this can induce a drop in housing starts and other investment demand, leading to a multiplied decline in income and output. Changes in the rate of interest have proven to be a powerful influence on aggregate demand in the U.S. economy.[10]

Equilibrium Income and the Interest Rate: The *IS* Schedule

The equilibrium level of income is different at a low rate of interest than at a high rate of interest. Another way of saying this is that *the goods market is in equilibrium with many different combinations of income and the interest rate.* In our example, the combination of a high interest rate and a low level of income (r_1,Y_1) gives goods-market equilibrium. But the combination of a low rate of interest and a high level of income (r_2,Y_2) also gives goods-market equilibrium. And, of course, there are many other combinations of interest rate and income in between that will give goods-market equilibrium.

The combinations of interest rate and income that generate equilibrium in the goods market make up what is known as the IS *schedule.* The **IS schedule** is shown in Figure 3–8. The pairs of values of the interest rate and income (r_1 and Y_1 at point E_1, and r_2 and Y_2 at point E_2) used in Figure 3–7 are identified along the *IS* schedule (points E_1 and E_2) in Figure 3–8. The *IS* schedule is downward-sloping because high interest rates discourage investment and therefore reduce equilibrium income.

IS schedule
The combination of interest rate and income that generate goods-market equilibrium.

---

10 When general business conditions are healthy, changes in the interest rate are more likely to affect investment demand than when general business conditions are suffering from recession or expectations of recession. A lower interest rate will be a weak incentive to invest when business prospects are poor. This helps explain why the Fed found it hard to stimulate the economy with low interest rates in 1992.

FIGURE 3–8
The IS Schedule

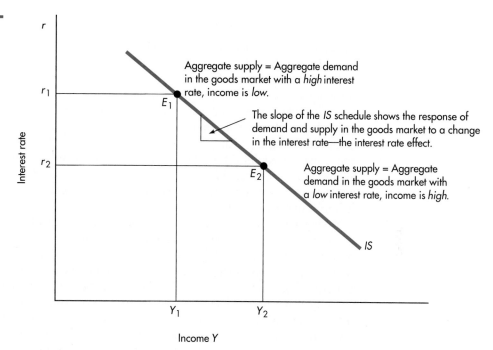

The *IS* schedule shows the combinations of income and interest rate that are consistent with goods-market equilibrium.

The slope of the *IS* schedule is important because it shows how much equilibrium income will change with a change in the interest rate. If a lower interest rate stimulates a large increase in aggregate demand, then the *IS* schedule will be flat. If a lower interest rate stimulates only a small increase in aggregate demand, then the *IS* schedule will be steep. In later chapters we look at the conditions that lead to large or small interest-rate effects.

Worked Example 3–3   In this example on page 87, we use the same consumption and investment functions used earlier in this chapter. But now we allow the interest rate to vary and solve for the IS schedule, rather than for a single level of equilibrium income.

Investment and Saving

The IS schedule gives points of goods-market equilibrium, but it gets its name from the fact that these are also points where saving equals investment. Households receive income in the form of wages, interest, and dividends from companies. Part of this income is used for consumption and (with no government or taxes) the remainder is saved. **Saving** is defined as income less consumption:

saving
Saving is the part of income that is not used for consumption.

$$S = Y - C \tag{3–15}$$

The condition for equilibrium in the goods market is that income equals aggregate demand. Using the definition of saving allows this condition to be expressed as follows:

$Y = C + I$, which implies $Y - C = I = S$ (3–16)

The condition for goods-market equilibrium is that saving (S) equals planned investment (I), and this tells us something important.

Production generates income in the household sector. Income is used partly for consumption, while some of it is set aside as saving. The part set aside for saving does not contribute directly to demand, so saving reduces aggregate demand. On the other hand, there is demand generated by businesses making investment. When the subtraction from demand (saving) equals the addition to demand (investment), then there is goods-market equilibrium. The amount of investment is influenced by the rate of interest, so *the IS schedule shows the points of goods-market equilibrium, where the interest rate encourages just the amount of investment by businesses that equals the saving being made by households.*

Saving represents income that does not become part of aggregate demand. This suggests that, when saving is relatively large, then consumption and hence aggregate demand will be relatively small. Indeed, if an economy is in a recession where demand is too low, saving is too high. If, for example, consumers suddenly decreased spending at all levels of income (a drop in C_0), there could be too much saving given the level of investment businesses plan to make. Then income would fall, lowering both saving and investment until the two are equal.[11] However, it would be wrong to think of saving as a detriment to the economy. By the act of saving, households refrain from consuming all of the goods and services produced. If business can gain access to those resources, perhaps by borrowing funds from savers, then business can make investments in capital goods that increase potential output. An economy's capability for growth is affected by its capacity for saving. If saving and investment can rise together, this will provide more capital resources for the long-run growth of the economy.

Increased saving can help the economy by freeing resources or it can hurt the economy by creating a shortage of demand. Which of the two cases applies depends on whether there is *coordination* between saving and investment. If higher saving is accompanied by higher investment, the economy is helped. If higher saving leads to a recession, the economy is hurt.

Saving—Investment Coordination

The idea that a failure of coordination between saving decisions and investment decisions could lead to recession is the major conclusion to be drawn from the work of John Maynard Keynes.[12] Keynes argued that saving could exceed planned-investment demand. In this situation, the result is excess supply of goods and services in the economy along with falling production and income. The equality of saving and investment is then restored, but only by a reduction of income as the economy goes into a recession.

---

[11] Starting from a position of $S > I$, equilibrium will be reached as long as saving falls by more than investment as income declines. Investment declines by $(I_1 \times \Delta Y)$. Saving declines by $(1 - C_1) \Delta Y$. As long as $(C_1 + I_1)$ is less than unity, saving declines by more than investment as income falls.

[12] J. M. Keynes, *The General Theory of Employment, Interest and Money,* 1936.

Prior to Keynes, economists had not considered that coordinating saving and investment decisions was a problem. The rate of interest was seen as the mechanism that brought the two into equality, without there being any fluctuations in income. And many economists still hold this view today. The view of Keynes has not been universally accepted by any means.

We have seen that changes in the rate of interest affect goods-markets equilibrium. The demand by business for new offices, factories, and equipment and the demand by households for new houses depends on the rate of interest. And this means that aggregate supply and demand will be equal at a higher level of income when the interest rate is low than when it is high.

To see how the rate of interest is determined, and then subsequently to see how monetary policy affects interest rates and the economy, we need to look at an analysis of a monetary economy and how the supply of and demand for money are equated to give money market equilibrium. But before we close that loop, first we want to see how the international sector of the economy influences demands and income. We will ask how the foreign sector affects the multiplier and how shifts in autonomous expenditure have an impact on the balance of imports and exports.

THE FOREIGN SECTOR: A FIRST LOOK

When consumers and firms can buy from overseas, part of consumption demand and planned-investment demand consists of foreign purchases. Thus, when the economy imports goods and services (*IM*), this is a subtraction from the total demand for domestically produced goods and services. On the other hand, when foreigners purchase goods and services from U.S. producers, these exports (*X*) are an addition to the demand for domestically produced goods. With a foreign sector, therefore, the condition for equilibrium income becomes:

$$Y = C + I + X - IM \tag{3-17}$$

We have already looked at what determines consumption and investment demand, so now we simply consider the factors that determine exports and imports. There are three main factors. The first is that the volume of imports depends on the level of domestic income. The more income that people have to spend, the more they spend on imports. The second factor is that the volume of exports depends on the level of income overseas. If Europe has a recession, U.S. exports decline. And third, both imports and exports depend on the prices of imports and exports. This last factor is reflected in the value of the dollar—the U.S. exchange rate relative to other countries' currencies. In this first look at trade we cannot take account of all three of these. Instead, we will only focus here on the *effect of domestic income on the demand for imported goods and services.*

Import Demand, Income, and the Trade Balance

In this discussion, the relationship between imports and income is simply described by a linear function much like the consumption and investment functions. Equation 3–18 shows the import function:

$$IM = IM_0 + IM_1 Y \tag{3-18}$$

marginal propensity to import (MPM)
The amount of increased imports (ΔIM) that results from an amount of increased income (ΔY) expressed as $\Delta IM/\Delta Y$.

In Equation 3–18, IM_0 represents the autonomous part of imports. IM_1 is the **marginal propensity to import,** which is positive and shows how imports increase as domestic income increases. Figure 3–9 illustrates the import function. The higher is income ($Y_A > Y_B$), the higher are imports ($IM_A > IM_B$). Since the exchange rate and foreign income are taken as fixed, the demand in other countries for U.S. goods and services (export demand) is predetermined. In this first look at trade, the level of exports doesn't change so that exports ($X = \overline{X}$) are shown as a horizontal line in Figure 3–9.

balance of trade
The difference between exports and imports.

Also shown in the figure is the **balance of trade,** the difference between exports and imports. Whenever the import line is above the horizontal export line (as when point A is above A'), there is a deficit—imports exceed exports. When the import line is below the export line (as when point B is below B'), there is a surplus. The trade balance is zero ($\overline{X} = IM$) when the import function crosses the export line (point C). The level of income (Y_C) at which the trade balance is zero is not necessarily an equilibrium level of income, nor is it a preferred target for equilibrium. Equilibrium can, and does, come about at levels of income that generate trade deficits or trade surpluses, and we would not argue that policy should be directed at changing the trade balance. We note, however, that one sure way to change the trade balance is to change the equilibrium level of income. A trade deficit can be converted into a trade surplus if the economy slides into a recession (point A to point B as income goes from Y_A to Y_B).

Goods-Market Equilibrium with Foreign Trade

We find the equilibrium level of income, accounting for foreign trade, by substituting the consumption, investment, export, and import functions into the expression for equilibrium income. As we did earlier in the chapter, we hold the interest rate constant at $r = \overline{r}$.

FIGURE 3–9
The Import Function and the Trade Balance

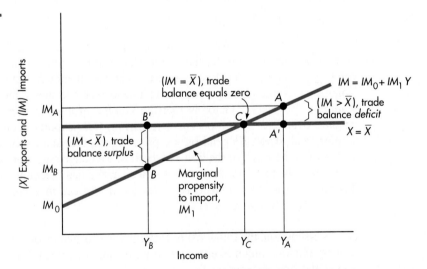

Exports can be larger or smaller than imports at different levels of income.

$$\begin{array}{rlll} \underset{\text{Income}}{\text{Equilibrium}} & = \text{Consumption} + & \text{Investment} & + \text{Exports} - & \text{Imports} \\ Y & = (C_0 + C_1 Y) + & (I_0 + I_1 Y - I_2 \bar{r}) + & (\overline{X}) & - (IM_0 + IM_1 Y) \end{array}$$
$$(3\text{--}19)$$

Collecting terms and solving for equilibrium income gives the equilibrium condition with a foreign sector:

$$Y = \frac{1}{1 - (C_1 + I_1) + IM_1} \times (C_0 + I_0 - I_2 \bar{r} + \overline{X} - IM_0) \qquad (3\text{--}20)$$

The multiplier is smaller as a result of the marginal propensity to import. To give an example, in our model, if IM_1 were 0.1 and the sum of the marginal propensities to consume and invest were 0.8 ($C_1 + I_1 = 0.8$), then the denominator of the multiplier expression would be 0.3 and the multiplier would be 3.3. In a closed economy, with no imports, the denominator of the multiplier expression is 0.2 ($1 - 0.8$) and the multiplier itself is 5. The presence of imports has reduced the size of the multiplier. Because a portion of the increase in income is spent on imports, a change in autonomous expenditure has a smaller effect on income with foreign trade than without it.

The successive rounds of expansion, following an increase in investment or consumption, have a smaller effect because *part of each increase in income "leaks" overseas in the form of demand for imports,* rather than adding to domestic demand.

The effect of trade on the multiplier is only one part of the effect of trade on income. Autonomous expenditure has also changed. Exports ($\overline{X}$) increase autonomous expenditures, while the autonomous portion of imports (IM_0) is a subtraction from such expenditure. In general, total exports will be larger than the purely autonomous part of imports. *Autonomous expenditure is increased as a result of the foreign sector.* The demand for domestic goods coming from overseas can benefit demand.

As a result of the foreign sector, the multiplier is smaller but the autonomous expenditure is larger. What is the overall effect of the foreign sector on equilibrium income? The answer can go either way. One way to think about the overall effect is as follows. Consider an economy with no foreign trade where the economy was in equilibrium. Then suppose that the country opened its borders and allowed imports and exports. If it were to turn out that export demand (demand by foreigners for U.S. goods) were just equal to import demand (demand by U.S. residents for foreign goods), then the presence of the foreign sector would have had no *net* effect on demand and, hence, on equilibrium income. In other words, if the trade balance is zero, then the foreign sector is neither boosting nor decreasing equilibrium income. Exports are adding to demand the same amount that imports are subtracting.

International trade among market economies is not constrained to be balanced. In practice, exports may be greater or less than imports, so that net foreign demand may raise or lower equilibrium income. In 1980 the United States had a surplus of exports over imports, so foreign trade was boosting U.S. demand and income, while in 1987 there was a huge deficit, so the foreign sector was reducing U.S. demand. There is a continuing trade deficit in the early 1990s.

Changes in Equilibrium Income and the Trade Balance

Suppose the economy starts out with exports and imports in balance as illustrated by the point where $Y = Y_C$ in Figure 3–9. Then suppose there is an increase in autonomous investment. The impact on equilibrium income follows from the new expression for the multiplier. From Equation 3–20:

$$\Delta Y = \frac{1}{1 - (C_1 + I_1) + IM_1} \times \Delta I_0$$

The change in equilibrium income is the new multiplier times the change in I_0. When equilibrium income changes, imports also change:

$$\Delta IM = IM_1 \times \Delta Y \tag{3–21}$$

Since exports are fixed, there is now a deficit on the foreign account (point A to Point A' in Figure 3–9) as imports exceed exports. *Starting from trade balance, an increase in income will result in a trade deficit.* And, of course, the same idea holds in reverse: *A fall in income will induce a trade surplus or reduce a preexisting deficit.*

The impact of income on trade is important in practice. One reason for the U.S. trade deficit in the mid-1980s was that the U.S. economy experienced strong income growth after 1982 and this pulled in imports. As the U.S. economy went into recession in 1990 and 91, this reduced U.S. imports.

> *Worked Example 3–4*   This example uses the same consumption and investment functions as prior worked examples, but adds an import function and exports. It examines the impact of international trade on the multiplier and equilibrium income. And it looks at the trade surplus or deficit. This example is worked out on page 87.

This concludes our first look at the foreign sector. We have shown how exports add to the total demand for goods produced in the United States. When U.S. consumers or businesses buy foreign goods, rather than U.S-made goods, this is a subtraction from U.S. demand. The net effect of the foreign sector on demand depends on whether we are running a surplus or a deficit in foreign trade.

We have also seen how changes in domestic income affect whether we run a trade deficit or a surplus. Strong growth in income tends to increase imports.

In the next chapter we return once again to a model of a closed economy—that is, one without foreign trade. We will be looking instead at how changes in the interest rate affect goods-market equilibrium (using the IS schedule) and then at the money market (using the LM schedule).

WORKED EXAMPLES

Worked Example 3–1

Determining Aggregate Demand and Goods-Market Equilibrium: Autonomous Expenditure and the Multiplier

Question   In a simple economy the consumption function is given as follows:

$$C = 600 + 0.7Y$$

Income (Y) and consumption (C) are in billions of dollars. The investment function is:

$$I_P = 250 + 0.1Y - 10r$$

In this expression the interest rate is expressed as an annual percentage.

    a. If the interest rate is 5 percent, what is the value of autonomous expenditure in this economy?

    b. What is the value of the multiplier in this economy?

    c. Solve for the level of income that gives goods-market equilibrium. What are the levels of consumption and investment at this level of income?

    d. If the MPC were to increase to 0.75, what would be the new multiplier and the new level of equilibrium income?

Answer   Always go to the condition that output equals aggregate demand. In our simple model, there is only consumption and investment demand, so we get:

$$Y_e = \underset{\text{(consumption)}}{600 + 0.7Y_e} + \underset{\text{(investment)}}{250 + 0.1Y_e} - 10r$$

$$Y_e = 600 + 0.7Y_e + 250 + 0.1Y_e - (10 \times 5)$$

Now collect all the terms with Y_e in them on the left-hand side and all the other terms on the right-hand side:

$$Y_e(0.2) = 800$$

Now divide both sides by the bracketed term:

$$Y_e = \frac{1}{0.2} \times 800$$

Part *(a)* asks for autonomous expenditure. The answer is 800. It is the sum of all the terms that do not contain Y_e. Part *(b)* asks for the multiplier, which in this model is $(1 \div 0.2) = 5$. The answer to part *(b)* is 5.

    The question then asks for the level of equilibrium income, and we can see that $Y_e = 4,000$. The first part of the answer to *(c)* is \$4 trillion. The level of consumption and planned investment are found by substituting back into the consumption and investment functions.

$$C = 600 + (0.7 \times 4,000) = 3,400$$
$$I_P = 250 + (0.1 \times 4,000) - 50 = 600$$

The rest of the answer to part *(c)* is that consumption is \$3.4 trillion and investment is \$600 billion.

    Part *(d)* of the question asks about the effect of increasing the MPC. This means there is a new consumption function:

$$C = 600 + 0.75Y_e$$

Substituting this function, rather than the original one, gives:

$$Y_e = 600 + 0.75 Y_e + 250 + 0.1Y_e - (10 \times 5)$$

We are assuming the interest rate stays at 5 percent. Collecting terms in the same way as before gives:

$$Y_e(0.15) = 800$$
$$Y_e = 1 \div 0.15 \times 800$$
$$= 5,333$$

The new multiplier is $(1 \div 0.15) = 6.67$, and the new equilibrium level of income is $5.33 trillion.

Worked Example 3–2

The Effect of Changes in Autonomous Expenditure

Consider the same simple economy that we used in the first example. We will look at the case where the MPC is 0.7. The consumption and investment schedules and equilibrium income in that case were:

$$C = 600 + 0.7Y$$
$$I_p = 250 + 0.1Y - (10 \times 5)$$
$$Y_e = 4,000$$

We are assuming that the interest rate remains at 5 percent throughout.

Questions

  a. What is the effect on equilibrium income of a decrease in autonomous consumption (C_0) from $600 to $550?
  b. What is the effect on equilibrium income of an increase in autonomous investment (I_0) from $250 to $300?

Answers   We will do this problem two ways. The long way is to solve for the new equilibrium income:

$$Y = 550 + 0.7Y + 250 + 0.1Y - (10 \times 5)$$
$$Y[1 - (0.7 + 0.1)] = 750$$
$$Y_e = \frac{1}{0.2} \times 750$$
$$= 3,750.$$

The answer to part *(a)* is that equilibrium income falls to $3.75 trillion. Now we do the problem the quick way.

$$\Delta Y_e = \text{multiplier} \times \Delta C_0$$
$$= 5 (-50) = -250$$

So the level of income goes from $4,000 to $3,750, the same answer we got doing it the long way.

  Finding the effect of an increase of $50 in the autonomous part of investment is similar to finding the effect of the increase in autonomous consumption. We could solve for the new equilibrium level of income, or we can use the multiplier. We will do it the quick way.

$$\Delta Y_e = \text{multiplier} \times \Delta I_0$$
$$= 5 \times 50 = 250$$

Equilibrium income rises by $250 billion.

Worked Example 3–3

Finding the *IS* Schedule

The *IS* schedule is derived from the same relation as the one we have been using to solve for equilibrium income. We find the *IS* schedule by equating output and aggregate demand. The difference is that we are now considering the interest rate as a variable rather than as a fixed number. This means that *instead of solving for Y, we will solve for the equation that shows how r varies with Y.* We will use the same investment and consumption functions that we used in the earlier examples:

$$C = 600 + 0.7Y$$
$$I = 250 + 0.1Y - 10r$$

We will now let the interest rate vary rather than being fixed at 5 percent.

Questions

a. With the relations just shown, what is the *IS* schedule?
b. What is the slope of this schedule?

Answers   Output equals aggregate demand gives the following:

$$Y = 600 + 0.7Y + 250 + 0.1Y - 10r$$

Now collect the terms with r in them on the left-hand side. And on the right-hand side collect two terms: one with the autonomous components of expenditure and the other with the terms involving Y. Notice that since the interest rate varies, it is treated separately. The interest-rate term is no longer included in autonomous expenditure:

$$10r = 850 + [(0.7 + 0.1) - 1]Y$$
$$r = 85 - 0.02Y$$

We have now answered part *(a)*. The preceding equation is the *IS* schedule. It is a linear— straight-line—relation and the slope is the coefficient on Y. The answer to part *(b)* is that the slope of the *IS* schedule is -0.02. This slope means that if we compare two points that are both in goods-market equilibrium, and the rates of interest differ by one percentage point, then the levels of income will differ by -50, as shown by the fact that $-0.02 \times (-50) = 1$.

Worked Example 3–4

The Foreign Sector and Aggregate Demand

We are going to take the same economy that was used in the earlier worked examples and add in the import and export functions. We get the following relations.

$$C = 600 + 0.7Y$$
$$I_p = 250 + 0.1Y - (10 \times 5)$$
$$IM = 50 + 0.1Y$$
$$\overline{X} = 450$$

Questions

a. What are the multiplier and equilibrium income in this economy?
b. Is there a trade surplus or deficit in equilibrium?
c. How do your answers change if exports increase to 510?

Answers   Use the condition that output equals aggregate demand, where demand includes exports and subtracts imports. We are assuming that the rate of interest remains at 5 percent throughout.

$$Y = 600 + 0.7Y + 250 + 0.1Y - (10 \times 5) + 450 - (50 + 0.1Y)$$
$$ \underbrace{}_{\text{Consumption}} \quad \underbrace{}_{\text{Investment}} \qquad \underbrace{}_{\text{Exports}} \quad \underbrace{}_{\text{Imports}}$$

Now collect all the terms involving Y on the left-hand side and all the autonomous terms on the right-hand side:

$$Y = (1 \div 0.3) \times 1,200$$
$$= 4,000$$

We have found that the equilibrium level of income is $4 trillion and the multiplier is $1 \div 0.3 = 3.3$. So we have the answer to part *(a)*. To find the surplus or deficit, we substitute the equilibrium level of income into the import function:

$$IM = 50 + (0.1 \times 4,000) = 450$$

Then the trade balance is equal to exports minus imports:

$$\text{Trade balance} = X - IM$$
$$= 450 - 450 = 0$$

The answer to part *(b)* is that there is no deficit or surplus, so trade is balanced. Actually, we knew it would come out this way because the level of equilibrium income, at $4 trillion, is the same as it was with no foreign trade.

To get the answer to part *(c)* we can use the long way and solve again for equilibrium income or we can use the multiplier. The multiplier is unaffected by the increase in exports, which are part of autonomous expenditure. We will just use the short way:

$$\Delta Y_e = \text{multiplier} \times \Delta \overline{X}$$
$$= (1 \div 0.3) \times 60$$
$$= 200$$

Equilibrium income increases from $4 trillion to $4.2.

The trade balance is affected both by the increase in exports and by the increase in imports caused by the increase in income:

$$\text{Trade balance} = 510 - [50 + (0.1 \times 4,200)]$$
$$= 510 - (50 + 420)$$
$$= 510 - 470$$
$$= 40$$

This completes the answer to part *(c)*. The trade balance did turn positive and equilibrium income increased as a result of the increase in exports. But the improvement in the trade balance was not dollar for dollar with the increase in exports. As income rose, this sucked more imports into the economy.

SUMMARY

- Aggregate supply and aggregate demand determine equilibrium income. In the short run the aggregate-supply schedule is fairly flat. Businesses are willing to supply the market demand at a given price. When production plans do not match demand, businesses will increase or decrease their inventories.

- Using the concepts of the National Income and Product Accounts insures equality between aggregate output and expenditure, but this is only an identity. It is true by definition, and the key definition that makes it true is that changes in inventory (positive or negative) are automatically counted as additions to or subtractions from investment.

- Goods-market equilibrium requires a more restrictive condition, namely that aggregate supply equals aggregate demand with no unplanned investment. This point of equilibrium is important because, if the economy is not in equilibrium, it will move toward it. Businesses will expand or contract their production, depending on whether inventories are piling up or running down.

- The consumption function relates consumption demand to the level of income using a simple straight-line function. The average propensity to consume, APC, is the average share of income devoted to consumption. The marginal propensity to consume, MPC, is the share of each additional dollar devoted to consumption.

- Planned investment demand is the amount businesses wish to add to their stock of capital goods and any planned increase in inventories. Investment demand depends positively on income and negatively on the rate of interest. The marginal propensity to invest is the change in investment demand resulting from a change in income.

- Equilibrium income can be determined with a given rate of interest. It is the level of income that equates supply and planned demand, using the consumption and investment functions to determine demand. Equilibrium income is equal to the multiplier times autonomous expenditure, and this same relation holds for changes in income. When there is a shift in autonomous expenditure, the resulting change in equilibrium income is equal to the multiplier times the change in the autonomous portion of expenditure.

- Income and interest rates combine to determine the demand for goods and services. Different combinations of interest rate and income generate different levels of aggregate demand, as shown along the IS schedule.

- Higher saving reduces aggregate demand but releases resources that can be used by firms for investment purchases. If firms buy capital goods with the resources released by saving, then saving will have increased the economy's ability to raise income by raising future potential output. An increase in saving that is coordinated with an increase in investment will maintain demand and help the long-run growth of the economy. If saving and investment are not coordinated, then the result will be income fluctuations and recessions.

- The foreign sector also affects aggregate demand. Exports are an addition to demand, while imports are a subtraction. A new expression for equilibrium income can be derived in which the multiplier is lower because of the marginal propensity to import, while autonomous expenditure is higher. The overall effect of the foreign sector depends upon whether exports exceed imports (raising income) or imports exceed exports (lowering income).

- Domestic income affects the foreign sector. If the economy expands, imports will increase but exports will not, so the effect may be a trade deficit.

KEY TERMS AND CONCEPTS

aggregate demand, p. 61

aggregate supply, p. 61

average propensity to consume, p. 68

balance of trade, p. 82

consumption function, p. 67

identity, p. 65

IS schedule, p. 78

investment function, p. 69

marginal propensity to consume (MPC), p. 67

marginal propensity to import (MPM), p. 82

marginal propensity to invest (MPI), p. 69

multiplier, p. 73

planned investment, p. 69

saving, p. 79

DISCUSSION QUESTIONS AND PROBLEMS

1. How does aggregate supply adjust to meet aggregate demand?

2. If the consumption function is represented by a straight line, how can the share of income spent on consumption goods decline as income rises?

3. Draw the investment function assuming a fixed rate of interest. How does it shift if the rate of interest increases or decreases?

4. Aggregate demand equals aggregate supply. In the simple model of the economy in this chapter, consumption and planned investment are the two components of aggregate demand. How can their sum exceed or fall short of aggregate supply?

5. Show graphically how equilibrium income is determined from the sum of consumption demand and investment demand. Show how a shift in autonomous expenditure leads to a multiplied shift in equilibrium income.

6. Discuss changes in economic behavior that would increase or decrease the multiplier. What effect would such changes have on equilibrium income?

7. How does the foreign sector affect equilibrium income? How would the trade balance be affected by a recession?

8. If saving is greater than investment at a given rate of interest, what happens to equilibrium income?

9. If autonomous spending increases by $50 billion and the multiplier is 3, what is the increase in equilibrium income? Assume that the interest rate is constant.

10. Canada has its exports equal to its imports. The U.S. economy goes into a recession. What happens to the Canadian trade balance?

11. The United States has its exports equal to its imports. There is a fall in autonomous expenditure in the U.S. economy. What happens to the U.S. trade balance?

12. Consider a closed economy (no foreign sector) without a government sector that is described by the following equations:

$$C = 700 + 0.6Y \qquad \text{(Consumption)}$$
$$I_p = 300 + 0.2Y - 40r \qquad \text{(Investment)}$$

Assume that the interest rate is fixed at 5 percent by monetary policy.

a. Calculate the magnitude of autonomous spending.

b. Calculate the multiplier and the level of income that gives goods-market equilibrium.

c. What is the level of saving in equilibrium?

d. If, for some reason, output was at the level 5,500, what would the level of unplanned inventory accumulation be?

e. If the level of autonomous investment, (I_0), were to rise to 400, what would the effect be on equilibrium income?

13. Consider an open economy (with foreign trade), but without a government sector described by the following equations:

$$C = 300 + 0.7Y \qquad \text{(Consumption)}$$
$$I_p = 110 + 0.1Y - 30r \qquad \text{(Investment)}$$
$$IM = 10 + 0.2Y \qquad \text{(Imports)}$$
$$\overline{X} = 250 \qquad \text{(Exports)}$$

Assume that the interest rate is fixed at 5 percent by monetary policy.

a. Calculate the multiplier in this open economy and the equilibrium level of income.

b. Calculate the balance of trade, $(\overline{X} - IM)$.

c. Assume that there is a reduction in export demand of 30 (i.e., $\Delta \overline{X} = 30$). By how much does equilibrium income change? By how much does the trade balance worsen?

d. If there were no foreign trade in this economy, what would the value of the multiplier be?

14. Consider question 12. Instead of a fixed interest rate of 5 percent, assume the interest rate can vary. Find the *IS* schedule.

INTEREST RATES, GOODS, AND MONEY-MARKET EQUILIBRIUM

INTRODUCTION

financial asset
A contract that gives the holder a financial claim on the issuer of the asset.

Money is obviously important in our economy. Without money we would be forced either to provide for ourselves without buying and selling in the market or to spend time and energy in bartering for goods and services. Money facilitates exchange. We will take a look at how money supports the working of individual markets in our economy and then turn our attention to the roles of money and the interest rate in the overall economy.

Interest rates are set in financial markets, where money is traded for many different **financial assets,** such as **U.S. Treasury bills** and long-term corporate bonds. These assets differ in how easily they can be resold and in how risky they are. Our first look at how the interest rate is determined will focus on the **money market** and the determinants of money demand and money supply. The money market is where people increase or decrease the amount of money they hold by selling or buying short-term bonds that carry very little risk of default, such as U.S. Treasury bills. The usefulness of this market is best illustrated by the actions of corporate financial officers, who buy and sell short-term bonds to strike a balance between the interest their companies can earn on Treasury bills against the company's need to hold money to pay its bills.

U.S. Treasury bills
A short-term bond issued and backed by the U.S. Treasury.

money market
The market is where people increase or decrease the amount of money they hold by selling or buying short-term bonds, such as Treasury bills.

What happens in the money market influences the real economy, but the real economy also influences what happens in the money market. Because of the two-way interaction between income and the interest rate, we need to combine the analysis of equilibrium in the money market with the analysis of equilibrium in the goods market.

Interest rates rise and fall on Wall Street. Jobs and production increase and decrease in the factories and offices around the country. How do the two parts of the economy affect each other? In this chapter we will use the equilibrium concept of the money and goods markets to provide an important part of the answer.

THE NATURE OF MONEY

money
Money is an asset that can be used to make transactions.

We know that money plays a large part in determining overall economic activity, but what is money? Is it the paper and coins in your pocket? Is it your credit cards or your bank balance? Is a savings account money? If so, what about a savings bond, common stock, a pension account, or an insurance policy? How about gold or silver or platinum? **Money** is used to make transactions. Because the role of money in transactions is so important we will now look at how money facilitates exchange in our modern economy.

Transactions and the Medium of Exchange

In modern economies, workers accept money in exchange for their labor, and firms accept money in exchange for goods and services they offer for sale. As long as businesses accept money for products, workers will accept money for labor. The usefulness of money in exchange is based on trust and the belief that money will be an acceptable form of payment for goods and services purchased. Money has value because of its ability to execute exchange, not because the money has any physical value as a product itself.

transaction
A single act of exchange of goods and services between a buyer and a seller, or a borrower and a lender.

Those who earn income receive a flow of payments in money; each receipt adds to the amount of money they have on hand. They also use money to buy things, and this depletes their holdings of money. At any particular time, *people and companies hold inventories or stocks of money.* The major reason why households, firms, and institutions hold stocks of money is to accomplish **transactions.** A transaction occurs whenever one person offers money in exchange for a good, a service, or an asset and another person accepts the money. There is a transaction when we buy food at the grocery store, and there is a transaction when your employer pays you at the end of the week or the month for the labor you have supplied. An important part of the role of money in the economy is that it serves as a **medium of exchange.** *Money is a medium of exchange.* It is an asset that is used for transaction purposes and it consists of currency and coin and any bank account or other financial asset that allows for the writing of checks.

medium of exchange
An asset that is used for transactions purposes.

demand deposits
Deposits that can be withdrawn on demand.

Bank accounts that allow for check writing are considered to be part of the money supply. These bank accounts are called **demand deposits,** because the funds in the account can be withdrawn on demand. Most checks are written on demand deposits.

| Unit of Account | It might be possible to work out a market trading system without money if everyone who received income did so in kind (shoe-factory workers, managers, and suppliers would receive shoes; umbrella factories would pay in umbrellas; and so on) and then they traded goods and services without carrying around an inventory of them. The trades would have to be recorded in an information bank and all the exchanges could be reconciled and cleared at the end of the day. People's holdings of shoes, umbrellas, and any other good or claim to service would then be recalculated. Even if supercomputers were capable of this daily relisting and clearing of what everybody owned, it would be a cumbersome project. To know where you stood at the end of the day, you would have to study the listed inventory of possessions and claims in detail. For accounting purposes, *it is much easier to convert all your assets into a common value or common units using the prices of all of the goods and claims on goods and services. Prices are stated in units of a commonly valued asset. Money serves this accounting function.* Money is a unit of account. It serves as the way in which we keep account of who has a claim on what resources. As a unit of account, money also allows for a common way of using prices to value wealth. |

The medium-of-exchange and the unit-of-account services provided by money are unique. Money also provides a value that is not unique; it is one of many vehicles for holding wealth. The amount of money you have is part of your total wealth, along with other types of financial and real assets.

FINANCIAL ASSETS AND MONEY

stocks

There are two separate definitions to be used in context. (1) Stocks are the plural of stock—a fixed quantity, as in the stock of money. (2) Stocks refer to corporate equities. The ownership shares of corporations.

A family that sits down to add up its economic assets and liabilities would include the value of tangible assets, such as a house or a car, plus the value of financial assets, such as **stocks** (ownership shares or claims on business and real assets), **bonds** (financial assets that pay a fixed dollar return to their owners over a specific time), and money—including bank accounts and cash. The sum of a family's economic assets is its **wealth,** and wealth is accumulated by saving over time. Household spending and saving patterns describe how much of their wealth people hold in various forms, such as stocks, bonds, real estate, and money.

Money is a financial asset. Financial assets are claims on the issues of the asset. People save, in part, by owning financial assets to store values for the future. Money is one kind of financial asset. Money, other financial assets, and tangible assets (also called "physical assets" or "real assets") are part of our total wealth.

Businesses also have assets and liabilities. The assets may include such tangible items as factories and inventory and financial assets, including money. Businesses are owned by shareholders, and the value of their shares becomes part of the wealth of the people who own them. Businesses, like households, also make independent decisions about how much money to hold along with a variety of other corporate assets.

The fact that money is one of many financial assets complicates the analysis of the monetary economy. The answer to the question *What is money?* is no longer obvious. There are ways of making purchases without an asset (e.g., credit cards). And there are assets that are very close to money (e.g., short-term bonds) that cannot be used directly to buy goods and services.

The Messy Problem of Defining Money

bond
A financial claim on an issuer with a specified interest payment and redemption value.

wealth
The net value of all assets.

Even were we to limit our definition of money to those assets that were held for medium-of-exchange or transactions purposes, there would be problems with any single definition of money, because some assets are used for transactions purposes more than others and because there are such mechanisms as *credit cards* for accomplishing, though not settling, transactions without using assets. This problem with the definition of money has become even harder in recent years, because the deregulation of banks and other institutions has led to the creation of new types of accounts. The most often used definitions of money are described next, and credit cards do not appear in any of them.

A purely transaction-based definition of money is $M1$. This includes *currency* plus accounts on which checks can be written (i.e., demand deposits) and *travelers checks.*

An almost purely transactions-based definition of money that includes some easily transferable savings accounts is $M2$. This consists of everything in $M1$, plus *overnight repurchase agreements* (RPs), U.S. dollar accounts held in Europe (*Eurodollars*) accounts held in *money-market mutual funds,* and *savings deposits,* including small *time deposits.*

A definition that gets even further away from pure transactions purposes is $M3$. This includes everything in $M2$ plus large time deposits and other accounts that are used less frequently for transactions purposes.

Based on the notion that money is the funds people can readily use for transactions, one might include unspent lines of credit on credit-card accounts (they are used all the time to make purchases) and exclude time deposits (which are bank accounts that, if used to make purchases quickly, must pay a penalty). In practice, the definitions of $M1$, $M2$, and $M3$ include items that are all *assets,* meaning individuals see them as part of their total wealth. Credit-card accounts allow people to borrow very easily, but then the bank that issues the card must hold money to pay the merchant that accepted the card. And the cardholder must then repay the bank. Credit cards certainly affect how much money people want to hold, but credit cards are excluded from the definition of money because they are not assets.

Time deposits are on the borderline. They are assets and can be used for transactions with only a little difficulty. They are included in one definition and excluded from another.

When we look at figures on money to assess monetary policy or judge whether there have been changes in the demand for money, we will look at both the $M1$ and the $M2$ definitions of money. $M1$ includes currency and bank accounts with checking privileges. It corresponds mostly directly to the idea of money held for transactions purposes. $M2$ includes everything in $M1$ plus small savings accounts and money-market accounts. Many of these accounts now have check-writing privileges also, so $M2$ can also be considered as mostly money.

$M3$ and the even broader money concepts are useful for some purposes, but do not really fit with the concept of money we are using here. They contain assets that are more like bonds. They can be converted into money but are not actually money themselves.

THE MARKET FOR MONEY

In macroeconomics we generally do not choose to study supply and demand in the market for any specific good or service. We do not look at supply and demand in the auto market or the insurance market. We study consumption, investment, government expenditures, and net exports, but these are categories of goods and services. We make an exception in the case of money, because it is different from other goods and services and it plays an especially large part in determining interest rates, inflation, equilibrium income, and overall economic activity.

The Demand for Money

It might seem strange to talk about the demand for money since we all want more money rather than less, but it is important to remember that money as we discuss it here is different from income or wealth. When people say they want more money, rather than less, what they generally mean is that they want more income or more wealth. They want to be richer or wealthier.

The demand for money has a narrower meaning: it is *the portion of our wealth we want to hold in the form of money.* The demand for money describes what motivates people to allocate their stock of wealth into a nonmonetary portion and a monetary portion. Big corporations may have billions of dollars of assets, and they allocate a few millions to money in the form of checking account deposits (demand deposits) and cash. Poor families may have some furniture, a car, some debts, and a hundred dollars in cash. When we study the demand for money, the decisions of the big companies are going to be quantitatively more important than the decisions of the poor family. But in both cases, the demand for money is the decision to allocate part of wealth to be held in the form of money. Businesses do not want to hold large amounts of money, because this portion of their wealth could be earning more interest if it were held in another form, such as another financial asset (e.g., bond).

Transactions and the Demand for Money

Since money is used to make transactions, if people, firms, and institutions are going to purchase more goods and services over a period, they will need more money. *When the number of transactions rises in the economy, the demand for money will rise.*

Many things will influence the number of transactions in the economy. For example, in a modern economy most goods are manufactured in several stages of production. Raw materials are turned into components and components are assembled into cars or computers. Money is used to facilitate the transactions at each stage of production, as component manufacturers buy raw materials and assemblers buy components. The number of transactions increases as the complexity of the economy increases.

However, changes in the way in which production is organized take place slowly. Institutions change gradually and the structure of markets changes slowly. In looking at the demand for money in a given year, the most important determinant of the volume of transactions is the level of income. The more income people have, the larger the volume of transactions they will want to make. A higher stock of money will be demanded to undertake a higher value of transactions. The demand for money increases as income increases.

A simple example of the relation between income and money demand is the following. An auto rental company that buys 1,000 cars every month must have $1.5 million in a checking account at the time of the purchase if the average cost is $15,000 per car. If the company increases its business and now buys 1,100 cars each month, it will need to have $1.65 million in its checking account for each monthly transaction.

The Price Level and the Demand for Money   The demand for money depends on the volume of transactions, but it also depends on the prices paid for the goods and services bought and sold in these transactions. The auto rental company that is buying 1,000 cars each month would need $1.575 million in its checking account each month if the average price of a car were to rise by 5 percent, to $15,750.

This example suggests that for the economy as a whole the demand for money will vary in proportion to the price level, holding constant real income and the interest rate. This result has been verified empirically. A 10 percent increase in the price level will increase money demand by 10 percent, other things equal. A fall in the price level of 5 percent will reduce money demand by 5 percent, other things equal. This result makes intuitive sense. Imagine two identical economies (they have the same real income and the same interest rate) except that prices and wages are twice as large in the second economy as they are in the first economy. The demand for money will be twice as large in the second economy.

Financial-Asset Holding and the Demand for Money

portfolio
The collection of assets and liabilities by size and type held by a household or organization.

portfolio choice
The decision about the proportions of different assets and liabilities held in a portfolio.

At any given time a household, individual, or organization has certain assets and liabilities. The net value of their assets is their wealth.[1] The household or organization's list of all its assets and liabilities is its **portfolio.** Since savers have a choice of vehicles for storing value—real and financial assets and their different types—they have to decide on the proportions of various types of assets in their portfolio. When people or firms decide how to allocate assets in a portfolio, they are making a **portfolio choice.** The decision about how much money to hold represents a part of the overall portfolio choice. For some people the choice may be whether to draw down the amount in a checking account to pay off a credit-card bill this month or, alternatively, to pay off only a minimum amount and maintain a higher checking account balance. For some firms, the choice will be whether to move money out of checking accounts and into brokerage accounts, so they can buy a variety of assets, such as stocks and bonds.

In deciding how much money to hold as part of their portfolios, individuals and companies will weigh the benefit of holding money against the cost of holding money. The benefit of holding assets in the form of money is the certainty that the asset can be

---

[1] The total net value of wealth includes the value of such assets as a house and stocks and bonds minus the value of liabilities, such as a mortgage or other debts.

quickly and readily used to purchase goods and services. The cost of holding money comes from the fact that money either earns no interest or has a very low interest rate.

Earlier we talked about an auto rental company that was buying 1,000 cars each month. At $15,000 per car this meant the company had to have $1.5 million in its checking account *at the time of purchase.* But this does not mean that the company needed this amount sitting in its checking account the whole month waiting for the purchase. The company will manage its portfolio of assets to have money in its checking account when this is needed for the auto purchases, as well as having money available for payroll and other payments that are part of its operations. Companies do not leave funds in checking accounts that are not needed for transactions. Households and individuals will also manage their portfolios to balance the need for funds to pay bills against the interest that can be earned by holding bonds.[2]

cash management
The adjustment of portfolios to minimize the amount of money needed and still provide the cash needed for transactions.

Other assets yield a higher return than money and this gives them an advantage over money. The disadvantage of holding these assets is that they cannot be used directly for transactions and when they are sold or converted into money this involves costs. There are costs, in the form of brokerage fees or even the time and trouble involved, when converting nonmoney assets to money.[3]

We will assume that households and firm managers choose between two alternatives: holding money or holding bonds. At any given interest rate on bonds, a balance is struck between the benefits of holding bonds and earning their interest and the benefits of holding money. When interest rates rise, the balance is upset because bonds appear relatively more attractive than money. A rise in the rate of interest tends to reduce the demand for money.

The Money Demand Function   Equation 4–1 expresses a money demand function showing the effect of changes in income, the interest rate and the price level on the demand for money.

$$M^d = (kY - hr)P$$

$$(4-1)$$

The demand for money (M^d) increases with increases in income (Y). The parameter (k) reflects the responsiveness of money demand to income changes. The demand for money decreases by an amount (h) for each percentage point increase in the interest rate (r). The use of money for transactions means that the demand for money is proportional to the price level (P).

-----

[2] Many wealthy families or individuals hold large sums in checking accounts, and often these families hold interest-bearing accounts in banks called "certificates of deposit." The banks often put these funds into Treasury bills or bonds or short-term commercial bonds. The banks are acting as the cash managers for these households.

[3] The cost of holding money is the difference between the interest that could have been earned on bonds or other alternative nonmoney financial assets and the interest that can be earned on money. The interest rate that can be earned on money varies from zero for holders of cash and owners of commercial demand deposits to competitively set rates on money-market accounts. When all money is taken into account, the interest rate earned on money is considerably lower than what is earned on any other financial asset. Moreover, when interest rates rise in the economy, the spread between the rates earned on money and on other financial assets increases.

It is often useful to divide both sides of Equation 4–1 by the price level, *P*, and express the money demand function as the demand for a *real stock of money*, (M^d/P). We will use his version of the money demand function, shown in Equation 4–2.

$$\frac{M^d}{P} = kY - hr \qquad\qquad (4\text{–}2)$$

Figure 4–1 illustrates a *money demand* schedule that responds to changes in income and the interest rate like the one shown in Equation 4–2. In the figure, the money demand schedules are so drawn that, at a given income level, money demand is a downward-sloping function of the interest rate.

Just as in the description of the transaction demand for money, a rise in the level of income will increase the demand for transactions and the demand for money. A rise in the level of income will increase the demand for money at all interest rates. Changes in income (*Y*) correspond to shifts of the money demands schedule (point *A* to *A′*). Changes in (*r*) are represented as movements along a given money demand schedule (points *A* to *B*).

FIGURE 4–1
The Demand for Money as a Function of the Interest Rate

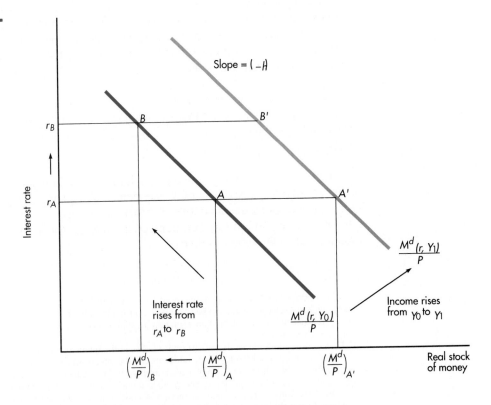

When income is constant, money demand is a negative function of interest.

The Velocity of Money A concept that has been important in the historical development of macroeconomics and one that is still seen by many economists as crucial in understanding the economy is the **velocity of money**. The velocity of money is defined as the ratio of income to the stock of money.

velocity of money
Measures the speed
with which the stock of
money turns over in the
economy.

$$V = \frac{Y}{M/P} = \frac{P \times Y}{M} \tag{4-3}$$

The velocity of money measures the speed with which the stock of money turns over in the economy. In 1992, the real GDP of the U.S. economy was about $5 trillion, while the stock of $M1$ averaged about $1 trillion over the year and $M2$ averaged about $3.5 trillion. This means that the velocity of money was 5 and for $M2$ velocity 1.4. According to the narrower definition of money, $M1$, the stock of money was turned over five times a year in relation to total GDP. People were making transactions and purchasing a much larger flow of output than the value of the stock of money available.

At one time, economists believed that the velocity of money was constant. This would mean that any change in the stock of money in the economy must lead either to a change in income (Y) or to a change in the price level (P). Based on empirical observation, we know that velocity of money is not constant. Both the $M1$ and the $M2$ velocity vary from year to year and the $M1$ velocity, in particular, has varied substantially over the past 30 years.

There is a substantial disagreement among economists about the relative importance of different sources of change in velocity, but most economists recognize that one important reason is the volatility of interest rates. Higher rates of interest encourage people to keep down their demand for money, allowing the same stock of money to be used for a larger volume of transactions. For example, suppose there is an increase in income in the economy but there is also an increase in the rate of interest. The demand for money could remain constant and the velocity of money will have risen.

Worked Example 4–1   In this example on page 108 a numerical money demand schedule is used to show how the velocity of money will change when the interest rate changes.

We have talked about the fact that a change in the rate of interest affects the demand for holding a stock of money, but to see how the demand for money interacts with the supply of money to determine the interest rate, we need to examine the determinants of the supply of money.

The Supply of Money

The supply of money in the United States, in common with most other nations, is determined by its central bank, the Federal Reserve (the Fed). The Fed works with private banks and other depository institutions to create and regulate the nation's money supply. The Fed has its headquarters in Washington, DC. There are 12 regional branches of the Fed located around the country in cities indicated on paper currency. The most important regional Fed is in New York near the Wall Street financial markets. Though the Fed is responsible for regulation of the nation's financial system, its primary responsibility is to secure the integrity of the money supply—not to allow the money supply to grow so quickly that the value of money declines and inflation ensues or not to allow a too slow growth of the money supply to constrain the growth of the real economy.

Because high rates of money and credit growth can be used by governments to avoid difficult decisions about taxes, revenues, and spending priorities, central banks are under considerable political pressure to err on the side of expansion of money and credit. Therefore, even though it is part of the executive branch of government, the Fed has been given considerable independence to increase the isolation of its policy making from political influence.

Checking account balances make up the greater portion of the money supply. U.S. banks and depository institutions issue checking accounts, and they are required to hold *reserves* that are a fraction of the amounts of checking accounts or other monetary accounts. Just as the Fed is the only legal entity in the United States that is allowed to issue currency, so, too, the Fed has the sole authority to create bank reserves. Since the Fed has control over both currency and the reserves that have to be held on checking accounts, *the Fed can control all of the assets that are part of the money supply, and it therefore controls the total supply of money available in the economy.* We will assume here that the supply of money is fixed by the Fed. (See Chapter 10 for a detailed description of the Federal Reserve system and the role played by banks and depository institutions in the creation and regulation of the money supply as well as the conduct of monetary policy.)

Money-Market Equilibrium

The Fed sets the supply of money, M^s, and since at this point in our analysis we are taking the price level as given, this means that the Fed is effectively choosing the real stock of money available to the economy—M^s/P. Money-market equilibrium occurs when the supply of money is equal to the demand for money. This condition is shown in Equation 4–4.

$$\frac{M^s}{P} = \frac{M^d}{P} = kY - hr \tag{4-4}$$

Since the supply of money is fixed, if the demand for money is higher or lower than the supply of money, then the adjustment has to take place in money demand. If there is less or more money demanded than available, the actions of moneyholders in trying to acquire or get rid of money will bring about a change in the rate of interest and hence in the quantity of money demanded so as to have moneyholders satisfied with holding the fixed amount of money available. In the money market, the interest rate adjusts to bring money demand into equilibrium with money supply.

Figure 4–2 depicts money-market equilibrium. The money supply is set by the Fed, so it is shown as a vertical line. Money demand is shown as depending on the interest rate, with the level of income, Y_0, taken as given. The figure shows that the supply of money and the demand for money are equal at the interest rate, r_0 (point A).

In Figure 4–2, when the interest rate is r_1 (lower than r_0), the amount of money demanded exceeds the amount of money supplied (point B to point B'), at the level of income (Y_0). We have an excess demand for money because the interest rate is too low. When the amount of money demanded exceeds the amount of money available,

FIGURE 4–2
Money-Market
Equilibrium

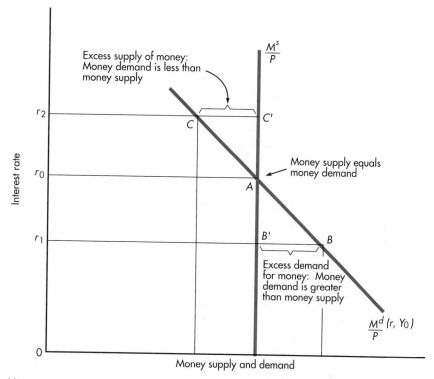

Money supply is fixed and money demand is for a given level of income (Y_o).

everyone wants more money than is available. Households and companies try to readjust their portfolios to increase the amount of money they have and reduce the amount of bonds. They can do this by selling bonds or by buying fewer bonds.[4] But since no more money is available, the only effect of this attempted readjustment is that the interest rate on bonds will rise.

If the level of income remains unchanged, the resulting rise in the interest rate *reduces* the excess demand for money. Money is like tickets for a popular concert. No matter how much excess demand exists for a particular show, that demand cannot create extra seats on the night of the concert. Ticket prices are bid up by those who want to attend, until demand is brought into line with the fixed supply and those who sell their tickets are willing to exchange tickets for money.

In the economy, if the total amount of money held does not change, the supply of money is fixed like the supply of concert tickets. If there is an excess demand for money, then the interest rate will rise and reduce the demand for money until people and firms are satisfied with holding the unchanged amount of money balances. In the

[4] The interest rate will change as asset holders manage their cash balances by selling financial assets to get money. When there are more sellers than buyers, the price of financial assets falls. When the price of financial assets falls, the interest rate rises.

figure, there is excess money demand when the interest rate is r_1. When the interest rate rises (r_1 goes back to r_0), the amount of money demanded declines. This process continues as long as the demand for money exceeds the supply. At point *A*, there is no longer any excess demand for money. Money demand equals money supply and there is a particular combination of interest rate (r_0) and income (Y_0) associated with money-market equilibrium.

> *Worked Example 4–2*   In this example on page 108 we use the same numerical money demand schedule that was in Worked Example 4–1 and put this together with a money supply schedule. With a given level of income, equilibrium in the money market determines the interest rate.

Income and Interest Rates in Money Markets: The *LM* Schedule

We have looked at equilibrium in the money market when the level of income remained unchanged. Now we are ready to see how changes in income bring about changes in the money market.

Starting with money demand equal to money supply, if income were to change, the value of transactions would go up or down—prices are assumed constant. Strictly speaking, an increase in income increases the *number* of transactions, which increases the demand for money and so would the size money balances demanded by asset holders. However, the supply of money is unchanged and, therefore, the increase or decrease in income creates either excess supply of money or excess demand for money. When there is equilibrium in the money market, money demand is brought into line with the fixed money supply and *there is a higher or lower interest rate associated with money-market equilibrium at a higher or lower level of income.*

In the diagram on the left-hand side of Figure 4–3, the money market is initially in equilibrium at point *A*, with income at Y_0 and the interest rate at r_0. An increase in income (Y_0 to Y_2) raises the quantity of money demanded (point *A* to point *B'*). Now there is excess demand for money. By the same process as was described before, the excess demand for money brings about an increase in the interest rate. The interest rate continues to rise (r_0 to r_2) until the demand for money is once again equal to the supply of money (point *B*).

When income went up, money demand went up, but there wasn't any more money. Asset holders held the same amount of money after income rose as before. *However, there was a change in the money-market equilibrium* that resulted from a higher income; namely, there was an increase in the desire to hold money because there were more transactions, and there was a decrease in the desire to hold money because the interest rate had gone up.

If the level of income fell, the analysis would run in reverse. At a lower level of income, the demand for money declines because transactions demand declines.[5] In the

---

[5] This is always a troublesome concept. How can firms and households want less money when income is falling? The way out of this puzzle is to remember that the demand for money is a demand for a portfolio or proportion of assets held in the form of money. Households and firms certainly want more *income;* but when income is falling, they want to hold a smaller portion of their wealth in the form of money. Because income is falling, cash managers need to hold smaller money balances and they buy bonds to increase earnings. Of course, every cash manager does the same thing so interest rates fall.

FIGURE 4–3   Changes in Equilibrium Income and Money-Market Equilibrium: The *LM* Schedule

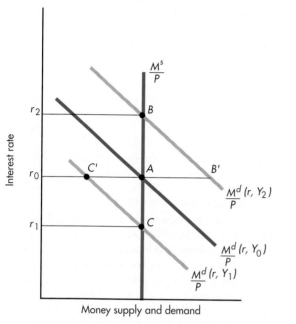

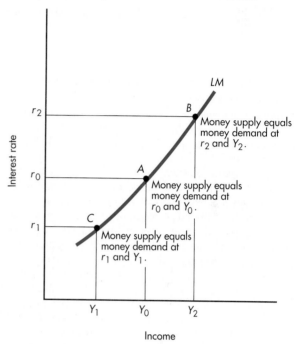

Money supply equals money demand at different levels of income and different interest rates.

The money market is in equilibrium at all points along the *LM* schedule.

diagram, the lower demand for money (*C′C*), which is illustrated by an inward shift of money demand, comes into equilibrium with money supply at a lower rate of interest (point *A* to point *C*).

There are now three levels of income (Y_0, Y_1, and Y_2) associated with three different interest rates (r_0, r1, and r_2). In all cases, the demand for money equals the supply of money. The diagram on the right-hand side of Figure 4–3 shows the pairs of equilibrium income and interest rate (points *A*, *B*, and *C*) along a line called the **LM schedule.** *The* LM *schedule gives all the combinations of income and interest rates where different levels of money demand equal a fixed money supply. The money market is thus in equilibrium everywhere along the* LM *schedule.*

LM schedule
Gives all the combinations of income and interest rates where money demand equals money supply.

Worked Example 4–3   This example on page 109 shows how equilibrium in the money market with a fixed supply of money determines the *LM* schedule.

The *LM* schedule is upward-sloping because the higher the level of income, the greater has to be the interest rate that will bring money demand back down into equilibrium with a fixed money supply. In general, starting with equilibrium in the money market (any given point on the *LM* schedule), an increase in income is

Keynes and Friedman: Shapers of Macroeconomic Ideas

John Maynard Keynes and Aggregate Demand in the Great Depression

Modern macroeconomics owes much to the revolution in thinking generated by the publication of the *General Theory of Employment, Interest and Money* by the British economist John Maynard Keynes in 1936.

The British economy suffered high unemployment after World War I and did not get back to full employment until the start of World War II, almost 20 years later. The economies of the industrialized world suffered their most severe business-cycle trough in the Great Depression of the 1930s. Keynes's theory was influenced by this experience and he argued that free-enterprise economies can become stuck in a recession or depression with no market mechanism strong enough to cure the problem. He argued that this can come about because aggregate demand can remain very low for a long enough period of time so unemployment becomes a persistent problem. He said that economies lack sufficient self-correcting mechanisms to stimulate aggregate demand and restore full employment. He argued, further, that an economy's central bank trying to expand output and employment by increasing the amount of money in the economy might not be effective. It might be necessary, he argued, to increase demand by bypassing the marketplace and increasing the amount of direct government spending in the economy. Keynes's ideas gained support among some American economists, such as Seymour Harris of Harvard, Paul Samuelson of the Massachusetts Institute of Technology, and James Tobin of Yale. They and the British economist John Hicks helped to sort out Keynes's ideas and develop them. Those ideas have remained controversial, however, particularly among political conservatives, who judge that Keynesian thinking rationalizes government intervention in free markets.

The high point for Keynesian views in the United States was the 1960s. Articulate advocates for these views, such as Walter Heller, who became the chairman of the Council of Economic Advisors under President John F. Kennedy, could point to the unprecedented suc-cess of the economy in the years following the development of Keynesian ideas. Unemployment was low, recessions were mild, and inflation was moderate. Economists even talked about fine-tuning macroeconomic policies to maintain full employment without inflation and judged that the big debate about macroeconomic policy was over. President Nixon, in the first Republican administration after the Democratic presidents Kennedy and Johnson, declared, "I am a Keynesian." Yet simultaneous with the ascendancy of Keynesian policies, the makings of a counterrevolution against Keynesian theory were already brewing.

Milton Friedman and Monetarism

Milton Friedman of the University of Chicago had never accepted the Keynesian framework. In 1963, with Anna Schwartz, he published the landmark volume, *A Monetary History of the United States,* which argued that the money supply is the primary engine determining fluctuations in aggregate demand.* As an advocate of monetarism, Friedman attacked the Keynesian idea that monetary policy is a weak or ineffective instrument. On the contrary, he said, monetary policy caused or contributed to almost all of the recessions he studied and was the prime cause of the Great Depression. Further, Friedman argued that the Great Depression of the 1930s did not demonstrate the failure of the free-enterprise system and the need for government to stabilize the economy. Rather, it demonstrated the failure of government economic policies, especially monetary policy as conducted by the Federal Reserve Board (the U.S. central bank). Where Keynes argued that a central bank is incapable of helping an economy get out of a depression, Friedman argued that the Federal Reserve was responsible for getting the U.S. economy into a depression.

Milton Friedman's prescription for macroeconomic policy is to avoid fine-tuning and to set a stable rate of growth of the supply of money. This will allow the natural stability of the economy to emerge, he says. The rate of growth of the money supply should be chosen to allow for the growth of GDP, without being large enough to accommodate inflation.

---

* Milton Friedman and Anna J. Schwartz, *A Monetary History of the United States* (Princeton, N.J.: Princeton University Press, 1963).

associated with a higher level of money demand. Since the quantity of money supplied to the economy is set by the Fed, the higher quantity of money demanded at a higher income cannot be realized. Thus, the increase in income creates an excess demand for money balances. A heightened demand in the presence of no increase in supply raises the price—in this case an increase in the rate of interest. The quantity of money demanded remains the same all along the *LM* schedule as the higher interest rate cancels the increase in demand due to higher incomes.

GOODS MARKETS AND MONEY MARKETS TOGETHER: THE *IS–LM* FRAMEWORK

We are now ready to answer the question left open in the previous chapter. If the *IS* schedule represents goods-market equilibrium at different rates of interest, what interest rate actually prevails and where is equilibrium? The answer comes from combining goods-market equilibrium (*IS*) with money-market equilibrium (*LM*). We will look at how the two markets interact to jointly determine income and the interest rate. We will also use the *IS–LM* framework to describe how changes in economic conditions drive the economy from one equilibrium to another.

Equilibrium Income and the Interest Rate

We can see how the goods-market and money-market equilibriums are jointly determined by combining the information contained in the *IS* and *LM* schedules. In Figure 4–4, *IS* and *LM* are shown together. The point of intersection of the *IS* and *LM* schedules (point A, with interest rate r_A and income Y_A) is the one combination of interest rate and income common to both schedules. This point is a very important one for the economy—it is the equilibrium point where both the goods market and the money market are in equilibrium.

In the figure we can see that a level of income higher than equilibrium ($Y_B > Y_A$) would require a higher-than-equilibrium rate of interest ($r_B > r_A$) along the *LM* schedule (point B). But at the same time, the higher level of income would require a lower-than-equilibrium rate of interest ($r_{B'} < r_A$) along the *IS* schedule (point B'). This inconsistency is because Y_B is a level of income that is in excess of equilibrium—one that cannot be maintained. At the equilibrium level of income (Y_A) the rate of interest (r_A) is consistent with equilibrium income in both the money market (*LM*) and the goods market (*IS*).

Worked Example 4–4   This example on page 110 brings together the *IS* schedule from Worked Example 3–4 and the *LM* schedule from Worked Example 4–3. Setting the interest rate along the *IS* schedule equal to the interest rate along the *LM* schedule gives the level of income for which both the goods market and the money market are in equilibrium.

The *IS* schedule gets its name from the simple condition that at all levels of equilibrium income, planned investment equals saving. The reason why *LM* is called *LM* is less clear. One explanation is that *M* stands for money supply and *L* for money demand—sometimes called "liquidity preference." The *LM* schedule then shows when money supply and demand are equal.

FIGURE 4–4
**Equilibrium in the
Goods Market (*IS*)
and Money Market
(*LM*)**

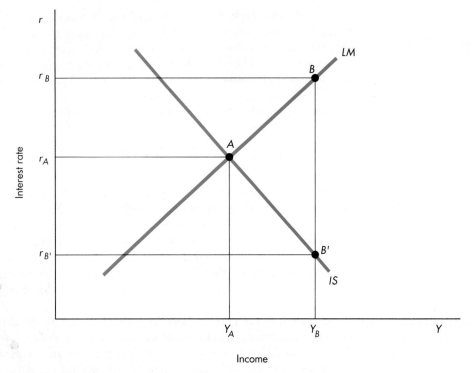

Both goods and money markets are in equilibrium at point *A*. If income were Y_B then the interest rate
consistent with money-market equilibrium (point *B*) is higher than the interest rate consistent with goods-
market equilibrium (point *B'*).

The Effect of a Change in Autonomous Expenditure

multiplier effect
The change in income that would occur following a shift in the goods market if there were no change in the rate of interest.

interest-rate effect
Following a shift in conditions in the goods market, the interest-rate effect is the change in income resulting from the change in the rate of interest.

When aggregate demand changes, the economy adjusts from one equilibrium to another and changes take place in both money markets and goods markets, thereby affecting both income and the interest rate. This is a different description of the impact of changes in aggregate demand from that set out in the multiplier process. In the description of the multiplier process, the rate of interest was taken as given.

It is useful to think of the effect on equilibrium income following a shift in the *IS* schedule as being comprised of (1) a **multiplier effect,** where changes in income result from shifts in goods markets with no change in the interest rate and (2) an **interest-rate effect,** following a shift in conditions in the goods market. The interest-rate effect is the change in income resulting from the change in the rate of interest.

We illustrate the multiplier and interest-rate effects in Figure 4–5. An increase in aggregate demand has occurred due to an exogenous increase in demand in the goods market. The impact of this increase in demand on equilibrium in the goods market is shown as an outward shift in the *IS* schedule (*IS* to *IS'*). If the rate of interest had not changed, then income would rise by the initial exogenous increase in expenditures times the multiplier, which is the full amount of the shift in the *IS* schedule—from point *A* to point *A'*. This change in income (Y_A to $Y_{A'}$) is the multiplier effect. In

FIGURE 4-5
The Multiplier and
Interest-Rate
Effects

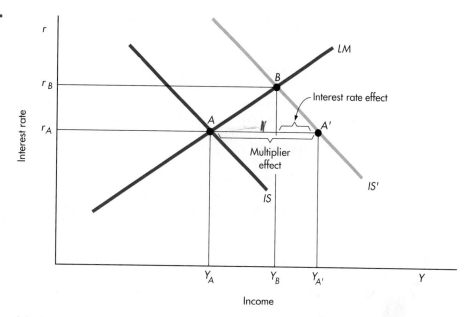

Adjustment to equilibrium takes place through the interaction of the multiplier with changes in the interest rate. The change in income at the initial rate of interest with no change in the interest rate is the multiplier effect. The reaction of income to changes in the interest rates is the interest-rate effect.

addition, in the absence of any other exogenous change, the increase in income will drive up the demand for money, resulting in a higher rate of interest (r_A to r_B). The higher rate of interest reduces the level of expenditure on investment goods below what it would be with no rise in the interest rate. Equilibrium takes place in the goods market at a lower level of income and production because of the higher interest rate. This reduction in income (Y_A' to Y_B from point A' to point B') is the interest-rate effect.

This concludes our introduction to the money market and to *IS–LM* analysis. We began our description of the economy by saying that, in the short run, changes in aggregate demand account for changes in the level of income. This idea still holds, but the analysis in this chapter has become more complex. We have to look to interest rates and money markets as well as goods markets to describe the state of aggregate demand. The determination of the interest rate was found in the money market, but the money market was also affected by the level of income.

In the next two chapters, we will use the *IS–LM* model to see how the government can stimulate or retard aggregate demand, thus affecting the level of income and interest rates. When the Fed changes the amount of money supplied to the economy, equilibrium will change in the money market and we will see the effect of that policy change in a movement of the *LM* schedule. When the government changes its level of expenditures or taxation, aggregate demand will change and we will see the effect of that policy change in a movement of the *IS* schedule.

WORKED EXAMPLES

Worked Example 4–1

How the Velocity of Money Is Affected by the Rate of Interest

Question   Consider the following demand-for-money schedule, where income is in billions of dollars and the interest rate is calculated as a percentage.

$$\frac{M^d}{P} = 0.4Y - 80r$$

a. What is the demand for money when income is $4 trillion ($4,000 billion) and the interest rate is 5 percent? What is the velocity of money?

b. When interest rates change in the economy, income often changes, also. Suppose income is $5 trillion ($5,000 billion) when the interest rate is 10 percent. What is the velocity of money now?

Answer   If we substitute the values for income and the rate of interest we get the following:

$$\frac{M^d}{P} = (0.4 \times 4,000) - (80 \times 5) = 1,200$$

The demand for money is $1.2 trillion. The velocity is the ratio of income to money:

$$\text{Velocity} = V = \frac{4,000}{1,200} = 3.33$$

If the rate of interest rises to 10 percent as income rises to 5,000 the demand for money remains constant:

$$\frac{M^d}{P} = (0.4 \times 5,000) - (80 \times 10) = 1,200$$

The velocity of money has now risen from 3.33 to 4.17. The velocity of money falls as the interest rate falls because corporations and individuals have less incentive to reduce their money holdings. The velocity rises as the interest rate rises, as money holders reduce their money balances in order to take advantage of the interest opportunity.

Worked Example 4–2

Money-Market Equilibrium

Suppose that the money-demand relation is the following:

$$\frac{M^d}{P} = 0.4Y - 80r$$

What is the rate of interest when the money market is in equilibrium? As before, we assume that income is $4 trillion ($4,000 billion). Suppose that the supply of money is $1.2 trillion ($1,200 billion). What is the rate of interest?

$$\frac{M^s}{P} = 1,200 = \frac{M^d}{P} = (0.4 \times 4,000) - 80r$$

$$80r = 1,600 - 1,200 = 400$$

$$r = 5$$

The solution is that the interest rate is 5 percent.

Suppose, however, that the interest rate were lower than 5 percent at the same level of income. If the interest rate were 3 percent, the quantity of money demanded would be:

$$\frac{M^d}{P} = (0.4 \times 4,000) - (80 \times 3) = 1,360$$

There would then be an excess demand for money of $160 billion.

$$\frac{M^d}{P} = 1,360 > \frac{M^S}{P} = 1,200$$

The $160 billion excess demand disappears when the interest rate rises by enough (from 3 to 5 percent) to drive the demand for money back into equilibrium with a fixed money supply of $1.2 trillion.

Worked Example 4–3

Income and Money-Market Equilibrium: The *LM* Schedule

We continue with the worked example used in 4–2 but we let income go up from $4 trillion to $4.3 trillion. We assume at the outset the interest rate is 5 percent. Money demand is now given as follows:

$$\frac{M^d}{P} = (0.4 \times 4,300) - (80 \times 5)$$
$$= 1,720 - 400 = 1,320$$

Since the supply of money is only $1.2 trillion ($1,200 billion), there is excess demand for money, $\frac{M^d}{P} > M^S$. This means that the interest rate must rise. When the interest rate has risen to 6.5 percent, the money market is in equilibrium again.

$$\frac{M^d}{P} = (0.4 \times 4,300) - (80 \times 6.5)$$
$$= 1,720 - 520 = 1,200$$

We have now found two points on the *LM* schedule:

1. $Y = \$4$ trillion, $\frac{M^d}{P} = \frac{M^S}{P} = 1,200$, $r = 5$ percent

2. $Y = \$4.3$ trillion, $\frac{M^d}{P} = \frac{M^S}{P} = 1,200$, $r = 6.5$ percent

If income falls from $4 trillion to $3.8 trillion, this drop in income of $200 billion causes the quantity of money demanded to fall by $80 billion ($0.4 \times 200$). With a rate of interest of 5 percent, there is an excess supply of money of $80 billion. As cash managers try to buy bonds, the interest rate falls until it drops from 5 percent to 4 percent. At the new lower interest rate, the amount of money demanded once more equals the amount supplied. This gives us a third point on the *LM* schedule:

3. $Y = \$3.8$ trillion, $\frac{M^d}{P} = \frac{M^S}{P} = 1,200$, $r = 4$ percent

Worked
Example 4–4

Solving for Equilibrium with *IS* and *LM*

Combining consumption and investment demands into aggregate demand equal to income gives an *IS* schedule as shown in Chapter 2:

$$Y = C + I$$
$$C = 600 + 0.7Y$$
$$I = 250 + 0.1Y - 10r$$

The *IS* schedule is:

$$r = 85 - 0.02Y.$$

The money-market relations in the previous worked examples were as follows:

$$\frac{M^s}{P} = \frac{M^d}{P}$$

$$\frac{M^d}{P} = 0.4Y - 80r$$

$$\frac{M^s}{P} = 1,200$$

$$1,200 = 0.4Y - 80r$$

If we put the interest-rate term on the left-hand side and divide by 80, this gives the equation for the *LM* schedule:

$$r = 0.005Y - 15$$

The point of intersection of *IS* and *LM* is found by solving for the level of income for which the interest rate is the same along both schedules:

$$85 - 0.02Y = 0.005Y - 15$$

Collecting terms gives:

$$0.025Y = 100$$
$$Y = 4,000$$

We have found that both the goods market and the money market are in equilibrium at an income of $4 trillion. The equilibrium rate of interest can be found from substituting into either the *IS* or the *LM* schedule. (Do both—it gives a good check.) Either way, we find that the rate of interest is 5 percent.

If income were higher, the *LM* schedule would require a higher interest rate; then equilibrium in the goods market would require a lower rate of interest than 5 percent. Investment would need more of a stimulus to sustain a higher level of income. The *IS* schedule would require a lower interest rate at a higher level of income. But if income were higher, equilibrium in the money market would require a higher rate of interest. The higher income would increase the demand for money. Since the supply of money is fixed, the interest rate would rise. Hence the goods market and money market could not both be in equilibrium. The same holds true for any other combination of interest rate and income level.

SUMMARY

- We go back to an economy without foreign trade to consider the effect of a change in the rate of interest. A shift in the rate of interest changes investment demand and this brings about a multiplied change in equilibrium income. There is a particular level of income that goes with each rate of interest. The *IS* schedule traces out the combinations of income and the rate of interest such that supply equals planned demand and the goods market is in equilibrium.

- The demand for money is derived from the services provided by money. Money facilitates *transactions* and avoids the need for barter.

- Money serves as *a medium of exchange.* Since transactions increase with income, the demand for money increases along with increases in income.

- For a given volume of transactions, the demand for money is proportional to the price level.

- Money is a store of value, one of several alternative assets. When the interest rate that can be earned on other financial assets goes up, the demand for holding money goes down. The demand for money will decrease along with increases in the interest rate.

- Since money is a financial asset, families have to decide on the proportions of assets in their portfolios. When people or firms decide how to allocate assets in a portfolio, they are making a *portfolio choice.* The decision about how much money to hold represents a part of the overall portfolio choice.

- Money consists of currency, coin, and any bank account or other financial asset that allows for the writing of checks. There is no ideal definition of money in practice. The *M*1 and *M*2 definitions of money are both useful. There are also extended definitions of money.

- The money supply is controlled by the banking system and the Federal Reserve. We take the money supply as fixed exogenously by the Fed. If the amount of money demanded exceeds the amount of money available, there will be an overall excess demand for money balances. The interest rate will rise until cash managers want to hold the amount of money that is available.

- The combinations of income and interest rates where money demand equals money supply are described along the *LM schedule.* Because higher levels of income increase the demand for money, higher levels of income are associated with higher levels of the interest rate. The *LM* schedule slopes up to the right.

- The point of intersection of the *IS* and *LM* schedules is the one combination of interest rate and income common to both schedules. This is the point where both the goods market and the money market are in equilibrium.

- The change in income that results from an exogenous shift in expenditure (a shift in the *IS* schedule) can be described as consisting of *a multiplier effect* (the change in income that would occur if there were no change in the interest rate) and an *interest-rate effect* (the change in income due to the change in the interest rate).

KEY TERMS AND CONCEPTS

bond, p. 94
cash management, p. 97
demand deposits, p. 92
financial asset, p. 91
interest-rate effect, p. 106
LM schedule, p. 103

medium of exchange, p. 92
money, p. 92
money market, p. 91
multiplier effect, p. 106
portfolio, p. 96
portfolio choice, p. 96

stocks, p. 93
transaction, p. 92
U.S. Treasury bills, p. 91
velocity of money, p. 99
wealth, p. 94

DISCUSSION QUESTIONS AND PROBLEMS

1. Along the *IS* schedule, when interest rates decline, equilibrium income rises. Why is this? Describe a circumstance when lower interest rates would not necessarily result in higher income?

2. Use the following consumption and investment functions to derive the *IS* schedule:

$$C = 700 + 0.6Y$$
$$I = 300 + 0.2Y - 40r$$

   Find the levels of income along the *IS* schedule for the interest rates, 3 percent, 5 percent, and 7 percent.

3. If the introduction of credit cards reduces the amount of money that people hold in order to make a given volume of transactions, how would this affect the *LM* schedule? How would it change the level of income in the economy?

4. Cash managers economize on money balances as the interest rate rises. Is there a limit on this process or could the velocity of money rise indefinitely?

5. When the demand for money exceeds the supply, what restores money-market equilibrium in the short run (before there is any change in income)? What happens to the interest rate as income changes?

6. Along the *IS* schedule, higher incomes are associated with lower interest rates, while along the *LM* schedule, higher incomes are associated with higher interest rates. If income increases, do interest rates rise or fall?

7. Describe the path of income and interest rates as the economy adjusts from one equilibrium to another following a shift in the *IS* schedule. Separate the change in income into the multiplier effect and the interest-rate effect.

8. Consider the following money-demand relation.

$$\frac{M^d}{P} = 0.6Y - 120r \quad \text{(Money demand)}$$

   a. What is the demand for money when income is $4 trillion ($Y = 4{,}000$) and the interest rate is 5 percent ($r = 5$)?
   b. What is the velocity of money?
   c. What is the velocity of money when the interest rate is 10 percent? 2 percent?

   d. Does the velocity of money rise or fall when income increases with a constant rate of interest?
   e. Suppose that the supply of money is $2.196 trillion $\left(\dfrac{M^s}{P} = 2{,}196\right)$ and income is $4 trillion ($Y = 4{,}000$). What is the rate of interest in money-market equilibrium?
   f. Suppose that the supply of money is $1.44 trillion $\left(\dfrac{M^s}{P} = 1{,}440\right)$ and income is $4 trillion ($Y = 4{,}000$). What is the rate of interest?

9. Consider now an *IS–LM* model. The money supply is fixed and the interest rate is determined in the model. The economy is now described by the following equations:

$$C = 950 + 0.65Y \qquad \text{(Consumption)}$$
$$I = 350 + 0.1Y - 20r \qquad \text{(Investment)}$$
$$\frac{M^d}{P} = 0.6Y - 120r \qquad \text{(Money demand)}$$
$$\frac{M^s}{P} = 2{,}196 \qquad \text{(Money supply)}$$

   a. What is the equation that describes the *IS* schedule?
   b. What is the slope of this *IS* schedule? What does the slope of the *IS* schedule show?
   c. What is the equation that describes the *LM* schedule (*Hint:* $2{,}196 = 12 \times 183$)?
   d. The equilibrium level of income is 4,760 and the equilibrium interest rate is 5.5 percent. Show how these values are obtained.

10. Use the following relations to derive the *IS* schedule:

$$C = C_0 + C_1Y$$
$$I = I_0 + I_1Y - I_2r$$

   Use the following relations to derive the *LM* schedule:

$$\frac{M^d}{P} = kY - hr$$
$$\frac{M^s}{P} \text{ is fixed by the Fed}$$

Solve for the equilibrium values of income and the interest rate in terms of the parameters of the equations and the magnitude of the real supply of money. Show that increases in autonomous expenditures, C_0 and I_0 will raise the level of equilibrium income.

Show that increases in the real stock of money will raise income and lower the rate of interest. Show that increases in the multiplier will raise income and the interest rate. What happens when k, I_2, and h change?

FISCAL POLICY, BUDGETS, AND EQUILIBRIUM INCOME

INTRODUCTION

fiscal policy
Government actions concerning tax revenues, transfers, and the amount of government purchases.

Fiscal policies determine the amount of tax revenue collected by the government and the amount and type of expenditures it undertakes. They influence which services the government provides and both expenditures and taxes affect the level of aggregate demand in the economy. **Fiscal policy** can help to offset recessions or restrain booms if it is used appropriately. However, chronic deficit spending of the kind that the federal government has made in recent years can do serious economic harm. The role of government in the economy is sufficiently large and different from the private sector's role so as to require our treating the government as a separate element of the economy. Fiscal policies describe the means by which government gets revenue and distributes transfer payments, and the amount and kinds of goods and services that the government purchases in the economy. We want to see how the government's fiscal decisions about the total amount of expenditures and taxation affect aggregate demand, income, and interest rates.

A part of government policy that we are either going to ignore or going to treat in a very simple way in this chapter is monetary policy. Through the actions of their monetary authorities (the Fed in the United States), governments affect the supply of money. In this chapter we look at money-market conditions only to the extent that they alter the effectiveness of fiscal policy. But before we look at how fiscal policy affects aggregate demand, we should look at government purchases, expenditures, and what goods and services the government is buying and why.

GOVERNMENT PURCHASES AND GOVERNMENT EXPENDITURES

**government purchases
of goods and services**
The goods and services
the government buys
from the private sector
plus the salaries of
government employees.

The size of **government purchases of goods and services** (including purchases by state, local, and federal agencies) measures the direct impact of the government on demand. In 1992, total government purchases were 19 percent of GDP. Of this total, about 40 percent represented federal purchases and the remaining 60 percent were state and local purchases. Government purchases include the salaries of government employees; this part is counted as government production—the government buys this production from itself. The remaining portion of government purchases (over 80 percent) consists of goods and services that the government buys from the private sector, everything from office-building rentals to missiles, school supplies, and computers.

Government purchases of goods and services were 2.6 percent of GDP in 1929 but rose above 40 percent of GDP during World War II (totaling 57 percent of GDP in 1944 during the height of the war). Military expenditures fell at the end of the war, so in 1947 government demand was only 17 percent of GDP. The Cold War and the growth of various federal programs pushed the percentage up again, so by 1955 government demand was 24 percent of GDP. This percentage has varied since then but fell in the 1980s and 90s, down to 18.3 percent by 1993.

**government
expenditures** or
outlays
The government's
purchases of goods and
services plus transfer
payments and interest
on government debts.

Total **government expenditures** or **outlays** exceed government purchases of goods and services because the federal, state, and local governments also pay funds directly in the form of transfer payments to people and institutions. Transfer payments include Social Security retirement and disability payments, unemployment insurance, agricultural subsidies, and interest on the government's debts. In 1992, total federal government expenditures were about three times the size of federal purchases of goods and services. Transfer payments (including interest on the national debt) make up the largest part of federal spending. However, transfer payments are a relatively small portion of state and local expenditures, which exceed the purchases of goods and services by only about 11 percent. States and localities devote their budgets primarily to providing goods and services. Over the past decade, total government expenditures have remained a fairly constant share of GDP. Total state, local, and federal outlays were equal to 13.9 percent of GDP in 1992.

The Treasury finances government expenditures by raising revenues, including direct taxes payable by individuals (such as federal and state income and local property taxes) and excise taxes (such as sales taxes and user fees). In the 1980s, there was an increase in the budget deficit (the gap between government receipts and government expenditures or outlays), which grew from 1.3 percent of GDP in 1980 to 3.4 percent of GDP in 1986. The deficit was 1.9 percent of GDP in 1989, but jumped up to 4.5 percent of GDP in 1992 as a result of recession. These deficits have been incurred by the federal government with small surpluses by state and local governments, partially offsetting the federal deficit. The large federal deficit has been financed by issuing federal government bonds (Treasury bills and bonds).

WHAT IS THE GOVERNMENT BUYING AND WHY?

State and local governments provide basic public services, such as schools, roads, and public libraries. They also provide some public welfare programs. Figure 5–1 shows how the state and local expenditure pie was divided in fiscal years 1980 and 1993. Over the intervening two decades, expenditures on education first rose and then fell—trends that have reflected the increased student population during the baby boom years and the fall in the number of students in recent years. Public welfare has risen in relative importance over the period.

The composition of federal expenditures is shown in Figure 5–2. During the 1980s, the federal government's expenditures on defense and interest on past debt had the most growth in their share of total expenditures, while education, energy, natural resources, agriculture, income security, transportation, VA benefits, and other expenditures had reductions in their shares. Defense expenditures rose as a result of the Reagan administration's commitment to strengthen the military. Military spending has fallen in the 1990s with the reduction in Cold War tensions. Social Security and interest payments on the debt have since risen. The rise in the share of expenditure going to pay interest came about because of the large budget deficits.

Public Goods, Income Distribution, and Merit Goods

Public goods are defined as those that have a special claim or merit, which requires that they be provided or subsidized by the government. Public goods are underproduced if production is left to the individuals in the marketplace. When provided publicly, they are often consumed in common. Examples include public health expenditures, cultural activities and national parks, basic scientific research, and national defense.

Individuals within the same country cannot be excluded from the benefits of the defense being provided for the country as a whole. And the amount of defense provided to one citizen does not subtract from the defense provided to other citizens.

FIGURE 5–1
State and Local Government Expenditures by Function, 1980 and 1993

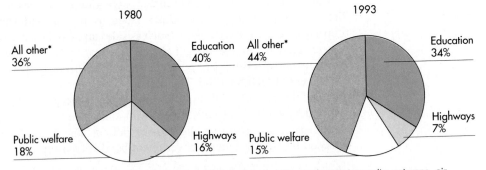

Note: "Other" includes expenditures for libraries, hospitals, health, employment security, veterans, air transportation, transit subsidies, police protection, fire protection, correction, and other expenditures.

Source: *Economic Report of the President 1994.*

FIGURE 5–2   Federal Government Expenditures, Fiscal Years 1980, 1988, and 1993 (billions of current-year dollars)

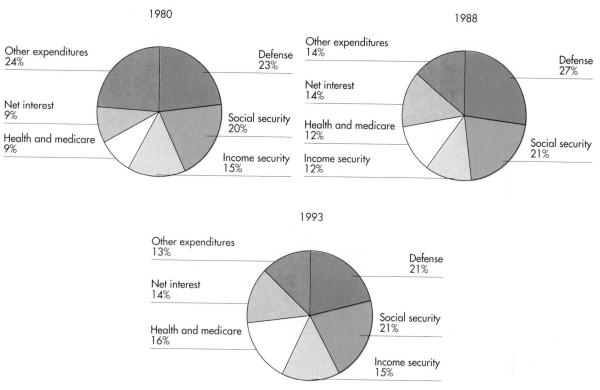

public goods
Public goods are goods and services provided or subsidized by government.

The private market does not work well for public goods, because public goods are by their nature consumable by everyone, regardless of whether any individual pays for the privilege. Therefore, a private market will result in much fewer payers than beneficiaries and in an insufficient supply of the public good provided by a private market. For example, since people benefit from their consumption of national defense irrespective of the amount they pay individually, it is unlikely that they will voluntarily pay for military services. If national defense were privately supplied and if only a very few were willing to contribute to its purchase, then too little would be supplied. Through the public provision of national defense we all contribute to its provision at a level that is determined politically.

Another major purpose for government expenditures is to provide income support for those in a society who are judged to be needy and deserving of public consideration: the elderly, the disabled, and others unable to support themselves. Leaving aside the intense debate over exactly which groups belong in this category and what the level of support should be, these social transfers are an important part of the mission of government, and these programs have become a large part of the federal budget.

Some public expenditures are for goods that are neither public goods nor for the needy, but they are still considered to have special value—these are merit goods. For instance, a small part of government expenditure helps support public libraries and art galleries. A major part of government spending goes for education. The main economic arguments for the public provision of education are that it provides opportunity for children whose parents lack the resources to educate them; and that it raises the overall productivity of the economy.

The process of deciding which goods have special merit and which do not is prone to abuse and partisanship. Most of us oppose pork-barrel projects that benefit special rather than public interests, although we often disagree on what these are. Citizens are also prone to put aside their objections to special-interest projects when the project in question benefits them or their neighbors. Many people argue that government expenditures are too large, but the issue of exactly which government expenditures should be cut is fraught with conflict and self interest. Even putting abuse and politics aside, the process of comparing the costs and benefits of competing public expenditures—hospitals versus highways, college loans versus head-start, libraries versus airports—is a highly subjective one. Surprisingly, macroeconomics does not ordinarily attempt to resolve these issues, because the choices among public expenditures usually do not affect the overall short-run performance of the economy.

We make a simplifying assumption about how government purchases of goods and services are determined as we study their aggregate-demand effects. We will assume that the total level of government purchases of goods and services, G, are autonomous expenditures fixed by policy. We ignore for now the specific programs which make up the total of government purchases.

TAXES, TRANSFERS, AND THE TAX FUNCTION

The government takes away part of the income of individuals and corporations in the form of taxes, and it contributes to the income of individuals and organizations in the form of transfer payments. By the amount of tax that households and institutions pay, the government affects private spending decisions and hence affects aggregate demand.

Gross and Net Tax Revenues

Taxes are levied to pay for government expenditures. Tax revenues are overwhelmingly the largest source (over 90 percent) of the funds used by the government to pay for its spending. Yet, because the federal government can spend in excess of, or less than, the amount collected from tax revenues, we will assume that *taxes are determined separately from expenditures*. The government can and often does run budget deficits and it has at times run surpluses.

The federal income tax, levied on households and corporations, generates the largest share of total tax revenue. Payroll taxes (such as the taxes used to support Social Security or unemployment compensation), sales taxes, state and local income taxes, and property taxes account for most of the rest of tax revenue. The total of all tax revenue collected by all forms of government is **gross tax revenue** (T_g).

gross tax revenue
The total of all tax revenue collected by all forms of government.

Transfer Payments

transfer payments
Income payments made by the government to households and institutions. Interest payments on the debt are included in transfers.

Along with its purchases of goods and services, the government allocates money to the private sector in the form of **transfer payments** (T_p). The decision to allocate these transfer payments is made as part of the budgetary process, and the payments are part of total government expenditures. In the newspaper you might find transfers and government purchases mixed together in a discussion of whether we can afford high levels of both defense spending (purchases) and Social Security payments (transfers). However, transfer payments affect aggregate demand differently than government purchases of goods and services. Transfers are an addition to the income of the recipient, rather than a direct part of aggregate demand. In the analysis of aggregate demand, income, and output, we cannot mix these two. How a transfer is spent and on what it is spent are determined by the recipient of the transfer and not by the government. We will treat transfer payments as an offset to gross tax revenues. They are negative taxes since, in total, the net amount we all pay to the government is equal to total tax payments minus the transfers that the government gives to the private sector.

Taxes and Income

net tax revenue
The total or gross tax revenue collected by the government minus transfer payments.

The government takes part of household income in the form of gross tax revenues (T_g) and adds to income the amount paid out as transfer payments (T_p). **Net tax revenue** (T) is the difference between these two, gross tax receipts minus transfers $(T = T_g - T_p)$.

Both components of net tax revenue (gross tax revenue, T_g, and transfer payments, T_p) have predictable relationships to the level of national income. During good economic conditions when national income is relatively high, more people are employed, wages per employee are high, and business profits are high. Since income taxes and payroll taxes are collected as percentages of wages, salaries, and profits, *when income is high, gross tax revenues are high.* For transfer payments, when income and employment are high, unemployment is low, so unemployment-insurance payments are low. When employment opportunities are good, people decide to delay retirement, reducing Social Security payments. In addition, a smaller portion of the population applies for welfare, lowering welfare payments. *When income is high, transfer payments are low.* The relationships between gross tax revenues and income and between transfer payments and income work together, so *net tax revenues rise when income rises and fall when income falls.*

The Tax Function

marginal propensity to tax
The change in net tax revenue, resulting from a change in income.

Equation 5–1 describes the relationship between net tax revenues and income via a *tax function*:

$$T = T_1 Y \tag{5-1}$$

The tax function says that net tax revenue is a fraction of income (T_1). If T_1 is equal to 0.2, then on average 20 percent of income is paid in net taxes. Since we have described a very simple tax function, T_1 is called the **marginal propensity to tax.** In the above example, 20 percent of any increase in income will go as additional tax payments. While the U.S tax code is very complex in practice, the tax function is an adequate approximation of the actual tax structure in the U.S. economy when we want to study changes in aggregate demand.

Disposable Income

disposable income
Income minus tax receipts.

The amount of income available for people to spend and save is the amount left over after transfers are added to income and gross tax receipts are subtracted from income. This net level of income is called **disposable income** (Y_d):

$$Y_d = Y - T_g + T_p = Y - T \qquad (5-2)$$

Disposable income (Y_d) is just total income (Y) less net tax payments (T).[1] When taxes are collected, *consumption expenditures are determined by the level of disposable income, not by the level of total income.* Because aggregate demand is affected directly by government expenditures and indirectly by net taxes through changes in consumption expenditures, we need to rework our description of goods-market equilibrium to account for the roles of government expenditures and net taxes.

GOODS-MARKET EQUILIBRIUM WITH TAXES AND GOVERNMENT SPENDING

We now incorporate taxes and government spending into the *IS–LM* framework. We start with the *IS* schedule, by including government purchases (G) in aggregate demand. Aggregate demand now includes consumption demand, investment demand, and government demand—which is equal to government purchases of goods and services—fixed by policy. The condition for goods-market equilibrium is:

$$Y = C + I + G \qquad (5-3)$$

Government adds to aggregate demand through its purchases of goods and services. It also reduces private consumption demand through its taxation. Since disposable income is the portion of income consumers are free to either spend or save, the consumption function has to be changed so *consumption depends on disposable income:*

$$C = C_0 + C_1 Y_d \quad \text{or} \quad C = C_0 + C_1(Y - T) \qquad (5-4)$$

We will assume that the inclusion of government does not change investment demand or its relation to income and the interest rate, so the investment function remains as described in Chapter 3, rewritten here as:

$$I = I_0 + I_1 Y - I_2 r \qquad (5-5)$$

We now replace the terms for consumption and investment expenditure (C and I in Equation 5–3) with the expressions for consumption demand (Equation 5–4) and

---

[1] In the National Income and Product Accounts disposable income excludes the profit income that businesses retain. We do not follow this procedure; instead, we assign all profit income to the owners of the businesses, because the income belongs to the owners and they take it into account when deciding how much to consume and how much to save.

investment demand (Equation 5–5). We show the substitutions that lead to the equilibrium condition in steps. First:

$$Y = C_0 + C_1 Y_d + I_0 + I_1 Y - I_2 r + G$$

Since disposable income is equal to total income minus net tax revenue:

$$Y = C_0 + C_1(Y - T) + I_0 + I_1 Y - I_2 r + G$$

Now replace net tax revenues (T) with the tax function. The result of these substitutions is the condition for goods-market equilibrium, when the government sector is included:

$$Y = C_0 + C_1 (Y - T_1 Y) + I_0 + I_1 Y - I_2 r + G \qquad (5\text{--}6)$$

Equation 5–6 can be rearranged to give an *IS* schedule, the combinations of income and the interest rate for which there is goods-market equilibrium. By moving the interest-rate term to the left-hand side and simplifying:

$$r = \frac{(C_0 + I_0 + G)}{I_2} - \frac{[1 - C_1(1 - T_1) - I_1]Y}{I_2} \qquad (5\text{--}7)$$

This is a complex expression that is not easy to interpret and you should not try to memorize it. It is worth going over Worked Example 5–1 to help understand the expression and to see how the IS schedule has been made steeper.

> *Worked Example 5–1*   This worked example on page 135 provides an alternative to the algebra of Equation 5–7. It shows how to find the *IS* schedule with a specific tax function and level of government purchases. We see that the introduction of a tax function has made the *IS* schedule steeper because the tax function reduced the multiplier.

Equilibrium with an Unchanged Interest Rate

We developed the idea of the multiplier in Chapter 3 by fixing the interest rate and we are going to do the same thing here. In practice, an unchanged interest rate in the face of a fiscal change would require the cooperation of the monetary authorities. The Fed would have to adjust monetary policy to maintain a constant interest rate, and it is not clear that the Fed would do this or even could do it. At this point, however, we are not concerned with how monetary policy is made. We are taking a step-by-step approach to understand the effects of fiscal policy. We can then take what we learn from this exercise and apply it later in the case where the interest rate varies.

With a given interest rate, equilibrium income can be determined from the goods-market–equilibrium condition—if the interest rate is known, then a particular point on the *IS* schedule is known, determining equilibrium income. By solving Equation 5–6 for the value of Y that just satisfies goods-market demands, we find equilibrium income. The solution involves collecting Y terms to the left-hand side and factoring out Y:

$$Y[1 - C_1(1 - T_1) - I_1] = C_0 + I_0 - I_2 r + G$$

Dividing both sides by $[1 - C_1(1 - T_1) - I_1]$ results in the following expression for goods-market–equilibrium income with a given interest rate ($\bar{r}$):

$$Y = \frac{1}{1 - C_1(1 - T_1) - I_1} \times (C_0 + I_0 - I_2\bar{r} + G)$$

(5–8)

| Equilibrium income | = | Autonomous-expenditure multiplier | × | Autonomous expenditure |

Rewriting the autonomous-expenditure multiplier using marginal propensities gives:

$$\text{Autonomous-expenditure multiplier} = \frac{1}{1 - \text{MPC}(1 - \text{MPT}) - \text{MPI}}$$

Equilibrium income in the goods market with a given interest rate is equal to the *autonomous-expenditure multiplier* times *autonomous expenditure,* and this has the same form as the solution for goods-market equilibrium that we had in Chapter 3 before we introduced government expenditures and taxation. However, when we introduced the multiplier in Chapter 3 we talked simply about "the multiplier." Now we are putting a specific label on this multiplier because there will be different multipliers, depending on which fiscal policy is being changed.

Looking at the autonomous-expenditure term, remember that, since we are holding the interest rate constant and focusing only on the multiplier effect, we have included as part of autonomous expenditures the portion of investment demand that is affected by the interest rate. The term that is new in the expression for autonomous expenditure is *government purchases.*

Taxes respond to income, so the marginal propensity to tax appears in the multiplier The autonomous-expenditure multiplier depends on the marginal propensity to tax (T_1 or MPT) as well as the marginal propensity to consume (C_1 or MPC) and the marginal propensity to invest (I_1 or MPI). Higher taxes reduce the level of disposable income left over from any increase in income. This effect is reflected in the multiplier, since the marginal propensity to tax *increases* the denominator of the expression for the multiplier and *decreases* the size of the multiplier.

Both autonomous expenditure and the multiplier have been changed by the introduction of the government sector. Autonomous expenditures have been increased, while the multiplier has been decreased. The government sector had offsetting effects on goods-market equilibrium, raising aggregate demand through government purchases and lowering demand through net taxation.

The Autonomous-Expenditure Multiplier and Government Spending The autonomous-expenditure multiplier shows how aggregate demand and income will change when there is a change in autonomous expenditure—be it a change in the autonomous parts of consumption, investment, or government purchases. The multiplier effect of a change in autonomous expenditure when there is a government collecting taxes is different from one with no taxation. If taxes are a function of the level of income, as they are in most modern economies, then there are **tax leakages** that reduce the multiplier. A boost in any autonomous expenditure will cause income to rise, but the rise in income drives up tax receipts, which, in turn, leads to smaller increases in expenditure in the subsequent rounds of the multiplier. We refer to tax

tax leakages
The increased net tax revenue associated with an increase in income.

payments as *leakages* because they drain off funds each time demand is recycled through the economy. The greater the leakage, the smaller the ultimate impact of any initial change. The effect of a change in autonomous expenditure on income is shown in Equation 5–9:

$$\Delta Y = \frac{1}{1 - MPC(1 - MPT) - MPI} \times \Delta(C_0 + I_0 - I_2\bar{r} + G)$$

$$
\begin{array}{ccc}
\text{Change} & = & \text{Autonomous-} \quad \times \quad \text{Change in} \\
\text{in income} & & \text{expenditure} \qquad \quad \text{autonomous} \\
& & \text{multiplier} \qquad \quad \text{expenditures}
\end{array}
$$

(5–9)

Since an increase in the marginal propensity to tax (the tax rate, T_1) reduces the multiplier, *the higher the tax rate, the lower the multiplier effect* on equilibrium income.

> *Worked Example 5–2*   This worked example on page 137 shows how a change in autonomous spending will affect income when the interest rate is fixed. It derives the autonomous-expenditure multiplier.

Changes in Government Purchases   There is an important implication of what we have found. *Since government purchases of goods and services are part of autonomous expenditure, a change in government purchases will change equilibrium income.* When the government increases its demand for aircraft or computers, this adds directly to total demand in the economy and there are then further increases in income as the multiplier works through the economy. When the government cuts back on its purchases, this will reduce demand in the economy and could trigger a recession. *An increase or decrease in government purchases will have a multiplier effect on income.*

A change in the level of government purchases in the economy will have the intended or unintended effect of changing income. In practice, the biggest changes in government purchases occur when there is a war. If the economy was at full employment before the war starts, then the wartime increase in government purchases will raise income above capacity and may well lead to inflation. Inflations have often accompanied wars. Alternatively, if the economy was in a recession when the war started, then the increase in income may be helpful economically. This was the case with World War II, when large increases in defense spending pulled the U.S. economy out of the high unemployment of the Great Depression.

Changes in income may be the unintended side effects of changes in government purchases that are made because of national defense or for other reasons, but there is also the possibility that *increases or decreases in government purchases may be used deliberately to affect income.* Policymakers may decide that they want to increase or decrease the level of income or employment in the economy and they can use government purchases as a way of achieving this.

The model we have used in this section, in which the government increases its demand and thus increases income and employment in the economy, was the one used by John Maynard Keynes to argue that government spending should be used to bring the British economy out of its long depression of the 1920s and 1930s[2] and his ideas still influence policy today.

Early in his administration, government expenditure increases were advocated by President Clinton as a way of ending recession. He argued that there was a need for government spending on roads and other projects and that this spending could also add to aggregate demand. Congress failed to support these initiatives and the stimulus package did not pass Congress.

As well as proposing increased government spending to alleviate recession, President Clinton had also proposed a cut in taxes. Tax cuts increase disposable income and encourage increases in consumption demand.

The Tax-Rate Multiplier

An important instrument of fiscal policy is to change the tax rate (T_1, or *MPT*). Tax-rate changes have an important characteristic—*the impact of any tax-rate change depends both on the amount of change in the rate and on the level of income in the economy before the change in the tax rate*. A given increase in the tax rate will bring about a larger increase in the amount of taxes paid and a larger reduction in the equilibrium level of income at higher levels of income than at lower levels of income (see Equation 5–10). This may seem puzzling, but notice that a change in tax rates affects the economy by changing the amount of tax dollars paid to the government out of different levels of income. If income in the economy is \$4 trillion and the tax rate rises by 5 percentage points, disposable income falls initially by \$200 billion. This is followed by a multiplier reaction that includes the increased tax leakage. However, if income were initially \$5 trillion, the same rise in tax rate would result in a \$250 billion fall in disposable income, followed by a multiplier reaction. The reduction in equilibrium income will be larger in the latter case where income was originally higher. The *tax-rate multiplier* gives the effect on income of a change in the tax rate, ΔT_1:

Effect on income of a change in the tax rate:

$$\Delta Y = \frac{-C_1 Y}{1 - C_1(1 - T_1) - I_1} \times \Delta T_1 \qquad (5\text{--}10)$$

| Change in = income | Tax-rate multiplier | $\times$ Change in tax rate |

Deriving this expression for the change in goods-market equilibrium requires the use of calculus, but Worked Example 5–3 provides an illustration of the effect of tax-rate changes.

Worked Example 5–3   This worked example on page 137 gives the expression for the tax-rate multiplier—the extent to which a cut in the tax rate will raise income. Keep in mind that multipliers give the increase in income only if the interest rate is taken as fixed.

---

[2] Keynes argued that there would be little or no change in the rate of interest following the increase in government spending because the economy has excess money during depression periods—the so-called *liquidity trap.* Most analysts have disagreed with this view. There is little empirical evidence to support the idea of a liquidity trap.

Monetary policy and money-market conditions often operate independently of fiscal-policy changes. There is no guarantee that the monetary authorities can or will so coordinate policies that a change in taxation or government expenditure occurs with a constant rate of interest. The changes in income that we computed holding the rate of interest constant were too large. We now use the *IS–LM* framework in which the interest rate adjusts along the *LM* schedule as goods-market equilibrium changes. The impact of a change in tax policy is the combined result of the multiplier effect and the interest-rate effect.

FISCAL POLICY AND MONEY-MARKET CONDITIONS

As we allow for changes in the interest rate, we will find that the time we have spent studying multiplier effects has not been wasted. Changes in fiscal policy will be represented by shifts in the *IS* schedule and the size of the horizontal shifts in the *IS* following a tax change or a change in government purchases of goods and services will be equal to the changes in income that we have just computed with a constant rate of interest (a similar result to the one we saw in Chapter 3). That is to be expected. The horizontal shifts in the *IS* schedule reflect the multiplier effect.

Fiscal Policy and Interest-Rate Effects

In Figure 5–3 we use shifts in the *IS* schedule to represent the effects of increases in government purchases and in taxes. The former shifts the *IS* schedule to the right (to *IS'*) and the latter shifts the *IS* to the left (to *IS''*).

Consider first the effect of the increase in government purchases of goods and services. In Figure 5–3, the shift from *A* to *B* describes the full multiplier effect of the increase in government spending. With no change in the interest rate, income would rise from Y_A to Y_B. However, with a fixed *LM* schedule, there is an interest-rate increase (r_A to r_C) that then leads to a partially offsetting decline in income (the interest-rate effect). The final increase in income (Y_A to Y_C) is less than the increase that is given by the multiplier effect alone.

The shift from *A* to *D* describes the full multiplier effect of the increase in the *MPT* (T_1). With a fixed *LM* schedule, there is a fall in the interest rate (r_A to r_E) that then leads to a partially offsetting increase in income (the interest-rate effect). The final decrease in income (Y_A to Y_E) is less than the decrease that is given by the multiplier effect alone.

We have found, therefore, that *the effectiveness of fiscal policy in bringing about changes in income is reduced by the movements of the interest rate that occur with an unchanged monetary policy*. If the fiscal-policy changes are being used appropriately in order to increase income when it is too low, or to decrease it when it is too high, then the interest-rate changes will work to offset the fiscal policy. Fiscal policy is then not as effective in bringing about an economic improvement. If the fiscal-policy change is made for other reasons (to fight a war, for example), then the mitigating effects of interest-rate changes may be helpful in preventing an overheated economy. The rise in the interest rate will reduce private spending and allow for the increase in public spending.

FIGURE 5–3
The Effects of an Increase in Government Purchases or an Increase in the Tax Rate

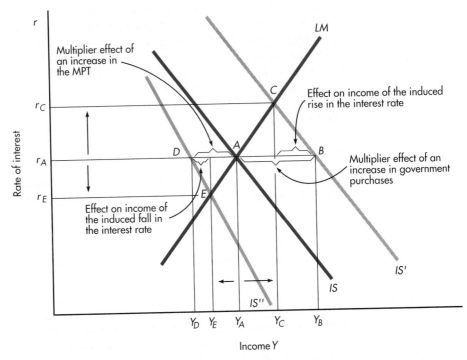

An increase in government purchases raises income (Y_A to Y_C) and the interest rate (r_A to r_C). An increase in the tax rate both lowers income (Y_A to Y_E) and the interest rate (r_A to r_C). Notice it also is described by a steepening of the *IS* schedule, because the higher tax rate reduces the size of the multiplier.

Figure 5–3 shows that a change in the tax rate will change the slope of the *IS* schedule, with an increase in the *MPT* causing the *IS* to become steeper. If we had shown the effect of a reduction of the *MPT*, we would have seen the *IS* becoming flatter.

The simplest way to understand why the *IS* schedule changes its slope as it shifts in this case is to look at Worked Example 5–1. We saw that introducing taxes that depend on income had the effect of making the *IS* schedule steeper. An increase in the tax rate (an increase in *MPT*) will strengthen this effect. Decreases in the tax rate will make the *IS* schedule more like the case with no taxes, so the *IS* is flatter. Another way to understand the result is to recall that the tax-rate multiplier changes with income. The multiplier and hence the horizontal shift of the *IS* schedule is greater at the combination of low rates of interest and high levels of income than at high rates of interest and low levels of income.

We have found that when the money supply remains constant (the *LM* schedule is fixed), the effectiveness of fiscal policy in altering income is reduced. Now we show that the extent to which this occurs depends on money-market conditions and the nature of money demand in particular. The way money demand responds to changes

FIGURE 5-4
The Effect of an Expansionary Fiscal Policy Depends on the Responsiveness of Money Demand

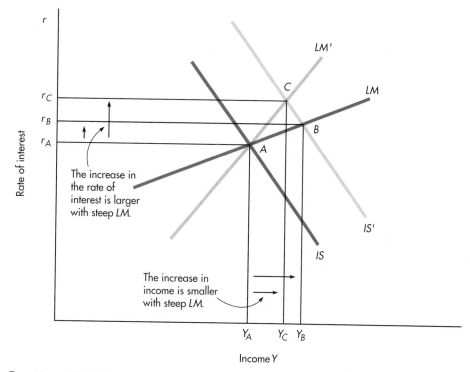

For a given shift in *IS*, the change in income will be smaller with a steep *LM* schedule.

in income and the interest rate has an important impact on the effectiveness of fiscal policy.

Money Demand and Fiscal-Policy Effectiveness

The way in which the demand for money responds to income and the interest rate depends mostly on how businesses and households adjust their money holdings. If people greatly increase their demand for money when income rises, and are unwilling to reduce their demand for money by much when the rate of interest rises, then an expansionary fiscal policy will have little effect on income. Let's see how this happens.

Figure 5–4 depicts an economy that is initially in equilibrium at point *A*. For this example only, we'll restrict fiscal expansion to higher government spending. There is then an increase in government purchases. The effect of this is depicted as a rightward shift of the *IS* schedule (from *IS* to *IS'*). Suppose that money-market conditions in this economy are represented by the *LM* schedule in the figure. In this case, the expansionary fiscal policy has increased income from Y_A to Y_B. As the fiscal policy increases demand in the goods market, there is an increase in the demand for money as people make more transactions—since the supply of money is fixed, the interest rate starts to rise. Money-market equilibrium is restored when people are content to hold the fixed money supply, even though they make more transactions. Provided the increase in money demand generated by the rise in transactions is not too great, and provided people are willing to change their money demand in response to a higher interest rate, the magnitude of the interest-rate (shown as the increase r_A to r_B in Figure 5–4 will not be very large.

Now suppose that money market conditions in this economy are represented by the schedule labeled *LM'* in the figure.[3] In this case, the fiscal expansion will still lead to an increase in income. But as income rises, either the transactions demand for money rises sharply or people are not willing to cut back on their money demand much when the interest rate starts to rise, or both. In this scenario, the only way to maintain money-market equilibrium in this economy is by a large increase in the interest rate (shown as the increase from r_A to r_C in Figure 5–4). The large increase in the interest rate then has a large negative effect on investment demand. This reduces the effect of the fiscal expansion on income. Income rises only from Y_A to Y_C in this case. The fiscal expansion has not been as effective in raising income.

Monetarist economists have criticized Keynes for his advocacy of fiscal policy as a way of pulling an economy out of recession. One reason for their opposition to fiscal policy is that monetarists do not think that money demand changes much when the interest rate changes. They claim that a steep *LM* schedule best represents the economy and thus fiscal policy is ineffective.

Crowding Out

crowding out
A reduction in private investment, resulting from an increase in government spending or a reduction in taxes.

An increase in government purchases increases aggregate demand, but it will also increase interest rates, as we have just seen. This is an important consideration if fiscal policy is being used to raise income. It is also an important consideration if government purchases are being increased to support government programs, good or bad. An increase in government purchases will raise the rate of interest and this will have an adverse effect on investment. This is called **crowding out.** Crowding out occurs when increases in government spending displace private spending, particularly private investment. Investment crowding out can also occur as a result of tax cuts. Tax cuts that increase disposable income and increase consumption will also cause the interest rate to rise and can have an adverse effect on investment.

---

[3] The demand-for-money relation we used in Chapter 3 was the following:

$$\frac{M^d}{P} = kY - hr$$

The case of a steeply sloped money-demand schedule is the same as the case of a small interest-rate effect on the demand for money balances (i.e., the value of the term h is small). A small interest-rate term in the money-demand equation leads to a steep *LM* schedule and a large interest-rate effect in the money market. When h is small, it takes a larger change in interest rates to bring about money-market equilibrium following a fiscal expansion than it does when h is large. The effectiveness of fiscal policy is dampened by a large interest-rate effect (small value of h) in money markets.

Estimates of the interest-rate effect in money markets comes from estimates of the demand for money balances. See John P. Judd and J. L. Scadding, ''The Search for a Stable Money Demand Function,'' *Journal of Economic Literature* XV, no 3 (September 1982).

The investment function (Equation 5–5) shows how investment demand depends upon income and the interest rate. If there is a fiscal policy change that results in changes in income and the interest rate, there will be a change in investment demand:

$$\Delta I = I_1 \Delta Y - I_2 \Delta r \tag{5-11}$$

The change in investment demand, ΔI, depends on the change in income, ΔY, the change in the rate of interest, Δr, and the magnitudes of I_1 and I_2. An increase in government spending or a cut in taxes will raise income and therefore raise investment demand. But an increase in government spending or a tax cut will also increase the rate of interest and this will lower investment demand. The extent to which crowding out is a problem depends on which of these two effects is more important.

We see that the problem of crowding out is closely related to our previous discussion of money-market conditions and the effectiveness of policy. If money demand is relatively unresponsive to changes in the interest rate (steep *LM* schedule), then this will mean that any increase in government spending or cut in taxes will raise income by relatively little and will raise the interest rate a lot. *Crowding out becomes a serious problem in this case.*

However, the nature of money demand is not the only factor. The responsiveness of investment demand to income changes and interest-rate changes is also important to an assessment of crowding out. Generally, it is thought that if the economy is in a recession and there are slack resources, investment will be fairly responsive to increases in income and not very responsive to changes in the rate of interest. *The crowding-out effect of increased government spending is not very serious if there is slack capacity in the economy in the first place. On the other hand, if income in the economy is already above potential output so that capacity is being overused, then adding the increased pressure of government demand is likely to crowd out private investment spending.*

GOVERNMENT FINANCE AND THE BUDGET BALANCE

Up until now we have assumed that taxes and government spending are determined separately. We talked about the effect of increases in government spending without saying where the resources are coming from to pay for the extra spending. In practice the relation between total spending and total revenues is an important one for the government and may affect fiscal-policy decisions. We now turn to an analysis of the government budget and the problem of the deficit.

The government raises tax revenues to finance its expenditures. If tax revenues always equaled expenditures, the budget would always be in balance. But often, actual revenues are either higher or lower than actual expenditures. When tax revenues exceed government expenditures, the result is a *budget surplus.* When government expenditures exceed net tax revenues, the result is a *budget deficit.* A budget surplus or deficit is defined, equivalently, as either the difference between net tax revenue (T) and government purchases of goods and services (G) or else the difference between

budget balance
The difference between government receipts and government outlays. There is a surplus when receipts exceed outlays, a deficit when receipts fall short of outlays.

gross tax revenues (T_g) and total government expenditures [government purchases (G) plus transfers (T_p)]. We refer to the surplus or deficit as the **budget balance** (B).

$$
\begin{aligned}
B &= T - G \\
&= T_g - T_p - G, \text{ or} \\
&= T_g - (G + T_p).
\end{aligned}
\tag{5–12}
$$

When the government balance (B) is positive, there is a surplus, but when B is negative, there is a deficit. Over the past several years in the United States, the cumulative effects of federal budget deficits have outweighed surpluses in some state or local budgets.

The Budget Deficit

Table 5–1 shows the combined receipts and expenditures of the federal, state, and local governments. These include government purchases, total tax receipts, and transfer payments. The table also notes the overall government balance, which was a deficit in each of the years shown. The figures are in current dollars, unadjusted for inflation. The table shows that government purchases, receipts, and transfers have all been rising, but that total receipts have not matched the sum of government expenditures and transfer payments. The result has been a deficit that widened until 1986. It fell a little after that and then ballooned in the recession. With recovery and deficit reduction efforts, it is now falling again.

The overall government deficit is a result of the fact that the federal government has been making expenditures greatly in excess of its receipts for several years now. How does it manage to do this?

Government Borrowing

One possible way in which the federal government can cover a deficit is that it can issue government bonds *and have the Fed buy the bonds,* thereby financing the deficit through an increase in the supply of money. Does this happen in practice?

In general, *the Fed does not automatically supply money to cover federal budget deficits.* And for good reason. The result would likely be inflationary. The main way in which federal deficits in the United States are financed is by borrowing from the public.

In the United States, federal government borrowing is generally done through the Treasury, which sells Treasury bills and bonds to the general public. (Treasury bills are just short-term bonds.) When the Treasury sells these bonds, the proceeds go to the government to close the gap between tax revenues and government expenditures. Some states and municipalities also borrow by using bonds, and this borrowing is included in the total of government borrowing. State and local levels of government have not been net borrowers in recent years, mostly because they are required to maintain balanced budgets by state laws and because they have been building up pension funds for their employees.

Once Treasury bonds have been sold, the federal government is obliged to pay the owners of the bonds an amount of *interest* every year and then to repay the loan or *principal* after a fixed amount of time. *There is a cost to the public from deficit*

TABLE 5–1
Federal, State, and
Local Government
Receipts and
Expenditures,
Calendar Years
1980–1993 (billions
of current-year
dollars)

	1980	1985	1990	1993
Receipts	$826	$1,217	$1,709	$1,969
Outlays	861	1,342	1,848	2,193
Surplus or Deficit (−)	−35	−125	−138	−224

financing. By borrowing, the government has covered its deficit in the short run without increasing taxes; but since the interest on the debts must be paid, this means that a larger fraction of future tax revenues must be devoted to debt service and not to public services.

There is much controversy surrounding the federal budget deficit: how harmful it is, and whether concerns about the deficit should limit the use of fiscal policy to increase income in recessions. The key point about budget surpluses and deficits is that they are a form of government saving or dissaving. *The government's decision to save or dissave affects the total of national saving in the economy. A budget deficit is a subtraction from saving, and the effects of this can be either good or bad.*

The Effect of the Budget Balance on Saving

private saving
The part of private income not consumed. It equals total income minus net taxes minus consumption.

With no government sector, equilibrium income occurs where saving equals planned investment. A similar condition relates saving and investment when we include government in the model. In Chapter 3 we assumed there was no government sector, so saving was defined as income minus consumption. Now we need to define two different concepts of saving, private saving and national saving. **Private saving** (S) is equal to disposable income (Y_d) minus consumption.

$$S = Y_d - C = Y - T - C$$

The goods-market–equilibrium condition is given by:

$$Y = \text{Aggregate demand} = C + I + G$$

Subtracting consumption and government spending from income gives:

$$Y - C - G = I$$

Then subtracting and adding net taxes gives

$$(Y - T - C) + (T - G) = I$$

or

$$S + B = I$$

national saving
The total of private saving plus the government's budget surplus (or minus the government's budget deficit).

Saving plus the budget balance equals investment. The sum of private saving and the budget balance is often called **national saving,** so *goods-market equilibrium occurs when national saving equals investment.*

When the budget is balanced ($B = 0$), government expenses are paid for by net tax revenues ($G = T$). In this case, the relationship between private saving and planned investment is the same as if there were no government sector.

If the budget is in surplus ($B > 0$), tax revenues exceed government expenditures ($G < T$) and this is the same as having the government save a portion of its tax revenue. The income received by the government is not all spent when it runs a surplus. This represents extra national saving that can then be used for investment, if there is enough investment demand to make use of it. National saving is larger than private saving in this case.

Finally, the most common case for the U.S. government is that it is running a deficit ($B < 0$), spending more than it earns in revenues ($G > T$). The resources of saving available for planned investment are lower than they would have been otherwise, because the resources devoted to meeting government expenditures exceeded the tax revenues collected to pay for them. Here, national saving is less than private saving.

The relationship between the budget balance, saving, and planned investment helps us to see both the pluses and minuses of using deficit spending to cure a recession.

Short-Term versus Chronic Deficits

When the economy is in a recession, there is inadequate aggregate demand. This can be due to a lack of coordination between the level of planned investment and the level of national saving. When planned investment falls below the amount of private saving generated in the economy and output are equal to potential output, there is a fall in income and the economy reaches a new equilibrium at a lower level of income.

In this situation, a cut in taxes or an increase in government purchases that creates a budget deficit provides a subtraction from private saving. Total national saving is then less than private saving; and if the difference is enough to bring national saving back into alignment with investment at full-employment income, then the lack of coordination between investment and private saving will have been overcome.

The use of deficits to solve the coordination problem should be seen only as a short-term approach, however. The coordination problem should not be used as an excuse to run chronic large deficits, since these shift the economy toward more government spending or more consumption as sources of aggregate demand and crowd out investment. If the economy has fallen into a recession because of inadequate investment, then it is better to reverse this and increase investment than to rely on demand fueled by deficit spending in the long run.

Since deficits can be either good or bad, policymakers need to have a correct view of whether or not there is a deficit problem. And it turns out that this is quite difficult to obtain, because *the deficit itself changes when the economy changes.* Lets see how this happens.

The Budget Deficit over the Business Cycle

We start the discussion of the effect of the economy on the deficit by looking at an economy that is about to go into a recession. Perhaps the recession begins with businesses becoming less optimistic about future sales and profits. Because of worsened expectations, firms target a lower level of planned investment. Production decreases, leading to further reductions in purchases of capital goods, and this reduction in investment is amplified throughout the economy through the multiplier process. If there are no offsetting positive changes in aggregate demand, the economy will go into a recession. Since income has fallen, tax revenues have fallen by an amount equal to the change in income times the marginal propensity to tax ($\Delta Y \times MPT$). If the budget was balanced before the recession ($B = 0$), the fall in income will move the government budget into deficit ($B < 0$). *Even if there is no change in policy, a recession by itself will create or worsen a deficit because of the dependence of tax revenues and transfers on income.*

Faced with this new, lower equilibrium income, what is the appropriate policy response? Should we cut government programs and raise taxes to cure the deficit, but worsen the recession? Or should we increase government programs and cut taxes to move the economy out of recession, but worsen the deficit? The basic problem is that *the budget deficit is giving a false indication of the status of the budget during recessions.* When the economy goes into a recession, it appears there is a deficit problem. The problem of giving false signals is not restricted to recessions. When the economy goes into a boom, it can look as though there is no deficit problem when in fact there is one. A way to avoid this problem is to define a concept called the cyclically adjusted budget.

The Structural Deficit

structural deficit
The budget deficit that would occur with current tax rates and expenditure programs if the level of output and income in the economy were equal to potential output.

cyclical deficit
The budget deficit minus the structural deficit.

The cyclically adjusted budget removes the impacts of cyclical changes in income. What remains provides a measure of the underlying or longer-term status of the deficit.[4] The **structural deficit** is defined as the budget surplus or deficit that would exist if the economy were at full employment; that is, if output were equal to potential output:

$$\text{Structural deficit} = G - T_1 Y^p \tag{5-13}$$

Of course, the level of net tax revenues that would occur at full employment has to be estimated.

Once the structural deficit has been estimated, the actual deficit in any year can be divided into two parts. If the cyclically adjusted budget is in deficit, then the economy has a structural deficit. The portion of the actual deficit which exceeds the structural deficit is classified as the **cyclical deficit:**

$$\text{Actual deficit} = \text{Structural deficit} + \text{Cyclical deficit} \tag{5-14}$$

In any given year, the actual deficit will be greater in magnitude than the structural deficit if output is less than potential output, and there will be a cyclical deficit. If output is greater than potential output, there will be a cyclical surplus.

Figure 5–5 shows the total budget deficit and estimates of the structural and cyclical components. The figure shows both the rising structural deficits in the 1980s and the substantial cyclical deficits in the early 1980s, particularly in 1982. The cyclical deficit grew again in 1990–92 and then fell as the economy recovered.

---

[4] The task of evaluating the status of the deficit and fiscal policy is discussed in Oliver J. Blanchard, "Debts, Deficits and Finite Horizons," and Edward M. Gramlich, "Fiscal Indicators." Both are working papers of the OECD Department of Economics and Statistics, April 1990, nos. 79 and 80, respectively.

FIGURE 5-5
Total Deficit as a Percentage of GDP—Fiscal Years 1979-1993

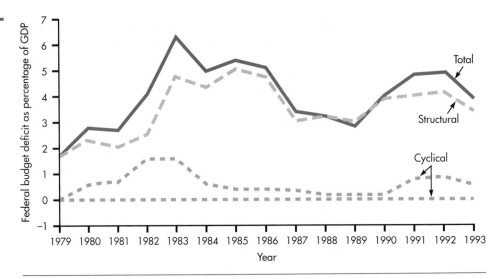

Source: Computed by the authors using data from the Bureau of Economic Analysis, U.S. Department of Commerce.

Cyclical Deficits and the Automatic Stabilizers

automatic stabilizers
Transfers and tax reductions that are activated when income falls, without the need for new authorizations or legislation from Congress.

The cyclical deficit is the amount by which the government budget is in deficit as a result of a level of output that is below potential output. In the view of many economists, including ourselves, policymakers should not worry too much about the cyclical deficits caused by recessions. Cyclical deficits are an indication that an economy has **automatic stabilizers** that are helping to offset recessions.

Automatic stabilizers consist of transfers and tax reductions that are activated in a recession without the need for new authorizations or legislation from Congress. Programs such as unemployment insurance help to support workers who are laid off by providing them with income. Laid-off workers who receive unemployment benefits continue spending, thereby bolstering aggregate demand. Other transfer programs, such as unemployment insurance, welfare, and Social Security, also help to sustain aggregate demand during a recession. By reducing the decline in equilibrium income and output, these transfer programs act as automatic stabilizers.

The fact that income and sales taxes also vary with the level of income and expenditure means that they, too, act as automatic stabilizers. The reduction in gross tax revenues during recessions helps sustain aggregate demand. The government is taking less income out of the economy. The combination of reduced taxes and increased transfers in recessions means that disposable income (Y_d) falls by less than income (Y).

The workings of the automatic stabilizers have already been incorporated into our analysis. When net tax revenues vary with income, this leads to a reduction in the tax-rate multiplier. This means that the changes in equilibrium income and the shifts in the *IS* schedule resulting from changes in autonomous expenditures (such as fluctuations in investment demand) are smaller in an economy with taxes and transfers.

In the short run, allowing the automatic stabilizers to work and even supplementing them with active adjustments to tax rates can improve economic stability without major cost. *Short-run cyclical deficits should not stop the use of fiscal policy when the economy needs an increase in aggregate demand.*

Structural
Deficits

The concerns over the deficit that started in the middle 1980s and continue into the 1990s were generated by an ever-increasing deficit during the economy's longest post–World War II expansion. During this time the long-term growth of government debt was more rapid than the growth of GNP. The economy was generating larger and larger structural deficits. This concern led to a movement to contain the deficit through formula, such as the Gramm-Rudman-Hollings deficit-reduction legislation, or through proposals for a constitutional amendment requiring a balanced budget.

The trouble with proposals to curb deficits with such formulas as the Gramm-Rudman-Hollings proposal is that these formulas may prevent the automatic stabilizers from working and discourage the use of tax-rate reductions to deal with severe recessions. But the reasons that these proposals are being made and supported are quite legitimate. The large structural deficits of the 1980s that seem to be continuing into the 1990s have done considerable damage to the economy and will continue to do damage. Large structural deficits crowd out investment. And as we will see in Chapter 7, they have disrupted our foreign trade and caused a large trade deficit.

Conclusions
about Fiscal
Policy

An expansionary fiscal policy will increase demand in the goods market (shift the *IS* schedule to the right) and will raise income. But the stimulation to aggregate demand from a purely fiscal expansion normally results in a rising interest rate and possibly crowding out private investment.

The problems that result from using fiscal policy to increase income are not terribly serious if the policies smooth out short-run variations of income over the business cycle. Since it is hard to mobilize both the administration and congress to take action on taxes or expenditures, the automatic stabilizers seem the ideal vehicle by which fiscal policy can improve the performance of the economy in the 1990s. There are good reasons to have in place such programs as unemployment insurance that support workers without jobs plus retirement and disability programs for those who cannot work. Maintaining or strengthening these income-supported programs because they help the needy will have the beneficial side effect of improving the overall stability of the economy.

Running a large budget deficit over several years can create serious problems. Indeed, deficits have created serious problems in the 1980s that continue into the 1990s.

In our discussions of fiscal policy we found that money-market conditions made a difference. We did not talk much about monetary policy. At this point we need to examine the role of monetary policy. This is the task of Chapter 6.

WORKED EXAMPLES

Worked
Example 5–1

Finding the *IS* Schedule with Taxes and Government Purchases of Goods and Services
We use the same investment function that appeared in earlier work examples, but *we have changed the consumption function.* Consumption now depends upon disposable income and we

have set autonomous consumption at \$80 billion, much lower than in the earlier worked examples.

$$C = 80 + 0.7Y_d$$
$$I = 250 + 0.1Y - 10r$$

There is a tax function as follows:

$$T = 0.2Y$$

The numbers used in these examples for marginal propensities and multipliers are illustrative only. Actual estimates vary over a considerable range and in many cases are smaller or larger than those used here.

We assume that there is \$1,080 billion of government purchases of goods and services:

$$G = 1,080$$

The condition for goods-market equilibrium is then:

$$Y = C + I + G$$
$$= 80 + 0.7Y_d + 250 + 0.1Y - 10r + 1,080$$
$$= 80 + 0.7(Y - 0.2Y) + 250 + 0.1Y - 10r + 1,080$$

Collecting terms gives:

$$Y = (80 + 250 + 1,080) + (0.56Y + 0.1Y) - 10r$$

Putting the interest-rate term on the left-hand side and the income terms on the right-hand side and dividing by 10 gives:

$$r = 141 - 0.034Y$$

This is the new *IS* schedule. What happens if the interest rate is 5 percent?

$$0.034Y = 141 - 5 = 136$$
$$Y = 4,000$$

We have used numbers that give the same level of income at the same rate of interest as the worked examples in Chapter 3. Notice, however, that the *IS* schedule is not the same. The constant term is higher (it was 85 in Worked Example 3–4 and now it is 141) and the coefficient on income is higher. (It was 0.02 in Worked Example 3–4 and now it is 0.034.) The new *IS* schedule is shifted to the right and is steeper than before. Why has this happened?

There is no rule that says that the *IS* schedule is automatically shifted to the right when the government sector is added. This result depended on the particular values we chose for taxes and spending. If we had set government purchases and taxes differently, we could have come up with a different result.

The *IS* schedule including a tax function is steeper than the *IS* schedule without a tax function because the schedule reflects the smaller multiplier effect caused by marginal taxes (see Worked Example 5–2, to follow).

**Worked
Example 5–2**

The Autonomous-Expenditure Multiplier with Tax Leakages

Question   Consider an economy where the marginal propensity to consume is 0.7 and the marginal propensity to invest is 0.1.

a What is the autonomous-expenditure multiplier when the marginal propensity to tax is zero?

b How does this answer change if the marginal propensity to tax is 0.2?

c What will be the increases in income resulting from an increase of $1 billion in autonomous expenditure in the two cases?

Answer   The autonomous-expenditure multiplier is given in Equation 5–9. Substituting in the values given in part *(a)* of the question leads to:

$$\text{Multiplier} = \frac{1}{1 - 0.7(1 - 0) - 0.1} = 5$$

Repeating this procedure for part *(b)* of the question gives:

$$\text{Multiplier} = \frac{1}{1 - 0.7(1 - 0.2) - 0.1} = 2.94$$

Equation 5.9 can also be used to answer part *(c)* of the question:

Change in income when MPT is zero = 5 × 1 = $5 billion

Change in income when MPT is 0.2 = 2.94 × 1 = $2.94 billion

A given increase in autonomous expenditure will result in a smaller increase in income ($5 billion versus $2.94 billion) in case *(b)* than in case *(a)*. This is because in case *(b)* tax payments rise along with the rise in income.

**Worked
Example 5–3**

The Tax-Rate Multiplier

We start with an economy before a change in the tax rate:

Income = $4 trillion ($4,000 billion)

MPC = 0.7, MPI = 0.1, MPT = 0.20

Then the tax rate is changed. MPT is reduced by 5 percentage points, to 0.15, so the change in the tax rate is −0.05.

$$\Delta Y = \frac{-C_1 Y}{1 - C_1(1 - T_1) - I_1} \times \Delta T_1$$

$$= \frac{(-0.7 \times 4,000)}{[1 - 0.7(1 - 0.2) - 0.1]} \times (-0.05)$$

$$= -2.06 \times 4,000 \times (-0.05)$$

$$= +412$$

In this example, with a constant rate of interest and with income initially at $4 trillion, a decline in the marginal tax rate from 20 percent to 15 percent of income would result in an increase of income of $412 billion.

If the initial level of income were lower, say $3,000 billion, then the change in income from the tax cut would also be lower. It would be derived in exactly the same way as the calculation just shown, except that 3,000 would appear instead of 4,000. The resulting increase in income would then be $309 billion.

SUMMARY

• The government purchases goods and services, which adds to aggregate demand. Government expenditures include transfers and are much larger than purchases. Transfer payments, including interest on the debt and Social Security, make up the majority of federal spending.

• Political pressures affect the spending decisions. Rationales for government spending include public goods, income support for the needy, and merit goods. The government raises tax revenues to finance its spending, but it often borrows to cover deficits.

• Net tax revenues, equal to gross tax revenues minus transfer payments, rise and fall with rising and falling income.

• Consumers make consumption and saving decisions based on disposable income (income minus net tax payments).

• Fiscal-policy changes include changes in the level of government purchases and changes in tax rates and transfers.

• With the government sector, equilibrium income is determined by equating aggregate demand ($C + I + G$) to output (Y). Taxes (T) affect consumption.

• Increases in government purchases boost aggregate demand and raise equilibrium income through the multiplier effect. Taxes that depend upon income reduce the autonomous-expenditure multiplier because of the leakages of income into tax revenues. The reduction in the multiplier results in a steeper *IS* schedule. Tax cuts raise aggregate demand.

• Increasing government purchases with a given money supply raises the interest rate. The interest-rate effect cuts into the expansion of aggregate demand.

• The interest-rate effect following a fiscal expansion can crowd out domestic investment.

• The government does not have to match expenditures with tax revenues. The difference between tax revenues and government expenditures is the government budget balance. When expenditures exceed revenues, the balance is in deficit. When revenues exceed expenditures, the balance is in surplus.

• Deficits can help cure recession; however, chronic deficits reduce the resources available for capital formation. Businesses may reduce investment in an economy with large chronic deficits. Deficits affect the amount of national saving in the economy.

• The budget balance can be adjusted for cyclical changes in income. The deficit can be split into cyclical and structural components. In the 1980s, the U.S. federal government ran large structural deficits. These are continuing in the 1990s.

KEY TERMS AND CONCEPTS

automatic stabilizers, p. 134

budget balance, p. 130

crowding out, p. 128

cyclical deficit, p. 133

disposable income, p. 120

fiscal policy, p. 114

government expenditures or outlays, p. 115

government purchases of goods and services p. 115

gross tax revenue, p. 118

marginal propensity to tax, p. 119

national saving, p. 131

net tax revenue, p. 119

private saving, p. 131

public goods, p. 117

structural deficit, p. 133

tax leakages, p. 122

transfer payments, p. 119

DISCUSSION QUESTIONS AND PROBLEMS

1. What determines which goods and services are supplied by government and which are supplied by private markets?

2. If increasing government expenditures leads to higher levels of equilibrium income, are we always better off when government expenditures are increased?

3. The federal government budget combines expenditures and transfer payments into a total government outlay. Why do we separate government purchases and transfer payments in our analysis?

4. Explain how an increase in government purchases brings about a shift in the *IS* schedule. How does the size of the shift depend upon the multiplier effect? How does the resulting increase in GDP depend upon the interest-rate effect?

5. Why is the multiplier different in an economy with government than in an economy without government?

6. Review the algebraic expressions for the following multipliers:
   a. Government purchases.
   b. Lump-sum taxes.
   c. Tax rates.

7. What is crowding out?

8. How is the effectiveness of fiscal policy affected by money-market conditions?

9. How can the government spend more than it receives in tax revenues? Who supplies the missing funds?

10. Is running a deficit ever a reasonable policy tool?

11. What is wrong with long-run deficits? What happens to national saving?

12. If government purchases and taxes increase by the same amount, what is the effect on:
    a. The budget balance?
    b. The equilibrium level of income?
    c. The share of GDP in the public and private sectors?
    d. Private saving, national saving, and the fraction of GDP that is saved?

13. The algebraic model of the economy is solved for equilibrium income by substituting functions for the terms in

$$Y = C + I + G$$

Why are taxes not included in this equilibrium condition?

14. Distinguish between government expenditures and government purchases. What part of government expenditures is an addition to aggregate demand and what part is an addition to national income? Use the following list of federal government programs to calculate the value of expenditures and purchases:

	$ Billions
Defense	200
Veterans benefits	30
Farm subsidies	20
Transportation	30
Social Security	150
Net interest payments	120

15. Calculate the values of the following: equilibrium income, the autonomous-expenditure multiplier, and the *IS* schedule for an economy described by the following relationships:

$$C = 100 + 0.8Y_d$$
$$I = 300 + 0.2Y - 20r$$
$$T = 0.25Y$$
$$G = 1,000$$

The interest rate is set by the monetary authority at: $r = 10$ percent. Compare the results you find with those shown in Worked Example 5–1. Which changes in the numerical values given in the above relationships compared to the value in Worked Example 5–1 contributed to increasing or decreasing equilibrium income and why?

16. Use the following consumption, tax, and investment functions to derive an *IS* schedule:

$$C = C_0 + C_1Y_d$$
$$I = I_0 + I_1Y - I_2r$$
$$T = T_1Y$$

G is set by policy

How does the *IS* schedule that you have found compare with the *IS* schedule with no government sector?

17. Combine the *IS* schedule from question 16, with an *LM* schedule derived from the following money supply and demand equations:

$$\frac{M^d}{P} = kY - hr$$

$$\frac{M^s}{P} \text{ is set by policy}$$

Show how to derive algebraic expressions for the level of income and the interest rate for which there is both goods-market equilibrium and money-market equilibrium.

MONETARY POLICY AND INFLATION

INTRODUCTION

This chapter examines how monetary policy influences the level of aggregate demand in the economy and hence the level of income. We see that the Fed can change the money supply, raise or lower the interest rate, increase or decrease the lending capacity of banks, and hence stimulate or restrain the demand for interest-sensitive and loan-sensitive expenditures, mostly on such investment goods as houses and office buildings.

In response to a recession, monetary policy can be used in conjunction with expansionary fiscal policies to increase aggregate demand while avoiding, in the short term, the increase in interest rates and the crowding out that is normally associated with a fiscal expansion. And monetary policy can be used alone to stimulate the economy through lower interest rates and through an increase in the availability of credit and loans offered by the banking system and in financial markets.

But these potential benefits of monetary expansion ignore an important problem, namely the inflationary consequences of such policies. In practice the Fed doesn't simply stimulate aggregate demand; often it restrains or contracts aggregate demand, because it regards controlling inflation as being its number one priority. Instead of working to reduce the severity of recessions and to stimulate the growth of income, the Fed has at times tolerated and sometimes initiated recessions as an unintended consequence of its desire to fight inflation.

In this chapter, we introduce inflation and examine the sources of inflation. We argue there is a trade-off between output and inflation over the short run, so increases in aggregate demand will bring about increases in output and income, but they will also increase the rate of inflation. Inflation is an important constraint on the use of expansionary policies, indeed, we conclude that such policies cannot raise output over the long run, though they can accelerate inflation.

CHANGING THE MONEY SUPPLY: MONETARY POLICY

When we studied fiscal policy, we found that an expansionary fiscal policy did not lead to the full impact on income that would be predicted from an analysis of the multiplier effect alone. This happens because the increase in income raises the demand for money, which drives up the rate of interest, and the interest-rate effect then reduces aggregate demand. This was represented by an outward shift of the *IS* schedule, leading to a new equilibrium occurring at a higher interest rate along a given *LM* schedule.

coordinated policy
Using monetary policy in concert with fiscal policy to affect income.

Fiscal policy does not necessarily have to be restrained by a higher interest rate. When both monetary and fiscal policymakers decide that the level of income should be increased, they can use a **coordinated policy** of fiscal and monetary expansion. In such a case, the increase in income may reflect the full impact of the multiplier effect.

Coordinated Monetary and Fiscal Policies

A coordinated antirecession policy is illustrated in Figure 6–1. Prior to any policy actions, the economy is in equilibrium in a recession (point *R*), with the interest rate at r_O and the level of income below potential output (Y_R). The government uses expansionary fiscal-policy tools (lowers taxes and/or raises government expenditures) to boost goods-market demand. The *IS* schedule shifts to *IS'*. At the same time the Fed increases the money supply—the effect of this being shown by a shift of the *LM* schedule to *LM'*. The result is an increase in income (from Y_R to Y_A) with a stable rate of interest.

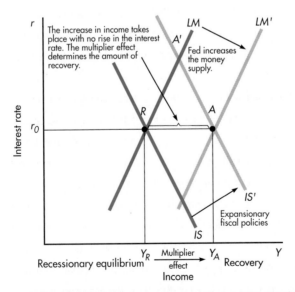

FIGURE 6–1
Using Monetary and Fiscal Policies to Cure a Recession

A coordinated change in both monetary and fiscal policies can change income while keeping the rate of interest stable. The increase in income could take place with no rise in the interest rate. The multiplier effect determines the amount of recovery.

Of course, coordinated policies also can be used to reduce demand. If the economy is in equilibrium at too high a level of income and is experiencing inflation that both the Fed and the fiscal authorities wish to curb, then a coordinated fiscal and monetary contraction will reduce the level of income while keeping the interest rate stable.

While there are great advantages to coordinated monetary and fiscal policies, in practice these policies are not always coordinated. In recent years, independent monetary policy has been a major force in the economy.

Independent
Monetary
Policy

Monetary and fiscal policies may not be coordinated because the Fed may decide that it disagrees with the fiscal-policy actions that are being made by the Congress and the administration. The Fed is often more concerned about inflation than is Congress, because the Fed sees itself as the protector of the value of the currency. Elected officials may be more concerned about high unemployment, especially those in Congress who face reelection every two years.

Since 1978, particularly, the Fed has asserted considerable independence of action, supported by the leadership of two strong chairmen: Paul Volcker, who held office from 1978 until 1987, followed by Alan Greenspan, the current chairman as of 1994. In 1979, Paul Volcker announced that the Fed was committed to a stable target for the money supply, regardless of changes in the interest rate. The reason for the change in policy was rapidly escalating inflation. Volcker was willing to see the economy go into the deep 1982 recession and to face strong criticisms from Congress.

In the 1990s, the problem of the budget deficit means that active fiscal policy is unlikely to be employed to any great extent to change the level of income, beyond the automatic stabilizers. In the absence of fiscal-policy direction, the Fed is left with the task of using monetary policy alone to influence the level of income and output.

We can see how an independent monetary policy works with the *IS–LM* framework as Figure 6–2 illustrates. The economy is depicted at an initial equilibrium (point *A*) with a level of income Y_A and an interest rate r_A. If the Fed then decides to increase the supply of money, this will initially result in an excess supply of money. As people then adjust their portfolios, the result is a fall in the rate of interest. The *LM* schedule shifts down or to the right, to *LM'*. The fall in the rate of interest stimulates investment, and over time the economy moves to point *B*, with a high level of income (Y_B) and a lower rate of interest (r_B).

The effect of a reduction in the supply of money is shown by the shift of the *LM* schedule from *LM* to *LM''*. There is an initial excess demand for money that leads to an increase in the rate of interest, and then a reduction in investment demand and a fall in income. The economy moves to point *C*, with income Y_C and interest rate r_C.

Even without a change in fiscal policy it is possible for monetary policy to affect the level of income and the interest rate. Independent monetary policy is an important instrument of control that can help the economy through sound policy actions or can hurt the economy through misguided actions.

Worked Example 6–1   In Worked Example 6–1 on page 171 we show how an increase in the money supply will reduce the rate of interest and increase the level of income. The example uses the *IS–LM* framework previously used in Chapter 5.

FIGURE 6-2
Changes in Income
and the Interest
Rate Resulting
from Independent
Monetary Policy

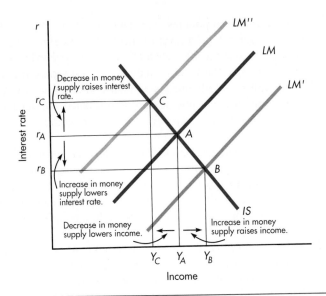

The Responsiveness of Investment to the Interest Rate and Credit Conditions

An expansion of the money supply stimulates aggregate demand by driving down the rate of interest and increasing the availability of credit. This encourages investment expenditures (an outward shift of the *LM* schedule and a slide down the *IS* schedule). The increase in investment then leads to higher income and output. This means that *the effectiveness of monetary policy depends on how much additional investment is induced by a given fall in the interest rate.* If the amount of induced investment demand is large, then monetary policy is an effective way of increasing income. If the amount of induced investment demand is small, then monetary policy is not an effective way of increasing income. With the slope of the *LM* schedule taken as given, *the effectiveness of monetary policy depends on the slope of the* IS *schedule.*

The case where investment expenditures do not respond by very much to a lowered interest rate is shown in the right-hand side (panel B) of Figure 6–3, where the *IS* schedule is steeply sloped. The shift in the *LM* schedule induces only a small increase in income. (The shift from Y_A to Y_B is small.)

The alternative case is illustrated in the left-hand portion (panel A) of Figure 6–3, where the *IS* schedule has a relatively flat slope. The expansion of the money supply is shown as a shift in the *LM* schedule, which raises income by more when investment is interest-rate–responsive *(Y_A to Y_B in panel A)* than when investment is not interest-rate–responsive *(Y_A to Y_B in panel B)*.

While some kinds of capital investment do not change much when the interest rate or credit conditions change (those kinds being the ones where the risks are high and the expectation of profits are more important than borrowing costs), there are others that are quite responsive (those long-term projects made by businesses in office buildings, shopping malls, and apartment buildings plus purchases of houses and cars by households).

FIGURE 6–3   The Effectiveness of Monetary Policy Depends on the Interest-Rate Effect in the Goods Market

A   A small drop in the interest rate generates a large increase in investment expenditures.

B   A large drop in the interest rate generates a small increase in investment expenditures.

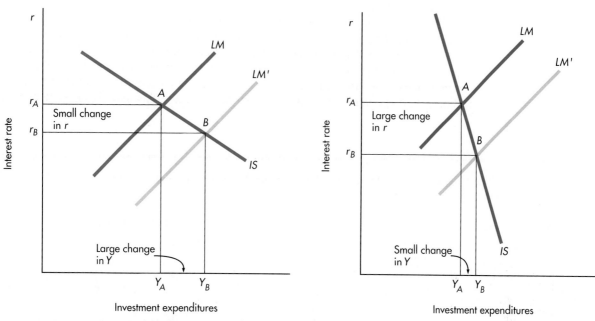

When the *IS* schedule is flat, monetary policy is an effective way of changing income. When the *IS* schedule is steep, monetary policy has a small effect on income.

The responsiveness of investment may also vary with general economic conditions. In an economic slump a reduction in the interest rate is not likely to stimulate much of an increase in expenditure on investment goods. Keynes argued that this was the case in the Great Depression[1] and that was a major reason why he claimed that monetary policy was ineffective during that period.

Monetary policy was used aggressively in the 1980s. The reaction of investment demand to monetary-policy changes was strong. This period, during which monetary policy was the sole instrument of economic policy, revealed the power of a restrictive monetary policy to slow income growth. By contrast, in 1991–92, the Fed followed a generally expansionary policy trying to stimulate growth, but the effects of the policy were weak and slow to act.

---

[1] J. R. Hicks, ''Mr. Keynes and the Classics: A Suggested Interpretation,'' *Econometrica* 5 (April 1937), pp. 147–59.

The
Interest-Rate
Responsiveness
of Money
Demand

In Chapter 5 *we found that the effectiveness of fiscal policy depends on the responsiveness of money demand*—the slope of the *LM* schedule. We will see now that the impact of a given monetary-policy change also depends on the responsiveness of money demand. The *LM* schedule gives points of money-market equilibrium and its slope depends on the response of money demand to changes in both income and the interest rate. Here we will focus primarily on the responsiveness of money demand to the interest rate.

When money demand is not very responsive to changes in the interest rate, the *LM* schedule is steeply sloped, as shown here in the right-hand panel of Figure 6–4. In this case, the response to a given increase in the money supply is a large fall in the rate of interest $(r_A$ to $r_B)$. The drop in interest rate stimulates investment and this then increases income. An increase in the supply of money leads first to an excess supply of money. As people try to reduce their money holdings, this increases the demand for

FIGURE 6-4   The Effectiveness of Monetary Policy Depends on the Interest Responsiveness of Money Demand (the slope of the *LM* schedule).

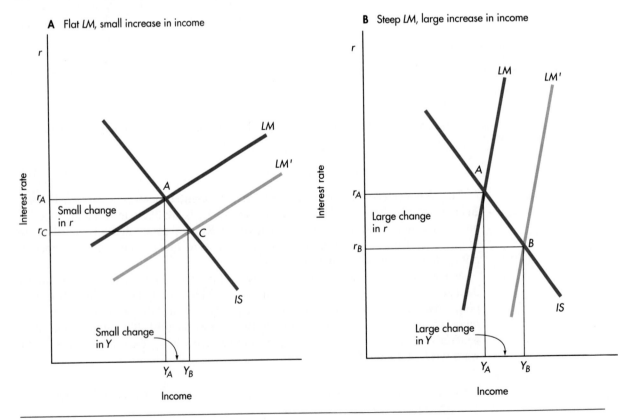

bonds or bills and drives down the rate of interest. Since, in this case, money demand is not very responsive to changes in the interest rate, it takes a large reduction in the interest rate to restore money-market equilibrium. Equilibrium income rises from Y_A to Y_B, moving along *IS* from point *A* to point *B*.

If a drop in the interest rate results in a large increase in the demand for money, then the *LM* schedule will be relatively flat. This case is shown in the left-hand panel of Figure 6–4, where the drop in the interest rate, from r_A to r_C, is a smaller reduction than in the former case. In this case, where the demand for money is quite responsive to changes in the rate of interest, the increase in the supply of money brings about a modest fall in the rate of interest. Hence, the stimulation to investment is also moddest. Income rises, but the gain in income from Y_A to Y_C is smaller than the gain from Y_A to Y_B.

We have found now that *the effectiveness of monetary policy in changing income also depends on the extent to which people change their demand for money when the interest rate changes.* To summarize the findings from this chapter and from Chapter 5:

- When people do not change their demand for money by much when the interest rate changes, then the *LM* schedule is relatively steep, and monetary policy is relatively effective and fiscal policy is relatively ineffective in changing income.
- When the demand for money responds strongly to interest rate changes, then the *LM* schedule is relatively flat and monetary policy is relatively ineffective and fiscal policy is relatively effective in changing income.

Worked Example 6–2   In Worked Example 6–2 on page 172 we show that monetary policy is more effective in changing income when money demand does not respond much to changes in the rate of interest—the *LM* schedule is steep.

The effectiveness of monetary policy is important; but perhaps more important to overall economic performance is the extent to which an expansionary policy will trigger an acceleration of inflation. In many situations, the economy languishes in recession even though some combination of monetary and fiscal policy would be quite capable of stimulating demand. But policymakers are unwilling to provide the stimulus when inflation is already too high, or when they are concerned about rekindled inflation.

THE TRADE-OFF BETWEEN OUTPUT AND INFLATION

Inflation is a rise in overall prices, an ongoing increase in the price level. In a dynamic economy, there are always changes in supply-and-demand conditions in individual markets that lead to increases in some prices and decreases in others and this does not necessarily result in any overall inflation. But when increases in prices outweigh reductions in prices and on average the economy experiences a rise in the overall price level, there is inflation.

Inflation is seen as a burden or a cost to the economy, especially when it surprises people. When you sell goods or services, when you offer your labor to an employer, or when you rent out capital assets to be used by others, you agree on an amount that you will be paid. An unexpected burst of inflation can lower the real value of wages received or other compensation, because the funds received for work done or for goods provided buy less when prices rise.

People appear to dislike inflation intensely even when there is no element of surprise. In part, this may stem from a misunderstanding. People often believe that increases in their wages or salaries are the result of their own efforts. They do not always realize that part of the increase they have received is attributable to general inflation. If wage increases are followed by increases in prices, wage earners may well see the inflation as undoing well-deserved gains, no matter that the inflation itself was a major reason for the higher wages. Even when there is no misunderstanding involved, however, there is still a cost of inflation—the added uncertainty in the economy that results from not knowing the real value of future revenues and returns.

The first place to look for a cause of inflation is aggregate demand. Higher demand in most of the markets in the economy brings about more output, but only at higher prices. Higher output raises production costs; higher demand means that producers can raise the prices that they charge while still being able to sell their output.

As well as increases in aggregate demand, other factors contribute to inflation. Inflation can be caused by inflation itself. Once inflation has been started, by demand or supply changes, it may generate its own momentum. The expectation of inflation may itself become a cause of inflation.

In addition, shocks to aggregate supply can cause inflation. An *inflationary supply shock* is a sudden and significant increase in the price level at which a given level of output is produced. The shock can be permanent, such as the long-run and possibly fundamental decline in productivity growth that started in the late 1960s. Or a shock can be temporary, such as the sudden OPEC–oil-price increases of the 1970s, increases that were largely reversed in the 1980s. A supply shock will generate a boost to inflation. The surge in inflation can then generate enough momentum to cause continuing inflation.

In this chapter, we concentrate on the aggregate demand side, together with the formation of inflationary expectations. We look at the implications for monetary policy of demand-induced inflation. In Chapter 12 we see how supply shocks can affect inflation and its implications for economic policy.

Shifts in Aggregate Supply and Demand and the Price Level

Looking at the simple model of aggregate supply and demand, we see how an increase in aggregate demand can raise the price level. In Figure 6–5, the rise in the price level is caused by the outward shift of aggregate demand along the rising portion of the aggregate supply schedule. In the figure, aggregate demand is increased twice, as shown by two successive shifts in the aggregate demand schedule. The first shift is from $AD(A)$ to $AD(P)$, and the second shift is from $AD(P)$ to $AD(B)$. The price level also rises in two steps along the aggregate supply (AS) schedule—first from P_A to P^P, followed by the increase from P^P to P_B.

The successive increases in aggregate demand (point A to point P followed by point P to point B) bring about increasingly larger increases in price, particularly as the level of income exceeds potential output (Y^P). The price level increases by more as income exceeds potential output because businesses are near full capacity. Increases in

FIGURE 6-5
**Aggregate Supply
and Demand and
the Price Level**

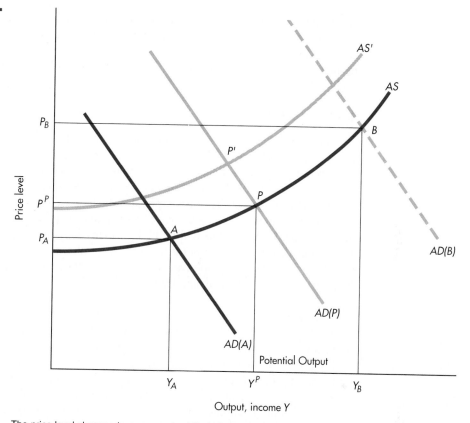

The price level changes in response to shifts in both supply and demand.

production raise costs by more when firms are operating near full capacity than when there is excess productive capacity.

The figure also illustrates how a rise in the price level can be caused by a shift in aggregate supply or a supply shock. The worsening of aggregate supply conditions *(AS* to *AS')* raises the price level with no change in aggregate demand conditions (point *P* to point *P'*).

The aggregate supply and demand model shown in Figure 6–5 provides a framework for illustrating the separate determinants of inflation. It suggests an important difference between inflation driven by increases in demand and inflation driven by shifts in supply. In the case of aggregate supply shifts, output falls as prices rise. In the case of aggregate demand shifts, there is an increase in output as prices rise. And this latter case suggests, in turn, the existence of an important trade-off. Increases in aggregate demand will induce higher levels of output, but at the cost of higher prices.

The simple model of Figure 6–5 is useful, but inflation is not about a one-time increase in the price level of the kind just described. Inflation refers to a continuing rise in prices over time and is measured by the rate of growth of prices. We want to understand why the rate of inflation increases or decreases and the consequences of these changes. That understanding comes from looking at the way in which higher demand leads to higher output and a higher rate of inflation—the output—inflation trade-off.

THE OUTPUT–INFLATION TRADE-OFF

output–inflation trade-off
The change in the rate of inflation associated with a change in the output ratio.

To understand the **output–inflation trade-off,** we start with the observation that the price level reflects the average of thousands of individual prices. In individual markets there is not always equilibrium between supply and demand; instead, *prices adjust at a rate that depends on the discrepancy between demand and supply.* In any given market there is a prevailing market price; if demand exceeds supply at this price, then the price will increase. If supply exceeds demand, then price falls. At a high level of aggregate demand, demand will be high in many individual markets. This will bring forth a high level of output; but it will also mean that there are also more markets for which demand exceeds supply, and hence there will be more prices that are increasing than prices that are decreasing. There will be inflation.

The Trade-Off with Competitive Markets

The economy has many different markets and the balances between supply and demand can be rather different from one to another. The goods and services produced in each industry or market require different kinds of labor that in turn are supplied in multiple labor markets.[2] Their technologies are different and the factories or offices that make up their capital inputs are distinct. This means there can be an excess of supply relative to demand in one market and, simultaneously, an excess of demand relative to supply in another. In Figure 6–6 we consider supply and demand conditions in two competitive markets in the economy. One of the markets is in excess supply and the other is in excess demand.

The two markets shown in the figure can reflect demand and supply conditions in different industries or geographic regions. Items produced in one market are not perfect substitutes for those produced in another market. Even though the firms and workers who are in the unfortunate position of being in excess supply are ready and willing to work more and produce more, these workers and factories cannot easily or quickly change production technologies and distribution systems so as to produce and sell the different products that are in excess demand. This division among markets is shown in the figure where the market shown in the right-hand panel indicates an excess demand for its products. Demand exceeds the supply at the going price (the distance AA') and there is a shortage of capacity and job vacancies. Output is equal to Q_A, constrained by the willingness of producers to sell at the going price. The market in the left-hand panel shows the opposite situation. There is an excess supply (the distance BB'); that is to say there is slack capacity and unemployed workers in this

---

2   Richard G. Lipsey, ''The Relation between Unemployment and the Rate of Change of Money Wage Rates in the United Kingdom, 1862–1957: A Further Study,'' *Economica* 28 (February 1960).

FIGURE 6-6   **Supply and Demand in Two Competitive Markets**

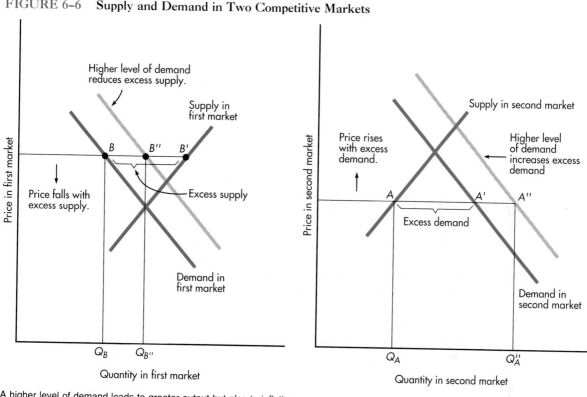

A higher level of demand leads to greater output but also to inflation.

region or industry. Output is at Q_B, constrained by the willingness of consumers to buy at the going price.

The prices will adjust in these markets. The price of the product and the workers' wages will be increasing in the market with excess demand and decreasing in the market with excess supply. When there is excess demand, prices and wages will increase as firms in these regions or industries bid against each other for the available pool of workers, and markups are increased. When there is excess supply, prices and wages will fall as workers compete for jobs and companies compete for customers. There will be no general inflation, however, as long as excess supply and excess demand balance out each other. Price increases in one market will offset decreases in the other. The economy is then in aggregate equilibrium. And individual prices are adjusting to equate supply and demand in both markets.

Consider now the case of a higher level of aggregate demand, so the demand schedules in both of the markets are above or to the right of the original demand schedules (shown as the shifted demand schedules in both panels). In the market that had an excess supply (the left-hand panel) output will be higher as firms can sell more (at Q_B''). In addition, the extent of the excess supply will be reduced. (It is now BB'', rather than BB'.) In the market that has excess demand, there is no change in supply; rather, the excess demand will be greater in the market (the distance AA'').

Comparing the case with a higher level of demand to the previous case, we find that the higher level of demand has resulted in a higher level of output through its impact on the market that was suffering from excess supply. But, as well as the impact of higher demand on output, there will also be an impact on prices. We assume that the price in the market with excess demand will rise faster following the increase in demand. The rate of price increase depends on the size of the gap between supply and demand; it depends on the amount of excess demand in the market. In similar fashion, we assume that the price in the market with excess supply will fall more slowly following the increase in demand. The extent of the excess supply has been reduced, and hence the rate of price decline is smaller.

Taking both markets together, therefore, we find that the increase in aggregate demand has changed the balance between price increases and decreases. *Price is rising faster in the excess demand market and falling more slowly in the excess supply market, so the average price (the price level) is now increasing; there is inflation.* The increase in demand has therefore shown us the trade-off between output and inflation. The higher level of aggregate demand has led to more output at the cost of inflation.

We have just considered the case of a higher level of aggregate demand, but we could just as easily have considered the case where aggregate demand was lower. A low level of aggregate demand will induce a low level of output as firms in the market with excess supply are able to sell less. And there will be deflation, as prices rise less rapidly in the market with excess demand and prices fall more rapidly in the market with excess supply.

This model of two markets can be extended to a model economy with many competitive markets. If this is done, the analysis (called "general equilibrium analysis") becomes extremely complex and it is hard to be sure exactly how individual prices or the overall price level will behave. But the intuitive lesson from such a model with many markets is that *there is an equilibrium level of aggregate demand and output for which there is no inflation (the price level is stable). Higher levels of aggregate demand will lead to higher levels of output combined with inflation. Lower levels of aggregate demand will lead to lower levels of output combined with negative rates of inflation (deflation).*

The equilibrium level of output where there is price stability is important. This level of output corresponds to what we have been calling "potential output." When output is equal to potential output, there is no inflationary pressure coming from excess demand in the economy as a whole. Once we take account of expected inflation, we will see that in the actual economy there can be (and usually is) inflation even when output is equal to or below potential output. But the idea of potential output as the point where the forces of excess supply in some markets balance out the forces of excess demand in others, remains an important one. When output is below potential output, there is net excess supply, and inflation will be decreasing. When output is above potential output, there is net excess demand, and inflation is increasing.

For any given level of output relative to potential output, the rate of inflation or deflation reflects the speed at which the markets in the economy adjust in response to the gaps between supply and demand. This speed of adjustment is something that economists do not agree on. One school of thought (the equilibrium–business-cycle theory discussed in Chapter 15) argues that the adjustment occurs very quickly indeed, so excess supply and demand are eliminated almost immediately. In that view, an increase in aggregate demand that results from an increase in the nominal supply of money will lead to a rapid proportional rise in the price level. The equilibrium level of output will be restored quickly, and any trade-off between output and inflation is only an extremely short-lived phenomenon.

However, if markets adjust slowly, as we believe they do, the situation is different. An increase in aggregate demand will induce a slow but persistent inflation and output will be above its equilibrium for some time. The mainstream view among economists is that the speed of adjustment is slow, so prices are sticky in response to changes in demand.

The Trade-Off with Sticky Prices

Few markets are perfectly competitive with completely flexible prices. Instead, many markets are dominated by companies that sell products that are unique; they have customers with loyalty to their brand; and they use extensive advertising to persuade existing and potential customers of the advantages of their products. Large companies, and many small companies as well, set the prices they will charge for their products, rather than simply taking a market price as given. And in many cases companies have established contractual arrangements with their suppliers and their customers. In addition, many companies maintain some slack capacity and they are almost always glad to sell more when demand increases.[3]

A firm that sets its price will try to anticipate what the response of its competitors will be and how its customers will then respond to what all the competing firms in the market have done. The two branches of economics that deal with the problem of how prices and wages are set are called *game theory* (named because choosing a pricing strategy is a bit like choosing a strategy in poker or chess) and *contract theory*. Unfortunately, these theories have shown us a lot about the complexity of the problem and not enough about the likely solutions. There are, however, some ways in which the lessons from the model of competitive markets should be modified once we take into account the way prices adjust in practice.

First, in the competitive market model pictured in Figure 6–6, an increase in demand will not lead to any increase in output in markets where there is already excess demand. In the actual economy, increases in demand will increase output in most markets. Second, many wages and prices are set either by formal contracts or by implicit understandings between buyers and sellers. Wage contracts are particularly important. These contracts—explicit or implicit—make prices and wages slow to

---

[3] Robert E. Hall, "The Relation between Price and Marginal Cost in U.S. Industry," working paper no. 1786 (Cambridge, Mass.: National Bureau of Economic Research, January 1986).

adjust to demand changes. And third, prices and wages are often stickier downward than upward. If firms cannot hire enough workers, they will increase wages, but they may not cut wages when there are layoffs.[4]

Relative to what might be expected from the model of competitive market adjustment, therefore, the output–inflation trade-off in the actual economy will be flatter, with inflation responding only a little to demand changes. And it will be flatter at low levels of output than at high levels. And since markets where there is excess supply will show little decline in prices due to **price stickiness,** while markets with excess demand will show increases in prices, it follows that there will have to be more markets with excess supply than there are markets with excess demand at the level of aggregate output where there is no inflationary pressure. This last point is important because it affects the way we think about potential output.

price stickiness

A characteristic of the economy wherein prices do not immediately and completely adjust to changes in supply or demand, or both.

Potential Output and the NAIRU

Potential output is a benchmark for the economy. It is the level of output that does not strain the available supply of labor or the productive capacity of the economy and hence does not lead to inflationary pressure. But to restrain inflationary pressures in the economy, it is necessary to maintain excess supply in many markets. When output equals potential output, there are many underutilized factories and many workers without jobs.

An economy that is producing at potential output generates a particular level of unemployment that we called the NAIRU, reflecting the fact that when the unemployment rate is equal to this level, there is no demand pressure to accelerate inflation. Potential output and the NAIRU are defined together, representing equivalent benchmarks for the economy. In the U.S. economy in the 1980s and the early 1990s, the NAIRU has been in the 5.5–6.5 percent range; and for much of that period actual output has been in fact equal or near potential. When the unemployment rate is equal to the NAIRU, the economy is said to be at *full employment,* but keep in mind that in 1990, when there was a 6 percent unemployment rate, there were 7–8 million people looking for work. It is unfortunate that our economy cannot reduce unemployment further without creating inflationary pressure. There is hope that the NAIRU will fall in the 1990s as we see a decline in the fraction of the work force that is made up of high-unemployment groups, such as teenagers.

We now summarize what we have found. The simple model of supply-and-demand adjustment suggests that the rate of inflation depends on the extent to which there is more excess demand than excess supply. This leads to the idea of a trade-off in which fluctuations in demand lead to changes in output relative to potential output and changes in the rate of inflation. This same idea can also be applied to the analysis of markets that do not have perfect flexible prices; but stickiness suggests a relatively flat trade-off, especially at low levels of output. In addition, when prices are sticky, the concept of potential output changes. When the economy is at potential output, this does not really mean that the economy is operating as efficiently as possible. Achieving a level of output above potential output leads to more jobs and more profits. The cost is higher inflation.

---

[4] Price and wage stickiness and the role of contract theory and implicit contracts are discussed in Chapter 15.

The Short-Run Output–Inflation Trade-Off

The **short-run output–inflation trade-off** for the aggregate economy relates the output ratio to the current rate of inflation. The short-run trade-off is shown in Equation 6–1:

$$\text{Current } \Delta P/P = H(Y/Y^P) \qquad\qquad (6\text{--}1)$$

The **output ratio** (Y/Y^P) was introduced in Chapter 1; it is the ratio of current output to potential output:

$$\text{Output ratio} = Y/Y^P = \text{Current GDP/Potential GDP}$$

It is usually expressed as a percentage. When current output is 5 percent higher than potential output, the output ratio is equal to 105 percent. When current output is 5 percent lower than potential output, the output ratio equals 95 percent.

In Equation 6–1, the letter H indicates a functional relation, where higher values of the output ratio cause higher values of inflation. This captures the idea that, when output is high relative to potential, there are many markets with excess demand, and prices are rising on average. Current inflation increases when the output ratio increases. The output–inflation trade-off given in Equation 6–1 is shown in Figure 6–7. The horizontal axis in the figure shows the output ratio, expressed as a percentage. The vertical axis shows the rate of price inflation. The figure shows a zero rate of

short-run output–inflation trade-off

The change in the rate of inflation associated with a change in the output ratio that takes place in the short run, before expectations of inflation are revised.

output ratio

The ratio of actual output to potential output.

FIGURE 6–7

The Short-Run Output–Inflation Trade-Off

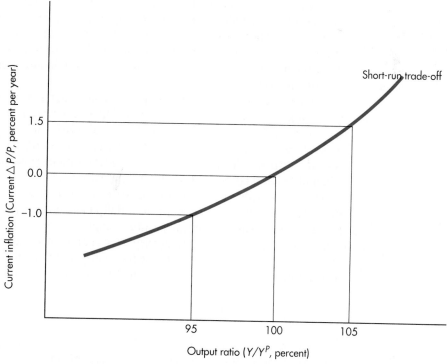

The trade-off is drawn assuming zero expected inflation.

inflation when the output ratio is 100 percent and positive and negative rates when the ratio is above or below this level. (This situation would only occur in practice if there were a zero expected rate of inflation.)

Since inflation rises with output, the output–inflation trade-off slopes up to right. The trade-off is also shown to be curved, getting steeper at higher levels of the output ratio. We discussed earlier how this property of the trade-off comes from the fact that excess supply may not reduce prices by much.

Shifts of the Output– Inflation Trade-Off

The concept of the output–inflation trade-off was introduced into U.S. policymaking discussion in the early 1960s.[5] Indeed, the behavior of the U.S. economy during much of the 1960s strongly supported the existence of the trade-off. As the output ratio increased, inflation gradually increased and there was almost a consensus among economists that policymakers could choose the combination of the output ratio and the level of inflation that was the best compromise and that they could use policy tools to reach that goal.

The consensus of support for the idea of a stable trade-off was short-lived however. Unfortunately for the well-being of the U.S. economy, the trade-off started to move around a good deal. During the 1970s, there was both more inflation and more unemployment than had been the case earlier. A new description of economic discomfort entered the national vocabulary—the *misery index* (the sum of the unemployment and inflation rates), with the index rising to new heights in the 1970s. The experience of rising inflation and falling income that occurred in the 1970s was called **stagflation,** the combination of stagnating or falling income and high inflation.

stagflation

A worsening of the output–inflation trade-off where the rate of inflation rises while there is a constant or reduced level of output.

The 1970s confirmed for many economists an idea that had been forming in the late 1960s—that the simple stable trade-off, as in Equation 6–1, was an incomplete description of the determination of inflation. The trade-off relation was shifting and the reasons had to be determined.

For a particular short-run trade-off a movement along the curve indicates that rising inflation is associated with rising output. The U.S. economy experienced such movements along the trade-off between 1963 and 1967. However, when the economy experiences increases of inflation with flat income, as occurred from 1967 to 1969, *then the trade-off is shifting up.* This was even more apparent from 1969 to 1970, when inflation increased with a falling output ratio.

The trade-off that we gave in Equation 6–1 was in fact a short-run trade-off. Over time, the trade-off itself may shift, so inflation and output worsen together. There are two main explanations for such shifts: supply shocks and changes in inflationary expectations. Changes in inflationary expectations can explain the shifts, because businesses set their prices based on what managers think other prices are going to be in the future. This means that, when there is an expectation of a higher rate of

---

[5] Paul A. Samuelson and Robert M. Solow, "Analytical Aspects of Anti-Inflation Policy," *American Economic Review* 50 (May 1960), pp. 177–94. In Chapter 16 we discuss the origin of the trade-off in the work of A. W. Phillips. The trade-off is often called "the Phillips curve."

inflation, current inflation can accelerate even though the growth of input is slowing down or even when output is falling. In this chapter we look to inflationary expectations as an explanation of the shifts of the trade-off.

INFLATION, OUTPUT, AND EXPECTATIONS

The current rate of inflation depends on what people think the rate of inflation will be as well as on the current level of income or output in the economy. If the expected rate of inflation rises, the current rate of inflation will rise even if income is equal to 100 percent of potential. In fact, if inflationary expectations are rising rapidly, inflation may increase even when income is below potential. This is what is meant by saying that changes in expectations lead to shifts in the short-run trade-off.

For example, when labor unions bargain for wages increases, the size of the increases they demand depends on how much inflation they expect over the course of the wage contract. The larger the expected rate of inflation, the greater the increase in revenues that will be expected by businesses, and so they will be willing to grant larger wage increases to union and nonunion workers alike. *As the expectation of inflation is built into actual wage contracts, this in turn raises costs and contributes to next year's actual inflation rate.* In addition, suppliers of materials have expectations about the amount of inflation that will occur over the duration of a contract to deliver goods over the coming year. The larger is the rate of inflation they expect, the higher is the price that they seek for deliveries. The rise in materials prices is then incorporated into the actual inflation in finished-goods prices.

The simple output–inflation trade-off shifts up or down depending on whether expected inflation increases or decreases. An increase in inflationary expectations can raise the current rate of inflation even though there is no change in the output ratio. This formulation is shown in Equation 6–2:

$$\text{Current}\Delta P/P = H(Y/Y^P) + \text{Exp}\Delta P/P \tag{6-2}$$

The current rate of inflation ($\text{Current}\Delta P/P$) is determined by the output ratio (Y/Y^P) and the expected rate of inflation ($\text{Exp}\Delta P/P$). As shown in Figure 6–8, increases in the expected rate of inflation lead to higher current rates of inflation for any given value of the output ratio. For example, at an output ratio of $(Y/Y^P)_A$ the rate of inflation will rise from the level at A to the level at A' and then to the level at A'', with successive increases in the expected rate of inflation. Similarly, if the output ratio is $(Y/Y^P)_B$, then inflation will be B, B', or B'', depending on expected inflation. The short-run trade-off shifts up (first from SR–TO:1 to SR–TO:2 and then from SR–TO:2 to SR–TO:3) with each increase in the expected rate of inflation.

The trade-off between current output and current inflation is still a valid concept for the short run. If the expected rate of inflation can be taken as given in the short run, then the current rate of inflation depends on the current output ratio; hence the short-run trade-off. But when people expect inflation to occur, there is no longer any guarantee that current inflation will be zero when the output ratio is 100 percent. U.S. inflation was in the range of 4 to 5 percent in early 1990 when output was equal to potential output.

FIGURE 6-8
Expected Inflation
and the Trade-Off

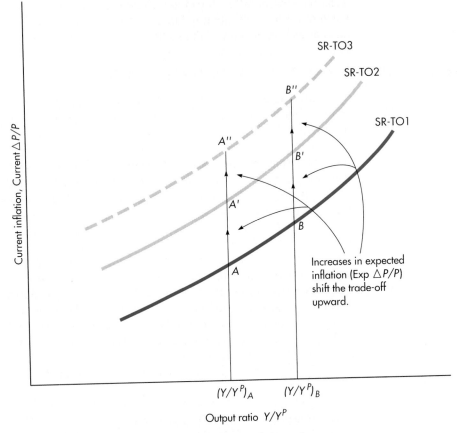

If expected inflation increases, the short-run trade-off shifts upward.

Worked Example 6–3   In Worked Example 6–3 on page 173, we use a numerical example to illustrate how current inflation depends on the output ratio and the expected rate of inflation.

The short-run trade-off still exists, but it may provide a treacherous guide to policy over the longer run. If increases in inflation in the short run result in increases in expected inflation in the longer run, the rate of inflation may increase in future periods even if output drops back. The key question, therefore, is: What determines expected inflation?

**Expectations
Formed by the
Past History of
Inflation**

If changes in inflationary expectations are an important reason why the U.S. economy suffered from stagflation, we need to know how expectations are formed and what causes them to change. Economists point to two primary determinants of inflationary expectations. The first is that expected inflation depends on past inflation. People have

adaptive expectations
Where the expected rate
of inflation is revised
over time as a result of
the experience of actual
inflation.

adaptive expectations, where they revise their view of future inflation as a result of
experience. The second is that expectations of inflation depend on a rational and
future-oriented view of supply-and-demand conditions in the economy. In practice,
both factors are important, but in our judgment the actual experience of past inflation
is the more important.

If inflation was high in the past, the expected rate of inflation will also be high.
People expect an established inflation to continue. Most economists who argue for this
view of the way expectations are determined believe that it is inflation experienced in
the economy over an extended period that is important. Increases or decreases in
inflation that are temporary have a small effect on the expected rate. For example, if
the rate of inflation has been running at about 6 percent a year for some time and then
it drops to 4 percent, the expected rate of inflation stays fairly close to 6 percent. If the
current rate of inflation then stays down at 4 percent for several more periods, the
expected rate gradually comes down, also.

An important variation on this idea is that past inflation gets into expectations and
hence into current inflation through a catch-up process. For example, if after a labor
contract is negotiated inflation turns out to be higher than was expected, then workers
will ask for larger wage increases to make up for the unexpected loss of buying power.

Past Inflation and Shifts in the Trade-Off

If inflationary expectations are formed from the prior history of the inflation rate, or if
workers and firms try to catch up with past inflation, then the expected rate of inflation
becomes a *built-in rate of inflation.* This means a certain rate of inflation gets built
into the economy and can only be removed by sustained changes in output. A built-in
rate of inflation alters the implications of the output–inflation trade-off.

When we first developed the idea of a trade-off, the analysis suggested that
inflation would cease as soon as output was below potential output. Once we take
account of expected inflation, this is no longer the case. Inflation will be reduced by
lowering output, but in the short run a level of output that is below potential output is
not sufficient to overcome the effects of high expected inflation. For example, if
inflation had been averaging 10 percent per year for 10 years, businesses and workers
would use 10 percent as a benchmark rate of increase for contracts for the next year's
products. Actual inflation in the 11th year would be somewhat higher or lower than
10 percent, depending upon whether output was above or below potential output.

According to this view of inflation, the problem of stagflation appears when output
is held above potential output for some time, the resulting acceleration of current
inflation is then gradually incorporated into increases in expected inflation. Then
higher expected inflation continues to drive up current rates of inflation, even after
output growth stalls.

The Vertical Long-Run Trade-Off

As long as output remains above potential output (as long as Y/Y^P is greater than 100
percent), there will be inflationary pressure in the economy and the acceleration of
inflation will continue. This argument has important implications. It means that there

vertical long-run trade-off
There is no trade-off between output and inflation in the long run.

is a **vertical long-run trade-off**; that is to say, *there is no trade-off between output and inflation in the very long run.* There is still a short-run trade-off in this case; but if output remains above potential output, the rate of inflation keeps on rising, as shown in Figure 6–9. In the figure, the combinations of output and inflation that are sustainable in the long run lie on the same vertical line. In this case *only one level of output is consistent with a stable rate of inflation: where output is equal to potential output.* Any sustained increase in aggregate demand that raises output above potential output will generate increases in inflation that are modest in the short run but keep on growing over time. This is shown in the figure by the movement from point *A* to *B* along a short-run trade-off (SR–TO:1). A sustained increase in aggregate demand will result in continuing acceleration of inflation, with ever-increasing inflation in the very long run (points *B'* and *C*). *Potential output is the highest level of output that can be reached without generating rising inflation in the very long run.*

FIGURE 6–9
The Vertical Long-Run Trade-Off

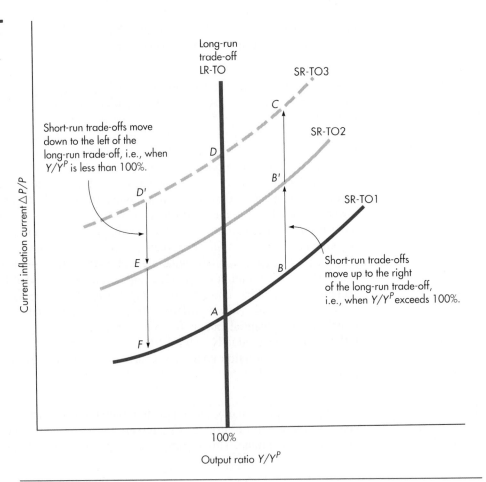

The process works in reverse for levels of output below potential output. If the economy starts at point *D,* and there is then a recession that reduces the output ratio, this will initially reduce inflation by only a small amount (point *D* to point *D'*). But at *D',* the current rate of inflation is below the expected rate of inflation and so the expected rate starts to decline. The short-run trade-off starts to shift down. In the long run, with the same level of output, the economy moves from point *D'* to *E* to *F.*

Worked Example 6–4   In this example on page 175, the short-run, intermediate-run and long-run trade-offs are examined with a numerical example. Expected inflation is assumed to equal the average actual rate of inflation over the two prior years. This assumption means that the short-run trade-off shifts more rapidly than we think is the case for the actual U.S. economy; but the example captures the idea of an increase in output leading to accelerating inflation over the long run.

The intuitive logic behind the idea of a vertical long-run trade-off was put forward by Edmund Phelps and Milton Friedman in the late 1960s.[6] Consider two economies that are the same in every way, except that in one the rate of inflation is 10 percent a year and in the other it is 3 percent a year. The people in the high-inflation economy have all become thoroughly used to the 10 percent rate. Why would the high-inflation economy have higher output? Does that make sense? Phelps and Friedman say no. Workers will have the same inflation-adjusted wages in the two economies and will work as long and as hard in the 10 percent–inflation economy as they do in the 3 percent–inflation economy. Producers will add 10 percent per year to their prices and consumers—having earned 10 percent more per year in dollars—will be buying the same real value of goods and services as their counterparts in the 3 percent–inflation economy. The real factors determining supply and demand will be the same in the two economies and so the level of output will be the same.[7]

The idea that the rate of inflation will keep getting larger if output is held above some critical point is plausible to most economists. In this sense, the Phelps-Friedman hypothesis of a vertical long-run trade-off has won broad acceptance.[8] As we discuss policies toward inflation, we will assume there is a vertical trade-off in the long run—that is, no effective trade-off in the long run. However, this does not eliminate the need to look at the impact of aggregate-demand policies on inflation and output in the

---

[6] Edmund S. Phelps, "Phillips Curves, Expectations of Inflation and Optimal Unemployment over Time," *Economica* 34 (August 1967), pp. 254–81; Milton Friedman, "The Role of Monetary Policy," *American Economic Review* 58 (March 1968), pp. 1–17.

[7] There is a complication that we are ignoring. With a high rate of inflation, the real return to money is large and negative. To the extent that money is substitutable for real assets, this will reduce the real money stock in the high-inflation economy.

[8] Many economists remain skeptical of the implications of the vertical trade-off hypothesis when output is below potential output. If output were sustained at, say, 98 percent of potential, the hypothesis says that this should first cause inflation to decline. Then price decreases will commence; and finally prices will start declining faster and faster. The idea of accelerating deflation seems implausible. However, Milton Friedman does not accept the trade-off framework in the form it has been presented in this chapter. He believes that an economy has a strong tendency to return to the natural rate of unemployment. The thought experiment of holding output at 98 percent of full-employment output is not one he would find valid.

short and intermediate runs. Policy is seldom pursued based on the very long run, and conditions never remain unchanged between the time a policy action is initiated and the time its long-run consequence appears.

Expectations Formed by Rational Forecasts of Inflation

The alternative view of inflationary expectations argues that they are formed by people's forecasts of the behavior of the economy. Past inflation may be used as an important guide to the future course of inflation, so, in practice, expectations may look as if they are based only on past inflation. But if there is some valid reason why inflation is likely to increase in the future, then expected inflation will increase also and will be different from past inflation. For example, if the Fed is expected to increase the rate of growth of the money supply, then people may expect this to increase aggregate demand and raise prices in the future. This will increase the expected rate of inflation, and this forecast of future inflation can increase current inflation even before there is any change in current income.

In this view, stagflation can come about as follows: When the Fed attempts to fight inflation by reducing the growth rate of the money supply, people do not believe that the Fed will stick to its guns—they think that the monetary contraction will be quickly reversed. Stagflation occurs because people expect aggregate demand to continue to expand, and thus they expect the inflation rate to continue to climb even though current monetary policy is restrictive. Monetary policy previously had been expansionary for several years, so, when tighter monetary policy is introduced, people believe the Fed will quickly give up its anti-inflationary policy and reinflate the economy.

In principle this view makes sense, but the problem with applying the rational-forecast model to the trade-off is that in practice it has not been found that the direct response of wages and prices to policy changes has been very large. Prices and wages are set in markets that are rather different from financial markets. Typical unions, businesses, employees, or customers do not adjust their wages and prices all that much in response to what they think the Fed will do.

Given this, we will continue to assume here that the expected rate of inflation that affects the current rate of inflation in labor markets and goods markets is based on the past history of inflation.

INFLATION, MONETARY POLICY, AND AGGREGATE EQUILIBRIUM

The *IS–LM* framework is used to describe the role of aggregate demand in determining equilibrium. By combining aggregate demand (from *IS–LM*) with aggregate supply (represented by the output–inflation trade-off), we now have a model of the macroeconomy where inflation is determined along with output and income. Inflation is determined within the economy along with other economic factors. Shortly we will see how to combine the *IS–LM* and trade-off frameworks. But first we must recognize that policy actions that change economic conditions also change the rate of inflation, and are themselves affected by inflation. If the money supply expands by 5 percent per year, is that a real increase of the money supply? The question appears to have an obvious answer, but what if the rate of inflation were 10 percent per year?

Inflation and the Real Supply of Money

Inflation erodes the size of the real stock of money for a given nominal money stock. Figure 6–10 shows the money market, where the demand for real money balances *(Md/P)* is initially equal to the real supply of money *(Ms/P)* at point A. Since inflation raises the price level *(P to P' to P" to P''')*, the real money supply declines, as shown in a series of shifts to the left of the schedule *(Ms/P', Ms/P", Ms/P''')*.

The demand for real money balances does not change as the price level changes, because the transactions demand for nominal money rises at the same rate as the increases in the price level (holding real income and the nominal rate of interest constant). Remember, a cash manager facing a 10 percent rise in prices will demand a 10 percent higher average cash balance to cover her firm's monthly purchases.

So if higher prices erode the real money supply and the demand for real money balances remains constant, then money-market equilibrium occurs at higher and higher short-term nominal rates of interest (points *B, C,* and *D). With a fixed nominal supply of money, an increase in the price level contracts the real money supply and shifts the* LM *schedule.* Figure 6–11 shows the shifts of the *LM* schedule *(LM', LM", and LM''')* that accompany inflation when the nominal money supply is unchanged.

Current and Expected Rates of Inflation

Earlier, when we looked at the way in which interest rates are adjusted for inflation, the inflation adjustment was for the *expected* future rate of inflation. Here, when we look at the role of inflation in changing the price level and the size of the real supply of money, we are looking at the *current* rate of inflation, and the two are not necessarily the same. When the rate of inflation has been constant for a long time, the current rate and the expected future rate of inflation are probably about the same. However, when

FIGURE 6–10
Inflation and the Real Money Supply

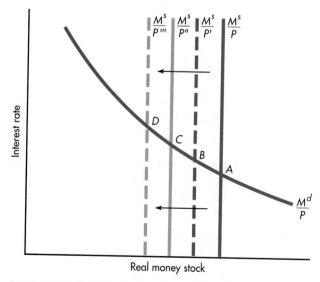

As the price level rises, a fixed nominal supply of money will lead to a declining real stock of money balances.

FIGURE 6–11
Inflation and the
***LM* Schedule with**
a Fixed Nominal
Money Supply

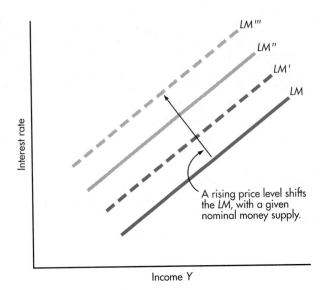

As the price level rises and the real stock of money declines, the *LM* schedule shifts up or to the left.

the current rate changes from year to year, then people will not usually expect that the future rate of inflation is going to be the same as the actual rate of inflation this year.

It is important, therefore, to keep the distinction clear between the expected future rate of inflation, Exp$\Delta P/P$, and the current or actual rate of inflation, Current$\Delta P/P$. The current rate of inflation is the rate at which the price level is actually changing over time. The expected future rate of inflation at any point in time is what people think inflation will be in the future.

Benchmarking
Monetary
Policy in an
Inflationary
Economy

When the Fed uses open-market operations to change the money supply, it can decide to increase, decrease, or keep constant the real money supply, even when there is inflation occurring in the economy. The Fed can choose to take an anti-inflationary position by maintaining a rate of increase in the nominal money supply that is less than inflation. It can even hold the nominal money supply constant or reduce it. In all of these cases the real money supply will fall. Alternatively, the Fed can offset the effect of inflation on the real money supply by increasing the nominal supply of money in proportion to the rise in the price level. This policy would maintain a fixed real supply of money. The Fed can even increase bank reserves and thus the nominal money supply faster than inflation and thus increase the real money supply. These alternatives are as follows:

A **contractionary monetary policy** occurs when $\Delta M^s/M^s <$ Current$\Delta P/P$. (The real money supply is falling.)

An **inflation-accommodating monetary policy** occurs when $\Delta M^s/M^s =$ Current$\Delta P/P$. (The real money supply is constant.)

An **expansionary monetary policy** occurs when $\Delta M^s/M^s >$ Current$\Delta P/P$. (The real money supply is increasing.)

Allowing for the Growth of Real Income

In the actual economy, potential output grows over time with increases in the labor force and the stock of capital and with gradual improvements in technology. And we have not taken this increase in potential output and income into account when we defined the monetary-policy alternatives. We certainly could incorporate the economy's growth trend into the discussion. The reason we have not done this is that there are already several different variables changing and lots of issues to deal with when we talk about policy, so adding complications is costly. The model becomes harder to understand.

When we apply the conclusions of our policy analysis to actual experience, however, it is helpful to keep in mind that potential output is growing. The Fed on average will aim for a rising real stock of money to meet the economy's increased need for transactions as the economy grows.

The *LM* schedule gives points of money-market equilibrium, and this means that if the Fed is following an inflation-accommodating policy, and there are no shifts in the money demand schedule, then the *LM* schedule will remain stationary. That makes the inflation-accommodating policy a useful benchmark. It means that the *LM* schedule will not be shifting because policy change has offset the effect of a rising price level.

If the Fed is choosing to increase the nominal supply of money more slowly than the actual rate of inflation, then this contractionary monetary policy will cause the *LM* schedule to shift upward and to the left. Alternatively, an expansionary policy will shift the *LM* schedule down to the right.

At different times the Fed has chosen each of the alternative policy options just described. For example, the Fed followed an expansionary policy in 1982–84 to combat the effects of the 1982 recession. A contractionary policy was pursued again in 1988–89 in order to restrain aggregate demand. Inflation had begun to accelerate in 1988–89, following a low level of inflation in 1987.

We are not saying which of the policy alternatives is more likely or more desirable. At this point, we are simply setting up the framework for policy analysis so that we can evaluate the appropriate policy actions. We summarize what we have found as follows:

A contractionary monetary policy reduces the real money supply and causes the *LM* schedule to shift up to the left.

An inflation-accommodating policy keeps the real money supply constant and causes the *LM* schedule to remain stationary.

An expansionary monetary policy increases the real money supply and causes the *LM* schedule to shift down to the right.

The Trade-Off and the *IS–LM* Framework Combined

When the *IS–LM* analysis of aggregate demand is combined with the trade-off analysis of aggregate supply, the resulting framework describes how aggregate supply and demand simultaneously determine the level of output, interest rates, and the current rate of inflation in the economy. The left-hand part of Figure 6–12 shows the

FIGURE 6-12   Output and Inflation Determined Together: Long-Run Equilibrium

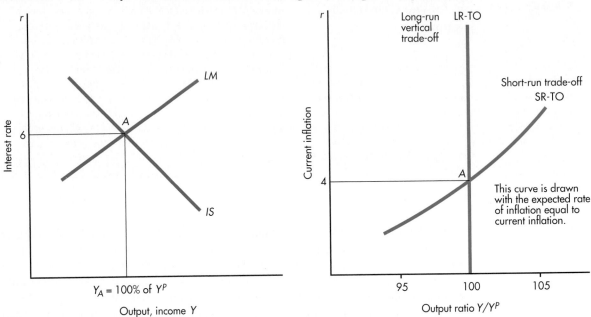

Bringing *IS–LM* and the inflation trade-off together shows how output, inflation, and interest rates are determined. The case shown is one of long-run equilibrium.

combinations of output and interest rate that are consistent with equilibrium. In this example, the economy is in *IS–LM* equilibrium (point *A*) at a point where income and output are equal to potential output. This means that the *IS–LM* equilibrium in this economy occurs where the output ratio is 100 percent. We use, as an example, a 6 percent rate of interest that corresponds to this level of income.

We have now described an economy in full aggregate supply and demand equilibrium. The *IS–LM* relations describe the demand equilibrium. The output–inflation trade-offs give aggregate supply equilibrium, with long-run equilibrium occurring where the trade-offs intersect.

In the equilibrium we have described, *there is only one level of output that lies on the long-run trade-off schedule.* Output must equal potential output if the economy is to be in long-run equilibrium. By contrast, we chose the rate of inflation arbitrarily. *Provided the Fed is willing to accommodate the current rate of inflation, whatever it is, full equilibrium can occur at many different rates of inflation.* This contrast between output and inflation in the long run seems to correspond to what we see in long-run historical data for the U.S. economy. We find that output does tend to fluctuate around potential output, but that inflation has been rather different in different time periods.

TABLE 6–1
Inflation, the Rate
of Change of the
Real Stock of
Money, and the
Output Ratio,
1979–1984

| Year | Current Inflation Percentage Per Year | | Rate of Change of Real Money Stock | | |
	CPI	GDP Deflator	M1/P	M2/P	Output ratio
1979	13.3	8.6	−1.7	−0.8	100.1
1980	12.5	9.5	−2.4	−0.5	97.2
1981	8.9	10	−2.9	0.0	96.8
1982	3.8	6.2	2.4	2.6	92.6
1983	3.8	4.1	5.6	7.6	94.0
1984	3.9	4.4	1.6	4.1	97.6

Of course, the fact that many rates of inflation have occurred does indicate that the Fed has been willing to accommodate these different rates of inflation. If the Fed had behaved differently, we could turn the model around and say that the only rate of inflation consistent with long-run equilibrium is where inflation equals the rate of nominal money-supply growth. But if the Fed had insisted on, say, zero inflation, then in our judgment, the economy would have spent long periods out of equilibrium with high unemployment.

The Trade-Off and Monetary Policy

When we first looked at monetary policy we made reference to a dilemma facing the Fed. If there is any trade-off between output and inflation, even if it is temporary, the Fed may have to choose between an expansionary monetary policy, which increases output and employment but leads to higher inflation, and contractionary policies, which reduce inflation at the expense of reductions in income and employment. This dilemma is posed even more starkly when there is no trade-off in the long run. Expansionary monetary policy that moves income above potential output not only generates a higher rate of inflation in the short run it also sparks a longer-run acceleration of inflation. In the short and intermediate runs, the Fed's choice is about the trade-off between income and inflation. In the very long run, the Fed's choice is only about the level of inflation in the economy and not about the level of output.

Fighting Inflation with Monetary Policy

Monetary policy is often employed to reduce a rate of inflation considered to be too high by the Fed. This was the case in the early 1980s when the Fed acted to undo the legacy of inflation of the late 1960s and the 1970s and stop the acceleration of inflation that was taking place in the early 1980s. Table 6–1 shows inflation, the output ratio, and the growth rate of the real stock of money for the U.S. economy for the years 1979–84. There are two measures of inflation shown: the rate of growth of the consumer price index (the CPI) and the GDP deflator. The CPI is an important indicator of how inflation is affecting consumers and it is used in wage contracts and to index various government programs. It shows the 1979–81 explosion of inflation. The CPI is rather volatile, reflecting the gyrations of food and energy prices over this period. Indeed, because of defects in the way it was computed at that time (defects since corrected), it exaggerated inflation over the period. The next column of Table 6–1 shows the growth rate of the GDP deflator as an alternative measure. It is less volatile, but it still reveals the seriousness of the inflation problem at the time.

According to the table, inflation fell to about 4 percent by 1984 and monetary contraction played a major role in this reduction in inflation. Since in the actual economy, potential output grows each year, the real money stock has to grow if it is to accommodate the increased demand for transactions. Over the years 1979–81, the real money stock fell, rather than rising. This put tremendous pressure on financial markets. The output ratio, shown in the last column in the table, fell from about 100 percent in 1979 to 92 in 1982. Notice two important facts, however. First, the fall in the real money supply came about because the Fed refused to accommodate the inflation, even though the nominal money stocks rose in every year. And second, there is a lag between the reduction of the money supply and the decline of the economy. The rates of increase or decrease in the money stocks are December-to-December values. That means, for example, that the real stock of $M1$ was 2.9 percent lower in December 1981 than it had been in December 1980. The economy had started to go into a recession in 1981, and then unemployment peaked in 1982 at 10.7 percent of the labor force in the fourth quarter of that year.

In 1978–79, the Fed initiated a gradual approach to fighting inflation. The real supply of money fell and there were credit controls enacted for a while in 1980 to induce some rationing of credit. The economy went into a very short recession in 1980, but then monetary policy was eased a little and the credit controls were relaxed. The economy actually started to recover again in late 1980. Inflation had jumped sharply in 1979; it rose again in 1980 and remained very high in 1981. The Fed decided it was not going to accommodate this inflation and it was prepared to accept the consequences of the cumulative decline in the real money stock from 1979 to 1981.

Events in the actual economy over this period were complex, reflecting the effects of supply shocks, fiscal-policy changes, and changes in the international sector as well as the monetary-policy changes that are our focus now. In particular, energy and food prices were rising sharply and driving up inflation through 1980. Then these prices fell back again. We will abstract from these supply shocks for the time being. In Figure 6–13 we look at a simplified analysis of the results of a monetary contraction.

Roughly in line with conditions that existed in the U.S. economy in 1979–80, the economy in its initial situation is shown in Figure 6–13 as having a very high expected rate of inflation, reflecting the fact there had been high inflation in the past and that the Fed was not expected to act dramatically to reduce inflation. We will assume an initial output ratio of 99 percent, so the current rate of inflation was slightly below expected inflation. (It is shown as $\left(\dfrac{\Delta P}{P}\right)_A$.) These initial conditions are reflected in points A in both panels of Figure 6–13.

We assume now that the Fed has a policy goal of reaching a new long-run equilibrium in which output is equal to potential output and the rate of inflation is going to be reduced to $\left(\dfrac{\Delta P}{P}\right)_C$. The policy goal used in this example is approx-

FIGURE 6-13   Short-Run Effects of a Sharp Monetary Contraction and Subsequent Recovery

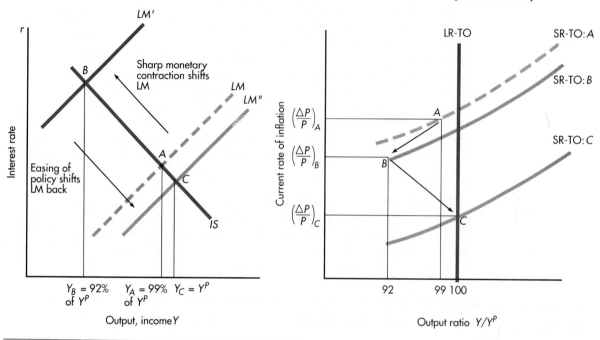

imately in line with the actual economic policies that were followed. Since the Fed wants to take a major step toward reducing inflation quickly, it sets a rate of growth of the money supply well below the current rate of inflation—the rate of growth of the real money supply is negative.

The drop in the real money supply increased the interest rate. This reduced output (point *A* to point *B*). This is shown as a large shift in the *LM* schedule *(LM* to *LM')* and a plunge of output to 92 percent of potential.

In the right-hand panel of Figure 6–13, the output ratio at point *A* was already slightly to the left of the long-run trade-off (LR–TO), the economy having moved a short distance along the short-run trade-off (SR–TO:A). In the following year, there is then a small downward shift of the short-run trade-off (SR–TO:A to SR–TO:B), a shift that occurred because inflationary expectations in the goods and labor markets dropped by a modest amount. The reduction of current inflation to $\left(\frac{\Delta P}{P}\right)_B$ then comes from the combination of the movement along the short-run trade-off and the downward shift of the trade-off (point *A* along SR–TO:A to point *B* along SR–TO:B).

This was a quick and substantial reduction of inflation, but it was achieved with a very large drop in output. Unfortunately, because of the sluggish response of wages and prices and the inertia built into expected inflation, this very large reduction in output only drove down inflation part way toward the long-run target.

Over the next few years output grew faster than potential output (the output ratio was increasing), but the level of output remained below potential (the ratio remained below 100). The economy was operating to the left of the long-run trade-off line, so expected inflation in the goods market and the short-run trade-off both fell. Current inflation was gradually reduced to the 4 percent range. Figure 6–14 depicts the adjustment. The Fed gradually eased monetary policy, allowing the economy to grow. This is shown by the down shifts of the *LM* schedule, from *LM′* to *LM″*. The short-run trade-off was also shifting down, from SR–TO:*B* to SR–TO:*C*, so that inflation was falling even though output and the output ratio were rising. The economy is depicted at point *C*, where it has reached a new long-run equilibrium, where the current rate of inflation and the expected rate of inflation Current$\left(\dfrac{\Delta P}{P}\right)_C$ are equal.

The Fed pursued a contractionary policy and the economy suffered through a period of tight money, high real interest rates, and falling aggregate demand. This is the classic "credit-crunch" scenario of an economy entering a slowing or a recession because of financial-market constraints initiated by the Federal Reserve. This drove the economy into a deep recession and a prolonged period where output was below

FIGURE 6–14   **The Economy Returns to Full Employment with Moderate Inflation**

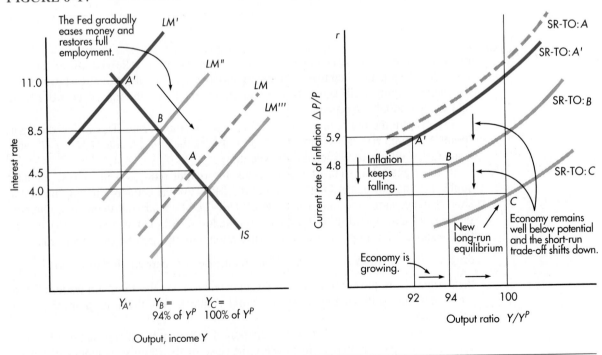

potential output. The Fed reduced inflation by engineering a severe recession and then re-expanded the real money supply to sustain a moderate recovery.

If, after 1979, the Fed had continued to pursue a gradualist strategy for reducing inflation by keeping output below potential output but not far below it, the time it would have taken to combat inflation would have been longer. On the other hand, the severe economic distress and bankruptcies of 1982 and 1983 might have been avoided. Although we have not talked here about instability, the choice between a short, sharp recession and a long, mild recession may be made in practice on the basis of concerns about unstable economic changes. Some members of the board of governors of the Fed considered the histories of extremely rapid inflations—such as those in Europe in the 1920s and in Argentina, Brazil, and Israel in recent times—and they worried about a repetition of these in the United States in the 1980s. If the Fed believes that a high rate of inflation is not stable, then a sharp reduction in money growth is indicated. This concern about inflation rising out of control influenced the Fed to use a sharp reduction of money growth. Some economists, such as James Tobin of Yale University, worried that too sharp a recession could have led to a repeat of the Great Depression of the 1930s. In mid-1982, the Fed actually eased off on its policy of tight money because it, too, was worried about a depression. The Fed wanted a sharp recession, but not a major depression.

Conclusions on Monetary Policy and Inflation

Monetary policy can be a potent tool to control the economy. In 1974–75 and again in 1981–82 we have seen the Fed act decisively to reduce the growth rate of the money supply, to allow interest rates to rise sharply, and to cut aggregate demand. These policy steps have been taken to reduce inflation. In the early 1990s, monetary policy has been used to help pull the economy out of a recession that was not caused primarily by tight money. And it was found that monetary policy was somewhat less effective than had been thought in this stimulative role. In addition, the Fed was restrained in its use of monetary policy by concern that inflation might accelerate again if too rapid an expansion of the economy was to result. We will be looking further at the role of monetary policy in the 1990–92 period in Chapter 8.

We have now seen how the *IS–LM* framework can be used to analyze the impact of policy when inflation is a concern. In the next chapter we reintroduce the foreign sector. The fact that the United States is an open economy and that the dollar is traded on international currency markets has an important impact on policymaking.

WORKED EXAMPLES

Worked Example 6–1

Monetary Policy: The Effect of Increasing the Supply of Money
In Worked Example 5–1 in Chapter 5 we found an *IS* schedule, given values for the components of demand in the goods market (the consumption function, the investment function, the tax function, and the level of government spending):

$$r = 141 - 0.034Y$$

The money-market relations used in Worked Example 4–4 in Chapter 4 were as follows:

$$M^d/P = 0.4Y - 80r$$
$$M^s/P = 1,200$$

The *LM* schedule then comes from setting money supply equal to money demand and rearranging terms:

$$r = 0.005Y - 15$$

To find the level of income at the intersection of the *IS* and *LM* schedules, we set the interest rates equal:

$$141 - 0.034Y = 0.005Y - 15$$

Solving this equation gives the equilibrium as $Y = 4,000$; that is, income is $4 trillion. Substituting back into either the *IS* or the *LM* equation gives the interest rate as 5 percent.

Question   Consider the economy just described. Suppose that the Fed now decides to expand the supply of money in order to increase income. If it increases M^s/P to 1,300 what happens to income?

Answer   The new *LM* schedule is given as follows:

$$M^d/P = 0.4Y - 80r$$
$$= 1,300 = M^s/P$$
$$r = 0.005Y - 16.25$$

The new *IS–LM* equilibrium is then given by:

$$141 - 0.034Y = 0.005Y - 16.25$$

Solving this gives a value for Y of 4,032. The level of equilibrium income has increased by $32 billion as a result of the monetary expansion. The rate of interest has dropped to 3.9 percent (check *IS* or *LM*) and this stimulated investment and raised income.

Worked Example 6–2

The Case of a Steeper *LM* Schedule

Take up the same model economy that was given in Worked Example 6–1. But suppose now that there is a different money-demand schedule, one for which the demand for money is less responsive to changes in the rate of interest. We assume also that the response to income is smaller. This new money-demand schedule is as follows:

$$M^d/P = 0.36Y - 48r$$

Questions

a. With this money-demand schedule and a money supply of 1,200, find the new *LM* schedule and show that it intersects the *IS* schedule at a level of income of 4,000 and an interest rate of 5 percent. How does the slope of this new *LM* schedule compare to the one in Worked Example 6–1?

b. What is the effect on income and the rate of interest of an increase in the money supply of $100 billion?

Answer: The new *LM* schedule is found by setting money supply equal to the new money demand:

$$M^s/P = 1,200 = 0.36Y - 48r$$

so that

$$r = 0.0075Y - 25$$

To show that $Y = 4,000$ and $r = 5$ are points on the new *LM* schedule, these values can be substituted in:

$$5 = (0.0075 \times 4,000) - 25$$
$$= 5$$

so that we have shown that this *LM* schedule passes through the same point as the original one. (That is why we made the income coefficient smaller when we made up the example.) The new *LM* schedule still intersects the *IS* where income if $4 trillion and the interest rate is 5 percent.

The slope of this *LM* schedule is 0.0075, rather than 0.005. This is a 50 percent increase in the slope. This completes the answer to part *(a)* of the question.

What happens if the Fed increases the money supply by 100 with this money-demand relation that is less responsive to the interest rate? The new *LM* schedule is:

$$M^s/P = 1,300 = 0.36Y - 48r$$

so that

$$r = 0.0075Y - 27.08$$

We then set the *IS* and *LM* interest rates equal:

$$141 - 0.034Y = 0.0075Y - 27.08$$

Solving this gives the result that $Y = 4,050$. Thus, *a given increase in the supply of money has had a larger impact on income with the steeper* LM *schedule.* (Income rose by $50 billion, rather than the $32 billion in Worked Example 6–1.)

Substituting into either *IS* or *LM* gives the interest rate. For the *IS:*

$$141 - (0.034 \times 4,050) = 3.3$$

The interest rate fell to 3.3 percent in contrast with a fall to only 3.9 percent in Worked Example 6–1. The greater decrease in the interest rate gives a greater stimulus to investment and a larger increase in income.

Worked Example 6–3

Current Inflation Depends on the Output Ratio and Expected Inflation

Consider the following relation for the determination of the current rate of inflation:

$$\text{Current}\Delta P/P = 0.2[(Y/Y^p) - 100] + \text{Exp}\Delta P/P$$

Suppose the output ratio and the expected rate of inflation take on the following values over an 11-year period:

Year	Output Ratio	Expected Inflation
One	100	0.0
Two	104	0.0
Three	108	0.8
Four	108	2.4
Five	104	4.0
Six	100	4.8
Seven	96	4.8
Eight	92	4.0
Nine	92	2.4
Ten	96	0.8
Eleven	100	0.0

Question

a. Evaluate the current rate of inflation for each of the 11 years.

b. In what years did the economy experience output and inflation moving in opposite directions? Did it ever experience the opposite case?

c. Comment on the relation between current and expected inflation in this economy. Are the values for expected inflation plausible

Answers   The answer to part *(a)* is worked out as follows:

Year	Trade-Off Relation	Expected Inflation	Current Rate of Inflation
One	0.2(100 − 100)	+ 0.0	= 0.0
Two	0.2(104 − 100)	+ 0.0	= 0.8
Three	0.2(108 − 100)	+ 0.8	= 2.4
Four	0.2(108 − 100)	+ 2.4	= 4.0
Five	0.2(104 − 100)	+ 4.0	= 4.8
Six	0.2(100 − 100)	+ 4.8	= 4.8
Seven	0.2(96 − 100)	+ 4.8	= 4.0
Eight	0.2(92 − 100)	+ 4.0	= 2.4
Nine	0.2(92 − 100)	+ 2.4	= 0.8
Ten	0.2(96 − 100)	+ 0.8	= 0.0
Eleven	0.2(100 − 100)	+ 0.0	= 0.0

The answer to part *(b)* is that output stayed the same from years three to four while inflation rose. Output actually fell from years four to five, while inflation rose. And output fell again from years five to six while inflation stayed the same. The years from three to six look pretty much like a perverse trade-off. The change from year four to year five certainly has output and inflation moving in opposite directions.

These were periods of stagflation, in that output stagnated or declined while inflation worsened.

The economy did experience the opposite case, where output grew but inflation declined or remained constant. This happened in years nine through eleven.

For part *(c)*, note that the numbers that are given for expected inflation in this example are actually the previous year's rate of inflation. In other words, the example used the following relation for expected inflation:

$$\text{Exp}\Delta P/P = \text{Actual inflation of the previous year}$$

Is this plausible? Expected inflation is probably not determined as mechanically as this. Expected inflation is based on the past experience of more than one previous year and may be based on other information, too. In the text we discuss the ways in which expected inflation is determined.

Worked Example 6–4

The Trade-Off in the Short Run, the Intermediate Run, and the Long Run
Consider the following relation for the determination of the current rate of inflation:

$$\text{Current}\Delta P/P = 0.2[(Y/Y^p) - 100] + \text{Exp}\Delta P/P$$

$$\text{Exp}\Delta P/P = 0.5(\Delta P/P \text{ of previous year}) + 0.5(\Delta P/P \text{ of two years prior})$$

Suppose that output in this economy has been equal to potential output and the rate of inflation has been 5 percent a year for several years. Then output increases to 105 percent of potential and stays there.

Questions
a. How does inflation evolve in this economy?
b. What is the slope of the short-run trade-off?
c. What is the slope of the two-year trade off?
d. What is the slope of the eight-year trade-off?
e. What is the slope of the long-run trade-off?

Year	Trade-Off Relation	Expected Inflation	Current Rate of Inflation
One	0.2(105 − 100)	+ (0.5 × 5.00) + (0.5 × 5.00)	= 6.00
Two	0.2(105 − 100)	+ (0.5 × 6.00) + (0.5 × 5.00)	= 6.50
Three	0.2(105 − 100)	+ (0.5 × 6.50) + (0.5 × 6.00)	= 7.25
Four	0.2(105 − 100)	+ (0.5 × 7.25) + (0.5 × 6.50)	= 7.88
Five	0.2(105 − 100)	+ (0.5 × 7.88) + (0.5 × 7.25)	= 8.56
Six	0.2(105 − 100)	+ (0.5 × 8.56) + (0.5 × 7.88)	= 9.22
Seven	0.2(105 − 100)	+ (0.5 × 9.22) + (0.5 × 8.56)	= 9.89
Eight	0.2(105 − 100)	+ (0.5 × 9.89) + (0.5 × 9.22)	= 10.55

Answers
a. The rates of inflation that evolve in this economy are shown over eight years in the table. The rates of inflation have been rounded. The calculations were made without rounding, so there will be small discrepancies if you check through the figures. We see that inflation gets gradually larger over time with a sustained increase in output.
b. The short-run trade-off gives the relation between output and inflation within the same year, taking the expected rate of inflation as given. The calculations just given indicate that the 5 percentage-point increase in output has raised inflation by 1 percentage point. The slope of the short-run trade-off is $1 \div 5 = 0.2$.
c. The two-year trade-off looks at the effect after two years of a change in the level of output that is sustained over the two-year period. The preceding calculations indicate that inflation

has risen by 1.5 percentage points after two years (6.5 − 5). Thus the slope of the two-year trade-off is 1.5 ÷ 5 = 0.3. This is steeper than the short-run trade-off.

    d. The eight-year trade-off looks at the effect after eight years of a change in the level of output that is sustained over the eight-year period. The preceding calculations indicate that inflation has risen by 5.55 percentage points after eight years (10.55 − 5). Thus the slope of the eight-year trade-off is 5.55 ÷ 5 = 1.11. We see that the slopes of the intermediate-run trade-offs are getting steeper as the time period increases.

    e. The long-run trade-off has a vertical slope. Inflation will continue to accelerate as long as output remains above potential output. Another way of understanding this is to see that the only way in which current inflation can equal expected inflation is if the output ratio equals 100.

SUMMARY

- Monetary expansion can stimulate aggregate demand and income. With a given level of income, an increase in the supply of money reduces the rate of interest and increases the availability of credit. This stimulates investment demand.

- Inflation is a continuing rise in the overall level of prices. It both affects economic decisions and is determined by economic conditions.

- An excessive level of aggregate demand, an increase in expected inflation, and shocks to aggregate supply (such as oil price increases) are the three main causes of increased inflation.

- If the concern about inflation is strong enough, the Fed will pursue contractionary monetary policies. These can be strong enough to stifle a recovery or even initiate a recession.

- When investment demand is not very responsive to lower interest rates and a higher availability of credit, such as when business prospects are poor, the *IS* schedule is relatively steep and monetary policy is less effective than when investment demand is responsive.

- When money demand is not very responsive to the interest rate, such as when income and transactions demands are high relative to the size of the money supply, the *LM* schedule is steep and it requires a large change in the interest rate to restore money-market equilibrium following a change in income.

- When output is equal to potential output, there is no inflationary pressure from aggregate demand. An excessive level of aggregate demand means that output is above potential output. This means there are more prices adjusting upward than there are prices adjusting downward, and the result is an overall inflation. Variations in aggregate demand lead to an output–inflation trade-off.

- The experience of the U.S. economy at the end of the 1960s and throughout the 1970s showed there is not a simple and stable trade-off between output and inflation. We characterize changes in the relationship between output and inflation as shifts of the short-run trade-off.

- The two major candidates for sources of shifts in the short-run trade-off are changes in the expected rate of inflation and changes in aggregate supply conditions.

- When policymakers try to reduce inflation, a decrease in output will bring about only a small reduction in inflation in the short run, but a much larger reduction in the long run.

- In the very long run, policy to change demand cannot change the level of output or unemployment in the economy.

- Monetary-policy changes will affect inflation directly through changes in aggregate demand and indirectly through changes in inflationary expectations.

- The existence of short-run trade-offs presents a difficult choice to monetary policymakers: inflation can be reduced, but the cost is a reduction in output.

KEY TERMS AND CONCEPTS

adaptive expectations, p. 159
coordinated policy, p. 142
output–inflation trade-off, p. 150
output ratio, p. 155

price stickiness, p. 154
short-run output–inflation
  trade-off, p. 155

stagflation, p. 156
vertical long-run trade-off, p. 160

DISCUSSION QUESTIONS AND PROBLEMS

1. Review the way in which the effectiveness of monetary policy changes with different slopes of the *IS* and *LM* schedules. Explain the differences in terms of the behavior of holders of money and firms deciding to purchase investment goods.

2. A rise in the demand for some goods and services drives up their prices. Why isn't there a fall in the prices of goods and services whose demand has not increased, leaving the price level unaffected?

3. What are some of the economic conditions that can fuel an increase in aggregate demand that leads to inflation? Which conditions are likely to be sustainable over time and which are likely to be self-limiting?

4. Why would stagflation be measured by a misery index? Why is stagflation so economically painful?

5. Stagflation can be described as a worsening of the short-run output–inflation trade-off. Show how such a short-run trade-off shifts in the face of stagflation. What could account for the shift?

6. What are the two contrasting views of how inflationary expectations are formed? How is the notion of a trade-off affected either way?

7. Which trade-off is steepest: short-run, intermediate-run, or long-run? Why?

8. What does the trade-off mean for the use of economic policy actions to:
    a. Stimulate the economy in a recession:
       (1) In the short run.
       (2) In the long run.
    b. Fight inflation:
       (1) In the short run.
       (2) In the long run.

9. "If there is no trade-off between output and inflation in the long run, it does not matter whether or not monetary policy is used to fight inflation or accommodate inflation." Comment.

THE EXCHANGE RATE, MACROECONOMIC POLICY IN AN OPEN ECONOMY, AND THE TRADE DEFICIT

INTRODUCTION

Worldwide economic policymakers, business managers, and the general public are well aware of the importance of the international economy. This awareness has developed relatively later in the United States than in the rest of the world. For much of U.S. history, especially during the period from 1945 until the 1970s, economic events overseas and across borders were of secondary importance to the United States. From the late 1940s through the late 1950s, the Japanese and European societies were struggling with recovery from the devastation of World War II. During that period, the United States dominated the world's economy.

The U.S. economy remains by far the largest national economy in the world, but U.S. GDP has dropped from approximately 50 percent of world output in the 1950s to below 30 percent in 1990. The Western European economy accounts for about 30 percent of world GDP, while the Japanese economy accounts for around another 10 percent. There has been a dramatic change in international economic relationships. The growth of Europe and Asia have challenged U.S. economic leadership. Many U.S. industries are now more concerned about foreign competition than about fluctuations in domestic demand.

In this chapter and Chapter 11 we will try to answer several questions about international economic relationships and the U.S. economy. What determines the exchange rate of the dollar for other currencies? Why does the value of the dollar fluctuate? Why did the U.S. economy change, going from a *net exporting nation* (one that sold more to the world than it bought from the world) to the reverse, a *net importing nation?* To pay for the excess of its imports over its exports, the United States had gone from being the leading creditor nation, lending more to other countries than any other nation, to being, by the late 1980s, the leading *debtor nation,* borrowing more money than any other. How did these changes in international economic relationships affect equilibrium income, economic performance, and economic policies?

International considerations add reality to our description of the economy. However, they also add significant complexity. To deal with this complexity, we focus on how international markets affect the domestic economy, rather than attempting to describe the workings of the world economy as a whole. We approach the role of trade in the domestic economy in several steps. First, we look at what determines imports and exports, taking as constant the level of income. This simplicity allows us to focus on the exchange rate of the dollar as a primary factor determining the balance of our trade.

We then look at the international purchases and sales of assets. These depend on interest rates and expectations about the future value of the exchange rate. The flows of exports and imports and the flows of capital assets are the major determinants of the demand for and supply of foreign currency, often called "foreign exchange," so in the second part of this chapter we turn the analysis around and look at how the supply of and demand for foreign exchange determine the exchange rate. Finally, we return to the *IS–LM* framework to look at the role played by international trade in macroeconomic performance and macroeconomic policy.

INTERNATIONAL TRADE AND FOREIGN EXCHANGE

foreign exchange
Foreign currencies that are exchanged in foreign-exchange markets.

Most international trade is accomplished by an importer who first obtains foreign currency and then uses foreign currency to purchase foreign goods. Foreign currencies (i.e., **foreign exchange**) are traded or exchanged for one another in international financial markets or, more specifically, *foreign-exchange markets*. Trades of foreign exchange facilitate and accompany the trade of foreign goods and assets. But the prices for currencies set in the foreign-exchange market also influences the amounts of goods and assets traded.

The decision to buy an imported good depends on many factors; but initially we will keep income and tastes constant, so we can focus on the *price* of a good being imported or exported. In general, therefore, *the volume of exports from the United States will be higher when the prices paid by foreigners for U.S. products is lower.* The price that is relevant is the price that foreigners pay in their own currency. By a similar argument, *the volume of imports into the United States will be higher when the prices paid by U.S. purchasers are lower.* And the price that is relevant is the price that importers pay in dollars. The prices of traded goods depend, then, on two elements: the domestic price of the goods and the terms on which currencies are traded.

For example, a decision by a non-U.S. airline to buy U.S.-made Boeing aircraft is certainly affected by many different economic and political factors (reliability and energy consumption, for example), but once those other factors are given, it is the price of, say, Boeing's 757 relative to the European Airbus that is most important. Further, even if the airline chooses Boeing, the number of planes imported is likely to be smaller in the case of a high price for Boeing airplanes than the number of planes imported when the price of U.S.-produced aircraft is low.

Boeing will offer to sell its planes to the foreign airline at a particular price in dollars. But to the managers of the airline, the price of Boeing aircraft (i.e., the price in marks, yen, lira, or whatever is the home currency of the purchaser) depends on how many dollars can be bought with its home country currency as well as depending on the price Boeing charges for its planes.

The Exchange Rate

exchange rate
The number of units of foreign currency that can be purchased for one unit of the domestic currency.

The number of units of one currency that can be purchased with one unit of another currency is called the *foreign-currency exchange rate* or simply the **exchange rate.** When referring to exchange rates it is important to be clear about how the rate is expressed. One can look at the exchange rate between any two currencies in two possible ways. For example, one can look at the number of German marks exchanged for one British pound or, alternatively, the reciprocal of this number is the fraction of a pound that can be purchased with a single German mark.

Foreign exchange rates are published daily in many newspapers; usually the exchange rates with the dollar are expressed both ways, such as number of marks per dollar, or fraction of a dollar per mark. But even so, the general practice in the United States is to express *dollar* exchange rates as so many units of foreign currency that can be purchased with one dollar—1.5 German marks per dollar, 100 Japanese yen per dollar, and so on. This means that if the amount of foreign currency that the dollar can buy falls (i.e., if the dollar becomes worth less in foreign-exchange markets), then the value of the dollar has fallen. *A fall in the value of the dollar is a decline in the exchange rate.* For example, if the dollar is exchanged for 90 yen, rather than for 100 yen, then the exchange rate of the dollar has fallen against the yen.

Changes in the Exchange Rate and the Flow of Trade

The exchange rates between the U.S. dollar and all other currencies are important in determining how much product from other countries is imported by U.S. buyers and how much U.S. product is exported to foreign buyers. For example, let's see how the exchange rate affects the choice of purchasing either a U.S.-made or German-made automobile. In the early 1980s the exchange rate between the U.S. dollar and the West German mark (deutsche mark or DM) was around two DM to the dollar. This means that during that time period, a German car that was sold to a U.S. dealer for DM60,000 by a German exporter cost $30,000 when purchased in the United States. At an exchange rate of two DM to the dollar, the U.S. import-car dealer had to pay $30,000 to purchase the DM60,000 needed to buy the German car. Of course, the dealer must also pay for shipping and for a small tariff that is levied on imported cars. (A tariff is just sales tax imposed by the government on imported goods.) The final customer in the United States might pay $40,000 to cover all these costs, including the dealer's markup. The number of BMWs or Audis that Americans would then buy depends on the comparison of these German cars at $40,000 with the alternatives facing car buyers in the United States.

In an earlier period, the dollar exchanged for four marks, so German automobiles that cost DM60,000 were substantially cheaper for U.S. customers. At four marks to the dollar it takes only $15,000 for a car dealer to cover the same factory costs in DM. For this example, let's assume that shipping costs and dealer markups stayed the same in all periods (approximately $10,000). Then an American customer would pay around $25,000 for the German car. As the value of the dollar fell to three marks, it took $20,000 for a car dealer to cover the factory cost in DM, so the American customer would pay around $30,000 for the German car. By 1992, the DM had risen to 1.55 DM to the dollar, and a DM60,000 automobile would have had a base price to U.S. dealers of $38,710 and a U.S. selling price of over $48,710 without any change in the price of the cars in marks. As summarized in the following tables, that sort of shift in exchange rates helped convert the BMW and Audi from upper-mid-priced cars to high-priced luxury cars in just a few years.

DM/$ Exchange Rate	Price of a German Auto in the U.S.*
4.00	$25,000
3.00	$30,000
2.00	$40,000
1.55	$48,710

* Including approximately $10,000 in U.S.-based charges. Assumes a fixed cost of DM60,000.

The same story runs in reverse for U.S. exports. U.S.-made aircraft or computers are expensive to foreign customers when the dollar is high and inexpensive when the dollar is low. It follows, therefore, that *an increase in the value of the dollar will encourage imports by making them cheaper, and it will discourage exports by making them more expensive.*

The Trade-Weighted Real Exchange Rate

The exchange rate of the U.S. dollar against the German mark affects U.S. trade with Germany, while the exchange rate of the U.S. dollar against the yen affects trade with Japan. In fact, these exchange rates also affect our exports to other countries where our companies compete for sales against Japanese and German firms. There are many different exchange rates, each of which has some effect on U.S. imports and exports, and they all change at different rates and in different directions. To characterize the average levels of all the different exchange rates, we need a summary measure of the exchange rates between the U.S. dollar and the currencies of our major trading partners.

Such a summary measure is provided by an *exchange-rate index.* The index is set equal to 100 in a base year and then changes over time, depending on the way in which the major currencies around the world move against the dollar. For example, if Canada accounts for 10 percent of U.S. trade and the U.S. dollar rises by 5 percent against the Canadian dollar, then the exchange rate index for the U.S. dollar rises by 0.5 percent (0.1 times 5 percent).

The Exchange Rate: Dollars for Yen or Yen for Dollars, Which Way Is It?

Readers be warned: international trade economists do it differently. One of the most confusing concepts in economics is the way in which the rate of exchange between two currencies should be expressed. As we indicate in the text, we choose to express the rate as the number of units of foreign currency that can be purchased with one dollar (e.g., let's say the yen is trading at 130 yen to the dollar). This approach is commonly used in the media and it squares with the intuitive idea of *appreciation* or *devaluation* of the dollar. When the exchange as we have defined it goes up (e.g., from 100 yen to 120 yen), the dollar buys more foreign currency—the dollar has appreciated. When the exchange rate goes down (e.g., from 100 yen to 90 yen), the dollar buys less foreign currency—the dollar has depreciated.

Unfortunately, this approach is the inverse of the concept that international trade economists focus on when they describe foreign-exchange markets. They define the exchange rate in terms of the price of foreign exchange, so the yen to dollar exchange rate is the cost of purchasing one yen with dollars. If the exchange rate in our terms is equal to 100 yen to the dollar, the inverse would be $0.01 (one cent) per yen. If the dollar appreciates, from 100 yen to 120 yen to the dollar (dollar purchases more yen), then the exchange rate, expressed as the cost of yen, declines in dollar terms, in this example dropping form $0.01 to $0.0083. The appreciating dollar means that yen purchased in foreign exchange markets are now cheaper to buy with dollars, exactly the concept that trade economists wish to show. But it also means that their definition of the dollar-exchange rate falls when the dollar appreciates! This is very confusing and so we define the exchange rate as yen per dollar, rather than dollars per yen. For those who go on to further studies in international economics, however, you will find that the trade economists' definition will usually appear in international economic texts and journals.

The exchange-rate index is designed to measure how, over time, movements in the dollar will affect U.S. imports and exports. And to do this well, the index must also take account of any differences between the rate of inflation in the United States and the rates of inflation in other countries. Suppose the rate of inflation were 10 percent a year in the United States but only 3 percent a year in Germany. The buying power of the dollar in the United States is falling 7 percent a year faster than the buying power of the German mark.

Now suppose that the exchange rate of the dollar declined by 7 percent from one year to the next against the mark. Then German buyers would be getting 7 percent more dollars for their marks; but the decline in the exchange rate would be exactly undone by the greater increase in prices in the United States than in Germany. The number of Mercedes that it took to trade for one Boeing 757 would be the same in the two years. (At least, this would be true on average for many goods.) This means that, when a change in the exchange rate simply compensates for differences in inflation rates, the relative prices of U.S. imports (from Germany) and U.S. exports (to Germany) do not change.

The best indicator, then, of how U.S. imports and exports are affected by changes in the prices of foreign goods relative to U.S. goods is an index number called the **real exchange rate,** and denoted by **rex.** Changes in the real exchange-rate index over time measure how the exchange rates of the U.S. dollar have changed, on average, against

real exchange rate index (rex) An index number that indicates how a domestic currency is exchanged for the currencies most important in the country's trade.

FIGURE 7–1
Real Exchange-Rate Index for the U.S. Dollar, 1973–1993

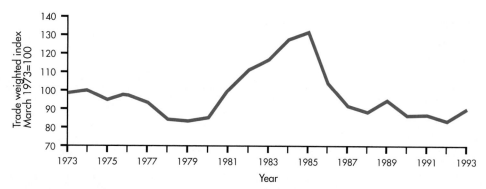

The U.S. exchange rate varies quite a bit from month to month and has shown sustained swings in value. The real and nominal exchange rates move together most of the time.

Source: *World Financial Markets*, various issues (New York: Morgan Guaranty Trust).

the major foreign currencies after adjusting for the difference between the inflation rate here and abroad.

Figure 7–1 shows the movements in the real exchange-rate index over the period 1973 to 1993. There have been some very large swings in the real exchange rate, with a large rise over the period from 1981 to 1985, followed by a rather abrupt decline in the dollar until 1988. The exchange rate has been waffling since then.[1] The large swings in the dollar have had an important impact on U.S. competitiveness in the global economy. A high dollar diminishes the ability of U.S. companies to sell overseas and enhances the ease with which foreigners can sell in the U.S. market.

Worked Example 7–1   In Worked Example 7–1 on page 214, we show a numerical example of how the nominal and real exchange-rate indexes are calculated and we give an algebraic definition of how the real and nominal exchange-rate indexes are related.

The Trade Balance and the Exchange Rate

We first introduced exports and imports in Chapter 3, where we showed how trade is affected by changes in income and how, in turn, trade affects aggregate demand. In doing so, we ignored the effect of changes in the exchange rate on the balance of trade. Here we are doing the opposite—we are looking at how a change in the exchange rate affects the trade balance, holding income constant. Obviously, in practice, both income and the exchange rate are important in determining trade. Before we are through we will take account of both effects and the interaction between them.

U.S. exports depend on how much foreigners have to pay for the goods and services that we offer for sales overseas, while U.S. imports depend on how much we have to pay for the things that foreigners offer for sale to U.S. customers. *Changes in a country's real exchange rate will, therefore, affect its balance of trade.*

---

[1] It is important in principle to take account of differences in rates of inflation between the United States and other countries; but in practice, when calculated for a large number of currencies, this does not have a major impact. A nominal exchange-rate index can be calculated that ignores inflation differences, and this index moves pretty much in step with the real exchange index.

FIGURE 7–2
With Income Given, Exports and Imports Depend on the Exchange Rate

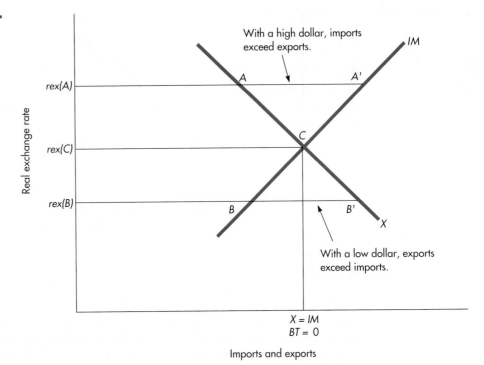

Import demand rises as the dollar buys more foreign currency, lowering the dollar cost to U.S. buyers of imports. Export demand rises as foreign currencies buy more dollars, lowering the cost to foreign buyers of U.S. exports.

In Figure 7–2 we illustrate the relationship between the real exchange rate and exports (X) and imports (IM). From the U.S. point of view, a high real exchange rate [$rex(A)$] means that imported goods are relatively inexpensive and imports are high (point A'). At the same real exchange rate, U.S. exports are relatively costly and exports are low (point A). At this high real exchange rate, $rex(A)$, imports exceed exports and the balance of trade is negative (point A − point A').

Conversely, at a low exchange rate, $rex(B)$, imports will be low (point B) and exports will be high (point B'). At this low real exchange rate the balance of trade is positive (point B' − point B). The figure shows that at some exchange rate [shown as $rex(C)$ in Figure 7–2] exports equal imports and the balance of trade is zero (point C). But the fact that the trade balance can be zero does not imply that in fact the exchange rate will necessarily so adjust that a country's trade balance will be zero. For instance, the U.S. balance of trade was positive through much of the 1950s and has been negative since the early 1980s. At point A in the figure, the negative trade balance means only that U.S. purchasers are buying more products from the world than they are selling to the world. *This deficit in trade could be balanced by other items, such as foreign purchases of U.S. assets. Thus, there is no guarantee that the trade balance (the international purchases and sale of goods and services) will be balanced over any particular period of time.*

What Figure 7–2 implies is that a fall in the real exchange rate will lead to a reduction in a trade deficit or an increase in the surplus, and vice versa for a rise in the real exchange rate.

As we have looked at trade and the impact of the exchange rate on the trade balance we have talked about trade in goods—trading aircraft for automobiles. But there is a lot more to trade and foreign exchange than this. There is an increasingly important trade in services. And there are foreign-held assets that yield flows of income to U.S. residents. We need to broaden our view of foreign exchange transactions. Imports and exports of goods and services and flows of income are tracked in a system of accounts called the balance of payments.

THE BALANCE OF PAYMENTS ON CURRENT ACCOUNT

balance of payments on the current account
The value of the trade balance plus the net balances of international items that affect income.

The best measure of aggregate economic performance in a given year is the total income generated in that year. In an open economy (one that trades internationally), this is still the case; but to determine income, we have to take account of the effect of the international sector. The effect on national income from the foreign sector includes traded goods and services, investment income, and other international transfers and receipts. The ways in which international transactions affect income are evaluated in the National Income and Product Accounts as part of the **balance of payments on current account.** We look at the components of the current account one part at a time.

The Balance of Trade

balance of trade
The part of net exports consisting of the net revenues from the sale of goods abroad.

The largest impact on income from the foreign sector consists of the revenues from the sale of goods abroad (merchandise exports) and the expenditures on goods purchased from other countries (merchandise imports). Total merchandise exports and imports also include trade in services, such as insurance and transportation. The value of merchandise exports less the value of merchandise imports is called the balance of merchandise trade or just the **balance of trade.**

The United States had a net surplus in merchandise trade every year from 1946 to 1970. During that period the biggest U.S. exports were agricultural products, chemicals, and capital goods, such as aircraft, communications equipment, and other machinery. There was a tremendous worldwide demand for U.S. capital goods in the 1950s and 1960s as other countries wanted access to U.S. technology and production methods. Traditionally the U.S. strength in exporting has been in high-tech products and this has remained the case into the 1990s, although the United States no longer has the dominant position it used to have.

The merchandise trade balance turned negative in 1971 and has been negative in almost every year since them. The deficit rose sharply in the 1980s, reaching a peak of almost $160 billion in 1987. It has been contracting since then, falling to $74 billion by 1991. It has started to rise again since then as the U.S. economic recovery strengthened. The deficit was $96 billion in 1992. The principal U.S. imports in the 1980s and 1990s have been oil, autos, machinery, agricultural products, semiconductors, other computer-related components, and consumer goods. These figures are all given in current dollars; that is, with no adjustment for inflation.

**Trade in
Services**

In recent years the United States has become a substantial net exporter of services, with education and tourism making major contributions (thousands of students and millions of tourists come to the United States each year). In 1991, net exports of services were almost $46 billion, rising to $56 billion in 1992. The positive U.S. net exports of services have partially offset the negative merchandise trade balance.

**Income Earned
on Foreign
Assets and
Transfers**

Because U.S. residents earn income on their ownership of foreign assets just as foreign residents earn income on their ownership of U.S. assets, the balance of merchandise trade does not account for all of the foreign effects on domestic income. For example, U.S. residents may hold bonds issued by foreign governments or foreign companies. They may hold foreign real estate or the stocks of foreign companies. In addition, many U.S. companies have foreign subsidiaries. These foreign assets yield a flow of income to their American owners. Similarly, foreigners own U.S. assets, bonds, stocks, real estate, and so on. These U.S.-based assets generate a flow of income to their foreign owners.

The United States has a substantial inflow of investment income, derived largely from the earnings of the foreign subsidiaries of U.S. multinational corporations. This source of income has continued to grow in recent years. Yet, what has changed is the tremendous growth in the outflow of investment income in the 1980s, as foreigners have purchased large amounts of U.S. bonds, stocks, and real estate and have acquired ownership of some companies previously owned by U.S. residents. In 1981, the United States had a $33 billion net inflow of investment income. By 1992, this had fallen to a net inflow of $6 billion.

Income flows are also generated by fees and royalties. U.S. companies hold key patents in many areas of technology and they license foreign companies to use the technology. This generates a flow of fees and royalties to the United States. There is a smaller reverse flow of payments by U.S. companies to foreign licensors. Books, movies, television shows, and other entertainment and media products also generate international income flows.

As well as the return on assets, payments known as *international transfer payments* are also made. Some of these payments stem from private financial transfers (i.e., gifts). There are many residents of one country who have ties to families in other countries. Monetary and in-kind gifts are sent in both directions, and the monetary transfers show up in the balance of payments. U.S. corporations and philanthropic institutions also make charitable contributions overseas. Other transfers result from the grants and aid that the U.S. government makes to foreign countries, most of it in the form of military assistance. In 1992 these transfers were substantial, a net outflow of $33 billion from the United States.

**The Current-
Account Deficit**

When the net balances of all these different items that affect income are added to the trade balance, the resulting figure is called the balance of payments on the current account, or just the current account:

$$\text{Current-account balance} = \begin{array}{l} \text{Balance of merchandise trade} + \\ \text{Balance of services trade} + \\ \text{Net investment income} + \\ \text{Net transfers} \end{array}$$

The current-account balance is reported regularly, along with the balance of merchandise and services trade, and these figures give a good indication of whether the U.S. economy overall is generating a positive or negative flow of income in its foreign activities.

Table 7–1 shows the U.S. Department of Commerce's current-account and figures for 1970, 1980, and 1992. In 1970, the balance of trade was in surplus, as was the current account. The nation exported $2.6 billion more to the rest of the world than it imported. The trade balance in services was very small. The United States transferred a little more than $6 billion net to the rest of the world, but it earned a little more than $6 billion on its foreign investment. In 1970, the balance of trade and the balance of payments were not seriously affecting income in the United States.

By 1980, the level of trade activity had increased and its composition had changed. The U.S. economy had switched from being a net exporter to being a net importer of merchandise. There was a deficit in merchandise trade (−$25.5 billion) and surplus in services trade ($6.1 billion) but an outflow of transfers (−8.3 billion). These deficits were offset by a substantial positive balance of investment income (+$30 billion), to give a positive current-account balance of $2.3 billion. By these measures, firms, households, and institutions in the United States purchased more from the world than they sold, but they more than paid for their excess purchases with income earned on foreign investments.

By 1992, foreign-investment income was no longer able to finance the rapidly rising level of net imports and large foreign transfers. The current account had swung into a substantial balance of payments deficit on current account of $66.4 billion. The main cause of the swing was the huge increase in the deficit on merchandise trade. American consumers preferred and demanded imported goods to a greater degree than ever before in the 20th century. Net investment income had become very small because foreigners had been investing heavily in U.S. assets. There has been a major

TABLE 7–1
The U.S. Current Account, 1970, 1980, and 1992 (billions of dollars)

	1970	1980	1992
Balance of merchandise trade	2.6	−25.5	−96.1
Balance of services trade	−0.3	6.1	56.4
Net investment income	6.2	30.1	6.2
Net transfers	−6.2	− 8.3	−32.9
Current account balance	2.3	2.3	−66.4

The Balance of Payments on Capital Account

We saw earlier that exports and imports of goods and services are recorded in the balance of payments on the current account. There is a similar account for asset flows called the *balance of payments on the* **capital account,** which is also called simply the *capital account.* The table below shows the capital account for the United States in 1970, 1980, and 1992. Comparing the balances on current account in Table 7–1 with the balances on capital account in the table below reveals that these balances add to zero. This is true in principle, because the inflows of goods and services and income to the U.S. economy represented by a current-account deficit have to be paid for by an outflow of dollars. To pay for the excess inflows of foreign goods and services reflected in the current-account deficit, there have to be sales of assets to the world economies in excess of purchases of assets from the world economies. *The deficit in the current account is balanced by a surplus in the U.S. capital account.*

Balance of Payments on Capital Account—1970, 1980, 1992 (billions of dollars)

	1970	1980	1992
Purchases of U.S.-owned assets held abroad [outflow (−)]	−9.3	−87.0	−51.0
Purchases of Foreign-owned assets held in U.S. [inflow (+)]	7.2	59.3	129.6
Statistical discrepancy	−0.2	25.4	−12.2
Balance on capital account	−2.3	− 2.3	66.4

Look at the relationship between the capital account and the current account in the United States in 1992. The current-account balance was a deficit of $66.4 billion. The sum of net private foreign investment and net foreign-government investment of $66.4 billion is by definition equal to the amount by which the U.S. economy ran a current-account deficit with the rest of the world.

U.S. private investment overseas represents an increase in the holdings of foreign assets by U.S. residents. It is a positive item in our national wealth. In the capital account, however, this capital flow is shown with a negative sign, because it represents the dollars supplied by U.S. investors in exchange for foreign currency used to purchase the foreign assets—an outflow of U.S. dollars to buy foreign capital (i.e., an outflow of U.S. capital).

Foreign private investment in the U.S. rose very rapidly in the 1980s, but has fallen somewhat since then.

The mix between long-term and short-term investments is different for foreigners investing in the United States than for private U.S. investment overseas. Traditionally, U.S. companies established products, brand names, and production technology within the United States and then engaged in *direct foreign investment*—setting up production facilities abroad to make and sell Ford cars, IBM computers, or Kellogg's corn flakes in overseas markets. Foreigners did relatively less direct foreign investment and purchased U.S. assets by buying short-term bonds in the United States. In the late 1980s, this pattern started to change as more foreign companies bought out U.S. companies or set up subsidiaries here.

The remainder of the capital-account balance—the remainder of the way in which the U.S. economy paid for its deficit—came from the large level of U.S. assets, (mostly financial securities and much of it Treasury bills and bonds) held by foreign governments. The governments of our trading partners financed our excess imports by purchasing U.S. financial securities.

Changes in foreign assets held by governments show that governments participate actively in current markets. Foreign-exchange intervention occurs as central banks conduct foreign-exchange open-market operations. They buy and sell foreign currencies in the exchange markets by increasing or decreasing their reserves of foreign-currency assets. In the 1980s there was very active intervention in foreign currency markets by foreign central banks, and, on occasion by the U.S. Fed. In 1987, for example, foreign central banks added over $45 billion to their U.S. dollar assets in an attempt to stabilize the value of the dollar.

Notice, however, one additional item in the capital accounts: the "statistical discrepancy." This item is very large in some years and warns us that much foreign currency trading occurs outside of the formal currency markets.

change in the international economic relationship between the U.S. economy and the economies of the rest of the world.

When the current account is in surplus, as it was in the United States in 1980, the nation is generating more income from its export sales and its foreign investments than it is paying out for imports and as returns to foreign investors. In the aggregate, international economic activities contribute to raising national income in any economy that is running a surplus on its current-account balance of payments. When the current account is in deficit (as it was in the United States after 1981), the nation is generating less income from its export sales and its foreign investments than it is paying out for imports and as returns to foreign investors. Overall, in an economy with a balance of payments deficit, the impact of the foreign sector on income is negative. Of course, this does not mean that the economy that is running a balance of payments deficit would be better off without trade, since consumers and firms benefited from their purchases of imported goods and services. Any artificial restrictions that might be placed on the import of foreign goods and services or the export of capital would raise the costs of acquiring comparable products and services along with increasing the cost of borrowing capital.

We have seen in the tabulation of the current account that foreign trade in goods services, flow of investment income, and transfers all involve foreign exchange as Americans buy Japanese cars or Japanese tourists visit Hawaii. There is another important ingredient in foreign exchange created by the purchases and sales of foreign assets.

INTERNATIONAL FINANCIAL ASSETS AND THE EXCHANGE RATE

Foreign currency is bought and sold to buy or sell foreign assets. U.S. companies and individuals buy foreign assets for much the same reasons as they hold domestic assets—they are balancing expected returns and anticipated risks. For example, some U.S. pension funds include foreign stocks and bonds in their portfolio of assets. U.S. multinational companies purchase factories and office buildings overseas. Pension-fund managers and multinational corporate treasurers may think that the returns to foreign assets are higher than the return to U.S. assets, or they may think that the overall risk of their portfolio of assets is reduced by diversifying and including foreign assets. Similarly, foreigners purchase U.S. assets, such as U.S. government securities, real estate in New York or Los Angeles, or factories in Ohio. All of these transactions involve foreign exchange. For example, a Japanese insurance company may decide to purchase an office building in Los Angeles. It deposits funds in yen into an account in a Japanese bank and the bank then arranges to exchange the amount in yen and transfer it into a deposit in a dollar account in a U.S. bank. These funds in dollars are then used to purchase the building. Because international investors require foreign exchange, international buyers and sellers of assets participate in foreign-exchange markets along with importers and exporters of goods and services.

In this section we examine the way in which international flows of capital are affected by interest rates and expectations about future exchange rates.

International Interest Rates and Expectations

Individuals and institutions that manage portfolios of assets look for the best combination of risk and return they can find. If the best opportunities are from buying financial assets in another country, then this is what they will do. Similarly, companies with profits to reinvest will weigh the returns from building a new factory at home against the returns from buying out a foreign company or expanding one they already own.

When people or companies hold foreign assets, there is an extra source of possible gain or loss, over and above the rate of interest or rate of profit earned by the asset itself. The extra risk comes from fluctuations in the exchange rate of the currencies involved. Gains or losses in the value of a foreign asset can be reversed or increased by changes in currency values, even when there is no change in the economic performance of the asset.

Consider specifically the return to holding a foreign financial asset, such as a government or commercial bond. The return on the bond will depend on the interest earned and on the future value of the bond when converted back to domestic currency. Since the rate of conversion that will apply to the future payments of interest and principal is the future exchange rate, the decision to purchase a foreign asset is affected by both the interest rate earned on the asset and expectations about the future value of the exchange rate.

The Interest Parity Condition and Capital Flows

Suppose an investor in the United States is considering buying a two-year bond. She could buy a German bond with an interest rate of 7 percent or a U.S. bond with an interest rate of 5 percent. Because the German interest rate is higher than the U.S. rate, it would seem to be an attractive opportunity to buy the German bond. However, she also believes that the German mark is very high and expects it to decline against the dollar over the next several years. Suppose the mark were expected to decline by 2 percent a year for the next two years. In this case, the U.S. investor would do no better by buying the German bond than she would by buying the U.S. bond. The interest-rate advantage of 2 percent for the German bond is just canceled out by the expected decline of 2 percent per year in the exchange rate of the DM versus the dollar. In this case, the investor would be indifferent between the two bonds.

The situation in which international investors are just indifferent among similar type bonds in different countries is both important and not at all unusual. It is described formally as the **interest parity condition,** and is shown below in Equation 7–1:[2]

interest parity condition
Holds, when the difference between foreign and domestic interest rate is just equal to the expected rate of change of the exchange rate.

$$r_{foreign} - r_{domestic} = \text{Exp}\,(\Delta rex/rex) \qquad\qquad 7\text{–}1$$

There is a tendency in international financial markets for interest rates and expected exchange rates to change in the direction of bringing about the interest parity condition. The interest parity condition will hold when investors, including large

---

[2] The condition given in Equation 7–1 shows the interest-rate differential as equal to the expected change in the *real* exchange rate; that is, the exchange rate adjusted for differences in inflation. In this case, we should also be talking about the *real* rates of interest, rates of interest that are also adjusted for inflation. We look at real interest rates in Chapter 8.

international companies, can choose freely where to place their funds around the world to earn the maximum return. If this condition does *not* hold, then investors will see higher returns in one country than in another and money will move—there will be **international capital flows** and these capital flows will work to bring interest rates and expected exchange rates closer to parity.

international capital flows
Funds from one country are changed into a foreign currency and used to purchase assets in another country.

In the example above, suppose the rate of interest in the United States were 7 percent, rather than 5 percent, and nothing else was different. Now there is no interest rate differential between the United States and Germany and yet the mark is expected to fall against the dollar. This will make U.S. bonds look more attractive than German bonds. Investors in Germany will buy U.S. bonds and there will be an international capital flow—a capital inflow to the United States.

International capital flows pass through the foreign-exchange market. If German or Japanese investors decide to buy U.S. bonds, as happened a lot in the 1980s, then they will supply marks and yen into the foreign-exchange market and demand dollars. *Capital inflows to the United States are a demand for dollars in the foreign-exchange market, and capital outflows are a supply of dollars.*

If the interest parity condition holds, then there is on balance no net incentive for capital to flow internationally. International investors may disagree among themselves about the likely changes in the exchange rate and hence there will probably be plenty of people moving money from one country to another. But when the interest parity condition holds, the international capital market is in equilibrium.

Changes in Interest Rates and Capital Flows   What happens, however, if there is a change in economic conditions? Specifically, suppose there is a change in the rate of interest in the United States. The interest parity condition had been satisfied, but now there is, for example, an increase in the U.S. interest rate. With no change in expectation about the future value of the exchange rate (holding the right hand side of Equation 7-1 constant), this will result in a capital inflow to the United States as U.S. bonds have become more attractive. *A change in the rate of interest in the United States will result in a change in the supply and demand conditions in the foreign-exchange market.* An increase in the U.S. interest rate reduces capital outflows and increases capital inflows; it raises the demand for dollars and lowers the supply of dollars.

Changes in Expectations and Capital Flows   The interest parity condition, Equation 7-1, also involves expectations of future movements in the exchange rate. If interest rates in the United States and overseas were to remain the same, but people became more optimistic about the value of the dollar in the future, then this would make U.S. bonds more attractive and induce a capital inflow to the United States.

The interest parity condition, therefore, tells us an important reason why there are large international capital flows. For the market to be in equilibrium there always has to be a balance between interest rate differences and expected exchange rate changes. When this balance is changed in any way, capital flows will occur until equilibrium is restored again.

Worked Example 7–2   Here we use a numerical example to show how the interest parity condition works and how changes in interest rates or expectations can lead to capital flows.

We now have examined how interest rates and expected future values of the exchange rate affect decisions to buy and sell foreign assets. We have seen in this and the preceding sections how trade flows and capital flows are affected by the exchange rate, by interest rates, and by the expected future exchange rate. *We are now going to refocus our discussion from one where the exchange rate affects trade and capital flows to one where capital flows, exports, and imports affect the exchange rate.* The supply of and demand for dollars in the foreign-exchange market are determined by trade and capital flows. Supply and demand then determine the exchange rate.

SUPPLY AND DEMAND IN THE FOREIGN-EXCHANGE MARKET

In foreign-exchange markets, currencies are traded at prices (exchange rates) that reflect supply and demand. The balance of trade and capital flows, both of which are affected by changes in the exchange rate, also contribute to determining the exchange rate.[3] The balances of trade and capital flows are also affected by fundamental economic factors, such as income, interest rates, and expectations. We will pull these factors together into a model of the foreign-exchange market.

We analyze the foreign-exchange market in terms of the supply of dollars being brought into the market by those wishing to purchase foreign currencies and the demand for dollars from those who are offering foreign currencies in exchange for dollars. Both the supply of and demand for dollars in the foreign-exchange market are derived from the demands for goods, services and assets that are involved in international transactions. From the U.S. vantage point, the supply of dollars is derived from the demand for foreign goods, services, and foreign assets by U.S. residents. From the foreign vantage point, the demand for dollars is derived from the demand for U.S. goods, services, and U.S. assets by foreign residents.

Equilibrium in the Foreign-Exchange Market

The exchange rates of the dollar against the currencies of America's major trading partners are determined in markets, where dollars are traded for yen and German marks and many other currencies. To maintain a manageable view of the foreign-exchange markets, we will assume a single consolidated market, where the value of the real exchange rate is determined by the total demand for and supply of dollars to be exchanged into all foreign currencies. This consolidated foreign-currency–exchange market is depicted in Figure 7–3. The supply of dollars rises with an

---

[3] Exchange rates are determined in foreign-exchange markets where the supplies of and demands for foreign exchanges are affected by a myriad of market forces. This characteristic of exchange rates makes the forecasting of changes in exchange rates subject to a very large degree of error. As a result of the inability of economists to forecast exchange rates, a recent body of research has emerged that argues that exchange-rate movements are indistinguishable from random events. (See Richard Meese, "Currency Fluctuations in the Post–Bretton Woods Era," *Journal of Economic Perspectives*, Winter 1990.) In this view, exchange rates are determined by everything and, therefore, by no individual factor in particular. This work highlights the complexity of the foreign-exchange market, and points to the conclusion that exchange rates reflect the impact of a host of international factors.

Exchange-Rate Risk and Foreign Assets

Consider a Japanese insurance company that bought a Los Angeles office building in 1985, expecting to take advantage of the real estate boom in southern California. In 1985 the dollar/yen exchange rate was approximately 250 yen to the dollar. If the Japanese investors looked at their investment in 1994, they would find that each dollar's worth of investment would only purchase about 100 yen in foreign-exchange markets. Even if the real estate market in Los Angeles turned out to be a booming market, doubling the dollar value of the same building in nine years, the building would be worth less in yen than

it was when it was purchased. A 100 percent appreciation of the value of the asset for a domestic investor would have netted a 20 percent loss to the foreign investor.

Even if the building was bought to be held for many years, rather than to be sold, and no account recognition was made of the changes in the market value of the office building, the Japanese insurance company would still suffer from the immediate effect of the decline in the dollar, because the flow of rental income from the property and the future value of leases would be much less in yen in 1994 than they were in 1985.

Foreign investments carry a significant currency risk, prompting many investors to hedge against risk using what are called derivatives.

FIGURE 7–3
Supply and Demand, the Real Exchange Rate, and the Foreign-Exchange Market

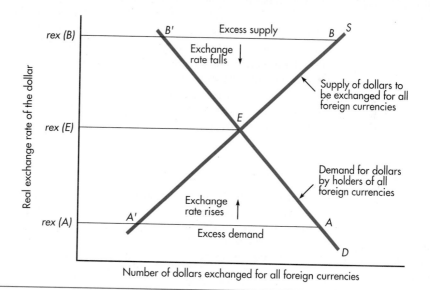

Number of dollars exchanged for all foreign currencies

increase in the real exchange rate, because imports in general become less expensive to U.S. residents. The demand for dollars by foreigners falls with an increase in the real exchange rate, because U.S. goods become more expensive to foreign residents. The equilibrium real exchange rate is determined at point *E*, where the schedules intersect. When there is excess supply of dollars or excess demand for dollars, then the exchange rate adjusts.

Changes in the Exchange Rate

Glancing at the financial pages of the newspaper over a time will reveal that exchange rates change frequently. Figure 7–1 showed there were large and sustained shifts in the real exchange rate of the dollar in the 1970s and 1980s. The direct causes of movements in the exchange rate come from shifts of supply and demand in the foreign-exchange market.

The demand for dollars by the rest of the world depends on the worldwide demand for U.S. goods and U.S. assets. Increases in the demand for either U.S. goods or assets will generate an outward shift in the demand for dollars. The supply of dollars is derived from the demand for foreign goods and assets; increases in either will be reflected in an outward shift of the supply of dollars. We describe the working of the foreign-exchange market by looking at the major sources of shifts of supply and demand. As a guide to the discussion, the connections between the domestic and foreign demands for goods and assets and the supply and demand for foreign exchange are summarized in Table 7–2. Up until this point in this chapter, we have assumed constant income, both at home and abroad, but we are now changing that assumption. In the table and in the discussion that follows, we are introducing changes in income into the analysis of the foreign-exchange market.

The Exchange Rate and Income

A rise in income in the United States generates an increase in the demand for imports (see Chapter 3). Since American customers want to purchase more foreign goods, they also increase their demand for foreign currencies. In the foreign-exchange market, more dollars are offered in order to purchase more foreign exchange. The effect of a unilateral increase in U.S. income on the foreign-exchange market is shown in Figure 7–4 as an outward shift in the supply schedule (S to S'). At the initial exchange rate, *rex (E),* the increase in U.S. income has increased the demand for imports and, therefore, increased (shifted) the supply of dollars being offered for foreign currencies. Since in this example there has been no change in the income of other countries,

TABLE 7–2

Changes in the Exchange Rate: Shifting the Supply of and Demand for Dollars

Factors affecting the supply schedule of dollars in the foreign exchange market:
　Outward shifts in the supply of U.S. dollars are derived from:
　　Increases in the demand for imports which are derived from:
　　　Increases in U.S. income.
　　Increases in the demand for foreign capital, real or financial, which are derived from:
　　　Increases in foreign interest rates and/or
　　　Decreases in the expected future value of the dollar.

Factors affecting the demand schedule for dollars in the foreign exchange market:
　Outward shifts in the demand for dollars are derived from:
　　Increases in the demand for exports, which are derived from:
　　　Increases in income in the rest of the world.
　　Increases in the demand for U.S. capital, real or financial, which are derived from:
　　　Increases in U.S. interest rates and/or
　　　Increases in the expected future value of the dollar

FIGURE 7–4
Income and
Exchange Rate

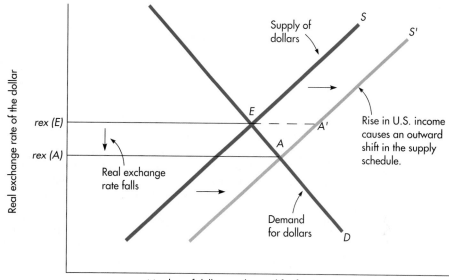

An increase in U.S. income leads to a fall in the real exchange rate.

the demand for dollars has not shifted. There is an excess supply of dollars (point A′ − point E) and the real exchange rate will fall.

The falling exchange rate makes imports more expensive, partially offsetting the increase in imports and hence partially offsetting the increased supply of dollars. And the fall in the exchange rate also increases the demand for U.S. exports and hence increases the demand for dollars by foreign buyers. The new equilibrium is established at point A.

The result of a rise in the level of U.S. income is a reduction in the real exchange rate of the U.S. dollar (ignoring other possible changes in the economy). And the process works in the opposite direction, also—*a fall in income in the United States will lead to a rise in the value of the dollar,* as U.S. residents cut their purchases of all goods, including foreign goods, and hence supply fewer dollars in the foreign-exchange markets.

The Exchange Rate and Capital Flows

Capital inflows and outflows have, especially in recent years, provided billions of dollars that flow through the foreign-exchange markets and affect exchange rates. Our analysis of these capital flows has been based on the interest parity condition given in Equation 7-1.

Interest Rates and the Exchange Rate   A change in the interest rate differential will affect the exchange rate. For example, if the differential changes because there is an increase in rates of interest in the United States that is unmatched by interest-rate changes in the other major economies, foreign investors will sell assets denominated

FIGURE 7–5
The Impact of U.S.
Interest Rates on
the Exchange Rate

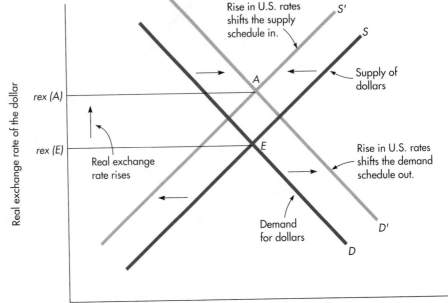

An increase in U.S. interest rates that raises the differential with foreign rates will increase the exchange rate.

in foreign currencies, buy dollars, and then buy U.S. assets. In Figure 7–5 this is shown as an outward shift in the demand for dollars (D to D'). At the same time, American investors will reduce or eliminate their purchases of foreign assets and in so doing bring fewer dollars to the market, seeking to exchange them for foreign currencies. This is shown as an inward shift in the supply of dollars (from S to S'). Both of these changes in behavior will raise the value of the dollar.

The impact of changes in interest rates on the dollar has been found to be very powerful, particularly in the mid-1980s when fiscal and monetary policy drove up U.S. rates. High interests rates in the United States attracted foreign investors and their demand for the dollar kept the real exchange rate high.

Expectations and the Exchange Rate   Changing economic circumstances lead to changed expectations about the future value of the dollar. There are many possible events that could change expectations. For example, predictions that U.S. manufacturers were losing their ability to develop new products might lead to the expectation of a reduced capacity to export and hence to the expectation of a lower future dollar-exchange rate. Or, a positive development, such as the discovery of a giant oil field in Alaska, might lead to the expectation of reduced oil imports and a higher expected value of the dollar.

For a given interest-rate differential, international financial markets are in equilibrium with a particular expected rate of appreciation or devaluation of each currency. (Recall the interest parity condition.) But if that expectation is altered, the interest-rate differential no longer makes up for expected changes in currency values and, in practice, large movements of capital around the world are generated because of changes in expectations.

For some given expectation about the future value of the dollar, an increase in today's value of the dollar has the effect of lowering the expected rate of increase of the dollar in the future. As the dollar rises, the market reaches a point where the rise in the current value of the dollar has a sufficient negative effect on the expected rate of appreciation of the dollar that expected returns are once again equalized between U.S. assets and assets in other currencies; the interest parity condition (Equation 7-1) holds once again.

Thus, for a given interest-rate differential, a change in the expected future value of the dollar will change the current value of the dollar until the expected rate of appreciation or depreciation has been restored and this has then restored the equality of expected returns to interest-bearing assets held in different currencies.

Interest Rates, Expectations, and Market Equilibrium   We have looked at the separate effects of changes in income, interest rates and changes in expectations about the exchange rate. In general, these things will be changing together. In particular, a change in the interest-rate differential between the United States and other countries will lead to capital inflows or outflows, to a change in the current exchange rate, and to a change in the expected rate of appreciation or depreciation of the dollar. For example, an increase in the U.S. rate of interest will cause a capital inflow to the United States that raises the current value of the dollar. As the current value of the dollar increases, people look at the likely future value of the dollar and decide that the expected rate of appreciation of the dollar has been reduced. The increase in the dollar today, means that there will be a smaller rate of capital gain in the future. International capital-market equilibrium will hold once again after the increase in the U.S. interest rate with a wider interest-rate differential between the United States and other countries and a smaller expected rate of increase in the dollar (or a larger expected rate of decrease).

The interest-rate differential between the United States and other countries did indeed widen in the 1980s, leading to capital inflows into the United States and a rising dollar. Gradually, the possibility of a dollar decline became greater, until in mid-1985 concern about the value of the dollar became strong enough to overcome the higher interest return to U.S. assets. The capital inflow began to slow and the dollar started to fall. The expectations of a fall in the dollar that had been building up were then realized and there was a continuing reduction in the real exchange rate of the dollar over the next three years.

In this chapter we have looked at how changes in prices and interest rates affect imports, exports, capital flows, and the exchange rate. In the rest of this chapter we apply what we have discovered about the working of foreign-exchange markets in order to extend our analysis of macroeconomic policies and the determination of equilibrium income in an open economy.

MACROECONOMIC POLICY IN AN OPEN ECONOMY

Aggregate income, interest rates, exchange rates, and inflation are all affected by the international economy. In the remainder of this chapter we continue the discussion of trade and capital movements and incorporate them into the analysis of income determination. In addition, we look at how monetary and fiscal policies operate in an open economy. Monetary and fiscal policies can change the trade balance and the exchange rate, which, in turn, influence the effectiveness of these policies in changing interest rates, employment, output, and inflation. Our analysis of macroeconomic policy is based on the current set of international monetary arrangements, which include the current system of fluctuating exchange rates that has been in place since 1971–73.

We start by reviewing the results of the simple income and expenditure model (introduced in Chapter 3) where exports add to demand and imports subtract from demand, assuming no changes in the exchange rate. We then describe the role of exchange-rate changes in determining equilibrium.

Aggregate Demand in an International Economy

Aggregate demand in an open economy is just the total of purchases by U.S. residents (regardless of where the goods originated) plus net exports:

$$Y = C + I + G + X - IM \qquad\qquad 7\text{--}2$$

To see how the foreign sector influences the level of income in the U.S. economy, we need to look at the determinants of net exports, just as we looked at the determinants of consumption and investment demand.

In the simple exposition offered in Chapter 3, we started out with an autonomously determined level of exports. On the import side, we assumed that a rise in domestic income raises overall expenditures, causing both the domestic and foreign components of consumption and investment to increase. This meant that imports increased as a result of a rise in income. The fact that imports rise when domestic income rises means that, with exports and the exchange rate fixed, *net exports decline as the level of income rises.*

Net exports are part of aggregate demand in the domestic economy, so a change in income will have a feedback effect on aggregate demand and income. The foreign sector, like consumption and investment, is influenced by income and also helps to determine income. When net exports are positive, the foreign sector provides a net addition to aggregate demand. Negative net exports are a net subtraction from demand.

We saw in Chapter 3 that the multiplier is smaller in an open economy than in a closed one. In an open economy, the increase in imports that occurs as income rises means that any increase in aggregate demand will leak partly into increased imports. Goods that are purchased from overseas do not generate increases in production and employment here in the United States, so the wage and profit income resulting from the production of these goods is not U.S. income. Imports are leakages like taxes or saving, in that they mitigate the multiplier effect of a given stimulus to income.

Goods-Market Equilibrium with a Foreign Sector   The *IS* schedule describes the combinations of the level of income and the long-term real interest rate that ensure goods-market equilibrium—where output equals aggregate demand. In an open economy, this *IS* schedule describes the same relationship as it does in a closed economy except that the foreign-trade multiplier is smaller than the multiplier in a closed economy. Therefore, taking the exchange rate as given, a reduction in the long-term rate of interest may generate the same initial increase in investment expenditure as in a closed economy but, because of import leakages, the increase in income is smaller. This means that, *with a given exchange rate, goods-market equilibrium in an open economy will be described by an IS schedule that has a steeper slope than the IS schedule that describes the goods market in a closed economy.*

Recall that the slope of the *IS* schedule has implications for policy. For example, monetary policy works by changing interest rates, which induces a change in investment and income. The effectiveness of monetary policy depends on the size of the interest-rate effect—the interest-rate responsiveness of expenditure changes as described by the slope of the *IS* schedule.

As well as affecting the economy's responsiveness to interest-rate changes, the foreign-trade sector can also affect the level of aggregate demand (shift the *IS* schedule). To illustrate, if U.S. firms are successful in bringing to market innovations in products that appeal to foreign customers, those innovations would increase the foreign demand for U.S. goods. Assuming no change in the exchange rate, U.S. exports will increase. And this will raise the level of autonomous expenditure. Figure 7–6 shows the effect of this increase in autonomous expenditure as a shift of the *IS* schedule from *IS* to *IS'*. As a result of an increase in foreign demand for U.S. exports, aggregate demand has increased. If the money supply is unchanged following the changes in export demand, the increase in export demand would raise income and the interest rate. As shown in Figure 7–6, the economy would move from point *A* to point *B*.

In the actual economy, changes in international economic conditions are seldom restricted to changes in the foreign demand for U.S. exports. Interest rates and exchange rates are likely to change as income and trade flows change. However, the effect of changes in the exchange rate on imports and exports can be slow in coming. A change in the exchange rate that is short-lived (i.e., the rate goes up for only a few months and then returns to its previous level) is not likely to have a marked effect on the flow of trade. To study the effects of the foreign sector within the *IS–LM* framework, we will use an *IS* schedule that is based on a fixed value for the level of exports and a given import function. *Shifts in net exports that are related to sustained changes in the exchange rate are shown as causing shifts of the IS schedule.*

A decrease in the exchange rate will eventually lead to a decrease in imports and an increase in exports. This means that *a sustained decrease in the exchange rate will cause the IS schedule to shift to the right.* Similarly, a sustained rise in the exchange rate shifts the IS schedule to the left.

FIGURE 7–6
The Impact of
Increasing Exports

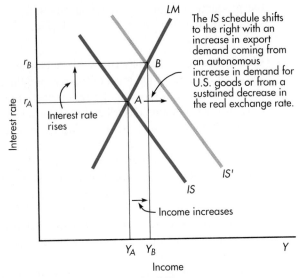

The *IS* schedule shifts
to the right with an
increase in export
demand coming from
an autonomous
increase in demand for
U.S. goods or from a
sustained decrease in
the real exchange rate.

Rising export demand shifts the *IS* schedule to the right.

Money-Market Equilibrium with a Foreign Sector   In an economy where goods, services, and financial capital are traded internationally, financial markets are affected by international market conditions, not just domestic conditions. Interest rates here in the United States are affected by interest rates overseas, with the effect of the international sector occurring primarily through the demand for money and other financial assets.

In terms of the *supply of money,* the Fed can still exercise control, if it chooses to do so. The Fed and the U.S. banking system, which is controlled by the Fed, are the only agencies that can supply U.S. money (money that can be used to make transactions in the United States). Of course, foreigners can go into the foreign-exchange market and buy dollars, but only by finding someone else willing to exchange those dollars. The foreign-exchange market allows dollars to be traded at varying exchange rates, but it cannot create dollars. *Fundamentally, therefore, even in an open economy, the Fed can maintain its control over the U.S. money supply.*

Even though the Fed can control the U.S. money supply, the ability of corporate cash managers to move money across international borders affects *money demand* and the nature of money-market equilibrium. The cash manager balances liquidity (given a firm's need for cash for transactions) against the return on T bills or other interest-bearing assets. In an open economy, cash managers can substitute foreign-currency assets for T bills. Although holding foreign assets usually involves greater risks because of exchange-rate fluctuations, if the return earned on the foreign assets is large enough, it will induce some cash managers to increase their holding of foreign assets and decrease their holdings of T bills. For example, a fall in short-term U.S. interest rates not matched by a similar fall in short-term foreign rates will make bills or notes denominated in foreign exchange look more attractive.

FIGURE 7–7
Money-Market
Equilibrium and
Foreign Interest
Rates

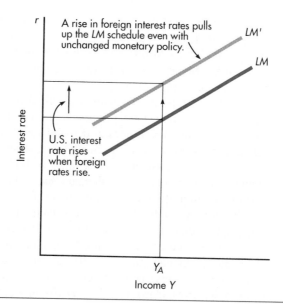

This same argument works for the counterpart to the cash manager in a foreign firm. Japanese corporate treasurers may hold a portfolio including U.S.-government T bills. A fall in the U.S. short-term nominal interest rate causes the Japanese cash manager to shift out of these U.S. assets and seek alternatives, including yen-denominated assets.

Because cash managers here and overseas can shift their portfolios into or out of U.S. T bills, U.S. money demand and hence financial-market equilibrium in the United States (as shown by the position of the *LM* schedule) will shift if foreign interest rates change. For example, if the interest rate on short-term Japanese government bills rises, then some cash managers will decide to reduce their holdings of U.S. T bills and increase their holdings of Japanese short-term assets. To bring the U.S. money market back into equilibrium, the interest rate on U.S. T bills will rise, too. This is shown as a shift from *LM* to *LM'* in Figure 7–7. At a given level of income, Y_A, the short-term interest rate will rise in the United States when foreign short-term rates rise. *There is an international transmission of interest movements that results from international capital flows.* The effect on the money market of an increase in foreign interest rates is shown as an upward shift of the *LM* schedule.

We have just said that there is an international transmission of interest rates, so, when foreign interest rates change, this leads to changes in U.S. rates (the *LM* schedule shifts). But the spillover from foreign interest rates to U.S. interest rates should not be overemphasized—the shifts in the *LM* schedule are not very great. One reason for this is that, when foreign interest rates change, a large part of the impact on the U.S. economy consists of changes in the dollar-exchange rate. A rise in rates of interest overseas will lead to a net capital outflow from the United States and a decline in the value of the dollar, as we saw earlier. *A change in the differential between the*

United States and foreign interest rates will change both the current value of the dollar and the expected rate of change of the dollar, as well as U.S. interest rates. The interest parity condition will be achieved partly by a change in the interest rate here in the United States and partly by a change in the expected rate of appreciation or depreciation of the dollar.

When we represent the economy with *IS* and *LM* schedules, we must take account of the fact that both money markets and goods markets are affected by the international economy. The domestic demand for goods and services is less responsive to changes in interest rates (*IS* schedule is steeper) because, for example, an increase in U.S. income or a fall in interest rates, or both, will raise the level of imports. That reduces the rise in aggregate demand that would have otherwise occurred. Changes in export and import demand can be the result of domestic or international recessions or booms or they can be the result of a change in the exchange rate of the dollar against other currencies, all of which affect the demand for U.S. goods and services.

If foreign interest rates change, this will have a direct, though small, effect on the U.S. money market (the *LM* schedule) because of the international transmission of interest movements that we described above. More importantly, *changes in either U.S. or foreign interest rates will upset the interest parity condition, encourage capital inflows or outflows, and lead to a change in the U.S. exchange rate.*

The analysis of equilibrium in an open economy is more complex than in a closed economy, and we are going to go over two of the more important situations where changes in the international economy affect domestic output, jobs, and interest rates. We start by looking at the effect of an increase in the demand for U.S. exports.

Increased Export Demand

An exogenous increase in export demand could have come about as a result of an increase in foreign income or a reduction in foreign-government restrictions (tariffs and trade barriers) on imports. Initially, an increase in export demand is like any other increase in autonomous expenditure—it will raise income and raise the interest rate. Imports will rise as the level of income rises, but, except under very unusual circumstances, imports will not rise by as much as the initial increase in export demand. So an increase in export demand will raise net exports, also. Since the increase in export demand has raised both interest rates and net exports, the result will certainly be an increase in the value of the dollar.

Over time, the increase in the value of the dollar will reduce exports and increase imports. This will reduce income and gradually eliminate the increase in net exports. An exogenous increase in export demand will gradually set off a self-correcting response (the rise in the dollar) that will tend to restore the original level of income and restore the original level of net exports. This adjustment process is shown in Figure 7–8. The economy is pictured initially at point *A* (the intersection of *IS* and *LM*). There is then an increase in export demand and this pushes the *IS* schedule out to *IS'*. The economy is now at point *B* and the level of income and the rate of interest are both higher. (Y_B is higher than Y_A, and r_B is higher than r_A.) Over time, the increase in the exchange rate reduces net exports, and hence the aggregate demand for goods and services. (The *IS* schedule drifts back to the left.) This is shown by the dashed lines in Figure 7–8. Eventually, the *IS* schedule will go back close to its original position. The

FIGURE 7–8
The Effect of an Exogenous Increase in Export Demand

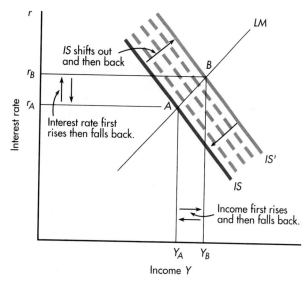

An increase in export demand is expansionary. But the dollar rises and reverses the initial impact.

exchange rate will remain higher in the long run, provided the factors that led to the initial increase in foreign demand for U.S. exports are sustained. *The long-run effect of a sustained increase in the demand for U.S. exports is that there will be little or no change in income or the interest rate in the United States. There will be an increase in the value of the dollar.*

A Rise in Foreign Interest Rates

In our analysis of a closed economy we found that interest rates change in reaction to changes in the goods market or the U.S. money market. The effects of changing market conditions on interest rates were described by shifts in the *IS* or the *LM* schedules. In an open economy there can be changes in interest rates even in the absence of changes in domestic conditions. There is an international transmission of interest rates that has an effect on domestic income. For instance, a rise in foreign interest rates will send capital out of the U.S. financial market and drive up U.S. interest rates, thereby affecting domestic aggregate demand. In Figure 7–9 we show the effect of such a foreign interest-rate increase through an upward shift in the *LM* schedule, from *LM* to *LM'*. Income falls from Y_A to Y_B as the rise in U.S. interest rates discourages domestic investment (the *LM* slides along the given *IS* schedule).

This is not the end of the story, however. So far we have looked at the effect of an increase in foreign interest rates on U.S. interest rates, while ignoring the impact on the U.S. exchange rate. When foreign interest rates rise, this will lead not only to some rise in U.S. interest rates but it will also change the international interest differential and lower the value of the dollar. The rise in foreign interest rates (which makes foreign assets more attractive) generates a capital outflow that lowers the exchange rate. If the rise in foreign rates is sustained, the fall in the dollar will increase our exports and decrease our imports. This response in the goods market to a change in the

FIGURE 7–9
The Impact of a
Rise in Foreign
Interest Rates

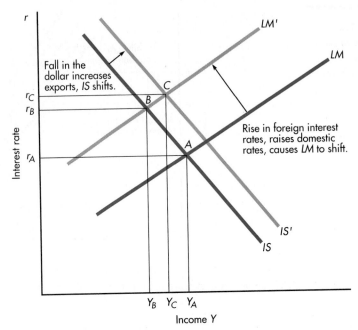

In this illustrative example, income is shown falling from Y_A to Y_B and then rising part way, to end up at Y_C.

exchange rate is shown as a rightward shift of the *IS* schedule (*IS* to *IS'*). Over the longer run, the initial negative impact on U.S. income of the increase of foreign rates is offset by the subsequent positive impact on income of the fall in the dollar. As income first falls back and then rises, the U.S. interest rate will rise further (to r_C in the figure).

Given the size of the U.S. economy, the impact on U.S. income from foreign interest-rate changes is likely to be fairly small. Nevertheless, when the changes are large enough, the effects may be more important. In 1992, German interest rates rose to very high levels as a result of government expenditures associated with German reunification. Interest rates rose in Germany and in other European countries as their monetary authorities reacted to events in Germany. The rise in rates made German and other European bonds attractive relative to U.S. bonds. There have been international capital flows coming to the United States for several years, but the rise in foreign interest rates tended to reduce these capital inflows to the United States. This, in turn, pushed down the value of the dollar exchange rate and helped to keep U.S. interest rates higher than they would have been otherwise.

Having seen a couple of ways in which events happening overseas can affect the U.S. economy, we turn now to see how policymaking in the United States is affected by the international economy.

Domestic Macroeconomic Policies in an Open Economy

The effects of domestic macroeconomic policy in an open economy are different from the effects in a closed economy—sometimes the foreign sector reinforces and sometimes the foreign sector works against policy actions.[4] Increases in aggregate demand that raise interest rates will cause capital inflows, changes in the exchange rate, and reductions in the balance of trade, all of which alter the effectiveness of policy actions.

Monetary Expansion and Capital Flows Expansionary monetary policy is designed to stimulate aggregate demand and the impact of a monetary-policy action on equilibrium is affected by the openness of the economy to international markets. First, the goods market is less interest-rate responsive in an open economy than in a closed economy. (The *IS* schedule is steeper.) A given decline in the interest rate induced by monetary policy has less of an effect on income in an open economy. Second, in an open economy, a reduction in the rate of interest also reduces the real exchange rate. The fall in the rate of interest changes the interest-rate differential between foreign and domestic financial assets. Financial managers will readjust their portfolios to hold more foreign assets and fewer domestic assets. This causes capital outflows, which reduce the real exchange rate. Initially, the lower real exchange rate will have little effect on the real volumes of exports and imports. Over time, however, net exports rise, adding to the increase in aggregate demand.

To summarize: Monetary policy has a different impact on income in a closed, rather than in an open economy. A monetary expansion lowers the rate of interest, which stimulates capital expenditures that in turn generate a multiplier process of increased aggregate demand. However, because of changes in the exchange rate and the international interest-rate differential, the story of the short-term effects of a monetary expansion in an open economy is somewhat different from the story in a closed economy. One difference makes monetary policy less effective (steeper *IS* schedule). But the second difference is more important over time. A monetary policy action also changes the exchange rate. *In an open economy, in the intermediate run, monetary policy becomes a stronger instrument for controlling income, because it works not only as a result of changing investment demand but also through changing the exchange rate and hence net exports.* This conclusion about the strengthening of monetary policy is one of the most important results obtained from the analysis of macroeconomic policy in an open economy.

---

[4] The basic framework for studying policy in an open economy is known as the Mundell-Fleming model. Robert Mundell, "Capital Mobility and Stabilization under Fixed and Flexible Exchange Rates," *Canadian Journal of Economics,* November 1963; and Marcus Fleming, "Domestic Financial Policies under Fixed and Floating Exchange Rates," *IMF Staff Papers,* November 1962. This framework has been extended by many authors since then. See, for example, Rudiger Dornbusch, *Open Economy Macroeconomics* (New York: Basic Books, 1980); John Campbell and Richard Clarida, "The Dollar and the Real Interest Rate," *Carnegie Rochester Conference Series* (Amsterdam: North Holland, 1987); Ralph Bryant et al., eds., *Empirical Macroeconomics for International Economies* (Washington D.C.: Brookings Institution, 1988); Paul de Grauwe, *International Money, Postwar Trends and Theories* (Oxford, England: Oxford University Press, 1989).

We look at this policy conclusion by starting with an economy producing at less than potential output. In Figure 7–10A, the *IS–LM* intersection (point *A*) describes an economy in a recession (Y_A). The Fed initiates a monetary expansion to stimulate aggregate demand and increase income, illustrated by an outward shift of the *LM* schedule (*LM* to *LM'*). The fall in the rate of interest will increase investment demand and hence income. (The economy is shown moving from *A* to *B*.)

Even before the fall in the interest rate has led to a change in income, there are effects in the foreign-exchange market. The drop in U.S. short-term interest rates starts a capital outflow. As dollar-denominated assets are sold and foreign-dominated assets are purchased, this increases the supply of dollars and reduces the demand. (*S* to *S'* and *D* to *D'* in Figure 7–10B). As a result, the real exchange rate falls (point *A* to point *B* in Figure 7–10B).

Over time, the fall of the real exchange rate works to improve the balance of trade, further stimulating aggregate demand, and reinforcing the effectiveness of monetary policy. In Figure 7–11A, the effect on aggregate demand of an improved balance of trade is pictured as an outward shift of the *IS* schedule (*IS* to *IS'*). The economy has moved to a higher level of income (Y_C is greater than Y_B) with some recovery of interest rates (r_C is greater than r_B but r_C is still lower than r_A) as the economy expanded.

In the foreign-exchange market, there has been some recovery of the value of the dollar. An increase in exports raises the demand for dollars, an effect that is reinforced

FIGURE 7–10   The Effect of a Monetary Expansion in the Short Run

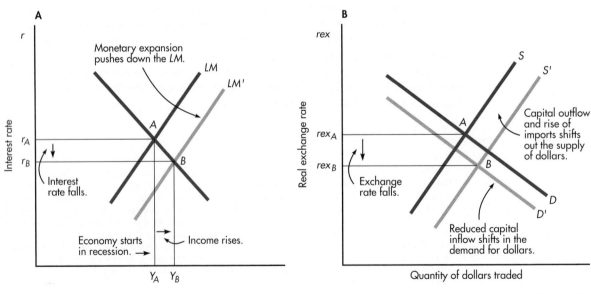

by the impact on capital inflows of the rise in interest rates. Decreasing imports, even in current dollars, reduce the demand for dollars, while the rise in interest rates also reduces capital outflows. In Figure 7–11B, these changes are shown by the shifts from S' to S'' and D' to D''. The exchange rate goes to rex_C.

Fiscal Expansion and Capital Flows Expansionary fiscal policy works by increasing aggregate demand directly (shifting out the *IS* schedule). In a closed economy in which the Fed pursues a policy that maintains the *LM* schedule in a fixed position, fiscal expansion raises the rate of interest. In an open economy, fiscal policy has an even smaller impact on income than in a closed economy. The rise in the rate of interest that results from the fiscal expansion causes capital inflows, which increase the real exchange rate, ultimately worsening the balance of trade and working against the expansionary policy. This is the second key aspect of macroeconomic policy in an open economy: *Fiscal policy becomes relatively ineffective over time in raising income; instead it generates a trade deficit.*

In Figure 7–12A we show how a fiscal expansion (*IS* to *IS'*) has increased aggregate demand (point *A* to point *B*). Output is higher at *B*, even though, for a given increase in government expenditures or reduction in taxes, the increase in output is smaller in an open economy than in a closed economy because of import leakages.

FIGURE 7–11   The Effect of a Monetary Expansion in the Intermediate Run

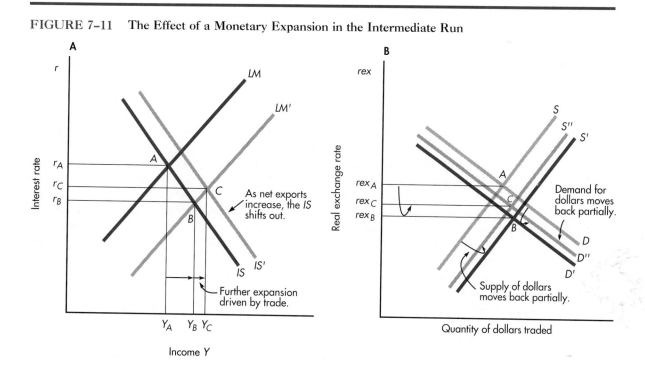

FIGURE 7-12   The Effect of a Fiscal Expansion in the Short Run and the Intermediate Run

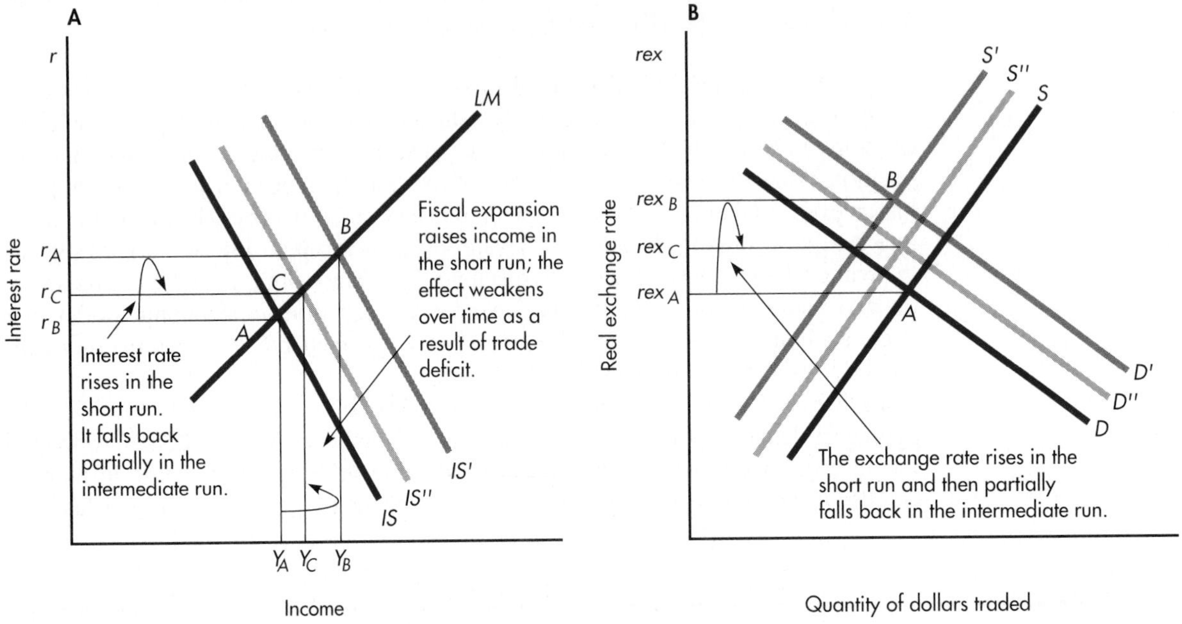

A

Interest rate

r_A
r_C
r_B

LM

B

C

A

Fiscal expansion raises income in the short run; the effect weakens over time as a result of trade deficit.

Interest rate rises in the short run. It falls back partially in the intermediate run.

IS'
IS''
IS

Y_A Y_C Y_B

Income

B

Real exchange rate

rex

rex_B
rex_C
rex_A

S' S'' S

B

A

D'
D''
D

The exchange rate rises in the short run and then partially falls back in the intermediate run.

Quantity of dollars traded

The growth of output has increased imports and has had a negative impact on net exports.

In the foreign-exchange market, the increase in the demand for imports raises the supply of dollars, which lowers the real exchange rate. However, the increase in the rate of interest brings capital flowing in, and this tends to decrease the supply of dollars and also to increase the demand for dollars. There are, therefore, offsetting changes at work in the foreign-exchange market. The experience of the United States, shown particularly by the period 1983–85, is that the overall effect of a fiscal expansion is to raise the exchange rate. Foreigners responded to higher U.S. interest rates by bringing in huge amounts of capital, more than enough to maintain the exchange rate. The shifts in supply and demand in the foreign-exchange market are shown in Figure 7–12B. (The supply of dollars shifts from S to S' and the demand for dollar shifts from D to D'.)

The initial effect of the fiscal expansion, therefore, is to increase income and bring about a rise in the real exchange rate as a result of capital inflows. Over time, however, the higher exchange rate works to reduce aggregate demand, undermining the effectiveness of fiscal policy.

The intermediate-run effects of the foreign sector on fiscal policy are also shown in Figure 7–12. The rise in the exchange rate has led to an increase in imports and a decrease in exports and so the *IS* curve has shifted back (*IS'* to *IS"* in Figure 7–12A), generating a level of income and rate of interest that are both lower than they were after the short-run reaction to fiscal expansion. (Y_C is lower than Y_B and r_C is lower than r_B.)

In the foreign-exchange market, capital inflows are still occurring, but they have slowed down as interest rates have dropped back. More importantly, over time the deterioration of the trade balance is increasing the supply of dollars and reducing the demand for them. The end result is that the supply and demand schedules have moved back in the intermediate run, bringing the exchange rate partway back toward its initial starting point. (The supply of dollars shifts out from S' to S'', the demand for dollars shifts down from D' to D'', and the exchange rate moves to rex_c.)

Comparing Policy Tools in an International Environment

Now that we have added the foreign sector, we have a different perspective on the effectiveness of fiscal and monetary policies. International capital flows place a constraint on policymaking. Policy that generates a rise or fall in interest rates while stimulating aggregate demand also generates inflows or outflows of capital and a rising or falling exchange rate. In an open economy, policymakers no longer have a captive financial sector.

The conclusion about monetary policy is that it is more effective in an open economy, because the change in the rate of interest brings about a response in capital movements that ultimately reinforces policy.

By contrast, on the fiscal-policy side, we find that *fiscal policy will have little effect on the level of aggregate demand in the intermediate or long run.* A fiscal expansion will lead to a rise in the exchange rate and a decline in net exports. However, fiscal policy should not be abandoned as an instrument for affecting aggregate demand. *In the short run, fiscal policy can have a major impact on demand if it is used forcefully; but in the long run, there is little leverage that can be applied through fiscal policies.* Keep in mind, also, that we are talking here about aggregate demand policies. Fiscal policy and the deficit will affect national saving and the long-term rate of growth of potential output in the economy.

The economic policies of the 1980s and early 90s have provided a sobering case study of the short-term and long-term effects of fiscal policy. We turn now to examine the impact of U.S. fiscal policy over this period.

The Budget Deficit, Trade Deficit, and Crowding Out

In Chapter 5 we examined the impact of fiscal policy in a closed economy, one without international trade. And we said that expansionary fiscal policy and budget deficits carry the danger of crowding out domestic investment. In the previous section of this chapter, we have said that the effectiveness of fiscal policy in changing income is reduced in an open economy because, for example, a tax cut will raise interest rates, raise the value of the dollar, and cause a trade deficit that reduces the aggregate demand for U.S. produced goods. When we look at the experience of the U.S. economy over the last 10 to 15 years, we see that, unfortunately, these predictions and ideas about the impact of fiscal policy on the trade deficit have been demonstrated.

Saving and Investment in an Open Economy   As we have seen earlier in this chapter, the condition that gives the *IS* schedule when there is international trade is as follows:

$$Y = C + I + G + X - IM \qquad (7\text{--}3)$$

This equation can be rearranged by subtracting consumption, investment, and government purchases from both sides, and by both adding and subtracting taxes from the left-hand side:

$$(Y - T - C) - I + (T - G) = (X - IM) \qquad (7\text{--}4)$$

Then, since income less taxes less consumption is simply private saving, and since taxes less government purchases is the budget balance, this condition becomes:

$$(S - I) + B = (X - IM) \qquad (7\text{--}5)$$

Since in practice the budget balance in the United States has been a large deficit (*B* has been negative), it is helpful to express this equation as follows:

$$(\text{Saving} - \text{Investment}) - \text{Government deficit} = \text{Net exports} \qquad (7\text{--}6)$$

In an economy with no government and no foreign trade, this equation says that saving minus investment is zero; that is, saving must equal investment. That was how we obtained the simple *IS* schedule. However, with a government sector, there can be a budget deficit that is effectively a subtraction from private saving. We saw in Chapter 5 that deficits can be helpful to alleviate recessions in the short run but can be harmful if they are large and sustained. Once we allow for international trade, there is a new element at work, as we have seen in this chapter, where changes in net exports can lead to shifts in the *IS* schedule.

To examine the way in which the budget deficit affected both domestic investment and net exports in the 1980s and early 90s, we show in Table 7–3 the three elements given above, saving less investment, the budget deficit, and net exports for selected years 1980–92. The table shows there were large variable budget deficits throughout the 1980s that are continuing into the 1990s. Net exports had a small surplus in 1980, which then ballooned into a large deficit in the middle 1980s before declining until 1991. In 1992, the foreign deficit again increased. To explain this pattern we divide the period into three parts: deep recession in the early 80s, recovery, and then recession again.

Sustaining Income in the Deep Recession of the Early 1980s

The economy went into a moderate recession in 1980 and made a partial recovery in 1981. Then in 1982, the economy went into a deep recession initiated by inflation and monetary policy and exacerbated by a collapse of business confidence. Table 7–3 reveals there was a substantial gap between private saving and domestic investment over the period 1980–83, a gap that sharply increased in 1982 after domestic investment fell by 13 percent between 1981 and 1982.

The budget deficits were both cyclical and structural, with the latter becoming more important after 1982. The tax cuts that came into effect in 1982 and 1983 were enacted because the administration argued that the burden of federal taxation was too great and

TABLE 7–3
Saving and
Investment, the
Government
Budget Balance,
and Net Exports,
1980–92 (billions of
1987 dollars)

	Excess of Saving over Domestic Investment (S−I)[a]	Government Budget Deficit (G−T) [b]	Net Exports (X−IM) [c]
1980	52.4	49.2	3.2
1981	44.7	38.4	6.3
1982	116.0	129.6	− 13.6
1983	109.3	160.3	− 51.0
1984	9.4	119.6	−110.2
1985	1.4	132.7	−131.3
1986	− 3.5	151.5	−155.0
1987	−55.6	111.7	−167.3
1988	−27.8	94.6	−122.4
1989	−22.2	71.4	− 93.6
1990	41.1	122.2	− 81.1
1991	159.6	166.7	− 7.1
1992	167.4	222.2	− 54.8

These figures give the three elements in the relation:
  (Saving − Investment) − Government deficit = Net exports

[a] Gross private saving minus gross domestic investment, computed as a residual
[b] Federal state and local deficits combined, deflated by the GDP deflator
[c] The balance on the current account, deflated by the GDP deflator. Note that this differs from net exports in the NIPA accounts.

was undermining incentives to work and invest. But as it happened, the timing of the tax cuts was excellent and they became a well-timed expansionary fiscal-policy change. The main effect of the budget deficits in these years was to help sustain aggregate demand, boost income, and help overcome the gap between private saving and domestic investment. Income still fell, but the 1982 recession would have been much worse without the expansionary effects of the deficit in these years.

In the early 1980s, there was a small deficit of exports relative to imports, so the foreign sector was not adding to aggregate demand.

Both income and investment started to rise rapidly after 1982. In fact, by 1984 domestic investment was 47 percent higher than it had been in 1982. The expansionary fiscal policy combined with an easing of monetary policy had generated a recovery, and the cyclical deficit was being reduced. It was time for fiscal policy to become less expansionary and to reduce the structural deficit. In practice, the total and structural deficits continued to grow, partly because the drive for tax reductions was so politically popular, while cutting expenditures was unpopular.

The Twin
Deficits in the
1980s Recovery

The growth of investment meant that *by 1984 the imbalance between saving and investment had been pretty much eliminated.* (See Table 7–3.) And that only left one way for the budget deficit to be offset. Net exports became very large and negative in 1984 and beyond. Table 7–3 shows that net exports went to $167.3 billion by 1987.

The structural deficits of the 1980s had the effect of inducing a very large trade deficit.

As the economy recovered after 1982, income grew strongly, and the increasing level of income led to increased imports. This effect of income on imports was part of our analysis in Chapter 3, where we saw that net exports will tend to turn negative with increases in income here at home. *Part of the reason that the U.S. economy had negative net exports in the 1980s was the strong recovery of income.*

This was by no means the whole story, however. The growing structural budget deficits, combined with monetary restraint, led to very high rates of interest in the U.S. economy. In our *IS–LM* model, we represent this by a rightward shift of *IS*, sliding along a given *LM* and driving up the rate of interest. And this meant that U.S. interest rates were very high compared to interest rates overseas. As a result, buying U.S. bonds became very attractive to foreign savers and they started to buy lots of them. There was, of course, no shortage of supply of U.S. bonds, because the federal government had a budget deficit and the Treasury had to issue huge numbers of bills and bonds to cover the shortfall of tax revenues compared to expenditures. *The United States started to finance its budget deficit by selling bonds to residents of foreign countries.* Saving made by foreigners was transferred to the U.S. economy in the form of negative net foreign investment from the perspective of the U.S. economy. Foreign saving was used to offset the U.S. federal government deficit.

When residents of foreign countries buy U.S. bonds, they write checks in their local currencies and give them to banks or other financial institutions to arrange the purchase of the bonds. The bank or other institution must then go to the foreign-exchange market and change the local currency into dollars. In effect, foreign residents demand dollars when they decide to buy U.S. bonds and this increases the demand for dollars. When the demand for dollars increases, this will drive up the foreign-exchange value of the dollar. In 1980, it took 1.81 German marks to buy one dollar, but by 1985 it took 2.94 German marks to buy a dollar. The change in the value of the yen was less dramatic, but still important. In 1980 it took 227 Japanese yen to buy a dollar, but by 1985 it took 238 yen. *The increase in U.S. interest rates encouraged residents of foreign countries to buy U.S. assets and this led to an increase in the value of the U.S. dollar.* In terms of this chapter, the rise in the U.S. interest rate changed the interest-parity condition and led to a capital inflow to the United States. This capital inflow that pushed up the dollar then reduced the demand for U.S. exports and increased U.S. imports. The result was the large negative shift in net exports that is shown in Table 7-3.

We have now traced how the budget deficits of the 1980s led to the trade deficits of the same period. The twin deficits together form one of the most serious economic problems of this period, one that is continuing into the 1990s. Many Americans believe that the trade problems of the U.S. economy are the result either of poor performance by U.S. firms or of protectionist policies overseas. But these views are not correct. It is certainly true there are U.S. companies that perform poorly as well as companies that perform well. And it is certainly true that many foreign countries protect their own industries much more than the United States does. And these factors may be important in determining which industries run deficits and which industries run surpluses. But all of these things were true in 1980, when net exports were not a problem. They cannot be blamed for the overall trade deficits of the 1980s. The real cause of the trade deficits has been the structural government budget deficits.

There were some changes in the fiscal situation in the second half of the 1980s. The continued growth of the economy in the 1980s and the Tax Reform Act of 1986 began to bring down the government deficit and hence to bring down U.S. interest rates relative to foreign rates.[5] There was a realization in foreign-exchange markets that the dollar had gone too high, and the dollar started to decline after 1985 (see Figure 7–1).

When President George Bush took office in 1989, he faced pressure to do something more about the deficit, and he reached an accord with Congress in 1990 to reduce some federal spending and raise some additional tax revenue. This was the right policy viewed from a long-term perspective, but the timing was not good. Unfortunately, the economy started to fall into recession by mid-1990.

The Recession of 1990–91

As the economy dropped into recession in 1990, the budget deficit started to increase again as a result of an increase in the cyclical deficit. The automatic stabilizers, like unemployment insurance, were helping the economy to avoid a deeper recession. This increase in the cyclical deficit, however, came on top of a preexisting large structural deficit and caused a massive total deficit for the economy—over $200 billion for 1992.

The growth of the deficit did not lead to an increase in the trade deficit in 1990 and 1991; on the contrary, there was a decline in the deficit of net exports. The reason for this is that, as the economy went into a recession, there was an excess of saving relative to domestic investment—just as there had been in 1982. The weakness in domestic investment in the recession meant that the budget deficit was no longer generating as large a foreign-trade deficit. Looking at Equation 7–5 or at Table 7–3 we see that the budget deficit can be accommodated without a large trade deficit as long as saving exceeds the level of domestic investment. By 1992, however, there were signs that the trade deficit was re-expanding.

Conclusions and Prognosis for the Future

We have seen in this chapter there are important interactions between the U.S. economy and the international sector. When economies change overseas—go into booms or slumps or change their interest rates—then this has an impact here in the United States.

As we have found that the effectiveness of domestic macroeconomic policy depends on the international economy. With a system of flexible exchange rates, such as we now have, monetary policy becomes somewhat more effective as a way of changing income. A tight policy raises U.S. interest rates and the value of the dollar and reduces net foreign demand. The reverse happens for a monetary expansion. In contrast to monetary policy, fiscal policy becomes less effective in an open economy. A fiscal contraction lowers the interest rate, lowers the dollar, and increases net

---

[5] The Tax Reform Act lowered tax rates further but eliminated enough deductions and loopholes that it actually raised some tax revenue.

foreign demand. The opposite case of an expansionary fiscal policy with a large budget deficit has been illustrated vividly by the U.S. experience over the past decade. Tax cuts in the early 1980s initially helped soften the impact of the 1982 recession; but then, as the economy grew, they had little effect on aggregate demand but led to a huge trade deficit.

By 1993 and 1994, the economy was recovering from the recession and the trade deficit was worsening again. We are repeating the experience of the 1980s. In order to bring the foreign deficit under control, policymakers must reduce the federal budget deficit.

WORKED EXAMPLES

Worked Example 7–1

Calculating the Nominal Exchange-Rate Index

The nominal exchange-rate index changes over time, depending on the overall or average rates of exchange of many currencies for one particular currency. This index is set equal to 100 in a base year and it then changes over time, depending on how the dollar moves, on average, relative to all the important foreign currencies. The computation uses a weighted average, where the weights are the relative importance of the countries in U.S. trade.

For example, if the United States traded with two countries (say, 40 percent of its trade with Germany and 60 percent with Japan) and the exchange rate of the dollar against the mark declined by 20 percent and the exchange rate of the dollar against the yen declined by 30 percent over some period since the base year, then the nominal exchange-rate index would have declined by 26 percent ($0.4 \times (-20) + 0.6 \times (-30) = -26$). The nominal exchange-rate index would then be $(100 - 26) = 74$.

Calculating the Real Exchange-Rate Index

Changes in the nominal exchange-rate index describe changes in the average exchange rate between dollars and foreign currencies, but this index does not necessarily reflect changes in the relative prices of U.S. and foreign products. Because inflation rates are different across countries, the nominal exchange rate can go off track as an indicator of how the prices of foreign goods sold in the United States are changing, relative to the prices of goods both produced and sold in the United States.

Since it is changes in relative prices that lead to changes in the demands for imports and exports, we want to find out how changes in the exchange rate affect the relative prices of internationally traded goods and services in general. We need a measure of exchange rates that is adjusted for the effect of any difference in the rates of inflation between the United States and its trading partners. We make the inflation adjustment between any two currencies by computing an inflation-adjusted exchange rate called the real exchange-rate index and denoted by the symbol *rex*. Changes in the real exchange rate (calculated as an index) indicate a change in the buying power of the currency in one country compared to the buying power of the currency in another. The computation of the change in the real exchange ate index for the U.S. dollar in relation to the other world currencies is shown in Equation 7–6.

$$
\begin{array}{ccccc}
\text{Percent change in} & & \text{Percent change in} & & \text{Difference between} \\
\text{the real exchange-} & = & \text{the nominal} & + & \text{U.S. and foreign} \\
\text{rate index} & & \text{exchange-} & & \text{inflation rates} \\
& & \text{rate index} & &
\end{array}
\qquad (7\text{–}6)
$$

$$
\frac{\Delta rex}{rex} = \frac{\Delta ex}{ex} + \frac{\Delta P}{P} - \frac{\Delta P_f}{P_f}
$$

The real exchange rate rises or falls whenever there is a change in the nominal exchange rate that is higher or lower than the difference between inflation rates across countries. For example, if the nominal exchange rate of the dollar were to rise by 5 percent from one year to the next, and over the same period the U.S. inflation rate were 3 percent higher than the average in other countries, the real exchange rate between the United States and the rest of the world would rise by 8 percent. For foreign purchasers of U.S. products and assets, the cost of buying dollars has gone up by 5 percent and the relative cost of goods and services in the United States has gone up by 3 percent.

Equation 7–6 uses the rate of change of the nominal exchange-rate index and the rates of inflation to calculate a rate of change of the real exchange-rate index. If we want to compare the price levels of traded goods and services in one economy and in the rest of the world, rather than rates of change (i.e., how expensive are U.S.-traded goods and services compared with those from the rest of the world), we can do so by computing the levels of the indexes. In Equation 7–7 we show that the real exchange rate (*rex,* shown here as an index), the U.S. price level (*P*), and the world or foreign price level (*P_f*), are related as follows:

$$rex = (P \times ex) \div P_f \tag{7–7}$$

In the preceding example, the nominal exchange rate had fallen from 100 to 74. If the U.S. price level had risen by 30 percent (to 130 or 1.3) and the average foreign price level had risen by 20 percent (to 120 or 1.2) over the same period, then the real exchange rate would have fallen to 80.2 as determined from $(74 \times 130) \div 120 = 80.2$.

Worked Example 7–2

The Interest Parity Condition and Capital Flows

In this example, an investor in Germany is considering buying a two-year bond. He could buy a German bond with an interest rate of 5 percent or a U.S. bond yielding 8 percent. Because of the 3 percent foreign interest-rate differential, the U.S. bond looks attractive. Indeed, many German and Japanese investors and pension funds bought U.S. bonds in the 1980s precisely because of the differential return. But for the German thinking of purchasing the U.S. bonds, the higher return had to be balanced against the expected change in the exchange rate. If the dollar were to fall by 6 percent over two years (approximately 3 percent a year), then the German purchasing the U.S. bond earning 8 percent would get the same return in marks as another German investor would earn if he had purchased a 5 percent bond at home. This example shows that, even though interest rates on similar assets may differ across economies, the expected rate of return on those assets can be equal. The condition under which expected returns are equalized is called in the text the "interest parity condition."

In the above example, from the perspective of a German investor, $r_{foreign}$ is the U.S. interest rate of 8 percent; $r_{domestic}$ is the German interest rate of 5 percent. Thus market equilibrium must imply an expected 3 percent a year increase in the (German) exchange rate, bringing the higher U.S. return back into line with the return available at home in Germany.

To German Investors

$r_{foreign} - r_{domestic} = Exp(\triangle ex/ex)$

U.S. 8% − German 5% = +3% expected annual increase in the German mark relative to the dollar.

By contrast, from the U.S. point of view, the dollar is expected to fall against the German mark (−3 percent per year) giving a 3 percent per year gain to U.S. holders of German currency. This expected gain from holding German marks converts the low 5 percent return on German bonds into an expected 8 percent return for U.S. investors, which is equal to what U.S. investors could earn at home.

To U.S. Investors

$r_{foreign} - r_{domestic} = Exp\ (\triangle ex/ex)$

German 5% − U.S. 8% = −3% expected annual decrease in the dollar relative to the German mark.

The interest parity condition can also tell us how investors will behave when there is *a change in the interest-rate differential*. Suppose at the outset that expected returns are equalized between U.S. and German bonds, but that the interest rate then rises in the United States. At first, the interest rate in Germany remains unchanged and the expected rate of change of the dollar with respect to the German mark also remains the same as it was before U.S. rates rose. This means that the expected returns are no longer equalized. For example, suppose that the U.S. interest rate rose from 8 percent to 10 percent, with the German interest rate remaining at 5 percent and the expected rate of change of the exchange rate remaining at a 3 percent rate of decline of the dollar. To both German and U.S. investors, the U.S. bonds now look more attractive.

To German Investors

$r_{foreign} - r_{domestic} > Exp(\triangle ex/ex)$

U.S. 10% − German 5% > 3%

From the point of view of a German resident contemplating an investment in U.S. bonds, the interest differential exceeds the expected improvement in the value of the mark. The German investor will want to sell German bonds and buy dollars so as to buy U.S. bonds.

To U.S. Investors

$r_{foreign} - r_{domestic} < Exp(\triangle ex/ex)$

German 5% − U.S. 10% < −3%

From the perspective of a U.S. investor contemplating investing in German bonds, the expected gains from holding a bond that pays off in marks (+3 percent per year, since the dollar is expected to fall by 3 percent per year) is not enough to overcome the advantage offered by the higher U.S. interest rate. U.S. investors will want to sell their German bonds and buy U.S. bonds.

Consider now the case where there is a change in the expected future value of the exchange rate. Take the example where initially there is expected-return equalization between U.S. and German bills, with an expected 3 percent decline in the dollar against the mark, matched by a 3 percent interest differential. If there was then a change in economic conditions that affected the German economy rather more adversely than the U.S. economy, then expectations about the decline of the dollar in terms of marks is expected to be only 1 percent lower next year instead of 3 percent lower. The comparison of U.S. and German bills would be:

To U.S. Investors

$r_{foreign} - r_{domestic} < Exp(\triangle ex/ex)$

German 5% − U.S. 8% < − 1% expected decline in the dollar.

To the U.S. holder of the German notes, the interest differential (3 percent advantage in holding U.S. T bills) is now greater than the loss that is now expected as a result of the expected decline in the dollar (− 1 percent). American financial investors will sell their German notes, exchange the marks they receive for dollars, and buy U.S. T bills. There will be a capital inflow to the United States as American investors move their assets back to the United States and also as German investors decide to purchase U.S. financial assets instead of German assets.

SUMMARY

- Modern national economies are not isolated from worldwide events. Rather than being closed economies, where economic activity is isolated within the country, modern economies are open and so are influenced by global economic circumstances.

- International trade is accomplished by an importer or investor (in cooperation with an international bank) first obtaining foreign exchange and then using the foreign currency to purchase foreign goods, services, or assets. The price of foreign currency is called the "exchange rate."

- In foreign-exchange markets, foreign currencies are traded at prices (exchange rates) that reflect the supply of and demand for foreign exchange.

- The demand for foreign exchange (foreign currencies) is derived from the domestic demand for imports and for foreign capital. The supply of foreign exchange is derived from the foreign demand for exports and domestic capital.

- Changes in income and interest rates as well as expectations about the future value of the exchange rate will cause shifts in the supply of and demand for foreign exchange and hence will cause changes in the current exchange rate.

- The value of merchandise exports less the value of merchandise imports is called the "balance of trade."

- When the net balances of items that affect income are added to the trade balance, the resulting figure is called the "balance of payments on the current account."

- When the current account is in surplus, international economic activities contribute to raising national income. When the current account is in deficit, the impact of the foreign sector on income is negative.

- Short-term financial capital will move internationally,

seeking the best return, until the interest rates earned on bonds of comparable quality in different countries differ by the amount of the expected rate of change in the exchange rate. There is, then, the condition of interest parity.

- Changes in the interest differential or in the expected rate of change in the exchange rate, or in both, will trigger capital flows into or out of a currency and a country's financial market.

- With flexible exchange rates, the Fed can still control the supply of money in an open economy. If the Fed tries to set the exchange rate, it will reduce or eliminate its ability to control the money supply.

- A change in U.S. monetary policy will change the U.S. interest rate and thus the differential between U.S. and foreign interest rates. This will change the exchange rate of the U.S. dollar.

- In an open economy with flexible exchange rates, domestic monetary policy is a stronger instrument for controlling income than in a closed economy. Monetary policy will lower interest rates, lead to a net capital outflow, lower the exchange rate, and increase net exports.

- In an open economy with flexible exchange rates, fiscal policy has a smaller impact on income than in a closed economy. A domestic fiscal expansion will raise interest rates, lead to a net capital inflow, raise the exchange rate, and decrease net exports.

- The main cause of the U.S. trade deficit since 1980 has been the federal budget deficit. The sustained expansionary fiscal policy experienced during the 1980s generated a government budget deficit. During that period the biggest impact of the large federal deficits was on the foreign sector.

KEY TERMS AND CONCEPTS

balance of payments on the current account, p. 185
balance of trade, p. 185
exchange rate, p. 180

foreign exchange, p. 179
interest-rate parity condition,
  p. 190

international capital flows, p. 191
real exchange rate index (*rex*),
  p. 182

DISCUSSION QUESTIONS AND PROBLEMS

1. How can a surplus in the balance of payments on the current account be reconciled with a deficit in the balance of trade for the same country in the same year?

2. What is the relationship between the current account and the capital account?

3. If there was a rise in the exchange rate between the U.S. dollar and the Japanese yen from 125 yen to 150 yen, would the yen become more or less expensive to holders of dollars?

   Assume that there have been no other changes except the exchange-rate shift just cited. Will Japanese products be more or less expensive for U.S. purchasers? Will U.S. exports be more or less expensive for Japanese customers?

4. Suppose that the value of imports to Canada are distributed as follows:

U.S.	60%
Japan	25%
Great Britain	15%

   and the exchange rates last year (the base year) for the Canadian dollar (C$) in terms of the currencies of its trading partners were:

   1 C$ = 0.85 U.S.$
   1 C$ = 125 yen
   1 C$ = 0.5 U.K. pound

   and the exchange rates this year are:

   1 C$ = 0.75 U.S. $
   1 C$ = 150 yen
   1 C$ = 0.65 U.K. pound.

   a. Did the Canadian-dollar trade-weighted exchange rate rise or fall? By what percent?

   b. What happened to the Canadian-dollar/U.S.-dollar exchange rate?

   c. What are you presuming about the allocation of Canadian imports among the three countries? Calculate the change in the Canadian-dollar trade-weighted index using different trading proportions from those previously indicated. Explain reasons why you expect the trading proportions to change in the direction you choose.

   d. If the rate of inflation in Canada was 6 percent per year while inflation was 5 percent per year in the United States, 1 percent per year in Japan, and 10 percent per year in Great Britain, calculate the percent change in the real exchange rate between the first and second years. Use constant trading proportions.

5. Explain how the balance of trade can worsen after a fall in the real exchange rate.

6. Suppose the rate of interest was 5 percent per year in Japan and 6 percent per year in Germany. Would investors necessarily prefer German securities to Japanese securities?

   a. If the treasurer of a multinational corporation were indifferent about holding short-term German government notes in marks or short-term Japanese government notes in yen, what does that indifference imply about the exchange rate between yen and marks?

   b. How would the expected returns to financial investment be related across economies if capital were perfectly mobile between nations?

7. If there is an increase in the rate of interest in the United States relative to the rest of the world, what is likely to be the effect on the demand for dollars in foreign-exchange markets?

   a. What would you expect to happen to the U.S. exchange rate?

   b. What other likely changes in the market could result in the exchange rate moving in the opposite direction from what you indicated in (*a*)?

8. Distinguish between domestic macroeconomic policies and international economic policies.

9. If monetary policy works through changing interest rates, how can monetary policy have any effect on an economy where interest rates are determined in worldwide financial markets?

10. Do you agree or disagree with the following statement? "The source of the U.S. trade deficit in the 1980s is closer to Washington and Detroit than it is to Tokyo?" Explain your position.

11. Suppose that domestic investment exceeds private saving by $10 billion and that government expenditure exceeds gross tax revenues by $20 billion. First, write down the relationship among private saving, domestic investment, government's budget balance, and net exports. Then find the numerical value for net exports.

AGGREGATE DEMAND, INFLATION, FINANCIAL RISKS, AND POLICYMAKING

INTRODUCTION

On February 4, 1994, Alan Greenspan, the Fed chairman, announced the first Fed-directed increase in the Federal Funds rate in over five years, by 0.25 percent from 3.0 percent to 3.25 percent. The news triggered a decline in the Dow Jones stock market index of almost 100 points. President Clinton responded by saying that a small increase in short-term rates would be good for the economy, keeping inflation in check and lowering long-term interest rates—those that are important for business borrowing and mortgages. In this chapter we recognize that in actual economies there isn't one interest rate that equilibrates money markets and goods markets, but many different interest rates and the differences are important.

When a household decides to purchase a new home or when a business decides to build a new office complex, each likely goes to financial institutions to borrow funds for these invest-ments. The cost and availability of those funds affects how much investment is made in the economy. New houses, factories, and offices are expected to last a long time; the return on these investments is subject to risk; and the assets being purchased are tangible—they are real assets, rather than financial assets.

In contrast with real investments and long-term financial decisions, when the Federal Reserve conducts monetary policy it does so by buying or selling bonds in the money market, and this has its most direct effect in the short-term money market affecting risk-free interest rates, such as the interest rate on Treasury bills.

The interest rate on a short-term safe bond differs from the rates on longer-term or riskier bonds, the latter rates being those that businesses or households face when they finance the purchase of tangible assets. And a further difference involves inflation. Short-term money markets operate using nominal rates of interest—the standard ones given in the newspaper or quoted by a bank—but long-term real investments are assessed using real rates of interest, rates that are adjusted for inflation.

How does a monetary policy shift, which moves the short rate, bring about a change in investment and aggregate demand? When the Fed attempts to slow down an inflationary economy, it drives up short-term interest rates, such as the rate on Treasury bills. But will the interest rate on mortgages or on 30-year corporate bonds go up? If not, firms and households may just continue to borrow and purchase investment goods and then the economy will not slow down. When the Fed attempts to stimulate an economy in recession, it drives down short-term interest rates, but the interest rates on mortgages or 30-year corporate bonds may not go down much. If this happens, firms and households may not be encouraged to borrow and purchase investment goods, and then aggregate demand in the economy will not recover out of the recession.

In this chapter we will look at the ways in which different interest rates move over the business cycle. The structure of interest rates, from short term to long term, is described graphically by what is called the yield curve. Preceding every U.S. recession since World War II there have been changes in the yield curve that signal a downturn. By looking at the pattern of interest-rate movements we will get a fuller understanding of the links between the real and monetary sectors of the economy. We start this examination by looking at the investment decision and how it depends on the cost of funds. To avoid excessive complexity we return to a closed economy.

INVESTMENT DEMAND AND THE COST OF FUNDS

Investment demand is that part of aggregate demand represented by expenditure on capital goods. When households or firms buy houses, autos, factories, and business equipment, they are making long-term investments in the productivity of these capital goods. In that sense, the household decision to purchase a house is similar to the business decision to buy an office building.[1] We describe all of the decisions to make investment expenditures as business decisions.

Business investment demand is the demand for capital goods and the planned accumulation of inventories. Firms invest to maintain or to increase profits. Capital

---

[1] A careful distinction between durable goods purchased by consumers (mostly houses, autos, and appliances) and durable goods purchased by firms (factories, equipment, and inventories) is deferred to Chapter 9, where the impact of a change in income on the desired capital stocks of households and businesses is discussed. There we explore the separate roles of the variability in household investment demand and business investment demand in contributing to fluctuations in economic activity.

goods allow the firm to initiate or increase production. The firm that can produce more and sell the increased product at a price that covers costs will maintain or increase its profitability.

How much to invest in new equipment, factories, and inventories depends primarily on the expectation of future sales. Higher sales are met by increasing production, which usually requires more capital goods. From the point of view of an individual firm, if capital goods were not purchased in the face of higher sales, the unit cost of increased production will rise, eroding profits.

At the aggregate level, when income is expected to rise in the economy, firms increase their level of planned investment because higher sales are expected. The role of income in our simple investment-demand function (described in Chapter 3):

$$I = I_0 + I_1 Y - I_2 r$$

was a rough approximation for the role played by expected income in determining investment demand. Income, including expectations of future income, is the most important determinant of investment demand, but it is not the only one. At this point we will focus on the interest cost of making the investment expenditure and how it affects investment demand. *Changes in the interest cost of capital spending provide the main link between the money market and monetary policy on the one hand and investment demand and the goods market on the other.*

The decision to purchase capital goods is first driven by the economic prospects facing a firm. There has to be a good business reason (such as increased sales or a change in technology) for the purchase. Beyond this, the decision to invest is a portfolio decision. A firm is deciding among several alternatives as it allocates the company's wealth. It could pay out funds as dividends to its shareholders or issue new shares. It could buy financial assets (such as bonds), retire some of the bonds it has issued in the past, or issue new bonds. It could buy out another company or buy a division or factory from another company. And finally, it could decide to purchase new capital goods. In making the decision to adopt some of these options, or others, the company's managers will examine the relative risks and returns from the alternative choices.

Which capital good to purchase and which corporate project to undertake are critical managerial decisions. These decisions go beyond simple portfolio considerations; however, as we study the level of investment demand in the total economy, most of the factors that are important for individual firms will average out, and the **cost of funds** becomes an important determinant of aggregate investment.

cost of funds
The effective interest cost that a company pays on its investment funds, taking into account the duration of the investment, its risk, and the impact of inflation.

Financing Investment

Corporations can finance capital purchases by borrowing from banks or other financial institutions and they can sell bonds. Alternatively, corporations can finance capital purchases by using corporate saving from past profits or by issuing new equity shares and selling them in stock markets, such as the New York or American Stock Exchanges or through private placement using investment bankers. When a corporation borrows from a bank or sells a corporate bond, it promises to pay a specific rate of interest on the liability it has assumed. Either way, the interest rate it will pay on its liability is the long-term rate of interest.

When a corporation issues equity shares (stocks), it must offer the buyers of these shares the expectation of a future return (dividends and capital gains). The exact amount of the payments is unknown in advance, but nevertheless the owners expect to gain a return, and that requirement for a return represents the cost of equity finance to the firm. When a company holds profits to invest, it is implicitly signaling its shareholders that the firm expects to earn an adequate rate of return on the investment—a return that will eventually benefit the shareholders.

Corporations, therefore, calculate an effective cost of equity finance that is analogous to the long-term rate of interest that they pay on debt finance. Even though there are important tax and risk differences between bond financing and equity financing, there is a relationship between the cost of equity finance and the rate of interest on long-term financial assets. Increases in the long-term rate of interest will raise corporations' overall cost of financing investment.

Small businesses often use loans to finance their operations. Small retailers finance inventory with loans. Many construction companies build condominiums or even single-family homes speculatively, without specific customers lined up. They rely on loans to pay for labor and materials before the first sales are made. Increases in interest rates, therefore, have a direct effect on these business investment decisions.

When a family or individual buys a house, the purchase is typically financed with a mortgage. The mortgage interest rate is a long-term rate of interest. When long-term interest rates rise, this increases the cost of financing a new home and has a negative effect on the demand for housing. The effect of increases in interest rates on housing demand is even exacerbated by the institutional rules of thumb that mortgage lenders use. A family has to qualify for a mortgage by showing that it has income of at least some fixed multiple of the size of the mortgage payment—the family income must be three to four times the mortgage payment. If the interest rate rises from 8 to 9 percent, this raises the annual interest cost of a $100,000 mortgage by about $1,000 and this in turn raises the income threshold for lending by a multiple of that amount, making it harder for families to qualify.

Opportunity Cost View of the Cost of Funds

opportunity cost of funds

The rate of interest on financial assets that could have been earned had the funds that were used for investment been used instead to purchase a financial asset.

When we talk about the interest cost of investment, we are assuming that financing investment out of corporate saving or using existing wealth to buy a house is similar to borrowing or issuing new shares. The concept of the **opportunity cost of funds** helps to clarify this idea. If a firm buys capital goods with its own funds, the firm is usually committing those funds for the life of the capital investment and it gives up the opportunity to invest those funds in financial assets.[2] The firm has chosen to invest in itself over a long term. In this case, the long-term rate of interest on financial assets represents the opportunity cost of investment. The same idea applies when a family cashes in its IRAs or CDs and uses the proceeds toward partial payment for a house. That family could have continued to earn interest on savings while financing a larger portion of the house purchase with a mortgage. The forgone interest represents the opportunity cost of financing the house purchase.

---

[2] Sometimes capital goods are resold before the end of their lives. In general, however, a firm assesses its investments over a long time horizon.

Discounted Cash Flow View of the Cost of Funds

discount rate
A measure of the extent to which funds available in the future are of lesser value than funds available now. The time value of money.

Another way to look at the impact of changes in the cost of funds on the decision to invest is to use discounted cash flow as a way of assessing the value of an investment project. In this approach, a company makes an estimate of the stream of profits that it expects to receive from a proposed investment project. It values this stream and then compares it to the cost of the project. This requires the company to put a value on profits earned one year from now, compared to profits earned two or more years from now. In general, dollars that will be received in the future are not as valuable as dollars received now, and the trade-off between present dollars and future dollars depends on the **discount rate** that is used for the discounting process. The discount rate is a measure of the extent to which funds available in the future are of lesser value than funds available now. The higher the cost of funds, the higher the discount rate and, as we shall see, the lower is the value of the stream of profits from the proposed investment.

To understand discounted cash flow, imagine that you have won $100,000 in the lottery. But under the terms of the prize you will receive $20,000 a year for five years. Being impatient, you decide that you want all you can get right away, not just the $20,000 that is the first payment. So you go to a bank and borrow against the future funds that have been promised to you. How much will the bank lend you? If the interest rate for borrowing is 10 percent, then you can borrow $18,182 against the second payment coming a year from now, because the $20,000 a year from now will just cover the principal and interest on the one-year loan.

The bank will also lend you against the other future payments. The amounts loaned are as follows:

Loan on the one-year away payment   = $18,182 since $18,182 \times (1.1) = 20,000$
Loan on the two-year away payment   = $16,529 since $16,529 \times (1.1)^2 = 20,000$
Loan on the three-year away payment = $15,026 since $15,026 \times (1.1)^3 = 20,000$
Loan on the four-year away payment = $13,660 since $13,660 \times (1.1)^4 = 20,000$
Total of four loans = $63,397

present value
Gives the current valuation of a stream of income or profits, where future profits are discounted using the discount rate.

The total amount that you are able to obtain today as a result of the prize is $83,397 equal to the initial $20,000 plus the $63,397 borrowed from the bank. *A $100,000 lottery prize spread over four years actually has a **present value** of only $83,397.*

The particular discount rate used in the above example [10 percent] generated a particular present value. In our example, the relevant discount rate was the borrowing rate charged by the bank, because the prize offered fixed dollar returns over a period of years. If the bank's borrowing rate were higher, say 15 percent, then the loans on payments in each future year would be worth less (e.g., the payment coming after one year will be worth $17,391, rather than $18,182, since $17,391 \times (1.15) = 20,000$) and as such the present value of the prize would be smaller at a higher discount rate. In general, the value of an investment project that pays off over time depends on the discount rate that is used to determine the present value of the future stream of returns.

For a company deciding on a new factory or retail outlet the discount rate it uses will be the company's cost of funds. And, as in the example, the higher is the cost of funds the smaller will be the present value of the returns from investment projects.

Increases in the cost of funds will tend to reduce the volume of business investment by reducing the present value of the payoffs from investment projects relative to the up front costs.

> **Worked Example 8–1**   This example on page 251 looks at a company deciding whether to open a new retail facility. It estimates the returns it will receive and uses discounting to compare these to the initial costs.

We have seen that the cost of funds to a company will affect its investment decision. Whether the company is using internal funds or borrowing funds, it will evaluate the profitability of an investment project by discounting the returns from the investment as they accrue in the future. We look now at the factors that companies will take into account in determining the cost of funds that they face. They will consider the time horizon of the investment project, the risk involved, the availability of credit, and the impact of inflation on the value of the project.

The Time Horizon of Investment Decisions   A factory is a very different kind of asset than are financial assets like money or short-term bonds. These latter assets are very "liquid," meaning they can be sold quickly without a serious penalty and with at most a small transaction cost. The costs of selling factories or offices or even houses are very large. A realtor will typically charge 6 or 8 percent of the sale price of a house, and the price you can get for a house will usually be lower if you have to sell the house quickly. Even for autos, the gap between the wholesale and retail prices at the dealers is large. Selling a used factory is difficult and the resale price is likely to be only a fraction of the initial cost of construction.

When a company decides to build a factory, it hopes and expects that this factory will operate for many years. Companies look for returns over the long term when they invest; they do not buy factories, offices, and retail stores as short-term investments. Of course, sometimes factories close after a year or so and are resold, but this is generally because the project has failed. Most factory closures or resales of factories that are not performing well will involve substantial losses.

Since they are buying an asset that has value only when used over a number of years, companies will want to borrow long term to finance the purchase. No company wants to renegotiate the mortgage on its office building every three months or even every year. And even when the investment in a factory or office is financed from internal funds, the company looks at how the return on this investment project compares to long-term alternatives. The opportunity cost view of the cost of funds tells us that *long-term interest rates are the ones that are relevant to discount returns from real investment projects.*

Inflation, the Real Rate of Interest, and the Cost of Funds   Virtually all economies have experienced inflation for a number of years and this means that an expected rate of inflation is built into economic decisions. People allow for the fact that prices will rise over time. In our analysis of consumption, investment, and other components of aggregate demand, we have been assuming that economic decisions are based on *real* values. And similarly, we need to understand, also, how financial decisions are affected by inflation, especially in the case of long-term borrowing and lending. When funds are loaned to a company to finance a long-term investment the lender needs to know how inflation erodes the value of the payment of interest and principal over the life of the loan. How should interest rates be adjusted for inflation?

The Real Rate of Interest

real and nominal rates of interest

The nominal rate of interest is the one reported by a bank or financial institution. It is denoted by the symbol, *i*. The real rate of interest is adjusted for inflation and is denoted by the symbol, *r*.

Along with nominal and real values for income, expenditures, and assets, there are nominal and real concepts of the interest rate. We will now use the letter *r* as the symbol for the **real rate of interest** and the letter *i* as the symbol for the **nominal rate of interest.**

Adjusting interest rates for inflation is more complicated than adjusting other nominal concepts. When someone buys a bond costing $100 that promises to pay $105 at the end of one year, then the bond is said to carry a nominal interest rate of 5 percent ($i = 0.05 = 5$ percent). If there is inflation in the economy, so the price level is expected to increase over the course of the year, then the $105 paid at the end of the year is not expected to buy 5 percent more goods and services. Depending on how much increase there has been in the price level over the year, part, all, or more than all of the 5 percent return will have been eroded by inflation. Notice that *it is the change of the price level, or the rate of inflation—not the price level itself—that counts here in assessing the real return.* And since the bond purchase will result in a return that will be paid in the future, and since the inflation that will occur cannot be known with certainty, *it is the expected rate of inflation that is relevant when people are deciding about buying or selling bonds.*

In general, the real rate of interest, *r*, is defined in terms of the nominal rate of interest, *i*, and the expected rate of inflation, *Exp$\Delta P/P$*, as follows:

$$1 + r = \frac{(1 + i)}{(1 + Exp\Delta P/P)} \tag{8-1}$$

In this equation, the values of the interest rates and the rate of inflation are not expressed in percentages. This means, as an example, that if the nominal rate of interest was 15.5 percent and the expected rate of inflation was 10 percent, then the real rate of interest of 5 percent is calculated as follows: $0.05 = [(1 + 0.155) \div (1 + 0.10)] - 1 = 5$ percent.

It is often useful to use an approximation for the real rate of interest. As shown in Equation 8–2, the real rate of interest is approximately equal to the nominal rate minus the rate of inflation:

$$r = i - Exp\Delta P/P \tag{8-2}$$

Worked Example 8–2   On page 252 we use a numerical example to show how the real rate of interest is computed. The exact formula is used and then compared to the simpler version that gives approximately the same answer.

This approximation is reasonably accurate as long as rates of interest and rates of inflation are not too large. If the nominal rate of interest is 5 percent and the rate of inflation is 4 percent, then Equation 8–1 gives a real rate of interest of 0.96 percent while the approximation gives the real rate as 1 percent. Equation 8–2 is also intuitive.

Real and Nominal GDP

In our analysis of the *IS–LM* framework we have described the decisions firms and individuals make about consumption and investment. These are decisions about the quantities of goods purchased and how they vary with income. They are decisions about *real* consumption and investment and how they depend on *real* income. Real income and real GDP measure the total value of income and output in the economy after adjusting for inflation. They are measured in the dollars of a given base year, 1987.

Expenditures and output denoted by the symbols *C, I, G,* and *Y* in our analysis referred to **real values** or inflation-adjusted values. Tax revenue, *T,* was also an inflation-adjusted or real value.

When we explicitly refer to a **nominal value** (for example, nominal income), we will precede the value with the symbol *P.* (For example, nominal income is shown as *PY.*) This particular use of symbols is consistent with the relationship drawn from aggregate supply-and-demand equilibrium:

P (the price level) × *Y* (real income)
= *PY* (the nominal or current dollar value of income)

Note, however, that we do not use this same notation for real and nominal money. The real stock of money is *M/P.*

It says that, to calculate the real return from holding a bond, one takes the nominal interest rate and simply subtracts off the part that must be used to compensate for inflation. We will generally use the approximation of Equation 8–2.

The real rate of interest is an important concept. *Rational economic decisions are based on real values, rather than on nominal values.* Investment decisions should be based on the real returns they are expected to yield over time, and we will see that the real rate of interest is the one that is most relevant for business decisions to purchase new investment goods.

Inflation and the Cost of Funds

To see how interest rates are adjusted for inflation, we will contrast two economies with different rates of inflation. In the first economy, there is no inflation and companies can borrow from the bank at 10 percent. In the second economy, there is 5 percent a year inflation but companies can also borrow at 10 percent (our example is to make a point; in the actual economy, interest rates will likely be different when inflation is different). In the first economy a company is deciding whether to borrow money to build a factory to produce auto parts. The price at which these can be sold will not change over time, in line with the general price stability in the economy. If its profits are a constant fraction of its sales, then profits will change only with the volume of sales.

In the second economy an equivalent company is making the same decision; but it knows that the price at which it can sell the parts will rise at 5 percent a year, in line with the general level of inflation in the economy. If its profits are a constant fraction of sales, then its profits will rise 5 percent a year independently of any changes in sales volumes. With the same nominal rate of interest, the investment project will look more attractive in the economy with inflation. In other words, in two economies with the same nominal rate of interest, inflation implies a lower real rate of interest.

Consider these same two economies and evaluate the decisions to buy a house in the two cases. If a household expects housing prices to be stable in the first economy and to rise at 5 percent a year in the second economy, then, with the same nominal mortgage interest rate, the purchase looks more attractive in the second economy where there is inflation. In general, for a given nominal rate of interest, the expectation of inflation makes borrowing to buy real assets more attractive, because the prices of the real assets will rise while the amount of the indebtedness does not rise.

In the actual economy, both borrowers and lenders will be aware that there can be inflation and they will have their own expected rates of inflation. When the decision is made to borrow from a bank or issue bonds to buy a real asset, a company should trade off the real rate on the borrowing against the expected real return from the investment project. *It is the real rate of interest or the cost of funds that affects the demand for investment*

Worked Example 8–3   On page 254 we revisit the business example in which a company is deciding whether to open a new retail facility. It now takes account of inflation.

Risk and the Cost of Funds

When the federal government borrowed from the public by issuing long-term bonds at the beginning of 1993, it had to pay an interest rate of 7.4 percent. At the same time, the large telephone companies (considered to be companies that are relatively unlikely to default) had to pay 8.5 percent interest on their long-term bonds, and households (with good credit histories) taking out mortgages to buy houses had to pay around the same rate. A company with a BAA rating from the Moody's Investors Services had to pay around 9 or 10 percent, and unrated ''high-yield'' or ''junk'' bond interest rates ranged from 15 to 20 percent, or even higher in some cases. An individual paying back on a credit card was typically paying somewhere between 15 and 20 percent interest.

risk premium
The extra interest or return that must be paid by a borrower to compensate the lender for the risk of default on the bond or loan.

There is a **risk premium** built into these interest rates, reflecting the fact that companies or individuals can default on their financial obligations. And the presence of these risk premiums is not surprising. In 1990 there were 60,400 business failures in the United States, involving assets of over $64 billion. And in the same year there were 725,000 bankruptcy petitions filed; 661,000 were personal and the remainder business. Since the late 1980s, many of our savings and loans and several banks failed or were forced into bankruptcy as a result of unwise or even fraudulent loans made to real estate and business ventures or of loans made to foreign governments that have defaulted on their repayments.

When a company decides to make an investment and it goes out to raise the funds to do this, it will have to take into account the risk premium that it pays on these funds. A small company going to a bank for financing will have to pay a rate of interest that is substantially higher than that paid by the Treasury for borrowing over the same time period (at the same maturity). *The cost of funds to a company includes a risk premium associated with the likelihood of default by that company.*

Credit Rationing and the Cost of Funds

A bank loan officer is evaluating a proposal from a small company. The owner wants to borrow to set up a small workshop to produce a new product that the owner has designed. The project looks very risky and the company has no other significant assets to use as collateral. The owner has little experience in production and the product has not been tested in the marketplace. There may be foreign competitors that can introduce a rival new product quickly and cheaply even if the product is a success. The loan officer's assessment is that the project is very risky indeed. It might pay off handsomely but it might very well fail altogether. The owner of the company is very confident of the success of this project and offers to pay a very high rate of interest to get the funds. Should the loan officer approve the loan at some very high rate of interest?

Obviously individual cases will vary, so there is no general answer to this question. But the loan officer may decide there is no rate of interest at which he can approve this loan. The probability of default is too high, because the underlying asset being financed with the borrowed funds, together with the fact there is no other collateral, makes this loan too risky. And in fact, the higher is the rate of interest, the greater is the cash flow that must be generated to service the debt and the greater is the chance that the borrower will default. *Rational decisions by banks will lead to a rationing of credit,* some prospective borrowers will be turned down.

The existence of credit rationing means the variations in interest rates that we see in the market may not reflect fully the changes that occur over time in the effective cost of funds. When the Fed institutes a contractionary monetary policy, it reduces bank reserves and forces banks to cut back on lending. This raises interest rates; but it also raises the requirements to get loans. Even without Fed action, banks may fear a worsening of business conditions and, on their own, raise the requirements for approving loans. This can lead to a full-scale credit crunch, where most banks drastically cut back on the volume of loans.

In practice, therefore, changes in the average cost of funds to all borrowers should reflect any changes in the *availability* of funds as well as any changes in the interest rate. When banks reduce availability and cut back on loans, this is a rise in the effective cost of funds.

The Cost of Funds: A Summary

Investment decisions by businesses and households are all affected by the cost of funds. Holding constant the level of income, the higher is the cost of funds the lower will be the level of investment demand. In summary:

- The cost of funds is based on the long-term interest rate, since investment goods are durable long-term assets.
- The cost of funds is based on the real rate of interest, since investment goods are tangible real assets.
- The cost of funds must incorporate a risk premium, since investment goods are risky assets.
- If there is tight money and a credit shortage, then the effective cost of funds will rise more than can be seen in increases in interest rates.

Investment demand is affected by the cost of funds, so, if the Fed is to influence investment, it must do so by changing the cost of funds. But *the Fed has no direct control over the cost of funds; it operates in the money market.* We look now at the money market.

THE MONEY MARKET AND THE SHORT-TERM NOMINAL RATE OF INTEREST

Billions of dollars of short-term bonds are traded every day in the New York financial markets. Many of these bonds are issued by corporations to cover short-term financing needs. The United States Treasury issues large numbers of such bonds as Treasury bills, or T bills. The demand for T bills and similar assets comes from corporate cash managers and wealthy individuals. This market is called the money market, and it is where money is traded for short-term bonds.

When the money market is in equilibrium, the supply of money is equal to the demand for money. Corporate cash managers are content, at the prevailing short-term interest rate, with the amount of money they have to pay bills and the amount of short-term bonds they are holding that pay interest.

In Chapter 4, we represented equilibrium in the money market with the *LM* schedule and the question we consider now is: which rate of interest were we talking about? Which is the rate of interest that affects the demand for money so that money demand can be brought into equality with money supply? The first answer to this is that it is a *short-term* interest rate. Cash managers buy and sell short-term bonds on a daily or hourly basis to ensure they can cover cash payments. They hold short-term bonds like T bills that mature quickly or that can be sold easily without any loss of principal. The demand for money depends on the short-term interest rate.

But what happens if there is inflation? Rational economic decisions are based on real values, taking inflation into account. What does this mean for money demand?

The Effect of Inflation on T Bills and Money

We have defined the nominal rate of interest as i, and we will assume now that this is the nominal or dollar return on holding a *short-term* bond, such as a T bill. The real rate of return to holding T bills is then (approximately) the nominal interest rate minus the expected rate of inflation.

$$\text{Real return to T bill} = i - Exp\triangle P/P \tag{8–3}$$

Someone holding T bills can expect this real return.

People hold money primarily because they want to make transactions. Money is an asset and the "return" to this asset derives from the fact that we can buy things with it or pay bills with it. But money also carries an implicit or explicit nominal rate of interest.

Some kinds of money carry negative rates of interest. For example, many checking accounts charge a fee and, if the fee were $5 a month and the average checking account balance is $500, then the monthly interest "earned" on this checking account would be −1 percent. With compounding, this amounts to −12.7 percent a year—a rather large negative rate of interest. Some banks offer more favorable terms than this; they charge no monthly fee if a minimum balance is maintained, and some even pay positive interest on the average balance. Such banks usually charge a per check fee, however, that eats up most of the interest. Cash is part of the money supply, of course, and it earns no interest. Cash also carries the risk of being lost or stolen.

By law in the United States, banks are not allowed to pay interest on checking accounts held by corporations; but larger corporations use accounts that minimize the balances in their accounts. Sometimes a company will agree to maintain an amount in its checking account to be granted other services by the bank, such as a line of credit.

In short, therefore, there is no simple answer to the question of what is the interest earned on money or paid on money. This varies widely, depending on how large the checking account is or how easy it is to make transactions with it. To keep things simple, we will assume that the effective nominal rate of interest earned on money is i_m. This can be thought of as the average of the positive and negative interest rates earned on all the different assets that make up the supply of money. We expect that this interest rate is less than i, the rate of T bills.

Given an average nominal rate of interest on money of i_m, what is the real return to holding money?

$$\text{Real return to holding money} = i_m - Exp\triangle P/P \qquad (8\text{--}4)$$

With some inflation being the norm, this return will generally be negative, because the nominal return to money, i_m, is small or even negative, but of course, this calculation ignores the benefit money provides as a means of making transactions.

<table>
<tr><td>

The Demand for Money and the Short-Term Nominal Rate of Interest

</td><td>

We are studying the demand for money as a choice between holding short-term bonds like T bills or holding money, and what is relevant for this choice is the *difference* in the real returns to the two assets.

$$\begin{aligned}
&\text{Real return on T bills} - \text{Real return on money} \\
&= (i - Exp\triangle P/P) - (i_m - Exp\triangle P/P) \qquad (8\text{--}5)\\
&= i - i_m
\end{aligned}$$

</td></tr>
</table>

When making a choice between money and T bills, the impact of expected inflation drops out. The *difference* in the rates of return simply reflects the fact that bonds carry a higher nominal rate of interest than do assets that are part of the money supply. If people are expecting inflation, they know that this will erode the real value of their holdings of T bills. But they also know that the inflation will erode the value of their money holdings. Both are financial assets that lose value as prices rise.

The choice between money and bonds, therefore, depends on the benefit provided by the money as a means of making transactions relative to the interest-rate advantage of the bonds. The demand for money, then, depends on the volume of transactions (which we assume is related to income, Y) and the short-term nominal interest rate on bonds, i, in relation to the implicit or explicit interest on money, i_m.

The average interest paid on money, i_m, has varied over time. Banks and other financial institutions were deregulated in the 1970s and began to compete more aggressively for funds. And there may even be some variation in i_m over the course of business cycle fluctuations in the economy. But it is a reasonable simplification to say that, whenever the interest rate on T bills rises, this makes these bonds more attractive relative to money. When the interest rate on T bills falls, this makes them less attractive relative to money.

$$\frac{M}{P} = L(Y, i) \tag{8–6}$$

We have modified the money demand relation by making it explicit that *the demand for money depends on the short-term nominal rate of interest.*[3]

The Fed controls the supply of money and, therefore, can affect equilibrium in the money market. It can drive up the T-bill rate or drive it down, that is to say, it affects the short-term nominal rate of interest, *i*. But how does Fed policy change the cost of funds for investment projects? As a first step in answering this question we look at how changes in short-term interest rates, like T bills, are related to long-term interest rates, like long-term Treasury bonds.

SHORT-TERM AND LONG-TERM INTEREST RATES

term structure of interest rates
The relationship among interest rates, depending on the maturity of the assets.

Many companies and financial institutions and households hold longer-term Treasury securities in preference to holding T bills. These longer-term financial assets usually have higher rates of interest than T bills and, therefore, yield a higher return; but there are some offsetting disadvantages to longer-term assets. The long-term nominal interest rate is not usually equal to the short-term nominal interest rate, and the two rates sometimes move differently. We want to ask now how the rate varies with the maturity of financial assets and how the gap between the long and short rates of interest varies with changing economic conditions. We are going to look at the **term structure of interest rates,** which describe the way in which interest rates vary, depending on the maturity of the assets on which the interest is being paid.

The first important link between the short-term and long-term interest rates is that long-term interest rates depend on expectations about future short-term rates. Leaving aside differences in the riskiness of different assets, the interest rate on long-term bonds reflects an average of current and expected future interest rates on short-term bonds. Let's see how this works.

Expected Future Interest Rates

The short-term interest rate today is the rate on a bill issued today that matures a few months or a year from now. These bills are being issued all the time, and new ones will be issued a year from now. What will the rate of interest be on these short-term assets a year from now? That is an important question for an investor deciding whether to hold a long-term bond. An investor thinking of buying a three-year bond could instead buy a one-year bill now and then another one a year from now and a third two years from now. How do these alternatives compare?

If there is no risk, then the return from holding a three-year bond must be the same as the return from holding three one-year bonds. Were the return to a three-year bond different from the return to three one-year bonds, investors would buy whichever had

---

[3] Because inflation erodes the real value of both bonds and money in equivalent ways, we have found that it is the nominal rate of interest that enters the money demand relation, not the real rate. But that does not mean inflation is irrelevant to the money market or to the use of the *LM* schedule to represent money market equilibrium. Recall from Chapter 6 that a rising price level will reduce the real stock of money unless the Fed follows an accommodating policy.

a higher return and sell whichever had a lower return—raising the price and lowering the interest rate on the higher-returning bond and lowering the price and raising the interest rate on the lower-returning bond. Trading in financial markets would tend to equalize returns. Suppose that the interest rate on one-year bonds this year, $i(1)$, is 7.2 percent. And the one-year rate is expected to be 7.0 percent next year and 6.8 percent the year after that. What is the rate of interest on a three-year investment, $i(3)$, that generates the same three-year return as these three one-year investments? One million dollars invested consecutively in three one-year bonds will earn a return as follows:

$$\$1,000,000 \times 1.072 \times 1.070 \times 1.068 = \$1,225,000$$

The three-year interest rate, $i(3)$, that yields the same return as three consecutive one-year investments is then given by:

$$\$1,000,000 \times [1 + i(3)]^3 = \$1,225,000$$

The three-year rate, $i(3)$, is 7 percent (since $1.07^3 = 1.225$). In general, the three-year interest rate, $i(3)$, and the current and expected future one-year rates, $i(1)$, are related as follows:

$$
\begin{aligned}
[1 + i(3) \text{ in year one}]^3 = \ &[1 + i(1) \text{ in year one}] \times \\
&[1 + i(1) \text{ expected in year two}] \times \\
&[1 + i(1) \text{ expected in year three}]
\end{aligned}
$$

This relation means that, ignoring risk differences, the long-term interest rate on a bond would be equal to the average of the expected short-term interest rates over the period until the bond matures.[4] And this result can be applied for two-year, four-year, and longer-term interest rates, also.

If expectations about future one-year rates were to change, then the current three-year rate would change, *without there being any change in the current one-year rate.* In the preceding example, if the expectation of the one-year rate in the third year fell from 6.8 percent to 5.3 percent, the current three-year rate [$i(3)$] would fall from 7 percent to 6.5 percent since:

$$(1.072) \times (1.070) \times (1.053) = (1.065)^3$$

The current short rate remains at 7.2 percent as the current longer rate falls. *A change in the expectation of a future short interest rate will change the relationship between current short rates and current long rates. Changes in interest rate expectations will change the term structure of interest rates.*

Interest-Rate Risk

We have looked at the relation between short-term and long-term nominal rates of interest without considering the difference in risk. In practice, more risk is associated

---

[4] Formally, this relation among rates is that the long rate is the geometric mean of the short rates. The geometric mean is an average taken by multiplying N elements and taking the Nth root of the product, in contrast with the arithmetic mean, which is taken by adding N elements and dividing the sum by N. For rates of interest that are not terribly large or do not change much over time, the simple average of the expected short rates is very close to the geometric mean.

with buying a long-term bond than in buying a short-term bond. Interest rates in the future are not known with certainty. Expectations about interest rates may not be realized.

Suppose a three-month T bill was purchased when the interest rate was 5 percent, and then rates double to 10 percent. The market price of the T bill would fall because it has to earn an equivalent return to newly issued T bills. But it will not fall by much since it is redeemed for its full face value very quickly.[5] So in the case of T bills, the loss of value that occurred with a rather large change in the rate of interest was not very great. The same is not true of longer-term financial assets, however.

At the opposite end of the spectrum from T bills are infinitely long-term government bonds called *consols* or *perpetuities*. These bonds are promises to pay a stated amount each year forever, but they are never redeemed. For perpetuities, there is a very simple relation between the interest rate and the price of the bond. Suppose a perpetuity promises to pay $100 per year forever. Then if its price is $2,000, its interest rate is 5 percent ($100 ÷ $2,000). If the price were $1,000, the interest rate on a consol would be 10 percent ($100 ÷ $1,000). The same change in the rate of interest that resulted in a small change in the value of a T bill would have led to halving of the price of a perpetuity. In general, long-term bonds lose much more in value than do short-term bonds, following the same size change in the rate of interest.

Long-term bonds have much more variability in price than do short-term bonds. Buying a long-term bond exposes the lender to much greater risk as a result of interest-rate changes than is the case when buying a short-term bond.

Risk and Term to Maturity

The fact that it is riskier to hold a long-term bond than a short-term bond means that interest rates on long-term bonds are usually higher than those on short-term bonds. In the normal case, savers get a risk premium in the form of a higher interest rate when they hold long-term bonds. This risk premium is not related to the likelihood that the Treasury will default on its bonds, rather it reflects uncertainty about future interest rates. For example, suppose the current rate of interest on T bills is 5 percent and this rate is expected to continue over the next three years; then with no risk premium, the interest rate on three-year bonds will also be 5 percent. But in practice the interest rate on three-year bonds might be 6.5 percent. The difference is a risk premium of 1.5 percentage points built into the three-year rate.

In the normal case in the bond market, holders of long-term bonds are receiving a higher rate of interest than the holders of T bills to compensate them for the extra risk they are taking. The holders of short-term bonds are receiving a lower rate of interest but have the compensating benefit of greater **liquidity** from holding T bills or other short-term assets. An asset is liquid if it can be sold quickly for close to its face value.

liquidity

The quick-resale characteristic of short-term financial assets. Assets that can be sold quickly for a value very close to the value that would be obtained by waiting.

---

[5]   T bills are so-called "zero coupon bonds." Rather than paying an explicit interest rate, they are sold at a discount below their face value. A T bill that is redeemed for $10,000 after three months will sell for $9,879 when first issued, if the interest rate is 5 percent (since $9,879 \times (1.05)^{0.25} = 10,000$). A rise in the interest will lower the price to $9,765 in order to generate a 10 percent interest rate (since $9,765 \times (1.1)^{0.25} = 10,000$). We discuss the T bill market in Chapter 10.

Not all situations in the bond market are typical, however, and there can be large variations in the interest rate on long-term bonds compared to the interest rate on T bills. Nevertheless, interest rates generally form a pattern that reflects the lower risks associated with short-term bonds and the higher risk associated with long-term bonds.

The Term Structure and the Yield Curve

yield curve
The array of interest rates on bonds by term to maturity.

normal yield curve
Where short-term rates are lower than long-term rates.

The relationship among the interest rates on the three-month T bills, six-month T bills, one-year Treasuries, two years, and so on up to 30-year Treasury bonds is called the "term structure of interest rates"—that is, how the different interest rates vary by the term to maturity of the bonds. A graph of the term structure of interest rates is called the **yield curve**—we will show actual yield curves later in the chapter.

There is a **normal yield curve** when the short rate of interest is below the long rate. The reason this is normal is that the interest-rate risk rises with maturity and the yield curve flattens out with increases in maturity. Long-term bonds are riskier and require a higher interest rate, but the differences in liquidity among medium-term bonds (2–10 years) and long-term bonds (10–30 years) is not usually very large.

If the short-term rate of interest is expected to remain constant into the future, then the rising yield curve simply reflects the rising interest-rate risk. However, interest rates are not always expected to remain constant.

Expectations and the Slope of the Yield Curve

inverted yield curve
Where short-term rates are higher than long-term rates.

If the short rate of interest is expected to change in the future, then the yield curve will reflect the impact of both interest-rate risk and the changes in expectations. *Holding the risk premium constant, an expectation that the short-term rate of interest will fall in the future will tend to reduce the current long-term rate of interest.* This was illustrated in the earlier example, where we found that, when the current short rate was expected to fall in successive years, then the long rate fell. While in the example the liquidity premium was taken as zero, the same result comes through even with the liquidity premium added in. It is even possible for the short-term rate of interest to be higher than the long-term rate, when expectational effects overcome the risk premium.

When the short-term rate of interest is actually higher than the long rate, we call this situation an **inverted yield curve,** because the normal relationship of higher long-term rates and lower short-term rates has been inverted. We will see that the inversion of the yield curve can be an important indicator that the Fed is following a contractionary policy.

THE INTEREST-RATE GAP AND EQUILIBRIUM INCOME

The interest rate that is determined in the money market is not the same as the cost of funds to businesses deciding whether to invest. By dealing with this issue, we can add something new to our analysis of aggregate demand. This analysis is based on an *IS–LM* framework that has been built until now on the assumption of a single interest rate. We now extend the *IS–LM* framework to take account of the gap between the money-market interest rate and the cost of funds. We will see that sometimes movements in the cost of funds are closely related to the movements in the money-market interest rate, but sometimes they are not.

FIGURE 8–1   The *IS* and *LM* Schedules Depend on Different Rates of Interest

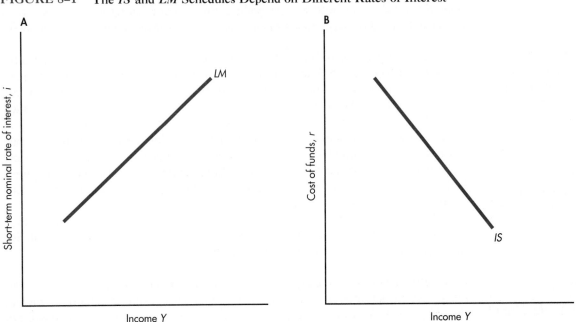

A

Short-term nominal rate of interest, *i*

LM

Income *Y*

B

Cost of funds, *r*

IS

Income *Y*

IS and LM with Different Rates of Interest

We have defined *i* as the short-term nominal rate of interest (the T-bill rate) and argued that equilibrium in the money market is represented by the *LM* schedule, giving combinations of income, *Y*, and the short-term nominal rate of interest, *i*, for which this market is in equilibrium. Figure 8–1A shows the *LM* schedule, which differs from the schedule in earlier chapters in that the vertical axis is now *i*, the money-market interest rate.

The *IS* schedule represents equilibrium in the goods market. It gives points where output is equal to aggregate demand, the sum of consumption demand, investment demand, government purchases of goods and services, and net exports. Earlier in this chapter we showed that investment demand depends on the cost of funds, *r*. This means that the *IS* schedule gives the combinations of income, *Y*, and cost of funds, *r*, for which the goods market is in equilibrium. The Figure 8–1B shows the *IS* schedule, drawn as in earlier chapters except *r* now stands for the cost of funds.

We have, in a sense, broken apart the *IS* and *LM* schedules. Equilibrium in the economy can no longer be described by the intersection of the *IS* and *LM* schedules, because *r* and *i* are not necessarily equal when the goods and money markets are both in equilibrium. We must account for the gap between the money-market interest rate, *i*, and the cost of funds, *r*.

The Interest-Rate Gap

We have identified four elements that separate the money-market interest rate and the cost of funds: (1) The slope of the yield curve, giving the gap or spread between long rates and short rates. The money market determines the short-term rate of interest

FIGURE 8-2
Equilibrium in the
Goods and Money
Markets, with the
Interest-Rate Gap

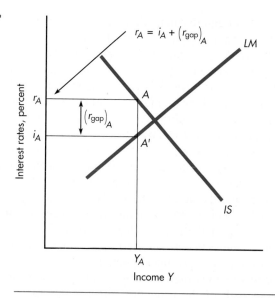

while companies borrow long term for investment. (2) The risk premium that arises when there is some probability of default on a loan or bond. The cost of funds for investment must incorporate such a risk premium. (3) The effective cost of funds will rise or fall to some borrowers if there are variations in the availability of credit. And (4) expected inflation—investment means buying real tangible assets, so the cost of funds reflects the real rate of interest.

To keep things simple, we will combine the effects of all of these elements into a concept called the **interest-rate gap,** r_{gap}.

$$r_{\text{gap}} = \text{Interest premium (from risk, yield curve, and availability)} - Exp\triangle P/P$$

This gives us the following relationship between i and r:

$$r = i + r_{\text{gap}} \tag{8-7}$$

Relative to the T-bill rate, the cost of funds is pushed up by increases in either the risk premium or a steeper yield curve (or both). If inflation is positive, then real rates of interest are below nominal rates, holding down the real cost of funds for a given nominal cost of borrowing.

The interest-rate gap is based on people's expectations about the economy. It reflects the risk premium and, hence, people's expectations about the likelihood of default and bankruptcy. It reflects the slope of the yield curve and, hence, people's expectations about the pattern of interest rates in the future. And it reflects expected inflation.

We can now introduce the interest-rate gap into the *IS–LM* framework. In Figure 8–2 the vertical axis simply gives percentage rates of interest, so we can draw both the *IS* and *LM* schedules. The interest-rate gap is shown, separating i and r. We show what we think is the normal case, in which the interest-rate gap is positive—the effect of risk and the positive slope of the yield curve outweigh expected inflation. Figure 8–2

interest-rate gap

The cost of funds, *r,*
minus the short-term
nominal rate of interest,
i. It depends on an
interest-rate premium
minus the expected rate
of inflation.

depicts an economy in equilibrium, where the level of income is Y_A, the short-term nominal rate of interest is i_A, and the cost of funds is r_A.

For points A and A' in Figure 8–2 to represent an overall equilibrium for the economy (both goods and money markets in equilibrium), the interest-rate gap that separates i and r must reflect people's actual expectations as they are revealed in the risk premium and the yield curve and the level of expected inflation.

The representation of equilibrium that is given in Figure 8–2 is a simple but important extension of the *IS–LM* model that we used earlier. It is built on a far firmer foundation, because it recognizes the existence of different interest rates and makes it clear that there is an interest-rate gap between the goods and money markets. And this gap can and will change in response to movements in the economy and to policy changes. To understand the determination of income or to predict what income will be, we need to understand or predict the interest-rate gap. And this is very hard indeed to do in practice. One of the reasons that economic forecasts are difficult and can sometimes be unreliable is that we do not have good ways of predicting changes in the expectations that are part of the interest-rate gap.

Figure 8–2 helps us to realize there are limits to how well macroeconomists can predict the future path of the economy, and it helps us to realize the limits that policymakers face in controling the economy. The Fed cannot control all interest rates and hence it cannot easily control investment.

The interest rate gap concept also has value for forecasting. The slope of the yield curve and other interest-rate changes can help predict the direction of changes in economic conditions. To see how this works, we next look at how changes in the interest-rate gap affect equilibrium income.

Worked Example 8–4   On page 255 we use a numerical example to show how to determine the level of equilibrium income when there are different interest rates.

A Monetary Contraction and the Interest-Rate Gap

In Figure 8–3 we depict the effect of a monetary contraction on the economy. The economy is initially in equilibrium at point A and A'. The level of income is Y_A, the money market is in equilibrium with an interest rate i_A, and the goods market is in equilibrium with a cost of funds r_A. The interest rate gap is $(r_{gap})_A$.

The Fed decides that inflationary pressures in the economy are too strong and it wants to cut aggregate demand and reduce income and output. It instigates a contractionary policy, shown by a shift in the *LM* schedule to *LM'* (the Fed sets the rate of growth of the money supply to be below the inflation rate, so the real money supply falls). The short rate rises sharply (from i_A to i_B), but the yield curve inverts and the interest-rate gap actually turns negative [$(r_{gap})_B$ is negative]. The cost of funds initially rises only from r_A to r_B and the level of income falls only to Y_B. The initial impact of the monetary policy is small.[6]

---

6 In actual situations, the level of aggregate demand in the economy may be rising with its own momentum, and the impact of the contractionary monetary policy would then be swamped and income would remain high. We could depict this in Figure 8–3 by showing an outward shift in the *IS* schedule; but we want to keep the analysis simple, so we are keeping the *IS* schedule fixed. The key point is that the Fed's contractionary policy has only a limited impact on aggregate demand in the short run.

FIGURE 8–3
The Effect of a
Monetary Contrac-
tion on Interest
Rates and Income

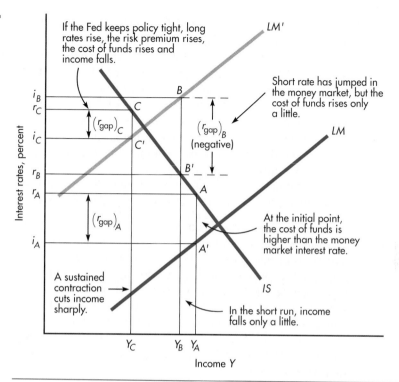

Provided the Fed sticks with its policy, the impact will increase over time. The sustained increase in T-bill rates will drive up long-term interest rates (the yield curve is no longer inverted). The banks restrict the growth of borrowing and the interest rate on short-term commercial paper rises, discouraging corporate borrowing. The realization that the Fed is serious in its efforts to depress demand may increase the risk premium and lower the expected inflation. We show the effect of these changes in Figure 8–3. The *LM* schedule does *not* shift, but the interest-rate gap gradually increases (there is now a normal positively sloped yield curve, the risk premium has risen and expected inflation has fallen, the interest-rate gap is now $(r_{gap})_C$), and the economy moves to a new equilibrium at point *C*, with income Y_C.

As the economy makes the transition described by the movement from Y_B to Y_C, we see that the interest rate in the money market and the cost of funds actually move in opposite directions. At income Y_C, the short rate has *fallen* from i_B to i_C.[7] Long-term risky interest rates and the cost of funds have *risen* (r changes from r_B to r_C).

Worked Example 8–5 On page 256 use a numerical example to show how equilibrium income is affected by a monetary contraction.

---

[7] This is still higher than the original rate at i_A.

The extension of the *IS–LM* framework has allowed us to see how a monetary contraction works over time to slow the economy in the normal case. The Fed can step in and have a quick and powerful effect on the money market. And then after time the effects of the contractionary policy will affect business borrowing and the cost of funds—it slows investment demand. This development of the *IS–LM* framework has also allowed us to see the predictive value of relationships among interest rates. If we observe that money market interest rates jump up above the long-term real cost of funds *an inversion of the yield curve* [as is shown in the example of Figure 8–3—points *B* and *B'*] that would be a strong signal that the real cost of funds was going to rise and that income was about to fall.

We have talked about policy and changes in the interest-rate gap without saying much about possible changes in expected inflation. We address that issue now.

Expected Inflation and a Contractionary Monetary Policy

Expectations about inflation in the economy are important, in part, because investment decisions are based on the cost of funds, which in turn depends on the real rate of interest. But unfortunately there is no easy way to observe the expected rate of inflation. This means that, though the real rate of interest is a key economic variable, in practice we do not know precisely what it is! Moreover, as we saw in Chapter 6 when we looked at the role of expected inflation in the output–inflation trade-off, there is little consensus among economists about how expected inflation is determined even in principle. Many economists believe expected inflation depends on the past history of inflation, while others argue that expected inflation is based on a rational forecast of the future.

This uncertainty about the rates of expected inflation and real rates of interest is a problem for economists who want to understand and test their ideas about the working of the economy, and it is a problem for policymakers who would like to estimate the real rate of interest when setting monetary and fiscal policy.

Fortunately there are some important conclusions that we can draw about how expected inflation and hence real interest rates change in response to a contractionary monetary policy. Such a policy will tend to reduce aggregate demand and reduce the inflationary pressure in the economy. Actual inflation is likely to be lower in the future as a result of such a policy, and people know this. So *the expected rate of inflation is reduced by a contractionary policy.* Virtually all economists will agree on this.

The more controversial question is about the extent to which expected inflation is likely to change in the short run. We argued in Chapter 6 that actual inflation is rather "sticky." It comes down only gradually when the economy goes into recession and increases only slowly when there is a boom. And people know this, so they do not change their expectations about future inflation quickly.

We think that a monetary contraction will not change the expected rate of inflation by much in the short run. But we agree with the rational-expectations view to the extent that a sustained and credible commitment by the Fed to inflation fighting will have a bigger effect on expected inflation than a contractionary policy that is seen as temporary or tentative.

- If the Fed adopts a contractionary monetary policy, this will reduce the expected rate of inflation, although not by much initially. The reverse holds true for an expansionary policy.

- If actions by the Fed are seen as part of a sustained and credible policy commitment to a reduction of inflation, then expected inflation will decline more than if the Fed actions are seen as either short-term adjustments of policy or as isolated changes.

And these statements lead to a conclusion about the way that a contractionary monetary policy will affect real rates of interest. Recall that the real rate of interest is equal to the nominal rate of interest *minus* the expected rate of inflation.

- If the Fed adopts a contractionary monetary policy, this will raise the real rate of interest by more than the increase in the nominal rate of interest.
- The above effect will be stronger if the Fed has a credible commitment to inflation fighting.

These conclusions about the effect of monetary policy are a help in understanding how monetary policy will affect real rates of interest and hence investment. We can observe nominal rates of interest rising following a monetary contraction, and we can conclude that real rates of interest will also have risen; in fact, in the normal case, they will have risen somewhat more than the rise in nominal rates, because the monetary contraction has lowered expected inflation.

Monetary Expansion and the Interest-Rate Gap

How does the interest-rate gap affect income when Fed policy is used to stimulate an economy where output is low and there is high unemployment? How did the economy get into this situation? Perhaps the Fed itself initiated a slowdown in the growth of aggregate demand. But once monetary contraction bit in, the economy may have continued to slide—there is usually a downward momentum that develops, and the economy can end up stuck in a recession with low income and high unemployment.[8] In such a case, the Fed's concern about high inflation will give way to a concern about lost output and jobs and there is a shift toward expansionary policy.

Figure 8–4 illustrates this case. The economy is initially at point *D*, with a low level of income. The Fed expands the money supply, represented in the figure as a shift in the *LM* schedule to *LM'*. The short-term nominal rate of interest drops from i_D to i_E. Initially, the yield curve becomes very steep, leading to an increase in the interest-rate gap. Long rates come down some, however. The risk premium will be reduced a little by the shift to expansion, and bank credit will become more available. Expected inflation is not changed much initially by the policy. Overall, the expansionary policy has a modest impact, pushing the economy to point *E*, with income Y_E.

Over time, the low rates of interest in the money market have an impact on long-term interest rates. They start to come down more and the interest-rate gap gradually declines. People gain more confidence in the prospect of economic recovery and the risk premium also declines. Expected inflation may rise some. These changes are represented in Figure 8–5 by the transition from point *E* to point *F*, with a rise in income from Y_E to Y_F. The *LM* schedule has not shifted; but, as the economy grows,

---

[8] As we will see in Chapter 9, there are usually fluctuations in the goods market (shifts in the *IS* schedule) occurring over the course of the business cycle. We have been concentrating here on shifts on the monetary side, so we have held the *IS* schedule constant to avoid excessive complication.

FIGURE 8–4
The Effect of a
Monetary Expan-
sion on Interest
Rates and Income

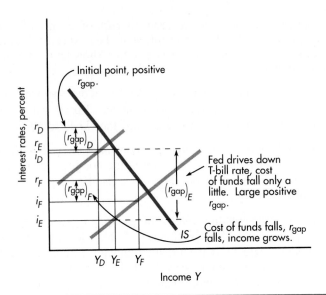

the short rate rises from i_E to i_F. The decline in the interest-rate gap means that the cost of funds has fallen, however, from r_E to r_F.

This case described the normal effects of an expansionary monetary policy. Initially only short rates fall; but after a lag, the cost of funds declines and investment is stimulated. This is just the opposite case to the earlier look at contractionary policy, where this policy, too, does not work immediately.

In actual situations, there are many pitfalls in the working out of policy, including the fact that the goods market, shown by the *IS* schedule, does not stay stable as we have assumed here. But we can see some of the effects we have shown here and some additional concerns facing policy makers by looking at monetary policy and interest rates from 1979 to 1983 and then again over the period 1990–92.

INTEREST RATES AND CONTRACTIONARY MONETARY POLICY: A CASE STUDY OF 1979–83

The economy was growing strongly in 1977 and 1978 but inflation was also heating up. The consumer price index increased by 9 percent from December 1977 to December 1978 and the Fed became concerned that inflation was moving out of control. It decided to move toward a more contractionary policy and moderated the growth of the money supply. The interest rate on three-month T bills averaged 5.3 percent in 1977, averaged 7.2 percent in 1978, and 10.0 percent in 1979. But the economy kept on growing and inflation kept increasing—the consumer price index increased 13.3 percent from December 1978 to December 1979. The Fed was finding the increases in short-term interest rates that it had engineered were not enough. Long-term interest rates had not risen as much as short-term rates and the risk premium remained moderate. Moreover, since inflation was rising, it is likely that expected inflation was also increasing, making it attractive for investors to borrow to buy tangible assets like houses and office buildings—expected inflation holds down real rates of interest.

The chairman of the Board of Governors of the Fed, Paul Volcker, had been appointed with a mission to reduce inflation and in October of 1979 he announced there would be a change in the operating procedures of the Fed. The growth rate of the money supply would be curbed, even if this resulted in very high rates of interest.[9] Short-term interest rates would be pushed even higher if that was needed to slow the economy; and he hoped to affect expectations, so the increase in short rates would translate into increases in the cost of funds. In the event, the Fed under Volcker did succeed in inducing a recession and slowing inflation, but there were large policy gyrations along the way.

Variations in Monetary Policy, 1979–82

Frustrated by the lack of a response to its gradual tightening of policy in 1978 and early 1979, the Fed decided to tighten further at the end of 1979. And it also imposed temporary restrictions on bank lending—the Fed acted directly to reduce the availability of credit. The reaction came quickly as the economy tipped into a recession in early 1980.

The Fed had succeeded in slowing the economy; but it suddenly got cold feet about what it had done and decided to ease its policy, fearing a very deep recession. This reinforced the view that the Fed was not willing to stick to a policy of fighting inflation—and growth quickly resumed. At the end of 1980, the recession seemed to be over; one of the shortest on record. Output and employment picked up again in 1980, but so also did inflation as the consumer price index rose 12.2 percent from December 1979 to December 1980.

The Fed again changed its mind and tightened policy at the end of 1980, and the economy turned down again in 1981–82, falling into the deepest recession that the U.S. economy has experienced since the Great Depression.

The vascillations of Fed policy are mirrored in the fluctuations of interest rates that took place over this time period. Rates rose when the Fed contracted and fell when it eased. But the different interest rates did not move exactly together, by any means.

The T-Bill Rate and the Yield Curve

The Fed reduces the growth of the money supply by reducing the growth of bank reserves. As the banks adjust to the lower level of reserves,[10] the supply of money declines and this changes the balance of supply and demand in the money market; that

---

[9] Volcker announced that the Fed would follow a more monetarist policy, targeting money growth, rather than interest rates. in practice this change was more cosmetic than real. The key policy change was the willingness to tolerate very high interest rates if necessary.

[10] The Fed uses open-market operations to do this, and so the first place that the contractionary policy is felt is the banks themselves. They find that they are short of reserves. If an individual bank is short of reserves, it sees first if there is another bank that it can borrow from, one that has excess reserves. This borrowing and lending among banks is carried out in what is called the "federal funds market," and so one of the first signs of a contractionary monetary policy is that the rate of interest on borrowed reserves, a rate that is called the "federal funds rate," starts to rise. As the banks adjust to the shortages of reserves—by selling T bills or reducing new lending—interest rates on T bills or other short-term assets start to rise. See the discussion in Chapter 10.

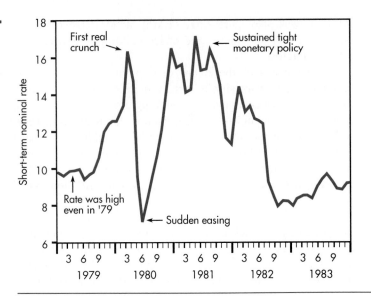

is, in the market for T bills. The reduced supply of money means that people do not
have as much money available to make transactions; they sell T bills to try and meet
their cash needs. The price of T bills falls and the rate of interest on T bills starts to
rise. Figure 8–5 shows how the interest rate on three-month T bills varied from 1979
through 1983, and we can see that indeed this interest rate did swing wildly up and
down as the Fed's policy changes interacted with a fluctuating economy. The T-bill
rate was already close to 10 percent in early 1979; then the Fed drove it over 16
percent in early 1980. The Fed eased and the T-bill rate dropped below 8 percent later
in 1980, before jumping again and staying very high indeed through 1981. It remained
over 10 percent until mid-1982, and then came down again as policy eased once more.

The interest rate on long-term bonds rises when the Fed contracts the money
supply, but not by as much as the increase in the T-bill rate and so the yield curve
flattens or inverts. Figure 8–6 shows a simplified yield curve for several dates over the
period 1979–83. The Fed had been moving toward a tight monetary policy since 1978
and there was already an inverted yield curve in October 1979 (yield curve *I*). This
inversion became more pronounced by March of 1980 (yield curve *II*) as the Fed
really tightened the monetary screws and both short and long rates rose.

When the Fed shifts to an easier monetary policy, T-bill rates come down again
very quickly and the yield curve once again has a positive slope—there was a normal-
shaped yield curve in June of 1980 (yield curve *III*). The pattern of tight money started
all over again and by December 1980 (yield curve *IV*) the yield curve was inverted
again and long and short rates were back up to their March levels.

We can see a clear pattern over this period. When the Fed decides to tighten
monetary policy, this drives up short rates and inverts the yield curve. In the normal
case this contractionary monetary policy will bring on a recession, and so *an inverted*

FIGURE 8–6
Simplified Yield Curve, Various Dates; 3 Month T Bill and 10 Year Bond

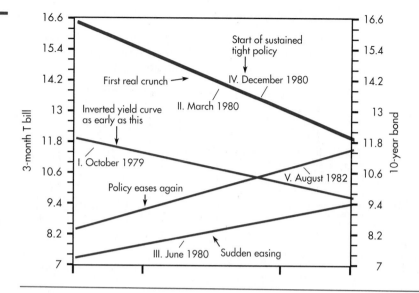

yield curve is characteristic of a period of tightening monetary policy and generally indicates a recession will be coming.

By mid-1982 the Fed decided it had tightened enough. Investment had fallen dramatically and the economy was in deep recession. The Fed eased its policy again in an attempt to avoid a still deeper recession. It now lowered the T-bill rate, so it was well below the interest rate on long-term bonds (yield curve *V*). Figure 8–6 shows that the yield curve was steep by August 1982. *A steep yield curve is characteristic of a loosening of monetary policy and generally indicates that the Fed is trying to stimulate the economy by lowering short-term interest rates.*

Even though there was a steep yield curve in the summer of 1982, both long and short interest rates remained very high. This was partly because inflation remained very high and bondholders were demanding some compensation in interest for the erosion of the value of their bonds by inflation. Partly it was because of the large structural budget deficit (see Chapter 5). The Treasury was issuing huge volumes of Treasury bills and bonds and the Fed was unwilling to ease money further.

The changing slope of the yield curve shows us that the Fed does not have direct control over long-term interest rates, and the effects of monetary policy changes on the economy are far from automatic. In 1978 and early 1979, the Fed was pushing up the T-bill rate, but the economy kept on expanding. Long-term rates had not risen enough to slow a strongly growing economy. In 1983, the Fed was pushing down the T-bill rate, but long rates stayed fairly high. The economy did recover in 1983—because the tax cuts and the deficit (expansionary fiscal policy) were also stimulating the economy at that time.

It does not always work out in the way we have just described. When we look at the 1991–92 period we will see a circumstance where, even with falling short-term rates,

FIGURE 8–7A   Interest-Rate Spread between BAA Bonds and 10-Year Treasury Bonds

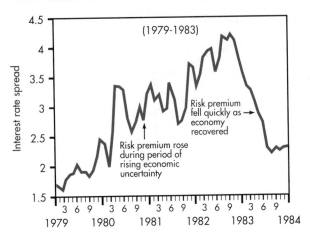

FIGURE 8–7B   Interest-Rate Spread between Three-Month Commercial Paper and Three-Month T Bill

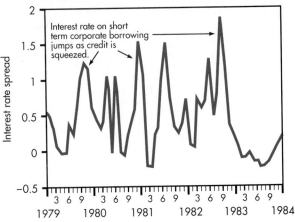

long rates did not fall enough to encourage investment. The Fed cannot control all markets, and sometimes it is frustrated in its efforts to use monetary policy to increase demand.

Changes in the Risk Premium and Credit Availability

As the economy fell into the deep recession of 1982, people became concerned about bankruptcies and defaults. Small businesses fail at very high rates in recessions and some large companies default on their debt payments or declare bankruptcy, and others are pushed close to default. The risk premium rose sharply between 1979 and 1983, and this is shown in Figure 8–7. Corporate bonds are rated for risk by two main investor services, Moody's and Standard & Poor's. A company rated AAA by Moody's is one with little chance of default, while bonds rated BAA have a greater risk, although they are still pretty solid. One measure of the risk premium is illustrated in Figure 8–7A by showing the gap between the interest rate on 10-year Treasury bonds and the interest rate on BAA corporate bonds. This measure of the risk premium was about 1.5 percent in 1979 but was over 4.0 percent by late 1982. *It is characteristic of recessions that the risk premium rises.* This usually happens as a recession unfolds; however, it does not typically happen before the recession starts. An increase in the risk premium has not been a frequent initial cause of recession, but a high or rising risk premium during periods of rising unemployment and economic uncertainty can discourage borrowing and exacerbate the recession. Usually the risk premium goes down again once the economy bottoms, and this pattern is clearly visible in Figure 8–7A. If the risk premium stays high after the economy has bottomed (as it did in the 1980s and again in the 1990s) it can slow an economic recovery.

Measuring the risk premium from the BAA bond rate understates what happens to credit conditions in the economy prior to and during recessions. As the Fed tightens monetary policy, banks start to restrict lending. At the same time, many companies, large and small, have a cash crisis. Their sales are falling below expectations and they have inventories piling up. They need funds as working capital and to cover the cost of the extra inventory. Just as the banks are trying to cut back on lending, the companies want to borrow more.[11]

Very large companies have a way out. They issue their own short-term bills—called "commercial paper"—as a way of raising funds to cover inventory or other short-term cash needs. There is often an increased flow of commercial paper issued into the financial markets as the Fed is tightening monetary policy and squeezing bank lending. The result is that the large companies that issue the short-term commercial paper end up paying very high interest rates on this form of corporate borrowing. Figure 8–7B illustrates what happens to the market for short-term commercial paper in periods of monetary tightening. The difference between the interest rate on short-term commercial paper and the interest rate on T bills is shown, and we can see that it jumped in late 1979 and then repeatedly through October 1982. Recall that T-bill interest rates were already rising sharply, so the figure shows that the interest rate on short-term corporate borrowing was rising even more. The widening spread shown in Figure 8–7B is characteristic of the U.S. economy, *the premium on commercial paper has jumped prior to several (although not all) U.S. recessions.*

Large companies have a tough time, because they end up paying high interest rates on their borrowing; but small companies have it even tougher. Their banks are restricting loans and it may be hard or impossible to find alternative financing. The small companies may be forced to cut back their activities or they may even be forced out of business. These companies are hard hit in recessions relative to large ones.

The fact that the risk premium and the availability of credit can both vary in response to changes in policy means there is another wedge or gap that is opened between the interest rate in the money market and the effective cost of funds for companies. In some ways, this allows the Fed to be more effective in its policies. When it reduces money growth, the Fed not only raises interest rates it also makes credit harder to find. This was illustrated in 1980 when the Fed reinforced its tight policy by imposing specific borrowing restrictions, and this had a quick and powerful effect on the economy.

On the other hand, the risk premium may vary for reasons that are not under the control of the Fed and that it may find hard to predict. If the Fed is trying to stimulate an economic recovery, it may drive down the interest rate on T bills but find that the interest rate on corporate borrowing remains very high. For example, in the Great Depression the interest rate on BAA bonds was very high, even though the T-bill rate was very close to zero. Low interest rates in the money market were no help to companies deciding whether to invest and to finance the investment by issuing bonds.

---

[11] Bank lending typically rises a little as the Fed contracts, probably as companies draw down their lines of credit. But it is still true that banks are trying to curb lending and are reluctant to finance expanding inventory accumulations.

Changes in Expected Inflation, 1979–83

Figuring out what expected inflation was over the specific period 1979–83 is not easy. Inflation was a very serious problem in the U.S. economy throughout the 1970s. The normal output–inflation trade-off was shifted at this time by increases in oil prices and other commodity prices. We will be looking at these "supply shocks" in Chapter 12. During this period, people had heard a lot of talk about how inflation was going to be curbed and they had then seen inflation accelerating, instead. As a result, when the Fed started to follow its contractionary policies in 1978, 1979, and 1980, people did not immediately think that there was going to be a drop in inflation in the near future. And this view did not change initially even when the Fed contracted again in 1981. *Expected inflation remained rather high in the early 1980s. Expected inflation was probably rising in 1978–79. After this, the contractionary monetary policies followed in 1979–81 lowered expected inflation a little, so the rise in the real cost of funds was somewhat higher than the rise in nominal interest rates, but probably not by much.* Expected inflation declined later in the 1980s.

A Summary of the Effect of Monetary Contraction on Interest Rates

Based on the *IS–LM* analysis and on what we have seen from this case study of the early 1980s, we can summarize the likely impact of a monetary contraction on interest rates.

- The Fed has control over the banking system and can reduce the money supply. This will increase the short-term nominal rate of interest (the T-bill rate). (There was very large increases in T-bill rates during the 1979–83 period.)
- As a recession actually unfolds, the risk of default rises and the risk premium rises. (The gap between the interest rate on BAA bonds and the rate on Treasury bonds widened sharply in 1982 and 83.)
- As the Fed squeezes the banks, companies find their ability to borrow is curtailed. Large companies sell their own short-term bonds, but find the interest rates they must pay jump even more than T-bill rates. (The rise in the "spread" between the T-bill rate and the commercial paper rate was very visible in the 1979–83 period.) Small companies may be squeezed even more when the Fed contracts and banks restrict lending.
- A contractionary monetary policy will lower expected inflation. This means that, following such a policy, the real rate of interest will increase by more than the observed increase in nominal rates of interest. In the short run, the reduction in expected inflation following a monetary contraction is likely to be small. (Expected inflation stayed high in the early 1980s.) A sustained and credible commitment to inflation fighting by the Fed will lower expected inflation by more than a contractionary policy that is seen as temporary.

The case study shows how difficult it is for the Fed to control the economy precisely. It can exercise pretty good control over T-bill rates; but it cannot control the cost of funds, and hence it may find investment and the economy moving in ways that are counter to its intent or it may find its policies having a bigger effect than it wants.

Expansionary Fed policies can misfire, also. The period 1990–93 provides a different and important illustration of what happens when the cost of funds in financial markets fails to respond to the Fed's push in money markets.

PUSHING ON A STRING: MONETARY POLICY, 1990–93

Helped by a sharp drop in oil prices, the inflation problem was finally brought under control in the mid-1980s and, by 1989, the U.S. economy had enjoyed one of the longest expansions on record. The Fed became concerned about the possibility of inflationary pressure building up, however, as the unemployment rate dropped below 6 percent. The Fed judged that the economy had reached the point where output was above potential output. It decided to try and reduce aggregate demand without actually bringing on a recession by using a contractionary monetary policy, but only a mildly contractionary policy. The yield curve flattened for quite a while starting in 1988 and continuing into 1990 as the Fed pushed up interest rates in the money market. And the experience of 1982 had effectively established the Fed's credibility—people now knew that the Fed was willing to tolerate high unemployment to control inflation. Hence this mild contractionary policy raised the cost of funds and slowed the growth of aggregate demand. The GDP grew at less than a 2 percent rate in the second quarter of 1989 and kept up a very slow pace of growth through the second quarter of 1990.

Since the Fed wanted to engineer a "soft landing," it eased its monetary policy as the economy began to slow and short rates fell, starting in the spring of 1989. Unfortunately, the policy did not work as intended, and the soft landing turned into a stall and the economy went into recession in 1990.

There are several possible reasons why there was a recession when the Fed had already eased.[12] First, it is very hard to engineer a soft landing in the economy, and the slow growth of output weakened investment demand—an accelerator effect that we describe more in Chapter 9. Second, there was a modest contractionary push from fiscal policy as the Congress and President Bush agreed to measures to reduce the budget deficit. Third, there had been excessive borrowing and excessive speculative building of offices and shopping centers in the 1980s. High vacancy rates discouraged further construction. Fourth, many banks had participated in the speculative building of the 1980s and were now facing bankruptcy as loans defaulted. They were unable to lend new funds. Fifth, Saddam Hussein invaded Kuwait and oil prices shot up. Twice before, recessions had followed jumps in oil prices, and consumers anticipated trouble this time and cut back their spending; auto sales were particularly weak.

GDP grew at only a 1 percent rate in the second quarter of 1990 and fell in the third quarter, and then fell more sharply in the fourth quarter of 1990 and the first quarter of 1991. The unemployment rate rose as output fell, but not as fast as in the recession of the early 80s. Unemployment seemed to hit a peak in June of 1991 at 6.8 percent, well below the peak of 10.6 percent in 1982.

Since recessions are defined as periods of declining output, the recession is said to have ended by mid-1991. But unfortunately this economic slowdown showed great

---

[12] See Olivier Blanchard, "Consumption and the Recession of 1990–91," *American Economic Review,* May 1993, pp. 270–74; Robert E. Hall, "Macro Theory and the Recession of 1990–91," *American Economic Review,* May 1993, pp. 275–79; and Allen Sinai, "What's Wrong with the Economy," *Challenge,* November/December 1992.

persistence and the worst had not yet come for unemployment. GDP increased after the first quarter of 1991; but its growth was very weak, so weak in fact that unemployment kept on rising. Increases in the labor force were not being absorbed into new jobs. The unemployment rate was 7.3 percent in December 1992 and employment was little changed from its low point in 1991. The weakness of the economic recovery (the so-called jobless recovery) contributed greatly to President Bush's defeat in the 1992 election.

The Fed had shifted its policy to become more expansionary once the recession hit; but this did not have the desired effect, because the economy grew in fits and starts, seemingly unable to really get moving again. Why was economic recovery so hard to come by, even though monetary expansion was in effect?

Interest Rates and the Slow Recovery, 1991–92

As we indicated above, there are reasons for the slow recovery of the economy after 1991 that can be found in the goods market (on the *IS* side). The overhang of unfilled space in office buildings and shopping centers and the decline in the price of residential housing in some parts of the country certainly discouraged investment in those sectors. We will look more at investment and the demand for consumer durables in Chapter 9. We want to concentrate here on the movement of different interest rates and how these shifts limited the effectiveness of monetary policy in getting the economy moving.

From June 1990 until the end of 1992 the rate of interest on three-month T bills fell almost 5 percentage points, going below 3 percent for the first time in many years. By contrast, the interest rate on 10-year Treasury bonds fell only about 2 percentage points and the rate on BAA bonds fell only 1.5 percentage points and stayed very high throughout 1991. Long-term risky interest rates fell less than the fall in the short-term money market interest rate.

The interest rate on new home mortgages fell about 2 percentage points over this period, also, but even this rather modest decline overstates the easing of conditions for home buyers. Many banks and financial institutions were experiencing financial difficulties and were limiting the amount they could lend. And all banks were tightening the rules for borrowing. There was an increase in the default rate on mortgages in the 1980s, and banks were demanding more credit checks and larger down payments. Some potential homeowners were unable to buy or they bought smaller houses than they would have wished.

Over the period 1990–92, the Fed eased monetary policy and brought down the short-term nominal rate of interest, as seen by the rate on T bills. But long-term interest rates and risky interest rates fell by much less. People were concerned that the Fed (having established itself as an inflation hawk) would soon turn around and raise rates again, so expectations of future interest rates worked to keep the yield curve steep. And people were concerned about the continued risk of default on loans. Given that investment demand was already rather weak and that consumers were hesitant to step up their purchases of consumer durables, the impetus to growth provided by the Fed was inadequate. Monetary policy was able to lower short-term rates but not lower the cost of funds enough to stimulate investment in the short run. This period again illustrates how Fed control of the money market limits its short-run control over investment.

CONCLUSION

In this chapter we have dropped our simple assumption there is one rate of interest in the economy, a single rate that influences the decision to hold money as well as influencing the decisions about purchasing real investment goods.

The Federal Reserve operates in the money market where the short-term nominal rate of interest is determined; and the Fed's policies affect that interest rate. In contrast, the movement of equilibrium income is driven by shifts in aggregate demand, which in turn is affected by business and household demands for real capital investments. This demand depends, in part, on the cost of funds, a cost that depends on risk and is strongly influenced by the long-term real rate of interest. The resulting gap among interest rates and, more importantly, the fact that these rates depend on the expectations held by the borrowers and lenders in different financial markets, explains one important reason why monetary policy may not always work as intended. Further, changes in the relationships among rates can be used to make inferences about changes in inflationary and business conditions, expectations, risks, and the course of monetary policy and thus be used to help economists predict trends in economic activity.

WORKED EXAMPLES

Worked Example 8–1

Evaluating an Investment Project

In this example, a firm is considering whether to expand its retail-distribution facilities by opening a new location. The future profits from the new unit's sales will have to be compared with the cost of opening the facility. The conditions surrounding this investment-project example are described as follows:

- *Opening a new retail operation costs $1,500,000*
  This covers the construction of the facility, buying equipment, putting in inventory, and other startup costs.
- *The firm plans to operate the facility for four years.*
  It is corporate policy to sell off the facility as a franchise operation after the first four years.
- *The firm's managers expect that the facility will generate a profit of $350,000 a year in each of its first four years.*
- *It is estimated that at the end of four years, the firm can sell the facility to a franchisee for $500,000.*

In Table 8–1, the present-discounted-value calculation for the distribution facility indicates that the retail-distribution-facility project has a present discounted value of just under $1.3 million. Since the project requires an investment of $1.5 million, this evaluation would lead to rejecting the project with a 15 percent discount rate.

TABLE 8–1
Present Value of the Distribution Facility (long-term interest rate = 15 percent)

	Return Estimates	Present Values
Year 1	$350,000 ÷ 1.15	= $ 304,350
Year 2	$350,000 ÷ (1.15)^2	= $ 264,650
Year 3	$350,000 ÷ (1.15)^3	= $ 230,130
Year 4	$350,000 ÷ (1.15)^4	= $ 200,115
Sale of facility to franchisee:		
Year 4	$500,000 ÷ (1.15)^4	= $ 285,875
Total present value		$1,285,120

TABLE 8–2
Present Value of the Distribution Facility (long-term interest rate = 5 percent)

	Return Estimates	Present Values
Year 1	$350,000 ÷ 1.05	= $ 333,333
Year 2	$350,000 ÷ (1.05)^2	= $ 317,460
Year 3	$350,000 ÷ (1.05)^3	= $ 302,343
Year 4	$350,000 ÷ (1.05)^4	= $ 287,946
Sale of facility to franchisee:		
Year 4	$500,000 ÷ (1.05)^4	= $ 411,351
Total present value		= $1,652,433

We used this example of an evaluation of an investment project to find how interest rates affect investment demand. In this case, the interest rate was so high that the project was rejected on a present-discounted-value basis.

What would the evaluation of the project look like if the long-term interest rate were lower? Table 8–2 shows the evaluation of the project when the long-term rate of interest is 5 percent instead of the previous 15 percent. With a lower long-term interest rate, the project has a present value in excess of $1.6 million, a figure that exceeds the initial investment cost of $1.5 million. At the lower interest rate, the evaluation of present discounted value leads to the acceptance of the project. *When the interest rate used to discount investment projects declines, there is an increase in the present discounted value of projects and an increase in the number of projects that are undertaken.*

Worked Example 8–2

Computing the Real Rate of Interest

Question   Consider a situation where it is expected there will be no inflation next year and a lender is considering lending $1 million for a year at 5 percent interest. In this case, the lender expects to be able to buy goods and services with a real value of $1,050,000 at the end of the year. The real rate of interest in this case is 5 percent, the same as the nominal rate of interest (with no inflation, $r = i$). Line 1 of Table 8–3 shows the simple case where $1,000,000 is loaned for one year at 5 percent and there is no inflation.

TABLE 8–3   Lending, Inflation, and Interest Rates

(a) Expected Inflation Rate This Year	(b) Loaned Funds	(c) Nominal Interest Rate	(d) Funds Repaid Next Year	(e) Real Value Next Year	(f) Real Rate of Interest
0%	$1,000,000	5%	$1,000,000 × 1.05 = $1,050,000	$1,050,000	5%
10%	$1,000,000	5%	$1,000,000 × 1.05 = $1,050,000	$1,050,000 ÷ 1.10 = $954,545	−4.5%
10%	$1,000,000	15.5%	$1,000,000 × 1.15 = $1,155,000	$1,155,000 ÷ 1.10 = $1,050,000	5%

Suppose now there were an inflation of 10 percent expected for the year. What will the real rate of interest be in this case, assuming no change in the nominal rate of interest? What will the nominal rate of interest have to be to yield a real rate of interest of 5 percent when there is 10 percent expected inflation?

Calculate the real rate of interest from Equation 8–2. When the nominal rate is 15.5 percent and the rate of inflation is 10 percent. How good is the approximation?

Answer   With 10 percent inflation expected, lenders will expect to lose 10 percent of the value of their loans when they are repaid. If the nominal rate of interest remains at 5 percent (i is still 0.05 = 5 percent), the lender receives $1,050,000 (the loan repayment plus interest) but, because of the 10 percent inflation, the loan repayment plus interest is worth 10 percent less than the nominal amount of the repayment. After the effects of inflation, the real value of the loan repayment plus interest is only $954,545 ($1,050,000 ÷ 1.10). In this case, the real rate of interest is −4.5 percent [r = −4.5 percent = −0.045 = (954,545 − 1,000,000)/1,000,000]. This is shown on line 2 of Table 8–3.

The lender loses purchasing value by making this loan. The real return to the lender is negative because, even after lending money at interest, the lender's investment buys a smaller quantity of goods and services after one year than could have been bought at the beginning of the year.

Suppose the lender expects 10 percent inflation and he wants his investment to be able to purchase 5 percent more goods and services after being loaned for one year. How high would the nominal rate of interest have to be to yield a real rate of interest rate of 5 percent? The answer is that, when there is 10 percent inflation, the nominal rate of interest has to be 15.5 percent (i = 0.155 = 15.5 percent) to yield a real rate of interest of 5 percent (r = 0.05 = 5 percent). This is shown on line 3 of Table 8–3, where the dollar amount of the loan repayment plus interest at an interest rate of 15.5 percent is $1,155,000. When this amount is reduced by the 10 percent expected rate of inflation, the value of the repayment plus interest is indeed $1,050,000 = $1,155,000/1.1, so the real rate of interest is 5 percent.

The approximation from Equation 8–2 generates a real rate of interest of 5.5 percent, rather than 5 percent. From Equation 8–2, 15.5 − 10 is equal to 5.5 percent. The approximation is more accurate for lower rates of interest and inflation.

TABLE 8–4
Present Value of the Distribution Facility with Future Returns Showing a 6.5 Percent per Year Rate of Inflation and Discounted at a 15 Percent Long-Term Nominal Interest Rate

	Original Estimate		Effect of Inflation		Discounting Future Values		Present Discounted Values
					New Return Estimate: Interest		
Year 1	$350,000	×	(1.065)	=	$372,750 ÷ 1.15	=	$ 324,130
Year 2	$350,000	×	$(1.065)^2$	=	$396,979 ÷ $(1.15)^2$	=	$ 300,173
Year 3	$350,000	×	$(1.065)^3$	=	$422,782 ÷ $(1.15)^3$	=	$ 277,986
Year 4	$350,000	×	$(1.065)^4$	=	$450,263 ÷ $(1.15)^4$	=	$ 257,439
Sale to franchisee:							
Year 4	$500,000	×	$(1.065)^4$	=	$643,233 ÷ $(1.15)^4$	=	$ 367,771
Total estimated *PV*							$1,527,499

Worked Example 8–3

Investment Demand, Inflation, and the Real Rate of Interest

In the distribution-facility example of Worked Example 8–1, suppose the firm's managers expect a particular rate of inflation over the life of the project. Taking inflation into account changes their estimate of future profits.

If the level of *real* activity remains constant (i.e., if the distribution facility is distributing the same volume of goods each year), then inflation will increase the dollar values of both future revenues and future costs of goods sold and hence increase their difference—future profit. When both sales and costs rise at the same rate as the rate of inflation, profit will also increase at the same rate as inflation.

Using a particular value for the expected rate of inflation, in this case 6.5 percent per year, we show in Table 8–4 how the present discounted value (*PV*) of the project is recalculated accounting for inflation. Notice this calculation assumes that the rise in the resale value of the facility to the franchisee has also mirrored the expected rate of inflation.

The verdict is that, even at a nominal interest rate of 15 percent, the facility looks like a good investment when adjusted for expected inflation. When inflation was ignored, the discount rate of 15 percent was high enough to make the project look undesirable. With inflation factored in, the project looks acceptable in spite of the 15 percent discount rate.

In Table 8–4, inflation is introduced by estimating its effect on the dollar returns from the project. The dollar or nominal values of the returns are then discounted, using the nominal rate of interest. From the point of view of the individual firm, that is the right way to do the calculation. When we analyze investment demand in the overall economy, we cannot introduce a specific inflation adjustment into the expected returns of all the separate investment projects. Rather, *we account for the effects of inflation on the future stream of profits by using an inflation-adjusted discount rate; that is, we use the real rate of interest.*

With an inflation rate of 6.5 percent and a rate of interest of 15 percent, the real rate of interest is calculated using Equation 8–1:

$$(1 + r) = \frac{1.15}{1.065} = 1.0798$$

The long-term real rate of interest, *r*, in this example is equal to approximately 8 percent. Using this value for the real rate to evaluate the distribution-facility project (shown in Table 8–5) results in the same estimate of the present value of the project that was obtained by calculating

TABLE 8–5
Present Value of
the Distribu-
tion Facility
Discounting with a
Long-Term Real
Rate of Interest of
7.98 Percent

	Original Return	Discounting Future Values		Present Discounted Values
Year 1	$350,000	÷	$(1,0798)$	= $ 324,130
Year 2	$350,000	÷	$(1,0798)^2$	= $ 300,173
Year 3	$350,000	÷	$(1,0798)^3$	= $ 277,986
Year 4	$350,000	÷	$(1.0798)^4$	= $ 257,439
Sale to franchisee:				
Year 4	$500,000	÷	$(1.0798)^4$	= $ 367,771
Total estimated *PV*				= $1,527,499

the nominal returns expected in future years (including the impact of inflation) and discounting these by the nominal interest rate.

Worked
Example 8–4

Equilibrium Income with Several Interest Rates

In the first worked example in Chapter 6, the *LM* schedule used was:

$$i = 0.005Y - 15$$

except the interest rate in Chapter 6 was labeled *r,* not *i,* because we were not making a distinction among rates. Now we have to keep track. The *LM* schedule relates the short-term nominal rate of interest rate and the level of income. In Chapter 4, Worked Example 4–6, we used the following *IS* schedule:

$$r = 141 - 0.034Y$$

The interest rate in this relation is the cost of funds. We will assume that the economy is in equilibrium, that the interest-rate premium due to risk and the slope of the yield curve is 5 percent, and that the expected rate of inflation is 3 percent.

Question

What is the interest-rate gap, the level of income, the short-term nominal rate, *i,* and the cost of funds, *r?*

Answer

$$r_{gap} = \text{Interest premium} - Exp\Delta P/P$$
$$= 5 - 3 = 2$$

The interest rate gap is 2 percentage points. The relation between *r* and *i* is then:

$$r = i + r_{gap}$$

So that

$$r = i + 2$$

We can then substitute the *IS* schedule for *r* and the *LM* schedule for *i* and we obtain the following:

$$141 - 0.034Y = 0.005Y - 15 + 2$$
$$\text{Hence} \quad 0.039Y = 154$$
$$Y = 3{,}949$$

The equilibrium level of income is $3,949 billion. This is lower than the level of income of $4 trillion that we found in Worked Example 4–6. The difference is the result of accounting for the interest-rate gap, which raised the cost of funds and lowered investment demand.

The cost of funds, r, can be found from solving from the *IS* schedule:

$$r = 141 - 0.034 \times 3{,}949 = 6.74 \text{ percent}$$

The short-term nominal rate can be found from substituting in the *LM* schedule or from using the fact that i and r differ by the amount of the interest-rate gap:

$$i = 0.005 \times 3{,}949 - 15 = 4.74 \text{ percent}$$
$$i = r - r_{gap} = 6.74 - 2 = 4.74 \text{ percent}$$

This example shows how equilibrium income can be determined if the *IS* and *LM* schedules are known and *if* (a big *if* in practice) the interest-rate gap is known.

Worked Example 8–5	### The Effect of a Contractionary Monetary Policy

We use the same starting point as in Worked Example 8–4. The economy is initially in equilibrium, with the following conditions:

$$(IS) \ r = 141 - 0.034Y$$
$$(LM) \ i = 0.005Y - 15$$

Interest-rate premium $= 5$, $Exp\Delta P/P = 3$, $r_{gap} = 5 - 3 = 2$ percentage points

We saw that equilibrium income was 3,939, r was 6.74 percent, and i was 4.74 percent.

Assume that the Fed contracts the money supply, so the *LM* schedule shifts as follows:

$$i = 0.005Y - 12$$

Assume that the expected rate of inflation does not change, but the yield curve inverts and the interest premium drops to only 2.5 percent.

Question

What happens to equilibrium income and to r and i?

Answer   Under these new conditions, r_{gap} is given as follows:

$$r_{gap} = 2.5 - 3 = -0.5$$

Solving for equilibrium income gives the following:

$$141 - 0.034Y = 0.005Y - 12 - 0.5$$
$$0.039Y = 153.5$$
$$Y = 3{,}936$$

The level of income has fallen only by a very small amount relative to the income (found in Worked Example 8–4) prior to the contraction of money. Substituting into the *IS* and the new *LM* schedules shows that the cost of funds, r, is now 7.18 percent, only a little higher than the prior rate of 6.74. On the other hand, the short-term nominal interest rate in the money market is now 7.68, much higher than before the policy change (from 4.74 percent to 7.68 percent).

Question
What happens if, after a while, the yield curve is no longer inverted and the risk premium rises, so the interest rate premium is now 4.5 percent? The expected rate of inflation has dropped to 2.5 percent.

Answer   Under these new conditions, r_{gap} is given as follows:

$$r_{gap} = 4.5 - 2.5 = 2.0$$

Solving for equilibrium income gives the following:

$$141 - 0.034Y = 0.005Y - 12 + 2$$
$$0.039Y = 151$$
$$Y = 3,872$$

Substituting into the *IS* and *LM* schedules shows that *r* is now 9.36 percent and *i* is 7.36 percent. In this new situation, income is sharply lower, the cost of funds is sharply higher, but the short-term rate in the money market is down a little (it is still much higher than before the policy change).

This example illustrates how the Fed can drive up money-market interest rates, but the effect of this on the economy is mediated by the expectations that are summarized by the interest-rate gap.

SUMMARY

- A company wishing to issue debt to finance investment or a household wishing to obtain a mortgage to buy a house will want to repay the debt over the long term. The long-term rate of interest will affect the decision to make debt-financed investments.

- The real rate of interest on a bond is approximately equal to the nominal rate of interest minus the rate of inflation that is expected over the lifetime of the bond.

- The present value of an investment project is the sum of the discounted flow of returns from it, using the cost of funds as the discount rate.

- An increase in the cost of funds will reduce the present value of investment projects. Compared with investment demand before the increase in the cost of funds, the number of projects undertaken or the size of some projects will be smaller.

- The cost of funds is influenced by financial risk and the long-term real rate of interest.

- Money demand depends upon the short-term nominal rate of interest. Money and T bills are both eroded by inflation.

- The relationship among the various interest rates on Treasury bills and bonds (government securities that are similar except for term to maturity) is called the "yield curve."

- Long-term bonds are riskier than short-term bonds, so the interest rate on long bonds will include a risk premium. Therefore, the yield curve is normally upward-sloping.

- During business-cycle peaks, the demand for money is high and the Fed is usually imposing a monetary restraint to cool off the economy. The short-term rate of interest is very high but is expected to fall. This can create an inverted yield curve, where short-term rates are higher than long-term rates.

- In recessions, short-term rates are usually much lower

than long-term rates and the yield curve is unusually steep.

- The short-term nominal rate of interest is determined in the money market at one end of the spectrum of assets (*LM*). The cost of funds affects investment and goods–market equilibrium (*IS*). The difference between the two rates is the interest-rate gap.

- When the interest-rate gap changes, the shift in the cost of funds will not be the same as the shift in the short-term nominal rate of interest. For example, a given change in monetary policy has a direct effect on money markets, but it has an equal effect on the real economy only when there is no change in the interest-rate gap.

- When the Fed undertakes a monetary contraction, there is a rise in short-term nominal rates—the *LM* schedule shifts up and the yield curve becomes flat or inverted. If this condition continues, the economy is likely to slip into recession.

- If the riskiness of business conditions increases, as happens in recessions, this can keep the cost of funds high, even though the Fed has pushed short-term interest rates down in the money market.

- The experience of interest-rate movements in the United States between 1979 and 1983 and the contrast with the period 1990 and 1992 illustrate how the effectiveness of monetary policy depends on changes in the interest-rate gap.

KEY TERMS AND CONCEPTS

cost of funds, p. 222

discount rate, p. 224

interest-rate gap. p. 237

inverted yield curve, p. 235

liquidity, p. 234

normal yield curve, p. 235

opportunity cost of funds, p. 223

present value, p. 224

real and nominal rates of interest,
  p. 226

risk premium, p. 228

term structure of interest rates,
  p. 232

yield curve, p. 235

DISCUSSION QUESTIONS AND PROBLEMS

1. How does a change in nominal interest rates affect the demand for real money balances?

2. If investors have a preference for liquidity, how can short-term interest rates ever exceed long-term rates?

3. Savers who deposit funds in a financial intermediary receive a lower rate of interest than the rate paid by families or companies who borrow from the intermediary. Why don't the savers lend directly to the borrowers?

4. Explain the different impacts of inflation on the returns from an investment project and the returns from a 30-year bond. Use your answer to explain why the real rate of interest affects investment demand.

5. If there is an increase in the supply of real money balances and a fall in the short-term nominal rate of interest, would investment demand rise? What might so change that investment was not affected?

6. Consider a firm's manager deciding whether to expand the firm's retail facilities by opening a new location. Suppose that opening this new facility costs $650,000. The firm plans to operate the facility for three years. The firm's manager expects that the facility will generate a profit of $200,000 a year in each of its first three years. The manager expects to sell the facility for $275,000 at the end of three years. Suppose that the long-term nominal rate of interest is 15 per-

cent. Also suppose that the firm's manager expects there to be an inflation of 2 percent per year over the life of the project. Further, the manager expects that the sales, costs, and resale value of the facility will rise at the same rate as the rate of the inflation.

a. What are the present discounted values of first year's, second year's, and third year's profit?

b. What is the total present value of this project? Should the firm undertake the project?

c. Now suppose that the rate of inflation turns out to be less than what the manager expected; it is 0 percent a year over the next three years. Would the project still have a present value greater than its cost? (Assume that the long-term nominal interest rate is still at 15 percent.)

7. If the Fed unexpectedly increased the rate of growth of the money supply, what would be the most likely immediate effect on short-term nominal interest rates? What would happen to the interest-rate gap?

8. If financial and business investors believe that there has been an increase in the riskiness of investments, can that change in expectations affect equilibrium output? How?

9. Consider an economy described by the following equations:

$$(IS) \; r = 70 - 0.0125Y$$
$$(LM) \; i = 0.004Y - 12.5$$

Assume that the interest premium is 6.3 percent and that the expected rate of inflation is 3 percent.

$$\text{Interest premium} = 6.3$$
$$Exp\Delta P/P = 3$$

Further assume that the Fed is following an accommodating monetary policy, so the real stock of money remains constant at the given rate of current inflation.

a. What is the interest-rate gap?

b. What is the equilibrium level of income?

c. What is the cost of funds, r, in equilibrium?

d. What is the short-term nominal rate of interest, i, in equilibrium?

e. Now suppose that expected rate of inflation declined from 3 percent to 1 percent. Assume that the interest premium and current rate of inflation are constant. What are the new equilibrium levels of income and the cost of funds?

f. Suppose that the expected rate of inflation goes back to its old level (i.e., to 3 percent), but the interest premium rises from 6.3 percent to 9.5 percent. What are the new equilibrium levels of income and cost of funds? What impact does the increase in the interest premium have on the short-term nominal interest rate?

ADVANCED TOPICS

9   Consumption, Capital Investment, and Economic Fluctuations

10   The Federal Reserve Banking System and Financial Crunches

11   External Balances and International Economic Policy

12   Supply-Shock Inflation and Economic Policy

13   Forecasting, Stabilization Policy, and the Variability of the Economy

14   Monetarism: Classical Roots and Contemporary Implications

15   Controversy in Macroeconomics: Equilibrium Models and the Neo-Keynesian Response

16   Employment Creation, Unemployment, and Earnings Distribution

17   Aggregate Supply, Long-Term Growth, and Productivity

The first part of this text provided a framework for income determination and macroeconomic analysis and as well an introduction to several important topics: long-term growth, the international economy, the financial sector, and fluctuations.

This second part expands on each of these topics while introducing new issues and dealing with others in more depth so as to answer a series of related questions:

- Why does the economic performance fluctuate? Why is there an apparent pattern of boom and bust?
- What causes imbalances in a nation's international trade and payments?
- How do changes in aggregate supply impact inflation rates or long-run growth rates?
- Can economists forecast periods of expansion and contraction.
- Can economic policies be organized so as to mitigate, if not prevent, these oscillations?
- Is monetary policy the driving force in macro-economic variability?
- Is policy ineffective because rational decision makers anticipate policy actions and incorporate their efforts in market prices?

- Is accelerating inflation inevitable if unemployment is too low?
- How does an economy create new jobs?
- Why are unemployment and earnings differentials a part of market economies?
- What are the determinants of long-term economic growth?
- How can we improve living standards over long periods through policy?

Investment demand is highly variable while consumption remains relatively stable. In Chapter 9 we ask why these patterns exist. This generates a richer picture of aggregate demand over time, and explains why these patterns resemble business cycle fluctuations. Chapter 10 picks up on work laid out in Chapters 4, 6, and 8 and addresses the operations of Federal Reserve policies and the role played by financial markets and in generating fluctuations. In Chapter 11, we extend the international discussions initiated in Chapters 2 and 7 and look at the balance of payments as a source of instability and as a measure of changing interest rates and policy actions. Chapter 12 carries the inflation story forward from the aggregate demand and policy issues introduced in Chapters 6 and 8 and looks at aggregate supply shifts as sources of sudden and sometimes lasting changes in the rate of inflation. In Chapter 13, we expand our discussion of several business cycle issues from Part 1 and Chapter 9—the pluses and minuses of attempting to forecast the macroeconomy, the effectiveness of policies designed to dampen fluctuations, and the question of whether or not the U.S. economy has become more or less variable as a result of the attempt to dampen fluctuations.

We recognize the disagreement in economics over some of the underlying assumptions as to how the economy works and, therefore, in Chapters 14 and 15, we describe two major alternative points of view concerning the workings of the economy—the sources of fluctuations over time and the implications for policy actions.

In Chapter 16 we take a more careful look at the labor market picking up on issues of productivity, competitiveness, and production introduced earlier in Chapters 2 and 14. Finally Chapter 17 returns to an issue that has the greatest impact on the long-run well-being of people in an economy—how to produce more per person and how to grow output and living standards.

CONSUMPTION, CAPITAL INVESTMENT, AND ECONOMIC FLUCTUATIONS

INTRODUCTION

The business cycle—consisting of periodic fluctuations in economic conditions, with recession and recovery—continues to be a feature of modern market economies. For example, the most recent cycle started with a stall in income growth at the end of the 1980s, moved through a decline in income during 1990 and 1991, and exhibited a slow recovery thereafter. Not only have business cycles persisted, they continue to be severe. During the period 1979 to 1982 the U.S. economy experienced the worst recession since the Great Depression of the 1930s. GDP fell 2.75 percent between the first quarter of 1981 and the third quarter of 1982, and unemployment rose rapidly.

One of the consistent features of business cycles in the United States and other industrial economies is that, even when the economy goes into recession, households tend to keep up their spending on nondurable goods and services. However, spending declines sharply in the purchases of *durable* goods, including consumer durables and new residential housing and producer durables—equipment and structures.[1] There are two contrasting patterns over the business cycle: the smoothness of consumption and the volatility of investment in durable goods. This chapter is devoted to a better understanding of these patterns.

In Chapter 8 we looked at how different interest rates move over the cycle and how these movements affect income and policy. We went deeper into the working of financial markets and enriched our analysis of the interaction between money and financial markets, on the one hand, and the goods market, on the other. In our representation of the economy we extended our

---

[1] Business inventories are also very volatile in recessions.

analysis of money and financial markets, the *LM* side of the *IS–LM* model. In this chapter we are going deeper into the determinants of consumption expenditure and investment demand; looking at aspects of the determination of aggregate demand other than interest rates or the cost of funds—the *IS* side of the *IS–LM* framework. Fluctuations in aggregate demand stemming from consumer durables and investment are very important contributors to the cycle of recession and recovery.

Since we will now be focussing on the variability of consumption and investment demand, we will move away from the expenditure categories as they were laid out in the National Income and Product Accounts, which separated consumers decisions from business decisions. Instead, we are now going to separate purchases of durable goods from the purchases of nondurable goods and services. We include all consumer purchases of durable goods as part of investment. Since residential housing is already included as part of business investment, we are simply adding consumer purchases of autos and appliances to investment as well.

When consumers buy durable goods, such as autos and houses, these decisions are similar to business investment decisions. A business decides to purchase machinery or buildings because these assets will yield a flow of productive services to the business over several years. Similarly, households buy consumer durables because they yield a flow of services to the households that own them over a period of several years. Buying a consumer durable, like buying a producer durable, involves an expected commitment over several years.

THE CONSUMPTION STANDARD OF LIVING

consumption standard of living

The value of goods and services consumed by households through current purchases of nondurables and from the flow of services obtained from consumer capital.

The material well-being of the average consumer is an important measure of economic performance. In common usage the *standard of living* has a simple meaning: the quantity and quality of goods and services available to the average consumer. Households consume goods and services through current purchases and through the flow of services that comes from using household ''capital'' purchased in previous years (i.e., homes, autos, appliances, and other consumer durables). We will define now the **consumption standard of living** as equal to *current* household purchases of nondurable goods plus the *flow of services* provided by the existing stock of consumer-durable goods and houses. This concept of consumption (based on nondurables and the flow of services from durables) is a good measure of consumer living standards.

Consumption Smoothing

Consumer purchases of nondurable goods and services and the flow of services from durables comprise the consumption standard of living. Through a typical U.S. business cycle, consumer purchases of nondurable goods and services are rather stable.

Consumption, Investment, and the Flow of Services in the National Income and Product Accounts

Even though consumer purchases of durable goods are similar to consumer purchases of houses and to business purchases of durable goods, the conventions of the national income accounts treat them very differently. The accounts assign consumer durables to consumption expenditures, while residential housing is considered to be part of investment, together with business investment. The value of the rental income paid on the existing stock of residential housing is included in GDP as part of consumption, including rent paid to landlords and the implicit rent paid by owner-occupiers to themselves. *Implicit rent* is an evaluation of the amount homeowners would have paid to rent the house they are living in if they did not own it. By contrast, there is no imputation made for the implicit rent that households pay to themselves for the flow of services provided by the autos or other consumer durables they own.

The conventions of the National Income and Product Accounts are rather arbitrary. In explaining household behavior, economists often reassign purchases of consumer durables and call them part of total investment and count the flow of services provided by the existing stock of dishwashers and autos as part of the flow of consumption. We are following this procedure as we examine the stability of consumption and the variability of investment. However, the flow of services from autos, appliances, and similar consumer durables does not appear as an observable measure that is included in the National Income and Product Accounts; it has to be imputed or estimated.

What of the other portion of the standard of living—the flow of services from durables? *The flow of services is likely to be stable from year to year even though the purchases of new consumer durables each year are quite variable.* The flow of services changes as the total stock of consumer durables changes. Changes in the stock of durables (more houses, autos, TVs, and appliances as well as newer and higher-priced and higher-quality products) change the flow of services. But the total stock of consumer durables available for use by households is large, and each year's purchases of consumer durables and houses adds only a small amount to the household's total accumulation of durables. If a household decided to delay or advance the purchase of a major new appliance, auto, or home, the total flow of services from consumer durables and houses would not change by much, even though there would be a large change in the amount of money spent on consumer durables in that year.

Combining the stability in the purchase of nondurables with the stability in the flow of services from durables means that, despite the fact that income varies quite a bit and the purchases of new consumer durables and houses vary quite a bit, *there is considerable stability in the consumption standard of living.* The fact that in a recession families maintain their purchases of nondurable goods and services and they do not quickly sell off consumer durables contributes to the overall stability of the aggregate economy. The slow response of households to recessions helps to reduce the size of recessions when they come.

When household incomes fall, people cut their consumption, but by less than the fall in their income. When consumers increase consumption by less than the rise in income and decrease consumption by less than the fall in income, they are smoothing

consumption smoothing

The decision to raise or lower consumption less than proportionally to swings in the level of income to moderate swings in the consumption standard of living.

the pattern of consumption expenditures over time—this is **consumption smoothing.** This behavior dampens fluctuations in aggregate demand and, to understand the variability of income, we want to know which economic factors affect the smoothing of consumption.

One explanation of consumption smoothing was put forward by James Duesenberry.[2] He argued that people become accustomed to a particular standard of living and so they choose to cut their saving or even dissave when their incomes fall, rather than cut back much on consumption. Further, it is both costly and difficult for people to quickly adjust many consumption expenditures. People who become unemployed do not want to leave their neighbors and disrupt their families by moving to lower-cost apartments. And even if they tried, breaking a lease, finding a new place, and moving are all costly, so the family stays put for awhile. Duesenberry described these ideas in institutional and sociological terms, and pointed out how people who suffer an economic reverse will go to great lengths to prevent that reversal from forcing them to change their lifestyles and fall behind their neighbors. Since Duesenberry's analysis, other important analyses of household-expenditure decisions used the more conventional and less sociological tools of economics to explain why households act to maintain their standard of living, even in the face of a fall in income.

Are people being irrational, stubborn, or simply motivated by social habit when they attempt to maintain their consumption living standards in the face of a decline? No. It is not just that in a downturn people do not want to reduce their standard of living. In many cases, they do not have to. They can take concerted action to smooth their consumption standard of living over time.

The Permanent-Income Hypothesis

In the book published in 1957 that still stands as a superb example of economic research, Milton Friedman developed and tested the *permanent-income hypothesis.*[3] His analysis emphasized the relation between the decision to consume and the decision to save.

The decision to save today is also a decision to consume more in some future period. *Saving and dissaving involve reallocating consumption from one period to another.* A major reason why people save in the first place is to allow themselves to smooth their consumption, so it is natural that saving, as a percentage of income, will go down during recessions and go up in booms. The permanent-income hypothesis argues that consumption is fairly stable, because consumers *can rationally obtain smooth consumption by varying saving and borrowing in the face of increases or reductions of income that are viewed as temporary.* A worker suffering a period of unemployment probably does not think that the resulting fall in income will last forever. A new job may be obtained or the old one might be restored.

---

[2] James S. Duesenberry, ''Income–Consumption Relations and Their Implications,'' in *Essays in Honor of Alvin H. Hansen* (New York: W. W. Norton, 1948), pp. 54–81.

[3] Milton Friedman, *A Theory of the Consumption Function* (Princeton, N.J.: Princeton University Press, 1957).

permanent income
The average level of income that households expect to receive over a period of years.

The average income that an individual or household expects to receive over a period of years is **permanent income.** For example, an increase in salary because of an increase in overtime pay is unlikely to change permanent income; however, a promotion coupled with advanced training is likely to change permanently the future course of income.

In Milton Friedman's analysis, the amount of consumption people make depends on their expectation of permanent income. Thus when a household suffers a drop in income in the current year, the family will not reduce its consumption proportionally, because its permanent income has fallen only a small amount. In this case, the household has a *transitory reduction in income*—its current-year income is below its permanent income.

permanent and transitory consumption
Permanent consumption is the average level of consumption that households anticipate undertaking over a period of years, given their permanent income. Transitory consumption is undertaken to meet unexpected needs, such as unexpected medical expenses.

The permanent-income hypothesis also leads to the concepts of **permanent consumption and transitory consumption.** A family that suddenly needs to buy braces for its children may well consume more than usual in that year. It may use up the saving it has made in the past. In response to the unusual need for dental expenditures, the family is making transitory consumption in excess of its permanent (meaning usual or average) level of consumption.

There is an important difference between transitory consumption for individual households and for the economy as a whole. The things that lead to individual transitory consumption are generally microeconomic. They depend on what happens to individuals, families, or small groups. *These shocks to the consumption standard of living will tend to average out over the economy as a whole, and they are not directly related to changes in income.* Of course, there are changes that lead to transitory increases or decreases in aggregate consumption, but it is unusual for aggregate consumption to be affected significantly by changes in the demand for particular goods or services.

By contrast, it is quite common for there to be aggregate changes in transitory income for the economy as a whole. While there is a substantial amount of individual variability of income, there are also important common fluctuations. A recession is a period when income is low in the aggregate, when many people have unusually low income, not just particular individuals or groups. A change in transitory income is more likely to be experienced economywide than a change in transitory consumption.

This analysis of permanent and transitory income and consumption led Milton Friedman to his version of the consumption function, a relation that helps explain why people maintain consumption levels over the business cycle.

The Permanent Income Consumption Function   This approach expands understanding of the consumption decision by separating the consumption expenditures of an individual household into two parts, permanent consumption and transitory consumption, and explaining each part separately. Permanent consumption, C_{perm}(household), represents the normal consumption standard of living for this household. Permanent consumption was assumed by Milton Friedman to be a fixed proportion, c, of permanent income, Y_{perm}(household). Under normal conditions, the higher is permanent income, the higher is the level of consumption that the household will normally undertake. In contrast, transitory consumption, C_{trans}(household), reflects unusual expenditures that a household might have to make if, for example, someone fell ill. The need for, or willingness to undertake, transitory consumption expenditures is driven by events that are randomly distributed across households. These relations are shown in Equation 9–1.

$$C(\text{household}) = C_{perm}(\text{household} + C_{trans}(\text{household})$$
$$C(\text{household}) = cY_{perm}(\text{household}) + C_{trans}(\text{household})$$

(9–1)

Across the nation, transitory consumption will generally average out to be small, with individual households going plus or minus. As a simplification, when we add up the consumption of all the households in the economy, we will take C_{trans} to be zero, so we can express total consumption as simply proportional to total permanent income:

$$C = cY_{perm}$$

(9–2)

The income of a household can also be divided into permanent and transitory parts:

$$Y(\text{household}) = Y_{perm}(\text{household}) + Y_{trans}(\text{household})$$

(9–3)

And there will be many fluctuations of income for individual households that are special to that family—a bonus adds to income or a dispute with the boss means being fired. When we add all household incomes in the economy, we get total income, and many of variations in income that affect individual households will average out in the total, just as was the case with transitory consumption. But not all of transitory income will average out. *During booms, income is unusually high* (Y_{trans} *is positive*). *During slumps, income is unusually low* (Y_{trans} *is negative*).

$$Y = Y_{perm} + Y_{trans} \text{ where } Y_{trans} \text{ is positive or negative}$$

(9–4)

We can now see how consumption smoothing takes place in this framework. During slumps, income in the economy is unusually low and current income, Y, is smaller than permanent income, Y_{perm}. Does consumption decrease in proportion to this decrease in current income? No, because consumption is tied to permanent income. The ratio of consumption to income (C/Y, the *APC*) will rise when income is low.[4] When the economy is in a boom, transitory income is positive—but when consumption is tied to permanent income and does not rise in proportion to current income—the APC will fall. Consumption is smoothed relative to income—precisely the pattern we observe in actual data.

Milton Friedman's analysis provided a powerful explanation of consumption smoothing. People do not follow the ups and downs of their current income by making proportional cuts in their consumption. They will save more when times are good and save less or dissave when times are bad—this is one of the reasons people begin to save. There is one important qualification to Friedman's model. His explanation of

---

[4] *C/Y* can be found by substituting Equation 9–2 into Equation 9–4. When transitory income is negative, the *APC* will be greater than *c*. When transitory income is positive, the *APC* is less than *c*.

consumption smoothing depends on the view that permanent income is less variable than current or year-to-year income. That makes intuitive sense, since permanent income is related to the average of one's income over a number of years. But that feature of Friedman's model has been questioned.

The permanent-income hypothesis emphasized that consumption can be smoothed in the face of the short-run fluctuations or uncertainties of income. But these short-run year-to-year variations in income are not the only important changes that occur in household incomes. Consumers face large but rather predictable changes in income associated with the different stages of life, particularly retirement. Taking these expected longer-term changes in permanent income into account has led to an important variation in the model of consumption smoothing. Changes in permanent income that are anticipated will lead to consumption smoothing that can be planned for through a particular pattern of saving behavior over people's life cycles.

The Life-Cycle Hypothesis

Franco Modigliani added a new element to the theory of consumption.[5] He demonstrated that *the amount households save is affected by the specific ways in which their income is expected to change over the future course of their lifetimes.* He formulated the *life-cycle hypothesis,* pointing out that one of the most important reasons for saving is for retirement.

When people retire they lose their primary source of income; their income from work. To maintain their consumption during retirement they draw down their savings accumulated during their working lives. The savings they had available in retirement was not generally the result of simple good fortune; rather, people anticipated their own retirement and provided for that time by saving.

In the early years of adulthood, many people are investing in education and many of them are borrowing to maintain their consumption and pay school fees. They are dissaving by piling up student loans or loans from family members. Then after leaving school most people get married and set up households at a time when their incomes are fairly low. They are usually accumulating a pension and making tax payments to the Social Security fund, but overall their net saving is low. As time passes, incomes rise and the peak expenditures of household formation pass, so net saving is larger. Incomes exceed consumption by a wider margin. At retirement, the situation changes. People's incomes drop and they draw on their pensions, collect Social Security, and draw on other assets to maintain their consumption during retirement. This pattern of saving over the life cycle is illustrated in Figure 9–1.

At age 18 (point *A*), income is low and many people are taking out student loans. At some point there is a crossover point (point *B*), where consumption levels and income continues to grow, generating positive saving. Families continue to make positive saving as they age and as their incomes rise toward peak income (point *C*).

---

[5] Franco Modigliani and Richard Brumberg, "Utility Analysis and the Consumption Function: An Interpretation of Cross-Section Data," in *Post Keynesian Economics,* ed. K. K. Kurihara (New Brunswick: Rutgers Univ. Press, 1954); and Albert Ando and Franco Modigliani, "The Life-Cycle Hypothesis of Saving: Aggregate Implications and Tests," *American Economic Review* LIII (March 1963).

FIGURE 9–1
Income and
Consumption over
the Life Cycle

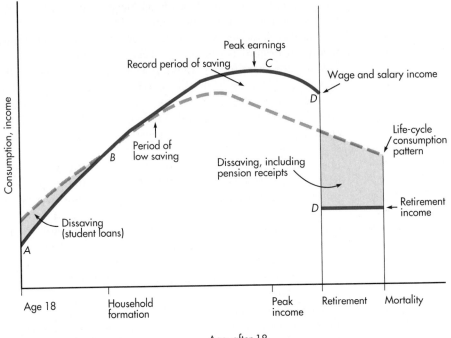

When people are young, earnings are low while consumption exceeds permanent income due to household formation. Earnings and saving peak in late middle age. At retirement, dissaving reappears due to low retirement income.

At retirement (points *D*) there is a downward drop in income as earned income is replaced by a lower level of retirement income. Families dissave again in the retirement years by drawing down their savings balances. (Pension income and Social Security income can also be considered as dissaving. See the following box.)

In testing his ideas, Modigliani argued that the consumption of a family will depend on the total wealth it has accumulated, representing the resources being held for consumption during retirement, and on demographic variables, such as age and the number of people currently in the family who need support. In the determination of aggregate consumption, Modigliani has stressed the importance of variations in aggregate wealth. For example, in Modigliani's model, a decline in the stock market leads to a fall in consumption.[6]

---

6 Empirical studies of the role of the stock market in consumption are in Barry Bosworth, ''The Stock Market and the Economy,'' *Brookings Papers on Economic Activity, 2:1975;* and Frederic S. Mishkin, ''What Depresses the Consumer? The Household Balance Sheet and the 1973–75 Recession,'' *Brookings Papers on Economic Activity, 1:1977.*

Saving for Retirement: Pensions and Social Security

For most people, saving for retirement is done through pension plans and through Social Security. In private pensions, a certain amount is set aside by employers and invested in stocks or bonds. Either a lump sum or an annuity is then paid on retirement, and the annuity may be adjusted for changes in the cost of living. Such plans provide protection against risk and allow people to reduce the costs associated with managing their own portfolios. However, there are certain sacrifices in terms of flexibility. Some employers give reduced benefits to employees who leave to change jobs. And if people suddenly need to dip into savings to meet an emergency, they may find it difficult to do this, or may face a penalty for withdrawal of contributions.

In the past, pension plans were not always funded by accumulating stocks and bonds from past contributions. Many plans used a "pay-as-you-go" approach, in which benefits for retirees are paid for by the contributions of employees still working. Such an approach was very attractive when pension plans were first being set up, because companies could offer the promise of future pension benefits without actually adding to current labor costs. Some years later these same companies have large hidden liabilities—the amount they owe to their retirees. Recent changes in federal legislation (the so-called *ERISA provisions*) now require private pensions to set aside amounts for retirees and provide federal insurance if companies or plans go broke.

The Social Security retirement program has used the same approach as the companies that failed to set aside contributions to retirement funds. The Social Security payments made to the early participants in the program greatly exceeded the contributions they had made to the plan, with the difference being made up with the Social Security tax payments made by those still working. At the present time, the program is running a surplus that is offsetting a big chunk of the federal government's budget deficit. But when the baby-boom generation retires, the burden on those who will still be working is likely to be very large.

One problem with pay-as-you-go plans, both private and public, is that they create a genuine asset for individuals. They are part of individual wealth. But they are not actually setting aside much saving themselves. The wealth created for any particular individual is largely a liability for taxpayers, not a net addition to national wealth. Such plans can reduce total national saving.*

* This issue has been discussed in Alicia H. Munnell, "The Impact of Social Security on Personal Saving," *National Tax Journal* 27, no. 4 (December 1974), pp. 553–67; and Martin S. Feldstein, "Social Security, Induced Retirement and Aggregate Capital Accumulation," *Journal of Political Economy* 82, no. 5 (September/October 1974), pp. 905–26.

There are important similarities between Modigliani's life-cycle hypothesis and Milton Friedman's permanent-income hypothesis. The permanent-income hypothesis argues that consumption decisions are made with reference to permanent income, while the life-cycle hypothesis argues that permanent income, over a lifetime, displays a rising and falling pattern that households anticipate. Both of these models place a strong emphasis on households making decisions on the basis of an expectation of future income and the use of saving and dissaving to smooth consumption over time. Most modern studies of consumption and saving combine elements of both approaches, and they indicate that the desire to smooth the consumption standard of living provides an important element of stability in the demand for nondurable consumption.

Recent Ideas on Consumption

The studies by James Duesenberry, Milton Friedman, and Franco Modigliani are the classic works on consumption behavior; but there have been several more recent studies, some of which have supported the old ideas and some of which have challenged them.*

Robert Hall of Stanford University has come up with an ingenious way of testing the permanent-income hypothesis. He pointed out that, if consumption depends on permanent income, changes in consumption should depend on changes in the estimates people make of their permanent income. Hall then shows that, if people are rational in computing their permanent income, changes in permanent income should be random—the only thing that will change the estimate is some new piece of information that was not available before. After taking the trend growth in income, new information will be random in its impact, being equally likely to raise or lower estimated permanent income. According to the permanent-income hypothesis the pattern of consumption should look like a *random walk*. In this case, consumption in the current period is equal to consumption in the preceding period plus a random error.

$$C_{current} = C_{last\ year} + \text{Random change}$$

Hall's analysis of U.S. consumption supported the idea that consumption is a random walk and hence he supported the permanent-income hypothesis. But his study sparked an explosion of additional research.

Criticisms of the permanent-income hypothesis and the life-cycle hypothesis have pointed to two concerns. The first is whether the permanent-income hypothesis can really explain consumption smoothing. When Hall suggested that consumption was a random walk, other people went out and found that income itself is close to being a random walk. And if that is true, *permanent income can be even more variable than current income.* The standard example that is used to illustrate a random walk is the sailor who should be heading back to his ship but he is so drunk that each step he takes goes in a random direction. As time passes, the sailor will not in general move closer to the ship. The uncertainty about his location rises over time. Similarly, if income is a random walk, changing by a random amount each year, then permanent income is not necessarily smoother or more predictable than current income.

A second concern is based on evidence from saving and consumption by individual households and whether it fits with the life-cycle model. One problem is that elderly people tend to save quite a bit while the young often save little. Young people don't think much about

The Constraints on Consumption Smoothing

The permanent-income hypothesis and the life-cycle hypothesis help explain how consumption smoothing affects consumption patterns in the economy. However, there are limits on most households' ability to smooth consumption. It should come as no surprise that households that suffer a significant reduction in income will not be able to completely maintain their standard of living. For most families, the largest share of permanent income comes from wages, so unemployment places constraints on the ability to smooth consumption. The family may be eligible for unemployment insurance and may be able to use credit cards or borrow from friends or family, but only up to a certain point. It is very difficult for some people to maintain their level of consumption through borrowing. An unemployed worker who went to a bank to explain that he wanted to borrow to cover the shortfall in his income resulting from his unemployment would receive a frosty reception. Banks have to lend on the basis of a borrower's future capacity to repay, not on the prospective borrower's need. Of course, prudent individuals who know that they may be laid off can set aside part of their income for saving, but many people fail to do this. Recent studies have found that

what will happen when they are old and they spend their current income. The elderly worry about becoming sick or needing nursing home care, so they save. A second finding from household surveys is that, across different households, there tend to be some who save a lot and some who save little, regardless of ages of the people in the households. Much of the variability in saving rates across households seems to come from differences in temperament (preferences), not from the fact that people are at different points in their life cycle. Households that save a lot end up passing their accumulated wealth to their children as bequests, not consuming it in retirement.

There has been no consensus as yet on some of these issues, but there are some general conclusions that we draw from the literature.

- Saving to smooth out the effect of the short-run variability of income and saving for retirement are important reasons why people save. There is a basic validity to the permanent-income and life-cycle hypotheses.

- It is hard to be sure what fraction of saving is made to make bequests to children, but it looks as if this is an important additional motivation for saving.

- A substantial fraction of the population consists of people who simply spend all of their current income. They do not make lifetime savings plans, other than to rely on Social Security, unemployment insurance, and company or union pension plans to provide for them in retirement or in the event of unemployment.

- Those people who make future-oriented plans and act on them, have a very strong dislike for variations in their consumption. This is basically what Duesenberry said many years ago. In current literature, this is described in terms of a low "intertemporal elasticity of substitution in consumption." The size of this elasticity reflects the amount of consumption people are willing to give up in one year to get more consumption in another year; studies find that the people will not give up much at all. They strongly prefer a smooth pattern of consumption.

* Robert E. Hall, "Stochastic Implications of the Life-Cycle-Permanent Income Hypothesis: Theory and Evidence," *Journal of Political Economy* 86, pp. 971–87, 1978; Alan S. Blinder and Angus S. Deaton, "The Time-Series Consumption Function Re-Visited," *Brookings Papers on Economic Activity*, 2:1985; John Y. Campbell and Angus S. Deaton, "Why Is Consumption So Smooth?" *Review of Economic Studies*, April 1989; John Y. Campbell and N. Gregory Mankiw, "Consumption, Income, and Interest Rates: Reinterpreting the Time Series Evidence," *NBER Macroeconomics Annual 1989* (Cambridge Mass.: MIT Press, 1989); Angus S. Deaton, *Understanding Consumption* Cambridge, Mass.: Oxford University Press, 1992.

consumption falls more during recessions than would be predicted by the permanent-income hypothesis.[7]

The ability of households to smooth their consumption during recessions will depend on the duration and depth of the decline in their incomes. A household's standard of living can be maintained during a short period of joblessness for one wage earner, but, after an extended period without work, or if the entire household is unemployed, consumption is bound to be adversely affected. The long recessions that occurred prior to World War II, when unemployment insurance was much more limited, were hard on people's standard of living. The economic difficulties experi-

[7] See Christopher D. Carroll, "The Buffer-Stock Theory of Saving: Some Macroeconomic Evidence," *Brookings Papers 2:1992,* pp. 61–135; and Robert E. Hall, "Macro Theory and the Recession of 1990–91," *American Economic Review,* May 1993.

enced over this period motivated the establishment of the modern unemployment insurance and Social Security programs.

We conclude, therefore, that, while consumption smoothing contributes to stability in the consumption standard of living, it doesn't guarantee that *consumption expenditures* remain unchanged in the face of a recession. Furthermore, aggregate demand is subject to fluctuations over and above the stabilizing effects that consumption smoothing has on the decision to continue to undertake nondurable consumption expenditures. Substantial variability in aggregate demand comes from other expenditure sources, including variations in consumption expenditures on durables and variations in business investment expenditures.

CAPITAL INVESTMENT AND ECONOMIC FLUCTUATIONS

A good deal of the instability in aggregate demand comes from the high degree of variation in the level of current expenditures on durable capital goods, particularly given that we are now defining capital investment to include all the investment purchases made by both businesses and households: machinery and equipment, structures, and inventories plus consumer purchases of new residential housing and consumer durables.

Businesses have a stock of capital on hand—the factories, equipment, and office buildings that they have been using to produce output. They assess whether the size and composition of their stock of capital will allow them to produce their products at the lowest cost and they then make investment purchases based on how large a capital stock they have, compared with how much capital they want to hold. They increase or decrease their investment expenditures to increase or decrease their current stock of capital. High business investment demand occurs when the current stock of capital is too low. Investment demand is low when the current capital stock is too high, relative to expected needs.

Although there are important differences between a household's decision to buy a new car and a company's decision to buy a new machine, we will group them together and focus on the similarities. Households look at the stock of durable goods that they have and decide whether this stock is large enough. If it is not, then they will purchase more durable goods. The household decision on when to buy a durable good is similar to the business decision on when to make a capital expenditure—both are based on a comparison of a household or firm's actual capital stock and what is called the *desired stock of capital.*

Capital goods wear out over time and have to be replaced. An important fraction of total gross investment consists of replacement investment. Businesses replace machines as they wear out or when better alternatives become available. Households buy new washing machines when the old ones wear out or when new models are sufficiently attractive.

The Variability of Total Capital Investment

Consumers smooth their consumption standard of living, but total purchases of all durable products by both business and households vary considerably over the course of a business cycle from recession to recovery. This tendency for the variability to be concentrated among durable products and buildings is a feature of business cycles that was studied many years ago, long before Keynes and the monetarists began developing the modern theories of the determination of output. For a long time it has been clear that there is something important about **durability.**

durability
A characteristic of capital goods. They last for more than one year, and they provide a *flow of services* over time.

The fact that capital goods last many years means that the stock of capital goods is large relative to both current investment and current income—business capital stock is approximately three times the level of business output. If businesses and consumers decide to maintain the size of the capital stock in relation to income, then small changes in income or production can lead to big changes in the amount of capital goods that have to be added to or taken away from the stock of capital. When a change in income triggers the desire to increase or decrease the capital stock, that change leads to large fluctuations in investment demand. This idea led to the development of a model called the *accelerator model of investment demand.*

The Accelerator and the Desired Stock of Capital

desired capital stock
The amount of capital businesses would like to have on hand, given current and expected economic conditions.

accelerator
The relationship between an increase in output and the level of investment demand.

The idea that investment demand depends on the way businesses vary the size of the capital stock leads to a simple model of variable investment demand. In this model, an increase in current output and income increases the **desired capital stock.** Since the actual capital stock was carried over from the past, there is then a discrepancy between the actual capital stock and the desired capital stock. The attempts to close this discrepancy lead to a large rise in investment demand. The model is known as the ''accelerator model of investment demand,'' because a small increase in output has a larger or accelerated effect on investment demand. Most empirical studies of the demand for consumer and producer durables start with some version of the **accelerator.**[8]

The simple accelerator model of the desired stock of capital assumes that, with a given production technology, it takes a fixed collection of capital goods—a particular amount of machinery, plant, and equipment—to produce a particular level of output. The amount of capital that firms want—the desired capital stock—is a fixed multiple of the level of output. The accelerator model can be applied to consumer purchases of durable goods. It says that, based on the level of their income, households also decide on a desired size of the stock of cars, houses, and appliances that they want to hold.

Equating income with output and combining the business and household desired capital stocks gives the following expression for the desired stock of capital:

$$K^d = vY \tag{9-5}$$

The desired capital stock is a fixed multiple of the level of income. The fixed multiple (v) is the ratio of the desired capital stock to output ($v = K^d \div Y$), called the **desired capital–output ratio.**

desired capital–output ratio
The ratio of the desired capital stock to the level of output.

If output is rising in the economy, investment demand is positive, because the actual capital stock is below the desired or required stock of capital. Firms and households demand investment goods in an attempt to adjust their actual stock of

---

[8] The history and development of the accelerator are surveyed in A. D. Knox, ''The Acceleration Principle and the Theory of Investment: A Survey,'' *Economica,* New Series, 19 (August 1952), pp. 269–97. Peter K. Clark, ''Investment in the 1970s: Theory, Performance and Prediction,'' *Brookings Papers on Economic Activity, 1:1979,* compares the performance of several investment models, including those based on the accelerator.

Net and Gross Investment

Consumer and product durables wear out over time. Cars last 5 to 10 years, so 10 to 20 percent of them are retired each year. Some others are lost to accidents. Computers become obsolete after only a few years, but houses and office buildings may last 50 or 100 years. Each year the U.S. Department of Commerce, the agency that constructs the National Income and Product Accounts, makes an estimate of the depreciation of the business capital stock and the stock of residential housing. This figure is called the **capital consumption allowance**. This figure is then subtracted from GDP to measure **net domestic product** (NDP). The same value is subtracted from *gross* business and residential investment to form the measure of *net* investment. In 1993, gross fixed private investment was $821 billion and net investment was $222 billion in 1987 dollars, so the majority of gross investment in the U.S. economy went to replace the capital that has worn out.

The fact that capital wears out means that investment demand can be divided into two parts: the demand for replacement capital and the demand for capital to increase the stock of capital (net investment). Of course, net investment demand can be negative. If companies decide they have too much capital, they will invest less than the amount necessary to maintain the size of their capital stocks. Individual companies can even sell off assets when they have too much capital—and these transactions happen quite frequently. And for the economy as a whole, used capital goods can be exported. There are substantial costs involved in trading second-hand capital goods, however. When a company buys capital goods, it will not usually plan to resell them except as a last resort.

capital with their desired or required stock of capital. The level of investment then depends on the amount needed to replace the capital that has worn out in the past year, plus or minus the amount to adjust for any changes in the level of income and output.

We define I_R as the amount of replacement investment, the investment that has to be made simply to keep the stock of capital from declining. Then if there is no change in the amount of output that firms want to produce, they will demand an amount of investment that simply replaces the depreciation. (I will equal I_R.) If there is an increase in the amount that firms want to produce, then the desired stock of capital will increase (I will be greater than I_R) and investment demand will be equal to depreciation plus the difference between the current desired stock of capital (K^d) and the desired stock in the previous period $[K^d_{\text{prior year}}]$:

$$I = K^d - K^d_{\text{prior year}} + I_R. \tag{9–6}$$

Combining 9–5 and 9–6 gives

$$I = vY - [vY_{\text{prior year}}] + I_R$$
$$I = v[Y - Y_{\text{prior year}}] + I_R \tag{9–7}$$
$$I = v(\Delta Y) + I_R$$

In the simple accelerator model, investment demand is equal to replacement investment plus the desired capital–output ratio times the change in income. The desired capital–output ratio (v) is the accelerator coefficient.

Even though it is so simple, the accelerator model can help us understand some important characteristics about the actual economy. In the actual economy, investment demand is much more variable than is income, as a whole, and the accelerator predicts this pattern because investment demand depends on a multiple of the change in income. In addition, we see in the actual economy that investment starts to decline once the growth of income slows down. Income is rising in a recovery, and this positive change in income keeps a high level of investment. Then as income growth levels off as the top of the boom approaches, the change in income decreases and investment demand actually declines, even though income may still be growing.

> **Worked Example 9–1** In this example on page 291 we show how variations in income can lead to much larger (accelerated) variations in investment demand.

While the accelerator model of investment demand gives us clues about why there is so much variability in the demand for durables, it is easily criticized as being too abstract. First, the desired capital stock will not remain a fixed proportion of income. The proportion will change with changing economic conditions. Second, following a change in income, firms and households do not attempt to close the gap between actual stocks and the desired stock immediately. Rather, adjustments take place gradually.

The Flexible Accelerator and Capital Investment

For considerable periods, firms and households can get along with a capital stock that is different from the one that fits exactly with their production needs. Businesses find that adjusting the size of their capital stock is very costly. While they will invest to bring the actual and the desired sizes into alignment, they will not close the gap completely in the short run. Companies have alternative strategies they can follow instead of investing in more capital. For example, they can temporarily hire more labor and take some time in adjusting their capital stock while still meeting production requirements. Given that they have this flexibility, firms that want to increase output look at the cost of building their capital stock quickly. The costs of rapid investment include technical adjustment costs, involving premiums paid for quick construction or delivery. So firms facing an increase in demand first use a combination of more labor (new hires, overtime, and temporary workers) and some more capital and then later undertake the remainder of the desired capital buildup. Adjustment costs are important in determining how the accelerator works in practice.

The fraction of the gap between the actual and the desired stocks of capital closed by investment in any particular period is the *rate of adjustment (d)* and this describes how rapidly firms react to changes in the desired capital stock. Of course in practice, the rate of adjustment is subject to change under varying economic conditions. A high rate of interest or a bout of pessimism about future sales will cause firms to delay their investments and adjust to the desired capital stock more slowly, lowering the rate of adjustment. But we will ignore the changing nature of the rate of adjustment for now by assuming that it is a constant value, and we will concentrate on how incomplete adjustment alone affects the accelerator model.

The lack of complete adjustment by businesses means that the actual capital stock in each period will not always equal the desired stock. *In this case, investment demand depends on the gap between the desired capital stock this period, the actual capital stock carried forward from the previous period, and the rate of adjustment.* The flexible accelerator is represented in Equation 9–8:

$$I = d[vY - K_{\text{prior year}}] + I_R \tag{9–8}$$

This equation says that net investment is a fraction *(d)* of the gap between the desired stock and the amount carried forward.

The effect of the partial adjustment is to smooth, over several periods, the impact of changes in output on investment demand, thereby sustaining investment demand even when output growth falls. This pattern of investment demand is more realistic than the explosion or contraction of investment demand implied by the simple model. The flexible-accelerator model predicts smoother investment patterns than the simple model, but it still explains the high degree of variability of the demand for durable goods.

> *Worked Example 9–2*   In this example on page 292 we show the working of the flexible accelerator. When income increases, businesses only make a partial adjustment to the new desired capital stock. Changes in income still lead to larger variations in investment, but the swings in investment are not as large.

The accelerator describes how changes in output lead to larger changes in investment demand. But in our analysis of goods–market equilibrium we have seen that an increase in investment demand will, through the multiplier, raise aggregate demand and output. What happens if we put these two ideas together?

The Multiplier–Accelerator Interaction

In a study that influenced decades of thinking about the business cycle and still does, Paul Samuelson combined a flexible-accelerator model with multiplier analysis into a model in which the increase in income generated by an increase in investment demand (through the multiplier) will lead to a larger increase in the desired capital stock (the accelerator). The higher desired capital stock then leads to a new increase in investment demand, and so on and so on until some maximum is reached. Then the slowdown in income generates a surplus of capital, investment demand drops, and the cycle works in reverse.[9] This interaction of the accelerator and multiplier helped Samuelson explain why the economy is prone to rapid expansions and contractions. The model predicted cycles under some conditions, and Samuelson suggested that business cycles in the actual economy might be the result of forces captured by the multiplier–accelerator model. We describe the working of his model and then use an example (Worked Example 9–3) to show how the path of output is traced out in a specific case.

---

[9] Paul A. Samuelson, "Interaction between the Multiplier Analysis and the Principle of Acceleration," *Review of Economic Statistics* 21 (May 1939).

In some versions of Samuelson's model, this process led to explosive growth in income, with income pushing investment even higher and then this pushing income even higher, and so on and so on. We know this does not happen in reality, because of rises in interest rates or shortages of workers or other constraints to expansion that prevent the explosive growth. These constraints would have to be incorporated into a more realistic model.

With some values for the multiplier and the accelerator, however, even the very simple model predicts that a boom will run out of gas and the economy will peak and start to turn down. The boost to investment increases income on the next round, but not by enough to increase the growth of income. This means income is growing still, but *the change in income is smaller,* so investment starts to fall. Investment expenditures decline even if the economy is growing, as long as the rate of growth is slower this period than last period. At that point, the loss of investment expenditure has a negative impact on aggregate demand. When aggregate demand falls, the actual capital stock exceeds the desired capital stock and investment demand accelerates downward, further driving down aggregate demand. The economy goes from boom to bust as the growth of output changes direction and turns over at a peak and heads for a trough.

The same process then works in the downturn. Provided the model is not unstable, there will be a point where the decline in income is less rapid, and then investment stops falling. Once investment stops falling, income stops falling and the bottom has been reached. Investment starts to rise again once income has stopped falling. This causes income to start growing and the economy moves into a recovery.

The accelerator–multiplier mechanism is illustrative of an important characteristic of actual economies: *if the growth of income begins to slow, the economy can move toward recession even while growth is positive.* For investment demand to remain strong, the rate of growth of output has to be sustained, and typically that does not happen. The economy approaches full employment and companies find hiring more difficult and anticipate slower growth, so the economy slows. Then falling investment demand may tip the economy toward recession.

The accelerator–multiplier interaction can also illustrate ways in which recovery takes place. Take an economy that has fallen into a recession. If the economy begins to recover, say as a result of policy action or an upward movement in consumer demand, output will begin to increase and the growth in output will generate a sharp increase in investment demand through the accelerator.[10] As investment demand comes back, this

---

[10] If the economy is using capital to capacity, as in a recovery or a boom, then the past year's capital stock will be insufficient to meet this year's need for production, and actual capital will be below the desired level.

    If output is rising as the economy is coming out of a recession, there is some question about actual capital being short of desired capital—what of all the capital that was not required or used during the recession, couldn't it be simply brought on line with no need for new capital expenditures? Not really, because if the recession were prolonged, actual capital could still be below desired capital because of past reductions in maintenance and technological obsolescence. New capital expenditures would also be needed if the industrial sectors leading the recovery are distinct from those that suffered the major effects of the recession.

will stimulate further increases in demand through multiplier effects, and the recovery is then well underway.

> *Worked Example 9–3*   In this example on page 293 we show how the multiplier and accelerator interact to generate a business cycle.

We have been grouping all kinds of durable goods and construction together in our analysis of the accelerator and the variability of investment. We have argued there are important common elements in the demand for consumer durables and housing as well as business investment. As we indicated earlier, we put off a discussion of changes in business inventories. Inventory changes are a volatile type of investment that we need to look at separately, and they play a particularly important role in the timing of cyclical fluctuations in economy.

Inventory Investment and the Inventory Cycle

Businesses use inventories in their production processes. Inventories are a capital good, like machinery and equipment, and are a costly necessity for a productive factory. While reducing inventory requirements is a reasonable goal for a firm as it attempts to improve its productive efficiency, at any given state of production technology there will be a necessary level of inventory associated with a level of output.

To the extent that inventories are simply a part of investment demand, changes in inventories can be analyzed using accelerator models. However, part of the purpose of inventories is to provide product for potential customers more quickly than by producing product on demand. This means that *expectations about future sales play an even more important role in determining inventory investment than other kinds of investment.* Inventory changes are observed to be more volatile than investment in fixed capital.

Inventories played an important role in the discussions of the multiplier and goods–market equilibrium in earlier chapters. We said that, in the short run, firms are willing to match supply to demand by allowing inventories to decline when demand exceeds current production or by letting inventories pile up when demand is weak. The change in inventories is partly a residual item—the amount of output that is produced but not sold. When demand is growing strongly, inventories become depleted. Then businesses step up production, both to meet demand and to rebuild the depleted stock of inventories. For a period at the peak of a business-cycle expansion, production exceeds demand. Once demand turns down, inventories pile up. Then businesses cut back production and lay off workers, both because of the fall in demand and to get rid of the excess inventories that have piled up. *Over the course of a business cycle, inventories actually add to variability. The variability of production in the U.S. economy is actually greater than the variability of sales.*[11] The effort to rebuild inventories pushes production above sales in cyclical peaks, while the effort to work off excess inventories pushes production below sales at troughs.

---

[11]   Alan S. Blinder, ''Can the Production Smoothing Model of Inventory Behavior be Saved?'' *Quarterly Journal of Economics* 91 (August 1986), pp. 431–53.

Inventories in Production: The Just-in-Time Innovation

While inventories may be necessary for production, actions taken to reduce that necessary level of inventories confer both cost benefits and production-technology benefits on a firm. The use of inventories in production is affected by managerial innovation. Better control systems are designed to make optimal use of inventories.

The just-in-time production method, developed in Japan by Toyota and now used worldwide, is a way of reorganizing production that not only uses fewer inventories but more importantly recognizes that the efforts made to reduce inventories reveal inefficiencies in production that were previously masked by the use of inventories as a buffer stock between stages of production or distribution. Correcting those inefficiencies not only reduces the need for inventories, it also increases productivity.

In the early chapters, we described a model of equilibrium in the goods market where businesses respond to declining inventories by increasing output following an increase in demand. They respond to rising inventories by decreasing output following a decrease in demand. This meant that in the income–expenditure model the economy was described as moving smoothly from one goods–market equilibrium to another. That was too simple, because it ignored the inventory rebuilding that is needed when inventories become depleted or the inventory liquidation needed when they pile up. The adjustment of inventories following a shift in demand can in practice involve some cycling (overshooting and undershooting) of the economy around a new equilibrium.

As the economy shifts from a period of inventory rebuilding in a business-cycle peak to a period of inventory liquidation in a trough, the shift in inventory investment can be very large.

Figure 9–2 shows the pattern of inventory investment over two periods of recession and early recovery, 1981–84 and 1989–93. The figure shows how the decline in inventory investment was both a result and a cause of the declines in output. As output growth slows, businesses find their inventories are piling up. They cut production and try to hold down their inventories. But since most businesses are acting in a similar way, the aggregate result is declining national production and income, declining employment, and declining demand. The shifts from positive to negative inventory investment both in 1981–82 and in 1989–91 were also causes of the overall decline in the economy.

Once the economy bottoms, businesses are able to work off their excess inventories. And then, provided demand starts to pick up again, firms will rehire workers, expand output, and begin to rebuild their inventories. The shift from negative inventory investment to positive inventory investment is an important part of the overall recovery in a typical business cycle and is seen clearly in 1983–84. The weak recovery in 1991–92 did not lead to a rebuilding of inventories until 1993. This was one reason for the fact that the economy became stuck in a slump.

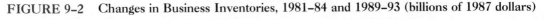

FIGURE 9–2   Changes in Business Inventories, 1981–84 and 1989–93 (billions of 1987 dollars)

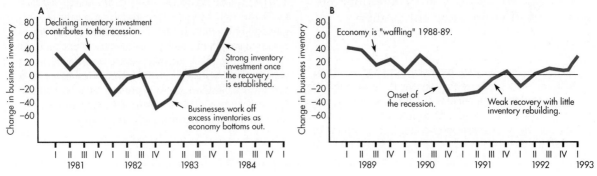

Expectations, Interest Rates, and Investment Demand	The flexible-accelerator model and its interaction with the multiplier, along with inventory adjustments, provide intriguing insights into the way investment and income might evolve over time. These models are based on the notion that firms and households face adjustment costs that affect the speed with which they match their actual capital stocks to their desired capital stock. Yet they still are lacking an important characteristic of investment demand, in that *the desired stock of capital itself changes as economic conditions change.* In practice, the investment decision is affected by factors that these models ignore: expectations and interest rates.

Expectations and Variability in Investment Demand

An important determinant of business investment demand is business expectations. The extent to which businesses adjust their investment demand in response to changes in output will depend on their expectations about future output. Is an increase in output going to last or not? Is an increase likely to be followed by a decrease? If so, why buy, build, or lease expensive capital this period only to be left with overcapacity next period?

One important reason why firms usually make only a partial adjustment to output changes is connected to their expectations about the duration of the change in demand. They do not necessarily think that increases or decreases in output will persist.[12]

If output is unusually low, then business managers may think it likely that output will rise, so they do not try to match their capital stocks exactly to the currently level of output; rather, they invest in excess of their current capital needs. They may continue to replace worn-out capital even though they will not need the replacement machinery right away. If output is unusually high, managers may think that output will fall, so they do not boost their investment by the full amount predicted by the simple

---

[12] This issue is discussed in Martin Neil Baily, ''Stabilization and Private Economic Behavior,'' *Brookings Papers on Economic Activity, 1:1978.*

accelerator. If families experience an increase or decrease in their income, they may see this as only temporary.

This discussion about expectations assumes that businesses or families will only partially adjust their investment following increases or decreases in output. If there is a recession and people believe that the economy will quickly return to full employment, then this belief actually helps to stabilize the economy. This is the normal case but it is not the only possibility. It presumes that businesses believe that reductions in output will be reversed fairly quickly. If businesses think, instead, that a fall in output will be prolonged or followed by a further fall, then the rate of adjustment can change rapidly and expectations may become destabilizing.

It is quite possible for a household to maintain its standard of living and still make fairly major changes in the timing of the purchase of a house or a car. Suppose the economy is in the early stages of a recession. Households are experiencing reductions in income, but they do not know at this point whether these income changes are transitory or permanent. They can decide either to postpone or go ahead with the purchase of a house or a car. Since they can manage perfectly well in the short run with the house or the car they have now, prudent behavior argues for waiting until they are sure about the nature of the income reduction. They decide to delay the capital expenditure. For example, the worker who thinks that layoffs are coming will not take on installment or lease payments for a new car but, rather, will continue to use the old car he already has. A middle-aged executive who hears that her company is planning to require early retirement among its staff will not buy a new house with a much larger monthly payment than the one she has now. An economywide postponement in auto, home, and appliance purchases may not initially affect living standards, but it will have quite large effects on aggregate demand.

On the business side, *in a single firm the timing of investment purchases can be changed without necessarily changing production.* For example, the decision to build a new factory could be postponed if a company suddenly decides that a recession is imminent and that demand will fall. A fall in demand would make it unprofitable to operate both the old and the new plants and it reduces the payoff to the investment project. If the company foresees a recession, it can continue to make do with the old plant for some time, *but an economywide postponement of investment will have a major effect on aggregate demand.*

As summarized next, the speed at which investment adjusts to changes in economic conditions can be quite different, depending on expectations.

- If the economy has been stable, where deviations around output are expected to be quickly reversed, a change in output will not lead to a big change in investment demand.

- If the economy is subject to large cycles, where major booms or slumps are expected to follow output changes, a change in output will lead to a larger change in investment demand.

- If businesses' expectations deteriorate such that they completely lose confidence in the economy, then investment can fall precipitously. One reason that the U.S. economy fell into such a deep depression in the 1930s is that business lost confidence in the economy, so gross investment fell almost to zero and net investment was negative.

In general, *the extent to which businesses and households are optimistic or pessimistic about future economic conditions will influence the current level of investment demand.* The fact that business investment and consumer purchases of durables vary with changes in expectations generates variability in investment and makes it hard to predict what investment will be.

The Interest Rate and the Accelerator

We assumed in earlier analysis that the interest rate of cost of funds affects investment. How does that fit with the analysis in this chapter, where investment depends on changes in the desired capital stock? We assume now that the cost of funds rate affects the size of the desired capital stock.[13]

In the flexible-accelerator model of investment demand, the effect of changes in the real rate of interest on the desired capital stock is captured by allowing the desired capital–output ratio (the accelerator coefficient, v) to depend on the cost of funds. A high interest rate will reduce the amount of capital that firms will choose to produce a given level of output.[14] For households, a high rate of interest will encourage them to economize on the amount of durable goods that they will choose at a given level of family income. This idea is expressed by:

$$K^d = v(r)Y \tag{9–9}$$

The desired capital–output ratio depends on the cost of funds, so the higher is the interest rate, the lower is v.

When the cost of funds is high over several years, as it was in the 1980s, this will lower the desired capital–output ratio, reducing the level of investment demand in each period from what it would have been otherwise. Inserting Equation 9–9 into the investment Equation 9–8 gives the following interest-sensitive version of the flexible accelerator:

$$I = d[v(r)Y - K_{\text{prior year}}] + I_R \tag{9–10}$$

In this version of the flexible-accelerator model of investment demand, the size of investment demand in a given period depends on the speed of adjustment and the desired capital–output ratio (which depends on income and the interest rate), the capital stock in the previous period, and the amount of replacement investment.

We use a simplified formulation of this flexible accelerator to see how these various factors affecting investment demand impact overall aggregate demand within the *IS–LM* framework. We concentrate on three variables in the interest-sensitive flexible-accelerator model—the level of income, the cost of funds, and the size of the capital stock in the previous period:

$$I = I[r, Y, K_{\text{prior year}}] \tag{9–11}$$

---

[13] In Chapter 8, we argued that, in an economy with inflation and uncertainty, investment demand depends on the cost of funds—a concept that takes these factors into account. For readers who have skipped Chapter 8, take the cost of funds to mean the interest rate that is most relevant for investment decisions.

[14] The classic study that brought the interest rate and other elements of the cost of capital into the accelerator framework was undertaken by Dale T. Jorgenson, "Capital Theory and Investment Behavior," *American Economic Review* LIII (May 1963).

This relation is now similar to the investment function that we introduced back in Chapter 3, except for the one additional term. It says that investment demand decreases with increases in the rate of interest and increases with increases in the level of income (just as before) and, in addition, *it decreases with the size of the capital stock carried over from the prior year.* Equation 9–11 summarizes the implication of the accelerator that we will apply to the *IS–LM* framework. If businesses and households already have a lot of capital, then investment demand will be weak, holding income and the interest rate constant.

THE CAPITAL STOCK, EXPECTATIONS, AND *IS–LM* EQUILIBRIUM

Introducing the flexible-accelerator model into our analysis provides a previously missing and important element of investment demand. Besides income and the real rate of interest, investment demand also depends upon the amount of capital that is already on hand, carried forward from the previous period.

Since investment demand is affected by how much of the capital stock is carried forward, equilibrium in the goods market is also affected by the size of the capital stock, and we must model the economy so *the position of the* IS *schedule depends on the capital stock.* Equation 9–12 illustrates:

$$Y = \underset{\text{Consumption}}{C(Y,T)} + \underset{\text{Investment}}{I[r,Y,K_{\text{prior year}}]} + \underset{\text{Government}}{G} \qquad (9\text{–}12)$$

The condition for goods–market equilibrium given in Equation 9–12 has become a fairly complicated expression, including fiscal-policy variables (G and T), the cost of funds *(r),* and a factor reflecting the capital stock in the prior year ($K_{\text{prior year}}$). We have omitted net exports from this equation, because we are not focusing on international aspects of the economy at this point.

The capital stock of the prior year was determined by economic conditions last year as well as by the capital stock in the year before that, while the capital stock in the year before that was determined by economic conditions in the previous year before and by the capital stock in the year before that, and so on and so on. *Over time, the goods–market equilibrium (the resulting* IS *schedule) shifts around depending on the past pattern of output and interest rates.*

Figure 9–3 uses two alternative *IS* schedules to illustrate this dependence on the carryover from past investment. When the capital stock carried forward is large relative to the desired capital stock, investment demand is small and the *IS* schedule (IS_A) is shifted inward to the left. The reverse is the case when the capital stock carried forward is small relative to the desired stock (IS_B). When there is a weak economic environment, firms are carrying forward a capital stock that is too large relative to the desired capital stock. They will face excess capacity, resulting in a reduced level of investment even with a low real rate of interest. Conversely, if the economic environment is strong with income rising or expected to rise, or both, firms will not have a capital stock equal to their desired capital stock. They will face a shortage of capacity and have trouble meeting demand. In this situation firms will invest in new capital even if the interest rate is high. This makes explicit what was only briefly described when we introduced investment demand in the *IS–LM* framework in earlier chapters.

FIGURE 9–3
Investment
Demand and
Income Depend on
the Amount of
Capital Carried
over from the Prior
Period

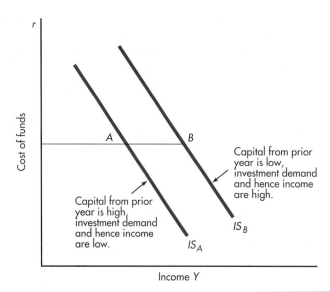

If economic conditions are such that income is falling, or if firms simply expect a reduction in demand, they will be reluctant to invest, even if the interest rate is low. At the same cost of funds, the level of investment demand is lower along IS_A (point *A)* than along IS_B (point *B*).

Consumer and business expectations are also important. If households think that a decline in the economy is going to get so worse that their own jobs are threatened, they will be very reluctant to invest in a new car. If people think that a recovery will come soon, they will not fear for their jobs and will be more willing to buy consumer durables.

In general, goods–market equilibrium as reflected in the position of the *IS* schedule will depend on both the past—the size of the existing capital stock—and on future expectations. *The demand for both producer- and consumer-durable goods will be greater (the* IS *schedule will be further to the right), the lower is the existing stock of these goods and the more optimistic people are about future income and sales. On the other hand, the larger is the existing stock of capital and the more people are pessimistic about the future, the smaller will be investment demand. (The* IS *schedule will be further to the left.)*

**Investment
Fluctuations
and the Cycle,
a Case Study,
1987–93**

We have discussed the way in which investment demand can be both a source of variability and can itself be affected by variability in the economy. We now look at the period from 1987–93, the most recent period of recession and recovery of the U.S. economy to see how this process works.

The Recession of 1990–91   In Figure 9–4 we show the main components of investment immediately prior to the 1990 recession and during the recession. The peak of the cycle occurred in the second quarter of 1990, while the trough occurred in the

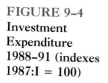

FIGURE 9–4
Investment
Expenditure
1988–91 (indexes
1987:I = 100)

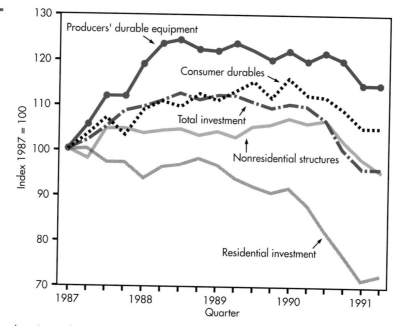

Investment plus durables equals gross private domestic investment plus consumer expenditure on durable goods.

third quarter of 1991. We have included consumer durables expenditure as one of the separate investment components, and included this expenditure as part of total investment.[15]

Over this period, we see total investment and most of its individual components rising and then falling as the peak is approached and then the economy turns down. The weakest component of investment over this period was residential housing (new single-family houses and condos), that had started to decline even before the recession was under way because of changes in tax laws. Other components of investment remained fairly strong through the summer of 1990 and then dropped in the third and fourth quarters—auto sales declined and businesses cut back on new offices, equipment, factories, and shopping centers.

What caused this pattern? In part it is exactly the kind of pattern we would expect to see over a business cycle based on the models of the accelerator that we have been describing. But there are also special factors in this recession, as there always are once we look at the actual economy.

One important aspect of the business that we have studied at length in earlier chapters but have ignored so far in this chapter is monetary policy and interest rates.

---

[15] Total investment includes changes in business inventories; but we have not shown this component separately, since these were shown already in Figure 9–2.

Several times in the U.S. economy in recent years the Fed has raised interest rates to slow the economy, and it was doing this in the late 1980s.[16]

In Chapter 8, we examined the impact of monetary policy on different rates of interest and on the cost of funds for investment. Since we are concentrating here on shifts in *IS*, we neglect these complexities (in terms of Chapter 8, we are setting r_{gap} equal to zero).

The accelerator model has shown us, however, that when the economy is growing slowly, even if it is still growing, this will lead to weakness in the demand for investment goods. And this lesson seemed to apply to the U.S. economy in 1990, because investment demand remained weak in early 1990, even though interest rates had declined. *The Fed's actions had left the economy in early 1990 on the edge of a recession.* At that point, however, a recession wasn't a necessity, only a possibility. What pushed the economy over the edge?

The most plausible explanation for the sudden drop in investment demand (and hence in GDP) in mid-1990 is that Saddam Hussein invaded Kuwait and the price of oil shot up. Consumers and businesses had experienced two such increases in oil prices before (1973 and 1979) and both times they were followed by recessions. Consumers and businesses expected hard times and cut back on their purchases of durable goods. There was a loss of business and consumer confidence. Concern about the effects of the oil price increase triggered the 1990 recession, through its impact on an economy that was already weak from the effects of Fed restraint and a banking crisis.

As demand fell, so did output, and then the fall in output further reduced the demand for capital goods and investment demand fell again and output fell again. The multiplier–accelerator model that we have studied is oversimplified, but it contains a kernel of truth about the actual business cycle as a self-reinforcing process of output and demand declines.

Figure 9–5 shows a way of modeling the decline in investment demand initiated by the rise in oil prices.[17] The loss of confidence would show in our models as a shift in the investment function that is depicted in Equation 9–11. As a result of the decrease in investment demand, the *IS* schedule shifts to the left, shown as a shift from *IS* to *IS'*, and income falls. Interest rates also fall as the intersection of the *IS* and *LM* shifts down (shown as a decline from r_A to r_B).

Once income falls there is too much capital in the economy relative to the level of output firms think that they can produce and sell—this is reported in the economic news as low "capacity utilization." In terms of Equation 9–11, the capital stock from the prior year ($K_{prior\ year}$) is too high for the current level of income and output. One

---

[16] An additional factor that can help explain the weakness in investment is that the crisis in the banking system was making it difficult for businesses to get loans to finance investment projects. And there is certainly some truth to this idea. But this possibility cannot explain the sharp drop in the economy that started in the summer of 1990, because there was no real change in the situation of banks or of savings and loans at that time.

[17] Since r_{gap} is being assumed to be zero, the equilibrium occurs where *IS* and *LM* intersect.

FIGURE 9–5
A Decline in Investment Demand Triggers Further Declines and Income Falls

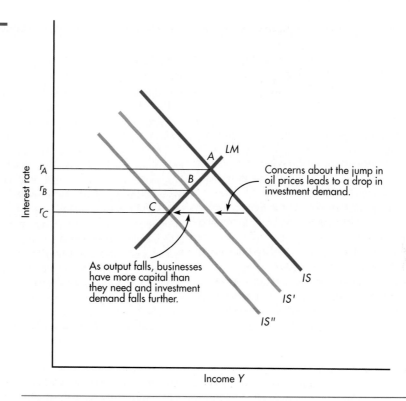

part of the capital stock that is often way too high in such a period is the level of inventories. Businesses want to cut back on unsold inventory. Investment demand (including inventory demand) falls again and the *IS* shifts further to the left (from *IS'* to *IS"*).

This process of decline eventually reaches a trough where businesses have adjusted to the lower level of output and, at that point, the forces of recovery start to work. This occurred in the U.S. economy in the second quarter of 1991.

The Slow Recovery of 1991–93   The normal cyclical pattern in the U.S. economy is that, once the recession ends, recovery is fairly rapid. Businesses work off excess inventories and output, and employment begins to recover. Demand picks up a little, and confidence starts to recover. Households that had postponed a new auto purchase find that the old clunker is giving too much trouble and they go out and buy. Businesses that were making do with their old PCs or their cramped office spaces, decide that they really need an upgrade. The Fed generally helps things along by keeping interest rates low with an easy monetary policy. (We would then model this process of normal recovery as a rightward shift of the *IS* schedule as the multiplier–accelerator process works in the upswing. The cost of investment funds will move down also with a successful expansionary policy by the Fed.)

Interest Rates and Investment Demand over the Business Cycle

The standard *IS–LM* model depicts a downward sloping *IS* schedule intersecting with an upward sloping *LM* schedule. A contractionary monetary policy is modeled as an upward shift of the *LM* schedule, causing high interest rates and a fall in income.

When students look at actual data for the U.S. economy, they find that interest rates are generally low during recessions and high during booms—exactly the opposite of what they expected from the *IS–LM* model. What is going on? What explains this puzzle?

The first issue is: What interest rate are we talking about? In Chapter 8 we argued that the cost of funds for investment is different from the short-term nominal rates

of interest that are determined in money markets. And the cost of funds is often high during recessions or periods of low output, even though short rates are low. So part of this puzzle was resolved in Chapter 8 when we examined the structure of different rates of interest. But that is not the whole story; there is also a second issue.

When the economy goes into a downturn, income and output fall, and so does investment demand, for reasons that we have described with the accelerator model. *In terms of the* IS–LM *model, the* IS *schedule will generally shift to the left as a recession unfolds.* Once we allow for the shift in the *IS* schedule, the *IS–LM* model suggests that low investment demand, low income, and low interest rates can easily go together. Indeed that is the pattern described in Figure 9–5, as the shifts in the *IS* schedule lead to declines in the interest rate—from r_A to r_B to r_C.

President Bush and many of his economic advisers were counting on these normal forces of recovery to operate in 1991 and 1992, but they and the rest of the country were disappointed. Investment demand increased from its level at the trough, but the recovery was very weak indeed. We show in Figure 9–6 the movement of investment starting from the trough of the recession. Residential housing grew strongly after the trough was reached, but recall that this component of investment had fallen the furthest. Even in 1993, this type of investment was only about back to where it had been prior to the recession. The increases in other types of investment were fairly weak, compared to prior recoveries. In particular, investment in nonresidential structures continued to fall even after the trough.

We discussed in Chapter 8 some of the reasons for the slow recovery. Because of the problems in the financial system and because of uncertainty about the Fed's intentions, the cost of funds for investment projects did not come down as fast as did short-term interest rates. And this inhibited growth in investment demand. In addition to these factors that affected the supply and hence the cost of funds, there was a weakness in business and consumer confidence that kept down the growth in investment for a while.

Fluctuations in investment demand are both a major cause of the overall business cycle and are themselves caused by fluctuations in output. In this chapter, we have looked at some economic models of investment demand to help understand this process better, and we have looked at the period 1988–93 as an example of shifts in investment demand and how they interact with the business cycle.

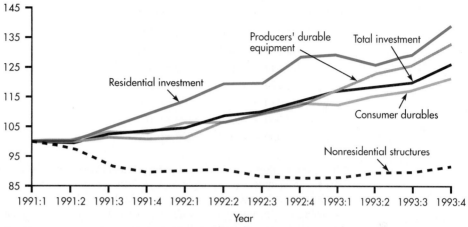

FIGURE 9-6
Investment
Expenditure
1991–93 (indexes
1991:I = 100)

Total investment equals gross private domestic investment plus consumer expenditure on durable goods.

Earlier in this chapter, we examined the opposite side of this coin—why consumers try to shelter their standard of living from the effects of the business cycle, and how consumer purchases of nondurable goods and services provide a source of stability for the economy.

WORKED EXAMPLES

Worked
Example 9–1

The Simple Accelerator Model of Investment
In this example we assume that production requires three units of capital to produce each unit of output. The accelerator coefficient, v, is equal to 3. Replacement investment in each year is equal to 400. The capital stock in year zero is equal to 12,000. The levels of output in the economy over eight years are as follows:

$Y_1 = 4,000$ $\qquad$ $Y_2 = 4,040$ $\qquad$ $Y_3 = 4,120$
$Y_4 = 4,140$ $\qquad$ $Y_5 = 4,120$ $\qquad$ $Y_6 = 4,080$
$Y_7 = 4,000$ $\qquad$ $Y_8 = 4,000$

Question Trace out the path of investment demand over this period.

Answer The desired capital stock in year one is equal to vY:

$K^d_1 = 3 \times 4,000 = 12,000$

The actual capital stock in year zero is also 12,000, so investment demand in year one will simply equal replacement investment:

$I_1 = 400$

In subsequent years, the level of investment demand is found by substituting into Equation 9–7:

$$I_2 = 3(4{,}040 - 4{,}000) + 400 = 520$$
$$I_3 = 3(4{,}120 - 4{,}040) + 400 = 640$$
$$I_4 = 3(4{,}140 - 4{,}120) + 400 = 460$$
$$I_5 = 3(4{,}120 - 4{,}140) + 400 = 340$$
$$I_6 = 3(4{,}080 - 4{,}120) + 400 = 280$$
$$I_7 = 3(4{,}000 - 4{,}080) + 400 = 160$$
$$I_8 = 3(4{,}000 - 4{,}000) + 400 = 400.$$

The example illustrates how volatile investment demand will be as a result of quite moderate changes in income. For example, income rose by only 1 percent from year one to year two (4,000 to 4,040), and yet investment demand grew by 30 percent (from 400 to 520). The following year income grew by about 2 percent (4,040 to 4,120) and investment grew by an additional 23 percent (from 520 to 640).

In years three to four income was still growing, but investment demand actually fell sharply—by 28 percent (640 to 460). Investment demand started to decline even before income started to fall. The subsequent declines in income from year four to year seven then sent investment demand way down until income had stabilized again (between years seven and eight), and investment returned to its original value (equal to replacement investment, 400).

Worked Example 9–2

The Flexible Accelerator

We will use the same starting point as we used in Worked Example 9–1. The capital–output ratio, v, is 3. In the initial year (year zero) output is 4,000 and the capital stock is 12,000. Replacement investment is 400.

Question   If the economy follows the same path of output that is given in Worked Example 9–1, show how the level of investment is determined with a flexible accelerator that has an adjustment coefficient of 0.3. Compare the results from the simple-accelerator model and the flexible-accelerator model.

Answer   The desired capital stock in year one is equal to vY with Y equal to 4,000, and the actual capital stock in year zero is 12,000. This allows the computation of investment in the first year, and then in subsequent years, by substituting into Equation 9–8:

$$I_1 = 0.3[(3 \times 4{,}000) - 12{,}000] + 400 = 400 \quad K_1 = 12{,}000$$
$$I_2 = 0.3[(3 \times 4{,}040) - 12{,}000] + 400 = 436, \quad K_2 = 12{,}036$$
$$I_3 = 0.3[(3 \times 4{,}120) - 12{,}036] + 400 = 497, \quad K_3 = 12{,}133$$
$$I_4 = 0.3[(3 \times 4{,}140) - 12{,}333] + 400 = 486, \quad K_4 = 12{,}219$$
$$I_5 = 0.3[(3 \times 4{,}120) - 12{,}219] + 400 = 442, \quad K_5 = 12{,}261$$
$$I_6 = 0.3[(3 \times 4{,}080) - 12{,}261] + 400 = 394, \quad K_6 = 12{,}255$$
$$I_7 = 0.3[(3 \times 4{,}000) - 12{,}255] + 400 = 323, \quad K_7 = 12{,}178$$
$$I_8 = 0.3[(3 \times 4{,}000) - 12{,}178] + 400 = 347, \quad K_8 = 12{,}125$$

These figures are calculated using unrounded numbers and then rounded, so there will be small discrepancies if you check some lines.

The most important difference between the flexible accelerator and the simple accelerator is that the predicted volatility of investment is smaller in the more realistic flexible model than in the highly abstract simple model.

With the simple accelerator, there was a peak of investment of 640 and a trough of 160. With the flexible accelerator, the same path of output led to peak of 497 and a trough of 323—a much narrower range. The acceleration effect has not disappeared, however. The percent changes in investment are still much greater than the percent changes in output. The reason the volatility is less is that the impact of a given change in output is spread over several periods. There is not a complete adjustment in the first period.

One important similarity carried over to the flexible model is that investment peaks before output peaks. Investment peaked in year three at 497, whereas output did not peak until year four.

Worked Example 9–3

The Samuelson Multiplier–Accelerator Model

We give here, with some adaptation, an example that Samuelson used to illustrate how the multiplier and the accelerator can interact. He used a simple consumption function and an investment function that was basically the simple accelerator, except that he used accelerator coefficients much smaller than the average ratio of capital to output, because of the kind of partial adjustment of capital that we incorporated here into a flexible accelerator.

His consumption and investment relations differed in one important way from the usual ones that we have used previously. *He allowed for time lags* between income and consumption and between the change of output and the demand for investment. The idea behind this was that consumers decide how much to buy based on how much income they received in the *previous* period. In the case of investment, it is often true that it takes a while for investment goods to be built and delivered, so investment this period depends on the decision to buy that was made in a prior period.

We will use the following consumption and investment equations together with a fixed level for government expenditure. Consumption, investment, and government expenditure in a given year are as follows:

$$C = 100 + 0.7Y_{\text{prior year}}$$
$$I = 0.6[Y_{\text{prior year}}] - Y_{\text{two years earlier}}] + 400, \text{ or alternatively}$$
$$I = 0.6[\Delta Y_{\text{prior year}}] + 400$$
$$G = 700$$

Question   Show that if income was 4,000 in both year zero and year one, then income in year two will be 4,000. Trace the path of income if government expenditure were to change to 900 in year three and then stay at the new higher level.

Answer   We write down the goods-market–equilibrium condition for this model economy in year two:

$$Y_{\text{two}} = C_{\text{two}} + I_{\text{two}} + G$$
$$= 100 + 0.7Y_{\text{year one}} + 0.6[\Delta Y_{\text{from zero to one}}] + 400 + 700$$

We can then substitute the value of 4,000 into this expression for the prior values of income and see what the current value of income is. Notice that income was constant at 4,000 during years zero and one, so there was no change in income from year zero to year one:

$$Y_{\text{two}} = 100 + 0.7(4,000) + 0.6(0) + 400 + 700 = 4,000$$

This confirms the first part of the answer. We now look at the case where the economy has been at 4,000 for some time, but then it is disturbed by the increase in government expenditure to 900. We trace out what happens to income:

$$Y_3 \quad = 100 + (0.7 \times 4{,}000) + 0.6(\quad 0) + 400 + 900 = 4{,}200$$
$$Y_4 \quad = 100 + (0.7 \times 4{,}200) + 0.6(\;200) + 400 + 900 = 4{,}460$$
$$Y_5 \quad = 100 + (0.7 \times 4{,}460) + 0.6(\;260) + 400 + 900 = 4{,}678$$
$$Y_6 \quad = 100 + (0.7 \times 4{,}678) + 0.6(\;218) + 400 + 900 = 4{,}805$$
$$Y_7 \quad = 100 + (0.7 \times 4{,}805) + 0.6(\;127) + 400 + 900 = 4{,}840$$
$$Y_8 \quad = 100 + (0.7 \times 4{,}840) + 0.6(\;\;35) + 400 + 900 = 4{,}809$$
$$Y_9 \quad = 100 + (0.7 \times 4{,}809) + 0.6(-31) + 400 + 900 = 4{,}748$$
$$Y_{10} \quad = 100 + (0.7 \times 4{,}748) + 0.6(-61) + 400 + 900 = 4{,}686$$
$$Y_{11} \quad = 100 + (0.7 \times 4{,}686) + 0.6(-61) + 400 + 900 = 4{,}644$$
$$Y_{12} \quad = 100 + (0.7 \times 4{,}644) + 0.6(-43) + 400 + 900 = 4{,}625$$
$$Y_{13} \quad = 100 + (0.7 \times 4{,}625) + 0.6(-19) + 400 + 900 = 4{,}626$$

$$\cdots \qquad \cdots \qquad \cdots \qquad \cdots \qquad \cdots \qquad \cdots$$

$$Y_{\text{long run}} = 100 + (0.7 \times 4{,}667) + 0.6(\quad 0) + 400 + 900 = 4{,}667$$

(These figures are calculated using unrounded numbers and then rounded, so you may note small discrepancies if you check some lines.)

FIGURE 9–7
The Path of Income over Time Following an Increase in Government Expenditure

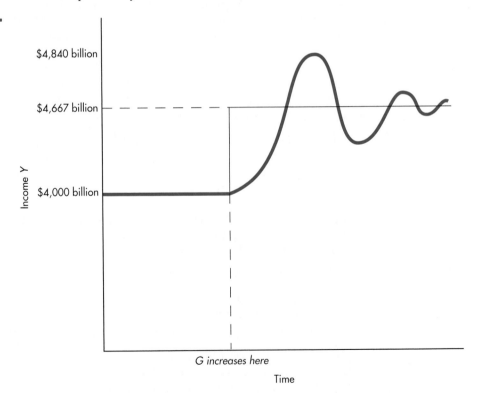

Note: Figure is based on a model adapted from Samuelson's multiplier–accelerator model.

The result of this multiplier–accelerator model, therefore, is that *income will rise and fall following an initial disturbance. The economy is actually tracing out a cycle.* This response of the model economy to the change in government spending is illustrated in Figure 9–7.

In the example we have used here, the up-and-down movements of the economy will die away and the economy will settle down to some long-run level of income. In fact, in this example the economy has come pretty close to its long-run value after 13 years.

The values used in this example insure that the economy will settle down to a stable value. (The system is convergent.) But other values would give different answers. The economy could behave in an unstable way with cycles that get larger and larger, or it could move to its long-run value without cycling.

SUMMARY

- The business cycle is described by a *peak,* the highest point reached before real GDP begins to turn down; a *recession,* when there is falling real GDP; a *trough,* the lowest point reached before GDP starts to turn up; and a *recovery,* where GDP is growing.

- Variability in aggregate demand in both the goods market and the financial market, due to domestic and international forces, contributes to the business cycle.

- The consumption standard of living is composed of household purchases of nondurable goods and services plus the flow of services provided by the existing stock of consumer-durable goods and houses.

- Consumers want to smooth consumption because they dislike large swings in the consumption standard of living. They are able to smooth consumption through borrowing, dissaving, and postponing capital purchases.

- Consumers form an expectation about their average or permanent income over their lifetimes. They set their normal or permanent level of consumption in relation to their permanent income.

- It is generally thought that consumption is smoothed because permanent income is more stable than year-to-year income. This idea has been questioned in recent research.

- Variability in the durable components of consumption and investment expenditure contributes to fluctuations in aggregate demand in the goods market.

- Because of variations in consumer expenditures on durables, together with variations in business investment, aggregate demand is subject to fluctuations in spite of the stabilizing effects of consumption smoothing.

- The stock of consumer-durable goods and houses along with the stock of businesses' equipment, inventories, and plant form the actual stock of capital.

- Businesses and households assess whether the size and composition of their actual stock of capital matches their desired stock of capital.

- Consumer expenditures on durables and business investment (net additions to the capital stock) take place when the actual stock of capital is below the desired stock of capital.

- The accelerator model of investment demand assumes that investment demand depends on the gap between actual stock and the desired stock of capital.

- In the accelerator model, an increase in current output and income increases the desired stock of capital. Since the actual capital stock was carried over from the past, there is a discrepancy between the actual capital stock and the desired capital stock. The attempts to close this gap led to a large fluctuation in investment demand.

- When the growth of income slows, investment starts to decline before the economy goes into a recession.

- Because of the interaction between investment demand and aggregate demand (the accelerator and the multiplier), income will rise and fall following an initial disturbance. The path of income in the economy can trace out a cycle.

- Inventories are a part of investment demand, and they are influenced by expectations about future sales. Expectations can change quickly and inventory changes are observed to be even more volatile than investment in fixed capital.

- The adjustment of inventories following a shift in demand can also contribute to cycling (overshooting and undershooting equilibrium) of the economy around a new equilibrium.

- When economic conditions change, firms and households can respond by changing their desired capital–output ratio.

- The flexible-accelerator model allows for a partial adjustment of the actual capital stock to a desired capital stock that is itself a moving target.

- The desired capital–output ratio and thus the desired capital stock are affected by expectations and interest rates. These changes in the desired capital–output ratio and the desired capital stock lead to changes in the level of investment demand.

- When interest rates are high/or when expectations dete-

riorate, or both, firms and households will economize on the amount of capital goods they require and they will postpone their expenditures on durable goods.

- The amount of investment in one year affects how large a capital stock is carried into the following year. Investment demand in the current year is affected by how much of the capital stock was carried forward.

- Equilibrium in the goods market is affected by the size of the capital stock. Since the capital stock that is carried forward each year reflects the economic conditions that existed in previous years, goods–market equilibrium shifts around depending on the past history of the economy.

KEY TERMS AND CONCEPTS

accelerator, p. 275

consumption smoothing, p. 266

consumption standard of living, p. 264

desired capital–output ratio, p. 275

desired capital stock, p. 275

durability, p. 275

permanent income, p. 267

permanent and transitory consumption, p. 267

DISCUSSION QUESTIONS AND PROBLEMS

1. Reconcile the stability of the consumption standard of living with the variability in consumers' purchases of durable goods and housing.

2. How can consumers smooth their income? Why don't they equalize consumption under all circumstances?

3. Does permanent income refer to income that doesn't change?

4. What types of expenditures add to the stock of capital?

5. Can net investment be negative? If so, what is happening to the stock of capital? What are some of the economic conditions that could lead to negative investment?

6. List reasons why actual capital stock can differ from the desired stock of capital?

7. In the simple accelerator model, what is being assumed about the desired capital–output ratio? Describe which behavior of business managers and consumers leads you to believe that those assumptions should be relaxed?

8. How does the discrepancy between actual and desired capital stocks lead to cyclical patterns of income?

9. The capital stock is made up of durable goods, which by their nature last from year to year. How does this durability contribute to variability in investment demand?

10. Why are changes in business inventories especially variable?

11. Consider an economy with the following investment equation:

$$I = 0.2[Y_{current\ year} - Y_{prior\ year}] + 500$$

Suppose income has been at 2,000 for several years and then increases to 2,500 and stays at the new level. Trace the pattern of investment over time.

12. Consider an economy with the following consumption function:

$$C = 800 + 0.6Y_{current\ year}$$

Investment is given by the relation shown in question 11. There is no government expenditure or foreign trade. If income is equal to 3,500 in year zero, find the level of income in year one and in subsequent years. Repeat your answer if income is 3,250 in year zero. Discuss your findings in relation to the results of Worked Example 9–3.

THE FEDERAL RESERVE BANKING SYSTEM AND FINANCIAL CRUNCHES

INTRODUCTION

Monetary policy is conducted by the Fed, and there is ample evidence from the last several years that Fed policies have an impact on the real economy. This is particularly the case for contractionary policies, where the Fed's efforts to fight inflation resulted in deep recessions in 1975 and 1982.

In earlier chapters we looked at the impact of monetary policy, using the framework of *IS–LM* analysis. But we have not yet explained how the Fed uses the tools of monetary policy. In this chapter we will explain how the Fed's instruments of monetary policy affect the banking system, the supply of money, and hence short-term rates of interest.

The traditional view of Fed operations has been that it works through commercial banks. However, because of a variety of changes within financial institutions, we need to broaden our view of the workings of Fed policy. Deregulation has allowed banks to pay interest on demand deposits. Savings and loans now offer many of the same services as commercial banks, and a variety of new financial instruments has been developed by banks and other financial institutions. The traditional role of banks and savings and loans has been altered by "securitization." Instead of holding a portfolio of loans themselves, banks resell these loans on the open market (issue securities). The banks or other financial intermediaries collect mortgage payments each month but no longer carry much of the risk from these mortgage loans.

One consequence of the changes in financial institutions is that it has become harder and harder to provide one single definition of the supply of money. Savings accounts have check-writing privileges, and large bank depositors have access to accounts that "sweep" funds out of checking accounts each day to ensure no interest earnings have been forgone.

It is still the case that the Fed and the banking system operate the payments system, the system that allows billions of transactions that take place each day. And because of its control over this payments system, the Fed can still control short-term interest rates. But a consequence of the changes in financial markets is that the Fed is now reducing its emphasis on the supply of money as an indicator of monetary policy. The Fed continues to use its traditional tools of monetary policy (notably open market operations), but it looks at short-term interest rates and credit conditions as guides to its actions. It does not set targets for the growth rate of the money supply.

Furthermore, the Fed's power to control credit conditions may have weakened in recent years. In today's deregulated financial markets, banks, other depository institutions, and a wide variety of financial intermediaries also play an important part in determining financial market conditions and aggregate economic performance.

Despite these changes that have taken place in financial markets, the best place to start our analysis of the working of monetary policy is with the traditional view of the money supply process and how the Fed is able to adjust the amount of money in the system. We describe how depository institutions contribute to the growth of the money supply through the transfer of funds among checkable deposit accounts. Then we look at how the Federal Reserve, which is the U.S. economy's central bank and monetary authority, controls the supply of money through the banking system. The supply of money is changed when the Federal Reserve changes the amount of reserves on which banks can draw to issue loans.

Having looked at the traditional view of monetary policy, we then turn to a broader discussion of the roles that credit crunches—both in financial markets separate from banks and in other institutions (including banks)—have played in several episodes of economic fluctuation in the U.S. economy. We conclude this section with a discussion of the role played by the Fed in the 1990–91 recession, with a special focus on the question of whether a banking sector credit crunch—independent of Fed policies—contributed to the downturn.

THE BANKING SYSTEM AND MONEY CREATION

The Fed conducts policy by affecting the money supply even though there is disagreement over which assets constitute the money supply! There are three alternative definitions of the money supply that are used by the Federal Reserve. The narrowest definition of money is $M1$, restricted to currency held by the public and to demand deposits and traveler's checks, assets that can readily be used to make transactions. A broader definition of money is $M2$ and this includes $M1$ plus money-market funds,

FIGURE 10–1
Alternative Definitions of the Money Supply

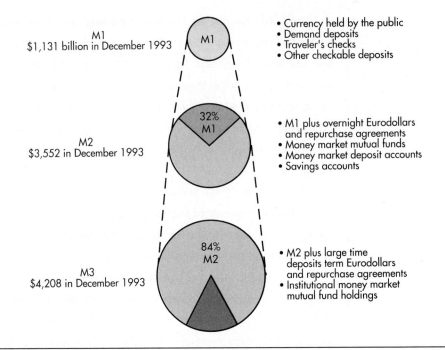

M1
$1,131 billion in December 1993

• Currency held by the public
• Demand deposits
• Traveler's checks
• Other checkable deposits

M2
$3,552 in December 1993

32%
M1

• M1 plus overnight Eurodollars and repurchase agreements
• Money market mutual funds
• Money market deposit accounts
• Savings accounts

M3
$4,208 in December 1993

84%
M2

• M2 plus large time deposits term Eurodollars and repurchase agreements
• Institutional money market mutual fund holdings

very short-term dollar accounts held in Europe (overnight Eurodollars) and small saving deposits. The broadest definition is *M*3 and, as well as *M*2, it includes large saving deposits and other less liquid financial assets. Figure 10–1 illustrates the alternative definitions of the money supply.

Rather than getting bogged down in debating among the alternative definitions of money, however, we will simply define the money supply, *M*, as currency plus demand deposits.[1] We recognize, however, that in today's economy it is very easy to transfer funds among the alternative financial assets, so, in practice, movements of all three measures of the money supply may be important.

commercial bank
A bank that is authorized to issue checking accounts to individuals and commercial customers.

A demand deposit is a liability of a **commercial bank** or other financial institution, such as a thrift institution or a money-market mutual fund. It is an asset of the customer who opened the account and deposited the funds. These private institutions, called "depository institutions," together make up the banking system. The liabilities of these institutions are the demand deposits that are part of the money supply. The currency portion of the money supply is provided by the Fed, the only supplier of legal tender in the United States.

For many years the different institutions that made up the banking system were distinguished by the kinds of assets that they held and by the ways in which they were

---

[1] We are using the term *demand deposits* to cover a broad range of assets that have some checking privileges. There is also a narrowly defined concept of demand deposits that includes only commercial-bank checking accounts.

savings and loan banks (S&Ls)
Prior to deregulation, they issued only savings accounts. Now they are similar to commercial banks.

regulated. For example, regulations formulated in the 1930s directed thrift institutions, such as credit unions, mutual saving banks, and especially **savings and loan banks** (S&Ls), to specialize in holding residential-mortgage loans as their primary asset. At the time, S&Ls were savings banks where customers held savings accounts, but these thrift institutions could not issue checking accounts. Commercial banks were free to hold a wider variety of assets, including consumer and commercial loans, and they could issue checking accounts.

Both S&Ls and commercial banks faced restrictions on the interest they could pay depositors, but S&Ls were allowed to pay a slightly higher interest rate than commercial banks, so S&Ls could attract deposits that were then used for mortgages. This regulatory environment remained unchanged from the 1930s through the 1970s. During that period, due to the regulations that affected them, the commercial banks issued most of the demand deposits included in the money supply.

In the 1970s and 1980s, following a period of inflation and fluctuating interest rates, the government undertook a policy of deregulation. Many of the regulations governing the composition of bank assets and the payment of interest on deposit liabilities were relaxed. S&Ls were no longer charged with the primary task of supplying mortgage credit. Commercial banks had to share the franchise for issuing checkable accounts with thrifts and money-market mutual funds. Financial institutions were forced to alter their strategies for competing among each other, and the differences among kinds of banks were reduced or eliminated. Following deregulation, the services provided by a checkable account (payment by check, fund transfer, or automatic teller machines) were very similar among different types of financial institutions.

As a result of the deregulation of depository institutions, there was a dramatic change in the composition of the money supply, with a rapid increase in checkable deposits held outside of commercial banks. But because of the similarity of services among depository institutions, *we will analyze the monetary system using commercial banks as representative of all depository institutions.* By describing how commercial banks create demand deposits we will explain the process by which the banking system and the Fed create money.

Money Creation, Loans, and Reserves

fractional reserve system
The system under which banks need only to hold a fraction of the funds deposited in the form of reserves.

Commercial banks are *financial intermediaries;* that is, they come between borrowers and lenders. They borrow from their depositors and use the funds to make business and personal loans and to buy other financial assets that yield returns. When banks purchase financial assets they are supplying credit—either through direct business and personal loans or through the purchase of financial securities, such as government bonds or corporate securities. In the process they "create money," because their liabilities are demand deposits that can be used for transactions, while their assets consist of a portfolio of loans that are not money. They are not creating wealth, for a bank's assets and liabilities are balanced. But by spreading risks over large numbers of different loans, they have, in a sense, transformed their assets (a portfolio of loans with various risks and maturities) into money (the demand deposits that are the banks' liabilities). A key element in the money-creation process is the **fractional reserve system.**

reserves
A depository institution's reserve-account balances held at the central bank (the Fed), plus cash held in the bank (vault cash).

Households and the cash managers of business firms deposit funds in bank checking accounts. These banks then want to use most of their funds to earn interest on them by making loans or buying other financial assets. However, banks must hold a fraction of the amount deposited with them as **reserves,** because their depositors may withdraw some of the funds that have been deposited. If your bank held no reserves of currency and you wanted to cash a check at the bank, the bank would not have any cash on hand. When you buy something and pay by check, the person from whom you buy the item will probably deposit the check in another bank, and so your bank will have to pay out funds to the other bank. Reserves are now held by banks in the form of U.S. currency (sometimes called *vault cash)* and special deposit accounts that banks have at the Fed (**reserve accounts).** These two parts of bank reserves are both liabilities of the Fed. Reserve accounts are like checking accounts that banks hold with the Fed; banks write checks to other banks using these accounts. Banks earn no interest on their reserve accounts in the United States. And notice that *bank reserves are not included in the money supply.* Cash held by the public is part of the money supply, but the cash and reserve accounts held by banks are not.

reserve accounts
U.S. Banks and other depository institutions hold funds in accounts with the Federal Reserve.

Deposits, Reserves, and Loans

To see how the banks and the fractional reserve system create money, we will use a simplified numerical example. A bank, First Newtown Bank, opens for business in a town that didn't have a commercial bank. The bank attracts a commercial depositor, a local restaurateur. This restaurant accepts only cash payments. The first deposit the restaurateur makes in the new bank is $10,000 in cash. The $10,000 is deposited in a checking account, creating a demand deposit *(DD).* The effect of the deposit on the bank's balance sheet is shown in Table 10–1.

At this point the amount of money supply has not changed. The cash has become part of the bank's reserves and, since bank reserves are not included in the money supply, $10,000 of cash has been subtracted from the supply of money. Offsetting this decrease in the money supply is the $10,000 demand deposit that represents an increase in the money supply. In other words, the money supply has not changed at this point, because the restaurateur has simply exchanged $10,000 in currency for $10,000 in a checking account. This is only the beginning, however.

For simplicity we assume that First Newtown sends all of the $10,000 in currency to be deposited in First Newtown's reserve account at the Fed. The bank intends to leave only a portion of the $10,000 in its reserve account and lend out the rest to earn interest. The portion of the $10,000 that the bank can lend depends on the level of reserves the bank holds. For U.S. banks, this is basically determined by the Fed.

The Reserve Ratio

reserve ratio
The ratio of total reserves to demand deposits.

The size of the loan that the bank can offer is limited by the **reserve ratio** *(Rr)* and, subject to a minor qualification, *the reserve ratio is set by the Fed;* it is the fraction of demand deposits held as reserves:

$$Rr = \frac{\text{Reserves}}{\text{Demand deposits}}$$

$$Rr = \frac{R}{DD}$$

(10–1)

If the Fed sets the ratio at 10 percent, then in our example First Newtown must hold at least $1,000 in reserves. Maintaining a $1,000 reserve means that First Newtown Bank can generate income by lending up to $9,000.

We assume a reserve ratio of 10 percent in our discussion here. The actual reserve requirements set by the Fed depend on the types of deposits (checkable and noncheckable), total size of all deposits, and the length of time the deposits are intended to be kept in a depository institution. If a large number of depositors decide to shift between checking accounts and savings accounts, the required reserve ratio changes to reflect the changing composition of deposits. This means that, in principle, the actual reserve ratio can and will change irrespective of any change in Fed policy. In practice the Fed adjusts its policy to make sure that, when the public shifts among different kinds of accounts, the money supply is not altered unintentionally. In December 1993, required reserves were 5.3 percent of the deposits included in $M1$ and 1.7 percent of the deposits included in $M2$.

The Banking System Creates Money

Returning to our example, the bank's credit manager finds that the local record store is interested in borrowing $9,000. When the loan is approved, a checking account with a $9,000 balance is issued to the record store. Table 10–1 is the balance sheet of First Newtown Bank after the loan approval but before the record store spends any loan proceeds.

The bank can make a loan, the borrower now has new money, and the restaurateur still has a deposit of $10,000. Now we see that, once the First Newtown Bank has made its first loan, the banking system has created money. The restaurateur owns a $10,000 demand deposit. She has the same amount of money she had before she deposited the cash in First Newtown Bank. There is also the record store's $9,000 demand deposit, which previously did not exist. The money supply increased by $9,000 when First Newtown Bank lent 90 percent of the restaurant owner's deposit to the record store.

The process of money creation does not stop with this first step. Of course, the record store did not borrow $9,000 to keep it in the bank. The record store purchases $9,000 worth of compact discs from a record distributor. The record distributor is located out of town and banks with City National Bank. City National Bank sends the check to the Fed. The Fed takes $9,000 out of First Newtown Bank's reserve account and credits it to the reserve account of City National Bank.

City National Bank now has a lending opportunity similar to what faced First Newtown Bank. City National Bank can lend 90 percent ($8,100) of its newly acquired $9,000 in cash reserves. City National Bank lends the money to an auto

TABLE 10–1
First Newtown Bank's New Balance Sheet

Assets	Liabilities
+$10,000 Reserves	+$10,000 *DD* (restaurant)
+$ 9,000 Loan (record store)	+$ 9,000 *DD* (record store)

**TABLE 10–2
Three Banks'
Balance Sheets**

Assets	Liabilities
First Newtown Bank	
+$1,000 Reserves	+$10,000 *DD* (restaurant)
+$9,000 Loan (record store)	
City National Bank	
+$ 900 Reserves	+$ 9,000 *DD* (record distributor)
+$8,100 Loan (auto mechanic)	
Second Country Bank	
+$8,100 Reserves	+$ 8,100 *DD* (tool manufacturer)

mechanic for tools, and the tool supplier banks with Second Country Bank in another city. The balance sheets of these three banks, as shown in Table 10–2, reflect the next stage of increases in the money supply.

In Table 10–2 the money supply has increased by another $8,100. This example started with a $10,000 deposit of cash in First Newtown Bank (the original +$10,000). There is now $27,100 of demand deposits in all three of these banks together. There was a $17,100 net increase in the supply of money as the banking system responded to the initial deposit. And the process is far from over.

The original cash deposit of $10,000 has not left the banking system; it has only been distributed among several banks. When these successive rounds of lending and interbank transfer of reserves is over, the original $10,000 will reside in the reserve accounts of many banks. But as long as no one takes cash out of the banks, the original deposit of $10,000 has added $10,000 to the reserves of the banking system. Table 10–3 is the consolidated balance sheet for the entire banking system, with the first three banks listed separately. By looking at the entire banking system, we see the banks' role in expanding the money supply.

**The Money
Supply and the
Amount of
Reserves**

Prior to the original cash deposit, the money supply includes $10,000 in cash. After the deposit, the cash becomes part of bank reserves and is no longer part of the money supply, so this reduces the money supply by $10,000. However, $100,000 of demand deposits has been created. There is, therefore, a net increase of $90,000 in the money supply. The simple act (by the restaurateur in this example) of rearranging the form in which money is held—from cash to demand deposit—changes the money supply, because the rearrangement adds reserves to the banking system. The $10,000 in cash deposited at First Newtown Bank becomes $10,000 in reserves. Eventually, this increase in reserves allows the banking system to expand the money supply by $90,000, balanced by an equal increase in loans.

Another way to see why the money supply rises by $90,000 in the example is as follows. Individuals and firms can choose to hold their money in the form of demand deposits *(DD)* or in the form of currency or cash *(Cp)*. The sum of these two is equal to the money supply:

TABLE 10–3
Consolidated
Balance Sheet for
the Banking
System

Assets	Liabilities
First Newtown Bank	
+$ 1,000 Reserves	+$ 10,000 *DD* (restaurant)
+$ 9,000 Loan (record store)	
City National Bank	
+$ 900 Reserves	+$ 9,000 *DD* (record distributor)
+$ 8,100 Loan (auto mechanic)	
Second Country Bank	
+$ 810 Reserves	+$ 8,100 *DD* (tool manufacturer)
+$ 7,290 Loan	
Another Bank	
+$ 729 Reserves	+$ 7,290 *DD* (another borrower)
+$ 6,561 Loan	•
•	•
•	•
Total Banking System Balance Sheet	
+$10,000 Reserves	+$100,000 Demand deposits*
+$90,000 Loans	

*The sum of $10,000 + $9,000 + 8,100 + $7,290 and so on is the same as $10,000 × [1 + 0.9 + (0.9)² + (0.9)³ + . . . (0.9)ⁿ + . . .]. This equals $100,000. The same figure can also be found from the value of cash brought to the banking system as new reserves divided by the reserve ratio (*R/Rr* = $10,000/0.1 = $100,000).

$$\text{Money supply} = \text{Demand deposits} + \text{Cash held by the public}$$
$$M^s = DD + Cp \tag{10–2}$$

The amount of demand deposits equals the amount of reserves divided by the reserve ratio. Substituting R/Rr for DD in the definition of the money supply yields:

$$M^s = Cp + \frac{R}{Rr} \tag{10–3}$$

The money supply depends on the cash held by the public *(Cp),* the amount of reserves *(R),* and the reserve ratio *(Rr).* In our example, cash held by the public decreased by $10,000 and reserves increased by $10,000 when the restaurateur deposited her cash. The reduction in cash held by the public was balanced by an increase in demand deposits. The initial increase in demand deposits of $10,000 ultimately led to an increase of $100,000 in demand deposits. The change in the money supply, shown in Equation 10–4, is the sum of the reduction of cash held by the public and the total increase in demand deposits:

$$\Delta M^s = \Delta Cp + \left[\Delta R \times \left(\frac{1}{Rr} \right) \right]$$
$$= -\$10,000 + \left(\$10,000 \times \frac{1}{0.1} \right) \tag{10–4}$$
$$= +\$90,000$$

The banking system, by keeping reserves that are a fraction of their banks' demand-deposit liabilities and lending out the rest, is able to take any increase in reserves and increase the money supply by a multiple of the increase in reserves. A small increase in reserves can lead to a large increase in the money supply.

Excess reserves   We have been assuming that banks expand loans to the maximum amount allowable. If that's the case, the reserve ratio is determined by the minimum reserve ratio set by the Fed. In reality there may be times when banks reassess the risks of lending and conclude that they exceed the return to loans. In this situation, the actual reserve ratio is higher than the minimum or required reserve ratio. The reserves held over and above the minimum amount required are called **excess reserves.** Since the total reserves *(R)* held by the banking system are equal to the Fed-mandated minimum or **required reserves** *(RR)* plus any excess reserves *(EX),* the reserve ratio needs to reflect both minimum reserves and excess reserves. The total reserve ratio is found by dividing the two parts of total reserves by demand deposits:

$$\frac{R}{DD} = \frac{RR}{DD} + \frac{EX}{DD} \quad \text{or}$$

$$Rr = RRr + EXr \tag{10–5}$$

When excess reserves are held, the reserve ratio is comprised of the **required reserve ratio** *(RRr)* and the **excess-reserve ratio** *(EXr).*

Banks attempt to keep their excess reserves to a minimum. During the 1970s, excess reserves fluctuated around 1 percent of total reserves, while during the 1980s the ratio rose close to 2 percent. The higher interest rates experienced in the earlier period may have contributed to the profitability of further squeezing down the level of excess reserves. On a day-to-day basis, fluctuations in deposits and withdrawals mean that often some banks have more reserves than they need (positive excess reserves) and some banks have less (negative excess reserves). On a very short-term basis, often overnight, banks that need reserves will borrow from the banks whose reserves are too high. These short-term borrowing and lending transactions occur in what is called the **federal funds market.**

In our bank example, the First Newtown Bank was shown as having excess reserves as it responded to the initial cash deposit. In practice, this bank would have lent these excess reserves in the federal funds market. In normal economic situations, the positive and negative excess reserves of different individual banks are channeled into the federal funds market and offset each other. This means that the banking system as a whole has a very low net excess reserve ratio.

On those rare occasions when the interest rate in the federal funds market is very low, or when banks are worried about a sudden wave of withdrawals by their depositors, or when banks are concerned about the riskiness of their assets, banks in general may decide to hold back on maximizing loans and the banking system will generate higher net excess reserves.

excess reserves
The amount of bank reserves held over and above the minimum amount required.

required reserves
The minimum level of reserves that must be held.

required reserve ratio
The ratio of required reserves to demand deposits.

excess-reserve ratio
The ratio of excess reserves to demand deposits.

federal fund markets
The market among banks for short-term borrowing and lending of bank reserves.

In our discussion of Equation 10–3 we assumed that the Fed directly controls the reserve ratio. However, because of excess reserves, the reserve ratio Rr and the required reserve ratio RRr may differ. But since excess reserves are so small, we can neglect this complication and use Equation 10–3 to see how the Fed changes the supply to money.

Changes in the Money Supply: Controlling the Monetary Base

The money supply changes when (1) there is a change in the required reserve ratio or (2) there is a change in the amount of cash held by the public or a change in reserves in the banking system. The Fed is the only issuer of currency and it can increase or decrease bank reserves (by a method we will describe shortly). This gives the Fed control over the money supply.

In practice, monetary policy is most often conducted without changing the required reserve ratio. Instead, policy is pursued by the Fed increasing or decreasing cash and/ or reserve accounts. The Fed changes the **monetary base.** Reserve accounts along with cash held by the public comprise the monetary base.

monetary base
The sum of bank reserves and cash held by the public.

$$MB = R + Cp \tag{10–6}$$

Of course, in exercising control over the monetary base and hence the money supply, the Fed will have to monitor the extent to which the public decides to use cash versus demand deposits. Households will increase the money supply if they decide to shift from holding cash to holding demand deposits. This was illustrated in the First Newtown Bank example given earlier, where the money supply and the supply of credit both increased when the initial deposit of cash led to an increase in the banking system's balances in reserve accounts. Banks issued new credit through the creation of new loans and the redepositing of those further expanded the supply of money and credit in the economy. In practice, however, changes in the public's propensity to hold currency is not a major factor in changing the money supply in normal times. Gradual changes in people's desires to hold currency relative to their holdings of demand deposits can be adjusted for by offsetting Fed actions.

The Fed is in the driver's seat in setting the money supply and that means that it can influence, or even control, short-term nominal rates of interest, such as the rate on T-bills. To see how changes in the money supply force changes in money demand and drive the interest rate up or down we look at equilibrium in the T-bill market.

T-Bill Prices and the Short-Term Rate of Interest

The rate of interest on a particular type of financial asset is determined through supply and demand in the market for this asset, while the effective rate of interest on an asset is directly linked to the price at which the asset is traded.

Consider the example of a financial asset consisting of an IOU that promises to pay $1,000 in one year. The IOU does not pay out anything until it is redeemed after one year. The borrower buys the IOU for less than $1,000 at the beginning of the year and then receives the $1,000 at the end of the year. The effective interest rate on the IOU depends on the price paid for it, relative to $1,000. The higher the price paid for the IOU, the less is gained after one year and, therefore, the lower is the rate of interest earned. Let's look at the effective interest rates on a $1,000 IOU payable in one year for different initial prices:

Initial price of the IOU	$600	$750	$900	$950	$990
Gain when the IOU is paid off	$400	$250	$100	$ 50	$ 10
Interest rate calculated by taking the gain as a percent of the price paid	66.7%	33.3%	11.1%	5.3%	1%

In this example, the interest rate was earned completely through the capital gain. A financial asset such as this is called a *zero coupon bond.* T bills are the most common example of such an asset.

Most other financial assets are not zero coupon bonds; they promise to pay a dollar amount each quarter or each year for a certain number of years. A bond then represents a claim on the interest as well as the repayment. For these assets, also, there is an inverse relation between the interest rate on the bond and its price. A dollar amount of interest to be paid per year (e.g., $100 per year) represents a higher return or interest rate when the bond is purchased for $500 than if the same bond paying $100 per year were purchased for $2,000. For all bonds—T bills, one-year bonds, 10-year bonds, perpetuities (bonds that are never redeemed) and so on—an inverse price/interest-rate relation exists.

We show in Figure 10–2 how equilibrium in the money market (panel A) is linked with equilibrium in the T-bill market (panel C). In panel B we show the relationship between T-bill prices and their interest rates. Numerical values from Worked Example 10–1 are shown in the figure.

In Figure 10–2C we show the supply (S_T) and demand (D_T) for T bills in equilibrium at a price, $P_T[A]$. Moving to Figure 10–2B, we see that this price of T bills implies a particular interest rate, i_0, on T bills. Then in Figure 10–2A, we see that equilibrium in the money market also occurs at the same rate of interest, i_A. The T-bill market and the supply of and demand for money are two sides of the same money market where cash managers trade money for T bills. Money supply and demand are equal at an equilibrium interest rate that corresponds to the equilibrium price of T bills. The relationship between the prices of assets and interest rates connects these two parts of the financial market.

If the price of T bills were above its equilibrium price (e.g., if the price of T bills were $9,879), then there would be an excess supply of T bills (Figure 10–2C). Tracking this back to Figure 10–2A, we see that this price of T bills corresponds to a short-term nominal interest rate of 5 percent, and this represents a situation of excess demand for money. The alternative case is also shown in Figure 10–2, where the price of T bills is $9,765, resulting in an excess demand for T bills and an excess supply of money.

Worked Example 10–1   We give a numerical example that shows how the price of T bills is related to the interest rate on T bills. This example shows how a price of $9,765 for a T bill corresponds to an interest rate of 10 percent and a price of $9,879 corresponds to an interest rate of 5 percent—these are the numbers shown in Figure 10–2.

Given its power over the money supply and its effect on interest rates, the Fed is very influential. How does the Fed operate?

FIGURE 10–2   Connecting Money Supply and Demand on the T-Bill

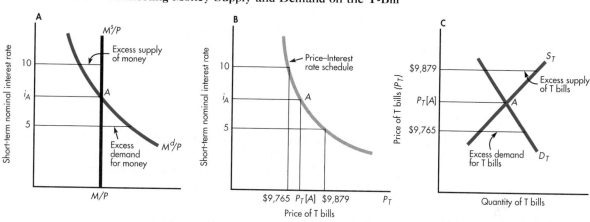

THE FEDERAL RESERVE SYSTEM

The manner in which monetary policy decisions are made is quite different from the way in which fiscal policy decisions are made. In the United States, fiscal policy is directed by the executive and legislative branches of government. Both the president and members of congress are elected and thus strongly influenced by electoral and political concerns, both regional and national. The conduct of monetary policy is carried out by an independent Federal Reserve that is much less influenced by political concerns.

The board of governors of the Fed has seven members appointed to 14-year terms by the president and confirmed by the senate. The board sets the overall policy goals for the Fed. The other primary decision-making group within the Fed is the Federal Open Market Committee (FOMC). The FOMC is composed of the seven members of the board of governors plus five members who are chosen in rotation from the 12 regional Federal Reserve banks. The FOMC determines what the Fed's monetary policy will be.

While there has rarely been unanimity of opinion about the direction of economic policy among members of the FOMC, in the past, the FOMC had been strongly influenced by the chairman of the board of governors. The Fed chairman is often, but not always, influenced by the economic-policy directions taken by the president. The Fed has a relation to economic policy not unlike the relationship of the Supreme Court to the body of U.S. law. The Fed's board members, as is the case with Supreme Court justices, are appointed by the president and they are not completely immune from political pressures, but they often make decisions that are not to the liking of the president.

TABLE 10–4
A Simplified
Typical Balance
Sheet of the
Federal Reserve

Assets		Liabilities	
U.S. Treasury securities	80%	Fed reserve notes	75%
		Bank and depository reserve accounts *(RA)*	15
Other assets	20	Other liabilities	10

**open-market
operations**
The buying and selling
of government securi-
ties; that is, Treasury
bills and bonds. They
are used to vary the
size of bank reserves.

The FOMC meets regularly every few weeks to consider the state of the economy and decide on the direction of its policy actions. It gives instructions to the staff of the Fed that have the effect of changing the money supply, either by changing the monetary base or by changing the reserve ratio. The main mechanism for monetary control is changing the monetary base through the control of reserves, using **open-market operations.** Open-market operations are the day-to-day purchases or sales of Treasury securities that are made by Fed staffers, mostly on the New York financial markets, following the directions given to them by the FOMC. We look at how this process works to change bank reserves.

Open-Market Operations

The Federal Reserve system actually consists of 12 regional banks, which means that each regional bank has its own balance sheet of assets and liabilities. But in Table 10–4 we show a simplified typical balance sheet for the Federal Reserve System as a whole, created by consolidating the balance sheets of the 12 regional Federal Reserve banks.

Since the Fed's assets consist primarily of U.S. government (Treasury) securities, for which there is a large and active market, it can buy and sell them in large quantities in the open market. Because the Fed acts through brokers, it participates in the market just like any other securities dealer. However, the Fed's motivation for buying and selling is quite different from that of the private purchaser. Private holders of Treasury securities want to earn interest on their investment, capture capital gains from changes in the prices of securities, or both. The Fed wants to control the money supply by changing the size of the monetary base.[2]

When the Fed buys securities (Treasury bonds or bills), its payment for those securities automatically increases the reserves of the banking system. *Open-market purchases of government securities increase reserves and hence the monetary base.* When the Fed sells securities, its payment for those securities automatically decrease the reserves of the banking system. *Open-market sales reduce the monetary base.* Increases or decreases in the monetary base then generate increases or decreases in the supply of loans and changes in the money supply.

---

[2] Jack M. Guttentag, "The Strategy of Open Market Operations," *Quarterly Journal of Economics* 80 (February 1960), pp. 1–30; Paul Mack, *U.S. Monetary Policy and Financial Markets,* Federal Reserve Bank of N.Y., 1982.

TABLE 10–5
Balance Sheets
Describing a Fed
Open-Market
Purchase

Assets	Liabilities
Federal Reserve	
+$1,000,000 Government bonds	+$1,000,000 Bank's reserve account
Corporation	
−$1,000,000 Government bonds	
+$1,000,000 Demand deposit	
Commercial bank	
+$1,000,000 Reserves	+$1,000,000 *DD* (corporation)
+$100,000 Required	
+$900,000 Excess reserves available for loans	

Open-Market Purchases: Increasing the Monetary Base

Table 10–5 illustrates how a Fed open-market purchase of securities raises the monetary base by showing the impact of an open-market purchase on three balance sheets: the Fed's, a private corporation's, and a commercial bank's.

In this example, the Fed purchases $1 million worth of government securities from a private corporation. The corporation sells these bonds to the Fed, because the Fed offers a high enough price for the securities to induce the corporation to sell. The Fed pays for the securities by writing a check on itself. By making this transaction, the Fed has increased its own assets by $1 million (the bond) and increased its own liabilities by $1 million (the check issued by the Fed). The corporation deposits the Fed's check into its corporate checking account. This Fed check is different from a check drawn on another commercial bank. When a check is deposited in one bank, it is usually drawn against another bank and the monetary base does not change. In this case the Fed's check is returned to the Fed, which accepts the check and credits the bank's reserve account at the Fed. Thus the check issued by the Fed has become part of the reserves of the banking system and *the net effect of the Fed's open-market purchase is an increase in reserves and hence an increase in the monetary base.*

Because reserve-account balances and currency are liabilities of the Fed, the Fed can increase the monetary base by simultaneously increasing its own assets and liabilities.[3] The $1 million open-market purchase has led to an increase in the reserve

---

[3] In the Fed balance sheet shown in Table 10–4, the Fed's liabilities were shown to be mostly Federal Reserve notes (cash) and the reserve accounts of banks and other depository institutions. All reserves and all cash (the components of the monetary base) are the liabilities of the Fed. The monetary base will increase or decrease when the liabilities of the Fed increase or decrease and the Fed can change the size of its liabilities. This is done when the Fed simultaneously increases or decreases both its assets and its liabilities. There is no mystery here. Any financial entity can simultaneously raise or lower assets and liabilities. When a corporation borrows money, its liabilities rise by the size of the debt and its assets rise by the size of the money balance and/or real assets purchased with the proceeds of its borrowing. What is different here is that changes in the firm's level of assets and liabilities do not affect the money supply—the lender's money balance goes down and the borrower's money balance goes up. In contrast, changes in the Fed's level of assets and liabilities in fact change the monetary base and ultimately change the money supply.

accounts of the banking system. If the reserve ratio is set at 0.1 then, following the open-market purchase and the deposit of the Fed's check with the bank, the bank's minimum or required reserves have increased by $100,000, while total reserves have increased by $1 million. There are $900,000 in excess reserves available for loans. When the bank lends those excess reserves, it creates a multiple increase in the amount of loans and money in the economy. The open-market purchase increases the monetary base and the increase of the monetary base leads to an increase of the money supply.

Open-Market Sales: Decreasing the Monetary Base

When the Fed wants to reduce the money supply, it sells Treasury securities. Private purchasers buy the securities by writing checks payable to the Fed. Instead of directly presenting those checks to the depository institution on which they were drawn, the Fed simply debits their reserve accounts. The reduction in reserves leaves banks with a shortage of required reserves. Banks react to the reserve shortage by building reserves. Reserves are accumulated when banks reduce the amount of new loans issued relevant to the amount of loan repayments it receives. Businesses find it harder to have lines of credit renewed, let alone continue or expand borrowing. The econ-omywide contraction of credit works in the opposite direction from the expansion of the money supply. The money supply is reduced. Tighter credit, along with an excess demand for money, drives up the interest rate and drives down the level of income.

The expansion or contraction of the money supply via open-market operations is both subtle and powerful. The Fed can vary its stance (i.e., expand or contract on a daily basis) to a small or large degree, depending on the size of its open-market purchases or sales. The power of open-market operations comes from the Fed's control over the monetary base.

This analysis of the way in which the Fed changes reserves has omitted one important qualification. The Fed has a commitment to the banks that they can actually borrow reserves if they are suddenly caught short. We take a look now at the question of *borrowed reserves*.

Borrowed Reserves

If an individual bank finds that it does not have enough reserves to meet its reserve requirements, it can enter the federal funds market to borrow reserves from another bank that has excess reserves. Banks charge each other for these loans at the federal funds rate. This market allows individual banks to avoid having to scramble to meet reserve requirements as a result of temporary increases in withdrawals of funds.

If, however, there is a shortage of reserves in the banking system as a whole, the federal funds market will not create new reserves. If the Fed tightens monetary policy, many banks are short of reserves and try to borrow in the federal funds market. The immediate effect of the Fed action is to increase the federal funds rate.

If a bank is short of reserves and cannot obtain extra from other banks, then it is allowed to borrow reserves directly from the Fed. The Fed is called the *lender of last resort,* meaning that banks only borrow from the Fed when, in the short run, they have no alternative. Banks have to comply with minimum reserve requirements, and those banks that have borrowed reserves must eventually reduce their loans and their demand deposits. The Fed's willingness to supply borrowed reserves enables banks to manage fluctuations in the withdrawal demands of their depositors without being forced to sell off their other assets too quickly and hence at a loss. It allows the banks to make a smooth transition when the Fed decides to change the money supply. In December 1993, borrowed reserves were $82 million out of total reserves of over $60 billion.

If borrowed reserves were freely available, this would undermine the Fed's control of reserves and hence its control of the money supply. This is why, in practice, *the Fed is willing to lend reserves only on a temporary basis.* The Fed will accommodate banks that are having difficulty coming up with enough reserves on a short-term basis. But it will not allow borrowed reserves to undermine its contractionary policies.

The Discount Rate

discount rate
The interest rate that the Fed charges on borrowed reserves.

When banks borrow from the Fed, they must pay interest. The interest rate that the Fed charges on borrowed reserves is called the **discount rate.** In principle, therefore, the Fed could control the amount of borrowed reserves by varying the cost of borrowing. In practice, the discount rate in the United States is not primarily used as a *direct* way of affecting the amount of borrowing banks do.

The Fed mostly uses the discount rate as a signal to financial markets about the direction of monetary policy. When the Fed raises the discount rate, it is signaling its intention to reduce the money supply. It is giving a warning to banks that they should start adjusting their loan activity accordingly. Banks read the discount-rate signal and they reduce their loan portfolios in anticipation of further Fed action. When the Fed lowers the discount rate, it is signaling its intention to increase the money supply.

Changing the Required Reserve Ratio

If the Fed decides to change the required reserve ratio, the result is an immediate change in the reserve position of the banks and other depository institutions. If the required reserve ratio is lowered, banks will have more reserves than they need to meet the new lower minimum requirements. Banks, finding themselves with unwanted excess reserves, will convert those reserves into loans or they will buy government or corporate bonds. Either way, bank credit has expanded economywide and the result is an increase in the money supply. The reduction in the required reserve ratio has left the amount of reserves unchanged; but the proportion of loans and money that can be supported by those reserves has increased—the money supply will increase.

Conversely, when the reserve ratio is raised, banks have insufficient reserves, which causes each bank to try to replace those reserves. Since there has been no increase in the monetary base, as the banks attempt to increase reserves, they do so by reducing the amount of loans and the money supply falls. Changes in the reserve ratio are rare. The Fed seldom changes the reserve ratio in such a dramatic fashion. On the rare occasions when the Fed has undertaken a significant change in the reserve ratio, the effect of such changes on the money supply has been substantial.

We have seen how the Fed can use its control over the open-market operations, the required reserve ratio, and the discount rate to exercise effective control over the money supply. And we have seen in earlier chapters how monetary policy can affect the economy. But as we said in the introduction to this chapter, changes in financial markets have made it difficult to define the money supply. What is it that the Fed is really controling and how can it operate in an era where many of the old regulations have changed?

The Usefulness of the Concept of the Money Supply

The money supply is difficult to define and currently there is no measure of the money supply that is used by the Fed as a rigid target for policy. Nevertheless, a complete analysis of monetary policy would look at all of the different financial assets in the economy, ranging from currency to demand deposits and private bills and bonds. We could in principle write down the demand for and supply of each of these financial assets and examine how the Fed's open-market operations change the whole range of short-term interest rates throughout the financial system.

We have not done this. It is too complicated and would not yield additional insights that are worth the complexity. The concept of the money supply provides a simple but useful exposition. By examining the supply of and demand for money and using the device of the *LM* schedule, we have cut through a lot of the complexity and preserved the central idea of how monetary policy works.

The Fed controls the monetary base, and on this base of currency and bank reserves is built the whole pyramid of other financial assets and liabilities. Through open-market operations, the Fed can squeeze the base of the pyramid and change the amount of liquidity in the financial system. Despite deregulation, the Fed is still the only entity with the authority to issue legal tender and allow the whole system of transactions to operate in the economy.

Fed Targets: Money Supply and Interest Rates

One important way in which deregulation of financial institutions has impacted the working of monetary policy is that it has changed the way the Fed sets targets. For many years the Fed presented targets for the growth of all three concepts of the money supply, $M1$, $M2$, and $M3$. The chairman of the Fed's board went before Congress regularly to present the Fed's forecasts for the economy and indicate ranges for the rates of growth of the money supplies over the coming year.[4]

Whatever the merits of the monetarist view may have been in the past, the Fed has been forced to reduce its emphasis on specific money growth targets, because deregulation has made them useless. People shift funds from one financial asset to another, leading to rapid growth of one concept of money and decline in another, with little significance for monetary policy or the economy. There are periods of a few years when the change in a particular measure of the money supply seems closely correlated with movements in the overall economy. But this correlation is found to be ephemeral and cannot be relied on in the future.

Because of the problems with money supply targets, the Fed now uses interest rates as a guide to help it decide whether its policy actions (usually open-market operations) are working as a brake on the economy or as a stimulus.

There are dangers to the use of interest-rate targets, however, dangers to which we pointed in Chapter 8. It is the cost of funds that affects investment and aggregate

---

[4] This approach had been urged on the Fed by monetarist economists, such as Milton Friedman. We will discuss the monetarist view in Chapter 14.

demand, and the Fed does not control this rate. And there is an important addition to the list of dangers that the Fed should be concerned with in assessing whether monetary policy is working the way that it should. There can be problems within the financial intermediaries themselves that may affect the real economy. Many people feel that credit crunches have been important in causing recessions in the past, and some people argue that a credit crunch has held back economic growth in the United States in the early 1990s despite efforts by the Fed to expand the economy.

FINANCIAL CRUNCHES

Shifts in financial markets have contributed substantially to fluctuations in the U.S. economy. Changes in financial-market conditions can affect wealth and consumption, the cost of capital, investment demand, and expectations. Financial-market crunches have the combined effect of raising interest rates and reducing the supply of credit available to borrowers. Such a contraction can occur endogenously within the economy (i.e., stock market crashes, banking panics, and credit crunches) or the contraction can stem from policy actions engineered by the Fed. The Fed can bring on a sharp contraction in the economy by contracting the real stock of money—raising interest rates and reducing the supply of loans available from depository institutions. Such a policy was used in 1974–75 and again in the early 1980s. Of course, the Fed induced those recessions to deal with inflation. The Fed's bringing on a deep recession as a result of its anti-inflationary policies is one type of **financial crunch** that contributes to economic fluctuations. A financial crunch occurs when there is a sudden drop in the availability of funds loaned by financial institutions. This may occur when the Fed is reducing bank reserves so rapidly that the banks are in danger of failing to meet their reserve requirements. Banks cut back sharply on new loans. A crunch may also occur when there is a loss of confidence in financial intermediaries, so depositors withdraw funds, once again forcing the institutions to make sharp cuts in lending. Finally, a credit crisis can occur if the financial intermediaries lose confidence in the firms or individuals they are lending to. They fear a rise in the default rate and so they cut back on lending.[5]

financial crunch
A sudden drop in the availability of funds loaned out by financial institutions.

The impact of a financial-market crisis on aggregate demand is heightened when there is an erosion in expectations—a loss of business confidence. As businesses revise downward their evaluations of the flows of revenue from investment projects and revise upward their estimates of the risks and costs of investment projects, the result is a drop in the demand for capital goods that reduces aggregate demand. As future business prospects worsen, the expected returns to investment projects deteriorate. Moreover, when stock prices fall, the cost of capital rises directly—firms generate less capital per unit of equity issued on the market. In such a crisis, where falling expectations are coupled with a rise in the cost of capital, the present dis-

---

[5] This section draws on Robert J. Gordon, ed., *The American Business Cycle: Continuity and Change* (Chicago: University of Chicago Press for the NBER, 1986); and Victor Zarnowitz, "Fact and Factors in the Recent Evolution of Business Cycles in the United States," NBER working paper no. 2865 (February 1989).

counted value of capital investment shrinks as expected future revenues fall and the discount rate rises.

Financial-Market Aspects of a Loss of Business Confidence

In the absence of any Federal Reserve policy changes, a loss of business confidence can contribute to a financial-market crisis even though there was no explicit reduction in the supply of credit made available by financial intermediaries.

Business managers expect to get higher rates of return on investments in real capital assets (new plant or equipment or real estate) than they could have gotten on safe financial investments, such as government bonds. A loss of confidence in the returns expected from real capital investment (a higher probability of loss on investment projects or a greater chance of default on bonds) increases the risk premium associated with those investments. We have seen there is a gap between the interest rate on short-term nominal assets, such as T bills, and the rate of return required by businesses to invest in real capital assets. This gap depends on expectations about inflation and about the future path of interest rates. But this gap also depends on the riskiness of the investment, and the riskiness of investment reflects businesses' expectations about future returns. *When there is a general loss of business confidence, the increased risk of investment raises the effective cost of funds relative to the short-term nominal rate of interest.*

The change in the interest-rate gap described was apparent in the Great Depression of the 1930s. The T-bill rate was about one-half of 1 percent while the interest rate on BAA bonds was 7.8 percent.[6] This difference of over 7 percentage points between the two nominal interest rates compares with a typical difference of 2 to 4 percentage points. The change in the T-bill rate relative to the long-term *real* rate of interest in the Great Depression was even larger. Prices had been falling from 1929 to 1933, so the expected rate of inflation was low or even negative.

The Great Depression was an extreme case, but it is common in even more moderate recessions for the interest-rate gap to change when there is increased uncertainty in the economy. For example, the difference between the T-bill rate and the BAA rate widened to 5.5 percentage points during the 1982 recession.

We have been considering how a financial crunch, through a loss of confidence, increases the long-term real rate of interest. The financial crunch in the case we described did not result either from a Fed policy change or from a crisis in the financial intermediaries themselves. It came from a change in expectations and a rise in the cost of capital. That scenario is quite different from a financial-market crisis where the supply of money and credit is contracted directly by Fed actions.

If the Fed initiates a contraction, it sells T bills to reduce the money supply, thereby contracting bank loans and driving up the short-term rate of interest. Yet, severe financial-market crises can occur even without Fed action, when there is a sizable reduction in the supply of credit made available by financial intermediaries.[7]

---

[6] These figures probably understate the true widening of the gap between rates that took place in the 1930s, because many bonds had their ratings downgraded.

[7] Ben Bernanke and Mark Gertler, ''Agency Costs, Net Worth, and Business Fluctuations,'' *American Economic Review* 79 (March 1989), pp. 14–31.

Financial Crises and the Supply of Credit

If financial intermediaries either are forced to reduce credit because of large withdrawals of funds or choose to do so because they reassess the risks of lending, then there is a rise in nominal and real interest rates coupled with a reduction in the quantity of credit available to borrowers. With the reduction in bank loans, many firms and consumers search for credit elsewhere; they pay a higher rate of interest if they can secure borrowed funds, or they are forced to reduce expenditures if they cannot. Banking panics and credit crunches that contributed to declines in aggregate demand and income have been part of the story of business-cycle fluctuations in the United States since the 19th century.

Bank Failures and Panics, 1873–1933

banking panic
Widespread occurrence of bank runs, where the rush to withdraw funds from one bank turns into a general withdrawal of funds from all banks, causing large numbers of *bank failures.*

Bank Failures and Panics, 1873–1933   In their monetary history of the United States, Milton Friedman and Anna Schwartz identify the downturns of 1873, 1884, 1890, 1893, and 1907 as banking panics.[8] There were **banking panics,** when banks could not convert demand deposits into currency. People lost confidence in the banks and refused to deposit funds in them.

Prior to the creation of the Federal Reserve, bankers voluntarily held reserves. Yet, the profit motives of banks caused them to minimize reserves and maximize loans. Most banks were managed by prudent bankers who held levels of reserves so the risk of running out of reserves was small. Unfortunately, a small number of ''wild cat'' banks (banks that attracted deposits and expanded loans without regard to the need for holding reserves or the need for prudent credit creation) contributed to a great deal of financial instability. Further, even if all banks had been well run, the absence of a system to increase reserves quickly in the face of sudden withdrawals meant that the banking system was subject to considerable instability. The economy was subject to repeated banking panics. If depositors feared that withdrawal demands could not be met, they would rush to take out their money; but since banks held only a fraction of their demand-deposit liabilities in the form of reserves, the rush to withdraw funds would create a self-fulfilling prophecy. Thinking that a bank could not meet its obligations caused people to take out funds, which caused a bank not to be able to meet all its obligations. This rush to withdraw further exacerbated the bank's position. The rush to take out funds from an individual bank is called a ''bank run.'' A run on an individual bank may be an isolated event; however, if many banks are unable to meet the needs of depositors who want to withdraw funds, then the run on a handful of banks would turn into a *panic,* with large numbers of banks failing. *Bank panics have the effect of rapidly reducing the money supply, because the general public shifts from demand deposits to cash—taking reserves out of the banking system.*

The reduction of the money supply brought on by the banking panic reduces the availability of credit, drives up interest rates, drives down investment expenditures, and pushes the economy into recession. Friedman and Schwartz point to the banking panics that occurred during 1930 and 1931 as having exacerbated the Great Depres-

---

[8] Milton Friedman and Anna J. Schwartz, ''Money and Business Cycles,'' *Review of Economics and Statistics: Supplement* 45 (February 1963), pp. 32–64; and *A Monetary History of the United States: Estimates Sources and Methods* (New York: NBER, 1963).

Deposit Insurance Prevents Bank Panics

The major reason panics no longer occur is that modern banks have their deposits insured by government-based deposit insurance. *Deposit insurance* convinces the public that their deposits are safe, so they should see no reason to rush to a bank and withdraw funds at the slightest hint of a banking problem. In 1933, after the banking crisis, Congress established the Federal Deposit Insurance Corporation, which currently insures deposits of up to $100,000 in commercial banks as well as in S&Ls. Most small depositors are completely covered. Even larger depositors are fairly safe, because the FDIC usually works to find a healthy bank willing to buy a failed bank and honor depositors' claims. Nevertheless, very big depositors will run from a bank in trouble. Because runs and bank closings are rare, the insurance funds do not have to hold enough funds to cover all or even most bank liabilities. Bank failures still occur, and they increased in frequency during the deregulated 1980s, especially among S&Ls. But they did not turn into panics. Banks do not hold large excess reserves, because they do not see bank panics as likely within the current system. Bankers do not guard against panics by holding excess reserves, because they are convinced that deposit insurance has removed the threat of panic.

As a result of increased bank failures in the last few years, the reserves set aside by the FDIC have been exhausted. Some people are concerned that this will undermine the stability of the banking system. However, it seems clear that the federal government will use general tax revenues to make up for any shortfall in FDIC reserves.

sion. During the 1930s, the economy suffered from a two-sided financial crisis—there was a loss of business confidence that reduced the demand for capital investment expenditures and banking panics that reduced the supply of money and credit. The combination of tight money caused by bank failures and increased business risks pushed the economy into the Great Depression, a period of unprecedented reductions in aggregate and income.

The Federal Reserve can prevent bank panics by supplying reserves to banks that are experiencing a run, but historically the Fed has not always done this. During the Great Depression there were runs on thousands of banks while the Fed waited for the crisis to pass.

Dealing with bank panics that have already started by providing borrowed reserves in a crisis is one way of dealing with the problem. But a better policy would prevent the panics from occurring in the first place. Insuring bank deposits against losses due to bank failures almost eliminates the rationale to withdraw funds from a troubled bank. There were 635 commercial bank failures from 1921 to 1929 and 2,274 between 1930 and 1933. After the 1930s, there were no bank crises for many years and the Federal Deposit Insurance Corporation (FDIC) is generally credited with having successfully reduced bank instability.

The Great Depression led to a large reduction in private debt and very conservative financial strategies by banks and other financial institutions. World War II led to a great increase in government-budget deficits and consequently the issuance of large amounts of government bonds. Banks and other institutions decided to hold large fractions of their portfolios in government debt and to avoid stocks and risky bonds.

Commercial banks made conservative business loans and S&Ls used real estate to give collateral for conservative mortgage loans. As a result of the salutary lessons from the 1930s, there were no crises in the banks or other financial intermediaries from 1945 until 1966. But crises caused by reductions in the supply of credit did not cease to affect the economy. What changed was that the crises were no longer generated by a withdrawal of bank deposits. From 1966 to 1982 there were mild financial crises, because the Fed started to use a more active monetary policy to control inflation. And in the past few years there has been concern that excessive borrowing has raised the possibility of a major financial crisis in the 1990s.

credit crunch
A mild financial crunch where there is a sharp reduction in the supply of credit that raises interest rates and reduces access to funds.

Credit Crunches, 1966–1982   A **credit crunch** is a mild financial crisis. It can occur separately from a Fed contraction or as a result of Fed policy. A credit crunch generally involves increases in interest rates, together with a reduction in the availability of credit. Whether a credit crunch causes a real economic downturn depends on the severity of the crunch and the availability of alternative sources of funds. First, we look at how a credit crunch develops and then we look at its impact on the economy.

In 1966, short-term nominal interest rates rose above the levels of previous years. Because the interest rates that banks could offer depositors were restricted by Fed regulation, the rise in market rates sparked a credit crunch. Because they had a competitive disadvantage (being regulated in a high–interest-rate environment), banks were unable to act as intermediaries for those funds. The lower risks and added convenience that banks offered depositors were overwhelmed by the higher returns available elsewhere. Banks suffered from **disintermediation**—depositors' withdrawals of funds to purchase higher-yielding financial-market securities. As savers looked for higher returns outside of banks, the flow of funds to banks fell along with the amount of funds that banks could make available for loans. The flow of bank credit to nonfinancial corporations fell by about 40 percent in the second half of 1966. Monetary policy had also become restrictive and the growth rate of the money supply fell sharply.

disintermediation
Withdrawals of funds from financial intermediaries and into direct investments, such as financial-market assets. Also used to refer to the withdrawal of funds from banks and S&Ls in the 1960s and 1970s.

There was not a major downturn in the economy at that time, since the funds that were being withdrawn from banks were still available through other financial institutions. However, mortgages and the housing market were affected, because at that time most mortgages originated at savings banks.

Following 1966, there were four credit crises or crunches occurring in 1969–70, 1973–74, 1978–80, and 1982–82. In each of these financial crises, the Fed was following a contractionary policy during which a crisis was triggered by a particular shock: The Penn Central railroad went broke in 1970, and the Franklin National bank became insolvent in 1974. In 1980, the First Pennsylvania bank had problems, there was turmoil in the silver market, and, for a brief period, the Fed introduced specific restrictions on bank lending. In 1982, there were bank failures, partly associated with energy-related loans, and concerns about the effect of loan defaults by less-developed countries. These financial crises were triggered by a loss of confidence in financial institutions.

The postwar credit crunches have sometimes but not always been associated with downturns in output. One typical pattern of credit crunch is that a business expansion leads to increased demands for borrowed funds by business for fixed investment and to finance increases in inventories. Then banks find their default rate rising on loans and they become more cautious in their lending strategies. This is particularly the case when the collateral is risky, as it is for loans to finance inventory. Businesses find it difficult to obtain loans from their usual lenders, while alternative sources of funds demand higher interest rates. They decide to cut production to reduce inventory and increase cash flow. If the Fed engages in restrictive monetary policy, this exacerbates the crunch.

The effect of the credit crunches has usually been to reduce investment and real output. Credit crunches can play an important role in the cycle of inventory investment that we described earlier, but this is not always the case. There were financial crises in the 1980s that did not slow the economy significantly. For example, the problems of the Continental Illinois bank in 1984 and the run on state-insured S&Ls in Ohio in 1985 had little effect. The collapse of the stock market in October 1987 did not bring on a recession, either, with many observers crediting the Fed's short-run expansion of the money supply and the bail-out efforts of the federal regulators with preventing a crunch. Just as a temporary spike in short-run interest rates fails to trigger a recession, because the impact is not transmitted to long-term real rates, a short-term crisis of confidence does not necessarily lead to a recession, because real investment expenditures are not immediately affected and, if the loss of confidence passes quickly, income and output are maintained. Furthermore, if the Fed offsets the impact of a financial crisis with expansionary monetary policies, the crisis will fail to lead to recession. If, on the other hand, it is the Fed that is driving the credit crunch with the aim of reducing output, then a recession is much more likely.

Fears of a Future Financial Crisis

A short-term loss of confidence does not necessarily lead to a recession. But a widespread collapse of confidence could certainly bring on a downturn. There has been increasing concern that the U.S. economy has built an excessive level of debt that threatens to initiate a financial crisis serious enough to affect output and employment. The savings and loan industry is going through an agonizing restructuring in which major bankruptcies are commonplace. Major commercial banks and other financial institutions hold loans made to developing countries in Latin America and elsewhere that are now in default or have been restructured. Is the economy threatened by the kind of instability experienced in the Great Depression?

An important difference between the 1930s and the 1990s is that the federal government insures commercial banks and savings and loans through the FDIC. This protects depositors and reduces the chance of sudden mass withdrawal of deposits when there is a threat of bankruptcy. But if the federal government stands behind the banks, who stands behind the federal government? The huge federal-budget deficits of recent years have created some popular concern that even the U.S. federal government might default on its obligations. The threat of default by the federal government is probably not realistic, but the fears of serious financial crisis look much more realistic when we consider the massive increase in corporate debt that has taken place.

Corporate Debt, Leveraged Buyouts, and Junk Bonds

leveraged buyout (LBO)
Firms repurchase their outstanding equity by issuing large quantities of debt borrowed with the company's own assets as collateral.

Concerns about financial instability are not limited to the banks and the federal government. During the 1980s, corporate indebtedness increased substantially. Financial restructuring of firms had been underway throughout the period. There was a wave of corporate **leveraged buyouts** (LBOs) where firms repurchased their outstanding equity by issuing large quantities of debt. Even companies that were not directly involved in buyouts or takeovers underwent major restructurings and took on large increases in debt to discourage takeovers. Financial innovations, such as the marketing of collections of high-interest, high-risk **junk bonds,** had facilitated a transformation of corporate capitalization from the use of equity shares to the use of debt. This debt had been successfully sold on two premises. The first is that a portfolio of junk bonds has lower risk than any single junk bond issue, because of risk pooling. Failure for one firm will be balanced out by success for another firm. The second premise is that corporate profits in general would continue to rise and the increased interest payments would be financed out of cash flow. For those investors who accepted these premises, junk bonds offered high returns and reasonable risks. Aggressive banks, insurance companies, and wealthy individuals bought many of them.

junk bond
High-interest, high-risk corporate debt often used to finance a *leveraged buyout* (LBO).

While the portfolio argument for junk bonds is valid, general business conditions can turn negative for all firms, so, instead of independent risks that are reduced by pooling, a portfolio composed largely of junk bonds is particularly vulnerable to a general economic downturn. A severe recession could strain the ability of corporations to cover their liabilities.

In the 1980s, the rise in corporate debt entailed paying out a larger fraction of cash flow in interest payments. This forces a kind of ''backs-to-the-wall'' management cycle. One view argues that this will lead to a deterioration in economic performance, because it encourages short-term decision making and discourages long-term investments and R&D. A more positive view holds that, when corporate managers finance expansion with retained earnings, they are prone to pursue their own interests, rather than serving the interests of the shareholders. The increased levels of corporate debt encourage managers to become more efficient and to pursue shareholders' interests.[9] While it is still uncertain what the final verdict will be on the wave of corporate restructuring that took place in the 1980s, the rising levels of corporate debts have increased uncertainty about financial stability in the 1990s.

Households in the 1980s and 1990s have also added to the growth of indebtedness and to the perceptions that the financial sector has become less stable. Consumer borrowing has increased along with a rise in the number of personal bankruptcies.

Have government, business, and households all gone on a borrowing spree and banks on a lending spree that could lead to a wholesale collapse of the financial sector? Or are the fears all overblown? So far the financial markets have remained

---

[9] Michael C. Jensen, ''Takeovers, Their Causes and Consequences,'' *Journal of Economic Perspectives* 2 (Winter 1988); and Martin Neil Baily and Margaret Blair, ''Productivity and American Management,'' in *American Living Standards: Threats and Challenges,* ed. Robert E. Litan and Robert Z. Lawrence (Washington, D.C.: Brookings Institution, 1988).

quite stable and the threats to stability are not as severe as feared. The fact that borrowing has gone up may or may not indicate a greater danger of financial crisis. We need to assess how large the increase in borrowing has been and whether there has been an increase in the risks associated with borrowing.

Assessing Excessive Indebtedness

Borrowing becomes excessive when the size of debt is so much larger than income that interest payments claim a significant portion of income. In the United States, has the ratio of debt to income risen to dangerous levels? Data presented by Robert Litan from government sources (Figure 10–3) show the ratio of debt to GDP for business, government, and households and for total debt.[10] It shows that, from 1950 to 1980, the ratio of total debt to GDP remained fairly flat at about 1.25. This was the result of a slight up trend in household and business debt and a slight down trend in government debt. After 1980, the trend in total debt shifted abruptly. Household and business debt continued to rise faster than GDP, but government debt reversed its trend and started to rise, also. The result was the sharp upward shift that is evident in the ratio of total debt to GDP.

The federal deficits of the 1980s are showing up in the form of an increased debt-to-income ratio, but it is notable that *the ratio of government debt to GDP at the end of the 1980s was still well below the level that existed in 1945.* Even if the federal deficits

FIGURE 10–3
Ratio of Credit-Market Debt to GDP (nominal) for Households, Businesses, and Government, 1950–1992

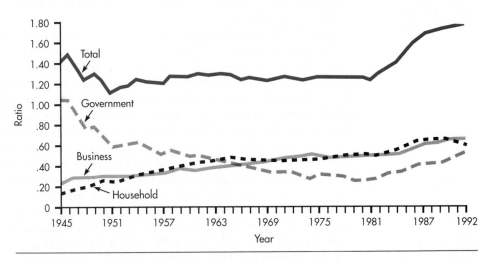

Sources: Board of Governors of the Federal Reserve System, *Balance Sheets for the U.S. Economy,* (Washington, D.C., various issues), *Flow of Funds Accounts: Financial Assets and Liabilities Year-End, (various issues); and Economic Report of the President* (Washington, D.C.: U.S. Government Printing Office, February 1994).

10   Robert E. Litan, ''The Risks of Recession,'' in *American Living Standards: Threats and Challenges,* ed. Robert E. Litan, Robert Z. Lawrence, and Charles Schultze (Washington, D.C.: Brookings Institution, 1988). Updated for this text.

continue for a number of years, they will not raise the ratio of government debt to income above the range it has had during the post-World War II period. The danger from the federal deficit is not that the government will go broke; rather, it is that the federal deficit is absorbing national saving, thereby reducing domestic investment leading to negative net foreign investment and thereby reducing future living standards.

The most plausible scenario for a serious financial crisis is that a wave of bankruptcies will strike businesses, households, or banks. How likely is this? Figure 10–3 shows the debt-to-GDP ratio, but the increase in private borrowing relative to GDP shown in the figure might be appropriate if assets had risen in line with borrowing. Insolvency will occur when there is a fall in asset values that pushes them below the value of liabilities. How close are private borrowers to insolvency? Figure 10–4 shows the ratio of assets to liabilities for nonfinancial corporations and households. It indicates that the ratio of debt to asset values has indeed risen as the debt-to-GDP ratio has risen, particularly for corporations. There is less of a margin of asset values over debt than there used to be.

The asset values used to construct Figure 10–4 reflect the historical cost of purchasing the factories, autos, and houses that provide the collateral for the loans. In the case of corporations, it is possible to use an alternative measure of solvency, the ratio of debt to equity. Figure 10–5 gives the debt–equity ratio for nonfinancial corporations, using the market values of both numerator and denominator. The figure shows some upward movement of the debt–equity ratio taking place in the 1970s and then a decline after that. The ratio is affected primarily by movements in stock prices. The stock market did poorly in the 1970s, particularly in 1974, and has done much better in the 1980s, even accounting for the 1987 crash. Using market values, therefore, suggests that the increases in indebtedness in the 1980s were perhaps not an unreasonable response by business to the increased market assessment of the value of their assets.

FIGURE 10–4
Nonfinancial-Business and Household Ratios of Total Liabilities to Total Assets, 1948–1992

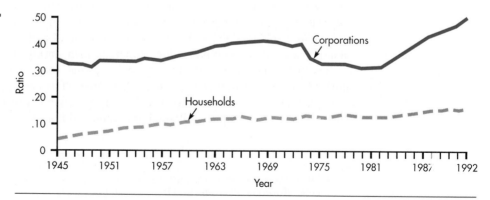

Source: Federal Reserve, *Balance Sheets for the U.S. Economy, 1948–87,* pp. 11–15, 21–25.

FIGURE 10-5
Ratio of Nonfinan-
cial Corporate-
Sector Debt to
Equity, Market
Value, 1961–1993

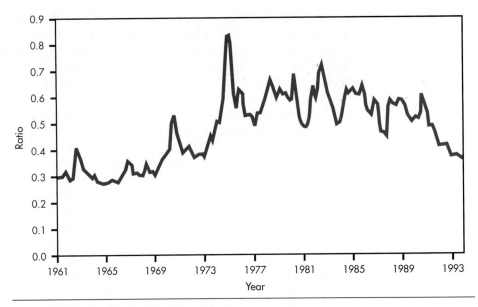

Source: Unpublished data from the Federal Reserve Board.

As a final indicator of the likelihood of financial crisis for households and nonfinancial businesses, we show in Figure 10–6 the ratio of the interest burden to income for households and businesses. This gives a measure of the ability of these groups to service the debt they have acquired. The figure gives some reason for concern. The fact that nominal interest rates have risen over the postwar period means that the debt-service ratio has risen faster than the debt-to-income ratio. The trend for business debt is striking, showing an increase in interest payments from less than 10 percent of cash flow to almost 40 percent. In a 1988 study of corporate indebtedness, Ben Bernanke and John Cambell predicted that if a severe recession, such as the 1981–82 recession, were to strike, it would leave about 10 percent of the large corporations with inadequate cash flows to service their debts.[11] Not all of these companies would then go bankrupt, but Bernanke and Cambell suggest that corporate bankruptcies would be much more numerous than during the 1981–82 recession. Figures 10–5 and 10–6, therefore, give somewhat conflicting evidence about the threat of corporate bankruptcies. The market values of assets suggest that the situation during the latter part of the 1980s was fine. The availability of income to service the debt does not look adequate, although the improved managerial efficiencies imposed

---

[11]   Ben Bernanke and John Y. Cambell, ''Is There a Corporate Debt Crisis?'' *Brookings Papers on Economic Activity, 1:1988,* pp. 83–125.

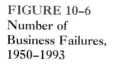

FIGURE 10-6
Number of
Business Failures,
1950–1993

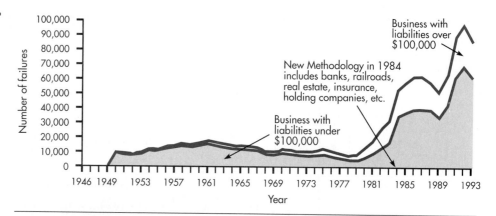

Note: The nonfinancial business measure is the ratio of interest paid to total cash flow. Interest burden of households is the ratio of household interest to disposable income.

Sources: U.S. Department of Commerce, Bureau of Economic Analysis, *National Income and Product Accounts of the United States, 1929–82* (Washington, D.C., 1986), pp. 63–70, 89–98, 392–93; and *Survey of Current Business* 68 (June 1988), pp. 5, 7.

by the debt load mitigate the danger of high interest burdens. The trade-off between debt and efficiency remained unresolved as takeovers and leveraged buyouts pushed up debt service–to–income ratios at the end of the 1980s. But the fears of a wave of bankruptcies are not purely hypothetical. Figure 10–7 shows the number of corporate bankruptcies over the 1945–93 period. The incidence of bankruptcy has risen sharply even though the economy had a long and steady period of economic growth.

The long economic recovery of the 1980s did not reduce the incidence of bankruptcy among industrial corporations, and it did not reduce the bankruptcies among banks and S&Ls, either. The FDIC [which in 1989 took over responsibility for its companion organization, the Federal Savings and Loan Insurance Corporation (FSLIC)] is a mixed blessing, because in recent years it has allowed some financial institutions to attract funds at low interest rates by offering security to depositors, and then lending out the money at high interest rates to borrowers undertaking very risky projects. This is a strategy that can yield high profits for the banks if all goes well, but puts the burden on taxpayers if the loans default. In some cases the risky loans have been made to friends or relatives of the managers of the banks.

The high-risk loans that have been made by banks and S&Ls have led to a tremendous increase in the bankruptcy rate in the 1980s for these institutions, as shown in Figure 10–8. Fortunately the number of bank failures has slowed in the 1990s.

Despite the weakness in the banking system, there has not been a wholesale banking crisis with a loss of confidence by the public. The reason is that the federal government has stood behind the banks. This has had major benefits for the economy; but there has been a major cost, too—the public costs of covering the shortfall and

FIGURE 10–7
Number of Business Failures, 1945–1993

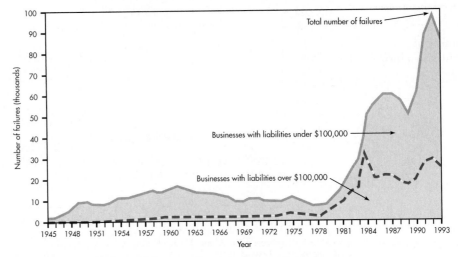

Data beginning in 1984 includes expanded coverage and is not generally comparable to earlier years.

Source: *Economic Report of the President* (Washington, D.C.: U.S. Government Printing Office, February 1988), p. 357.

FIGURE 10–8
Bank Failures, 1934–1993

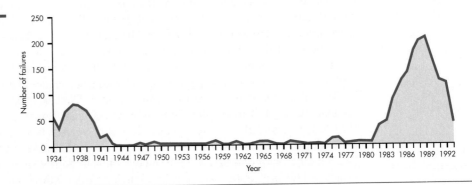

Source: Federal Deposit Insurance Corporation, *1987 Annual Report,* p. 49.

reimbursing depositors. The cost to taxpayers was $29 million a day in the last quarter of 1989.[12] Some estimates of the total cost of the crisis exceed $300 billion.

Banking Sector Credit or Capital Crunch in the Early 1990s

The S&L crisis of the 1980s may not have a direct effect on financial markets, but the change in the regulators that that crisis induced may have had a subsequent influence on the economy by contributing to the financial crisis and recession of 1990–91 and the slow recovery of the economy after that recession. In many sectors of the economy, businesses reported increasing difficulty in borrowing funds. The recession that began in July 1990 appears to have worsened and deepened, if not initially caused, by a reduction in credit availability. Most of the reported difficulties surrounding the supply of credit were centered around changes in lending practices or lending capability of commercial banks.[13]

Bank lending slowed during the 1990–91 recession, by more than usual for downturns. Most of this drop was in commercial and industrial loans, and it was concentrated in particular regions, mostly New England and the West Coast. The interesting question, as yet not fully answered, is why the decline occurred.

When bank lending declines, this could be because businesses are facing weak business conditions or they fear conditions will worsen, and so they are reluctant to borrow for expansion. This would show up as a decline in the *demand for bank loans,* and if this were the case we would not say that a recession was caused by a credit crunch. On the other hand, if businesses were looking for loans but the banks were not willing or not able to provide them, then this is a decline in the *supply of loans* and is what we mean by a credit crunch.

It is hard to evaluate which of these two cases applies to the 1990–91 period, but it appears that there was some decline in the supply of loans. This was a genuine credit crunch. And importantly, this decline in the supply of credit was not necessarily the result of Fed policy. There is little evidence that the Fed was tightening monetary growth immediately prior to or during the recession, the most typical cause of a financial crunch. This means that the credit crunch of 1990–91 was the result of the behavior of the banking system. Banks decreased lending on their own and this exacerbated the recession. Moreover, the difficulties that the banks experienced continued beyond 1991 and slowed the recovery.

There is still one more puzzle: Did banks reduce lending because they perceived an increase in the riskiness of lending or were they forced into reduction because of other

---

[12] Values released by federal regulators, reported in *The New York Times,* March 27, 1990, p. A1.

[13] As of the writing of this chapter there is still controversy over the degree of or even existence of a credit crunch that took place in 1990–91. The most complete discussion of the credit crunch appears in Bernanke and Lown, from which much of this section is drawn. They find some evidence of a credit crunch centered on inadequacy of bank capital, though they are dubious about the extent of the impact. We take a somewhat stronger position: that there was a crunch and that it contributed to the recession. See B. Bernanke and C. Lown, "The Credit Crunch," in *Brookings Papers on Economic Activity,* 1991, no. 2, (Washington, D.C.: Brookings Institution).

factors? The other factors include regulatory zeal following the S&L crisis and inadequate bank capital. The evidence, overall, favors the view that bank capital was a problem.

A bank has inadequate capital when it suffers losses on its loans. Banks always set aside loan-loss reserves to cover mortgages and business loans that default. During the early phase of the 1990–91 recession, there was a rapid drop in real estate values and an increase in defaults, particularly from real estate developers and from household mortgages. Some large banks also faced losses on foreign loans. This forced banks to take real estate loans off their books in amounts that greatly exceeded the loss reserves that had been set aside. The banks were forced to take funds from their own capital to make up the difference. This reduction in bank capital has the same effect as an increase in Fed reserve requirements, because it reduces the amount of new loans that can be sustained for any level of demand deposits.

This episode was an unusual example of how changes in the economic status of financial institutions can have independent effects on the supply of credit and can interfere with the policy intentions of the central bank.

The reduction of lending caused by the increase in nonperforming loans in the early 1990s was similar to, although less severe than, the crunch of the 1930s. One big difference is that bank depositors were protected by federal bank insurance and did not rush to withdraw deposits when a bank found its capital depleted. There were bank failures but few runs on banks.

CONCLUSION

Banks and other financial intermediaries play a crucial role in the working of modern economies, so important in fact that all of the industrial economies closely regulate their activities. Despite all the movement toward deregulation of U.S. financial intermediaries, the Fed still has a lot of control over financial markets. It can use its power over the monetary base to determine the money supply and affect or even determine short-term interest rates.

Despite its power, the Fed may find that changes in the financial status of banks can affect the supply of credit independently of short-term interest rates. When many banks had nonperforming loans in the early 1990s, they were forced to curtail lending and this discouraged investment and hence reduced aggregate demand.

WORKED EXAMPLES

Worked Example 10–1

When There Is a Change in Money Demand, How Does the Change in the Short-Term Interest Rate Come About?

Question   A three-month Treasury bill is an IOU issued by the U.S. Treasury. At the end of three months the U.S. Treasury promises to pay the owner of the T bill a fixed amount, say $10,000. When the bill is first issued, it will sell in the money market at a price below $10,000.

For example, if the T bill sold for $9,765, the owner would gain $235 after three months. When expressed as an annual rate of interest, this gain is 10 percent. How is this interest rate calculated? What is the interest rate if the price of the T bill is $9,879?

Answer   First calculate the percent gain or return after three months.

Purchase Price	Redemption Value	Gain
$9,765	$10,000	$235

3-month gain = ($235 ÷ $9,765) × 100 = 2.41 percent

Then the annual interest rate is calculated by assuming that the proceeds from the redemption are reinvested every three months in T bills at the same interest rate. The result of doing this is calculated as follows:

Value of Holding Three-Month T Bills for Four Periods in Succession with Reinvestment

1st: $ 9,765 × 1.0241 = $10,000
2nd: $10,000 × 1.0241 = $10,241
3rd: $10,241 × 1.0241 = $10,488
4th: $10,488 × 1.0241 = $10,741

Annual Gain

($10,741 − $9,765) ÷ ($9,765) × 100 = ($976 ÷ $9,765) × 100 = 10 percent

The interest rate on an annual percent basis in this example is just 10 percent. In general, the annual rate, i, is found by compounding the three-month rate (i_3) four times:

$$1 + i = (1 + i_3) \times (1 + i_3) \times (1 + i_3) \times (1 + i_3) = (1 + i_3)^4$$
$$i = (1 + i_3)^4 - 1$$

Applying this formula in the example gives

$$0.1 = 1.0241^4 - 1$$

Thus $i = 0.10$ or 10 percent. This completes the answer to the first part of the question.

The same method can be used to calculate the interest rate when the price of the T bill rises to $9,879. In this case, the three-month return is given by:

$$(1 + i_3) = 10,000 \div 9,879 = 1.0122$$

Then the annual interest rate is given by

$$0.05 = 1.0122^4 - 1$$

Thus i in this case is 0.05 or 5 percent.

This worked example has confirmed, therefore, the inverse relation between the price of T bills and the annual percent rate of interest. The increase in price of the T bill from $9,765 to $9,879 meant that the interest rate fell from 10 percent to 5 percent.

SUMMARY

- Monetary policy is conducted by the Federal Reserve acting through the banking system.

- Changes induced by the Federal Reserve in the supply of money are normally brought about by the Fed's increasing or decreasing the monetary base.

- The monetary base is comprised of bank's reserve account balances held at the Fed bank's vault cash and of cash held by the public.

- The banking system consists of depository institutions that offer checkable deposit accounts. Most checkable account balances are held in banks. A bank's assets include reserves, which must be a minimum fraction of the amount of checkable deposit accounts in the bank. The remainder of the bank's assets are loans.

- The Fed has control over the money supply by setting required reserves and by managing open-market operations.

- Open-market operations are purchases and sales of government securities. The amounts are determined by the Federal Reserve's Open Market Committee (FOMC). These purchases are designed to affect the level of reserves in the banking system.

- When the Fed sells government securities, it takes reserves out of the banking system and thus reduces credit and reduces the money supply. When the Fed buys government securities, it adds reserves to the banking system, which allows banks to increase credit and thus increase the money supply.

- Financial crunches are periods of contraction of money and credit, often initiated by Fed policies, which bring about reductions in real economic condition.

- A financial crisis can arise without Fed actions as a result of a loss of confidence. If depositors lose confidence in the banks, the demand for cash will increase and the money supply will decrease. Loss of confidence in the profitability of business investment can lead to an increase in the risk premium, an increase in the long-term rate of interest, and a decline in income.

- A credit crunch is a mild financial crisis where there is a rapid reduction in the availability of loans from financial intermediaries. Whether a credit crunch reduces aggregate demand and initiates a financial crisis depends on the reaction of the central bank.

- The possibility exists that the financial markets of the 1990s have become more prone to instability, because of an increased level of indebtedness among all sectors of the U.S. economy.

- Corporate debt outstanding has risen relative to the value of assets. The loan portfolios of banks and S&Ls have become riskier. Bankruptcy rates have risen sharply for both banks and corporations.

- The ratio of federal debt to GDP is high but not as high as in 1945, and consumer confidence in the financial system remains adequate. The debt–equity ratio for corporations is not unusually high, but interest payments have become a very large fraction of corporate cash flow in many companies.

- In the face of a serious recession, there would likely be a wave of corporate and bank bankruptcies that could erode confidence and worsen the recession. But it is unlikely that the crisis would get out of hand and lead to a repeat of the 1930s.

- Nevertheless, the recession that began in July 1990 appears, if not initially caused by, to have been worsened and deepened by a reduction in credit availability. Most of the reported difficulties surrounding the supply of credit were centered around changes in lending practices or in lending capability of commercial banks.

- The decline in the supply of credit was not necessarily the result of Fed policy.

KEY TERMS AND CONCEPTS

banking panic, p. 317

commercial bank, p. 300

credit crunch, p. 319

discount rate, p. 313

disintermediation, p. 319

excess-reserve ratio, p. 306

excess reserves, p. 306

federal funds market, p. 306

financial crunch, p. 315

fractional reserve system, p. 301

junk bond, p. 321

leveraged buyout, p. 321

monetary base, p. 307

open-market operations, p. 310

required reserve ratio, p. 306

required reserves, p. 306

reserve account, p. 302

reserve ratio, p. 302

reserves, p. 302

savings and loan banks, p. 301

DISCUSSION QUESTIONS AND PROBLEMS

1. How does the Fed control the monetary base?
2. Describe the role of banks in increasing the money supply.
3. When the Fed buys or sells securities, what happens to the monetary base?
4. Suppose currency held by the public is $400 billion and bank reserves are $72 billion. What is the monetary base? Suppose that the reserve ratio is 9 percent (0.09). How large are demand deposits? How large is the money supply? What happens to the money supply if reserves are increased to $75 billion and there are no other changes? What happens to the money supply if the monetary base rises to $475 billion and cash held by the public is always one half of the size of demand deposits?
5. What does the Fed have to know about economic conditions, bank behavior, and the public's preferences to know how large an increase in the monetary base is necessary to bring about a targeted increase in the money supply?
6. Comment on whether debt levels contribute to financial-market instability. How can financial-market instability contribute to fluctuations in the real economy?
7. Compare a banking panic with a credit crunch. Do they have different effects on aggregate demand and instability?
8. *(A)* In a financial crisis driven by contractionary monetary policy, the short-term nominal rate of interest rises much more than the long-term rate. *(B)* In a private-sector financial crisis driven by a loss of business confidence, the cost of funds rises much more than the short-term nominal rate. Compare the way in which both of these two very different effects contribute to a decline in aggregate demand.

EXTERNAL BALANCES AND INTERNATIONAL ECONOMIC POLICY

INTRODUCTION

Many people were shocked in the late 1980s when the United States ran huge trade deficits. From the end of World War II through 1970, the U.S. economy ran surpluses—selling more to the rest of the world than was imported. The U.S. balance of payments was in deficit through most of the 1970s and early 1980s, but the deficits increased in magnitude and became a serious concern by the end of the 1980s. What had happened to the world's most powerful economy?

In 1987, the U.S. economy had a deficit in its current account of over $160 billion, representing about 4 percent of GDP. The deficit in its foreign transactions has fallen since 1987 but remains high in the first half of the 1990s. The United States over the past 15 years or so has had difficulty maintaining what is called **external balance.**

external balance
An economy is in external balance when its balance of payments on current account is neither in deficit nor surplus.

The United States is not alone in experiencing these difficulties. France, the United Kingdom (U.K.), Italy, and many other countries have experienced balance of payments difficulties. Balancing these deficit countries there are economies that have run up frequent current account surpluses. For example, Japan and Taiwan have had large and persistent trade and current account surpluses.[1]

The worldwide system of international trade and payments exhibits large external imbalances, where some countries have current account deficits and others current account surpluses.

---

[1] A current account deficit means that a country is importing more than it is exporting and borrowing overseas to pay for the excess of imports. This must mean that another country has a current account surplus and is lending the funds needed. When we examine the current accounts of all the countries around the world, however, we find that they do not add up to zero. Is the world as a whole in deficit? An impossibility. There are trade and financial flows that are not captured by official data, possibly because the people involved do not want to report their actions to government agencies.

After the end of World War II, the then leading industrial nations, led by the United States, built an international monetary structure designed to deal with the problems caused by large external imbalances and the impact those imbalances would have on foreign-exchange markets. For a while it worked. The international conference held at Bretton Woods, New Hampshire in 1944, established a system for international trade and exchange in which exchange rates were held constant as far as possible. The United States pledged to maintain a fixed relation between the dollar and gold (holding the price of gold at $35 an ounce and agreeing to sell gold at this price to foreign central banks). And other countries pledged to hold their own currencies in a fixed relation to the dollar, except for periodic devaluations or revaluations. These periodic exchange-rate changes were intended to be infrequent and to occur only as a large resort if a fixed parity to the dollar could not be maintained.

The Bretton Woods system came under stress many times in the 25 years after the war as various nations were unable to maintain fixed parity of their currencies to the dollar. And the system broke down altogether 1971–73 as the United States abandoned its commitment to a fixed price for gold (gold rose to over $800 an ounce at one time) and other currencies began to fluctuate in value against the dollar. Since 1973, the world economy has moved toward a system of market-determined exchange rates, although central banks around the world still intervene in foreign exchange markets.

Foreign-exchange markets since 1973 have been characterized by very great volatility. As we saw in Chapter 7, there have been large swings in the value of the U.S. dollar in relation to an average of other currencies. And as Figure 11–1 shows, there are even large month-to-month variations in individual exchange rates. The replacement of exchange rates set by international monetary arrangements with exchange rates set in foreign-exchange markets did not lead to stability. Instead, exchange rates have been subject to tremendous volatility and uncertainty.

Both fluctuations in exchange rates and the emergence of external deficits and surpluses give rise to a call for government intervention. Domestic producers facing foreign competition want the government to "cure the trade imbalance" while export firms that have to deal with the vagaries of revenues received in foreign exchange want government to "stabilize exchange markets." Even the policy leaders in the international community have regular summit meetings, like the G–7 meetings (seven major industrial economies), designed to explore what they can do to deal with imbalances and fluctuations.

This chapter addresses these two related issues. First, the problem of external imbalances. Why do persistent trade and current account surpluses and deficits emerge? Should policy-makers be concerned about these imbalances and what if anything should they do about them?

FIGURE 11–1
The Exchange Rate between the U.S. Dollar and the Japanese Yen

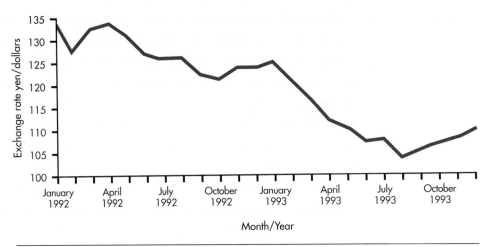

Second, the volatility of exchange rates. Why do these rates fluctuate so wildly? Should policymakers try to stabilize exchange rates, and, in general, what type of exchange rate system should there be?

Does government have a role in stabilizing exchange rates or is economic performance enhanced when exchange markets are free and unfettered from government intervention?

WHAT IS THE PROBLEM WITH AN EXTERNAL IMBALANCE?

The United States has had a current account deficit and a trade deficit for many years now and the economy has not fallen apart. Why should we worry about an external imbalance? There are three reasons to be concerned. First, if there is an external imbalance with a current account deficit, then this is usually accompanied by a trade deficit. A U.S. trade deficit means that we are buying more from overseas than we are selling. While that sounds attractive from a consumer point of view (i.e., being able to consume more than we produce) might it not also mean that, on balance, the United States is losing jobs to foreign workers? Second, a current account deficit could be a drain on national wealth as assets leave the country to pay for the imbalance. Third, if the external debt becomes too large, then couldn't there be a loss of confidence, triggering an economic crisis?

Loss of Jobs

One of the most common questions in the U.S. policy debate is: Is America ever going to get back all the jobs that have been lost to workers overseas? There is a widespread perception that U.S. jobs have disappeared in manufacturing as a result of our excessively open trade policies. Many people believe that the United States has such a large trade deficit, because of unfair competition, particularly from countries with

FIGURE 11–2
The U.S.
International Asset
Position—
1983–1992

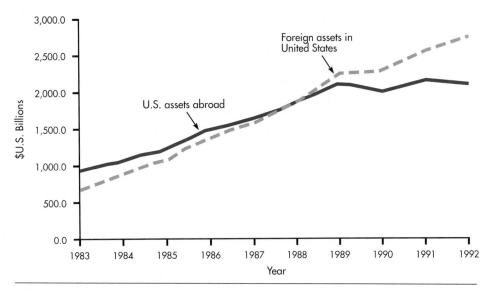

Source: *Economic Report of the President*, February 1994.

very low wages. This is an important issue that we have touched in earlier chapters. In this chapter, we examine critically the case for managed trade as a cure for the U.S. trade deficit and the alleged loss of manufacturing jobs.

Loss of Wealth   As we saw in Chapter 7, there is an accounting identity between the current account and the capital account. If the United States is importing more goods and services than it is exporting, then it must be getting the funds from somewhere—there must be an offsetting capital inflow. This means, in practice, that foreign residents are buying U.S. bonds (private or government), or they are buying up our real estate or factories or some other assets.

We believe it is not a problem for the United States if foreigners buy some of our assets. A foreign-owned company that buys a U.S. factory or service company and makes it more efficient is helping productivity in the U.S. economy. And, after all, U.S. companies and individuals have been buying foreign assets for years and years. As the world becomes increasingly integrated, such capital flows are to be expected and even encouraged. But there is a problem if the balance is off. If the United States is constantly running a current account deficit, then this must mean that foreign claims on U.S. assets are growing faster than U.S. claims on foreign assets.

Figure 11–2 shows this is indeed the case. In 1983, foreign assets in the United States were just over $800 billion, compared to over $1 trillion of assets held by the United States overseas. By 1992, this situation had changed dramatically. Foreign-owned assets in the United States exceeded U.S.-owned assets overseas by more than $600 billion.

In calculating the wealth of the U.S. economy, U.S. assets held overseas are an addition to our national wealth and foreign assets held in the United States are a subtraction from our wealth. The fact that the United States has become a net debtor means that our national wealth is diminished. If large current account deficits continue into the indefinite future, the extent of our foreign indebtedness will be a significant drag on our wealth and on our living standards. Overseas investors will only hold U.S. assets provided they are paid a return on them that is comparable to the return they could earn elsewhere in the world. That return must be paid out of the national income generated here in the United States. Our net foreign indebtedness is a liability that we will have to service indefinitely or repay eventually.

Crisis of Confidence

If foreign indebtedness grows without limit there may also be a crisis created. If foreign-asset holders become increasingly concerned about the size of the U.S. overseas debt, they will wonder if a collapse in the value of the dollar is likely in the near term. For foreign holders of U.S. debt, a large U.S. imbalance can even raise fears that the U.S. debtors may default on their obligations. The very fear of such a collapse or default could then trigger a panic sale of U.S. assets that would bring about the very crisis that has been feared.

Such a foreign-exchange or default crisis is unlikely to happen soon for the United States, because the U.S. economy is so large and the size of the government debt is not so large that it cannot be serviced. But it has happened in the past for some countries, and it may happen to other countries in the near future. In the 1970s, the U.K. had borrowed large amounts to preserve the value of its currency, and investors began to be concerned about default or currency crisis. The U.K. was forced to undertake drastic policy changes, which led to sharp recession, and there was a large fall in the value of the pound. In 1993 and 1994, Canada had a very large and growing foreign indebtedness and investors were concerned about default or a sharp drop in the Canadian dollar. The Canadian government was forced to pay premium interest rates on its borrowing to compensate foreign investors for the risks they took by buying Canadian bonds.

WHAT IS THE PROBLEM WITH FLUCTUATING EXCHANGE RATES?

The price of strawberries goes up in December and down in June and no one worries too much about it. If the exchange rate of the dollar fluctuates against the yen or the mark, why should we worry about that? There is concern when the price of any really important commodity varies by large amounts. When the price of oil went up in the 1970s and 80s, this contributed to major recessions and inflations. We discuss the consequences of these supply shocks in Chapter 12. And the exchange rate is an important price, like the price of oil. If a U.S. company is selling a significant fraction of its output in Europe and the dollar rises, then the profit it derives from these sales will decline.

The exchange rate is important for the United States, but exchange rates are even more important for small countries. A company in Holland might be selling three-quarters of its output to Germany. If the exchange rate of the Dutch guilder were to vary by 10 percent against the German mark, this could turn a profitable company into one running deficits. And since the exchange-rate drop plays out similar effects across most of the firms in Holland, which relies heavily on exports, the rate drop could easily send a strong economy into recession.

Exchange-rate fluctuations were a serious problem for the United States in the 1980s. The U.S. auto industry was already feeling new competitive pressures from the Japanese and German industries by the end of the 1970s. Then the dollar rose. In the 1990s, the exchange rates have swung in the other direction. The Japanese recession of the early 1990s is being made more difficult for Japanese companies as they try to compete internationally when there are about 100 yen to the dollar.

Planning production and sales—deciding where to produce and the types of cars to produce. These decisions become very difficult when exchange rates vary so widely.[2]

The member countries of the European Union (formerly the European Community) believe that currency fluctuations within the union are so serious a problem that they have tried to fix exchange rates to one member country against the others. This is seen as a necessary step toward a fully unified market. And in setting this goal, the European Union is repeating the history of the American colonies that decided to adopt a single currency with the formation of the United States of America.

Exchange-rate movements also greatly affect capital flows. The Japanese companies that bought U.S. real estate in the 1980s have taken a double hit in the 1990s. Not only have real estate prices in dollars been weak but also the fall in the exchange rate of the dollar against the yen has meant that many Japanese investors have taken huge losses on their U.S. investments.

The problem of persistent external imbalances and the problem of exchange-rate fluctuations are linked. Adjustments in the exchange rate should work to maintain external balance (reduce current account imbalances). When a country runs an external deficit, its currency should fall in value in exchange markets. The lower price of its exports and higher price of its imports should trigger just the changes in demand that move the deficit toward surplus. But imbalances and exchange rates don't work this simply. Surprisingly, external balances do not move quickly to equilibrium even though there are flexible exchange rates that can adjust quickly. Rather, trade flows adjust very slowly to changes in the exchange rate, and the trade balance can even move perversely for a period after an exchange-rate change.

WHY DO EXCHANGE-RATE CHANGES FAIL TO BRING ABOUT EXTERNAL BALANCE?

We find the answer to the sluggish response of the external balance to changes in exchange rates by taking a careful look at the factors that determine exports and imports. Figure 11–3 illustrates the relationship between the real exchange rate (*rex*) and exports (*X*) and imports (*IM*) that was first shown in Chapter 7. From the U.S.

---

[2] In recent years it has become popular for companies to protect themselves against exchange-rate fluctuations by using what is called the "derivatives market." The availability of this insurance is a big help to companies, but buying this kind of hedge through insurance can be expensive. We discuss forward exchange contracts later in the chapter.

FIGURE 11–3
With Income
Given, Exports and
Imports Depend on
the Exchange Rate

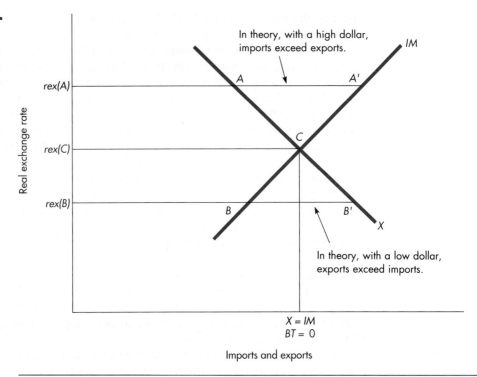

point of view, a high real exchange rate [*rex(A)*] means that imported goods are relatively inexpensive and imports are high (point *A'*). At the same real exchange rate, U.S. exports are relatively costly and exports are low (point *A*). At this high real exchange rate [*rex(A)*], imports exceed exports and the balance of trade is negative (point *A* − point *A'*).

Conversely, at a low change rate [*rex(B)*], imports will be low (point *B*) and exports will be high (point *B'*). At this low real exchange rate the balance of trade is positive (point *B'* − point *B*). The figure shows that at some exchange rate [shown as *rex(C)* in Figure 11–3] exports equal imports and the balance of trade is zero (point *C*). But the fact that the trade balance can be zero does not imply that in fact the exchange rate will necessarily so adjust that a country's trade balance will be zero. For instance, the U.S. balance of trade was positive through much of the 1950s and was negative in the 1980s. At point *A* in the figure, the negative trade balance means only that U.S. purchasers are buying more products from the world than they are selling to the world. *This deficit in trade could be balanced by other items, such as foreign purchases of U.S. assets. Thus there is no guarantee that the trade balance (the international purchases and sale of goods and services) will be balanced over any particular period of time.*

What Figure 11–3 implies is that a fall in the real exchange rate will lead to a reduction in a trade deficit or an increase in the surplus, and vice versa for a rise in the real exchange rate. Does this relation shown in the figure hold in actual practice?

Figure 11–4 gives data for the real exchange rate and the balance of merchandise trade in the U.S. economy since 1977. There is some support for the relationship

FIGURE 11–4
The Real
Exchange-Rate
Index and the Bal-
ance of Trade for
the United States,
1977–1993

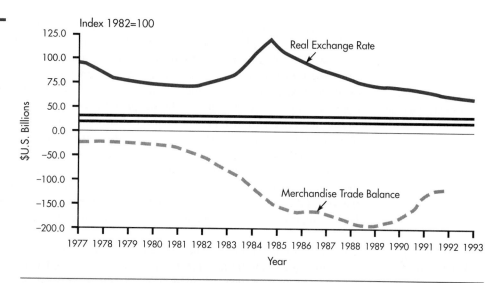

Source: *Economic Report of the President* (Washington, D.C.: U.S. Government Printing Office, February 1994).

between high exchange rates and trade deficits. There is a tendency toward reductions in the deficit associated with periods of decline in the exchange rate, while during periods of a rising exchange rate there is a tendency toward increases in the trade deficit. For example, the exchange rate fell after 1977, and this was followed by a decline in the trade deficit in 1979 and 1980. This same pattern occurred again after 1985, as the deficit had begun to fall by 1988.

However, this pattern does not hold at all times and, when the exchange rate falls, the balance of trade does not immediately improve. In fact, *when the exchange rate falls, there is a clear tendency for the trade deficit to get worse before it gets better.* This can be seen in 1978, 1986, and 1987. This same pattern also sometimes works in reverse, when the exchange rate rises. For example, the deficit fell in 1989 even though the exchange rate rose.

Trade Adjustment Lags and the J-Curve

J-curve
The pattern of the trade balance following a re-duction in the exchange rate, where the trade balance first worsens and then improves.

The trade balance often worsens at first following a reduction in the exchange rate. The balance of trade traces what is called a **J-curve**.[3] There are several reasons why the balance of trade may not always improve when the exchange rate falls. One reason is that both domestic and foreign income can and will change. But aside from income changes, the most important reason is that it takes time for changes in the exchange rate to bring about shifts in the real flows of exports and imports, while changes in the exchange rate immediately change the dollar or nominal value of imports—even before there is any change in the real volume of imports.

---

[3] The J-curve and the adjustment of trade flows are discussed in Rudiger Dornbusch and Paul Krugman, "Flexible Exchange Rates in the Short Run," *Brookings Papers on Economic Activity* 7, no. 3 (1976), pp. 558–66; Jeffrey D. Sachs, "The Current Account and Macroeconomic Adjustment in the 1970s," *Brookings Papers on Economic Activity* 12, no. 1 (1981), pp. 201–68; and Paul Krugman, "The J-Curve, the Fire Sale and the Hard Landing," *American Economic Review* 79, no. 2 (May 1989), pp. 31–35.

trade adjustment lag
In international trade, the time delay between a change in the exchange rate and changes in the volumes of imports and exports.

The increase in exports and the decrease in imports that follow a reduction in the exchange rate take place with a considerable time delay or **trade adjustment lag.** To increase sales abroad, exporters must expand the number of dealers or retailers that carry their products; they must advertise and convince foreign customers of the availability and reliability of their products. On the import side, when the dollar falls, imports become more expensive. But people will have grown to like Japanese cars and stereo equipment, Danish furniture, and Italian wines and they keep buying these and other imports even as their prices rise in the United States. Suppliers of imports, having established a market share in the United States, lose that market position rather slowly. Foreign suppliers would rather suffer a reduction in markups than allow all of the change in the exchange rate to be reflected in higher prices of imports in U.S. markets. Of course, neither the preference for imports nor the reductions in profits for foreign suppliers can be maintained indefinitely if the real exchange rate keeps falling.

The Trade Balance and the J-Curve

The value of the trade balance shown in Figure 11–4 is in current dollars—the nominal value of the trade balance. This current dollar balance is important, because it reflects the contribution of trade flows to the supply of and demand for foreign exchange. But we must now take account of the fact that this dollar trade balance can change when prices and the exchange rate change, whether or not the physical qualities of goods exported and imported change.

The dollar value of exports (PX) *equals the physical volume of exports* (X) *times the U.S. price level* $(PX = P \times X)$. This is the amount of dollars that are demanded by foreigners to buy U.S. goods. On the import side, *the dollar value of imports* (PIM) *equals the physical volume of imports* (IM) *times the foreign price level* (P_f) *divided by the nominal exchange rate* $(PIM = IM \times P_f \div ex)$. This is the amount of dollars that U.S. importers will convert into foreign currencies to buy foreign goods. For example, if the U.S. imports 1 million Japanese autos at 2 million yen per auto and the dollar–yen exchange rate is 100 yen per dollar, then the U.S. import bill is $20 billion $(1,000,000 \times 2,000,000 \div 100 = \$20 \text{ billion})$.

A decline in the exchange rate has the effect of making a given quantity of foreign goods more expensive for Americans to buy. This means that the current-dollar cost of imports will rise as a result of the fall in the exchange rate, even if the physical quantity of imports remains unchanged. Suppose that the value of the dollar drops to 90 yen with no change in the yen price of Japanese autos and suppose further that the number of autos imported does not change in the short run; then the U.S. import bill will increase to $22.22 billion $(1,000,000 \times 2,000,000 \div 90 = \$22.22 \text{ billion})$. *A constant physical volume of imports represents a higher dollar cost of imports when the value of the dollar declines (an increase in the value of the yen).*

In general, the demand for Japanese imports in the United States is not perfectly inelastic, meaning that the volume of Japanese goods purchased in the United States will decline as the prices of these goods increases. But in practice it is quite inelastic, especially in the short run. This means that the demand for imported products does not change very much when their prices change. Given this, the auto-import bill would rise even is Japanese auto manufacturers lowered their yen prices somewhat to remain competitive in U.S. markets and even if the Japanese automakers lost some sales because of the price rise. For instance, suppose there were a fall in the value of the dollar from 100 yen per dollar to 90 yen per dollar, imported car prices in yen dropped to 1.8 million yen per car, and sales volume fell by 2 percent to 980,000 vehicles. The import bill in current dollars would still rise (from $20 billion a year to $20.69 billion) because the *dollar price* of cars would go up by more than the reduction in volume of cars bought (the price rise is 5.5 percent, $20,000 to $21,111, compared to the 2 percent fall in quantity).

The effect on the current-dollar balance of trade of a drop in the exchange rate (a decline in the dollar) is, therefore, the outcome of the following effects:

1. The physical volume of U.S. exports will rise because they are now cheaper for foreigners to buy. U.S. exporters may also decide to raise the price in dollars of their foreign sales after a dollar decline, so the value of U.S. exports will rise more than the volume. This effect improves the trade balance.
2. The physical volume of U.S. imports declines because imports are more expensive. Foreign companies may also decide to trim their profit margins. Both of these effects improve the trade balance.
3. A given physical volume of imports requires more dollars to pay for the foreign currency needed to buy imports, even if import prices may have come down somewhat. Following a decline in the exchange rate, there is a decline in the terms at which U.S. goods exchange for foreign goods, as measured by a fall in the price of exports relative to the price of imports. This effect is called a decline in the terms of trade and this decline worsens the current-dollar trade balance.

In practice, for some time after the decline in the exchange rate the third factor dominates the first two. The current-dollar trade balance traces out a J-curve following a fall in the exchange rate. Figure 11–5 shows the J-curve, where the trade balance first falls (worsens) and then rises (improves) above the initial level.

Even though we are taking a simplified view of changes in trade flows, we can see the workings of the J-curve in the actual economy. For example, the dollar exchange rate started to fall in 1985, fell in 1986, and declined again in 1987. But the current-dollar trade balance continued to deteriorate until late in 1988. One consequence of the trade adjustment lags and the J-curve is that policymakers, and perhaps traders in international markets, can become confused about the fundamental relationships between exchange rates and trade flows. For example, a country running a trade deficit experiences a decline in its exchange rate. At first, this worsens the deficit; sophisticated policymakers and market traders know why and are patient, waiting for the improvement in the balance of trade. However, some in the policy arena may lobby for protection of domestic producers in the form of import quotas in part because the decline in the currency is not working to reduce the trade deficit.

Some international investors may lose confidence in the currency and speculate on further declines in the currency. Policymakers and decision makers need to understand adjustment lags and the J-curve to make sound decisions about international trade.

The slow adjustment of exports and imports to changes in the exchange rate is only one of the reasons why it is difficult to eliminate external imbalances. A second reason is that income varies domestically and abroad.

FIGURE 11–5
The J-Curve

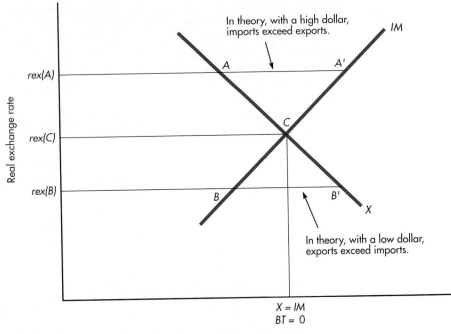

The J-curve describes a deficit worsening before improving following a fall in the dollar.

Income
Changes and
the Trade
Balance
in the Early
1990s

The U.S. current account deficit began to decline in the late 1980s and by 1991 it had almost fallen to zero. Was this the result of the relatively weak dollar at this time? In part it was, but only in part. An important reason why the U.S. current account deficit improved so much from 1990 to 1991 is that the U.S. economy went into a recession and then experienced a very slow recovery.[4] In Europe, however, there was no recession in 1990 and 1991; while in Japan, there was a continued boom, fueled by the rapid rise in real estate prices and the stock market.[5] The fact that the United States was out of phase with the economies of Europe and Japan meant that U.S. imports were down because all U.S. spending was down, and U.S. exports were up because spending overseas was up.

By 1992 and into 1993 the situation was different. Europe had fallen into a deep recession and the bubble economy had burst in Japan. Meanwhile the U.S. economy was finally picking up steam and spending was rising. This meant that, even though the dollar remained pretty low, especially against the Japanese yen, there was an increase in the U.S. current account deficit in 1992 and 1993.

---

[4]   The current account deficit was so low in 1991 in part because of payments made to the United States for costs incurred in the Gulf War.

[5]   The rise in real estate prices encouraged a lot of construction spending, while the rise in the stock market meant that companies could finance investment at very low cost and this encouraged investment (the rise in the stock market lowered the cost of funds).

The countervailing effects of income movements and exchange-rate movements are summarized in Equation 11–1. Exports and imports depend on the real exchange rate, *rex*, and foreign and U.S. income (Y^{for} and Y^{US}).

$$\text{Current account} = X - IM$$
$$= X(rex,\ Y^{for}) - IM(rex,\ Y^{US}) \tag{11–1}$$

- When *rex* declines this increases exports and imports decrease (when *X* goes up, *IM* goes down). But this happens slowly.
- When foreign income increases, this raises U.S. exports (when Y^{for} goes up, *X* goes up).
- When U.S. income increases, then U.S. imports increase (when Y^{US} goes up, *IM* goes up).

The U.S. current account is the difference between exports and imports (with foreign income payments included as part of imports and exports). When the exchange rate declines, foreign goods and services are more expensive and domestic goods and services are less expensive, so exports increase and imports decrease; but this response is fairly small in the short run, as we indicated in the discussion of the J-curve. In contrast with exchange-rate effects, the effects of income changes are much quicker. A drop in income in Europe and Japan will reduce U.S. sales overseas within a few months. And a rise in U.S. income will increase imports very quickly also.

Summary of the Effects of Exchange Rates and Income

We can now give an important part of the answer about why current account imbalances often fail to respond to the changes in the exchange rate that are expected to correct them.

- When an exchange rate falls, this will worsen the current account deficit in current dollars in the short run (the J-curve effect). And the reverse is also true. A currency appreciation will increase a current account surplus in the short run.
- Changes in income at home or abroad will have large and relatively quick effects on the current account that may offset the impact of a change in the exchange rate. (Of course, sometimes these income changes can reinforce the effect of an exchange-rate change, but the point is that there is no assured response to an exchange-rate change.)

We are examining the issue of why changes in exchange rates do not act quickly to eliminate external imbalances. For example, why didn't the fall in the dollar after 1985 solve the U.S. trade and current account deficits? And we have summarized here an important part of the answer. Exchange-rate changes can act perversely for a while. And their impact may be offset by cyclical changes in income here or abroad. But actually, these answers give only part of the story. To complete the answer, we need to return to another point introduced in Chapter 7: The fundamental cause of an external imbalance is a gap between national saving and investment.

The Iron Law of the External Imbalance

In Chapter 7, we showed how the budget deficit reduces national saving and we repeat the basic identity here:

$$S \quad + \quad T - G \quad = \quad I \quad + \quad X - IM$$

Private saving   Budget balance   Investment   Net exports
(current account)
(net foreign investment)

The budget balance turned sharply negative (a large deficit) in the 1980s and, since there was no offsetting increase in private saving, national saving was also sharply reduced (National saving $= S + T - G$). Investment has been affected by both interest rates and cyclical variations, but it had not fallen to the point of equality with national saving. The result has been an external imbalance (a deficit on current account matched by an inflow of capital; that is to say, by net foreign investment).

As a result of modest efforts during both the Bush and the Clinton years, there had been some reduction in the structural budget deficit.[6] But despite these efforts, the structural deficit remained large and is likely to cause a continued trade and current account deficit for the United States. *As long as there is an imbalance between national saving and domestic investment, the exchange rate will not move to the value that would be necessary to eliminate the external imbalance.* Estimates made in 1993 indicated it would have taken about a 10 percent decline in the dollar to restore external balance once the long term (i.e., once the J-curve effect) had passed. The reason the United States has a chronic external imbalance is that neither voters nor politicians really want to do what is necessary to balance the federal deficit.

Raising taxes or cutting expenditures, or both, are the right ways to deal with a persistent trade deficit. But since these alternatives are unpopular and since most people do not connect the budget and trade deficits, there are often political pressures to avoid the economic pain of reducing government deficits and, instead, policy-makers and the public turn to trade policies. They look to policies that will restrict the free flow of goods, services, and funds to cure the external balance. These policies appear to be costless and simple: If we're buying more from the rest of the world than we're selling, why not fix the external balance problem by just slapping on a tariff or, even better, make sure foreign goods don't get in, so why not invoke a quota? We'll explore whether such restrictions can provide a useful solution to the external balance problem.

Even when there is not a trade deficit, there may also be calls for trade restrictions. International trade leads to job losses in particular industries even when exports and imports are balanced. There have been many arguments made that the United States should use a variety of restrictions and international agreements to "manage" its trade. Does managed trade make sense?

---

[6] During the 1990–92 period of recession and slow recovery, the level of investment demand in the United States was low and this gave temporary help to the overall saving-investment imbalance and led to a dip in the current account deficit. This is the same point that we made above, about the effect of income variations on the trade deficit.

USING TRADE POLICIES TO ACHIEVE EXTERNAL BALANCE

Why do countries engage in international trade? They do so because all countries can be better off by trading with each other than they can by going it alone. The theory of comparative advantage explains the rationale for trade.

The Theory of Comparative Advantage

comparative advantage
A country has comparative advantage in those goods and services in which it is *relatively* most productive.

The theory of comparative advantage grew out of the notion of specialization— advantage accrues to those who concentrate on doing what they do best. Instead of attempting to be self-sufficient, specialization requires markets where producers can trade what they make for what they want and need. For example, as market economies developed, someone who was a skilled carpenter found that he or she was better off to work full-time as a carpenter, sell the furniture or other wood products, and use the proceeds to buy food. This was more efficient than trying to spend part of the time farming and part of the time working as a carpenter. The market allows people to specialize in the activities for which they have a **comparative advantage.** People then trade goods and services to friends and strangers and everyone can be better off.

It is not necessary to be the best carpenter in the world to find that a person can be better off to concentrate on carpentry. (In other words, a person need not have an *absolute advantage* in carpentry.) Comparative advantage simply means that carpentry is the best way for the person to spend his or her time, relative to other possibilities and given the market value of the wage paid to carpenters.

For countries, comparative advantage has a similar market test. Provided there is an equilibrium exchange rate, countries should export those goods and services where they can sell profitably at world prices (i.e., where it has comparative advantage) and import those goods and services where they can buy more cheaply abroad than they can produce at home (i.e., when it has comparative disadvantage). Such a policy allows countries to produce more of the things at which they are relatively efficient in producing and move out of the production of those things they are relatively inefficient at producing. A country's trading partners are doing the same thing and world efficiency and productivity is maximized.

This theory of the advantages of trade was developed by the economist David Ricardo in 1817, using a very simple model with goods produced only with labor. But the central idea holds for more realistic frameworks, and it is an idea that still makes common sense today.[7] An important implication of the theory, however, is that *trade rearranges production.* It reduces production and employment in some industries and increases it in others. Trade leads to structural change in the economy; in fact, the benefits of trade are only realized if there is such change.

The theory of comparative advantage, however, requires some strong assumptions to reach its conclusions, and these can be questioned. First, it assumes that economies always have fully employed resources. It does not deal with the possibility of weakness in aggregate demand with output below potential. We will ask first whether

---

[7] For the development of the theory of comparative advantage, see, for example, Paul Krugman and Maurice Obstfeld, *International Economics: Theory and Policy,* 3rd ed. (New York: Harper Collins, 1994).

a country can increase aggregate demand and hence output through trade either via increased competitiveness or via restrictive trade policies.

Second, the theory assumes that the relative efficiencies or productivities with which countries produce goods are given and unchanging. At an individual level, this might mean that, if someone had a comparative advantage in washing dishes, then one should do this full time. In fact, this person might realize that, by going to school or acquiring skills on the job, he or she could change the comparative advantage and obtain a more skilled and better paid job. For countries, this same idea might mean building up industries to achieve comparative advantage even if initially these industries did not have it. This twist on comparative advantage points to the dynamic nature of trade and production, arguing that it matters which industries a national specializes in—maybe it makes a difference to the quality of life and living standards whether an economy specializes in potato chips or computer chips; or maybe not. We explore in this section whether the dynamic nature of comparative advantage provides a justification for trade restrictions.

Trade Policies

Increases in net exports will increase aggregate demand. This means that trade policies, including restrictions on imports can, in principle, be used to increase income and employment. We look now at this issue. Will policies that raise the trade balance as opposed to autonomous improvements in the trade balance raise real income temporarily or permanently? Is there any difference between the effect of a gain in net exports from autonomous increases in sales abroad spawned by improved business practices and a gain in net exports brought about by national economic policies directed at reducing imports? First, we will look at increases in exports that stem from improved competitiveness. Second, we will look at an artificial circumstance, where imports are restricted.

Competitiveness and Increased Exports   If exchange rates are allowed to adjust freely in response to market forces and trade is unrestricted, selling to the rest of the world requires firms in a country to design, produce, and market products or services that can compete effectively in world markets. During the 1980s, there was concern that many U.S. firms had lost their ability to compete effectively in international markets. But in the past few years, the manufacturing sector of the U.S. economy has increased its rate of productivity growth and worked more effectively than in the past to increase its competitiveness. Some of this improved competitiveness has come from investment by foreign companies in the United States. These foreign companies have brought technology and new management methods into the U.S. economy. Both the efforts of domestic companies and the investment by foreign companies have helped U.S. exports and reduced U.S. imports for any given exchange rate. Overall competitiveness has improved and this has had a beneficial effect on U.S. income.

The effect of an improvement in competitiveness on aggregate demand was shown in Figure 7–6. We saw there that the initial effect of the increase in exports is to raise aggregate demand and raise income. In the U.S. economy in the last few years, this has indeed been the case, where a falling trade deficit has helped to sustain the growth of aggregate demand. As we noted in the discussion of Figure 7–6, however, the longer-run effect of increases in competitiveness is to increase the value of the dollar relative to where it would be otherwise. The increase in the real exchange rate then gradually eliminates the aggregate demand effects of the increased demand for exports, by restraining exports and encouraging imports.

The gradual elimination of the aggregate demand effect of improved competitiveness does not mean there are no long-run benefits. The increases in efficiency that have taken place in the manufacturing sector, partly in response to foreign competition and foreign investment, have improved overall productivity and efficiency; this translates into higher living standards for Americans.

Increasing competitiveness helps the trade balance and income in the short run and improves living standards in the long run. But some policymakers suggest benefits can also be gained from restricting trade.

Protectionism, Tariffs, and Decreased Imports　　The trade balance can be improved by protectionist policies, such as restricting imports through the use of tariffs. Placing a tariff on imports raises the prices of imports and import substitutes. Imports decline as the balance of trade improves. The effect on the level of aggregate demand of the imposition of trade restrictions is similar to the effect of an increase in the demand for U.S. exports, although the specifics are different. Initially, the trade restrictions will reduce imports and have no effect on exports. The *IS* schedule shifts to the right initially as a result of the increase in net exports, and income and the interest rate rise. But the trade surplus and the higher interest rate then lead to an increase in the value of the dollar and there is a gradual reduction in exports and an increase in imports. Over time, the *IS* schedule shifts back to the left again. *The effect of trade restrictions on aggregate demand is temporary,* just as the effect of an increase in export demand was temporary.

In terms of the long-run effects on real income, however, trade restrictions and increased competitiveness are very different in their impact. Increasing competitiveness will expand trade, encouraging exports and then using the foreign-exchange resources to buy more foreign goods. By contrast, the trade restrictions have reduced both imports and exports. Typically, trade restrictions are imposed because of the loss of jobs in industries that compete against imports. And the restrictions can succeed in doing this, at least temporarily. But the unseen effect of the restrictions is to reduce exports, also, which means fewer jobs in exporting industries. The efficiency of production is reduced as a result of the restrictions.

The Costs and Benefits of Tariffs　　Based on traditional approaches to trade theory, we cannot say unequivocally, however, that tariffs would reduce real income in the United States. The U.S. economy is very large and foreign companies that sell in the U.S. market face very competitive conditions. A tariff on imported goods might force foreign companies to cut the prices they will receive for their goods in the U.S. market. The price we pay as consumers would go up, but the tariff revenue would help pay our taxes. The United States can use its large size as a way of getting better terms in international trade, just as monopolists can make a profit by restricting output. Of course, other countries will suffer as a result and they may then retaliate. Trade restrictions that are unilaterally placed on imports by one country often lead to *retaliation,* whereby the affected country places tariffs on imports from the initiating country. A trade war can ensue, resulting in lower trade for all countries.

Moreover, raising import restrictions eventually leads to import substitution that has a longer-run repercussion effect. When domestic buyers finally move away from the higher-priced imports, the income of other countries falls, causing them to demand fewer exports. As we indicated earlier, this repercussion effect has not been traced as the primary cause of recessions in the United States, but it has been seen as the basis for severe contraction in economies where trade is a much larger share of national income. During the 1930s in the midst of the Great Depression, most European countries attempted to improve their own trade balances and their domestic aggregate demand by passing legislation or enacting policies sharply restricting imports.[8] In Europe a downward spiral of the level of trade contributed to the deepening of the depression.

Quotas   When policymakers become concerned about the overall trade deficit, or the level of imports of specific products, such as automobiles or computer memory chips, they often impose quotas. These quotas sometimes take the form of "voluntary" restraint agreements, or VRAs. For example, in response to the rising imports, the U.S. and Japanese governments negotiated a VRA on Japanese-made autos. The European Union has used VRAs extensively to protect its industries against Japanese and other South East Asian competition.

The disadvantage of a U.S. quota or VRA from the viewpoint of U.S. consumers is that instead of generating revenue for the U.S. government, which would help pay the tax bill, the quota will allow foreign producers to earn a rent or excess profit on each unit they sell in the United States. Figure 11–6 illustrates this point. The world price of the good is P_w, but after the quota is imposed, the price in the U.S. rises to P_{US}. This allows U.S. producers to sell more and be more profitable, but foreign producers can also sell at P_{US} and earn rents, shown by the shaded box in Figure 11–6.

So why do policymakers often use quotas or VRAs, rather than tariffs?[9] Partly this is because there is a mistrust of the effectiveness of tariffs in reducing imports, but also they are used precisely because there is a payoff to foreign producers. This payoff makes the foreign companies and governments more willing to accept the quota without retaliation.

This assessment of the costs of tariffs and quotas is based on a static perspective, which assumes that production costs and industry productivity levels are constant and are not affected by trade. More recent research has taken into account the dynamic

---

8   Philip Friedman, "The Welfare Costs of Bilateralism: German–Hungarian Trade, 1933–1938," *Explorations in Economic History* 13, no. 2 (January 1976), pp. 113–25; and "An Econometric Model of National Income, Commercial Policy and the Level of International Trade: The Open Economies of Europe, 1924–1938," *Journal of Economic History* 37, no. 1 (March 1978), pp. 148–80.

9   In the case of the motor vehicle industry, both restrictions have been used. There is a VRA on cars and a 25 percent tariff on light trucks. Charles P. Kindleberger *The World in Depression, 1929–39* (U.S. Berkeley Press, 1973).

**FIGURE 11-6
The Case of
Improved
Productivity as a
Result of Trade**

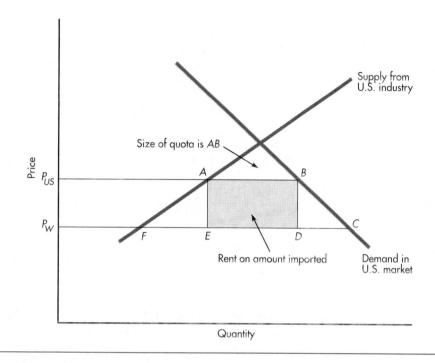

effects of trade and competition over time on the efficiency of production itself. There are two opposing viewpoints.[10]

**Dynamic
Arguments for
and against
Trade
Restrictions**

The first view says that trade restrictions could actually help a country's efficiency over time by increasing production volumes. For example, when a new computer memory chip is introduced, the unit (or average) cost is very high. As production volumes increase and the companies learn how to produce the chips more efficiently, costs per unit fall rapidly. There is a "learning curve" at work, as shown in Figure 11–7.

If learning curves are important, then there is a case for trade restrictions that allow a domestic industry to increase its production volumes as much as possible to drive down its costs. It has been argued that Japan has protected its domestic market, allowing it to drive down costs, and then its companies have been able to outcompete U.S. companies who are never able to move as far down the learning curve.

The second view argues that facing international competition actually forces a domestic industry to become more efficient and productive. Managers and workers are often resistant to change and fail to adopt the most productive business practices unless they compete directly against companies that are themselves using best prac-

---

[10] For a discussion of these issues, see Paul Krugman and Maurice Obstfeld, *International Economics;* and Laura D'Andrea Tyson, *Who's Bashing Whom? Trade Conflict in High Technology Industries* (Washington, D.C.: Institute for International Economics, 1993).

FIGURE 11-7
The Relation
between Unit Cost
and Volume
Produced: A
Learning Curve

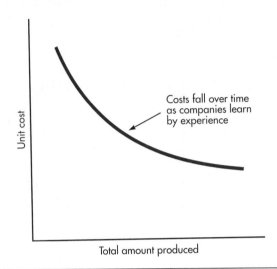

Unit cost

Costs fall over time
as companies learn
by experience

Total amount produced

tices. The pressure of worldwide competition forces change and eliminates slack in companies. Trade restrictions can slow the process of change and adjustment.

This idea is illustrated in Figure 11-8. At point *A* a protected domestic industry has a supply schedule *SS* for a particular product. The demand schedule is *DD*, the price is P_A and the output of the domestic industry is Q_A. Then trade restrictions are removed and the price of this product falls to P_B. Initially, the output of the domestic industry falls to Q_B and there are imports equal to the segment *BC* to meet the total demand in the market of Q_C.

Over time, however, there is a response from the domestic industry. Companies start to increase their own productivity, and there may also be transplant production by foreign companies bringing best practice methods with them. These transplants then become part of the domestic industry. The supply schedule shifts down to *S'S'* and, in the figure we have shown the case where the output of the domestic industry is restored. In practice, imports could be reduced more or less than this.

The Evidence
That Trade
Improves
Productivity

Do trade restrictions help industries grow and develop under the protection of tariffs and quota or do trade restrictions prevent the competitive pressure required to bring about efficiencies in production? Economists disagree about this, but we favor the pro-trade argument that competition increases productivity. Increased foreign competition either forces the domestic industry to improve its own performance—supporting the dynamic case for free trade—or else the domestic industry contracts or closes down and resources are freed for other uses—a result that we would expect in many cases, based on the theory of comparative advantage.

A recent study of manufacturing productivity in the United States, Germany, and Japan found that forcing domestic companies to compete against international best

FIGURE 11–8
A Shift in Supply
as a Result of
Increased
Competition

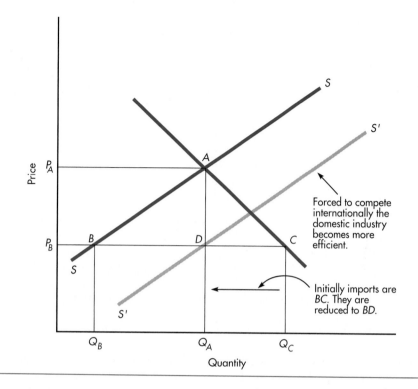

practices has a positive effect on productivity.[11] The study showed the importance of the pro-trade view in practice. The study covered nine industries for the three countries (a total of 27 examples) and productivity was calculated to see which country had the highest level of productivity in each of the nine cases. Actually there were 10 first-place finishers because of two that tied for first. For the remaining 17 industries that were below the productivity leader, a "globalization index" was constructed measuring the extent to which the industry competed head to head with the leader. This head-to-head competition could occur through trade and also through transplants from companies in the best practice industry. Figure 11–9, drawn from the study, indicates those industries that faced substantial competition from trade or transplants that were using best practice were forced to improve their own productivity so that it was close to the level of the best practice industry.[12] We can illustrate this idea by looking at the auto industry.

---

[11]   McKinsey Global Institute, with the assistance of Martin Baily, Francis Bator, Robert Solow, and Ted Hall, *Manufacturing Productivity* (Washington, October 1993).
[12]   In Chapter 17 we discuss some of the reasons why productivity differences occur and how competition can eliminate them.

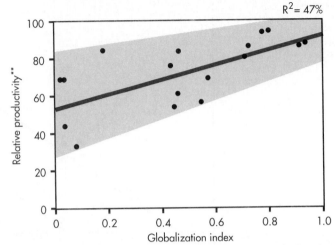

FIGURE 11–9
Globalization vs.
Relative
Productivity*

$R^2 = 47\%$

* Data points are nine case study industries in countries without productivity leading edge.
** Relative to industry leader at 100.

Source: Manufacturing Productivity, McKinsey Global Institute, 1993.

**Example:
The Effect of
Competition on
the U.S. Auto
Industry**

The U.S. industry was by far the strongest and most productive in the world in the 1950s and 60s. U.S. companies set up transplant operations in the U.K., Germany, and elsewhere. They brought best practice methods with them and this encouraged domestic European companies, such as Volkswagen and Mercedes-Benz, to improve their own efficiency and product quality. And indeed these companies began to export back to the U.S. market in specific product segments.

The Japanese auto industry was protected in the 1950s and 60s and as result it was slower to become productive. But despite that protectionism, there was a strong orientation toward the international market, and Japanese auto companies began to compete in the U.S. market in the 1970s against the U.S. companies that were still best practice companies at the time. The Japanese companies did not face international competition at home, but they sought that competition overseas.

As a result of process innovations and product design innovations, the Japanese industry gained on the U.S. industry in productivity and actually overtook it in the 1980s. Coupled with an overvalued dollar in the 1980s, this led to rising market shares for Japanese imports in the United States.

After ignoring the Japanese threat for many years, the U.S. companies finally got the message and began to increase their own productivity and to improve product quality. By the early 1990s such cars as the Ford Taurus and the Chrysler Concorde and the Saturn line of General Motors had achieved product quality that was as good as the Japanese and were produced with comparable productivity. Moreover, the Japanese companies are now making their cars in highly productive transplants in Ohio, Kentucky, and elsewhere, adding to the average productivity of the domestic industry.

By contrast, the German auto industry delayed its own response to the increasing competitive challenge. The European market in the 1980s was largely protected from Japanese competition by quotas.[13] With the exception of the United Kingdom, European governments were not enthusiastic about bringing in Japanese transplants. As a result, the German auto companies did not restructure and adopt the innovations in product and process design that the Japanese industry had pioneered, and by 1990 their productivity was well below that of the best U.S. and Japanese companies. As recession hit Europe in the early 1990s, and Japanese transplants from the U.K. began to produce for the European market, the German industry has been forced to lay off workers and become more productive.

Like most real-world examples, this case is not as clear-cut as we would like. The United States restricted trade in motor vehicles, putting a VRA on Japanese imports and a tariff on light trucks. But on balance this example shows the benefits of international competition. Imports had reached a large fraction of the market before the VRA was imposed. The Japanese companies effectively undermined the impact of the VRA by building transplants to produce standard sedans and pickups and using their quota of imports to sell luxury cars like Lexus and Infiniti.[14] Once the dollar fell against the yen in the late 1980s, the VRA was no longer binding. The result of this increased competitive intensity in the U.S. market was to create a more productive U.S. auto industry, including the transplants as part of the U.S. industry.

The case study of the auto industry suggests the benefits of open competition. But what about situations where learning curve effects may be more important?

Do Learning Curves Make a Case for Trade Restrictions?

There is no question that learning curves are important for computer memory chips—unit costs are estimated to drop by 28 percent for each doubling of the cumulative output produced in a plant.[15] And there other examples where either there are learning curves or there are large fixed development costs that then have to be spread over long production runs.[16]

It is far less clear that these effects can be used to justify trade protection. The problems that the U.S. steel, auto, and consumer electronics industries had with competition from Japan were not because they could not move down learning curves. The problems were the result of weaknesses in product and process designs. The United States has a very large market and large companies that are well-positioned to exploit learning curves or to spread development costs over long production runs.

---

[13] Mercedes and BMW were able to export very successfully to the United States and elsewhere in the luxury car market, a segment that the Japanese had not stressed. Once the Japanese companies entered the luxury segment, the market share of the German producers was cut back outside of Europe and they have had to respond quickly to the challenge by cutting costs.

[14] There is an interesting question about whether a temporary VRA can be justified as a way of buying time for domestic companies to adjust. Arguably, Chrysler would not have survived without the VRA. On the other hand, General Motors might have adjusted more quickly without the VRA.

[15] See Kenneth Flamm, ''Semiconductor Dependence and Strategic Trade,'' *Brookings Papers on Economic Activity, Microeconomics, 1:1993,* (Washington), pp. 249–334.

[16] When auto companies introduce a new model, they estimate there is a learning curve effect for a period of about six months. This is based on interviews with auto assembly plant managers.

To give this argument for trade restrictions its best shot, however, let's look at the case of computer memory chips.

Example: U.S. Trade Policy and the DRAM Market

In 1986, the U.S. government concluded a semiconductor pact with Japan, and, in 1991, this was followed by the Semiconductor Trade Arrangement, which set out a framework for trade and investment in the industry. The motivation for these agreements, or at least the purported motivation, was the concern by U.S. policymakers that, because of the importance of large fixed development costs and learning curve effects, the Japanese industry would be able to take over the market. The U.S. semiconductor industry might be driven out of business completely, leaving U.S. manufacturers of computers or other users of semiconductors (including the Defense Department) vulnerable to a Japanese semiconductor cartel.

The semiconductor agreement came after years of arguing among the Japanese government and the U.S. government, and the producers in both countries going back to disputes over transistors starting in 1959.

The general pattern of this argument was that the Japanese producers would reduce prices below that of the U.S. companies. The U.S. industry would claim that the Japanese were trying to drive them out of business to form a cartel and raise prices. The spectre of a "semiconductor OPEC" was often raised. Trade restrictions would be put in place that had the predictable effect of raising semiconductor prices in the U.S. market. Whereupon the industry would argue that its story about a cartel was vindicated, even though the high prices were a result of U.S. policy not of a cartel. Of course, Japanese producers were not averse to taking advantage of the U.S. trade restrictions to sell at higher prices in the U.S. market (see the earlier discussion of quotas).

High U.S. semiconductor prices as a result of trade restrictions eventually led to complaints from U.S. companies that were buying the chips: they were being penalized in the production of computers or other products. Ordinary consumers do not have an effective lobby against quotas; but when other U.S. companies are the customers, there can be effective political pressure brought against them. As a result of this countervailing pressure, the semiconductor restrictions were usually relaxed when prices got too high, or else a new generation of chips would come along that was not yet subject to a quota.

Chip demand was weak in 1985–86 relative to capacity, and U.S. chip prices fell dramatically. The Commerce Department announced a preliminary finding of dumping of 64K DRAMs in response to a suit brought by Micron, a U.S. manufacturer, and this was followed by a determination of dumping for 256K DRAMs (and other products were also being considered for similar action). Against this backdrop, the Semiconductor Trade Arrangement was concluded in 1986. The dumping cases were suspended in return for an agreement by the Japanese chip manufacturers to abide by price floors. There was also a "secret" side agreement that the United States would be given a 20 percent share in the Japanese market.

The Japanese government held down chip production and pressured its companies to reduce capacity investment. By 1988, there was a shortage of DRAMs and prices soared, leading to complaints about the trade arrangement by U.S. semiconductor users—a repeat of the usual pattern. U.S. chip producers responded, of course, that prices were rising because of a Japanese cartel that was exploiting its earlier success in predation.

Ironically, however, U.S. trade policy may have actually brought about the cartel it was supposed to prevent. It did not lead to a resurgence of the U.S. memory chip industry and there are signs of Japanese collusion in 1989 as the boom and bust cycle of chip prices took another downturn. Demand weakened in 1989 and Japanese companies appear to have made coordinated cuts in output to sustain prices. Kenneth Flamm, an expert on the industry, interviewed Japanese semiconductor executives in 1989 and they were frank about their plans to cut production to sustain prices.[17] Prices stayed above the floor levels of the trade arrangement despite the weakness of demand. And one semiconductor executive told a U.S. official that the Japanese industry had moved from competition to market sharing. The Semiconductor Trade Arrangement may have been the institutional mechanism that *facilitated* a Japanese cartel, rather than being the policy that protected the United States from a Japanese cartel.

The silver lining to this story is that learning curves do not in fact allow Japanese companies or anyone else to form a sustained cartel. South Korea is now a significant producer of DRAMs and it is unlikely that anyone can really maintain a high price for this product. Indeed the real irony of the DRAM industry is that it is probably not a good industry for U.S. companies to be in, anyway. Development and capital costs are very high and yet the chips become commodities very quickly with no product differentiation. It has been very hard for any company to make money making DRAMs except for brief periods. Such U.S. companies as Intel have done well in the more profitable parts of the semiconductor industry.

In summary, one can in principle make a case for trade protection on the grounds there are learning curves or large development costs that have to be spread over long production runs. And perhaps one can make a case in practice for these trade restrictions for developing countries that can benefit from protecting "infant industries" until they become large enough to compete in the world economy.[18] But for a large advanced economy like the U.S. economy, it is very hard to justify trade restrictions on these grounds. The example of U.S. trade policy in DRAMs does not suggest that restrictions are effective or necessary. They are likely to have adverse effects. Protecting a domestic industry is much more likely to induce sluggish productivity growth and high prices than it is to induce learning curve effects and low prices.

Trade Restrictions to Protect Jobs in Specific Industries

We have suggested that industries will respond to increased international competition by becoming more productive. An alternative outcome is that a domestic industry will collapse. And this is not a remote possibility. The U.S. machine tool industry and the U.S. consumer electronics industry are now very much smaller than they once were. The only U.S.-owned company making television sets is RCA and its sets are made in

---

[17]   Kenneth Flamm, "Semiconductor Dependence."

[18]   Japan in the 1960s may be a good example of this, although the dangers of protection even in developing countries are well-illustrated by Latin America, which stagnated under protectionist policies and is now moving toward greater openness.

Mexico. And the U.S. share of the DRAM market is very small despite the trade agreement. Shouldn't the U.S. protect its domestic jobs?

We have already examined the case for protectionism to sustain aggregate demand and argued that the case is very weak, because such policies would work only temporarily and at the expense of other countries (see earlier Protectionism section).

In this section we are looking at the case for preserving existing jobs in specific industries, such as consumer electronics. We review the arguments as follows, and reject most of them.

There is no way U.S. workers can compete against developing countries with wages that are only a fraction of the U.S. wage.   There is a reason that wages are much lower in developing countries. These countries do not have the skills, the transportation systems, the electric power, the service industries, or the capital that a rich country like the United States has. Their productivity is much lower than productivity in the United States. They need low wages to compete at all. And in practice, our largest trade deficits during the 1980s were with Japan and Europe, where wages were not that different from U.S. wages. During the 1993 NAFTA debate, we had a manufacturing trade surplus with Mexico. During 1993 and 1994, South Korea has started running a trade deficit.

Other countries do not abide by the same rules that we do.   Clearly this is correct. The United States is by no means free of trade restrictions, but generally it is easier for foreign producers to obtain easy access to the U.S. market than it is for the United States to obtain access to many foreign markets. In part this is because Americans are willing to buy goods made anywhere, whereas many foreigners have very strong preferences for goods made at home. What is less clear, however, is whether we should use this as an excuse to restrict imports. Maintaining relatively free trade is in our interests. We are not doing this as a concession. Despite our openness to trade and despite our own macroeconomic policies that reduced national saving and led to the trade deficit, manufacturing employment in the United States has remained steady over the last 20 years, whereas in Europe manufacturing employment has fallen. Some U.S. jobs have been lost in some manufacturing industries and gained in others. Over the period 1977 to 1987, 4.5 million new jobs were created in newly opened plants in U.S. manufacturing.[19] Restrictions that attempt to preserve existing jobs often fail and they often discourage the creation of new jobs.

We need restrictions as a lever to force open foreign markets.   There is a case to be made on these lines. Perhaps our restrictions should be taken down only on a reciprocal basis. If this is an effective way to ensure freer trade worldwide, then there is something to be said for it. The argument is an odd one coming from those who deplore the impact of trade on U.S. jobs, however. Opening the Japanese market, for example, would greatly benefit Japanese consumers. It would benefit some U.S. producers and farmers. *It would also result in a lower value of the yen and more imports from Japan as well as more exports.* Remember the iron law of the current account deficit. We cannot cure our deficit by opening foreign markets, even though we can increase the volume of trade in both directions.

---

[19]   Martin Neil Baily, Eric Bartelsman, and John Haltiwanger, ''Downsizing and Productivity: Myth or Reality?'' working paper, University of Maryland, January 1994.

We are losing vital technologies needed for the military.   There are a few products where we need to preserve the expertise and the production capacity for defense needs. But this argument is often used in situations where it is not applicable. It is relatively rare that the Defense Department actually says that it needs to maintain production capacity. And in those cases, the Defense Department is often willing to support the industry by purchasing from domestic suppliers. Most of the time, the national defense argument is invoked merely as a device to justify protection.

We believe that the debate over trade and its impact on jobs in the United States or other industrial countries is misinformed. The main reasons why some manufacturing industries have lost jobs, particularly production workers jobs, are to be found here at home. Foreign trade is an easy scapegoat for people who have lost well-paid jobs in traditional industries. Their losses are real and painful, but do not convince us to turn away from a commitment to free trade.[20]

Negotiations have just been completed among the trading countries reworking the General Agreement on Trade and Tariffs (GATT), which has regulated trade and trade barriers. This was part of "the Uruguay Round" of negotiations. The new agreement has established the World Trade Organization (WTO) to regulate international trade. In the last few years the greatest threat to free trade in the United States has come from antidumping cases. A U.S. producer goes before the International Trade Commission and claims that a foreign producer is selling in the U.S. market at a price below the price it charges at home and has damaged the U.S. industry. As yet these cases have not overturned our basic openness to trade. But the threat is there.

The rules under which the antidumping cases are heard are outrageously unfair to foreign companies trying to sell in the U.S. market. And no congressman or woman facing reelection can criticize the prosecution of "unfair" trade, so the rules are not changed. The only thing that may preserve free trade in the United States is that other countries are enacting statutes like the U.S. statutes. Since the United States is the largest exporter in the world, our own companies have a lot to lose if they are forced to operate the way we have made some foreign companies operate. For example, how would Boeing feel if it was told to provide office space for investigators from some South East Asian country and to create a complete new set of accounts for its company using the rules and tax laws of that country. That is what we are making foreign companies do. Eventually, the rules on antidumping cases will have to be negotiated as part of the WTO. We hope that this backdoor to trade protection is not allowed to flourish.

Conclusions on Trade Restrictions

We have argued strongly in this book that there should be free trade. We do not see trade as a zero-sum game in which the United States has allowed foreign countries to steal our jobs and wealth. Trade benefits both parties. It allows customers to choose from the best selection of products at the best prices worldwide. It increases the competitive intensity at home and forces companies to increase productivity. It leads

---

[20] We will look at the problems of the labor market, including the problems of manufacturing, in Chapter 16.

our economy to abandon some plants and industries where we are not productive or where costs are too high for some other reason.

Trade is one source of change in the economy, and responding to change can be tough for workers and managers and owners. But no one in today's economy can take a job and expect to keep it for 30 years. Industries rise and fall, companies rise and fall, plants rise and fall, and skills that are needed in one time period are not needed in another. This is true with trade, but it is also true without trade. We conclude, therefore, that the use of trade restrictions to cure external imbalances is ineffective and causes economic damage.

We turn now to exchange-rate policy. Why do exchange rates fluctuate so much? Should governments try to maintain fixed exchange rates or intervene at all in foreign-exchange markets?

ECONOMIC POLICIES TOWARD THE FOREIGN-EXCHANGE MARKET

Currency exchange rates have been driven increasingly by market forces since the early 1970s. And experience has shown two rather troubling things. First, there are large swings in exchange rates lasting for periods of several years. For example, in 1985 Americans going to Europe found everything cheap. Only a few years later it seemed that a cup of coffee in Europe cost more than a whole meal in the United States. Second, exchange rates are very volatile in the short run and seem subject to speculative swings as money managers move funds around the world in huge amounts seeking short-term gains. What are the reasons for these problems and what should policy do in response? One possibility, of course, is that policy is the source of the problems.

The Sustained Swings in Exchange Rates

In Chapter 7 we looked at the reasons for the dollar's increase in the early 1980s. And we argued that the answer lies in capital flows that can swamp trade (the flow of goods) as a source of exchange-rate change. We argued that the budget deficit pushed up interest rates in the United States and led to an appreciation of the dollar from 1980 to 1985. But after 1985, the dollar came down again. What explains this? We can better understand the drop in the dollar after 1985 by returning again to the interest-parity condition: The interest-rate differential between the United States and the rest of the world is equal to the expected rate of change of the exchange rate. This condition helped us to understand that a fiscal expansion increases U.S. interest rates and the size of the differential. The resulting capital inflows then led to an increase in the value of the dollar. The new equilibrium is reached with U.S. interest rates above foreign interest rates, and with a high value for the dollar, *but with the dollar expected to fall in the future.* In other words, the fact that the dollar declined in the late 1980s was something that was built into expectations in the early 1980s when the dollar was rising—although the exact timing and magnitude of the swings in the dollar were not necessarily well-anticipated.[21]

---

[21]   One economist who predicted (or overpredicted) the sharp decline in the dollar was Stephen Marris, *Deficits and the Dollar: The World Economy at Risk* (Washington, D.C.: Institute for International Economics, 1985).

exchange-rate overshooting
Exchange-rate movements away from long-run equilibrium.

Exchange-Rate Overshooting   The fact that the dollar rose as much as it did in the early 1980s and fell sharply after 1985 has been described as **exchange-rate overshooting.** The exchange-rate swings were much larger than many people expected. The capital inflows and outflows in response to changes in fiscal policy and the resulting changes in the international interest-rate differential were very large indeed. How large are the swings in the exchange rate that we should expect from a fiscal-policy change and how long will they last? We will try to give an answer to this question; but keep in mind that if we or anyone else could really predict exchange-rate movements precisely, we would not be writing textbooks. We would be sitting in the sun in the Bahamas enjoying the profits of our speculations in the foreign-exchange market.

Suppose the interest rate on foreign short-term securities is, say, 5 percent and a fiscal-policy change (or indeed some other change in the U.S. economy) has pushed up the interest rate on one-year Treasury bills to 10 percent. Suppose that the U.S. exchange rate was 100 initially and investors judge that this is the long-run equilibrium value for the U.S. dollar. The key question now is how long U.S. interest rates will remain above world rates. Suppose investors think that U.S. rates will remain at the high level of 10 percent for one year and then fall back to 5 percent. In order that investors be indifferent between holding U.S. Treasury bonds and foreign government bonds, the exchange rate must then be expected to fall by 5 percent over the next year. Since the long-run value of the dollar is 100, it follows that the exchange rate will rise to 105 when U.S. interest rates rise to 10 percent. That way the dollar can fall by 5 percent over the coming year and end up back in equilibrium.

Now let's think about the case where U.S. interest rates are expected to rise to 10 percent and stay there for two years. For investors to be indifferent between holding U.S. and foreign bonds, the value of the dollar must be expected to fall by 5 percent a year for two years. And if the long-run equilibrium value of the dollar is still 100, this means that when U.S. rates rise to 10 percent and are expected to remain at this level for two years, then the exchange rate will rise by about 10 percent (to 110.3). That way the dollar can fall 5 percent a year for two years and still end up in equilibrium (back at 100). An interest differential of 5 percentage points for five years will cause an immediate jump in the exchange rate of 28 percent (5 percent compounded for five years).

If investors see policies instituted that they expect to lead to high U.S. rates of interest that persist over several years, then the exchange rate will rise dramatically. In other words, *when short-term and long-term interest rates rise together,* this will be accompanied by large changes in the exchange rate. In the early 1980s, when fiscal expansion was instituted in the United States, it was not done as a short-run measure to stabilize the economy. It was done as part of the Reagan program of tax reduction. Investors reasoned, correctly, that the United States would have a budget deficit and high interest rates for several years. Consequently, there was a large rise in the value of the dollar. By 1985, however, the natural growth of tax revenues plus the measures taken to raise Social Security taxes were forecast to gradually reduce the deficit and bring down interest rates. So after 1985 the dollar started to fall also. (See Figure 11–10.)

**FIGURE 11–10
Interest Rates on
10-Year Govern-
ment Bonds in the
United States, Ger-
many, and Japan,
1981–1993 (*annual
average percentages*)**

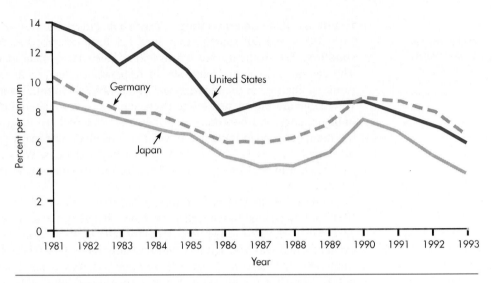

Source: *Federal Reserve Bulletins.*

Of course, in practice investors do not know how long policies will last or how long interest rates will stay high. Once investors decided that the interest-rate differential was not enough to sustain the very high value of the dollar, and once that view became widespread, the dollar started to fall quickly.

In the period since 1988 the dollar has fluctuated, probably as a result of a reassessment of the interest-rate situation. Japan has maintained a conservative fiscal policy and kept interest rates low, while Germany (as a result of reunification) has developed a budget deficit that is worse than the United States. Germany's interest rates have gone above U.S. rates.

We would argue, therefore, that large swings in the value of the dollar over the past 15 years were in large part the predictable consequence of the domestic fiscal and monetary policies of the period. But it is also likely that the fluctuations in the dollar, including the large day-to-day fluctuations in currency values, are being driven not by the fundamentals of real interest-rate differentials but by short-term speculation. If the dollar starts rising, some traders buy expecting further increases and quick profits. Foreign-exchange speculation adds another element to understanding exchange-rate movements.

**Short-Term
Exchange-Rate
Swings and
Foreign-
Currency
Speculation**

A financial investor who was convinced that the dollar was going to depreciate in the very near future would anticipate making a profit that was solely due to the change in the currency value. Any interest-rate differential would be small relative to the potential gain from guessing correctly the coming depreciation. With access to credit, an investor could speculate in currencies without having any assets herself.

Consider the case of a speculator who believes the dollar will fall against the yen in the next few months. He can borrow money in dollars and then exchange the dollars for yen and buy an interest-bearing asset in Japan, such as a short-term bond. Then he can wait until the dollar falls and bring the money back to the United States at a profit.

Suppose he borrows $1 million at a 10 percent rate of interest in New York, changes this into 100 million yen (at 100 yen to the dollar), and holds a Japanese government security paying a 3 percent rate of interest. If he waits one month and the dollar falls to 90 yen to the dollar, he can sell the yen (receiving approximately 100,254,000 yen, including the one month's interest), move the money back to New York, and receive approximately $1,114,000. After paying the interest on the loan (about $8,000), the speculator has made a return of almost $106,000. But, of course, this return was made on a highly risky and speculative transaction. If the exchange rate had risen to 110 yen to the dollar over the course of the month, he would have been facing a loss of $96,000. Foreign currency is itself a foreign financial asset and investors who buy foreign currencies so they can convert back to dollars at a profit are engaging in **currency speculation.**

currency or foreign exchange speculation Buying and selling foreign exchange and foreign exchange futures contracts for the purposes of profiting from changes in exchange rates.

Speculation can be beneficial for the economy. When shifts in supply and demand occur in currency markets, there can be temporary inbalances between supply and demand. Currency traders are willing to bridge the gap between supply and demand in the short run; they gather information, take risks, and do what is called "making the market" in foreign exchange. This means that they help maintain a smoothly functioning market where people can make the currency transactions they need to finance trade.

Because importers and exporters want to alleviate some of the risks of doing business in foreign currencies, speculation is a necessary consequence of international trade under a flexible–exchange-rate system.

Exchange Risk and Hedging   All firms operate in the face of risk. Demand for their product can fall off, the cost of production can increase, and as a result profits are uncertain. Firms generally are willing to pay for insurance to reduce the risks associated with their foreign exchange transactions. The profit of a U.S. firm that buys materials or components from abroad and sells products internationally is subject to *exchange risks*. Its foreign accounts receivable and accounts payable will change in value when the exchange rate shifts. Companies find themselves becoming speculators in foreign currencies even though they do not want to do this.

foreign-exchange forward contracts A contract to buy or sell a quantity of foreign currency at a set future date, but at a price known today.

One of the benefits of having foreign-exchange speculators is that they provide firms with the ability to insure against exchange risk. If an importer has accounts payable (monies it owes for purchases that it expects to pay in the near future) denominated in foreign currency, the importer can insure against or *hedge* the exchange risk by entering into a contract with a financial institution. The contract would obligate the financial institution to exchange a fixed amount of foreign currency for a fixed amount of dollars at a point in the future. The financial institution charges a fee for offering the contract. Such a **foreign exchange forward contract** provides insurance, because the importer will know with certainty how much it will cost in dollars to obtain the foreign currency needed to pay his bill. The existence of futures contracts helps to facilitate international trade. Those who want to shed the

Setting the Price of Gold, the Bretton Woods System, and Fixed Exchange Rates

Prior to World War II, President Roosevelt fixed the dollar by setting the price of gold at $35 an ounce. The president instituted the fixed–exchange-rate system (actually he reinstated the system, since international financial arrangements have alternated between fixed– and flexible–exchange-rate systems throughout the 19th and 20th centuries) because he believed that exchange-rate movements governed purely by private market forces would be large and possibly unstable. Large swings in the values of currencies can be very disruptive for businesses engaged in trade or competing with overseas competition. Based on what had happened with flexible exchange rates during the Great Depression of the 1930s, President Roosevelt judged that speculation in foreign currencies had exacerbated currency fluctuations.

As World War II ended, the Allies established a new international economic system that would avoid both the excessive rigidity of the old international monetary system, under which gold was the international currency, and the instability that was associated with the flexible–exchange-rate system of the 1930s.

The United States and Britain drew up a proposed plan, and delegations from the 44 main industrial countries met in 1948 in Bretton Woods, New Hampshire, to discuss and ratify this proposed new currency system.

The Bretton Woods plan designated two key currencies: the U.S. dollar and the British pound. Roosevelt had set $35 equal to an ounce of gold, and this value was to be maintained after the war. The British pound was set by making £12.50 equal to an ounce of gold.

The United States and the United Kingdom were to hold gold reserves and maintain their currencies at the fixed values. Other countries could exchange their dollars (or pounds) for gold bars at the fixed rates. Their exchange rates were set in relation to either the dollar or the pound and fixed values were to be maintained as far as possible. Each country's central bank held reserves of dollars or pounds and would buy or sell their own currencies for dollars or pounds to maintain their fixed rates. *Chronic* payments deficits or surpluses were to be cured by devaluations or revaluations of the currencies. Thus the system was never meant to be one with completely fixed nominal exchange rates; it was meant to provide the best mix of stability and flexibility.

The system worked reasonably well for 20 to 25 years—why? After World War II, U.S. monetary policy did not use expansions and contractions of the money supply in a forceful way to maintain full employment. The

risks associated with exchange rates can find speculators who, for a price, will enter foreign-exchange markets and accept exchange-rate risks.

Destabilizing Speculation

A free market with a system of fluctuating exchange rates worries many policymakers because they fear that speculation may not always be beneficial. They believe that speculation may drive exchange rates away from equilibrium. If speculation causes unnecessarily large swings in exchange rates, the benefits of flexible exchange rates may be outweighed by risks. Speculation can be destabilizing if changes in the exchange rate fuel further changes in the same direction. We look at two possible sources of destabilizing speculation.

Self-Fulfilling Prophecy   If a rumor can lead to a fall in the exchange rate and the fall in the rate is taken as evidence that the rumor is correct, causing the rate to

Fed was trying to maintain stable nominal interest rates, a policy consistent with a stable exchange rate. To the extent that the Fed varied interest rates, this did not create major problems with the exchange rate because the U.S. economy was so large relative to the rest of the world. The United States determined the world interest rate, rather than the other way around.

By the late 1960s the system was in trouble. This Fed policy was causing problems as inflation rose. The real rate of interest was diverging from the nominal rate. As the Fed began to play an active role in controlling the domestic economy, it was difficult to maintain its pledge to keep the exchange rate constant.

Under the Bretton Woods plan, countries with chronic trade surpluses were supposed to revalue their currencies, allowing the dollar to fall against other currencies. But the plan failed to specify how and when currency realignments were to take place. The countries with undervalued currencies did not adjust them upward, preferring to run trade surpluses. Key currencies, therefore, tended to become overvalued.

The dollar remained strong for a longer period and, ultimately, took over as the lone key international currency. However, by the late 1960s, the United States was in trouble. The currencies of Japan, West Germany, and France were set very low at the end of World War II

to compensate for wartime devastation. But these economies recovered, grew rapidly, and began to export very successfully. They piled up surpluses and refused to revalue their currencies; instead, they demanded that the United States make good on its pledge to maintain the relation of the dollar to gold. U.S. gold reserves held in Fort Knox were falling and potentially, could run out. Moreover, U.S. manufacturers were complaining about the effects of low-cost foreign competitors.

Under the Bretton Woods system, citizens of the United States, Britain, and other countries were forbidden from holding gold coins or gold bars. But some countries permitted gold holdings. As people saw the U.S. gold reserves falling, they began to speculate on a sharp rise in the price of gold. The worldwide demand for gold increased, as speculators added to the demand by foreign bankers.

In 1971 President Nixon abandoned the commitment to a gold price of $35 an ounce, as part of a package of economic measures that included wage and price controls. Over a two-year period, the Bretton Woods system was effectively abandoned and a flexible–exchange-rate system was adopted. Gold was demonetized and American citizens can now hold gold coins or gold bars. The price of gold shot up to a peak of $850 an ounce, 24 times its old official value, before falling back.

continue to fall, we have the makings of a self-fulfilling prophecy.[22] In earlier examples, we showed that investors would sell a currency if its expected rate of depreciation worsened. The rumor of an impending depreciation changes the expected rate of depreciation, which in turn generates a capital outflow from the country whose currency may decline. The exchange rate then actually falls, confirming everyone's suspicion about the rumor, so even more capital leaves, and the situation continues.

Expectations are affected by the confidence that investors have in the future value of a currency. If confidence in a currency decreases, investors revise downward their estimates of future values. This creates still less confidence and a further fall.

---

[22] Self-fulfilling behavior in international markets is discussed by Maurice Obstfeld, "Rational and Self-Fulfilling Balance of Payments Crises," *American Economic Review* 76 (March 1986).

Conversely, a gain of confidence leads to a rise in the currency and further self-fulfilling increases in the exchange rate. Speculation that feeds on itself can create a *"bubble"* (in which the exchange rate for a currency shoots up in a speculative frenzy) or a *panic* (when sales generate falling exchange rates that drive sales further down).

Not everyone believes that self-fulfilling prophecies exist or are important. Their key argument is that such speculation loses money, because it involves selling currencies when they are too low and buying them when they are too high. People who lose money by speculating will stop doing it, leaving the market to those who buy when a currency is too low and sell when it is too high—this will make the rate more stable. A similar argument is made by economists who endorse the assumption of rational expectations. They apply this assumption to the currency market and argue that, if exchange-rate speculation simply feeds on itself, then this implies that speculators are ignoring information about the fundamentals that determine the exchange rate. Why would such information be ignored, they say?[23]

The J-Curve and the Demand for Foreign Exchange   Speculation may be destabilizing in the short run, because the quantities demanded of imports and exports do not change immediately following changes in the exchange rate. The J-curve described the implication of the lags that exist in trade. A fall in the exchange rate between the dollar and the yen lowers the price of U.S. exports and raises the price of Japanese cars in the United States. In the short run there is little change in the volume of U.S. exports. Also, the U.S. demand for Toyotas, Nissans, and Hondas is quite inelastic, meaning that people keep buying them even at a higher price. Since the price of yen has gone up, it takes more dollars to buy the amount of yen needed to purchase nearly the same number of Japanese cars. In the face of a higher price for foreign exchange, consumers only slightly reduce the quantity of imports they demand; rather, they demand more foreign exchange.

When trade, rather than capital flows, have the dominant influence on the exchange rate and the J-curve is in operation, short-run movements in foreign currencies can be destabilizing. When the exchange rate rises, and foreign currencies become less expensive, the short-run response is not to import more. The demand for foreign currency falls, but at the lower price of foreign currency, there is more foreign currency available for sale than currency traders wish to buy, and the price of foreign currency falls even more. If the impact of destabilizing expectations as we described them earlier is added to this scenario, the potential for large swings in the exchange rate, away from equilibrium, could be substantial.

The fact that exchange rates fluctuate so widely creates problems for businesses that have to operate in foreign markets. This has led to two responses. The first is a private-sector response—private businesses buy insurance and mitigate their exchange risk through hedging. The second is that the government intervenes to smooth the fluctuations.

---

[23] There is a lively discussion among economists on whether speculative bubbles can be consistent with rational expectations. See Krugman and Obstfeld, *International Economics*.

While hedging goes some way toward solving the problems created by exchange-rate fluctuations, private insurers do not have the capacity to provide insurance for large long-term currency swings. This is a task that only governments have tried to take on. When governments have committed themselves to international arrangements for determining currency prices, they have done so in an attempt to eliminate the problems created by fluctuating exchange rates.

Fixed– and Flexible–Exchange-Rate Policies

fixed exchange rates
Prices of foreign currencies set in relationship to each other. Central banks agree that they will intervene in foreign-exchange markets to keep exchange rates from changing.

flexible exchange rates
Exchange rates that can change values in response to changes in supply and demand for currencies in foreign-exchange markets.

Up to this point we have described the working of the foreign-exchange market as if it were a free market where the exchange rate was determined by the forces of supply and demand, unimpeded by government actions or regulations.

From before World War II until 1971, governments intervened heavily in determining foreign-exchange rates by committing to a system of **fixed exchange rates.** Exchange rates were fixed by arrangements among central banks around the world. The central banks pledged to maintain the value of their currencies against another key currency. From 1948 to 1971 the dollar was the key currency, which required the United States to pledge to maintain the value of the dollar against gold.

Fixed–exchange-rate systems are attractive to policymakers when they fear ''excess'' fluctuations in exchange rates. Fixed–exchange-rate systems tend to break down when the established fixed rates fail to reflect the underlying economic relationships among economies. Following a period in the late 1960s and early 1970s of rising inflation and an escalating outflow of capital, President Nixon, over the period 1971–73, uncoupled the U.S. dollar from the fixed–exchange-rate arrangements that were maintained among central banks.

The current **flexible–exchange-rate system** evolved at that time; but even though the new system allowed for fluctuations in exchange rates, it has not been the case that international financial markets were free from government intervention. Foreign central banks, and on occasion the U.S. Fed, still pursued exchange-rate policies. There is central bank foreign exchange intervention. Rather than trying to fix rates, they engaged in the buying and selling currencies in an attempt to influence the value of exchange rates.

In the 1990s, based on arguments that currency speculation is generating wild swings in exchange rates, policymakers are considering whether or not, after 20 years of flexible rates, they should return to a fixed-rate system. The case for or against switching to a fixed–exchange-rate system to avoid currency swings turns on the question of how currency speculation works, its benefits, and some of the problems it creates.[24]

---

[24] The basic case for flexible exchange rates was given by Milton Friedman, ''The Case for Flexible Exchange Rates,'' *Essays in Positive Economics* (Chicago: University of Chicago Press, 1953). This same view was put forward more recently by Martin S. Feldstein, ''Let the Market Decide,'' *The Economist* December 8, 1988. See the box on the breakdown of ERM.

A long-time critic of speculation and a supporter of fixed exchange rates has been Charles Kindleberger, *Manias, Panics and Crashes* (New York: Basic books, 1978). Recent empirical assessments of the effect of speculation are Jeffrey Frankel and Richard Meese, ''Are Exchange Rates Excessively Variable,'' *NBER Macro Annual,* 1987; David M. Cutler, James Poterba, and Lawrence Summers, ''Speculative Dynamics,'' working paper no. 3242 (Cambridge, Mass.: National Bureau of Economic Research, January 1990).

A Fixed–
Exchange-Rate
System

The great advantage of fixed exchange rates is that they encourage trade. The United States has achieved its very high standard of living in part because of the large size and diversity of its economy. Companies in California must compete with companies in New York and bright engineers or managers can learn from working in Boston and take this experience to North Carolina. The fact that the United States has one currency has played a role in this success. There is not a separate dollar for California with a separate fluctuating exchange rate for the dollars of every other state.

One way to get the benefits of reduced uncertainty in the international market is to adopt a government policy of fixed exchange rates. Under this system, the Fed holds reserves of foreign currencies and it buys and sells dollars and foreign currencies to maintain equilibrium with supply equal to demand at a fixed exchange rate.[25]

The problem with fixed exchange rates is that maintaining the system is pretty much impossible unless countries are willing to give up their independent control over monetary policy. To see why this is the case, we look at the impact of monetary and fiscal policy in a fixed-rate system.

Monetary Policy with a Fixed Exchange Rate   If exchange rates are really fixed, the expected rate of change of the exchange rate is zero. This means that investors holding U.S. T bills must get the same interest return as they could get from a German short-term asset, because there is no exchange-rate risk. *With fixed exchange rates, there will also be interest-rate equalization.* And because of this, it turns out that monetary policy cannot do anything whereas fiscal policy can! Figure 11–11 illustrates this. The economy is initially shown at point *A*, where the *IS* and *LM* intersect at the world interest rate.[26] Suppose now that the Fed decides to conduct an expansionary monetary policy and it increases the money supply (moves the *LM* schedule to *LM'*). The economy starts to move toward a new equilibrium (intersection of *IS* and *LM'* at point *B*). But the falling U.S. interest rate generates a capital outflow and this puts downward pressure on the dollar.

The Fed is commited to maintaining the value of the dollar, so it must supply foreign currencies from its own reserves and accept dollars. Foreign-currency trading is carried out through the banking system, so the Fed is selling foreign currencies from its own reserves and is accepting dollars from banks. Banks buy foreign currency from the Fed and pay by reducing their reserve accounts held by the Fed. This reduces the number of dollars available as reserves of U.S. banks. The Fed is automatically reducing the monetary base as it maintains the value of the dollar.

The money supply, therefore, starts to decline and domestic interest rates rise back toward equalization with the internationally determined foreign interest rate. (The *LM* schedule starts to go back from *LM'* to its initial position. The economy moves from

---

[25] Policy can go even further toward fixing rates by using gold-backed currencies. See Robert Flood and Peter Garber, "Gold Monetarization and Gold Discipline," *Journal of Political Economy* 92 (February 1984).

[26] To keep things simple we have assumed that the interest rate gap (r_{gap} from Chapter 8) is zero. We could make the same point in a more complete (and more complex) figure that allowed for the gap between the short-term nominal rate of interest and the cost of funds.

FIGURE 11–11
Monetary Policy
When the Fed
Tries to Fix the
Exchange Rates

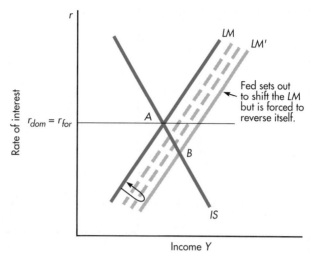

The Fed cannot bring about sustained changes in interest rates and also fix the exchange rate.

point *B* back toward point *A*.) In fact the process must continue until the old equilibrium is restored, since the economy must return to the world interest rate and goods–market equilibrium has not changed. (The *IS* schedule has not shifted.) *The Fed has found that it cannot maintain a fixed value for the currency and also make independent decisions about domestic monetary policy.*

Fiscal Policy with a Fixed Exchange Rate   Somewhat surprisingly, the reasons that made it impossible to follow an independent monetary policy with fixed exchange rates also make fiscal policy rather effective. Figure 11–12 illustrates how this works. The economy is shown at an initial equilibrium at point *A,* just as before. Now there is an expansionary fiscal policy. (The *IS* schedule shifts to *IS'*.) The interest rate starts to rise as the economy wants to move to point *B*.

The rising interest rate leads to capital inflows and there is upward pressure on the dollar. The Fed finds that, to maintain the exchange rate, it must supply dollars to the foreign-exchange market and take in foreign currencies as part of its foreign-currency reserves. As the Fed supplies dollars to the currency market, this automatically increases the U.S. monetary base. With the Fed committed to a fixed exchange rate, a fiscal expansion automatically triggers a monetary expansion (shown in Figure 11–12, as a shift from *LM* to *LM'*).

The use of a fiscal-policy expansion in a fixed–exchange-rate system has trapped the Fed. Since the Fed is committed to keeping the exchange fixed, Fed policy cannot help but accommodate the fiscal expansion. Since the U.S. interest rate must be the same as the world interest rate, this monetary expansion must continue until interest rates are equilized, as they are in the new equilibrium (point *B* to point *C*). The combination of fiscal expansion and monetary accommodation has also generated a higher level of income.

FIGURE 11–12
A Fiscal Expansion
While the Fed is
Targeting a Fixed
Exchange Rate

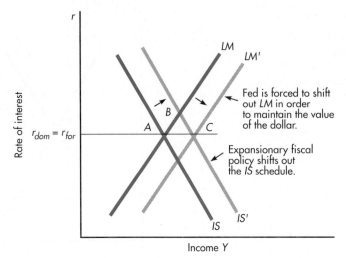

The Fed is forced to respond to the fiscal expansion by increasing the money supply in order to prevent a rise in the dollar.

The inflationary implications of this sort of policy trap for the Fed are serious. To maintain a fixed–exchange-rate system, the key-currency country must have a disciplined fiscal policy. If fiscal policy is allowed to be too expansionary (as it was in the U.S. economy in the late 1960s and early 1970s), that expansion will generate an increase in inflation. The Fed will be forced to choose between maintaining a fixed–exchange-rate system (i.e., accommodate the fiscal expansion with a monetary expansion) and fighting inflation. Faced with that choice, any government may well have to abandon its commitment to fixed exchange rates. (See the box on the near breakdown of the European Exchange Rate Mechanism (ERM).)

Policy Intervention with Flexible Exchange Rates

For the most part, the current international currency system is one of flexible exchange rates. However, many countries intervene in currency markets. Some developing countries and socialist economies also fix exchange rates and exercise considerable direct control over foreign trade and capital movements. These countries maintain balance of payments ''equilibrium'' with a fixed exchange rate by restricting imports if necessary. Often black markets in currency develop to circumvent the restrictions. Sometimes there are special stores where only foreign currency is used, as in the former Soviet Union. As these socialist countries move toward greater liberalization of their economies, they are planning to develop foreign-exchange markets for their currencies and reduce currency restrictions.

Major countries, such as Japan, Germany, Britain, and France, do not set fixed rates; but they, along with the United States, intervene to influence the values of their currencies. Central bankers have decided that short-term capital movements have driven their currencies away from their underlying equilibrium values, so they intervene to change their values. For example, the German central bank has reserves of

The Near Breakdown of the European Exchange-Rate Mechanism

There's a strong but by no means unanimous view among economists that monetary union—a single currency—makes sense for Europe today.

In the early 1800s in the United States, there were separate currencies circulating in the various states. Traders and merchants kept lists of different monies and their relative value one to the other. This confusion and impediment to commerce ended with the establishment of national banking and a single currency. Almost two hundred years later the economies of Western Europe are facing the same issues today.

For decades Europe has been caught in a policy struggle over the issue of foreign exchange regulation and currency reform. Should such highly interdependent economies have separate currencies and suffer the costs of constant fluctuations in exchange rates? Or should European economies give up on monetary autonomy in order to gain the stability and certainty found in a single currency?

The solution to the currency dilemma has been a series of unhappy compromises—fixed rates that burst under the pressure of excess supply and demand; floating rates that are capped, pegged or that crawl but that need to be managed by central banks; sharp limitations on the flow of capital across borders that sometimes limit international capital investment but more often are evaded, avoided and overcome by market forces; and a host of central bank to central bank arrangements for providing stability to exchange rate fluctuations without giving up national sovereignty over monetary policy last for awhile but ultimately break under the assault of currency speculation.

The latest effort is the European Exchange Rate Mechanism (ERM) an agreement among the central banks of the European Community to link currencies. The ERM was designed to bridge the unworkable arrangements of the past with monetary union and a single currency in the future. Now, the strength of any bridge is tested in a storm. On September 16, 1993, a hurricane struck the ERM. There was a massive selling off of the British pound. The ERM works by central banks driving interest rates up and down in order to defend exchange rates. A rise in short-term rates by 5 percentage points was needed in order to attract investors back to sterling. Unfortunately, the U.K. was in the midst of a recession and that kind of rate hike—the steepest one day increase ever experienced—was more than they could handle. Within hours the British reneged on the rate hike and left the ERM (temporarily). Italy also had similar shocks which forced it out of the ERM. Both Spain and Sweden were nearly lost as well but they managed to hang on through large devaluations or interest rate jumps. The ERM bridge almost collapsed.

Was this September storm evidence of the folly of monetary union or evidence of the need to complete the passage to a single currency?

The causes of the large-scale movements of foreign exchange in Europe and the resulting pressure on exchange rates and the ERM stem from the rise in German interest rates and the fall in U.S. interest rates. German rates went up because German reunification forced the new government to borrow heavily. U.S. rates went down because the Fed wanted to sustain the sluggish recovery at the end of the 1991–92 recession. Currency traders wanted more marks and fewer dollars and exchange rates started to move. If a European country's economy was linked to either the United States or to Germany, either that country's exchange rate changed or its monetary policies had to adapt to the new environment.

Wouldn't the European community have been better off with completely floating rates so that currency realignment could take place whenever external interest rates flipped around? Not necessarily. Not if the goal in Europe was to forge a single, functioning economy. Could the ERM have been strengthened by imposing controls on the flow of capital? No, controls on capital flows tend to be useless because governments manage them poorly. Or, if the controls work to a degree, they interfere with exactly the kind of trans-border capital investments required for an integrated economy.

A key lesson from the storm of September 1993 is that the ERM is a poor substitute for a single currency. With a single currency, there is no means by which a single state can opt out of the currency arrangement. Capital moves from market to market inside the integrated economy, but interest rates stay the same and exchange rates disappear.

FIGURE 11–13
Foreign-Exchange
Reserves and Daily
Foreign-Exchange
Trading Volume

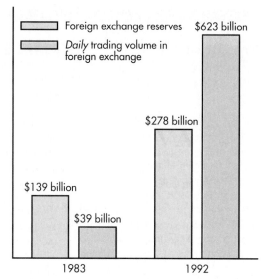

Reserves were larger than trading volume in 1983, but were much smaller than trading volume in 1992.

Source: International Monetary Fund and the Bank for International Settlements. Trading volume is for New York, London, and Tokyo. Reserves are for the United States, United Kingdom, Japan, Germany, and Switzerland.

dollars and other foreign currencies. Perhaps the mark is falling, but the bank believes it is already too low and wishes to keep the rate from falling further. It will use its reserves to supply dollars and other currencies and to buy marks in exchange.

sterilized intervention
A central bank buys and sells foreign currencies to influence its exchange rate. At the same time, it neutralizes the domestic money supply effects of its actions.

To maintain an independent monetary policy while intervening in the foreign-exchange market, central banks have used a strategy called **sterilized intervention.** When the German central bank buys marks, the German monetary base is decreased, but this is accompanied by an open-market purchase that increases the money base and offsets the domestic monetary consequence of the exchange-rate intervention.

Many economists doubt the ability of such sterilized intervention to support a falling currency even temporarily. The volume of private-sector currency transactions is now very large and makes foreign-currency reserves look small (see Figure 11–13). Monetarists argue that such exchange-rate intervention has an effect only if it also changes the domestic money supply.[27] Exchange-rate intervention will only raise the real exchange rate, they argue, when it is allowed to bring about a domestic–monetary-policy contraction, not when it is a simple exchange of currencies with no change in the equilibrium conditions in the economy.

Conclusions on
Exchange-Rate
Policies

Flexible exchange rates create uncertainties and difficulties for trading countries, but the post-World War II fixed–exchange-rate system broke down because the key-currency economy (the United States) lost control of domestic inflation and other

<hr>

[27] Milton Friedman, ''The Case for Flexible Exchange Rates.''

countries subsequently lost control of their monetary policies. Our current system of flexible exchange rates has probably helped the free economies of the world weather the economic storms of the 1970s and 80s. But exchange-rate gyrations have caused problems. We have to make a choice.

The only way to obtain the advantages of fixed exchange rates worldwide is to adopt a system with one currency controlled by one world central bank. Such a system would encourage the growth of trade and eliminate certain kinds of uncertainty. But the single central bank would not be able to use different monetary policies to meet the conflicting needs of all the different countries, some of which might have full employment and some of which might have recession.

In this chapter, we have looked at the effectiveness of monetary and fiscal policies with fixed and with flexible exchange rates and we found rather striking results. With flexible exchange rates, monetary policy becomes more effective and fiscal policy less effective. With fixed exchange rates, the story is reversed. These results may help us understand how the policy environment has changed since World War II. In the 1950s and 1960s, the emphasis was on using fiscal policy, and the automatic stabilizers were seen as an important tool that contributes to economic stability. Starting in the 1970s, monetary policy took over the task of maintaining economic stability. In the light of our discussion in this chapter, this shift in policy strategy does not look like an accident. Once we shifted to a flexible–exchange-rate system, monetary policy was free to act independently and fiscal policy became less effective. In fact, fiscal expansion mostly led to a trade deficit.

In the next two chapters, we will look further at the sources of economic instability and the role of stabilization policy.

SUMMARY

- Countries run trade and payments surpluses and deficits. Combined, they are described as the external balance.

- Deficits in the external balance are seen as a problem for policymakers, because of concerns over domestic wealth and jobs.

- Exchange-rate fluctuations are also seen as a source of concern by policymakers, because of the risks imposed on work trade.

- Exchange-rate changes fail to immediately bring about external balance, because of adjustment lags and because of international income fluctuations.

- The primary sources for external balance deficits are found in domestic savings inadequacies, and in government budget deficits.

- Policymakers often turn to direct trade restrictions or managed trade to deal with external balance deficits.

- There is no consensus about whether managed trade helps or hinders long-run economic performance, but we find that the case for free trade is very strong.

- Governments often turn to intervention to foreign-exchange markets to mitigate exchange-rate fluctuations or to prevent sudden and significant shifts in the real exchange rates.

- Exchange-rate intervention rarely works well. Policies that change interest rates will also change the exchange rate.

- In a fixed-exchange environment, monetary policy becomes ineffective and fiscal policy becomes more effective.

KEY TERMS AND CONCEPTS

comparative advantage, p. 345

currency or foreign-exchange
  speculation, p. 361

exchange-rate overshooting,
  p. 359

external balance, p. 332

fixed exchange rates, p. 365

flexible exchange rates, p. 365

foreign exchange forward
  contracts, p. 361

J-curve, p. 339

quotas, p. 348

sterilized intervention, p. 370

trade adjustment lag, p. 340

DISCUSSION QUESTIONS AND PROBLEMS

1. If monetary policy works through changing interest rates, how can monetary policy have any effect on an economy where interest rates are determined in world-wide financial markets?

2. Is long-run interest-rate equalization necessary to conclude that fiscal policy is ineffective when exchange rates are flexible?

3. What sort of policy options does the Fed have when it wants to control exchange rates and the domestic money supply?

4. Do you agree or disagree with the following statement? "The source of the U.S. trade deficit in the 1980s is closer to Washington and Detroit than it is to Tokyo." Explain your position.

5. List and compare arguments in favor of a system of fixed or flexible exchange rates.

6. What are the arguments for and against tariffs and quotas.

SUPPLY-SHOCK INFLATION AND ECONOMIC POLICY

INTRODUCTION

Inflation and unemployment were both higher in the U.S. economy in the 1970s than in any comparable period after World War II. The adverse experience of that decade changed people's views about what could be expected from the performance of the economy and it changed people's views about the success of economic policy. Living standards grew very slowly over the decade and even declined in some years. Consumers, workers, and business people all found this a difficult period. Old ideas of how the economy works had to be discarded or modified.

Besides economic effects, the bouts of very rapid inflation over this period and a worsened output–inflation trade-off had important social and political consequences. The defeat of President Gerald Ford by Jimmy Carter has been linked to the burst of inflation in 1974 followed by the recession in 1975 and 1976 that resulted from fighting the inflation. Four years later, it was President Carter's turn to face voters' anger over inflation, as he was defeated by Ronald Reagan, partly because of the burst of inflation of 1979–80 and the recession of 1980.

During the 1980s, inflation was brought under control and President Reagan's popularity over that period was due in part to the fact that voters credited him with bringing greater price stability to the U.S. economy. This popularity carried over to President Bush, who was elected in 1988 after several years of moderate inflation. Inflation was not a major issue in the 1992 election, although jobs and the economy were. During 1993, U.S. inflation was around 3 percent, at a low compared to recent U.S. experience.

In Chapter 6 we saw that inflation can be initiated by high levels of aggregate demand, and then inflation may develop a momentum as people come to expect inflation. Once inflation is established, workers and firms change the conditions under which they are willing to supply output: They change their price-setting and wage-setting behavior. Expected inflation causes the output–inflation trade-off to shift up. But in the analysis in Chapter 6, it was aggregate demand that initiated the process.

The acceleration of inflation that occurred in the 1970s was not initiated primarily by aggregate demand. Inflation was much worse in the 1970s than can be explained either directly by demand in that decade or by the legacy of excess demand from the 1960s. And there are other cases where changes in the rate of inflation have occurred that were not initiated by demand changes. Inflation declined in 1986 even though the economy was growing strongly and output was not far from potential output.

There have been sharp rises and falls in inflation caused partly or wholly by abrupt shifts in aggregate supply that were not directly related to past inflation or demand. These shifts have come to be called **supply shocks.** In this chapter we explain the increases in inflation that took place in the 1970s and we look at how the reversal of those shocks helped to reduce inflation in the 1980s and whether further shocks are likely in the 1990s. When an inflation is initiated by a supply shock, the output–inflation trade-off worsens, because higher costs drive up prices with no offsetting increases in output. Rather, the economy experiences both worsened unemployment and worsened inflation. Supply shocks are an important part of the explanation for stagflation.

When a shock occurs, inflation rises and output falls, confronting policymakers with a dilemma that is similar to the dilemma created when expected inflation builds up. Either policies can be anti-inflationary, which will make the reduction in output even worse, or policies can focus on increasing output and employment, but at the cost of further fueling inflation. The fact that policymakers have to choose between two unpleasant options is why political leaders of either party become unpopular when supply shocks hit.

supply shock
A change in supply conditions, often associated with large and rapid changes in the relative prices of commodities or raw materials.

SUPPLY SHOCKS AS A CAUSE OF INFLATION

Supply shocks can take different forms and not all of them are alike. But the supply shocks that have been the most important in affecting U.S. inflation involve large changes in the relative prices of certain key commodities. When the supply conditions for a particular product change, so its price relative to the price of other goods goes up enough to affect the overall price level, the economy is experiencing an **adverse supply shock.** A large reduction in the relative price of a key commodity will have the opposite effect and reduce the overall price level. This is a **favorable supply shock.**

A supply shock comes about when at least two circumstances exist in the economy. First, the national expenditure on the product suffering the supply shock is a large enough portion of GDP so the increase in price measurably affects the price level.

adverse supply shock
A large and rapid increase in the relative prices of key commodities.

favorable supply shock A large and rapid reduction in the relative prices of key commodities.

Second, in the case of an adverse supply shock, there has to be enough downward rigidity in wages and other prices so the effect of the shock is not canceled by the fall in other prices. If these conditions are met, then there will be an increase in the price level in the economy for any given level of output; that is, there will be an upward shift in the aggregate supply schedule. Mostly when we refer to supply shocks we will be talking about adverse shocks.

The increases in the price of imported oil that were initiated by the Organization of Petroleum Exporting Countries (OPEC) in 1973 and again in 1978–79 provide the clearest examples of adverse supply shocks. U.S. energy producers suddenly faced very different market conditions for their products. The world price of oil had jumped so U.S. energy producers were able to sell their own production at a much higher price, despite some price controls. This was true for U.S. oil producers and also for natural-gas and coal producers whose prices were linked to the price of oil. Since energy production is a significant part of GDP and nonenergy prices did not fall, the increase in the price of energy led to a significant increase in the overall price level.

In Figure 12–1, the economy is represented at an initial equilibrium at point A, with a level of income Y_A and a price level of P_A. A supply shock is shown as an inward movement of aggregate supply (AS to AS'). With the aggregate demand curve unchanged, the economy will move to a new equilibrium (point A to point B) with a lower level of income (Y_A to Y_B) and a higher price level (P_A to P_B).

FIGURE 12–1
Output and the Price Level Following a Supply Shock

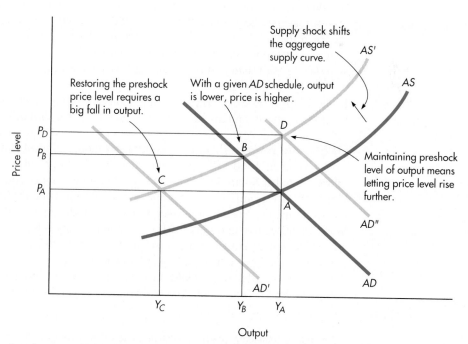

An adverse supply shock raises the price level and lowers output. Shifting aggregate demand can raise output at the expense of higher prices or reduce output to cut prices.

There is a limited amount that policymakers can or should do in the short run to change the conditions that lead to the supply shock. The rise in the market price of oil is already giving a signal to increase production and decrease demand. These market responses will take time to work and policy should probably leave the market to work in its own way. This means in practice the main decision policymakers have is whether to alter *aggregate demand.* They could increase aggregate demand to increase the level of output but with more inflation, or they could decrease aggregate demand to reduce inflation but also further reduce output.

Given that the supply shock has occurred and the economy now has lower output and a higher price level, policymakers face a dilemma. We illustrate the policy dilemma in Figure 12–1. Policymakers could reduce aggregate demand (AD to AD') and further reduce output (Y_B to Y_C) to bring the price level back down to its original level. Alternatively, they could stimulate aggregate demand (AD to AD'') to restore the original level of output and thereby further increase the price level (P_B to P_C). Both of these alternatives are unattractive.

In their effect on inflation, adverse supply shocks are similar to increases in expected inflation, in that they shift the aggregate supply schedule and create serious dilemmas for policy. But in an important respect, adverse supply shocks are much worse. When OPEC raised the price of oil and domestic energy producers raised their prices, this had an adverse effect on the cost of living of the average American. We commented earlier that the cost of a pure monetary inflation may not be terribly high. But there is no problem in identifying the costs of supply-shock inflation; there is a loss of real income. After adjusting for inflation, workers' wages were only slightly higher in the 1990s than they were in the late 1960s, because of the various adverse changes in supply conditions that have occurred. Workers saw supply-shock inflation as reducing their standard of living, and they were right.

Adverse Supply Shocks in the 1970s

In the 1970s a series of dramatic supply shocks hit the economy. These shocks were from a variety of sources, mostly from increases in commodity prices.[1]

OPEC and Energy Prices   The Organization of Petroleum Exporting Countries was formed in 1960. Though dominated by the large oil-producing Arab nations, OPEC included South American and African producing countries as members, all of which faced very different economic conditions and which subscribed to very different economic ideologies. Moreover, not all oil producers joined OPEC. At first OPEC had little influence on oil prices; it was an attempt by oil-exporting countries to get a somewhat better deal from the western oil companies that then dominated the world energy market. Given the diversity of its membership, it was not at all clear that OPEC could form a cartel that would successfully raise the price of oil higher than the competitive market price and keep oil prices stable at that higher level. Yet, in fact, the

---

[1] The role of commodity prices in inflation in the 1970s is discussed in Barry Bosworth and Robert Z. Lawrence, *Commodity Prices and the New Inflation* (Washington, D.C.: Brookings Institution, 1982). To some extent these relative price increases were subsequently reversed, but they caused serious economic difficulties along the way.

OPEC cartel was successful in raising the price of oil by enforcing production quotas on its membership, and the price quadrupled in 1973 and rose again in 1979 and 1980.[2] (See the following box, "Oil Shocks.")

The increases in the price of imported oil in the 1970s had an impact on overall inflation in the United States, because both the domestic supplies of oil and the domestic demand for oil were inelastic—neither demand nor supply in the United States could easily be changed in response to the changes in the price of oil. On the supply side, the flow of oil that can be drawn from a given base of reserves cannot easily be changed without impairing the longer-run productivity of the field. U.S. oil producers could not quickly respond to the price rise with quantities that were sufficiently high to undo the impact of a reduction in foreign supplies. Also, the supplies of alternative sources of energy, such as natural gas, could not be quickly increased by enough to matter. On the demand side, oil is a significant part of total raw-material use in the economy, and it was hard to reduce energy use quickly. Reducing the amount of oil used per dollar of GDP takes time because energy efficiency is generally built into the existing stock of machines, furnaces, motor vehicles, and appliances. Improvements in energy efficiency came about slowly as these capital goods were replaced. Other oil-consuming countries, most of which had no production of their own, were also faced with seizes in inflation.

In 1973, the United States used 17.3 million barrels of oil a day. Refined petroleum products rose in price by about $5.50 a barrel as a result of the OPEC price increase in 1973, so an oil "levy" of $35 billion was imposed on oil users—about 2.5 percent of GDP. The second price increase in 1979 was much bigger. Oil rose in price to about $21 a barrel, imposing an oil levy of $144 billion on users—about 6.5 percent of our GDP.[3] In addition, the price of competing fuels, such as coal and natural gas, also rose when the price of oil increased, adding to the levy on energy users.

Eventually, however, the cartel unraveled as new suppliers came into the market and some OPEC members exceeded their production quotas and sold oil at lower prices. The price of oil adjusted for inflation fell throughout the 1980s, especially in 1986, providing a positive supply shock that helped the reduction of inflation in the 1980s.

Agricultural Shocks and Food Prices   The prices consumers paid for food rose by 15 percent in 1973 and by 14 percent in 1974. Food is an important component of the cost of living and hence has a large weight in the consumer price index (CPI). These price increases (coming on top of rising gasoline prices and utility bills) cut living standards and left many households fearful about the future. Food is, of course, purchased on a frequent and regular basis, so noticeable increases in food prices may be perceived by many as evidence of general inflation.

---

[2] Facts about energy prices and uses are given in Robert L. Loftness, *Energy Handbook,* 2nd ed. (New York: Van Nostrand, 1984), and in Congress of the United States, Office of Technology Assessment, *Energy Use and the U.S. Economy* (Washington, D.C.: U.S. Government Printing Office, June 1990).

[3] These figures are taken from Alan S. Blinder, "Anatomy of Double-Digit Inflation in the 1970s," in *Inflation Causes and Effects,* R. E. Hall, ed. (Chicago: 1982).

Oil Shocks, Wage and Price Controls, and Stagflation: The 1970s

What happens when the price of a raw material necessary in the production of a large share of output and consumption sharply rises? This is precisely what happened during the 1970s—not once but twice. In the first instance, it happened during a time of full employment.

The inflationary effect of the first oil price shock during this era was complicated by President Nixon's surprising introduction of price and wage controls in August 1971. The president reacted to what was then perceived as evidence that inflation was heating up. Based on prior U.S. experience, the 6 percent annual inflation rate *was* scary. The wage and price controls he imposed held prices down to the 3.9 to 4.3 percent range in 1971–72 and resulted in shortages.

From 1972 to 1974, the price of Saudi Arabian oil increased from $1.90 per barrel to $9.76 per barrel. This price was instigated by an Arab oil embargo and an increasing degree of market control among OPEC members. In the United States the price hike quickly filtered to gasoline pump prices, which jumped nearly 40 percent from September 1973 to May 1974. The second oil shock came during 1979 and was related to the war between Iran and Iraq. It resulted in an oil price increase from $12.70 to $28.67 per barrel during 1978–80.

The abrupt and steep price hikes destabilized the economies of most of the oil-importing industrial countries. In the case of the United States, real GNP declined by 0.6 percent and 1.2 percent during 1974 and 1975, respectively, and by 0.4 percent during 1980. Unemployment rose in each period. This was the stagnation; the "flation" part of stagflation came from the jump in inflation from 5.7 percent in 1973 to 9.3 percent by 1975 and from 8.6 percent in 1979 to 9.4 percent in 1981. The term *stagflation* was coined to characterize what happened in the wake of the oil shocks.

Meanwhile, what had been happening to price and wage controls? President Nixon gradually removed the controls in 1973 and 1974, precisely at the time of the first major oil price shock. Workers were pushing for the higher wages denied by wage controls, and firms raised markups in an attempt to catch up with the profit losses they suffered during the price freeze. This "catching up" not only accelerated the inflation rate but also increased the expected rate of inflation.

At the same time, nominal wages in the United States were *downwardly* rigid. Thus the leftward shift in aggregate supply from the higher cost of production due to higher oil prices was not offset by falling wage costs. Instead, output and employment fell. A nonaccommodating policy by the Fed and a tight fiscal policy in 1973 reinforced the shock-induced decline in output. The "Great Recession" of 1974–75 was the result.

One possible explanation for the strong U.S. recovery between the two 1970s price shocks, relative to the European experience, was the decline in U.S. real wages. U.S. unions have fewer wage contracts with wages indexed to inflation than do European labor unions. For this reason, the Fed followed the same tactics after the 1979 oil shock with the same result—recession, hopefully to be followed by lower inflation and economic recovery. This time unemployment rose so rapidly that Fed policy was prematurely reversed before subduing inflation. Inflation accelerated again and the Fed held down the monetary brakes for a much longer time in 1981 and 1982. Then came the steepest and most prolonged recession since the Great Depression.

The economic drama of the 1970s and early 1980s is not due entirely to oil on troubled waters. The wage and price controls were poorly handled, and monetary policy itself was quite unstable.

Food prices are set in world markets, where small differences in supply and demand generate large fluctuations in price. The variability of individual food prices is normal; the rapid rise in overall food prices was the shock. These agricultural price shocks were preceded by bad weather conditions. The Soviet Union made major grain purchases that reduced the supply of grain in the rest of the world and contributed to the run-up in grain prices. And since fertilizers are made from oil and gas, the energy crisis also had an impact on food production and prices.

Food prices are also affected by government actions. In the United States, until the early 1970s, farm policy included acreage restrictions and grain reserves in an attempt to stabilize prices. By 1973, the stabilization program had been abandoned and the grain reserve had been depleted, so, when the Soviets entered the market as a major grain purchaser, the effect on prices was dramatic. Food-price hikes coupled with oil-price hikes comprised a devastating series of price and supply shocks that impacted the entire economy.

Since the early 1970s, there have been other adverse events that have affected agriculture; notably the midwest floods in 1993. None of these has been large enough to affect world-wide agriculture prices greatly.

Slowdown in the Growth of Labor Productivity   Labor productivity describes the amount of output per unit of labor input.[4] If labor productivity grows, workers are producing more per hour than before, so they can be paid more per hour without necessarily raising prices. The growth in labor productivity allows for a gap between the rate of growth of wages and the rate of inflation.

A productivity increase means that it takes fewer hours of labor to produce a unit of output, so *increases in productivity lower unit labor costs.* The wage rate is the amount an employer has to pay for each hour of work, so *increases in wages raise unit labor costs.* As shown in Equation 12–1, the growth of unit labor cost (*ULC*) is equal to the difference between the rate of wage increase and the rate of growth of labor productivity:

$$\text{Growth of } ULC = \text{Growth of wages} - \text{Growth of labor productivity} \tag{12–1}$$

Unit labor costs are constant when the growth of wages equals the growth of labor productivity; they increase when wages grow faster than labor productivity. This means that *a decrease in the rate of productivity growth will add to the rate of increase of unit labor costs, unless it is offset by a decline in the rate of growth of wages.*

Productivity growth slowed in the late 1960s and then slowed sharply after 1973, so, to avoid an acceleration of unit labor costs, the rate of wage increase would have had to slow, also. In practice, the rate of growth did not slow, at least not for several years, so unit labor costs accelerated. Then, with costs rising for most firms in the economy, business managers were able to pass on the cost increases in higher prices. The acceleration of unit labor costs led to an acceleration of price inflation.

Supply Shocks and the Price Level

Supply shocks have a direct effect on the price level. When the prices paid for U.S. agricultural output and energy output rose sharply relative to other prices, this raised the overall U.S. price level. The increases in the relative prices of the agricultural and

---

[4]   Labor input is often measured as hours worked. Output per unit of labor is a measure of total output per hour. This is often compared with wages measured as wages per hour. The hourly wage includes fringe benefits and payroll taxes prorated on an hourly basis. The hourly wage figure is often referred to as *hourly compensation.*

energy sectors are shown in Figures 12–2A and 12–2B. The 1971–85 period is shown in the figure, split into two parts. In Figure 12–2A, we show the price indexes over the 1971–78 period for the output of the agricultural and the mining sectors of the U.S. economy, together with the price index for all of GDP except for these two sectors. These price indexes normally have 1987 as a base year; but we have divided the indexes by their 1971 values, so all three are set equal to 100 in 1971, instead of in 1987. This is done to show more clearly how prices evolved after 1971.

Figure 12–2A shows how the price of agricultural output rose very rapidly between 1972 and 1973. After that, agricultural prices fell back a little until there was a second milder price increase in 1978.

The price of the output of the mining sector in the United States primarily reflects the prices of crude oil, natural gas, and coal. The combined effect of the price increases in these energy-producing sectors was a massive jump in the price of mining output between 1973 and 1974. Following the OPEC price increase, the price of U.S. energy output would have occurred earlier than it did, except that price controls on energy products were in effect in that period.

The price of mining output continued to increase more rapidly than other prices even after 1974. The United States is gradually exhausting its most available sources of oil and gas, so costs of drilling and extraction have risen. The supply schedule for the U.S. industry has been moving up. If foreign energy had remained cheap and available, this would have led to a fall in U.S. output. Since, in fact, foreign energy became more expensive and was at times limited in supply, this kept U.S. energy output and prices high during this period.

Figure 12–2B repeats the same exercise over the 1978–91 period. We have reset the price indexes again, this time to equal 100 in 1978. This figure shows that prices in the agricultural sector did not contribute to the increase in the overall 1979–81 price level. On the contrary, increases in agricultural productivity have lowered costs in the 1980s and have helped to keep the price level down.

The price of mining output rose faster than the price of other goods throughout the 1970s, and then there was another massive price boost between 1979 and 1981 that pushed up the overall price level. At that point, U.S. energy prices began to fall as a result of the breakdown of the OPEC cartel and the cumulative effects of increased efficiency by consumers and the increase of supply by non-OPEC energy sources. The relative price of mining output then fell after 1982.

The agricultural and mining sectors made up 4.7 percent of total GDP in 1972. The combined price index for these two sectors went up by 64 percent between 1971 and 1974, so, in the absence of any offsetting declines in other prices, this price shock added about 3 percentage points directly to the overall price level ($0.047 \times 0.64 = 0.0299 = 3$ percent). In 1979, the mining sector was 2.9 percent of total GDP and the price index for this sector went up by 84 percent between 1979 and 1981. Leaving aside changes in other prices, this added 2.4 percent to the overall price level.

We have found, therefore, that large price changes in important sectors of the economy can have an impact on the overall price level. But if this had been the end of the story, the overall effect on inflation would not have been that bad. Adding 3 percent to the price level over a two-year period means adding about 1.5 percent to

FIGURE 12–2
The Price of
Agricultural
Output, the Price of
Mining Output, and
the Price of GDP
except for These
Two Sectors

A.   Price indexes, 1971–1978, set equal to 100 in 1971.

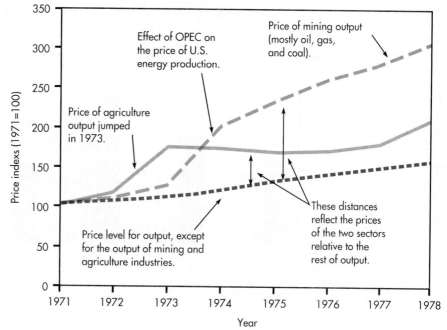

B.   Price indexes, 1978–1991, set equal to 100 in 1978.

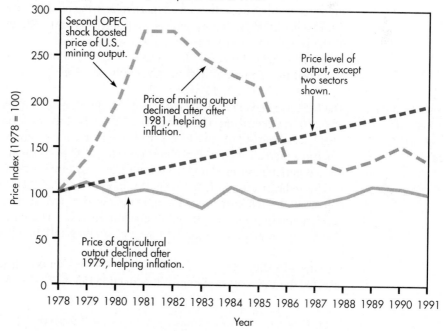

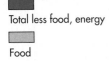

FIGURE 12-3
The Average
Annual Rate of
Growth of Food
Prices, Energy
Prices, and Prices
of Other Items in
the Consumer
Price Index,
1965–1993

Total less food, energy

Food

Energy

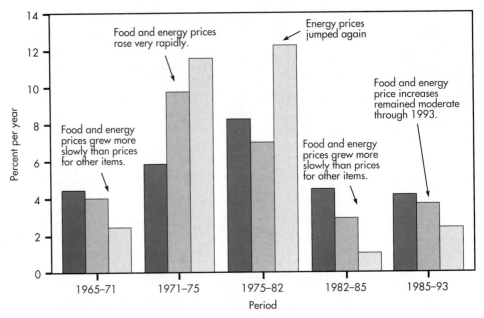

Note: The figures for 1965–71 are the averages of the annual growth rates for each of the six years. Other periods' figures were calculated similarly.

the annual inflation rate for two years. Of course, there were other adverse changes in supply conditions over this period (particularly the productivity-growth slowdown), so the total effect of the supply shocks was larger than this. But even so, the *direct* effect of the supply shocks on the price level was not huge.

Unfortunately, however, this was not the end of the story. We have not yet examined the indirect effects of the supply shocks.

Supply Shocks, the Cost of Living, and Wages

The U.S. price level reflects the price of U.S. production.[5] When OPEC raised the cost of oil, this affected the U.S. price level directly only as a result of the shift in the supply schedule of U.S. producers. But when the cost of energy and food rose sharply, this had a dramatic effect on the cost of living of U.S. consumers. U.S. consumers buy oil and agricultural products from both U.S. and foreign producers.

The indirect effect of the adverse supply shocks is that when the cost of living increased, this led to an acceleration in the rate of wage increase. And then, finally, the acceleration of wage growth led to general inflation. The initial impact of the supply shocks on the price level turned into a continuing inflation problem.

Changes in the U.S. Cost of Living   The way in which food and energy prices affected the U.S. cost of living is illustrated in Figure 12–3. The figure shows the rates

---

[5] The GDP deflator measures changes in the prices of U.S. produced goods and services. It does not include the prices of imported goods.

of increase of three parts of the consumer price index averaged over various periods. Recall that the CPI is an index that changes over time as a weighted average of the rates of change of the various goods and services that are purchased by a representative consumer. Figure 12–3 shows these sources of growth in the CPI over a 20-year period: first, the price of food (16.3 percent of the total); second, the price of energy (7.4 percent of the total); and third, everything else (76.3 percent). The price of food at the consumer level reflects prices at grocery stores and restaurants. The price of energy is computed by seeing how much consumers spend on energy through such items as their electricity and natural-gas bills and their gasoline purchases.

Over the 1965–71 period, food and energy prices rose more slowly than the prices of other goods and services in the CPI. This situation changed abruptly from 1971 to 1975, when both food-price and energy-price increases were much greater than other price increases. From 1975 to 1982, the situation was a little different again as food prices rose somewhat more slowly than other goods' and services' prices, but this time energy costs were jumping. After 1982, costs of both food and energy went up much less than the costs of other items, so these sectors were holding down the overall increase in the cost of living in the 1980s, as they had in the 1960s.

The supply shocks that drove up food and energy prices had an important impact on the cost of living faced by U.S. consumers. One consequence of this was political. U.S. voters were angry at the erosion of their living standards and demanded change. Another important consequence is that workers demanded higher wage payments in an attempt (fruitless, as it turned out) to offset the run-up in food and energy costs.[6]

The Cost of Living and Wage Increases   Increases in the prices of imported and domestically produced food and energy were bound to have an adverse effect on the cost of living of the average consumer. The supply shocks represented a real cost to the average American. There were different ways in which the costs could have been paid, however. One possibility is that wages, salaries, and corporate profits could have been reduced in dollar terms following the supply shocks. In this case, the prices outside of mining and agriculture would have fallen following the supply shocks. The shocks would not have increased the price level as there would only have been changes in relative prices. A second possibility is that wages and other prices might have been unaffected by the supply shocks. They could have increased by the same amount that they would have increased without the shocks. In this case, the effect of the shocks would have been to increase the price level and increase the cost of living,

---

[6] The main supply shocks in the 1970s stemmed from food prices, energy prices, and the slowdown in productivity growth, as we have described. But there were two other factors. First, as the value of the dollar fell after 1971, this raised the prices that U.S. households paid for imported goods and reduced their standard of living. In addition, it allowed U.S. producers competing with foreign companies to raise their own prices. Second, the way in which the CPI was measured in the 1970s exaggerated inflation, because of the way home ownership costs are computed. Mortgage interest payments are counted as a cost of owning a home, so, when mortgage interest rates increased in the 1970s, this increased the CPI. But the method of computation assumed, incorrectly, that all homeowners were taking out new mortgages each year, while in fact only a small proportion of homeowners were actually paying the high mortgage rates. The incorrect CPI was then used to index wage payments and other contracts, pushing up actual inflation.

but there would have been no persistent effect on inflation. There would have been a short-term boost to inflation, of course, just to raise the price level, but the inflation would have stopped quickly.

Unfortunately, neither of these possibilities is what actually happened. Instead, the increases in the cost of living that were the result of the supply shocks then led to increases in money wages. Figure 12–4 illustrates what happened. From 1965 to 1971, the rate of increase in hourly compensation (wages plus fringe benefits) was already high. Over this period, there had been a very strong demand for labor and very low unemployment. The expected rate of inflation had increased in the 1960s, as we saw in Chapter 6, and this increase in the expected rate of inflation had been built into wage increases. Then after 1971 the rate of increase of hourly compensation began to grow even more rapidly in response to the increases in the cost of living. This is a particularly striking fact for the 1975–82 period, when the rate of increase of hourly compensation accelerated even though the demand for labor was very weak and the rate of unemployment was much higher than it had been for 20 years or more previous to that.

The most straightforward explanation of the acceleration of wages is that the supply shocks created a problem of catch-up. Workers found their real wages had been reduced unexpectedly by the increase in energy and food prices, and they wanted

FIGURE 12–4
Average Annual Rate of Growth of Hourly Compensation for Workers in the Business Sector, 1965–1993

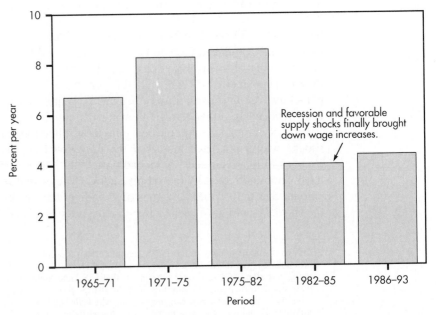

Hourly compensation includes employer payments for fringe benefits. The figure for 1965–71 is the average of the annual growth rates for each of the six years. Other periods' figures were calculated similarly.

to be compensated. For union workers with contracts that included cost-of-living adjustments, this compensation happened automatically. Then, employers were willing to grant similar wage increases to nonunion workers, because it was equitable and because they expected every other firm to do the same.

The supply shocks initiated a process that is sometimes called a **price–wage spiral.** Prices rose in some sectors of the economy and for imported goods, and this led to increases in the cost of living and then to increases in wages. The increases in wages then led to an increase in prices throughout the economy. We can explore how this price–wage spiral works using the identity between output and income.

price–wage spiral

The ongoing process whereby increases in wages raise unit labor costs, contributing to a higher rate of inflation and still higher wages.

The Price–Wage Spiral

There is an identity that relates income and output and we have used this identity many times. This identity holds for real output and real income and also for nominal output and nominal income. We have used the former relation up until now, but to see the impact of a supply shock we now make use of the identity in nominal terms:

$$\text{Nominal value of output} = PY = \text{Nominal value of income}$$
$$= \text{Nominal wage income} + \text{Nominal value of payments to capital} \quad (12\text{--}2)$$

Equation 12–2 simply states that the value of output is paid out either to workers or to the owners of the businesses for which they work. Of course, in practice there are many small businesses where the owner and the worker are the same. And some of the capital here will include agricultural land and reserves of oil and gas. But these complications do not change the overall identity.

If we now take the identity in Equation 12–1 and divide through by real output *(Y)* we obtain the following:

$$\frac{PY}{Y} = P = \frac{\text{Wage income}}{Y} + \frac{\text{Capital income}}{Y}$$
$$\text{Price level} = \text{Unit labor cost} + \text{Unit payments to capital} \quad (12\text{--}3)$$

Equation 12–3 tells us that the price level is equal to the amount paid to labor per unit of output produced and the amount paid to capital (including the amount paid to the owners of land and natural resources).

The first term on the right-hand side of Equation 12–3 reflects the cost of wages for labor used to produce, distribute, and market the goods and services produced in the economy. The second reflects two elements. There are costs associated with the purchase, rent, or lease of the plant, equipment, and land, plus the carrying costs of inventory that are used in production and distribution. These capital costs are often viewed as a return to capital investment and are included in profits in company accounts. But on top of this, there may be an additional markup added to unit costs that reflects the generation of an economic profit, a return over and above the normal return to capital. If any particular firm is making less than a normal return on its capital, then its price is less than full cost and its ''additional'' markup is actually negative.

Equation 12–3 is an identity, because the total payment to capital is defined as whatever is left (positive or negative) after paying the labor costs.[7] When the average markup is positive for the economy as a whole, this means companies are earning returns greater than the normal return on capital. In a competitive economy, such excess profits will attract new firms or cause the expansion of existing ones, or both. This increased competition drives down any excess return and eliminates the markup. When the markup is negative on average, this will encourage firms to shift their production into other lines or to close down plants. The reduction in capacity reduces supply and prices rise to restore the normal return on capital. Of course, at the time that a supply shock hits the economy, there will be substantial changes in "markups" in the affected industries. Farm incomes rose and the profits of energy producers increased significantly in 1973–74. But once the shock has passed, market adjustments will mean that prices in most industries will stay fairly close to the sum of labor and normal capital costs. This means that, *when the price of labor rises, this cost increase is seen as a general increase in the cost of doing business and is passed along into final prices.*

Notice the importance of the productivity-growth slowdown at this point. When productivity growth slowed, this meant that any given increase in wages would lead to a higher rate of growth of unit labor costs and hence a higher rate of price increase. The only way to avoid an upward movement of inflation is to cut the rate of wage growth. In practice the opposite happened in the 1970s. *The slowdown in productivity growth that started in the 1970s coupled with an acceleration of wages translated into an even larger acceleration of price inflation.*

We have now given a descriptive analysis of how the supply shocks have resulted in a broader inflationary surge. The cost of living increased and this led to a push by workers to try to recoup some of the decline in their living standard. As workers demanded higher wages, firms were willing to grant the increases, knowing that every other firm was doing the same. The general increase in wages took place despite a decline in the growth of labor productivity and so it led to a general increase in prices. We will now return to the model of inflation and the trade-off that we introduced in Chapter 6 and see how the effect of the supply shocks can be incorporated into this analysis.

---

[7] We define the cost of capital as the price a firm would have to pay to lease or rent plant and equipment to produce its products. Even if the firm owns its own capital, the cost of capital figures into the cost of a product, because the firm must pay for its capital out of revenues. The owners of a company own all the assets of the company, and so they usually own much of the capital used by the company in production. They receive as their return the residual income after labor costs, material costs, and rental payments for capital not owned by the company have been paid. This residual return includes both an implicit payment for the capital owned by the company plus any markup beyond the cost of capital.

Sometimes the markup can be negative for a time for a company that is not able to earn the normal return on the capital that it owns—price is less than average unit cost. Sometimes the markup is large for a short time for a company producing a product for which there has been a short-run increase in demand—price is then greater than unit cost.

SUPPLY SHOCKS AND THE SHIFTING TRADE-OFF

An adverse supply shock initially pushes up the price level. This means it has an effect that worsens the short-run output–inflation trade-off. It causes a temporary upward blip in the trade-off. Equation 12–4 gives a modified version of the short-run trade-off described in Chapter 6. Here, the current rate of inflation depends on the output ratio $[H(Y/Y^P)]$, the expected rate of inflation $[Exp(\Delta P/P)]$, and the direct but temporary effect of the supply shock on inflation *(SS)*:

$$\text{Current inflation } \Delta P/P = H(Y/Y^P) + Exp(\Delta P/P) + SS \qquad (12\text{–}4)$$

We can see what this specification implies by using an example of an increase in both agricultural prices and energy prices. Suppose there is a 4 percentage-point increase in the price level as a result of these supply shocks and it happens over a single year. This means the rate of inflation is increased by 4 percent for one year as a result of the direct effect of the changes in the relative prices of these commodities. This means *SS* is equal to 4 in the year in which the supply shock strikes and is then zero thereafter. This example obviously is simplified relative to the actual supply shocks, but it captures the main idea.

Figure 12–5 illustrates the short-run impact of a supply shock, assuming no changes in other prices or changes in expectations. Initially, the economy is experiencing stable inflation at full capacity (output ratio at 100 percent). This is shown as a point (point *A*) along a short-run trade-off (SR–TO:1). The economy then experiences a supply shock. The impact of the shock shifts the short-run trade-off upward (SR–TO:1 to SR–TO:2 by the amount *SS*). In general, we would expect output to fall in the short run following the supply shock. The price level has been increased and, unless the Fed takes specific action in response to this, the real stock of money will fall. If output falls (point *C*), then the economy faces the situation of stagflation, where both output and inflation are worse following the supply shock. However, the recession has mitigated the inflationary effects of the supply shocks $[(\Delta P/P)_C < (\Delta P/P)_B]$. The fall in the real stock of money following the supply shock induces an offsetting fall in output, which helps to reduce the impact of the shock on inflation.

If it is possible for the Fed to act very quickly to restore the real money supply so it maintains the same level of output (output ratio remains at 100 percent), then the new level of inflation is shown along SR–TO:2 at point *B*. Current inflation has increased by the full amount of the supply-shock effect $[(\Delta P/P)_B = (\Delta P/P)_A + SS]$.

And finally it is possible, although unlikely, that the Fed is so anxious to avoid recession that it overshoots and increases the real stock of money. Then income will increase above potential (to point *D*) and the economy will experience an even greater increase in inflation than that caused by the direct effect of the supply shock $[(\Delta P/P)_D > (\Delta P/P)_B]$. The increase in output above potential generates an aggregate-demand–driven inflation that exacerbates the inflationary effects of the supply shock.

Figure 12–5 gives the alternative outcomes for the economy in the year that the supply shock actually hits. Policy can react by accommodating the resulting inflation surge, fighting it, or even exacerbating it. Once the initial shock has passed, however, the question then becomes: What next?

FIGURE 12–5
The Short-Run
Effect of a Supply
Shock on Inflation

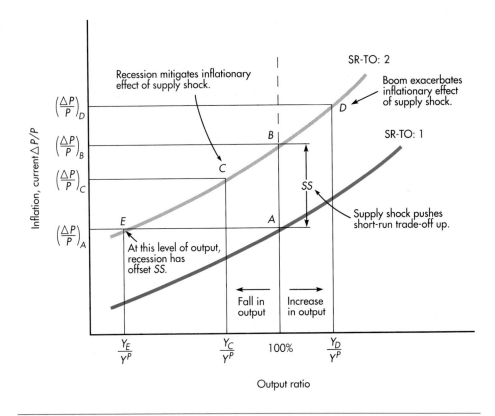

A supply shock will turn into a continuing inflation problem if expected inflation increases as a result of the shock. In the earlier part of this chapter we suggested that this is exactly what happened as a result of the price–wage spiral that was precipitated by a supply shock. In Figure 12–6, we illustrate the case in which the supply shock leads to an increase in expected inflation, so the short-run trade-off does not return to its original position even after the supply shock passes.

We assume, just as in Figure 12–5, that the supply shock has initially shifted the short-run trade-off from SR–TO:1 to SR–TO:2. We assume further that the rise in the price level is not accommodated by the Fed, so there is a reduction in the real stock of money and hence in the output ratio. The economy moves from point A to point C.

We consider now the period following the supply shock. The economy improves after the supply shock has passed, but it does not immediately return to its preshock equilibrium. In Figure 12–6, the new short-run trade-off is represented by SR–TO:3. The trade-off is better than it was when the shock first hit (SR–TO:3 lies below SR–TO:2), but worse than before the shock hit, because the shock has increased expected inflation (SR–TO:3 lies above SR–TO:1).

The particular combination of inflation and output experienced along the shifted short-run trade-off depends on aggregate demand conditions following the shock. In

FIGURE 12–6
Inflation and the Trade-Off Once the Supply Shock Has Ended

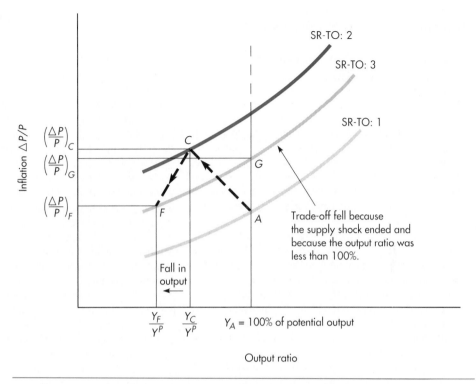

the case shown in Figure 12–6, income continues to fall $(Y_C$ to $Y_F)$ in the year following the shock. This case means the inflationary effects of the supply shock have been almost eliminated. The economy has experienced a fairly severe recession, but only a temporary surge in inflation.

Supply Shocks and Expected Inflation   We have argued that the supply shocks of the 1970s increased the expected rate of inflation. This meant the shocks resulted in a persistent inflation problem, not just a one-time increase in the price level, followed by a serious recession to offset the inflationary effect of the shock. And we would argue that the opposite situation happened in the 1980s, when the decline in energy and food prices helped to reduce expected inflation.

The idea that supply shocks will change expected inflation is controversial. Rational-expectations economists argue that changes in the relative prices of food and energy do not lead directly to changes in expected inflation. They say that, if there was a legacy of higher expected inflation as a result of the relative price changes of the 1970s, then this must have been because of the way policymakers reacted to the shocks. If the Fed accommodates supply shocks, then people will make a rational judgment that inflation will be higher in the future. But if the Fed had not allowed money growth to increase, then there would have been no increase in expected inflation.

Potential Output and Supply Shocks

Some schools of thought represent potential output differently from the way we describe it. Some economists contend that supply shocks reduce potential output. Therefore, noninflationary full employment must be redefined as whatever rate of unemployment it takes to avoid any increase in inflation, no matter how high the unemployment.

In Figure 12–5 the supply shock is assumed not to alter potential output; rather, any reduction of output is a temporary drop below potential. Why? An oil-price hike does not change the economy's capacity to produce goods and services by very much in the short run.

When there is a jump in the price of an essential raw material, the business firm passes along the extra cost of production to the final customer. For example, since chemical fertilizers are made from petroleum by-products, a successful naval blockade of the Persian Gulf will lead to higher fertilizer prices for American farmers. This, in turn, will lead to higher food prices. The fertilizer firm will use the same amount of crude petroleum as before, and the farmer will use almost the same amount of fertilizer. In the short run, businesses do not change their production recipes by much. Rather than change the mode of production, they raise prices and maintain production at former levels.

Over time, chemical firms and farmers can take steps to reduce their use of crude petroleum. Some of these kinds of changes contributed to the decline in American productivity growth during the 1970s and 1980s. If inno-vations lead to production processes in which petroleum is no longer an essential input, productivity would increase. Nonetheless, supply shocks are the hares, and changes in production processes are the tortoises.

Now we come to the alternative view. Suppose the economist defines potential output as the level of output just sufficient to keep the acceleration of inflation at zero. Then when the oil-price shock comes, potential output will fall dramatically and unemployment will rise in the same year the supply shock hits. In Figure 12–5, the economy would have to operate at point E to avoid any acceleration of inflation. Compared to an unchanged level of potential output, the output ratio that precludes any increase in inflation would be at Y_E/Y^P. At this newly defined level of potential output, output would equal 100 percent of potential.

We do not agree with this alternative definition of potential output as a benchmark. The high unemployment rate at point E, perhaps as high as 14 percent for a large supply shock (like the one in the example where SS is 4 percent) would be only temporary. By this awkward definition, potential output would suddenly shoot way up the following year when the supply shock had run its course!

We prefer instead to define potential output and the unemployment rate that prevails when output equals potential (the NAIRU) as the level of output that will not lead to accelerating or decelerating inflation *in the absence of supply shocks*. We would prefer to estimate potential output from benchmark levels for unemployment and factory utilization plus the long-run trend of growth in the capacity of the economy.

We disagree with the rational-expectations perspective on this. We argue that expected inflation, as it affects price and wage setting, is strongly affected by the actual experience of past inflation. And in the case of the supply shocks, there was also a push by both union and nonunion workers for catch-up wage increases. But the rational-expectations economists are certainly correct to stress the role of monetary policy in determining the course of inflation following a supply shock. *If a supply shock leads to persistent inflation, then it must be the case that monetary policy is accommodating the inflation.* Next we examine the role of policy.

SUPPLY-SHOCK INFLATION AND ECONOMIC POLICY

If there is no change in monetary policy and no increase in the nominal supply of money following a supply shock, then the increase in the price level will generate a lower real stock of money that will in turn reduce real income. Unless the Fed follows an inflation-accommodating monetary policy, there will be a fall in income following the supply shocks. Such a fall was described in Figure 12–6 *(Y_A to Y_C to Y_E)*. In the *IS–LM* framework we would describe this decline in the real money stock $[(M^s/P)$ falls as P rises] as an inward shift of the *LM* schedule.

If the Fed does respond to a supply shock, it has two very different policy alternatives. First, the Fed can accommodate the inflation by increasing the rate of growth of the money supply to match the new, higher rate of inflation. Inflation accommodation would maintain the level of the real money stock, thus allowing income and output to return quickly to their preshock levels. Alternatively, the Fed could refuse to accommodate the inflation by keeping the growth of the nominal supply of money below the rate of inflation. This would mean that income continues to fall after the supply shift and stays below potential until inflation has gone back to its preshock level.

In practice, when adverse supply shocks hit, policymakers were continuously torn between the two goals of maintaining income and employment on the one hand, and reducing inflation on the other. At different times, the Fed embraced both inflation-accommodating and anti-inflationary policies. Indeed, policy oscillated as first inflation and then unemployment was thought to be the greater problem. Given the trade-off, it is not obvious that the Fed could have or should have tried to immediately eliminate any inflationary consequences of the supply shocks. Nevertheless there was a higher inflation rate during the period than would have been experienced had an anti-inflationary policy been applied consistently. Prior to reviewing the rather confusing and inconsistent policies that were actually followed during this period, we will look at the two very different options that confronted policymakers: accepting the higher inflation to drive output toward potential output or bringing inflation back down to its preshock level and accepting the loss of income and the increase in unemployment. Combinations of these two policies made up the actual course of policy actions in response to the adverse supply shocks of the 1970s.

Targeting a Return toward Potential Output

When policymakers are more concerned with sustaining income and keeping down unemployment than with controlling inflation, their policy response following a supply shock will be to use economic policy actions that are targeted at income. The initial effect of the supply shock has been to initiate an inflationary spiral, reduce the real stock of money, and lower real income. Following this, expansionary fiscal or monetary policy, or both, could be used to bring output back toward potential output. Fiscal policy could be used to lower taxes or increase government expenditures, or both, and monetary policy could expand the rate of growth of the money supply. The result of this policy of stimulating aggregate demand is to drive income up toward potential output, but with a higher long-run rate of inflation than existed before the combination of supply shock and the expansionary policy actions. In Figure 12–7 we

FIGURE 12-7   Inflation and a Quick Return to Full Employment Following a Supply Shock

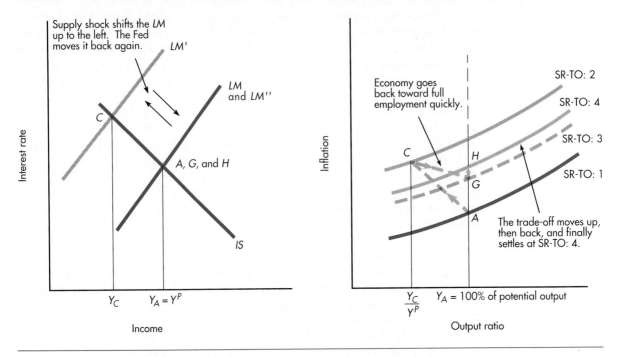

return to the *IS–LM* framework and the output–inflation trade-off to show the case where expansionary monetary policy is used after a supply shock to stimulate aggregate demand. The initial effect of the shock is shown as a movement from point *A* to point *C* in both panels of the figure. The right-hand panel shows the shift of the trade-off from SR–TO:1 to SR–TO:2, just as in Figure 12–6. The left-hand panel shows the shift in the *LM* schedule that accompanies this change. The rise in the price level has reduced the real money supply *(LM to LM′)*, but then the Fed accommodates the inflation, so the real money supply grows again. (The *LM* schedule moves back to its previous position and *LM″* coincides with *LM*.) The trade-off has moved down following the end of the supply shock (to SR–TO:3, the same as in Figure 12–6). The economy has returned to the level of employment that existed before the supply shock, in this case to potential output (points *G* in both panels; points *A* and *G* coincide in the left panel).

In subsequent years, the Fed maintains the level of output by adjusting the nominal money supply. This avoids any additional cost in jobs and production, but there is a long-run boost to inflation. The new long-run equilibrium is shown at point *H* on SR–TO:4, where the economy has had to accept high chronic inflation. Point *H* coincides with points *A* and *H* in the left panel.

To keep things simple, we have taken the interest-rate gap as zero. In practice we would expect that in the new equilibrium at point *H,* the cost of funds would be the same as at point *A,* but expected inflation and nominal interest rates would be higher.

In the example shown in Figure 12–7, the Fed has returned the economy quickly to potential output and has accepted a long-run legacy of higher inflation. The short-run trade-off is above its preshock position.

> *Worked Example 12–1*   Here a numerical example shows how a supply shock can boost inflation over the long run unless there is an anti-inflation policy.

We have seen that, if the Fed decides to accommodate the supply-shock inflation, then there will be a higher rate of inflation indefinitely. The alternative strategy is to allow the increase in inflation to reduce the real stock of money and hence to bring on recession.

Reducing Inflation to Preshock Levels

The strategy of allowing the real stock of money to decline following the supply shock and then living with the resulting deep recession describes Fed policy in the 1980s, and we examined this approach to policy in Chapter 6. The benefit of this strategy is that inflation is eventually brought under control. The cost of it is the lost output and employment that may persist for several years.

> *Worked Example 12–2*   A numerical example shows how a sustained recession can be used to reverse the impact of an adverse supply shock.

Our discussion of policy responses to a supply shock indicates that neither of the two responses considered so far looks terribly appealing. This is just what one would expect, given that policy actions cannot immediately replace the loss of output the economy suffered. There is either going to be an increase in inflation that could last indefinitely, or there is going to be a sustained recession. No wonder that, in practice, policymakers oscillated between the two alternatives for several years. Adverse supply shocks are hard to deal with.

The Sacrifice Ratio   Our Worked Example 12–2 illustrates how the anti-inflationary policies of the 1970s created a substantial cost. The economy operates for some time at a lower level of output and with a higher level of unemployment than it would have had if the policy of contraction had not been followed. One measure of that cost is called the **sacrifice ratio,** which is calculated as the number of percentage points of lost GDP per year given up for each percentage-point reduction of inflation. Robert J. Gordon has estimated the sacrifice ratio for the U.S. economy as about six.[8] This means that it takes an output ratio of 99 for six years or a ratio of 94 for one year to bring about a long-run reduction of 1 percentage point in the inflation rate. In our

sacrifice ratio
The loss in GDP, measured as a percentage, associated with a 1 percent reduction in the rate of inflation.

---

[8] Robert J. Gordon, ''Inflation, Exchange Rates and Unemployment,'' in *Workers, Jobs, and Inflation,* Martin Neil Baily, ed. (Washington, D.C.: Brookings Institution, 1982).

example, the inflation rate started at 8 percent and ended up at 4 percent. This translates into 24 percent of lost GDP (4 percent of GDP for six years). This is quite a price. It is more than a third of consumption in a given year, and this will be painful whether it comes about through a short, sharp recession or through a longer, but milder recession.

Another even more drastic approach has been suggested by rational-expectations economists, namely that the Fed should establish credibility in its anti-inflationary policies by taking a very hard line: Allow almost no increase in inflation at all, restore the economy to the preshock inflation rate very quickly, and reap the benefits of a faster drop in inflation as a result of a downward shift in inflationary expectations. This is a result of establishing policy credibility.[9]

Extreme Anti-Inflationary Policies and Policy Credibility

If there is a belief that the Fed will choose to pursue a very hard anti-inflationary policy following a supply shock, then that policy could result in inflationary expectations that were lower than those that would be calculated based on past inflation. The improvement in expectations (a drop in Exp $\Delta P/P$ unrelated to past rates of inflation) should contribute to the effectiveness of anti-inflationary monetary policy.

Unfortunately, to maintain credibility by employing draconian policies, the Fed may have to contract the money supply severely, perhaps bringing about a very deep recession. Whether this credibility-building approach to inflation fighting—kicking inflation cold-turkey—is worthwhile depends on just how much of a reduction in expected inflation is brought about by the establishment of anti-inflationary credibility. If a cold-turkey policy works, then inflationary expectations will be reduced in each year by more than would have occurred in the absence of the credibility-building policy. The **credibility effect** is a reduction in inflationary expectations due to the belief that the Fed will be committed to restoring the preshock inflation rate as quickly as possible. *The greater the reduction in expected inflation due to credibility effects, the milder will be the recession necessary to restore inflation to its preshock level.*

credibility effect
The reduction in inflationary expectations that comes from being convinced that the Fed is in fact following a tight anti-inflationary policy.

Worked Example 12–3   In this example, we present a numerical illustration of how a cold-turkey approach to reversing a supply shock could reduce the total amount of lost GDP required to restore low inflation, that is, it may reduce the sacrifice ratio.

KEEPING INFLATION UNDER CONTROL IN THE 1980s AND 90s

The double recession of 1980–82 and the sustained high unemployment of the early 1980s resulted in a reduction of inflation. Output in the U.S. economy was below potential output for several years, and the short-run output–inflation trade-off was moving down. The Fed was able to establish considerable anti-inflation credibility over this period; although not all economists agree that this increase in credibility is an important factor in shifting down the trade-off. Credibility was enhanced because the

---

[9] The credibility-policy suggestion does not require that there be strictly no initial increase in inflation, but rather that inflation is eliminated quickly and that the anti-inflationary policy is sustained.

Fed pursued a contractionary policy and the economy suffered through a period of tight money, high real interest rates, and falling aggregate demand. This is the classic ''credit-crunch'' scenario of an economy entering a slowing or a recession because of financial-market constraints initiated by the Federal Reserve. This drove the economy into a deep recession and a prolonged period where output was below potential output. The Fed reduced inflation by engineering a severe recession and then re-expanded the real money supply to sustain a moderate recovery.

If, after 1979, the Fed had continued to pursue a gradualist strategy for reducing inflation by keeping output below potential output but not far below it, the time it would have taken to combat inflation would have been longer. On the other hand, the severe economic distress and bankruptcies of 1982 and 1983 might have been avoided. Although we have not talked here about instability, the choice between a short, sharp recession and a long, mild recession may be made in practice on the basis of concerns about unstable economic changes. Some members of the board of governors of the Fed considered the histories of extremely rapid inflations, such as those in Europe in the 1920s and in Argentina, Brazil, and Israel in recent times, and they worried about a repetition of these in the United States in the 1980s. If the Fed believes that a high rate of inflation is not stable, then a sharp reduction in money growth is indicated. This concern about inflation rising out of control influenced the Fed to use a sharp reduction of money growth. Some economists, such as James Tobin of Yale University, worried that too sharp a recession could have led to a repeat of the Great Depression of the 1930s. In mid-1982 the Fed actually eased off on its policy of tight money, because it, too, was worried about a depression. The Fed wanted a sharp recession, but not a major depression.

Favorable Supply Shocks, 1981–1988

Not all supply shocks are adverse, and not all of the reduction in the rate of inflation in the 1980s can be traced to the recession and the change in monetary policy. Some of the reduction was due to the good fortune of positive shifts of supply. When there is a sudden reduction in the price of commodities or materials, the economy experiences a favorable supply shock. In terms of the output–inflation trade-off, *SS* becomes negative and the current rate of inflation is lower, because of the direct effect of the shock. Of course, this boon to the economy in the form of a lower price level has exceptional effects, just like (though in the opposite direction from) those that occur under stagflation.

Through much of 1980s, energy and food prices fell and this was an important source of the drop in the price level. There was a downward shift in the short-run trade-off. Food and energy prices fell in real terms by from 1 to 4 percent per year form 1981 to 1986 and oil prices collapsed in 1986, falling by more than 20 percent in real terms that year. Another positive supply shift in the United States was the upward movement in the foreign-exchange value of the dollar, a trend that continued along with falling energy and food prices until 1985. By putting downward pressure on the prices of imports sold in the United States, the revaluation of the dollar contributed to overall lower prices.

The positive supply shocks also contributed to a decline in inflationary expecta-tions. As the built-in rate of inflation came down, the short-run trade-off slowly fell.

From 1981 to 1988 the annual rate of inflation was low and the rate of real output growth was high.

Adverse Oil Shocks in the 1990s?

Since the supply of oil in industrialized economies is declining, should there be concern about the return of oil shocks in the 1990s?

The Gulf War   By 1988 and into 1989, the Fed was once more concerned about accelerating inflation. Monetary policy was tightened, although only by a little. The Fed was trying to engineer a ''soft landing,'' in which aggregate demand and output growth both slowed and the upward pressure on prices was eased. As we have seen in earlier chapters, the Fed was unsuccessful in bringing about the soft landing and there was recession in 1990–91 and a subsequent slow recovery.

Oil shocks played an important part in the onset of the recession. Iraq invaded Kuwait, triggering the Gulf War. The oil supplies from these two countries was no longer available on world markets. There was a very sharp spike in oil prices. Consumers and businesses feared a repeat of what had happened during 1979–82 and they cut back expenditures, bringing on the very recession they had feared.

Fortunately, the brief oil shock was not translated into supply-side inflation problems. World oil markets had changed over 10 years. New supplies of oil had been developed and users of oil had found ways to reduce consumption or switch into alternative fuels. In addition, Saudi Arabia, the largest oil supplier, used its spare capacity to make up for much of the shortfall from lost Iraqi and Kuwaiti supplies. The spike in oil prices was short-lived and inflation did not get a new boost in the 1990s. The sluggish recovery of the early 1990s has not been the result of persistent inflation problems.

Concerns about New Oil and Food Shocks   The supply of oil in the United States is gradually declining and will continue to do so unless there are dramatic increases in the world price of oil (or unless there is some surprising discovery). The growth rate of oil use has slowed, but oil consumption is still rising.

Some people believe that shortages will occur around the world of food and other commodities, as total world population continues to grow. There is concern, therefore, about a gradual tightening of oil supplies as the U.S. oil imports rise and about rising food prices, because limited resources are inadequate to feed the ever-increasing population. Similar stories are told for other commodities.

Reason tells us there must be a limit to the production of food in the world and that oil supplies will eventually run out. But careful assessments of resource availability indicate that commodity shortages are not likely to occur at any time soon, barring new wars or the mismanagement of resources. New oil discoveries outside the United States and energy conservation should keep supply and demand in the oil market in balance with moderate prices for the rest of this century. In particular, there is great scope to expand oil production in Russia and countries of the former USSR. Also these countries have squandered energy in the past and are likely to become more energy efficient.

There are, of course, areas of the world where there is starvation; but this problem is the result of bad resource management, not because it is impossible to produce more food. Many developing countries have kept food prices artificially low and this has discouraged farming. Other areas, as we have seen in Somalia, have political and social problems that prevent economic development and lead to the destruction of natural resources. Shortages of oil, food, and natural resources, up until now, have been the result of bad social and policy choices. If we see a new adverse supply shock in the 1990s, it will be because of such choices in the future, not because such a shock is inevitable.

WORKED EXAMPLES

Worked Example 12–1

The Effect of a Supply Shock on Inflation with Inflation-Accommodating Monetary Policy (Output Returns Quickly to Potential Output)

Consider the following particular output–inflation trade-off when there is a supply shock, *SS:*

Current $\Delta P/P = 0.2[(Y/Y^P) - 100] + \text{Exp } \Delta P/P + SS$

coupled with the following relationship, which determines inflationary expectations based on past rates of inflation:

Exp $\Delta P/P = 0.5(\Delta P/P$ of previous year$) + 0.5$ $(\Delta P/P$ of two years prior$)$

Question   Suppose that output in this economy has been equal to potential output and the rate of inflation has been 5 percent a year for several years. Then there is a supply shock of 6 percent for one year. (*SS* equals 6 for one year and is then zero after that.) Output falls to 95 percent of potential in the year of the shock and is then restored to 100 percent in subsequent years. Show how inflation evolves in this economy.

Answer: The rates of inflation that evolve in this economy are shown as follows over the eight years starting with the initial shock. The rates of inflation have been rounded, but the calculations were made without rounding, resulting in small discrepancies.

Year	Short-Run Trade-Off Relation	+	Expected Inflation	+	Supply Shock	=	Current Inflation
0	0.2(100 − 100)	+	[(0.5 × 5.00) + (0.5 × 5.00)]	+	0.00	=	5.00
	Supply shock starts:						
1	0.2(95 − 100)	+	[(0.5 × 5.00) + (0.5 × 5.00)]	+	6.00	=	10.00
	Supply shock ends:						
2	0.2(100 − 100)	+	[(0.5 × 10.00) + (0.5 × 5.00)]	+	0.00	=	7.50
3	0.2(100 − 100)	+	[(0.5 × 7.50) + (0.5 × 10.00)]	+	0.00	=	8.75
4	0.2(100 − 100)	+	[(0.5 × 8.75) + (0.5 × 7.50)]	+	0.00	=	8.12
5	0.2(100 − 100)	+	[(0.5 × 8.12) + (0.5 × 8.75)	+	0.00	=	8.44
6	0.2(100 − 100)	+	[(0.5 × 8.44) + (0.5 × 8.12)]	+	0.00	=	8.28
7	0.2(100 − 100)	+	[(0.5 × 8.28) + (0.5 × 8.44)]	+	0.00	=	8.36
8	0.2(100 − 100)	+	[(0.5 × 8.36) + (0.5 × 8.28)]	+	0.00	=	8.32

The rather mechanical way that expected inflation is formed as a two-year average is giving an up-and-down movement to inflation. But despite this, the example provides an important lesson. It illustrates the way in which the shock feeds back into expected inflation.

With no sustained recession to offset the supply shock, there is a long-run boost to inflation. Inflation will settle indefinitely at a rate that is about 3 percent higher than the rate it started at, as a result of the one-time supply shock (inflation started at 5 percent and ended at just over 8 percent). The shock gave an initial boost to inflation of 6 percent; that was partly offset by a one-year decline in output.

In this example, monetary policy is playing an important role in the background by accommodating the increase in inflation to restore the level of output.

Worked Example 12–2

Anti-Inflationary Policy: A Sustained Recession

We assume the same output–inflation trade-off and expectation formation with a supply shock that we have used previously.

$$\text{Current } \Delta P/P = 0.2[Y/Y^P) - 100] + \text{Exp } \Delta P/P + SS$$
$$\text{Exp } \Delta P/P = 0.5(\Delta P/P \text{ of previous year}) + 0.5(\Delta P/P \text{ of two years prior})$$

Question   Suppose that output in this economy has been equal to potential output and the rate of inflation has been 5 percent a year for several years. Then there is a supply shock of 6 percent for one year. (*SS* equals 6 for one year and is then zero after that.) Output falls to 95 percent of potential in the year of the shock and is then held at this level until the increase in inflation has been eliminated. What rates of inflation are generated in this economy?

Answer: The rates of inflation that evolve in this economy are shown below. The rates have been rounded; but the calculations are made without rounding, resulting in small discrepancies.

The level of output for year 6 was calculated as the level needed to reduce inflation just to 5 percent. Expected inflation in year 6 was 5.72 percent $[(0.5 \times 5.56) + (0.5 \times 5.88)]$. This had to be reduced by 0.72 percent and this gave the figure of 96.4 percent for the output ratio $[0.2(96.4 - 100) = -0.72]$. A similar calculation is used to find the figure of 98.6 for year 7.

This example illustrates the substantial price that must be paid to restore the old level of inflation. Inflation jumped to 10 percent in the year that the supply shock hit. This was reduced to 5 percent by holding output to 95 percent of potential during years 2 through 5 and at 96.4 percent of potential in year 6, and at 98.6 percent of potential in year 7. This was a loss of 25 percent of GDP over the four years.

Year	Short-Run Trade-Off Relation	+	Expected Inflation	+	Supply Shock	=	Current Inflation
0	0.2(100 − 100)	+	[(0.5 × 5.00) + (0.5 × 5.00)	+	0.00	=	5.00
Supply shock starts:							
1	0.2(95 − 100)	+	[(0.5 × 5.00) + (0.5 × 5.00)]	+	6.00	=	10.00
Supply shock ends; recession is continued:							
2	0.2(95 − 100)	+	[(0.5 × 10.00) + (0.5 × 5.00)]	+	0.00	=	6.50
3	0.2(95 − 100)	+	[(0.5 × 6.50) + (0.5 × 10.00)]	+	0.00	=	7.25
4	0.2(95 − 100)	+	[(0.5 × 7.25) + (0.5 × 6.50)]	+	0.00	=	5.88
5	0.2(95 − 100)	+	[(0.5 × 5.88) + (0.5 × 7.25)]	+	0.00	=	5.56

After inflation rate is restored to preshock level, monetary policy expands to allow for an increase in output:

6	0.2(96.4 − 100)	+	[(0.5 × 5.56) + (0.5 × 5.88)]	+ 0.00	= 5.00
7	0.2(98.6 − 100)	+	[(0.5 × 5.00) + (0.5 × 5.56)]	+ 0.00	= 5.00
8	0.2(100 − 100)	+	[(0.5 × 5.00) + (0.5 × 5.00)]	+ 0.00	= 5.00

This loss of GDP is a sacrifice made to tame inflation. See discussion of the sacrifice ratio above.

Worked Example 12–3

Establishing Anti-Inflationary Credibility via a Cold-Turkey Approach to Dealing with a Supply Shock

The output–inflation trade-off with a supply shock is defined as:

$$\text{Current } \Delta P/P = 0.2[(Y/Y^P) - 100] + \text{Exp } \Delta P/P + SS$$

In this example, inflationary expectations are formed out of past inflation. However, to illustrate the potential benefits of credibility, we assume that the expected rate of inflation is reduced by 1 percentage point when there is a credible anti-inflationary policy in effect.

$$\text{Exp } \Delta P/P = 0.5(\Delta P/P \text{ of previous year}) + 0.5(\Delta P/P \text{ of two years prior})$$
$$-1.0 \text{ if the anti-inflation policy is credible}$$

Question   Suppose that output in this economy has been equal to potential output and the rate of inflation has been 5 percent a year for several years. Then there is a supply shock of 6 percent for one year. (*SS* equals 6 for one year and is then zero after that.) Monetary policy is used to keep the inflation rate from rising by more than 3 percent in spite of the supply shock. How large a reduction of output is needed and what subsequently happens to inflation in the economy?

Answer   The rates of inflation that evolve in this economy are shown as follows over the four years starting with the initial shock:

Year	Short-Run Trade-Off Relation	+	Expected Inflation with Credibility	+	Supply Shock	=	Current Inflation
0	0.2(100 − 100)	+	[(0.5 × 5.00) + (0.5 × 5.00)]	+	0.00	=	5.00

Supply shock starts; monetary contraction keeps the current inflation rate from reflecting more than one-half of the supply shock:

Year	Short-Run Trade-Off Relation	+	Expected Inflation with Credibility	+	Supply Shock	=	Current Inflation
1	0.2(85 − 100)	+	[(0.5 × 5.00) + (0.5 × 5.00)]	+	6.00	=	8.00

Supply shock ends; the deep recession coupled with the relatively mild increase in the inflation rate makes the Fed's anti-inflationary policy credible:

Year	Short-Run Trade-Off Relation	+	Expected Inflation with Credibility	+	Supply Shock	=	Current Inflation
2	0.2(97.5 − 100)	+	[(0.5 × 8.00) + (0.5 × 5.00) − 1.00]	+	0.00	=	5.00
3	0.2(97.5 − 100)	+	[(0.5 × 5.00) + (0.5 × 8.00) − 1.00]	+	0.00	=	5.00

Inflation has been restored to preshock levels and the economy has been restored to the preshock equilibrium:

Year	Short-Run Trade-Off Relation	+	Expected Inflation with Credibility	+	Supply Shock	=	Current Inflation
4	0.2(100 − 100)	+	[(0.5 × 5.00) + (0.5 × 5.00)]			=	5.00

Output is equal to 100 percent of potential and inflation is 5 percent in subsequent years. In contrast with the previous example, where output was not allowed to fall below 95 percent of potential output, a serious enough contraction, in this case the initial contraction in output was down to 85 percent of potential. If this example described an actual event, a recession of that depth would exceed any that has been experienced in the United States since the 1930s.

The figures for output in years 2 and 3 were the levels needed to reduce inflation to 5 percent. In both years, expected inflation would have been 6.5 percent [(0.5 × 8.00) + (0.5 × 5.00)] if there were no credibility effect. In this example, expected inflation in those years, including the credibility effect, was 5.5 percent. Inflation had to be reduced by 0.5 percent and this meant an output ratio of 97.5 percent [0.2(97.5 − 100) = −0.5]. Output would have had to be reduced by less if the credibility effect were stronger, and it would have had to be reduced by more if the credibility effect were weaker. In practice, the impact of credibility is not known.

This example illustrates the depth of the recession that must be endured to reduce inflation so quickly. In this example, the loss of GDP totaled 20 percent over three years in this cold-turkey case versus 25 percent over six years in the sustained-recession case. The cold-turkey approach benefits from the credibility effect, but, though the recession is shorter, it is nevertheless much deeper. While the total loss of GDP is somewhat less here than in the more gradual approach, there are significant dangers in using so drastic a cut in output. We have assumed here and in the discussions in the text that goods–market equilibrium (the *IS* schedule) will remain stable as the Fed hits the economy with a recession. In the real economy, investor or consumer confidence might be broken by a recession as deep as the one just described, leading to an unstable decline in output.

SUMMARY

- Inflation can be initiated by shifts in aggregate supply as well as by increases in aggregate demand.

- If there are large changes in the relative prices of important commodities and no offsetting changes in other prices, then these relative price changes will change the overall price level. The result is called a "supply shock."

- For supply shocks to contribute to an increase in both the overall price level and the rate of inflation, the national expenditures on the products suffering the supply shocks have to be large portions of GDP and there has to be downward rigidity in other prices, particularly real wages.

- The relative prices of energy and agricultural products have changed sharply; the price of both groups of commodities rose in the early 1970s. Energy prices rose again in the late 1970s. Both relative prices have fallen subsequently. These changes were important supply shocks. A supply shock, such as the OPEC price increase, means that we have to pay more for foreign oil. There is no simple way to avoid the costs that this imposes.

- The productivity slowdown and changes in the value of the dollar were supply shocks of a somewhat different kind. The slowdown in the growth of labor productivity led to a rise in the unit labor costs. Since there was no offsetting reduction in the rate of growth of wages, this also contributed to inflation. The changes in the value of the dollar changed the cost of living as foreign goods became more or less expensive.

- In a supply-shock inflation, the economy experiences an initial increase in the price level as the price of the output of U.S. producers in affected sectors increases. The cost of living increases, because of both the increase in the price of domestic output and because of the rise in the prices of imported commodities. The increased cost of living then affects wages, and the acceleration of wage inflation leads to increased price inflation. There is a price–wage spiral.

- In terms of the output–inflation trade-off, an adverse supply shock results in an initial upward shift in the trade-off. The subsequent price–wage spiral then results in an increase in expected inflation.

- In the absence of any offsetting action by the Fed, a supply shock will raise the price level and reduce the real stock of money. This will reduce output. The Fed can choose to sustain the real money stock and avoid the contractionary effects of the shock.
- A supply shock confronts policymakers with a dilemma—once the shock has occurred, inflation rises. Aggregate demand policies can then be directed either at fighting the rise in inflation (thereby making the reduction in output worse) or policies can stimulate aggregate demand to return output and employment to their preshock levels (at the expense of making inflation worse).
- Once the impact of the supply shock has passed, inflation will fall and then subsequent increases or decreases in aggregate demand will determine whether there is a continuing or even a worsening legacy of inflation or whether income expands toward potential.
- When anti-inflationary policies are chosen, these involve reducing aggregate demand.
- If the Fed takes a completely tough line and seeks to

bring inflation back to its original level right away, then it will create a major reduction in the real money supply and a very serious recession, though inflation will eventually start to decline and output will return to potential.
- The effectiveness of the anti-inflationary policy is enhanced to the degree that the Fed is able to establish its credibility as an inflation fighter, thereby reducing inflationary expectations.
- In practice, policymakers vacillated between the goal of fighting inflation and the goal of reducing unemployment. The result was that, during the 1970s, the economy oscillated between very high inflation and very high unemployment. Then, in the 1980s, a determined course of inflation fighting was chosen.
- Supply shocks can be positive. In the mid-1980s such positive supply shifts occurred because of a collapse of oil prices and a decline in the prices of imported goods.
- Positive supply shocks, combined with an anti-inflationary monetary policy, drove down both inflation and inflationary expectations in the 1980s, but the rise in oil prices in 1990 threatens a new adverse supply shock.

KEY TERMS AND CONCEPTS

adverse supply shock, p. 374

credibility effect, p. 394

favorable supply shock, p. 375

price–wage spiral, p. 385

sacrifice ratio, p. 393

supply shock, p. 374

DISCUSSION QUESTIONS AND PROBLEMS

1. Contrast the explanation for stagflation that is based wholly on inflationary expectations with the explanation based on supply shocks.
2. How is a supply shock different from the normal process by which relative prices change in the economy?
3. What are the choices that policymakers face when confronted with a supply shock? List some costs and benefits of alternative responses.
4. Use the following relationships:

   The output–inflation trade-off with a supply shock

   Current $\Delta P/P = 0.3[(Y/Y^P) - 100] + \text{Exp } \Delta P/P + SS$

   The formation of inflationary expectations

   Exp $\Delta P/P = 0.75(\Delta P/P$ of previous year$) + 0.25(\Delta P/P$ of two years prior$)$

   to trace out the reaction of the economy over several years to a supply shock of 4 percent for one year. Inflation has been stable at 3 percent per year prior to the shock. In the absence of an overt policy response, output falls to 98 percent of potential in the year of the shock.

   a. Assume that the output ratio returns to 100 percent the year after the shock has passed and stays at 100 percent. What has been the long-run effect of the supply shock on inflation?

   b. Assume that the output ratio stays at 98 percent until inflation is brought back to 3 percent a year or less. How long does this take?

FORECASTING, STABILIZATION POLICY, AND THE VARIABILITY OF THE ECONOMY

INTRODUCTION

The business cycle consists of recurring fluctuations of income and output over time. Evidence shows clearly these fluctuations are not regular and some are severe and some are mild. Economists, business managers, financial investors, and government policymakers generate macroeconomic forecasts, attempting to predict the ups and downs of the economy. They use a variety of methods and have had a mixed record of success and failure. In this chapter, we look at how forecasts are made and how well they work. We also look at the attempts by policymakers to use forecasts in support of policies designed to ameliorate economic fluctuations. Finally, we discuss the track record of stabilization activities.

Governments are nearly universal in their desire to moderate economic fluctuations. Boom and bust cycles are seen as costly, they force society to bear risks and in the down-cycle they generate unemployment and bankruptcies, which create both economic and political pains that governments would rather avoid.

The aversion to economic variability can be taken to extremes. Economic vitality requires some risk taking, and without winners and losers there would be no economic progress. The industry of firms that survive a recession are often better prepared for longer-term growth than the collection of companies that sprung up in the growth phase of the recovery. Nevertheless, economic well-being is improved if the extremes of the business cycle can be avoided.

Policymakers intending to stabilize the economy need to rely on forecasts, because there are lags between the time when actions are taken and the time they have an effect on the economy. For stabilization to work, policy actions have to be undertaken *before* changes are observed in economic conditions. Based on forecasts of where the economy is going, policy makers sometimes make changes in monetary and fiscal policy, and the record of these policy changes and their outcome make up the history of stabilization policy—the policy response to the continuing fluctuations of the business cycle.

We have already spent a lot of time looking at the impact of policy actions directed at particular economic circumstances; for example, a rise in expected inflation or a decline in aggregate demand. We look now at the overall strategy of policies designed to maintain stability. Rather than asking whether any individual policy action is or is not appropriate, we want to know what constitutes a well-working collection of policies invoked over long periods. What makes for a good policy regime?

There are pluses and minuses to using stabilization policy, and a real question for many economists is whether the effect has been beneficial. One crude test of effectiveness is to see whether the economy has actually been more stable since the advent of active stabilization policies.

FORECASTING THE MACRO ECONOMY

Forecasts are used implicitly or explicitly by almost all participants in the economy. Company managers who are scheduling production over the coming year, or who are deciding whether to go ahead with a plant expansion, will look for forecasts of how the macro economy will perform over the coming year or more. For such industries as autos, household appliances, or machine tools, knowledge of the business cycle is crucial in predicting what their sales will be. When we looked at investment demand in Chapter 9, we argued this is determined by the difference between the actual capital stock and the desired stock of capital. The desired stock of capital, in turn, depends on expected future demand and output. It is the anticipation of increases in demand, *based on a forecast,* that convinces households and firms that they have inadequate stocks of capital and they need to invest more.

When the Fed's open-market committee meets to decide the direction of monetary policy, the members base their decisions on forecasts. The Fed has to come to a conclusion about whether it thinks the economy will grow rapidly, leading possibly to an acceleration of inflation, or whether it will stagnate, resulting in an increase in unemployment.

In recent years, fiscal policy has not been used routinely to stimulate or restrain aggregate demand, because of the pressures created by the budget deficit. Nevertheless, both the president and the Congress pore avidly over forecasts of the economy to determine whether fiscal policy changes are necessary, despite the deficit.[1] And since

---

[1] And, of course, the president and the Congress also pore over the forecasts to assess their re-election chances.

the deficit itself depends on the growth of the economy, forecasts of the economy are needed to estimate what taxes and expenditures will actually be.

Forecasts are made of almost every economic and financial variable, but particularly real GDP, inflation, unemployment, and interest rates. In this section we look at forecasting methodologies as they are used to make such forecasts. Three approaches are in common use.

First, there are surveys that ask business managers what their plans are for production and investment, and there are also surveys that ask consumers whether they are planning to buy a car or a new house.

Second, there are forecasts that build on the pattern of past experience but do not rely on a formal model of the economy. One of the simplest and most widely used tools in this last category is the index of leading economic indicators issued by the Department of Commerce.

Third, there are formal econometric models that use statistical methods to estimate economic performance from past experience and are then used to predict the future.

Surveys of Business Managers and Consumers

Survey data from business managers and consumers are collected regularly and reported by a number of institutions, including the Institute for Social Research at the University of Michigan, the Consumer Research Center at the Conference Board in New York, and McGraw-Hill, Inc.

The strength of this approach to forecasting is that it is very direct. You want to find out what people are going to do, so you go and ask them what they are going to do. There is no need to construct an elaborate model of how the economy works, and no need to assume that the past pattern of movements in economic data will continue in the same way in the future. The weakness of this approach is that people frequently do not know what they are going to do, even when they are honest about their intentions. Managers are themselves trying to make forecasts of the economy and decide how much to invest. They may respond to a forecast question that they are planning to build a new plant in the next 12 months; but if the economy starts to weaken, they will quickly change their minds and postpone or cancel their plans. Similarly, consumers may say they are confident about the future and are planning to buy a new car. But if the boss suddenly starts to talk about cutbacks, then the plans are changed.

On balance, surveys have not proven to be the most reliable way to forecast the economy. They are useful as a supplement to other methods to indicate when there is a change in direction of the economy that breaks the usual pattern. And surveys of consumer confidence can give guidance about the likely pattern of consumer durable goods purchases. But other ways of looking at the data are needed.

Surveys of Forecasts

Any single forecast or forecaster is unlikely to be consistently accurate. A collection of forecasts will provide a consensus measure that provides an improvement over any individual source. At any time there will be a number of business and financial economists working to generate macroeconomic forecasts that are based on a variety of methodologies. Surveys of forecasts are reported quarterly in *The Wall Street Journal* and *Business Week*. On a monthly basis, the *Blue Chip Economic Indicators*[2] presents both the individual and the consensus forecasts drawn from over 50 separate sources, including university research groups, public and private forecasting companies, and individual business economists.

Table 13–1 reproduces an excerpt from February 1994 *Blue Chip Economic Indicators,* which gives forecasts for the 1995 rate of growth of real GDP and the consumer price index (CPI) as well as forecasts of short-term and long-term nominal interest rates and the unemployment rate for 1995. High and low forecasts are noted along with the average or consensus. By the time you are reading this, you may be able to check on the accuracy of these forecasts or see how the forecasts for 1995 have changed over time.

Leading Indicators

lagging indicators
Variables that move just after a turning point.

coincident indicators
Variables that change along with peaks and troughs.

leading indicators
Forecasting variables that move prior to a turning point in the economy.

index of leading economic indicators
An index based on leading indication, it usually rises prior to periods of economic growth and falls prior to recessions.

One of the pioneers of the study of the business cycle in the United States was Wesley Mitchell.[3] Even before the Great Depression of the 1930s, he worked at finding a means of predicting changes in economic conditions. Later in the 1930s, along with Arthur Burns at the National Bureau of Economic Research, the work was refined into a search for economic variables that would systematically change value around the time of turning points—peaks and troughs in the business cycle. Variables that moved just after a turning point were called **lagging indicators;** those that changed direction along with peaks and troughs were called **coincident indicators;** and the forecasting variables were those that moved prior to a turning point in the economy—**leading indicators.**

The rationale behind the search for leading indicators was based on two notions. First, it was believed there is a pattern to movements in the economy. For example, an increase of capital-goods orders precedes an increase in production. Leading indicators were sought because they were thought to be early indicators of conditions that were already in place but were in the process of rolling through the economy. Second, there are variables that reflect expectations, and people's expectations about the future may have value in predicting the future.

Beyond any explicit rationale, however, leading indicators were sought in an opportunistic manner—a search for what works. In practical terms, the forecasting ability of any one leading indicator is rather weak, though a collection of many such indicators is better. When compiled as a group, these indicators are called the **index of leading economic indicators.** They have been reported monthly by the Department of Commerce in the *Survey of Current Business* since 1961.[4]

---

[2] *Blue Chip Economic Indicators,* Robert J. Eggert, editor, 1993, Capital Publications, Alexandria, Va.

[3] Wesley C. Mitchell and Arthur Burns, *Statistical Indicators of Cyclical Revivals,* Bulletin 69 (New York: National Bureau of Economic Research, 1938); Wesley C. Mitchell, *Business Cycles and Their Causes* (Los Angeles: University of California Press, 1941); Geoffrey Moore, *Business Cycles, Inflation & Forecasting,* 2nd ed., NBER Studies in Business Cycles (Cambridge, Mass.: Ballinger Publishing, 1983).

[4] Research on leading indicators is still being conducted by Geoffrey Moore and others at the Center for International Business Cycle Research at Columbia University.

TABLE 13-1   Blue Chip Economic Indicators—1995 Real GDP Consensus Estimate Rises to **2.8%**

| February 1994 Forecast for 1995: Source | Percent Change 1995 from 1994 | | Average for 1995 | | |
	Real GDP	Consumer Price Index	Treas. Bills 3-mo.	Corp. Aaa Bonds	Unempl. % Labor Force
UCLA Business Forecast	3.6H	2.3	2.8	6.6	5.7
Chemical Banking	3.5	2.5	3.4	6.9	6.2
Conference Board	3.4	4.3H	4.3	7.7	6.1
Georgia State University	3.4	3.5	4.4	7.5	6.0
Chrysler Corporation	3.4	3.5	4.4	7.9	6.1
Robert Genetski & Assoc., Inc.	3.3	4.0	5.7H	8.3H	6.0
Morris Cohen & Associates	3.3	3.5	4.5	8.0	6.1
Sears Roebuck & Co.	3.2	3.5	4.6	7.6	6.0
Prudential Insurance Co.	3.1	2.2	2.5L	6.5	6.0
For Motor Co.	3.0	3.4	4.6	—	6.0
Northern Trust Company	3.0	3.4	4.5	7.2	6.2
Bankers Trust Co.	3.0	3.0	—	—	6.5
Dun & Bradstreet	3.0	3.6	3.6	7.8	6.0
PNC Bank	3.0	2.7	3.8	6.7	5.9
Merrill Lynch	3.0	2.9	3.9	6.9	6.4
Wayne Hummer & Co., Chicago	2.9	3.5	3.8	7.5	6.2
Eggert Economic Enterprises, Inc.	2.9	3.4	3.8	7.3	6.6
U.S. Trust Co.	2.9	3.5	4.3	7.7	5.9
Brown Brothers Harriman	2.9	3.3	3.6	—	6.5
Morgan Guaranty Trust Co.	2.9	3.3	—	—	5.7
First Interstate Bancorp	2.8	3.3	3.9	7.2	6.4
Reeder Associates (Charles)	2.8	3.1	3.7	7.2	6.4
NationsBanc Capital Markets, Inc.	2.8	2.0L	4.0	6.7	6.0
Comerica	2.7	4.1	4.1	7.6	6.4
Shawmut National Corp	2.7	3.5	3.7	7.1	6.7

Because the index of leading economic indicators is based on an opportunistic search for economic variables, the composition of indicators in the index changes over time. The current list is comprised of:

- Average weekly hours of production workers.
- Average initial claims for unemployment insurance.
- Manufacturers' new orders (real dollars) for the consumer goods and materials industries.

| February 1994 Forecast for 1995: Source | Percent Change 1995 from 1994 | | Average for 1995 | | |
	Real GDP	Consumer Price Index	Treas. Bills 3-mo.	Corp. Aaa Bonds	Unempl. % Labor Force
Metropolitan Life Insurance Co.	2.7	3.8	4.3	7.7	6.2
DuPont	2.7	3.5	3.7	7.2	6.2
Bank of America	2.7	3.2	4.0	7.4	6.2
Laurence H. Meyer & Assoc.	2.7	2.8	3.8	6.6	6.1
Evans Economics	2.7	3.5	3.6	7.2	6.4
National Assn. of Home Builders	2.7	2.9	3.8	6.5	6.1
U.S. Chamber of Commerce	2.7	2.5	3.3	6.7	5.9
Econoclast	2.6	4.0	4.1	7.6	6.2
First National Bank of Chicago	2.6	3.5	3.6	8.0	6.5
Bostian Economic Research	2.6	3.4	3.8	7.0	6.5
CoreStates Financial Corp.	2.6	2.7	4.5	7.3	6.2
Turning Points (Micrometrics)	2.5	3.5	3.8	7.5	6.1
Mortgage Bankers Assn. of Amer.	2.5	3.0	4.7	7.2	5.8
General Motors	2.5	3.5	3.6	7.2	5.9
Fairmodel	2.5	2.4	3.6	6.2L	5.3L
Nat'l. City Bank of Cleveland	2.4	3.2	3.9	7.6	6.3
Cahners Economics	2.3	3.7	4.0	7.5	6.3
Chase Manhattan Bank	2.3	3.2	3.2	7.0	6.7
Standard & Poors	2.2	3.1	3.2	7.0	6.0
SOM Economics, Inc.	2.1	3.3	4.2	7.1	6.0
Motorola, Inc.	2.1	3.2	3.6	—	6.0
Inforum—Univ. of Maryland	1.0L	2.9	2.6	6.4	7.2H
1995 Consensus:					
February Avg.	2.8	3.2	3.9	7.2	6.2
High 10 Avg.	3.3	3.8	4.6	7.8	6.6
Low 10 Avg.	2.2	2.5	3.2	6.6	5.8
January Avg.	2.7	3.3	3.8	7.2	6.2

- Vendor performance, a measure of the slowness of deliveries.
- Contracts and orders (real dollars) for plant and equipment.
- Building permits for new private housing units.
- Change in manufacturers' orders (real dollars) for durables.
- Change in sensitive materials prices.
- Standard & Poor's 500 Stock Average.
- The real stock of money ($M2/P$).
- The Conference Board's index of consumer confidence.

The business press regularly reports changes in the index of leading indicators, and business managers and financial investors pay attention. There is a special focus on them when they appear to be signaling a turning point. Though generally the index tracks along with the business cycle, it often does not give much advance warning. Further, the index has a history of false prediction. The index fell for seven months in a row in 1984 and five months in a row in 1987 and the recession did not start until late 1990. As with the surveys, this approach to forecasting is far from perfect.

Econometric Forecasting Models

Starting before World War II, economists started to build detailed models of the economy that allows them to use statistical techniques with economic data in order to understand past behavior and to forecast where the economy was moving. The first Nobel prize in economics was given to Ragnar Frisch and Jan Tinbergen for their pioneering efforts to construct an econometric model of the economy. It was the development of high-speed computers, however, that allowed the estimation of complex models of the economy, especially once the National Income and Product Accounts provided reliable data over many years.

In the United States, econometric forecasting models were built by academic economists and became more and more complex and sophisticated in the 1960s and 70s. Leading models were developed by Lawrence Klein and colleagues at the University of Pennsylvania, by Otto Eckstein at Harvard, and by Franco Modigliani at MIT. In important ways, the economics profession and the business community have judged these efforts to have been successful. Klein and Modigliani have both won Nobel prizes for their modeling and other work. The Klein model is now operated commercially as the Wharton forecasting model. The Modigliani model focused on financial markets and has been used by Fed for many years as part of its forecasting effort. The Eckstein model has been the most successful commercially, as he and his colleagues spun off their venture into Data Resources, Inc., which was subsequently sold to McGraw-Hill in a multimillion-dollar deal.

The Strength of the Models   Writing down an econometric model provides a discipline to the process of understanding the economy and forecasting it. Economists trained in the rigorous world of economic theory are fond of constructing narrow models that show some very striking result. They may even pull together some data to suggest this result is important in the real world. But they never have to ask whether the phenomena they are describing could really be important relative to other factors. And sometimes they ignore some other implications of what they are doing. One of the strengths of the macro econometric models is that they force economists to put the whole picture together and see how it all fits.

Just writing down the identities in the economy can be instructive. For example, James Tobin was an adviser on an early attempt to construct a macro model. He worked on the demand for assets, such as money, bonds, and capital. He realized there is a simple identity that says that total wealth is equal to the sum of the values of all of these assets. Since wealth is given at any given moment in time, an increase in the demand for one asset must be equivalent to a decrease in the demand for another asset—a simple point that had been ignored.

Putting together all the pieces to explain consumption, investment, government, and net foreign demand can show the relative importance of the different elements. How much does the change in inventories contribute to the overall variation of the economy? What are the possible channels by which monetary policy could affect the economy?

Ultimately, however, the value of the econometric models is demonstrated by results. Do they forecast well? The record as a whole shows that they do provide valuable information about the future path of the economy. As a simple market test, the models have been able to sell their forecasts to many corporations. These companies would not keep buying the forecasts unless they had value.

Problems with the Models   To say that the forecasting models have value, however, is not to say that they have always been reliable. They have had some serious problems.

Prediction Failures at Times of Major Changes   The period from 1973 to 1975 was a very difficult one for the economy and the forecasting models. As we saw in Chapter 12, there were large supply shocks, notably the increases in energy and fuel prices. As inflation soared, policymakers and the Fed, in particular, shifted to a policy of restraint to bring the inflation rate back down. The economy was slowing by early 1974, but had not dropped into recession; and the main econometric models forecast then that income growth into 1975 would be over 2 percent a year. The policymakers responded by a sharp contraction in monetary policy that led to a fall in the real stock of money.

The forecasts of the economy were way off. A model is only as good as the theory behind it. The models were built on the assumption that the only alternatives for output and inflation were along a trade-off—since prices were rising, unemployment had to go down. Remember, this was before the mechanisms behind supply shocks and a worsening trade-off were fully understood. In contrast to the forecasts, real GDP fell by almost 4 percent over a year, rather than rising by 2 percent. The credibility of the forecasting models was damaged.

The period 1979–82 was another difficult one for both the economy and for the forecasters. The continued growth of the economy in 1979 was surprising; the sharp fall of the economy in 1980 was not well forecast; the quick turnaround in the second half of 1980 was a surprise; and then the collapse of the economy in 1981–82 was not forecast.

Not all of the errors have come in trying to forecast recessions. The forecasters were too pessimistic about the recovery after 1982 and were too optimistic in predicting recovery in 1991 and 1992.

In general, the models have difficulty forecasting important changes in the economy. And that is a serious problem. Those are precisely the predictions we would like to have, because they are times when business managers, households, and policymakers need to respond to changing circumstances.

Why Have the Models Had Trouble at Times of Change?   The first problem the models had with these episodes of change is that they cannot really predict what the policymakers will do. The more the policymakers believe the predictions of the models, the more they may work to change the actual outcome of the economy. For example, if the models predict strong growth in GDP, this will encourage the Fed to follow a contractionary policy to curb the economy and inflation. It was in part the predictions of economic growth in 1974–75 that caused the Fed to squeeze the economy.

The second problem that the models had was the impossibility of forecasting changes in the structure of the economy. Models are based on both data and theory, but even theory is set in a historical context. During the episodes described above, the economy was hit by changes, such as supply shocks, that had not been captured well in the equations of the models. Supply shocks, such as oil price increases, were not a concern for the United States until we became a major oil importer. In general, the international economy has become much more important over time. The nature of financial markets has changed. After 1979, the Fed was willing to see interest rates at 15 to 20 percent. These rates were unheard of in the 1950s and 60s. In general, it is hard to use time-series data from the economy to infer economic behavior when the structure of the economy changes over time.

One of the reasons that Otto Eckstein's model forecast so well for many years is that Eckstein had an intuitive sense of when the forecasts made good sense and when they did not. He would make ''adjustments'' to the variables and then rerun the forecasts. He did not simply take his model as gospel. In a changing economy, he thought it was better to use a combination of intuition and econometrics, rather than using the model by itself.

Order or Chaos   One of the interesting developments in applied mathematics in recent years has been chaos theory. And this development grew out of work with forecasting models. Large-scale forecasting models have been constructed for the weather, which incorporate knowledge of fluid dynamics, evaporation, and other elements that go into determining the pattern of rainfall or the likelihood of hurricanes. These models have become increasingly sophisticated, to the point where they need supercomputers to carry out their projections.

It was discovered in the course of building these models of the weather that they are exquisitely sensitive to the initial conditions that are assumed. A typical model run specifies what the temperatures and the weather patterns are around the world at some point in time. The computer then runs the model forward to forecast what conditions will be 24 hours later or a month later. It was found that, if the intial temperatures entered into the model are varied only very slightly, the resulting predictions could be wildly different. Small initial differences are often blown into large final differences, rather than being attenuated over time. A small variation in the initial conditions can change the predicted path of a hurricane from striking land to moving harmlessly out to sea.

Exploring the reasons behind this surprising result, the mathematicians discovered that even quite simple systems of equations, provided they are not linear, are extremely sensitive to initial conditions, to the point that long-range predictions become impossible. At that point, the process is described as *chaotic*. Based on this work, it is suspected that many natural phenomena will have to be understood by using chaos theory.

Large-scale econometric models are rather like models of the weather, so it is possible that the economy itself is a nonlinear chaotic system and that, like the weather, the economy is intrinsically very hard to forecast. At this point we do not know whether the economy is chaotic, using the term as the mathematicians use it; but chaos theory provides an important lesson for economic forecasters. Previously, it had always been assumed that macro econometric models have had trouble forecasting, because they did not have the correct equations. It was thought that the models must be wrong. Chaos theory found that, even in artificial models that were correct by assumption, it was impossible to predict very far into the future. This implies that, even if the econometric models were improved and the equations provided a good approximation to actual behavior, they might still have trouble forecasting over periods longer than a few quarters.

Expectations   Finally, macro econometric models have problems with expectations. All of the models have to make assumptions about the way expectations are formed. If people in the economy use all of the information available to them in a rational way to make forecasts, the models will break down, because people will constantly revise their behavior in reaction to the forecasts and by doing so make invalid the assumptions about expectations that were used in the model. This problem is called the *Lucas critique.* Lucas argues that, if any model was really as good as is claimed, then everyone would use the model to forecast the future and base their decisions on these forecasts. But if that happened, their behavior would not be the way that it is described in the model. So if the model is right, it will soon be wrong![5]

This criticism is a very trenchant one in principle, and it went a long way toward discrediting the econometric models among economists. In practice there is little evidence that this criticism has been important in explaining any of the forecasting failures that the models have experienced.

Despite our skepticism of the strong assumptions that Lucas makes, we think he has an important point in stressing the role of expectations in the models. The predictions of the models depend heavily on what people expect to happen and the difficulty of modeling how expectations are formed has contributed to the failures the models have had.

The Statistical Analysis of Leading Indicators

The inconsistent performance of macroeconometric models lead economists to reconsider simpler approaches enhanced by modern methodologies. Two econometricians, James Stock and Mark Watson, tried to improve on the forecasting ability of the index of leading indicators.[6] They reasoned that the index had been put together in a very ad hoc fashion before the days of high-speed computers, and there was scope to test the predictive power of large numbers of economic time series.

---

[5] We discuss this point further in Chapter 15.
[6] James Stock and Mark Watson, ''New Indicators of Coincident and Leading Economic Indicators,'' *NBER Macro Annual,* 1989.

Stock and Watson particularly wanted to explore the fact that the Department of Commerce index ignores interest-rate variables, perhaps because the opportunistic approach to leading indicators overlooked the importance of interest-rate differences. Many Wall Street economists have been using the slope of the yield curve for years as a way of predicting recessions. Inverted yield curves often precede recessions for several reasons; a rise in short rates could signal a tightening of monetary policy and/ or a fall in long rates could indicate an increase in long-term bond purchases in anticipation of even larger rate reductions and increases in bond prices, because a recession along with a decline in borrowing demand is expected.[7]

Stock and Watson looked at a large number of interest-rate measures, including a measure thought to reflect business risk—the spread between the interest rate on short-term commercial paper (short-term corporate bonds) and the rate on T bills. The Harvard economist Benjamin Friedman had found that this interest-rate spread rose prior to the 1974–75 recession and prior to the recessions of 1980 and 1981–82.

Stock and Watson started with a list of 280 economic time series, and these were initially screened to see which ones exhibited simple correlations with the old Department of Commerce index. A few were retained on the grounds that economic theory suggested they should be important. This initial screening dropped the number down to 55 series. They then screened further by running the variables in batches, looking for ones that showed up consistently as adding some independent predictive power to their regressions.

At the end of their search process, they had a list of 7 time series and a new index of leading indicators. Their variables were new housing starts, the growth of unfilled manufacturers orders, the change in the exchange rate, the change in part-time work, the change in the interest rate on 10-year Treasury bonds, the spread (or interest-rate gap) between the six-month commercial paper rate and the six-month T-bill rate, and the spread between the rate on one-year Treasury bonds and 10-year bonds (the slope of the yield curve).

Their tests indicated, based on past history, that their new index would provide much more reliable predictions of recessions than the old Department of Commerce series. Much of the power of the new index came from the inclusion of the new interest-rate variables.

Stock and Watson had an early opportunity to test their index. In late 1989 and early 1990, many forecasters and the old Department of Commerce index of leading economic indicators were suggesting that a recession was probably coming. The Stock and Watson index, on the other hand, was showing a fairly robust economy six months ahead. Based on their index, they estimated that the probability of recession over the next six months was very low. As history testifies, the economy went into a sharp recession in 1990 and Stock and Watson had to go back to the computer.

---

[7] In Chapter 8 we made a case for the predictive nature of the interest-rate gap. By looking at the difference between short-run nominal rates and the cost of funds, we focused on inflationary expectations and the risk or maturity premium, both of which indicate the direction where the economy was heading.

Many economists (especially those lacking the computer and econometric skills of Stock and Watson) took satisfaction in seeing the old leading indicators do better than the high-powered computer-assisted model. It was like the old John Henry story. The more interesting question is why such a careful and skilled study, which found variables that did a good job of ''predicting'' in the past, failed so badly the first time they were used to make a real prediction.

The Stock and Watson index was a powerful predictor in the 1970s and 80s because the recessions in that period had a key element in common: *They were all triggered by contractionary monetary policy responding to excessive inflation.* The Fed squeezed credit, pushed up short-term interest rates, and changed the slope of the yield curve. In the late 1980s, the Fed started to tighten credit to slow the economy, but by the end of 1989 it had eased. The interest-rate spreads fell and so did the Stock and Watson index. The trigger to the recession was probably the Gulf War or perhaps a private sector credit crunch unconnected to Fed policies.[8] In any case it was not the Fed tightening policy. The new index was powerless to predict the 1990 recession, since that recession was not caused by the same factors that caused the earlier recessions. As we said before, it is hard to use time-series data from the economy to infer economic behavior when the structure of the economy changes over time.

Forecasting, and Lessons for Stabilization Policy

Based on this review of forecasting methods, we have learned of the need to be cautious. It is very had to know exactly what the state of the economy is and whether it is about to fall into recession or to grow strongly. Some economists conclude it is hopeless to use monetary and fiscal policy to try and smooth the effects of the business cycle. We disagree. But we think that stabilization policy has to be designed and executed in a way that both recognizes the problems of forecasting and attempts to build a relatively stable policy regime without trying for excessive fine-tuning and control. The policymakers do not know at once that the economy is in difficulties. Then there is a lag before policies take effect. Will the policies start in time, will they still be needed when they start to work? Even worse, will the wrong policy hit the economy at the wrong time—even with the best intentions? Should policy change on the basis of small-scale short-run information? Or should only changes in large-scale long-lasting trends trigger policy reactions? We examine those issues next.

STABILIZATION POLICY

As the world economy emerged from World War II, the greatest fear was there would be a recurrence of the high unemployment of the 1930s or, if not that, then a return to the rather severe and frequent business-cycle fluctuations that occurred throughout the 19th and 20th centuries. Although there was concern about inflation, the principal goal of stabilization policy in the postwar 1950s was to maintain the level of output close to

---

[8] A private sector credit crunch would show as a rise in the risk premium across types of securities, but would not be reflected in differences in rates among short-term and long-term government securities.

potential output—to ameliorate the effect of the business cycle. By the 1960s, this goal was being compromised by the need to control inflation. And since 1970, there have been several periods during which economic policymakers have tolerated or even induced a recession to reduce inflation. **Stabilization policy** today means trying to form a reasonable compromise between the often conflicting goals of full employment and moderate inflation. A major motivation for delving into the structure of the economy has been to understand how policy could be pursued to achieve this reasonable compromise.

stabilization policy
A systematic program of monetary and fiscal policies designed to lessen the severity of business cycle fluctuations.

In this section, we will analyze the effectiveness of stabilization policy in tackling a recurring business cycle. We focus particularly on the critical issue of the timing of policy actions. Stabilization policy can fail when the direction of the economy changes more quickly than policy can respond and more quickly than policy actions have their effect.

We also review the performance record of stabilization policy by looking at the history of the business cycle. If the stabilization policy that was applied over the past decades is to be judged successful, then it should have reduced the degree of fluctuation and made the economy more stable.

Hitting a Moving Target When Visibility Is Bad

Stabilization policy requires policymakers to steer a very large and sluggish ship with better information about where it has been than where it is currently. The ship has limited controls, with long lags between changes of course and visible reactions. And finally, policymakers are faced with controversy over the appropriate direction in which to steer the ship. At a given point in time, there is reasonably good information available about last year's GDP, inflation, and unemployment. There is only preliminary information about these variables during the previous nine months and there are imperfect forecasts of the future.

An ideal stabilization policy would have policymakers acting in advance of the onset of the recession and certainly in advance of the time when the experience of a recession is certain. Since policymakers cannot be certain about upcoming change in the direction of the economy, and since it takes time for policymakers to react even when they have come to a conclusion about a policy direction, *policy actions are subject to lags between the time that policy actions should be initiated and the time that policy actions are in fact initiated.* There is a **recognition lag** between the time an economy starts into a downturn and the time policymakers really know about it, and there is a **decision lag** between the time that the need for policy action is recognized and the time that the levers of policy are actually changed.

recognition lag
The time it takes for policymakers to recognize that economic conditions have changed.

Policymaking is not carried out by individuals but by groups. In a democracy, a majority of decision makers have to be convinced that action is needed and then take the action, and this process takes time. In the case of fiscal policy, that lag can sometimes be very long. Both houses of Congress have to vote on tax and expenditure policies and the president has to sign a bill. Often there is no action taken.

decision lag
The time it takes for policymakers to initiate a change in policy following their recognition of the need for a policy action.

In the case of monetary policy, the process is typically much shorter. The Fed's governors (who control the Fed) are not elected officials and there are only a few of them. This can provide an advantage in speedy action. However, even the Fed will take some time to decide its actions, because the open-market committee has to meet and vote to change a policy stance. Further, while the Fed is operationally free to pursue monetary policy, it may well be affected by current political constraints so even Fed policy is subject to lags. The recognition lag and the decision lag together make up what is called the **inside lag**—the time it takes the policymaking apparatus to move.

Following the inside lag, there is an **outside lag**—the time before the policy actually takes effect. A tax cut will only boost demand once people know their paychecks will be affected. Monetary policy has to change interest rates and then change investment expenditures. The full effects of monetary and fiscal policy will depend on the working through of the multiplier and financial-market adjustments.

The outside lag also depends on expectations. We saw in Chapter 8 that, if participants in financial markets do not think that a change in monetary policy is going to last very long, then long-term interest rates may not change by very much when short-term interest rates change. If this is the case, then the effect of a monetary-policy change on investment and output will be small until expectations have changed and long-term rates have moved. Expectations can also affect the fiscal-policy lag. If people know that legislation has been passed to cut taxes, they may even go out and spend more before the policy has actually altered their disposable incomes. If, on the other hand, people believe that a tax cut is only going to be temporary, then they may regard it as a change in transitory income and not change their spending much at all. Since the outside lag depends on expectations, it will be variable and uncertain.

The combination of inside and outside lags makes it difficult to fine-tune the economy. A boom or a slump will certainly have some time to develop before offsetting policy actions can be taken, even assuming that such action is taken. But the problem may be even more severe than that. There is a real risk that, by the time a policy change is activated, it hits the economy at exactly the wrong time.

Timing Problems   An expansionary policy may just be beginning to kick in when the economy has already turned around and is heading back to full employment on its own. The policy action may then precipitate too strong a boom and an acceleration of inflation. Figure 13–1 illustrates the potential problem caused by lags. The dark line traces a stylized cyclical fluctuation in output, and we assume that the economy would follow this path over time in the absence of any policy intervention. Suppose that, at a point in time, the economy is already in a recession with actual output below potential output (point A in the figure). Making the most favorable case for stabilization policy, we assume that an ideal policy would drive actual output toward potential output more quickly and with a less severe recession than if the economy were left to itself.

The alternative paths of adjustment are shown in the figure. If there were no stabilization policies invoked, actual output would reach potential output at a later time (solid line from point A to point C) and with a greater loss of output than it would with an ideal policy (dashed line from point A to point B).

Unfortunately, the inside lag means the recession has continued and worsened (point A to point D) before an expansionary policy has been enacted. The outside lag means policy actions taken too late (at point D) do not have a major impact on the economy until well after the business cycle has caused actual income to recover

---

inside lag
The time it takes for policymakers to initiate a policy change following a change in economic conditions that requires policy action. This is the sum of the recognition lag and the decision lag.

outside lag
The time it takes for a policy action to take effect after it has been initiated.

FIGURE 13–1
Lags in
Recognition and
Implementation
Can Lead to
Policies That
Worsen
Fluctuations

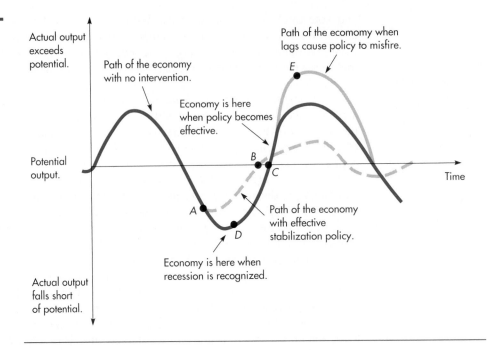

through potential output (point *C*) and beyond. The effect of the policy is to generate a boom (beyond point *C* to point *E*) where output greatly exceeds potential and inflation accelerates. This is a larger and more costly expansion than would have occurred without policy. The effect of policies that misfired is that attempts at stabilization policy have actually increased the amplitude of the business cycle.

How serious is this problem of policy misfiring? In the past, policies have been applied at the wrong time. When John F. Kennedy was elected, he proposed an expansionary fiscal policy to move the economy out of recession. Part of this took effect fairly quickly; but the tax cuts that he proposed did not take effect until 1964, after his death and after the time that they were needed. The 1964 tax cut was one factor pushing the economy into the inflationary boom of the later 1960s. In 1992, President Clinton was elected on a promise to improve the economy. He proposed a stimulus package to Congress in 1993, but Congress voted it down because of concerns about the budget deficit. It turned out not to be needed, since the economy grew strongly without the package.

In general, fiscal policy requiring legislative change is difficult to use for counter-cyclical purposes, because of the lags involved and the dangers of making the cycle worse. The lag problem is less severe with monetary policy. The Fed can act quickly, its board members are regularly briefed on the state of the economy, and Fed actions will have immediate effects on interest rates and fairly quick effects on the economy. If recessions turned around quickly on their own, then it would be a mistake to try and offset them with stabilization policy. But since recessions often lead to persistent excess unemployment, it makes sense to use some combination of monetary and fiscal policies to restore full employment. However, since most of the burden for stabilization policy will fall on monetary policy, the Fed's freedom of action is constrained by the need for inflation to be kept at an acceptable level.

automatic stabilizers
Statutory provisions that automatically vary taxes or expenditures in response to changes in the economy.

Automatic Stabilizers   Policies that require actions by policymakers are called "discretionary policies." And the recognition lag and the decision lag that make it difficult to regularly use discretionary fiscal policy can lead to policy misfiring. Moreover, fiscal policy has been caught up in the debate over the deficit and the appropriate size of the federal government, so there is little prospect of using discretionary fiscal policy to stabilize the economy, even if such use were warranted. That does not mean that fiscal policy has no role to play. There are statutory provisions that automatically vary taxes or expenditures in response to changes in the economy. These automatic fiscal stabilizers operate without requiring action by policymakers and they help the economy to avoid booms and slumps. There are two main types:

1. *Automatic changes in tax receipts.* People with very low incomes pay little federal income tax, so, as their incomes rise, tax receipts rise. To the degree that the personal income tax is progressive, the fraction of income paid in taxes rises as income rises. This means that a boom will automatically raise federal tax receipts and act as countercyclical fiscal policy. When we studied the multiplier, we saw that its size is reduced by income taxes. This reduction of the multiplier reflects the automatic stabilization of the economy through taxes.

2. *Unemployment compensation and other transfer payments.* In a recession, unemployment rises along with the fall in income. Unemployed workers receive unemployment insurance. This transfer payment, which partially sustains income, is an automatic countercyclical fiscal policy.

In 1978–79, when unemployment was fairly low, about $9 billion a year was paid in unemployment benefits. During 1982, when there was a deep recession, nearly $24 billion was paid.

Aside from workers who are laid off, there is a constant flow of people in and out of the labor force. Mothers with children may decide to look for work. Retirees may find that they need more money and come back into the labor force to look for part-time work. During recessions, it is harder for these labor-force entrants to find jobs. But there are transfer programs that are designed to help them—welfare and Social Security. During recessions, more people will rely on these transfer programs to sustain their incomes.

In 1989, all transfer payments by government were equal to 11.7 percent of GDP. In 1992 this figure rose to 14.1 percent, providing a significant offset to the weak demand and slow growth of that year.

Goals and Instruments   If stabilization policy is going to be effective, policymakers need to have control over the policy tools or instruments necessary to achieve their goals. Since policymakers are required to deal with a number of different goals for the economy (reduce unemployment, fight inflation, lower interest rates, encourage saving, raise or lower the real exchange rate, and so on) they need to have control over more than one policy instrument (i.e., bank reserves, income taxes, budget expenditures). There has to be a match between goals and instruments, because a policymaker cannot cause one instrument (say, the growth of bank reserves) to both increase and decrease at the same time. The classic example is one that is already very familiar. Keeping inflation low may require monetary policymakers to reduce the growth of bank reserves, ultimately driving the level of output below potential output. But the goal of stabilizing output and employment may require an expansionary monetary policy that would cause the Fed to increase the growth of bank reserves.

Many suggestions have been offered over the years for adding an additional instrument to solve the trade-off dilemma. The most popular has been wage-and-price guidelines or controls. In the early 1960s, President Kennedy introduced wage-and-price guidelines, hoping to prevent inflation from accelerating. He had a major showdown with the steel industry and persuaded its management to roll back price increases, even though he had no power to force a change. A few months later the industry restored the price increases.

In 1971, President Nixon introduced mandatory wage-and-price controls and kept them in force until 1973, although he loosened them even before this. These mandatory controls were very effective in reducing inflation temporarily, but they failed badly in the longer run as inflation bounced back as soon as the controls were relaxed. Since then there have been proposals to give incentives for wage-and-price restraint—so called tax-based incomes policies. But there has not been much recent support for such ideas.

The Fed and President Reagan decided that it was better to pay the prices of high unemployment as the way to reduce inflation. Economists in the Bush administration accepted the idea that a compromise or trade-off between conflicting goals was the only way to deal with the problem of using stabilization policy when there are more goals than instruments.

Given the difficulties associated with forecasting and policy lags, however, not to mention the problems created by inflation, it is clear that trying to fine-tune policy is difficult or impossible. There are bound to be fluctuations in the economy that the policymakers cannot eliminate. Rather than trying to do this, they should concentrate on creating a good policy regime, one where their actions are seen as consistent and sustained. This will make the policy actions more effective when they are taken and allow policy do what it does best, namely help the economy to avoid serious recessions or excessive inflation.

We turn next to a discussion of what is needed to create a successful policy regime.

CREATING A POLICY REGIME FOR STABILITY

In the next section of this chapter, we will argue that attempts to give a "quick fix" to macroeconomic policy may have worked for a while during past periods when private decision makers were less sophisticated or less informed. But in today's economy where information is widely disseminated such policies will not work well.

In making this case we draw together elements from prior chapters. In Chapter 8 we looked at the working of monetary policy when there are different interest rates. We use this analysis now to show how monetary policy will be ineffective when it is temporary, but much more effective when it is credible and sustained. In Chapter 9, we showed how consumption depends on permanent income and not on temporary income. We will see here this leads to the conclusion that temporary fiscal policies will be ineffective. In Chapters 6 and 12 we saw that short-term policies to fight inflation were ineffective. There is no need to go over that point again here. We simply note that it reinforces the conclusion we have already drawn about the importance of credible and sustained policies.

The Policy Regime

policy regime
Describes the general pattern of policy actions that are taken in response to varying economic conditions.

In much of this book, we have examined the impact of isolated policy changes, looking, for example, at what happens following an increase in taxes, or a decrease in the money supply. But we have also explored the importance of expectations. These affect long-term interest rates, permanent income and the position of the output–inflation trade-ff. And people's expectations take into account what policymakers are likely to do in the future—that is to say, the nature of the policy regime.

The **policy regime** is a way of describing the pattern of policy actions that are taken in response to varying economic conditions. For example, if there is an increase in inflation, perhaps this normally leads to some tightening of monetary policy. If there is an increase in unemployment, perhaps this normally leads to some expansionary move on fiscal policy. Based on observing policy actions over time, people form expectations about future policy. Some sophisticated players in financial markets may follow Fed policy in excruciating detail to determine the nature of the policy regime. Many ordinary citizens have little interest in policy actions, although they may have a general sense that steps will be taken to counter adverse movements in inflation or unemployment.

If a single policy action is analogous to the weather over a short time, then the policy regime is analogous to the climate. One hot summer does not make us change our expectations about next year's summer weather, but several hot summers in a row and we start to worry about whether the climate is changing. Similarly, if the Fed were always to follow expansionary policies when the unemployment rate was above 7 percent, then this will create the expectation that such a response has become part of the normal policy regime.

Since we have seen in Chapter 8 that long-term interest rates depend on people's expectations about future short-term rates, it follows that the effectiveness of monetary policy depends on the nature of the policy regime. We see now how that works.

The Ineffectiveness of a Policy Change That Is Expected to Be Temporary   It is widely believed that, if the Fed tries to fine-tune the economy (make small adjustments in aggregate demand that keep income near some target level of income) by using short-term monetary contractions or expansions, then it will find that its efforts are not effective. Why is that?

Suppose the economy has been experiencing relative stability for some time—income, inflation, interest rates, and the rate of growth of the money supply have undergone only minor fluctuations. Now suppose that, in this stable environment, the Fed wants to trim back aggregate demand. The Fed decreases its open-market purchases of T bills, thereby bringing about a reduction in the growth of the nominal money supply. Since there is no immediate change in the rate of inflation, the slowdown of the growth of the nominal money supply means there has been a contraction of the real money supply.

With a stable economy, investors, cash managers, and many other members of the economy could easily believe that this action does not mean the Fed has decided to pursue a sustained contractionary monetary policy. Rather, there could be an expectation that the monetary contraction is only temporary. There has been no perceived change in the policy regime.

The policy regime is like the climate. It indicates the way in which the Fed normally responds to economic situations. People form expectations about the climate on the basis of fairly long-run experience. An unusual turn in the weather, such as a hot day in winter, does not change people's view of the climate. Similarly, if people have learned that the Fed normally tries to maintain a full-employment economy, a shift to monetary contraction in an otherwise stable economy does not change their view of the policy regime. They will expect the Fed to reverse and change policy rather quickly.

Given that the policy is seen as temporary, what will happen to the economy? The monetary contraction will certainly affect the money market. There will be a rise in the short-term nominal interest rate. But the rise in this rate will not necessarily generate a corresponding increase in the long-term rates and the cost of funds. Let's see why.

First, since the monetary-policy contraction is seen as temporary, higher short-term rates will not change expectations about future short-term nominal rates of interest in the economy. Bondholders will see the current rise in short-term rates as a spike and not a sustained increase. They will not attempt major adjustments in their portfolios and so the interest rate on long-term Treasury bonds will rise only a little.

Second, a monetary contraction that is seen as temporary is unlikely to have much effect on the risk premium. While risk premiums are hard to predict, it is unlikely a policy change that is seen as temporary will bring on a major or prolonged recession or a financial crisis.

Third, a contractionary monetary policy may lead to some small reduction in the expected rate of inflation. But as we saw in Chapter 6, the expected rate of inflation changes only slowly in response to policy moves, and it will change hardly at all in response to a temporary policy contraction. There will likely be little change in inflationary expectations as a result of this temporary policy shift.

Since neither long-term nominal rates nor expected inflation changes by very much, *the temporary monetary contraction does not have much effect on the cost of funds.* The *LM* schedule moves as a result of a temporary monetary contraction but the cost of funds changes very little. A small change in the cost of funds can still have some effect on investment demand. There will be some projects that are postponed as a result of even a small change in the cost of funds. But since the purchase of capital goods involves a long-term commitment and is financed with long-term borrowing, *the effect of a small change in the cost of funds will itself be small.*

FIGURE 13–2
A Monetary Con-
traction Expected
to Be Temporary

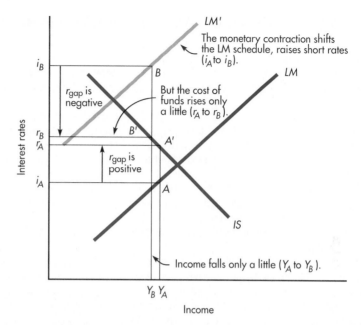

A temporary monetary contraction has only a small effect on income.

Temporary gyrations of the money supply will cause gyrations in short-term interest rates but will not have much effect on investment demand or on income.

Figure 13–2 illustrates how a monetary contraction that is seen as temporary may have little effect on income. We use the concept of the interest-rate gap that was introduced in Chapter 8. The economy is initially in equilibrium at points A and A', with income Y_A. The interest-rate gap is positive, the cost of funds is r_A, and the short-term nominal rate of interest is i_A.

The contractionary monetary policy shifts the LM schedule to LM' and raises the short-term nominal rate of interest to i_B. But since this increase in short rates is seen as temporary, the cost of funds rises only slightly (to r_B). The economy is now in equilibrium at points B and B' and income has fallen only a little to Y_B. A large increase in short rates has not had a large effect on either the cost of funds or on income.

The Effectiveness of a Policy Change That Is Expected to Be Sustained   The conclusion about the ineffectiveness of a temporary shift in monetary policy can be contrasted with the effectiveness of a monetary contraction that is believed to be sustained. Consider the case where the Fed has established a policy regime under which monetary contractions are not quickly reversed, even if a contraction results in recession. When there is a reduction in the real money supply, people will believe that the contraction is just the beginning of a sustained policy of tight money. As a result,

Expectations Are Sometimes Revised Quickly in the Capital Market

The recession of 1990–91 was followed by a very slow recovery. During this recovery, the Fed was following an easy money policy that pushed the interest rate on three-month Treasury bills to 3 percent or even below. At first, the bond market was skeptical of the Fed's intentions, believing that short-term rates would soon be increased because the Fed would again become concerned about inflation. The interest rate on 10-year Treasury bonds stayed close to 8 percent.

After short-term interest rates remained low through 1993, however, bond markets began to believe that rates would stay low and the 10-year bond rate fell to 5.33 percent in October of 1993. This belief in low rates was not held with great confidence, however. In late 1993 and early 1994, bond markets were looking every day for signs of increasing inflation or signs that the Fed was going to raise rates.

The markets did not have long to wait. The economy grew very strongly in the last quarter of 1993 and continued to grow well in the first quarter of 1994. The Fed Chairman Alan Greenspan announced that he was concerned about the potential for inflation and he was raising short-term interest rates, albeit only by a little. The bond market reacted very strongly indeed. Long-term bond prices fell and their interest rate jumped to over 7 percent. The rise in the long rate was actually more than the rise in the short rate! In response to the rise in interest rates, the stock market tumbled.

Today, the Fed has the power to raise long rates just by announcing its intention to change to a more contractionary monetary policy. This in contrast to 1991–92 when the Fed was trying to get the economy moving and long rates remained high. The Fed can change expectations rather quickly in financial markets when it *increases* interest rates. Its ability to lower long-term rates is much weaker. It has established itself as an inflation fighter, not as a promoter of growth.

the policy will be effective. One or more of the three conditions linking a rise in short-term nominal rates with a rise in the cost of funds will hold. Expected future short rates will likely rise along with the current short-term rate. In financial markets, all securities will trade at a lower price/higher interest rate, because everyone expects higher interest rates to last. Thus, in this case, the rise in the current short-term rate of interest will be accompanied by an increase in expected future short rates with no tendency for the yield curve to flatten.

In terms of the risk premium, a policy of monetary contraction that is expected to be sustained will raise concerns about a recession and a possible financial crunch and will increase the probability of defaults—both for businesses and for household mortgages.

As a result of the stability of the yield curve and the increase in the risk premium, therefore, the interest rate premium will not fall and may well rise in response to a sustained monetary contraction. The cost of funds will rise along with the short-term nominal rate.

In terms of expected inflation, a strategy of long-term monetary restraint will certainly reduce expected inflation somewhat. Some economists believe that expected inflation will fall quickly if the Fed follows a credible policy of sustained monetary contraction. We think this view is overly optimistic, but at the least there would be some decline in expected inflation in this case.

TABLE 13–2
The Links between a Rise in the Short-Term Nominal Rate of Interest and a Rise in the Cost of Funds

	A Monetary Contraction That Is Expected to Be Temporary	A Monetary Contraction That Is Expected to Be Prolonged
Short-term nominal interest rate	Rises	Rises
Expected future short rates	No change	Rise
Risk premium	Falls	Rises or stays the same
Expected inflation	Little Change	Falls
Cost of funds	Little change	Rises

It follows, therefore, that *in the face of a sustained monetary contraction, the increase in the long-term nominal rate of interest will probably result in an increase in the cost of funds.* The belief that the monetary policy will be sustained, contributes to the transmission of the Fed's policy action from the money market to the goods market. Table 13–2 summarizes the different effects of a policy-induced rise in short-term nominal rates that is perceived as temporary with one that is perceived to be sustained.

Figure 13–3 illustrates how a monetary contraction that is seen as sustained will have a large effect on income. The economy is initially in equilibrium at points A and A', with income Y_A, just as in the case shown in Figure 13–2. The interest-rate gap is positive, the cost of funds is r_A, and the short-term nominal rate of interest is i_A.

The contractionary monetary policy shifts the *LM* schedule to *LM'* and raises the short-term nominal rate of interest to i_c. But since this increase in short rates is seen as sustained, the cost of funds also rises to r_B. The interest-rate gap has become smaller, but remains positive. The economy is now in equilibrium at points C and C' and income has fallen substantially, to Y_C.

Comparing this case to the previous one, the monetary contraction that is seen as sustained has increased the cost of funds much more, inducing a larger reduction in investment demand and a larger reduction in income than when the contraction was temporary.

When it formulates its policies, the Fed needs to take account of expectations. If financial-market participants come to learn that changes in the direction of monetary policy will be reversed quickly, then they will regard any policy move as merely temporary. This will make the Fed's policies relatively ineffective. But, if financial-market participants learn that when the Fed embarks on a change of direction for monetary policy, the Fed usually makes a commitment to sustain the change over a considerable period or until the Fed's objectives (e.g., reducing inflation or stimulating demand) have been realized, then financial markets will take Fed actions seriously and these actions will become more effective. The Fed must establish the credibility of its policies for those policies to be effective.

**FIGURE 13–3
A Monetary
Contraction
Expected to Be
Sustained**

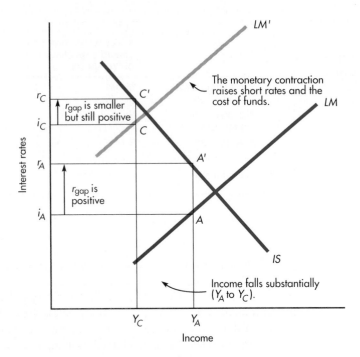

A sustained monetary contraction has a substantial effect on income.

Permanent and Temporary Fiscal Policies

We have used a framework for understanding fiscal policy in which government purchases of goods and services go directly into aggregate demand, while tax policy affects disposable income and hence consumption demand. We have already pointed to some pitfalls in using fiscal policy for stabilization purposes. In particular, we noted that fiscal policy today is largely frozen by concerns over the budget deficit. Moreover, we found that in an open economy the increase in aggregate demand caused by an expansionary fiscal policy will eventually be dissipated into a trade deficit.

In principle, fiscal policy can make use of either changes in government purchases of goods and services or changes in tax rates. But generally it is difficult to use variations in government purchases as part of a systematic stabilization policy. Coming up with ways for the government to spend money just for the sake of it is a recipe for wasteful programs. Generally, it will be changes in tax rates that are part of the regime of stabilization policy, if any fiscal policy is to be used systematically for this purpose. If that is the case, will it matter whether tax-rate changes are thought to be temporary or permanent? We use the permanent income framework to examine that question.

The Effect of a Temporary Tax Cut   As we saw in Chapter 9, people do not base their consumption decisions just on the income they receive in a single quarter or a single year. Instead, they form an expectation of their own permanent income, a concept that roughly corresponds to the long-run average level of income they expect to receive. The word *permanent* is the one usually used, but it is a bit misleading. Nobody really knows what their income will be over their entire lifetime, and so most people form an expectation of what their income will be over the next few years, and they base their consumption on that. In practice, households often look at what their incomes have been over the past few years and extrapolate that forward.[9]

To give a simple example, suppose that a household bases its consumption on the average level of income it expects over the next three years; that is, the next 12 quarters.

$$Y^{\text{perm}} = 1/12 \ [Y_1 + Y_2 + \ldots \ldots + Y_{12}]$$

In this equation, Y_1 is the expected income in the next quarter, Y_2 is the expected income in the quarter after that, and so on. To make the example specific, suppose the household expects to receive on average a disposable income of $16,000 per quarter, so the household's permanent income is $16,000. Assuming this family consumes 85 percent of its income, with the rest applied to a pension fund or other saving, consumption will be $13,600 a quarter.

Congress now passes a tax cut to stimulate the economy; but it is not clear how long the tax cut will remain in effect. Some taxpayers may not consider the likely duration of the tax cut; but for those who do, their expectations matter for stabilization policy. For example, if the public perceives the tax cut to be temporary—in effect for only one-quarter of one year—they will expect only a one-quarter boost to disposable income. The effect will be more like receiving a bonus instead of an increase in salary. A tax cut thought to be very short run was enacted in 1975 in an attempt to alleviate the recession the economy was in at the time. In our example, assume that the tax cut will increase the household's disposable income by $600 for one quarter.

What does the permanent income theory tell us about the impact of the tax cut? Averaged over 12 quarters, the increase in permanent income works out to be only $50 a quarter ($600/12). With a propensity to consume of 0.85, this would boost consumption by only $42.50 a quarter. Even added over millions of families, the boost to aggregate demand will be modest.

The Effect of a Tax Cut Thought to Be Sustained   Suppose now that Congress decides to cut tax rates and makes it clear that the rates will remain at the new lower level for three years. Assume for our example, that the tax cut will increase disposable income by the same $600 per quarter that we used earlier. In this case, however, the permanent income of the household will be perceived to rise by the full $600 and consumption will rise by $510. Added over millions of households, this would give a significant boost to aggregate demand.

---

[9] Of course, for someone forced into early retirement or someone who has just made partner at a law firm, past income may not be a good guide to the future path of income.

We have found that a tax cut seen to be of long duration will have a much bigger impact on aggregate demand than a tax cut seen to be only temporary.[10] But it is important to remember that, to maintain the credibility of a sustained tax cut, the cut has to actually remain in force for a considerable time. This is much more expensive than a temporary cut in its impact on the budget and the deficit. The sustained tax cut is providing a boost of $7,200 to the household in our example over the 12 quarters ($600 × 12). Added over millions of households, that would create a large increase in the budget deficit and the total federal debt. It is not surprising that the effect is bigger. The real lesson here is that there is no cheap way to give a quick boost to aggregate demand by a very short-term tax cut. Congress signaled that the cut was going to be temporary in 1968 and again in 1975 and the policies were largely ineffective in both cases.[11]

If tax cuts are ever to be part of the regime of policy responses to recession and high unemployment, then the tax cuts will end up being expensive. The more temporary a tax cut is, the bigger it has to be to have a significant impact on aggregate demand. The more sustained a tax cut is, the more effective it is, but the greater is its impact on the budget deficit.

We have given in this chapter some of the reasons why stabilization policy is difficult. It is hard to know where the economy is and where it is going. And when a policy change is decided, it cannot be a quick fix—it has to be a sustained and credible policy. Given this, one can ask whether stabilization policy is worth it. One way to look at this is to see if the economy has become more stable since such policies were introduced. We turn to this issue now.

HAS THE ECONOMY BECOME MORE STABLE?

Many problems are involved in using stabilization policy, including lags, disagreement over direction, and the conflict between inflation and unemployment. Sometimes policymakers find themselves deliberately adding to the variability of the economy by trying to push the economy into a recession to combat inflation. Despite these considerations, it is important to make a broad-brush comparison of the economy before and after the initiation of stabilization policy. The Employment Act of 1946 specified that policy should be used to maintain price stability and full employment. In spite of the apparent contradiction embedded in the act, this date is generally taken to be the starting point of stabilization policies. Is there any evidence that the economy has actually become more stable? Since we are looking at historical data, we look at the Gross National Product (GNP) rather than the Gross Domestic Product (GDP).

---

[10] Suppose we had been unaware of the permanent income hypothesis, and we had used a simple consumption function like the ones we used in the first half of this book. If the marginal propensity to consume had been taken to be 0.85, we would expect a boost of $510 in consumption following the tax cut. In other words, our discussion of fiscal policy in earlier chapters implicitly assumed we were talking about tax-rate changes that the public thought to be permanent.

[11] The cuts in tax rates that were made in the early 1980s were seen as sustained and these helped the growth of the economy. The problem with these tax cuts, however, was that they created a structural deficit that is with us still.

The Barro Hypothesis: No Effect of Tax Cuts

Harvard economist Robert Barro has suggested that, if the permanent income hypothesis is carried to its logical conclusion, tax cuts will have no impact on aggregate demand.* His idea was first suggested by David Ricardo in the 19th century and is sometimes called the "Barro–Ricardo hypothesis." Barro bases his hypothesis on the assumption that people estimate their permanent income not just on their expected income for a few years into the future but for their expected incomes over their lifetimes. In fact, he argues that people even think about the incomes their children will earn and how large the bequests will be that they leave to their children. Households consume today, he says, based on the whole future path of their own incomes and their families' incomes.

Take Barro's assumption and see what it implies for the impact of tax cuts. If Congress passes a tax cut with no other change in policy, then this will increase the deficit. This raises household disposable income today, but in the future the government will have to pay interest on the bonds that have been issued to finance the deficit. And households are liable for the taxes that will have to be collected in the future to pay the interest or to pay off the bonds. Cutting taxes today, says Barro, is equivalent to raising taxes tomorrow. And since people look at their permanent income over the very long term, they will realize that the tax cuts today have not raised their permanent income at all.† Once we open the door to the permanent income hypothesis, Barro argues, we conclude that tax cuts have no effect on aggregate demand.

Is Barro correct?‡ We think not. First, it is very implausible to assume that households routinely look far, far into the future when making decisions about current consumption. Many people concern themselves with the future only to the extent of participating in a company pension plan, if at all, and simply spend the rest of their income. It is already a strong assumption to suggest that people look three years ahead. Second, even for those people who in fact carefully revise their notions of their permanent income, that revision is more likely to be based on changes in one's own circumstances, such as a promotion or an inheritance, rather than on changes in governmental policies. How many families have their own in-house policy wonk? Finally, Barro's model of the economy is very different from the one we have used in this book (he has supported the equilibrium business-cycle approach that we describe in Chapter 15). Barro assumes that a tax cut today must leave people with lower income in the future. But we have argued that recessions are times of market failure, so a successful fiscal policy that moves the economy out of recession will raise people's future income by putting more people to work and raising GDP closer to potential GDP. In fact if the economy starts with a large output gap, a package of monetary and fiscal policies can actually mean lower future budget deficits.

Despite our disagreement with Barro's conclusion, his work has influenced our discussion of fiscal policy. When we criticize structural deficits during periods of high employment, we do so because, as Barro has pointed out, these deficits do not reduce the real tax burden, they simply postpone the need for higher taxes. And his emphasis on evaluating fiscal policy when households look at permanent income has led us to conclude that very short-term tax cuts will have little impact on aggregate demand.

---

* Robert Barro, "Are Government Bonds Net Wealth?" *Journal of Political Economy,* November/December 1974.

† Permanent income in the Barro formulation is based on the present value of all future income receipts—equal to a household's current wealth. If the discount rate used in calculating the present value is equal to the interest rate on government bonds, then the deficit, he argues, will not change the present value of household wealth. His hypothesis is sometimes stated as "government bonds are not net wealth."

‡ Evidence on the Barro hypothesis is reviewed in Lawrence Kotlikoff, *What Determines Saving?* (Cambridge, Mass.: Harvard University Press, 1989).

FIGURE 13–4A
Real Gross National Product, Percentage Changes, Quarterly 1875–1918

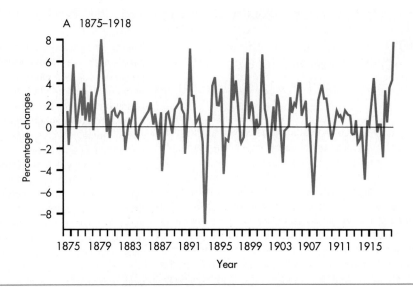

A   1875–1918

Source: Victor Zarnowitz, "Fact and Factors in the Recent Evolution of Business Cycles in the United States," NBER working paper no. 2865 (February 1989). A similar figure was used to illustrate the effects of stabilization policy in Martin Neil Baily, "Stabilization Policy and Private Economic Behavior," *Brookings Papers on Economic Activity,* 1:1978, pp. 11–59.

FIGURE 13–4B
Real Gross National Product, Percentage Changes, Quarterly 1919–1945

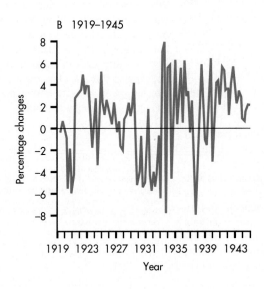

B   1919–1945

Source: Same as for Figure 13–4A.

FIGURE 13-4C
Real Gross National Product, Percentage Changes, Quarterly 1946-1993

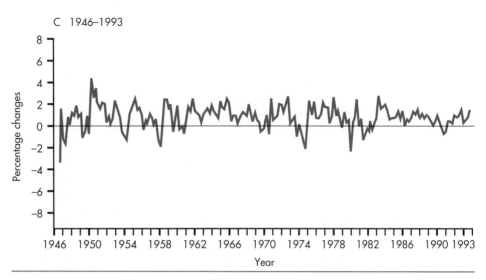

C   1946-1993

Source: Same as for Figure 13-4A.

The magnitude of fluctuations in real GNP provides one indicator of the stability or instability of the overall economy. In three parts, Figure 13-4 shows the rate of growth of GNP over different periods from the 19th century until the 1980s. The reduction in the size of the fluctuations in GNP is dramatic. The period of the Great Depression in the 1930s stand out, but the fluctuations in earlier periods were large, also. The period from 1946 to 1983 is much more stable, despite the problems in dealing with inflation in the 1970s and 1980s.

The simple conclusion from these figures is that stabilization policies, despite their problems, have worked. This conclusion has been challenged on two grounds.

Christina Romer has argued that problems with the data are distorting the results.[12] There were no National Income and Product Accounts prior to World War II and so the figures for real GNP have been pieced together from a variety of different data sources. Romer argues that the way the data were constructed introduced a spurious amount of variablility. If variability in the early figures is due to data problems and not to actual variations in GNP, that suggests instability is the exception rather than the rule for an economy, even one without stabilization policy.

---

[12] Using a highly original approach, she constructs GNP data for the post-1946 period, using the methods that were used for the earlier years. She then compares her new post-1946 numbers with the earlier numbers and concludes that the economy was unstable *only* during the Great Depression. Christina Romer, "Spurious Volatility in Historical Unemployment Data," *Journal of Political Economy* 94 (February 1986), pp. 1–37; "Is the Stabilization of the Postwar Economy a Figment of the Data?" *American Economic Review* 76 (June 1986), pp. 314–34.

Romer's conclusions have themselves been subject to criticism. For example, Charles Schultze looks at several economic series that have been collected continuously over many years and finds that they all individually show sharp reductions of variability after the war. And Nathan Balke and Robert Gordon construct their own estimates of prewar GNP and find that it varies just as much as the official series.[13] The basic conclusion from Figure 13–4 turns out to be correct: The economy has become much more stable.

A second criticism of the conclusion that stabilization policy has reduced economic variability runs as follows: While variability may have been reduced, it was not stabilization policy and certainly not discretionary policy that caused the greater stability. And there is some force to this argument. A detailed examination of the policy actions that were taken show that policy was often misguided.[14] It is argued that the economy has become more stable as the result of a changed economic structure, in spite of mistaken policy actions. The large service sector of the economy, including the government bureaucracy itself, has increased stability.

Conclusions on Stabilization Policy

There is little doubt that the economy is much more stable than it used to be. There are five main reasons for this conclusion. (1) Federal deposit insurance has protected the banking system and the money supply from banking panics. (2) Automatic stabilizers generate fiscal policies that sustain disposable income during recessions and that restrain the growth of disposable income during booms. (3) The structure of the economy has so changed that a smaller fraction of it is in durable-goods manufacturing and agriculture, where fluctuations are most severe. (4) Government policymakers have stepped in on many occasions to offset the cycle, and, even though mistakes have been made, probably they have been smaller or fewer in number in the period since 1946. (5) As a result of all of the preceding reasons, businesses and households have learned that fluctuations are smaller and so their expectations have become more stable and hence so has their behavior.

We have reached three important conclusions in this chapter, and they point in rather different directions. We have found that the economy has become much more stable over time, suggesting the value of stabilization policy. We have found that forecasting the movements of the economy is very difficult and that stabilization can go off track if the timing is wrong. This suggests that policymakers can easily get into trouble. And finally, we have found that short-term temporary policies are not very effective. Policymakers need to establish credibility for sustained policies, so expectations of future interest rates or future tax rates or future inflation rates will work to

---

[13] Charles L. Schultze, *Other Times, Other Places* (Washington D.C.: Brookings Institution, 1986). Nathan S. Balke and Robert J. Gordon, "The Estimation of Prewar Gross National Product: Methodology and New Evidence," *Journal of Political Economy,* February 1989. Another critic of Romer's conclusion is David Weir, "The Reliability of Historical Macroeconomic Data for Comparing Cyclical Stability," *Journal of Economic History,* June 1986.

[14] George L. Perry, "Stabilization Policy and Inflation," in *Setting National Priorities: The Next Ten Years,* ed. Henry Owen and Charles L. Schultze (Washington, D. C.: Brookings Institution, 1976), pp. 271–321.

support the policies and not weaken them. On the one hand, it is easy to make a mistake about policy. On the other hand, it is unwise to change the direction of policy too frequently.

To resolve this conflict, we believe that policymakers should avoid efforts to counter every up and down of the economy. A good and active stabilization policy involves dealing with the serious problems. If there is a serious problem of accelerating inflation, then this becomes evident even without ideal forecasting models, and a credible and sustained policy of contraction can be followed. If the economy is in free-fall in a severe recession then this, too, is evident and a sustained expansionary policy can be followed.

To the extent that policy can do more than deal with the serious problems, it should enhance the working of the automatic stabilizers and should find ways to increase the intrinsic stability of the economy. Automatic stabilizers work even when the forecasters make mistakes. And banking policy, while it should encourage competition, should also maintain safeguards against banking crises.

SUMMARY

* Economists, business managers, financial investors, and government policy makers generate macroeconomic forecasts, attempting to predict the ups and downs of the economy.

* Forecasts based on surveys of business managers and consumers are simple and direct but subject to error, because intentions do not necessarily translate into actions.

* Surveys of forecasts produce consensus predictions, which are more reliable than individual predictions.

* Leading indicators are economic variables that have a history of changing before business-cycle turning points. They have the weaknesses that they do not forecast very far in advance and they sometimes give false predictions.

* An attempt to improve the effectiveness of leading indicators using new statistical methods was a failure, because the 1990 recession was not induced by monetary contraction.

* Econometric forecasting models of the macro economy are based on the statistical estimation of data organized in multiple equations in an attempt to model the workings of the whole economy.

* Problems with forecasting models include failure due to structural changes in the economy as well as difficulties with capturing the effects of expectations.

* Stabilization-policy actions are subject to lags. There is an inside lag, comprised of a recognition lag plus a decision lag. There is an outside lag. The combination of inside and outside lags makes it difficult to fine-tune the economy.

* The timing problem can cause policy to misfire, when it is activated at the wrong time. It can then exacerbate, rather than stabilize, the business cycle.

* Automatic stabilizers avoid some of the problems of discretionary policies. They come into effect more quickly and are automatically tied to the state of the economy.

* The general pattern of policy actions that are taken in response to varying economic conditions is a policy regime. Successful policy regimes must establish the credibility of policy changes, by using sustained policy actions.

* In spite of the mixed record of stabilization policy in practice, the U.S. economy has improved its stability in the period since World War II compared to the prior period.

KEY TERMS AND CONCEPTS

automatic stabilizer, p. 417

coincident indicators, p. 405

decision lag, p. 414

index of leading economic
  indicators, p. 405

inside lag, p. 415

lagging indicators, p. 405

leading indicators, p. 405

outside lag, p. 415

policy regime, p. 419

recognition lag, p. 414

stabilization policies, p. 414

DISCUSSION QUESTIONS AND PROBLEMS

1. Explain the three main approaches to forecasting and assess their strengths and weaknesses.

2. How well did the *Blue Chip* forecasters do in predicting the economy in 1995?

3. Review the series used in the Department of Commerce's index of leading economic indicators. Explain why each might provide information about the future course of the economy and how they might give misleading information.

4. Explain how an econometric forecasting model could go off track if it fails to model expectations correctly.

5. What are the lags that make stabilization policy difficult? Which is likely to be the most important?

6. Temporary monetary policies and temporary fiscal policies are not very effective. Are the reasons the same or different for the two types?

7. Are people in the United States today aware of the problem of the budget deficit? Do they adjust their own saving in response to the deficit? If not, why not?

8. Can we conclude that stabilization policy has made the economy more stable?

MONETARISM: CLASSICAL ROOTS AND CONTEMPORARY IMPLICATIONS

INTRODUCTION

Monetarism
A model of a self-correcting economy. Changes in the money supply are the primary cause of inflation and short-run fluctuations in output.

Monetarism is a view of the aggregate economy that stresses the primacy of changes in the money supply in determining inflation and short-run output fluctuations.[1] A higher growth rate of the money supply means a higher rate of inflation. Monetarists argue that fiscal policy is ineffective as a means of stimulating aggregate demand. Monetarists also argue that expanding the money supply to increase employment and real income is mistaken policy, because, fairly quickly, the only result will be more money chasing the same amount of goods and services— more money simply generates higher prices. They believe that the economy is self-correcting and will insure full employment on its own, and they conclude that government had best pursue a monetary policy that is predictable and unchanging.

The major difference between Monetarism and the models we have presented so far is found in their different assumptions about the short-run behavior of the economy, about the time for the economy to return to full employment following a recession, and specifically about the time it

---

[1] Monetarism is associated most closely with the work of Milton Friedman. See this chapter's box titled ''Monetarism and the Monetarists: Milton Friedman and the Monetary Revolution.'' See also Milton Friedman and Anna J. Schwartz, *A Monetary History of the United States* (Princeton, N.J.: Princeton University Press, 1963); *A Monetary History of the United States: Estimates, Sources and Methods* (New York: NBER, 1963); *The Great Contraction* (Princeton, N.J.: Princeton University Press, 1965); *Monetary Trends in the United States and the United Kingdom* (New York: NBER, 1982). See also Milton Friedman, ed., *Studies in the Quarterly Theory of Money* (Chicago: University of Chicago Press, 1956); Friedman, *A Program for Monetary Stability* (New York: Fordham University Press, 1959); and Friedman, *The Optimum Quantity of Money* (Chicago: Aldine, 1969).

takes for markets to react to changes in the growth of the money supply. The Monetarist model assumes that prices and wages are not very sticky, so markets clear fairly quickly and smoothly.

Monetarism developed in the 1960s and 1970s as an alternative to the Keynesian analysis that had come to dominate macroeconomics following the publication of Keynes' *General Theory* in 1936. Whereas Keynes had rejected the classical model in which output in the short run is wholly determined by equilibrium in the labor market, Monetarists instead built their analysis on classical roots. Whereas some Keynesian writers had emphasized the impact of fiscal policy and played down the importance of monetary policy, Monetarists instead stressed the importance of money and minimized the role for fiscal policy. Since Monetarism is based on classical roots, we begin our discussion of Monetarism by looking at the classical model.

THE CLASSICAL UNDERPINNINGS OF MONETARIST THEORY

classical model
A model of the economy in which all markets clear. Supply and demand in all markets either are in equilibrium or, if disturbed, come quickly back into equilibrium.

The **classical model** is a model of supply and demand where all markets for goods and services are competitive and clear at some set of prices. Similarly, there are competitive markets for the inputs into the production process, and in particular labor is traded like any other commodity at an equilibrium price (the wage rate). The amount of employment is determined in the marketplace and this then determines the amount of production in the economy. Goods and services are produced in factories, office buildings, stores, shopping malls, and all the small and large businesses in the economy. The amount of output that firms can produce, as distinct from how much they choose to produce, is determined by (1) the productive resources that the firm has on hand (including capital, labor, purchased materials, and energy); and (2) the way in which those resources are managed and allocated. In those businesses that buy materials and convert those materials to other products, labor and capital costs are in fact a relatively small fraction of the total cost of production. However, the materials that are so processed were produced by labor and capital in the factory that supplied the materials. There is a chain of production where raw-materials suppliers (e.g., mining operations supplying iron ore) sell to firms that fabricate semifinished goods (e.g., steel mills and metal-stamping companies) which in turn sell to firms that manufacture finished goods (e.g., autos, appliances, and metal furniture). Each firm adds value to the materials it buys from supplying firms. In the aggregate, GDP is the sum of the values added by each firm, and purchased materials are intermediate goods that net out of GDP. The economy's productive capacity (potential output) depends on how much capital and labor are available for production and on the technology used in production. If more capital and labor are used in production, more output can be produced. The classical model of production starts with this relation between output and the inputs used to produce it, a relation described in Chapter 2 by the aggregate production function.

Equation 14–1 shows the aggregate production function under classical assumptions:[2]

$$Y = F(K, N, T_{ECH}) \tag{14-1a}$$

where output (Y) is produced in firms using capital (K), labor (N), and technology (T_{ECH}). Technology refers to the methods used to organize and manage production as well as the technical aspects of the capital equipment used in production.

In this analysis of how the level of output is determined in the short run, capital and technology are held constant and only the labor inputs varies:

$$Y = F(\overline{K}, N, \overline{T}_{ECH}) \tag{14-1b}$$

In this case, the production function relates total output to the total amount of labor employed. Since capital and technology are assumed constant, we can drop them from the function for simplicity:

$$Y = F(N) \tag{14-1c}$$

Output (Y) rises with increases in total employment (N) subject to diminishing returns. As shown in Figure 14–1, this assumes that more workers are required to produce more output—increases in employment lead to increases in output (point A to point B, point B to point C) along the production function. Furthermore, because of diminishing returns, the gain in output that results from more labor (N_0 to N_1 to N_2) declines as firms employ more labor. This is shown in the figure by seeing that ($Y_2 - Y_1$) is smaller than ($Y_1 - Y_0$).

The Demand for Labor

While the production function describes how much labor is needed to produce a certain level of output, it does not describe the decision about how much labor to hire. That depends on how much labor costs and how much output the firm wants to produce. In the classical model, the amount of labor demanded and the amount of output firms wish to produce are determined together, depending on the contribution of labor to the profitability of the firm.

Classical economists assumed that firms are competitive profit-maximizers. This means they decide how much to produce by comparing the extra (marginal) revenue from additional output with the extra (marginal) cost of production. Selling more output increases a firm's revenue and, for firms in competitive markets, marginal revenue is simply equal to the price charged per unit of output times the number of units. If an extra unit of output is sold for $10, then the marginal revenue from one extra unit of output produced is $10. If two extra units are produced, the marginal revenue is $20. (For firms that are not competitive, the price will change with the level of output. Marginal revenue is then no longer equal to price.)

---

[2] This is the same equation we used in Chapter 2 (Equation 2–1), except that in this chapter, the assumption is made that output (Y) and potential output (Y^P) are equal, even in the short run.

FIGURE 14-1
The Aggregate Production Function

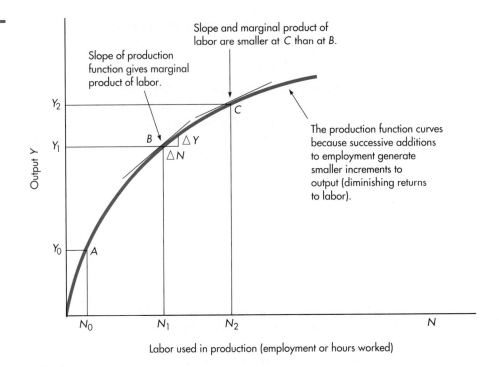

Labor used in production (employment or hours worked)

By producing and selling more, firms can increase their revenues. But firms do not attempt to hire more and more workers and produce as much as is possible, because of diminishing returns to labor. Hiring more workers adds to total labor costs, and the increment to employment generates progressively smaller increments to output. This eventually eliminates any additional profit from further hiring. The marginal cost of production is the amount of wages paid to produce one extra unit of output. Marginal costs rise with successive increases in hiring and output, because the labor requirement per unit of output rises.

As long as marginal cost is less than the price of the product, more output is produced and more labor is hired. If marginal cost is above price, then the firm has hired too much labor and will cut its employment and output. When marginal cost equals price, then the firm has hired just the amount of labor and is producing just the amount of output that maximizes its profit.

We can illustrate how this condition determines the demand for labor with a figure and equations. In Figure 14-1 we showed the relation between additions to employment and additions to output. If at any level of output (such as point *B*), employment increases (ΔN), then the increment to output (ΔY) is the difference between the amount of output at two points along the production function. The ratio of the two is the **marginal product of labor** (*MPL*), which is the additional output that results from hiring additional labor. For small changes in employment, the marginal product of labor is approximated by the slope of the line through point *B* in the figure. The

marginal product of labor
The additional output that results from employing additional labor.

flattening of the slope as employment rises illustrates the declining marginal productivity of labor due to diminishing returns. Equation 14–2 also shows the marginal product of labor as the ratio of the increments to output and labor:

$$\text{Marginal product of labor} = MPL = \frac{\Delta Y}{\Delta N} \tag{14–2}$$

For a competitive firm the increase in revenue received from hiring extra labor is equal to the extra output produced by the extra labor times the price per unit ($P \times \Delta Y$). The marginal cost incurred in producing the increment to output is equal to the extra wages paid out ($W \times \Delta N$). Equation 14–3 shows the condition under which a firm will have hired the amount of labor that maximizes its profit:

Increase in revenue from producing ΔY of extra output	$= P \times \Delta Y$
Increase in cost from adding N to employment to product ΔY	$= W \times \Delta N$
Condition for profit maximization	$= P \times \Delta Y = W \times \Delta N$

Dividing by P and by ΔN gives an equivalent condition for profit maximization:

$$\frac{\Delta Y}{\Delta N} = \frac{W}{P} \tag{14–3}$$

A firm has set the level of employment that maximizes its profit when the marginal product of labor ($\Delta Y/\Delta N$) *equals the real wage* (*W/P*). Whenever the marginal product exceeds the real wage, the firm hires more workers. For example, a bicycle company sells bikes at a price that yields $100 over and above material cost. Hiring another metal worker adds five bikes per week to production. The firm has hired to the profit-maximizing–output level if metal workers earn $500 per week. The real wage is $500/$100 or five bikes per week, which is just equal the marginal product of labor. The bicycle company hires workers until the last worker it hires adds five bikes per week to production and costs the firm wages worth five bikes per week. Having reached this point, the bicycle company then stops hiring.

The condition given in Equation 14–3 describes the hiring decision of a particular firm. In the classical model, this relationship is taken as representative of the economy as a whole and used to determine the aggregate demand for labor in the economy. Total employment increases and the marginal product of labor falls until it equals the real wage prevailing in the economy. The *aggregate demand for labor, N^d,* simply depends on the real wage:

$$\text{Labor demand} = N^d\left(\frac{W}{P}\right) \tag{14–4}$$

A low real wage is required to induce firms to hire a lot of labor. A high real wage will lead firms to keep their employment low. *In the classical model, the quantity of labor demanded in the economy increases when the real wage declines. The quantity of labor demanded decreases when the real wage increases.*

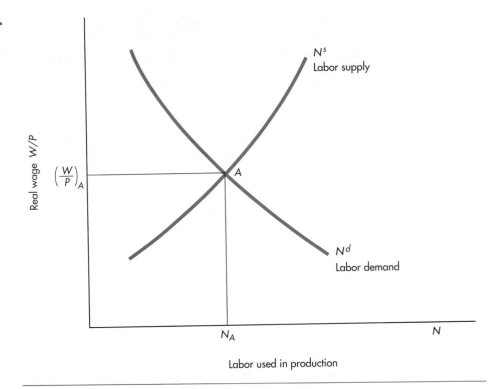

FIGURE 14–2
The Supply of and Demand for Labor and Labor-Market Equilibrium

In Figure 14–2, the labor-demand relationship in the labor market is illustrated by a downward-sloping demand schedule, N^d. Firms hire workers by paying them the value of their marginal contribution to output. The value of labor's marginal contribution to output (the wage paid) and the amount of labor employed depend on how labor is supplied as well as on the demand for labor services.

The classical model of the demand for labor is oversimplified because, among other things, it assumes firms are perfectly competitive and can sell all the output they want at some given market price. But despite this, the model has direct relevance to a modern economy. If real wages rise with no offsetting improvements in technology and productivity, then employment will in fact suffer.

The Supply of Labor

The classical economists used a labor-supply model based on the decisions individuals make about whether to participate in the labor force—that is, whether to look for paid employment. In that model, people decide if they wish to seek work in the market for a wage or do something else—such as looking after their homes without receiving a wage or simply pursuing other activities. The classical model of labor supply argues that higher wages induce more people to decide to seek work in the marketplace, or, for hours worked per employee to increase.

When people are making their decisions about work, at what wage do they look? Wages are expressed in dollars per hour (nominal wages). But people are not interested in working for dollars just for the sake of dollars; they want to buy goods and services with those dollars. *Workers who are making rational decisions about work will look at the money or nominal wage* (W) *in relation to the price level* (P). Specifically, if the price level were to double, then the nominal wage would have to double to induce the same supply of labor. This construction assumes that potential workers have an accurate measure of the price level that they use to adjust the **nominal wage** so they can react to a **real wage.** As shown in Equation 14–5:

nominal wage
The average wage measured in current dollars.

$$\text{Labor supply} = N^s\!\left(\frac{W}{P}\right) \tag{14–5}$$

In the classical model the supply of labor depends on the real wage. The quantity of labor supplied increases when the real wage increases and decreases when the real wage decreases. In Figure 14–2, the labor-supply relationship is shown as the upward-sloping supply schedule.

real wage
The average wage measured in constant dollars; that is, after adjustment for inflation.

When this classical model of labor supply is applied to a modern economy in the Monetarist or equilibrium–business-cycle models, the decision about *when* to work is stressed. If wages are good in a particular year, some people will decide to work in that year and quit the next year. These intertemporal choices about labor supply are also relevant for seasonal employment changes. Employment and output are much higher in the period up to and including Christmas. Job opportunities are good then, and many people who are not regularly employed take short-term employment.

Equilibrium Output and the Labor Market

The labor market clears (comes into equilibrium) when labor supply equals labor demand at the equilibrium real wage. Even in equilibrium, some workers remain voluntarily unemployed, because the market wage is lower than the wage they require to enter employment. In Figure 14–2 an equilibrium real wage $[(W/P)_A]$ and level of employment (N_A) are described by the intersection of labor supply and demand (point *A*). This model does not say how the wage level and the price level are determined separately; rather, the classical model of the labor market only determines the ratio of the nominal level of wages and the price level (i.e., the real wage). While there may be people who are able to work but who choose not to work at the prevailing wage, there is no involuntary unemployment in this model. It is assumed that wages adjust until all those who want to work at the going wage will work and all those not working are choosing not to work.

The equilibrium level of employment in the labor market implies an equilibrium level of output. Firms demand labor because the output that the workers produce will be sold and generate profits. In terms of the model, the level of output is determined by the amount of labor employed and the production function.

$$Y_A = F(N_A) \tag{14–6}$$

In the classical model, labor supply is determined by people's willingness to work in relation to the real wage. The demand for labor is determined by the marginal productivity of labor in relation to the real wage. *Unless there are changes in the willingness to work or the productivity of labor, then the equilibrium level of output will not change.* In particular, forces that bring about a change in aggregate demand, such as an increase or decrease in the money supply, should not affect either the willingness to work or the productivity of labor and, therefore, they do not affect employment or output. It is in this sense that the classical model implies there is a set level of real output determined by a set equilibrium level of employment. This is shown in Equation 14–7:

$$Y_A = Y(\overline{N}_A) = \overline{Y} \tag{14–7}$$

This view of the labor market is derived from the view that variations in production are solely determined by variations in employment and the assumption of perfectly competitive, quickly clearing product and labor markets. There is no involuntary unemployment in this model, because excess supply in any market leads to immediate reductions of the wage rate. Some additional workers choose not to work now that the wage rate is lower.

Unemployment in a Classical Labor Market   The classical model of the labor market can generate unemployment, but it has to result from institutional arrangements that prevent workers from reducing their nominal wage in the face of a reduction in the demand for labor. A source of unemployment that stems from such an institutional change is the unemployment created by a minimum wage. Distortions in the labor market, such as the introduction of minimum-wage legislation, unemployment insurance, welfare support programs, and unions, will produce level of output and employment that is lower than the level achieved with unrestricted labor markets. Minimum-wage legislation has a direct effect in putting a floor under wages. Such programs as unemployment insurance may lead to the same effect by making workers unwilling to accept wages below a certain minimum level. The effect of a minimum level to the real wage is illustrated in Figure 14–3, where the minimum wage creates an excess supply of workers, where the number wishing to work (point *B*) is greater than the number demanded by firms (point *A*) given the minimum wage. The excess supply of labor does not lead to a reduction in the real wage in this case, since minimum wage will only lead to unemployment if it exceeds the market-clearing wage.

The classical model of the labor market suggests, therefore, that unemployment is caused only by institutional restraints, such as minimum wages. Many economists blamed the unemployment of the Great Depression on unions or minimum wages that were said to be preventing wage adjustment.

When the classical model of the labor market is used to provide a basis for Monetarism, the simple classical model is modified to take account of the fact there is not perfect information available about jobs and wages. Workers are then unemployed because they are searching for the best available job. Variation in overall unemployment can occur if workers' expectations about the likelihood of getting a better wage change over time.

In the classical model, the labor market determines the aggregate supply schedule. The aggregate demand schedule is based on the classical quantity equation.

FIGURE 14–3
Unemployment Resulting from a Minimum Wage in the Classical Model

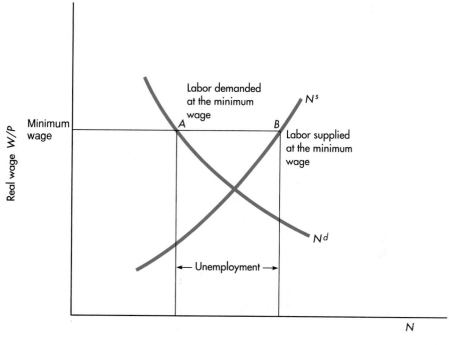

The Classical Basis for the Quantity Equation

The classical labor market, with full employment and supplier output fixed in the short run, sets the stage for aggregate demand and nominal income. Nominal income is output times the price level, and the price level depends on the quantity of money. In the classical model there is a very simple money-demand relation in which money demand is proportional to income. A key feature of classical money demand is that it does not depend upon the rate of interest. When the money market is in equilibrium, money demand equals money supply ($M^d = M^s = M$), giving the following relation:

$$M = k \times PY$$

velocity of money
V in the *quantity equation*. The ratio of *nominal income (PY)* to the money supply.

Then, since k is assumed to be a constant, the **velocity of money,** V, is also a constant ($V = PY/M = 1/k$).

Substituting for velocity then gives the famous classical **quantity equation:**

$$M \times V = PY \tag{14–8}$$

quantity equation
The money supply times velocity equals nominal income.

To the classical economists, velocity was a constant with respect to short-run fluctuations in the economy, even though, in the long run, velocity might change slowly as a result of such things as increases in the speed with which banks clear checks.

FIGURE 14–4
The Quantity
Equation and the
Aggregate Demand
Schedule

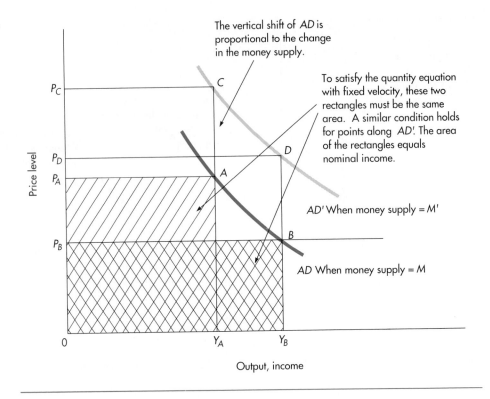

The quantity equation with the assumption of a constant velocity of money is the classical aggregate demand relation. An increase in the nominal supply of money (an increase in M) must translate into a proportional increase in nominal income, with velocity taken as given. The quantity equation in the classical model takes the place of the *IS–LM* plus trade-off framework.

Figure 14–4 illustrates the aggregate demand schedule in the classical model. When the money supply is equal to M, then the schedule is AD. The points A and B on this schedule must then both satisfy the quantity equation:

$$P_A Y_A = P_B Y_B = MV$$

With fixed velocity and money supply, the aggregate demand schedule is curved in the way shown in the figure. (It is a hyperbola.)

If the supply of money were to increase to M', there would be a new aggregate demand schedule, AD'. Points along AD' would also have to satisfy the quantity equation:

$$P_C Y_A = P_D Y_B = M'V$$

A given percent increase in the money supply (M to M') raises nominal income by the same percentage.

AGGREGATE SUPPLY AND DEMAND IN THE CLASSICAL MODEL

The characteristics of aggregate supply and demand equilibrium in the classical model are different from those in the *IS–LM* trade-off model in the short run. In the *IS–LM* trade-off model, increases in demand lead to increases in both output and inflation. Producing more requires hiring more labor at a higher unit cost. The higher unit costs generate an increase in the price level. In terms of the aggregate-supply/aggregate-demand diagram, the aggregate-supply schedule is upward-sloping but not vertical.

In the classical view, output does not change as aggregate demand changes; rather, the effect of an increase in aggregate demand is solely an increase in the price level. The aggregate supply schedule is vertical, derived from the classical model of the supply and demand for labor and not from the short-run trade-off of output and inflation. This same classical approach will be carried over to the Monetarist framework.

The Role of Aggregate Demand and the Price Level

Since in the classical model the labor market sets the equilibrium amount of labor supplied, which in turn fixes the supply of goods and services, the aggregate supply schedule is vertical. This is shown in Figure 14–5, where output ($\overline{Y}$) is set by equilibrium in the labor market. The price level is set by the level of aggregate demand intersecting the vertical aggregate supply.

Changes in aggregate demand simply lead to changes in the price level at a set level of output ($\overline{Y}$). An increase in aggregate demand (*AD* to *AD′*), resulting from, say, an increase in the money supply, raises nominal income, but real income remains unchanged. As shown in the figure, ($P_B \times \overline{Y}$) at point *B* is greater than ($P_A \times \overline{Y}$) at point *A*. The increase in aggregate demand simply raises the price level from P_A to P_B.

The classical model seems to have left no room for changes in a aggregate demand to affect output. Hence the classical model implies there are no changes in output that results from changes in aggregate demand policy, nor are there business cycles or fluctuations in equilibrium output that result from changes in aggregate demand. Consider, for example, whether there would be a rise or fall in output resulting from an increase or decrease in taxes. Since output only changes when there is a change in the amount of labor and there is no mechanism in the classical model by which changes in consumption demand can lead to changes in the real wage, output does not change. Tax-rate changes will only affect output to the extent to which they change the willingness to work or have some other supply-side effect.

If aggregate demand fell (shifted down or inward), equilibrium would be maintained in labor markets without reducing output. In the goods markets, supply would temporarily exceed demand. The excess supply of goods and services would drive down prices and nominal wages. There would be a fall in both the price level and the wage level, but no change in the real wage. With no change in the real wage, there is no change in the level of employment nor in the amount of output produced. This is why, in the classical model, real output, the real wage, and employment are determined independently of fluctuations in aggregate demand.

The classical model does not consider the adequacy of aggregate demand nor whether the output level will actually be purchased. The classical model accepts **Say's**

FIGURE 14–5
Aggregate Supply and Aggregate Demand in the Classical Model

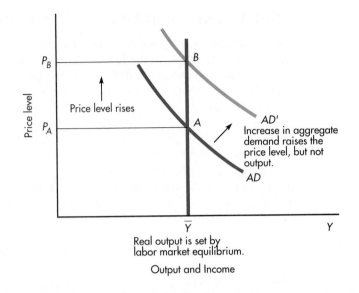

Say's Law

Supply creates its own demand. Production always generates enough income so that those who receive the income can purchase all that is produced.

Law. This states that the income flowing to suppliers always creates enough demand to match the available supply, so there will always be an adequate level of aggregate demand. The value of production always generates an amount of income equal to the amount of output, with such leakages as saving being offset by such injections as investment.

The classical model implies that even short-run changes in aggregate demand are ineffective in affecting aggregate real output. The model implies that only the price level is affected by changes in aggregate demand. This classical link between aggregate demand and the price level provides a foundation of the Monetarists' view that changes in the money supply are the primary cause of inflation. With a vertical aggregate supply schedule, an increase in the nominal supply of money will lead to a proportional increase in the price level and no change in the real supply of money—an important Monetarist idea.

MONETARISM, AGGREGATE DEMAND, AND INFLATION

Monetarists do not take over all the assumptions of the classical model in its most extreme form. They recognize that changes in aggregate demand have an effect on output as well as on prices. But they have used the classical model as a key starting point to develop their view that the role of money and monetary policy is of primary importance in determining inflation and economic conditions. The Monetarist analysis has provided an important alternative to Keynesian analysis, and their ideas have been incorporated into modern macroeconomics.

Just how much does money matter in determining the performance of the macro-economy? In the early 1960s, when the combination of the Phillips curve and the

Keynesian income–expenditure model dominated the general view of macroeconomics, the importance of money and monetary policy were little emphasized. At the time, the view held by some economists and policymakers in the United States and in Britain was that, because of the vast range of financial assets that are close substitutes for money, a central bank, such as the Federal Reserve Board or the Bank of England, would be relatively powerless to influence the pace of economic activity in an economy.[3] Trying to control inflation by restricting the money supply, it was argued, is like trying to control alcoholism by restricting the supply of whiskey. People will quickly switch to gin or vodka.

Monetarists used the classical model and the quantity equation to develop arguments to balance the Keynesian focus on fiscal policy as the most important tool of economic policy. To counter the view that money does not matter, the Monetarists argued that money is all that matters. This went too far, but they made a forceful case for the importance of the money supply in determining equilibrium income in the short run and inflation in the long run. Money does matter, even if it is not the only thing that matters.[4]

The Monetarists are right to say that money matters. The view that money does not matter has turned out to be fundamentally incorrect. Money matters because there is no ready substitute for it. The Federal Reserve Board's actions in controlling the monetary base are maintained or strengthened, not diluted, as they work through the extended financial system. Indeed, Monetarists have made an important contribution to the mainstream view of the economy.

The Basic Monetarist Framework

Monetarists work with the quantity equation, just as the classical economists did, but they recognize that velocity is not a strict constant. The quantity equation itself is an identity, and so it always holds, but the value of V may change. Moreover, since they apply the Monetarist framework to analyze inflation, Monetarist ideas can often be understood more easily when the basic quantity equation is transformed into a monetary-growth relation. The quantity equation (14–8) implies that the rate of growth of the money supply plus the rate of change of velocity equals the rate of inflation plus the rate of growth of real income. Equation 14–9 shows what this means:

The Quantity Equation in Growth Rates
$$M \times V \equiv PY$$
$$\frac{\Delta M}{M} + \frac{\Delta V}{V} \equiv \frac{\Delta P}{P} + \frac{\Delta Y}{Y} \tag{14–9}$$

By subtracting the rate of growth of velocity from both sides of Equation 14–9, the identity is restated so as to allocate the growth of the money supply into its growth

3 J. G. Gurley and E. S. Shaw, *Money in a Theory of Finance* (Washington, D.C.: Brookings Institution, 1960); Committee on the Workings of the Monetary System (generally known as the Radcliffe Committee), *Report* (London, England: Her Majesty's Stationery Office, 1959).
4 Franco Modigliani, "The Monetarist Controversy or, Should We Forsake Stabilization Policies?" *American Economic Review* 67 (March 1977), pp. 1–19.

Monetarism and the Monetarists: Milton Friedman and the Monetary Revolution

We have only occasionally referred to Keynes and we have avoided use of the term *Keynesianism* to describe the income–expenditure approach to understanding the economy. Today, the *IS–LM* trade-off model has been changed and developed substantially since Keynes did his original work. By the same token, Monetarism is a collection of different ideas and theories developed by different people, each of which can be judged on its merits. Many economists (including Karl Brunner, Allan

Meltzer, Bennet McCallum, Phillip Cagan, Anna J. Schwartz, and William Poole as well as the research staffs of several Federal Reserve banks, especially the Fed bank of St. Louis) have contributed to the modern development of Monetarism. However, of these, Milton Friedman has undoubtedly been the most creative and influential advocate of the Monetarists' ideas. Apart from his own contributions to economic literature, Friedman has exercised enormous influence on generations of students and colleagues at the University of Chicago and on public opinion also, through his popular writings and his public-television series. Milton Friedman's name will always be associated with Monetarism.

---

monetary-growth equation
The growth version of the quantity equation, where the growth of the money supply equals the inflation rate plus the growth of real income less any change in velocity.

components. As shown in Equation 14–10, this describes a **monetary-growth equation**:

The Monetary-Growth Equation

$$\frac{\Delta M}{M} \equiv \frac{\Delta P}{P} + \frac{\Delta Y}{Y} - \frac{\Delta V}{V} \tag{14–10}$$

The rate of growth of the money supply must equal three terms: the rate of growth of prices plus the rate of growth of real income less the rate of growth of velocity. The monetary-growth equation changes from an identity to a substantive tool for analysis when assumptions are made about the relationship of money growth to velocity, prices, and output.

The classical economists assumed that velocity is an institutionally determined constant, so the change in velocity is zero ($\Delta V/V = 0$). In this case, any given rate of growth of the money supply will determine the rate of growth of nominal income:

$$\frac{\Delta M}{M} = \frac{\Delta P}{P} + \frac{\Delta Y}{Y}$$

$$= \frac{\Delta PY}{PY} \tag{14–10a}$$

However, the classical model also assumes a vertical supply schedule with equilibrium in the labor market (full employment), which means that real income grows at a rate equal to the rate of growth of potential output ($\Delta Y/Y = \Delta Y^p/Y^p$). This means that changes in the rate of money growth will go one-for-one into changes in the rate of inflation.

The Monetarists' version of the monetary-growth equation differs from the classical version, in that Monetarists realize that velocity and output fluctuate around their trends; but they argue nevertheless that the classical assumptions of fixed velocity and constant growth of income are good approximations of the actual behavior even over periods of a year or two. According to the Monetarists, fluctuations in velocity and output are short-lived and they return to their long-term trends rather quickly.

Short-Run Variations in Output   The Monetarist version of equilibrium is different from the classical version, because of the recognition that wages do not react immediately to changes in the inflation rate. Consequently, in the Monetarist framework an increase in the growth of the money supply will, in the short run, lead to temporary changes in the growth rate of real output, as well as to changes in the inflation rate.

The Monetarists recognize there are many changes going on in the economy as part of its normal operations and that these changes will lead to some frictional unemployment, even when the labor market is in equilibrium. Milton Friedman defined the **natural rate of unemployment** as the rate that occurs as a result of the usual microeconomic changes as workers leave jobs and look for other jobs, even though there is no aggregate disequilibrium.

natural rate of unemployment
Unemployment that results from the normal changes taking place in the labor market.

To see how Monetarists analyze the way in which changes in the rate of growth of the money supply affect the real economy, we look again at the classical labor-market model. As shown in Figure 14–6, the economy is initially in equilibrium with output equal to potential output and unemployment at the natural rate (point *A*). The labor market is in equilibrium; the real wage has adjusted to equate the supply of and demand for labor; and the only unemployment is the result of normal frictions and adjustments. Then, suppose that the rate of growth of the money supply is reduced. In the Monetarist framework, this causes an excess demand for money and the price level starts to grow more slowly. This reduction in the rate of increase of prices is unexpected. Firms find that the prices of the products they sell are rising more slowly than expected. There would be no real effect from the deceleration of inflation if the growth of wages slowed at the same rate, but wage growth does not slow. Monetarists assume that workers do not realize that the prospective reductions in nominal wage gains are going to be offset by lower-than-expected prices. Workers are making decisions based on nominal wages only. In the short run, as firms cut back on employment, *nominal* wages may fall, but the *real* wages paid to workers are still rising. The unexpected decline in the inflation rate, unmatched by a reduction in nominal wages of the same magnitude, has made labor more expensive (W_A/P_A grows to W_C/P_C even though W_A has fallen). Yet workers do not recognize their good fortune and fewer workers seek employment as employers cut back on nominal wages—labor supply shifts inward (N^s_A to N^s_C). Fewer workers are employed at the higher real wage (point *A* to point *C*).

The result of the increase in the real wage is that production is cut back and output and employment fall. (Employment declines from N_A to N_C.) Thus in the Monetarist model, the impact of an unexpected reduction in the growth of the money supply is partially transmitted into an unexpected drop in inflation and partly brings about a drop in real output.

FIGURE 14–6
Unexpected Changes in Inflation Leading to Changes in Employment

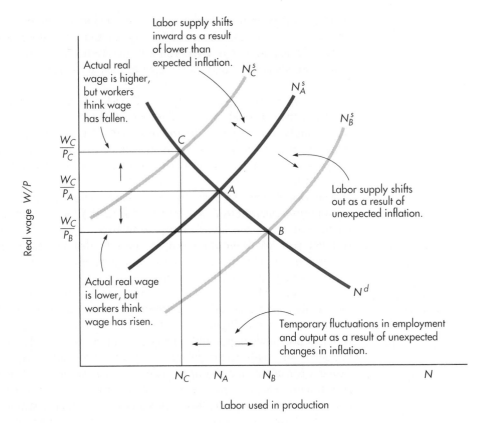

Labor supply shifts inward as a result of lower than expected inflation.

Actual real wage is higher, but workers think wage has fallen.

Labor supply shifts out as a result of unexpected inflation.

Actual real wage is lower, but workers think wage has risen.

Temporary fluctuations in employment and output as a result of unexpected changes in inflation.

Labor used in production

In the reverse case, an increase in the growth rate of the money supply will appear to firms as an increase in revenue. The apparent increase in demand generates new hiring and a rise in nominal wages. Workers work more hours at the higher nominal wage ($W_B > W_A$) even though the real wage falls ($W_B/P_B < W_A/P_A$). The supply of labor shifts out (N^s_A to N^s_B) and employment rises from N_A to N_B. More workers are employed at a lower wage (shown by the shift from point A to point B).

Changes in employment in the Monetarist model depend on differences in perceptions by workers and firms. Firms immediately recognize that a lower price for their own products means less revenue, so the real cost of any nominal wage has increased; but workers see only their own nominal wages and do not see immediately there has been a general fall in prices. These differences of perceptions cannot be maintained for long, however. Eventually everybody catches on to reality. This is why the effects of real income only take place in the short run.

The Monetarist Link from Money to Prices   In the *IS–LM* framework, an increase in the money supply causes a readjustment of portfolios between bonds and money. Prices are affected when the bidding for bonds drives down the interest rate, and this in turn raises aggregate demand. The increase in aggregate demand increases the purchases of goods and services, which stimulates increases in production. Higher levels of production generates higher costs and markups that increase the price level.

The Monetarists argue that an increase in the money supply causes individuals to buy more goods and services, which will directly raise the price level. They infer a relationship between money and prices, because almost all goods trade for money and the price level of goods is related to the price of money. The price of goods is how much money is needed to buy a given amount of goods; the price of money is the amount of goods that have to be given up to obtain a given amount of money. In a very simple economy, with only one good (bread) and money (dollars), the price of bread is the reciprocal of the price of money. If one loaf of bread costs one unit of money ($1), the price of bread is $1 per loaf and the price of money is one loaf per dollar. If one loaf of bread costs two units of money ($2), the price of bread is $2 per loaf and the price of money is one-half a loaf per dollar.

Generalize from one good to the many goods and services in the economy, and the price level sets the terms on which money and goods are exchanged. How much money has to be given up to buy a given market basket of goods and services? The answer is proportional to the price level. The higher the price level (P) the greater is the amount of money needed. The reciprocal of the price level ($1/P$) can be thought of as the price of money.

With this Monetarist frame of reference, a simple supply-and-demand analysis leads us to expect that an increase in the quantity of money will lead directly to a decrease in the price of money. Since a lower price of money (declining $1/P$) means that the price level rises, increasing the quantity of money leads to inflation. With a given supply of goods and services, an increase in money will create an excess supply of money, and the response of any market to excess supply is to lower the price of the item in excess.

Inflation is popularly characterized as ''too much money chasing too few goods.'' In our judgment, this phrase confuses an effect (inflation) with one of its causes (too much money). To Monetarists, that popular statement is exactly on target. Inflation is the direct consequence of an excess supply of money. Whether to view inflation as a wholly monetary process or as a partially monetary process is a central question posed by the Monetarist controversy.

We now discuss that question by taking a more careful look at the quantity equation and the Monetarist view of the stability or predictability of velocity.

The Stability or Predictability of Velocity   In the classical model the rate of growth of velocity was zero and the rate of growth of output was constant. The link from money to prices was simple and direct. In the Monetarist framework, output growth can fluctuate temporarily and velocity will change.

Figure 14–7 shows annual values for the rate of growth of the velocity of money. The growth of velocity has not been zero. This is true of either the $M1$ or $M2$ version of velocity—it varies from year to year and even changes direction in different periods.

FIGURE 14-7
The Rate of
Growth of Velocity,
1970-1993

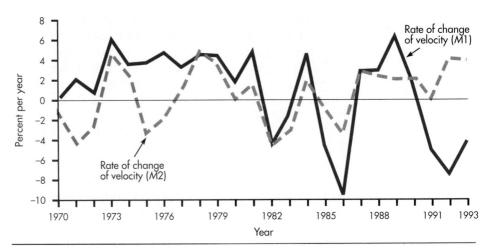

Source: *Economic Report of the President,* 1994.

Milton Friedman confronted the issue of the stability and predictability of velocity by formulating a more sophisticated version (Equation 14–11) of the quantity equation in which velocity is no longer a constant, but is instead a predictable function of other economic variables:[5]

$$PY = M \times V\,(r,\ \mathrm{Exp}\Delta P/P) \tag{14–11}$$

In this restatement of the quantity theory, the velocity of money depends on the real interest rate, r, and the expected rate of inflation.

Written in this way, Milton Friedman's restatement of the quantity theory is very similar to the money-demand specification used in the *IS–LM* trade-off model. But in his interpretation, Friedman is able to give an *exclusive* role to monetary policy: The supply of money affects both income and inflation in the short run and affects only inflation in the longer run. He explains his theory by asserting that the real interest rate is constant and that the expected rate of inflation is determined by the expected rate of growth of the money supply. In other words, his response to the criticism that velocity does in fact vary is that *variations in velocity are all caused by changes in monetary policy*—all the sources of variation in the price level are driven by changes in the

---

[5] Milton Friedman included other variables than those given in Equation 14–11 in his article, "The Quantity Theory of Money: A Restatement," in *Studies in the Quantity Theory of Money,* ed. Milton Friedman (Chicago: University of Chicago Press, 1956). This issue of predictability as distinct from stability is one of the forecasting accuracy of econometric models of velocity. Though some versions of forecasting models are better than others and some definitions of velocity result in more predictability than others, velocity has in general not proven to be as stable or predictable a macroeconomic variable as is indicated by the Monetarists' models of the economy.

money supply. The link between money and prices is maintained and inflation is still always and everywhere a monetary phenomenon.[6]

According to Friedman, the real rate of interest is a constant, because it is tied to stable real factors, such as individuals' attitudes toward consumption now versus consumption in the future (called the "rate of time preference") and the rate of profit or marginal productivity of capital. The second assumption is that the expected rate of inflation depends *only* on monetary policy.

While the Monetarist bottom line is that the quantity equation works, modern Monetarism differs from the classical framework in its capacity to take account of the observed variability of output and velocity; but it does so in a way that preserves the primacy of money and monetary policy as determinants of inflation.

Monetarist Monetary Policy

Monetarists argue that a monetary policy that changes the rate of growth of the money supply to deal with current economic events should not be used to manage the economy. The Monetarist view is that fluctuations in real output are short-lived because the economy is self-correcting, and that the growth of the money supply is the primary determinant of nominal income and inflation. This leads them to conclude that an active use of monetary policy will not improve economic performance. Monetarists hold the position that the economy will do better without government action. Attempts to fine-tune the economy through marginal changes in the money supply will only disrupt the economy, resulting in unnecessary fluctuations in inflation and output.

In the face of real shocks to the economy, it may take a while before prices and wages adjust to restore full-employment equilibrium, but not that long. In this view of the world, the private economy is fundamentally self-correcting—it is a stable system that will return to equilibrium quickly unless it is continuously disturbed. Therefore, to Monetarists the best monetary policy is a stable and predictable rate of growth in the money supply—one that is matched to the long-run growth of potential output.

Milton Friedman's Constant–Money-Supply-Growth Rule   In his most famous policy prescription, the **constant–money-supply-growth rule,** Milton Friedman argued that setting a target of constant percent growth in the money supply would insure price stability; that is, roughly a zero rate of inflation.[7] He arrived at that rule by using his assumptions about velocity and the rate of growth of real output and

constant–money-supply-growth rule
The policy of setting the rate of growth in the money supply equal to the long-term rate of growth of potential output.

---

[6] Milton Friedman, "A Theoretical Framework for Monetary Analysis," *Journal of Political Economy,* March/April 1970, p. 217.

[7] "The precise rate of growth, like the precise monetary total, is less important than the adoption of some stated and known rate. I myself have argued for a rate that would on the average achieve rough stability in the level of prices of final products, which I have estimated would call for something like a 3 to 5 per cent per year rate of growth in currency plus all commercial bank deposits or a slightly lower rate of growth in currency plus demand deposits only." [Milton Friedman, "The Role of Monetary Policy," *American Economic Review* LVIII (March 1968), pp. 1–17.]

applying them to the monetary-growth equation (Equation 14–10). He assumes that the growth of velocity will be close to zero, because the main cause of fluctuations in velocity (namely, fluctuations in the growth rate of money) has been eliminated. In this case (shown in Equations 14–12a and 14–12b), the desired growth rate of money is equal to the desired rate of inflation plus the desired growth rate of real output:

$$\text{Since } \frac{\Delta M}{M} \equiv \frac{\Delta P}{P} + \frac{\Delta Y}{Y} - \frac{\Delta V}{V} \tag{14–12}$$

then, if the change in velocity is zero, this gives:

$$\text{Desired } \frac{\Delta M}{M} = \text{Desired } \frac{\Delta P}{P} + \text{Desired } \frac{\Delta Y}{Y} \tag{14–12a}$$

Then, if the desired rate of inflation is zero and the desired rate of growth of output is the growth rate of potential output, this gives:

$$\text{Desired } \frac{\Delta M}{M} = \text{Constant growth rate of potential output} \tag{14–12b}$$

The workings of such a rule-based policy are illustrated in Figure 14–8. The economy is initially pictured at point A, where output is equal to potential output (Y_A is equal to Y^P), aggregate demand is shown by the AD_0, and the price level is P_A. Over the

FIGURE 14–8
Unexpected
Variations in
Velocity with
Friedman's Money-
Growth Rule

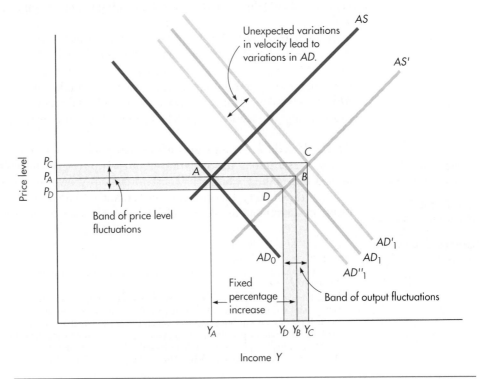

course of the next year, potential output grows by a fixed percentage, based upon the trend of potential output (*AS* to *AS'*). The increase in the money supply by the same percentage is just enough to increase aggregate demand from AD_0 to AD_1, assuming no change in velocity or no change in the price level.

Friedman recognizes that in practice there may be some change in velocity as a result of all the shocks and changes that go on in a diverse economy. If velocity grows a little, then, instead of having aggregate demand of AD_1, there will be aggregate demand of AD'_1. This unexpected increase in velocity will push up the price level (to P_C) and the resulting unexpected inflation will lower the real wage and raise output above potential. (The economy goes to Y_C, moving along the short-run aggregate supply schedule *AS*.) Similarly, an unexpected decrease in velocity will lead to aggregate demand of AD''_1, an unexpected decrease in the price level (to P_D), and output below potential (at Y_D).

Because the uncertainty of monetary policy has been eliminated, the fluctuations of velocity will be small and so the range of fluctuations of prices and output will be small. The cyclical fluctuations in the economy will have been greatly reduced. Figure 14–8 shows the bands that should cover output and price-level variations, assuming only small changes in velocity.

The analysis could also be extended to cover the possibility of short-run changes in potential output. Small economic fluctuations might take place as a result of changes in technology, consumer preferences, or foreign trade and these could lead to a band of variation around the aggregate supply schedule. This would broaden the range of possible output fluctuations that would be experienced in practice; but the business cycle still would be largely attenuated—given Friedman's view that most of the variability in output in the past has been caused by variable monetary policy. Figure 14–9 illustrates the case where there is a band of variability around both the aggregate demand and the aggregate supply schedules. The shaded diamond area indicates the sizes of the price and output variations that would occur with a money-growth rule.

According to the Monetarist view, the shaded area between the aggregate supply and demand schedules in Figure 14–9 represents the highest level of performance and the most stability that the economy is capable of obtaining. The unexpected changes in velocity or the unexpected changes in supply conditions cannot be corrected by policy, because the policymakers do not know any more about them than the private sector knows. Policy changes that drive the rate of growth of the money supply above or beyond the constant growth rate of potential also drive equilibrium to be temporarily outside of the shaded area. The failure to hold a constant rate of growth in the money supply and the subsequent erratic fluctuations in monetary policy are seen by Monetarists as the main sources of the historical business cycle.

There is an important situation where Monetarist ideas are clearly applicable. There have been many episodes in the past where governments have been unable or unwilling to raise enough taxes to finance the level of government spending and where they have been unable to borrow enough to pay for the resulting budget deficits. If central banks are then forced to increase the supply of money more and more rapidly, the result is a **hyperinflation.**

FIGURE 14–9
The Range of Price and Output Variations with Unexpected Variations in Velocity and Supply Conditions with Friedman's Money-Growth Rule

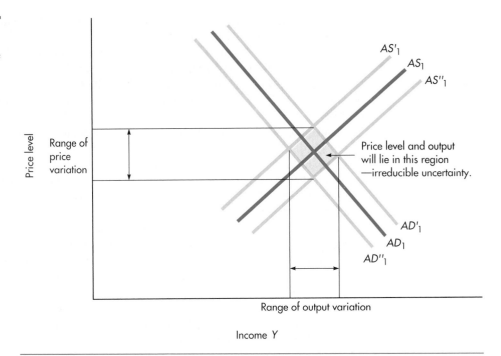

Income *Y*

---

hyperinflation
Rapid, escalating inflation. Defined technically as an inflation where the price level rises at a rate in excess of 50 percent per month for at least one year.

Hyperinflation   Rates of inflation experienced in the United States in the 20th century have rarely exceeded 10 percent per year. In an economy that experiences any annual growth in real income, inflation rates that remain below 10 percent per year can be attributed to both monetary and nonmonetary causes. But not all inflations are as mild as these. There have been economies that have experienced extraordinarily higher rates of inflation. In those economies inflation has been shown to be a purely monetary phenomenon. This is because the extraordinarily large increases in the money supply overpower all other causes of inflation.

Phillip Cagan, a Monetarist who studies rapid inflation, defined hyperinflation as an inflation where the price level rises by more than 50 percent per month or well over 1,000 percent per year.[8] In economies suffering from hyperinflation, the explosive acceleration in the price level is almost completely monetary in nature. The rate of inflation accelerates as the rate of growth of the money supply increases. The growth of the demand for money follows quite closely what would be predicted by Friedman's version of the quantity equation. There is a rapid growth of velocity as money-supply growth increases and people come to expect rapid inflation. People want to spend money as quickly as possible, because its value is falling: the opportunity cost of holding money is rising rapidly. The growth of income and other nonmonetary

---

[8] Phillip Cagan, "The Monetary Dynamics of Hyperinflation," in *Studies in the Quantity Theory of Money,* ed. Milton Friedman (Chicago: University of Chicago Press, 1956).

variables has little impact on inflation compared to the effect of the increase in the money supply. The most well-studied hyperinflation took place in Germany from May 1921 to November 1923. Prices and the stock of money in Germany at the end of the hyperinflation had increased by more than one billion times what they were less than two years before. Had such an inflation occurred in the United States in modern times, the price of a loaf of bread would have risen from $1 to $1 billion and the price of a midsized automobile from $12,000 to $12 trillion, all in a very brief 30 months.

The most amazing hyperinflation took place in Hungary in 1945–46, where the price level rose by over one octillion times (5.20×10^{27}) in 13 months. While at the peak of the German hyperinflation, prices were rising at over 300 percent per month, or 5 percent per day; in contrast, during the Hungarian hyperinflation, prices were rising at almost 20,000 percent per month, or almost 40 percent per day! As evidence there was a rapid increase in velocity that exacerbated the inflationary effects of rapid monetary expansion, German and Hungarian workers demanded to be paid every several hours, since the purchasing power of their wages was eroding during the day.

All of the hyperinflation started with a continuing acceleration of the money supply. The hyperinflations typically ended with budgetary reforms to reduce the budget deficits and hence reduce the pressure to expand the money supply. These were also accompanied by the initiation of a currency reform. The growth of the money supply was drastically curtailed and inflationary expectations were rapidly reduced. Following the end of the hyperinflations, people returned to holding money, velocity fell, and the economies stabilized. Yet stopping hyperinflation was not painless; several of the economies in central Europe went through severe economic downturns, because of the credit crunch that followed the steps taken to end the inflation.

The relationship between the money supply and the price level described by the quantity equation works best in a hyperinflation where the growth of the money supply is so large as to dominate all other economic concerns. But the lessons from hyperinflations do not carry over to the United States. U.S. inflation has had both monetary and nonmonetary causes. The fact that excess money growth is the cause of hyperinflations does not mean that the Monetarist model can be applied to the U.S. economy in normal times. In our judgment there are serious difficulties with the Monetarist position.

Assessing the Monetarist Model

There is no question that Monetarism has contributed to our understanding of the macroeconomy. Indeed, the importance of money to long-run inflation is an idea that has been incorporated in the analysis of earlier chapters. Our emphasis in this book on financial markets and expectations owes a lot to the Monetarist revolution. The major differences between the Monetarist model and the *IS–LM* trade-off model have to do with the degree to which money is either important or all important, the time it takes for the economy to adjust to equilibrium, and the extent to which wages and prices are flexible in the short run. The trade-off model of inflation has several nonmonetary elements (output, adaptive expectations, supply shocks) that influence inflation, while the Monetarist view is that inflation is always and everywhere a monetary phenomenon.

Brazil's Harsh Attack on Inflation Is Risking Deep Economic Slump

SAO PAULO, Brazil—When Fernando Collor de Mello took office in March, he said he had "only one shot" to halt Brazil's hyperinflation. But instead of firing a bullet, the new president dropped a bomb.

"The monetary contraction we imposed on society is fantastic," acknowledged Ibrahim Eris, one of the architects of the harsh anti-inflation plan and now the president of the central bank. "It's probably the first time in the world that a country in time of peace has practically destroyed its monetary standard and replaced it."

Under the plan, Mr. Collor didn't just restrict credit or cut spending, as other governments here have done. He froze about 70 percent of the money circulating in the economy for 18 months, until the fall of next year, and also replaced the old currency, the cruzado novo, with a new, strictly controlled one, the cruzeiro. If money causes inflation, the thinking goes, then removing money removes inflation.

Fast Medicine

The results have come faster than it takes to say hyperinflation. Inflation, which reached 84.32 percent in March alone and totaled 4,854 percent in the 12 months through March, halted completely—in fact, prices fell—in the month following the unveiling of the plan, the government says. (However, some trade unions and economists disagree, charging that the index is based on an incomplete basket of goods.)

But in stopping inflation, the government has also stopped the economy. "To kill the cockroach, they set the apartment on fire," complains former Economic Planning Minister Antonio Delfim Netto.

Deprived of cash, consumers stopped buying, companies stopped producing, and exporters stopped exporting. Then, afraid that it had paralyzed the country, the government started reinjecting money into the system to the point that some feared a revival of inflation, and the government closed the tap again. Although the government terms all this as only a short, predictable phase and says economic activity is picking up again, many economists and businessmen think that Brazil has simply traded inflation for recession—and could end up with both if the government errs in its efforts to revive the economy. . . .

"We're walking on a very narrow road," the central bank's Mr. Eris concedes. "On one side is the precipice of recession; on the other is inflation. Today, society thinks we're walking close to recession, but the road is so narrow we could fall the other way. Our problem today is trying to administer this so we don't fall on either side."

Mr. Eris also admits that the plan "has implications that aren't clear. Talk of recession or depression and talk of an explosion of demand prove the economy hasn't found its equilibrium." Inflation, he says, "has been knocked down, and the judge has counted to three. When he says 10, we'll be in another world." But both he and Economics Minister Cardoso are confident of steering the economy through the twin perils of inflation and recession.

If they succeed, economists say, they will have laid the foundations to allow Brazil, at long last, to live up to its huge potential. If they fail, Brazil will have "exhausted the economic encyclopedia" of ways to cure inflation, Mr. Langoni says. The results, all agree, won't be clear for at least another couple of months.

"We're going to have a terrific decade," Abril's Mr. Civita says, "All we have to do is get over the next two months. I'm sure there's a promised land at the end of the desert. The question is: Is there enough water in the canteen to make it across?"

Money and Prices   There is a problem with the Monetarist analysis of the link between money and the price level. The price level is the aggregate result of thousands of individual price and wage decisions made by firms and workers on the basis of the supply and demand for goods and services. The price of a pair of shoes is not set on the basis of the proportion of the shoe manufacturer's wealth he or she wants to hold in the form of money. When demand increases, each producer sets its own price relative to the prices of other manufacturers and relative to import prices. Inflation increases as a rise in aggregate demand filters down to the individual price and wage decisions. Each decision maker tries to raise his or her relative price, and all prices go up. Similarly, wage rates are set by firms based on wages in other companies, the cost of living, and the state of the labor market. Wages rise more rapidly if companies experience problems in hiring, nor directly because cash managers are holding larger checking-account balances. Inflation accelerates as a result of increased aggregate demand for goods and services, and this demand depends on income and the rate of interest, not particularly on money, which is a tiny fraction of total wealth.

It is misleading to say that the reciprocal of the price level is *the* price of money and hence that changes in the quantity of money will lead directly to changes in the price level. Any durable good has two prices, the purchase price and the rental price; and this is true for money, also, in that money can be "rented" by borrowing at the prevailing rate of interest. It is the rental price of money (the interest rate) that adjusts directly when the quantity of money is varied. When the Fed expands the money supply, this leads to an excess supply of money in the money market, where T bills and other short-term assets are traded; and the excess supply of money is then eliminated by a change in the short-term nominal rate of interest. Over time, the change in the interest rate may lead to a change in aggregate demand and hence to a change in the price level.

Real Wages over the Cycle   The Monetarist model argues that changes in real output are the result of changes in the real wage. When the price level increases, the real wage falls and employers hire more workers and produce more output. When the price level falls, this raises the real wage and firms cut back on employment. If this model is correct, it should be possible to look at data on real wages and see their cyclical pattern. Figure 14–10 shows data on the real wage with business-cycle fluctuations marked on the figure. There is no clear tendency in the data for wages to be below their trend during booms and above trend during recessions. Real wages do not seem terribly sensitive to cyclical variations in the economy.

If there is any cyclical pattern to real wages visible in the data, it is a tendency for wages to fall in recessions, suggesting that recessions are periods where product demand is low and employers lay off workers and hold down wages. This does not fit with the Monetarist model in which employment losses are driven by high wages.

The behavior of wages over the business cycle is a problem for other models as well as for the Monetarist model. In the *General Theory,* Keynes also assumed that the real wage would fall in booms; the rational-expectations model that we will discuss in Chapter 15 has the same problem. The reason all of these models have the same difficulty is that they assume perfectly competitive markets with flexible prices. In a

FIGURE 14–10
**The Real Wage
over the Business
Cycle**

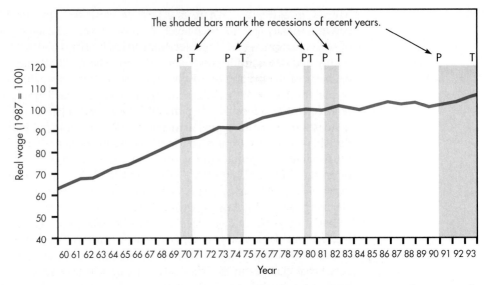

The real wage has increased over time as productivity has increased. It fell with the oil-price increases and other suppply shocks. It has not shown much systematic relation to the business cycle.

perfectly competitive market, employment and output are determined by the relation between wage cost and product price. Once we recognize the importance of imperfect markets and other market conditions, this is not so. We will return to this issue in Chapter 15.

Monetary Aggregates and Economic Activity   There is general agreement among economists of different schools of thought that monetary policy has played an important role in business-cycle fluctuations. But the Monetarist position that money growth dominates all other factors is hard to accept. The surge in inflation in the 1970s is hard to explain without allowing for the OPEC price increase and other supply shocks. And as another counter-example to Monetarism, in the 1980s there was a rapid growth of the money supply that was not accompanied by any surge in inflation. This period also does not fit well with the Monetarist view.

The movements of monetary aggregates are important in explaining the course of economic events, but they are not as all important as a Monetarist model assumes. In the *IS–LM* model, the power of monetary policy comes from its impact on nominal and real interest rates and on credit conditions, not through a direct link from money to prices. There is room for monetary and nonmonetary influences on the economy.

Even if one disagrees with the Monetarist model, however, there is more to Monetarism than this. Monetarist economists are not simply developers of an alternative model of the macroeconomy. Much of the literature of Monetarism is taken up with reviewing historical economic policy with a very critical eye and with criticizing the Keynesian income–expenditure model for its mechanistic structure, for its excessively constrained role for money and financial markets, and for the imprecision of its forecasts and its policy prescriptions.

Monetarist Criticisms of the Income–Expenditure Model

In the simplest Keynesian models, exogenous shifts in investment or government expenditure lead to large changes in final output, because of the induced changes in consumption, investment, imports, and government expenditures, net of taxes. The allocation of expenditures using national income accounting led many to believe that the induced change in consumption was the largest contributor to the growth of final output. In those models that described changes in income as a multiplier process, the marginal propensity to consume was a crucial component of the multiplier. The Monetarists' fiercest criticisms of the simple income–expenditure model were directed toward the multiplier. The criticisms had some validity, since the multipliers generated by those models were subject to much more variation than the early Keynesians had realized. The marginal propensity to consume is not a constant; rather, the relationship between short-run changes in income and short-run changes in consumption vary a great deal. The permanent-income hypothesis indicates that families engage in consumption smoothing, so an increase or decrease in income induces only a small change in consumption.

Monetarists were, and continue to be, very critical of economic-stabilization policy. Such policy is unnecessary, they argue, because the economy is self-correcting. Stabilization policy is unwise because government actions historically have only made things worse. Milton Friedman argues it was the collapse of the money supply after 1929 that led to the Great Depression. In general, he judges that counter-cyclical policies directed against recessions have performed poorly.

At the heart of the Monetarist criticism of stabilization policy is the argument that, even though the Fed can affect the economy through changes in the growth of the money supply, the Fed is incapable of timing changes so as to match up with the need for intervention. Policy goes wrong so often, not because of bad intentions, but because of bad timing. We never know where the economy is today, only where it was some months ago. Monetarists have argued that, even if fiscal policy had an effect on the economy, the problem of timing would almost guarantee that stabilization policy would have the government executing the wrong policy at the wrong time.

Monetarist Criticism of Fiscal Policy   Monetarist criticism of fiscal-stabilization policy extended with the argument that cutting taxes will not induce any increase in consumption. The argument is that households know that a cut in taxes without a corresponding cut in government expenditures will increase their disposable income only temporarily. Suppose the government budget starts in balance, and then there is a stimulative tax cut that generates a budget deficit. Monetarists point out this deficit must be covered by issuing government bonds. And either these bonds must be repaid in the future or interest payments must be made indefinitely to service a permanent increase in the national debt. Either way, taxpayers will face higher future tax payments. They will prepare for these payments now by saving the proceeds of the original stimulative tax cut, rather than spending it. Thus there is no stimulus to current private expenditure. We discussed the proposition that fiscal policy is ineffective in Chapter 13, where we said that the Monetarist proposition requires individuals to take account of changes in the federal budget deficit when making private-expenditure decisions. While a sudden rise in the federal deficit may well have a direct impact on financial markets, a similar direct effect of the deficit would be hard to find in consumers' decisions to purchase automobiles and vacations.

Monetarist criticisms of stabilization policy were the precursors of even more fundamental attacks on the standard models. While Monetarism has classical underpinnings, and concludes that stabilization policy is inadvisable, the equilibrium–business-cycle theorists use an approach that is based even more heavily on the classical model, and they conclude that systematic stabilization policy has no effect on output and employment.

SUMMARY

- The main core of Monetarism holds that: (1) The rate of inflation is strictly determined by the rate of growth of the money supply. (2) The economy is self-correcting, so full employment will be restored fairly quickly in the absence of government intervention. (3) Government policies have contributed to business-cycle fluctuations and were the main cause of the Great Depression. (4) Government should set monetary policy, so the growth of the money supply equals the growth of potential output.

- Most economists agree that in the long run the economy will behave in the way that the Monetarist/classical model describes. The disagreements concern the behavior of the economy over the short and intermediate runs.

- Monetarism has its basis in the classical model of the economy, where real output is determined by supply and demand in labor markets that clear fairly quickly and smoothly. The Monetarist model rejects the notions of extended price and wage stickiness.

- The classical model is based on the following elements: (1) Output changes come about through changes in the quantity of labor employed. (2) In the short run, capital and technology are held constant and only variations in the amount of labor employed bring about changes in output. (3) Employers determine the demand for labor based on the condition that the marginal product of labor equals the real wage. (4) Workers decide how much labor to supply, based on the real wage.

- Changes in aggregate demand, such as an increase or decrease in the money supply, should not affect either the willingness to work or the productivity of labor and, therefore, they do not affect employment or output.

- Changes in aggregate demand simply lead to changes in the price level at a set level of output. With a constant velocity of money, an increase in the money supply will lead to a proportional increase in the price level.

- In the Monetarist model, changes in aggregate demand have an effect on output as well as on prices. A change in the supply of money leads to a change in the price level and hence in the real wage. These changes in the real wage are only temporary, and so the deviations of output from potential output are also only temporary.

- Monetarists recognize that velocity changes, but they argue that these changes are the result of changes in the expected rate of growth of the money supply.

- Monetarists say that the role of money and monetary policy is of primary importance in determining inflation and economic conditions.

- Monetarists say that the economy will do better without government action. Attempts to fine-tune the economy through marginal changes in the money supply will only disrupt the economy, resulting in unnecessary fluctuations in inflation and output.

- There are several objections to the Monetarist model. Changes in the supply of money may lead to changes in the rate of interest, rather than leading directly to changes in the price level. Real wages do not vary over the business cycle in the way that the Monetarist model predicts.

KEY TERMS AND CONCEPTS

classical model, p. 434
constant–money-supply-growth
 rule, p. 451
hyperinflation, p. 454
marginal product of labor, p. 437

Monetarism, p. 433
monetary-growth equation, p. 446
natural rate of unemployment,
 p. 447
nominal wage, p. 439

quantity equation, p. 441
real wage, p. 439
Say's Law, p. 444
velocity of money, p. 441

DISCUSSION QUESTIONS AND PROBLEMS

1. Why does output not change in response to aggregate-demand changes in the classical model?

2. List reasons why labor markets in an actual economy would or would not resemble the classical labor market. Does the time horizon matter? Why?

3. What is the role of aggregate demand in the classical model?

4. If potential output is determined by aggregate supply, what guarantees that all of potential output will be produced and purchased?

5. Describe the connection between the quantity equation in a classical model and Monetarism.

6. Fill in the blanks in the following table.

Growth of Nominal Money Supply	Rate of Inflation	Growth of Velocity	Growth of Real Income
5	5	0	—
5	10	0	—
10	—	5	5
0	10	0	—
0	0	5	—
20	—	5	5

7. Discuss the pros and cons of a fixed rule for the growth of the money supply. What do you have to assume about the economy to endorse or reject such a policy?

8. It has been suggested that, instead of setting a fixed rate of growth of the money supply, the Fed should vary the rate of growth of money, depending on whether nominal income is growing faster or slower than some target rate of increase. Comment on this proposal.

9. During the period 1980–81, the Keynesian economist James Tobin used the monetary-growth equation to argue there would be a sharp recession as a result of the Fed's policy of monetary contraction. Try to reconstruct Tobin's argument. Recall that the monetary-growth equation is an identity.

CHAPTER 15

CONTROVERSY IN MACROECONOMICS: EQUILIBRIUM MODELS AND THE NEO-KEYNESIAN RESPONSE

INTRODUCTION

Expectations of future prices, interest rates, exchange rates, and policy actions affect the behavior of the modern economy. Everyone interested in macroeconomic policy agrees that expectations are important, but there is significant disagreement over how they are formed and the degree to which they affect income and inflation.

rational expectations
Expectations made without bias using all available information.

In the 1970s, a group of economists developed a **rational-expectations** model of the economy, in which they saw expectations formed on the basis of a rational forecast of economic conditions. This model accepted many, but not all, of the ideas of Monetarism and also relied even more strongly than previous models on classical assumptions about market behavior in the economy. By combining classical assumptions about the quickness with which markets reach equilibrium with the idea that expectations are formed solely on the basis of rational forecasts of economic conditions, the rational-expectations economists developed alternative views of the source of fluctuations in the economy and the impact of policy changes.

choice-theoretic framework
Models of the economy where the actions of economic agents result from the rational choices they make, based on maximizing their self-interest.

This approach to the analysis of the cycle was developed largely in response to what was seen as a failure of Keynesian analysis. Charles Plosser, a leading advocate of equilibrium–business-cycle models, describes the problem: "The essential flaw in the Keynesian interpretation of macroeconomic phenomena was the absence of a consistent foundation based on the **choice-theoretic framework** of microeconomics." He argued that Keynesian macroeconomics, by focusing on aggregate behavior, ignored microeconomic decision making.[1] And he would certainly make the same criticism of the *IS–LM* trade-off model that we have used in this book. Equilibrium–business-cycle economists argue there is no fully rational model of behavior that is consistent with sticky wages and prices.

As we work through the equilibrium models, their implications will be startling: Government will have no systematic policymaking role in controlling aggregate demand, because everyone will know what the effect of an anticipated policy action will be and they will buy or sell goods or assets so as to insulate themselves from its effects. In the view of the rational-expectations economists, output will deviate from potential output only in the short run and only as a result of unexpected shocks. Full employment will quickly be restored without the need to use policy—indeed, systematic policies will have no effect and unexpected policy actions will have adverse effects.

In equilibrium models, systematic stabilization policy is irrelevant with regard to the real economy, but government can affect nominal values. It can quickly raise the rate of inflation by increasing the rate of growth of the money supply and it can quickly reduce the rate of inflation provided it establishes policy credibility; that is, provided that the government's commitment to reducing the rate of inflation is believed.

If expectations are rational, this means they are formed using all the available and relevant information about the economy, and further, people do not *consistently* form overestimates or underestimates of future inflation, output, or other economic variables. In this view of the economy, people do not consistently think that inflation is going to be lower or higher than it actually is. Rational expectations result from a knowledge of supply and demand and inferences about the effect of changes in markets on future equilibrium conditions. If supply and demand conditions are such as to generate economic equilibrium, then participants in the economy will know that that is true and they will act as if they expect supply and demand mechanisms to work accordingly.

In the past few years some of those who advocated the equilibrium–business-cycle approach have even concluded that fluctuations in output cannot be explained by unexpected changes in demand. To be consistent with the classical assumptions of their model, anticipated fluctuations in the money supply (or in aggregate demand, in general) should only lead to changes in the price level and not to fluctuations in real output even in the short run. These economists began developing models of the business cycle that were strictly classical. In these

---

[1]   Charles I. Plosser, ''Understanding Real Business Cycles,'' *Journal of Economic Perspectives* 3 (Summer 1989), pp. 51–78.

models, called *real–business-cycle theory,* fluctuations in real output come about because of shifts in aggregate supply as a result of changes in technology or individual preferences, not because of shifts in aggregate demand.

The complaints voiced by the equilibrium theorists about Keynesian analysis generated a response in a body of theory that is now called *neo-Keynesian analysis.* These models attempt to explain the kind of wage and price stickiness that are assumed in the *IS–LM* analysis and that seem to exist in the actual economy in a way that is consistent with rational behavior. We conclude this chapter with a review of these models.

We begin the discussion of the rational-expectations point of view in the same way that these models were developed, by reconsidering how inflationary expectations are formed.

INFLATIONARY EXPECTATIONS

adaptive expectations
Expectations that are revised, based on how closely past expectations conform to reality.

In some of our earlier analyses, we assumed that expectations of the future were formed out of a memory of past inflation in such a way that individuals adapt their expectations to any changes they observe over time in the actual rate of inflation. Under **adaptive expectations** the expected rate of inflation is changed from one period to the next if there is a difference between what was expected last period and what actually happened last period. Adaptive expectations assume that people adapt their beliefs on the basis of how closely they conformed to reality the last time.

In 1961, John F. Muth offered a strong argument that the adaptive-expectations model is inconsistent with people acting in their own self-interest (i.e., it was irrational).[2] He said that rational economic behavior would lead people to form their expectations by looking at whatever relevant economic information is available. And all of this information is incorporated efficiently into unbiased expectations about the future. Muth found support for his idea in the behavior of agricultural prices.

Applying Muth's approach to the macro economy suggests that past inflation is not directly important in forming inflationary expectations. Rather, expectations of future inflation are formed by looking forward, using the economic conditions that generate the future rate of inflation. Past inflation is only important to the extent that it forecasts future inflation. If people have reason to think that future inflation will be very different from the rate that has prevailed in the past, then expected future inflation will not simply be an extrapolation of past trends.

---

[2] John Muth, "Rational Expectations and the Theory of Price Movements," *Econometrica* 29 (July 1961), pp. 315–35.

The Output–
Inflation
Trade-Off with
Rational
Expectations

In Chapter 6, we described a trade-off relation (reproduced here as Equation 15–1), in which current inflation is determined by the current level of output relative to potential and the current state of inflationary expectations:

$$\text{Current } \frac{\Delta P}{P} = H\left(\frac{Y}{Y^P}\right) + \text{Exp}\left(\frac{\Delta P}{P}\right) \tag{15–1}$$

While we previously described the two factors that determine how those expectations could have been formed—by either past history or forward-looking forecasts—we developed the trade-off analysis based on the assumption that the past history of inflation is a major determinant of expected inflation. What characteristics of inflation would be implied by an inflationary process where current inflation is related to forward-looking forecasts, rather than to past inflation?

First, forward-looking forecasts ought to produce self-fulfilling prophecies. If everyone thinks that inflation will be high in the current and future periods, then it will be. In terms of Equation 15–1, if the expected inflation rate were to rise, then actual inflation would rise, even if output were to remain equal to potential output. Each individual firm would anticipate larger price increases by all other firms and so would raise its own prices more, even though there was no excess demand in the economy. Second, this purely future-oriented inflationary process should offer the possibility of reducing even a long-entrenched inflation without incurring the cost of prolonged low output. If expectations of a future inflation could somehow be reduced, then actual inflation would fall even if output did not fall below potential output. A reduction in the level of inflation in the economy would come about because each individual firm would anticipate smaller price increases by all other firms. To remain competitive, each firm would have to reduce its own price increases, bringing about the reduction in inflation even though there was no excess supply in the economy.

If inflation can really be reduced without a prolonged recession, why has past experience with reducing inflation been so painful? Robert Lucas, an economist whose work was instrumental in forming the equilibrium–business-cycle model, has argued that the trade-offs between output and inflation that have been observed in the past were the result of the public's skepticism about the commitment of policymakers to reducing inflation.[3] For example, if the Fed restricts credit in the face of a high rate of inflation, this will not reduce inflation by much if few people believe that the Fed will stick with tighter credit over the long term. In terms of Equation 15–1, even at a current level of output different from potential, if there has been no change in inflationary expectations, there will be little change in current inflation.

When expectations of inflation are formed on the basis of future forecasts, then the public's understanding of which policy regime is in force is a more important part of

---

[3] Robert E. Lucas, Jr., "Some International Evidence on Output–Inflation Tradeoffs," *American Economic Review,* June 1973; and R. E. Lucas, Jr., ed., *Studies in Business Cycle Theory* (Cambridge, Mass.: MIT Press, 1981).

their rational expectations than is the current or past experience with the actual rate of inflation. The credibility of policymakers becomes a primary factor in determining the current rate of inflation.

Credibility Issues   According to the rational-expectations view in the face of a higher-than-desired rate of inflation, a credible change in policy could reduce inflation without reducing output. If somehow policymakers could convince the private sector that the policy change toward a slower rate of growth of the money supply was a clean break between past inflation and future policy actions, then the reduction in the rate of inflation would be fully expected by everyone. Price increases in the private economy, including wage increases, would slow down, reflecting these new expectations. The rate of inflation would in fact decline, with no reduction in employment or output! The key to making such a break, it is argued, is to introduce *credibility* into anti-inflation policy. If policymakers can convince individuals that monetary and fiscal policies will not be adjusted to accommodate inflation, then expectations will change and inflation will end without recession, without output being below potential output.

In the early 1980s, President Reagan and his advisors wanted to benefit from using a credible anti-inflationary strategy to lower expected inflation. Some economists in his first administration promised that inflation would melt away without recession. Here the prediction of the absence of a trade-off was not borne out. There is some indication that inflation fell a little more quickly in 1983 and 1984 than would have been predicted from past experience. But a major recession was still necessary to bring the inflation down.

Credibility in anti-inflationary policy probably helps, but, judging by experiences in the United States and in other countries, it cannot be established by simply announcing a firm policy. The Reagan administration was unrealistic about what could be achieved through the direct effects of policy on inflationary expectations. Despite this, there is wide acceptance of the idea that both past inflation and policy anticipations affect inflationary expectations. Even economists who emphasize the importance of inertia and past trends in forming expectations about inflation concede that a firm commitment to inflation control can bring down the expected rate of inflation more quickly than would be predicted from past experience with half-hearted inflation control.

The rational-expectations view of credibility was maintained without assuming that markets are neoclassical; that is, competitive and quick to come to equilibrium. It can be argued that expectations are formed rationally but that prices are sticky. If government regulations fix prices, if private institutions set wages or prices with long-term contracts, or if prices or wages are simply adjusted based on past procedures in some markets, then it is perfectly rational to base expectations of inflation on this behavior. After all, if prices are in fact sticky, it is rational to expect them to be sticky.

However, most rational-expectations economists argued that their view of expectations formation should be combined with the assumption of flexible prices and market equilibrium. The resulting models led to a revolutionary movement in macro-economics.

COMBINING RATIONAL EXPECTATIONS WITH MARKET CLEARING

Equilibrium–business-cycle economists reject the Keynesian ideas that money wages and prices are rigid and that a recession is a period of excess supply for either goods or labor. The reason they give for rejecting these ideas is that, if there is price stickiness, so there is excess supply or demand in a market, then there are opportunities to buy and sell that would be profitable, but these profit opportunities are not being exploited. In this view, markets are always in equilibrium and such opportunities cannot exist, at least not for long, because people will come along to take advantage of any profit that is around.

The claim is made that, since the price of a product reflects the terms of a voluntary transaction between two parties, if either party objects to the terms, it can look for a better price. If the transaction goes through, then both parties presumably accept that the price is appropriate. If that price causes no further changes in supply or demand, it is an equilibrium price. The same logic applies to wages. If a company experiences a decline in the demand for its product and lays workers off, then this is the choice of the company and its workers. The parties could always agree to reduce the wage and keep employment higher. Workers who are laid off must prefer this to offering to work at a lower wage. In a sense, they choose to be laid off. Here institutional arrangements matter very much. In most corporations when downsizing is contemplated, the alternative of reducing wages isn't usually offered to employees. However, the growth of temporary or contract workers in the 1990s (often the same workers who were previously let go) may be a version of just the phenomenon described here—continuing employment at a lower real wage.

It is acknowledged that declines in wages and prices (outside of agricultural prices) have been relatively rare in the period since 1948, but it is argued that price-flexibility was much greater before World War II. The wholesale price index fell from 158 in 1920 to 102 in 1922. It fell from 100 in 1929 to 74 in 1932. Equilibrium–business-cycle economists claim that the greater apparent stickiness in the postwar period is the result of a change in the policy environment, not because of any change in the structural characteristic of the economy.

Equilibrium Business Cycles

equilibrium–business-cycle model
Where fluctuations in output occur as a result of unexpected shocks, especially unexpected money supply changes.

In the **equilibrium–business-cycle model** of the macro economy, fluctuations in output occur, but only as a result of unexpected shocks that temporarily drive the economy away from full employment. Individual markets remain in equilibrium over the course of the cyclical fluctuations—hence the name. The unexpected shocks are typically thought to be unexpected changes in the supply of money.

The economy reacts quickly to eliminate any profit opportunities that result from fluctuations in markets, and this has the effect of quickly reversing any deviations from potential output. The result is a pattern in which output oscillates around potential and full employment is quickly restored. In a paper that develops his business-cycle models, Robert Lucas describes his main goal in developing his view of the business cycle:

In all of the models discussed in the paper, real output fluctuations are triggered by unanticipated monetary-fiscal shocks. The first theoretical task—indeed, the central theoretical problem of macroeconomics—is to find an analytical context in which this can occur and which does not at the same time imply the existence of persistent, recurrent, unexploited profit opportunities.[4]

Robert Lucas pictured the economy as made up of separate businesses, each of which is on its own island.[5] A business is affected by what happens on other islands but no company knows exactly what other companies are doing right away. There is *incomplete information* in the economy.

To make his framework easier to understand, Lucas says that one can think about a representative worker-producer—a firm consisting of one person. And at the outset, suppose that the aggregate price level is constant. Over a given time period, the representative worker-firm finds out what the market price is for her product, a product that requires a fixed number of hours of work for each unit produced. She then determines the amount she wishes to produce, given this price, and thus how many hours she wishes to work that period. In return for the output she makes, she receives money that she then spends on a variety of goods over some time.

Suppose that the representative worker-firm starts work one day and finds that the price of her product is now 10 percent higher than it had been the previous day. She does not know why this price increase has occurred, and neither does any other individual worker-firm. Nor does she know how long it will last. Lacking complete information, she makes her best choice, either work more and gain income from the price increase or work less and take more leisure at the same income. If she suspects that the price is only high temporarily, she'll likely respond with more work and increase in output. She will want to cash in on a temporary price hike while it lasts.

Now suppose there is not a constant price level, but, instead, prices throughout the economy may be changing and the overall price level may change. What happens now when the worker-firm finds that the selling price of her product has risen 10 percent? She does not have complete information about the rest of the economy, so she does not know how much of this increase in her own price is paralleled by an increase in the price level. She must form some expectation about what is happening to the price level and what she will be able to buy with the dollars that she earns by working and producing the output. Because she operates in a competitive environment, she cannot control prices; she can only react to price changes by changing output. How much she changes her work hours and output depends on whether she thinks the rise in price was specific to her product or to a general increase in the price level. She will change her work and output depending on how her own actual price compares to her expectation of the overall price level.

---

[4] Robert E. Lucas, Jr., "An Equilibrium Model of the Business Cycle," *Journal of Political Economy* 83 (December 1979), p. 1114.

[5] Robert E. Lucas, Jr., "Understanding Business Cycles," in *Stabilization of the Domestic and International Economy,* ed. Karl Brunner and Allan H. Meltzer, Carnegie-Rochester Series on Public Policy (Amsterdam: North-Holland, 1977), pp. 7–29. The parable of separate islands was first introduced by Edmund S. Phelps in the introduction to the volume he edited, *The Microeconomic Foundations of Employment and Inflation* (New York: W. W. Norton, 1970).

FIGURE 15–1   The Labor Market and Aggregate Supply in the Equilibrium–Business-Cycle Model

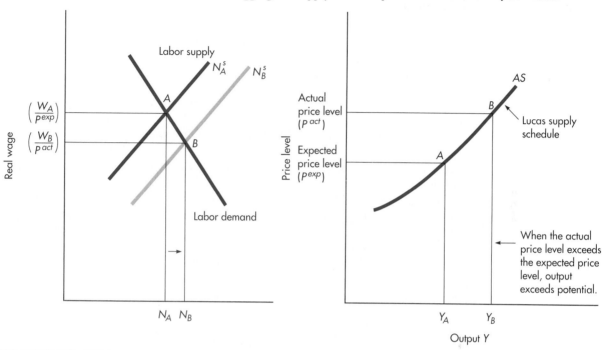

The case of a single worker-firm is obviously just a parable, but the equilibrium–business-cycle theorists apply the same idea to the aggregate economy and to the aggregate labor market specifically. Wages are assumed to be flexible, and they react quickly to changes in the supply of and demand for labor. Workers expect a particular inflation rate in the future, and they base their decisions about how much to work on the nominal wage they are being paid and their expectations about inflation. Figure 15–1 shows the equilibrium–business-cycle labor market in the left panel. The labor-supply schedule (N_A^s) is based on workers' expectations about the price level (P^{exp}). This labor supply reflects the amount workers would choose to work based on different levels of the real wage only if the price level turns out to be what workers expect it to be. In that case, the economy will operate at point A and the level of employment will be N_A.

If the actual price level (P^{act}) turns out to be higher than the expected price level (P^{exp}), then the actual real wage (W/P^{act}) will be lower than the real wage workers expected (W/P^{exp}). The labor-supply schedule (N_B^s) is based on the actual price level and not on the expected price level being realized. It is shifted out compared to the supply when expectations were fulfilled. The economy operates at point B, where the nominal wage is higher than at point A, but the real wage is lower.

The unexpected increase in the price level has raised employment. Workers have worked more because the nominal wage was higher, and they thought this increase would be reflected in an increase in their real wage. They were faced with the unpleasant surprise of being fooled about how much they would earn in real terms. When they discover the price level is higher than they expected, they find that they have worked more than they wanted. They expected to earn a high real wage and in fact they ended up with a low real wage.

The Lucas Supply Schedule   Based on the idea of a labor force that offers more labor when workers *mistakenly* believe their real wage is going to rise, Lucas proposed an aggregate-supply schedule—the **Lucas supply schedule.** The Lucas supply schedule is related to the one proposed by Milton Friedman, where output differs from potential output only when the actual price level differs from the expected price level.

Lucas supply schedule
An aggregate supply schedule proposed by Robert Lucas where an unexpected high price raises output.

When the price level turns out to be higher than expected, this drives down the real wage and firms demand more labor and produce more output. The right-hand panel of Figure 15–1 shows how output will be affected by movements of the actual price level relative to the expected price level. If the actual price level turns out to equal the expected price level, then the economy will produce output equal to potential (Y_A at point A). When the price level is above the expected price level, output exceeds potential output (Y_B at point B). Similarly, when the price level is below the expected price level, then the level of output will be below potential output. For any given level of the expected price level, therefore, increases in the actual price level will lead to higher levels of output. This relation is shown in Figure 15–1 as the Lucas supply schedule.

One important feature of the Lucas aggregate-supply schedule is that its position depends upon the expected price level. When people are expecting a high price level, then the price level must turn out to be high to avoid a recession. This idea is illustrated in Figure 15–2. The aggregate-supply schedule shifts up when the expected price level shifts up (AS'). The price level shifts down when the expected price level shifts down (AS''). When people are expecting a low price level, then the price level must turn out to be low to avoid a boom.

The shifts in the aggregate-supply schedule shown in Figure 15–2 are similar to the shifts in the output–inflation trade-off that we saw in Chapter 6. When the expected rate of inflation is high, there will be large expected increases in the expected price level. An upward or downward shift in the Lucas supply schedule parallels the upward or downward shifts in the trade-off analysis.

While the discussion of the trade-off in Chapter 6 was influenced by the equilibrium–business-cycle model, there is, however, an important difference. In the equilibrium–business-cycle model, the expected price level is based on rational, forward-looking forecasts by workers and firms. There is no such thing as an entrenched inflation. The only reason that the price level is expected to rise is the expectation that future economic conditions will generate a higher price level. The case is usually made in reference to expectations about monetary policy. *The price level is expected to increase when the Fed is expected to increase the money supply.*

FIGURE 15–2
The Aggregate-
Supply Schedule
Shifts Up or Down
Depending on
Changes in the
Expected Price
Level

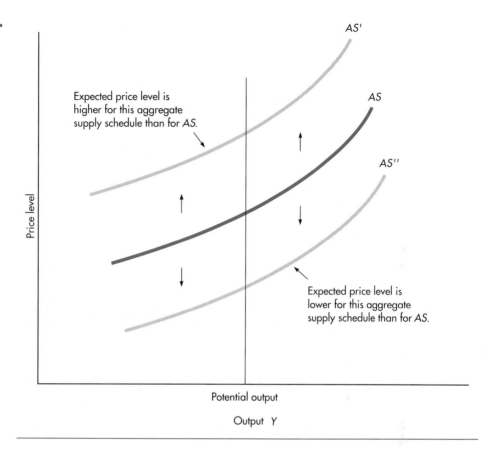

We may observe periods that look as if there is an entrenched inflation. But that is simply because the Fed has followed a pattern of generating inflation through excessive money growth.

Output Changes and Unrealized Expectations of the Price Level   What could cause the price level to turn out to be different from the expected price level? In equilibrium–business-cycle models, either a supply or a demand shock (e.g., an unexpected increase in the money supply) will cause the actual price level to differ from the expected price level. Then the Lucas supply schedule indicates that output will deviate from potential output. For example, an unexpected increase in the money supply leads to an increase in output.

This description of the business cycle may be hard to follow, given that it is being assumed people have rational expectations. Since expectations are formed rationally, how can expectations fail to be realized? The point is that having rational expectations does not mean that people know exactly what is going to happen. Rather, it means that they make the best use of the information they have available at the time. The

The Variability of Prices and the Slope of the Lucas Supply Curve

The Lucas supply schedule is based on the assumption that firms and workers do not have complete information. And the slope of the Lucas supply schedule depends on the difference between the information people have about the prices of the products they produce and the overall price level. This is why Lucas uses the parable of people being on separate islands. They know much more about their own island than what is going on in the whole archipelago.

When a worker-firm finds the price of its own product has increased, it has to decide to what extent this is an increase in the *relative* price of what it produces; that is, the extent to which its own price has risen relative to the overall price level. For simplicity we will ignore persistent inflation for the present and simply consider increases or decreases in both individual prices and the overall price level.

If the movements of a firm's own price are highly correlated with the movements in the overall price level, the firm can expect that a given increase in its own price is only a very small increase in its relative price. For example, if, on the average, a 10 percent increase in its own price will be associated with a 9 percent increase in the overall price level, then the firm will expect only a 1 percent increase in its relative price when its own price rises by 10 percent. In this situation the firm will increase its output only very little.

On the other hand, in a firm where changes in the price of its own product are usually unrelated to changes in the overall price level, an increase in its own price will be seen primarily as an increase in its relative price. For example, if, on the average, a 10 percent increase in its own price will be associated with only a 1 percent increase in the overall price level, then the firm will expect a 9 percent increase in its relative price when its own price rises by 10 percent. In this situation the firm will increase its output a lot.

Differences among firms in a given economy will lead to differences in short-run responses to price changes. And it may also lead to overall differences among different economies. In an economy that always maintains stability in its overall price level, firms come to expect that changes in the prices of their own products must be changes in the relative prices of those products. In this case, small price changes will lead to large changes in output. If the money supply were to be increased in such an economy and the overall price level were to rise, the result would be a large increase in aggregate output as most firms would assume that their own prices have increased. The Lucas supply curve will be very flat in such an economy. If there has not been much inflation in an economy, then a sudden burst of inflation will fool people into raising output.

The opposite will hold in an economy with a great deal of variability in the general price level. Firms will assume that changes in the prices of their own products are mostly the result of gyrations in the overall price level and they will not respond by changing their production. In such a situation, an increase in the money supply will not result in much increase in aggregate output. The Lucas supply curve will be very steep. A sudden burst of inflation will have very little effect on output.

Lucas has used this analysis to help understand why the relations between output and inflation might be different in different countries. Those with a wide variability of inflation will have steep supply schedules with small increases in output resulting from a given increase in the inflation rate. Those with stable rates of inflation will have flat supply schedules. Lucas found some support for his model in his sample of 18 countries.[*]

To understand his argument, however, it is important to remember that it is the *variability* of inflation that is important, not the level of inflation. We assumed earlier there was no persistent inflation, but that is not generally the case in practice. In the Lucas model, where people have rational expectations, any stable rate of inflation will simply be factored into people's calculations and should not affect the slope of the supply curve. The Lucas supply curve's slope will not necessarily be different in economies with different average rates of inflation. This will only be the case if higher average inflation is also associated with greater variability of inflation.

---

[*] Robert E. Lucas, Jr., "Some International Evidence on Output–Inflation Tradeoffs," *American Economic Review* 63 (June 1973), pp. 326–34.

fluctuations of output around potential output reflect the fact that people's expectations are not always realized even though they are formed rationally. A higher-than-expected price level must have resulted from a shock or disturbance to the economy that could not have been foreseen by a rational evaluation of the economy. Only an *unexpected* shock or disturbance to the economy can cause actual prices to so exceed expected prices that actual real wages are lower than the real wages workers expect to receive. Workers, therefore, work more and output exceeds potential output.

The assumptions of rational expectations and flexible prices and wages play an important role in the analysis. The movement of output above potential output will be only temporary. In the next period, workers make full use of available information to form a new expected price level. And since their expectations are rational, they will not consistently overestimate or underestimate the future price level. In any given period, *there is the same likelihood that the actual price level is above the expected price level as below it, and so output in any period is as likely to be above potential as below it.* Deviations of output from potential output occur randomly.

The Monetary Basis of Aggregate Demand and Equilibrium   In the rational-expectations model, aggregate demand is a monetary phenomenon determined by a quantity equation—the price level times output is equal to the stock of money times velocity. Provided the actual money supply and velocity turn out to be equal to their expected values, the expected price level will prevail and, by assumption, this price level is the one that will result in output equal to potential output.

Changes in aggregate demand (changes in the money supply or in velocity) come about because of unexpected events. If monetary policy takes an unexpected turn or if velocity changes, the money stock and velocity will differ from their expected values. The result will be that the price level will differ from the expected price level and output will be affected.

In Figure 15–3 aggregate equilibrium is shown at potential output (point A) that occurs when expectations about the price level are realized. This occurs when the money stock times velocity (MV) is equal to the expected price level times potential output ($P^{exp} \times Y^P$). There are no surprises in the growth of the money supply or in the velocity, so the actual price level in this case (P_A) turns out to be equal to the expected price level. The aggregate-demand schedule, AD, is drawn for this case.

When there is an unanticipated increase in the money supply or velocity, actual aggregate demand is higher than expected and the economy comes into temporary equilibrium (point B) with output exceeding potential. This is shown by the aggregate-demand schedule, AD'. The actual price level in this case (P_B) turns out to be above the expected price level.

The shocks that cause variations in the price level and output occur because of *monetary surprises*—unexpected changes in the money supply or velocity, or both. Like the Monetarists, equilibrium–business-cycle economists see policy gyrations and **monetary shocks** as the main causes of the business cycle. Monetary shocks are unexpected changes in aggregate demand; changes in the money supply times velocity (changes in $M \times V$). At times monetary shocks can originate in the private sector; for example, if people's preference for holding money changes, then velocity may

monetary shock
An unexpected change in the money supply or velocity, or both. Also called a monetary surprise.

FIGURE 15-3
The Split between
Nominal and Real
Effects in an Equi-
librium Business
Cycle

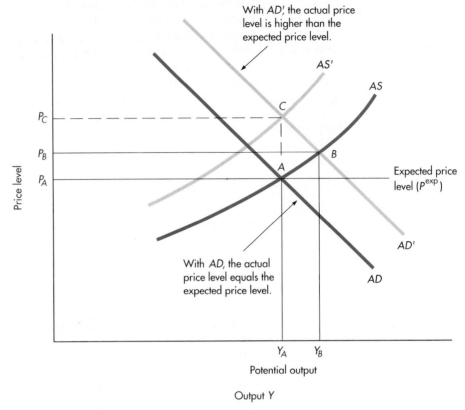

Unexpected changes in the money supply or velocity, or both, lead to short-run changes in output and the price level. In the long run they lead to changes in the price level only.

change. But mostly, monetary shocks come from the inconsistent and highly variable nature of shifts in the money supply brought about by the way in which the Fed uses monetary policy for stabilization. To illustrate, in the face of an increase in the rate of inflation, the Fed will initially take an anti-inflationary position; but it has often switched to an inflation-neutral or inflation-accommodating policy position. The Fed has even moved back and forth from one monetary stance to the other as the goals of Fed policy change. As such, Fed policy actions are often unanticipated—the Fed itself may not know in advance how it will react to economic circumstances.

The Effect of Monetary Shocks on Real Output and Inflation   In all of the different macroeconomic models, the effect of monetary shocks can be separated into nominal effects (changes in the price level and inflation) and real effects (changes in output and employment). If the effects are all nominal, there is no real impact of a fluctuation on the economy; this is the purely classical result. If the effects are all real, economic fluctuations exact a very large toll in lost output and employment; this is the purely Keynesian result. The *IS–LM* model uses the output–inflation trade-off to predict how a given change in aggregate demand will be split between changes in output and changes in inflation.

The Monetarists used the monetary growth equation to describe aggregate demand, which says that the rate of change of aggregate demand is equal to the rate of change of real income plus the rate of inflation:

$$\frac{\Delta M}{M} + \frac{\Delta V}{V} = \frac{\Delta (MV)}{MV} = \frac{\Delta Y}{Y} + \frac{\Delta P}{P} \tag{15–2}$$

And in the Monetarist model it was assumed that changes in aggregate demand would fall in part on real output $\left(\dfrac{\Delta Y}{Y}\right)$ in the short run. The changes might be unexpected and it is assumed that there is some short-run stickiness of prices so the increases in $\dfrac{\Delta (MV)}{MV}$ are larger than the increase in $\dfrac{\Delta P}{P}$.

In contrast, the equilibrium–business-cycle model assumes no price stickiness beyond the very short-run gap between an unexpected demand increase and realization that inflation will follow. The *only* reason that changes in aggregate demand will affect real output is if the changes are unexpected. After such an unexpected change, the economy quickly responds to an aggregate-demand shock through readjustments of expected prices. As shown in Figure 15–3, in the long run, as the higher actual price level (P_C) once again is equal to a higher expected price level, equilibrium occurs at potential output (point C). The effect of the shift in aggregate demand only raises the price level.

If aggregate demand (MV) is equal to its expected value, then the rate of growth of real income just equals the rate of growth of potential output and the rate of inflation equals its expected rate. If the rate of change of aggregate demand differs from what is expected, then this will split into real effects (output changes) and nominal effects (price changes). The exact shares of the increase going to real income and to inflation will depend on how much more labor is employed when firms see real wages temporarily drop. The responsiveness of output to the aggregate-demand surprise is illustrated by the shape of the aggregate-supply schedule and the speed with which aggregate supply reacts (*AS* to *AS′*) to the rise in the price level over time.

The equilibrium–business-cycle model is a complete model, therefore, in which aggregate demand and supply interact to determine real output and inflation. It combines the assumption that expectations are formed by making a rational evaluation of future economic conditions with the assumption that the economy is composed of markets that clear quickly in a classical manner. The equilibrium–business-cycle model provides a clear alternative to the other models we have described. We have argued that the systematic use of economic policies, both monetary and fiscal, affects economic performance. In the equilibrium–business-cycle model, changes in aggregate demand and, therefore, changes in fiscal- and monetary-policy actions have no effect on the economy unless they are unexpected.[6]

What kind of a business cycle is predicted by this equilibrium model? If this model describes the actual economy, we would expect to see random short-term fluctuations in output. Given that prices and wages are very flexible and move quickly toward equilibrium, the economy can only maintain a level of output that exceeds potential as long as shocks to the economy continue to boost actual prices above expected prices. It would require a series of shocks, all in the same direction, to maintain output either persistently above or persistently below potential output. This is possible but unlikely. Coins do not come up heads many times in a row very often. Therefore, the rational-expectations model predicts that persistent or sustained recessions or booms are unlikely.

THE RATIONALIST CRITIQUE OF STABILIZATION POLICY

The implications of rational-expectations theory for policy are really a strong form of the Monetarist position. Monetarists start with the view that the economy is basically stable, but they allow that frictions and even temporary price stickiness can slow the adjustment back to full employment. Monetarists argue that stabilization policy is undesirable, because it is so mistake-prone and subject to lags and inaccuracies. The rational-expectations theorists go further than this. They assume that the private economy is very efficient indeed and that information, including information about economic policy, is incorporated into expectations and acted on. Economic policies then become a totally ineffective way to stabilize the economy.

The Policy-Ineffectiveness Theorem

In an economy with rational expectations, people will form expectations about which policy actions governments will take under different circumstances. And they will adjust their behavior in the light of these expectations. If the government's response to a particular set of economic conditions is predictable, then the government is said to be following a program or regime of *systematic policymaking*. Systematic policymaking will be incorporated into expectations and there will be no unexpected policy shocks. Since, in the rational-expectations view, only an *unexpected* shock can cause output to differ from potential, systematic policy is ineffective as a tool for raising or lowering output.

The notion that policy that is anticipated is policy that is ineffective comes from the work of Thomas Sargent and Neil Wallace.[7] They developed the **policy-ineffectiveness theorem.** This theorem says that any systematic stabilization policy

---

[6] While the rational-expectations model allows for the possibility that policy could have an effect if it affected aggregate supply, there do not appear to be any supply-side policy instruments (subsidies to education and R&D, immigration policies, changes in tax incentives) that can be made into effective tools for the stabilization of the business cycle.

[7] Thomas Sargent and Neil Wallace, "Rational Expectations, the Optimal Monetary Instrument and the Optimal Money Supply Rule," *Journal of Political Economy* 83 (April 1975), pp. 241–54.

policy-ineffectiveness theorem
If only unexpected changes in policy affect output, systematic or expected changes in policy cannot affect output and, therefore, stabilization policy is ineffective.

designed to mitigate the business cycle will be ineffective. The theorem is based on the idea that meaningful stabilization policy must be directed at some end or goal and thus it cannot be random or totally unexpected. Then the equilibrium–business-cycle model predicts that a policy that is anticipated is ineffective. Thus the conclusion is that stabilization policy is impotent.

To explain the theorem further, suppose that the Federal Reserve followed a systematic policy rule of setting the growth rate of the money supply at 2.5 percent a year in normal times to accommodate the trend growth in potential output. Whenever the unemployment rate goes 1 percentage point above or below the natural rate of unemployment, the Fed will expand the money supply at an annual rate higher or lower than 2.5 percent. This policy rule could be either explicitly stated or observed over time. Either way, the policy would be anticipated and incorporated into the expected change in the money supply.

Suppose unemployment actually rises. There will be an expectation that aggregate demand will rise, reflecting the anticipation that the Fed will react to the rise in unemployment by increasing the rate of growth of the money supply. The increase in the expected growth of the money supply leads to an increase in the expected rate of inflation. When the increase in the growth of money supply actually occurs, the subsequent actual rise in the price level will equal the expected rise in the price level. Since output and employment only rise when the actual price level exceeds the expected price level, the result of the application of the policy rule will be that output and unemployment are no different than they would have been in the absence of the policy rule. Inflation will certainly be higher as a result of the attempt at recession fighting. And this is a pure cost, for nothing was gained.

In the equilibrium–business-cycle model, the Fed's stabilization policy would only have been effective in increasing output if the Fed had engineered a much larger than anticipated increase in the money supply; but that would mean the Fed chose not to follow its systematic policy rule—rather, it engineered a surprise. Of course, that would only work as long as the policy is unexpected. Repeating the same policy in reaction to the same circumstances would surprise no one.

Some critics of the policy-ineffectiveness theorem argue that in practice policy is not made according to a systematic rule that market participants can learn. But this criticism misses the point. If you accept the underlying assumptions of the equilibrium–business-cycle model, the theorem shows it is only the random or unexpected part of policy that will affect real output. And since stabilization policy by its nature implies that government is expected to take expansionary actions during recessions and contractionary actions during booms, there is no sensible case to be made for a stabilization policy based on always doing the unexpected. A sensible stabilization policy will be contractionary in booms and expansionary in recessions and people will come to expect that pattern. The importance or validity of the policy-ineffectiveness theorem follows directly from the equilibrium–business-cycle model. The validity of the theorem turns on the validity of that model.

In the face of policy ineffectiveness, the equilibrium–business-cycle model gener-ates a policy prescription, a prescription similar to that offered by the monetarists.

If a stable policy regime were followed, such as Friedman's constant–money-supply–growth rule, then cyclical fluctuations would be greatly reduced. There might still be cyclical fluctuations in the economy, because there are some shocks to the velocity of money originating in the private sector of the economy. But these fluctuations are unavoidable, because the government has no way of knowing about them any sooner than does the private economy. The private economy will do a better job of offsetting these shocks than will the policymakers.

Taxation and the Deficit   In terms of effectiveness, fiscal policy designed to control aggregate demand fares no better than does monetary policy under rational-expectations theory. Consider the following fiscal-policy action. The government attempts to stimulate aggregate demand by cutting taxes, but not expenditures. To finance this deficit, the government must issue new debt. Since under a rational-expectations view of the world, everyone knows that the debt repayment will raise taxes in the future, saving goes up in anticipation of future tax liabilities. There is no net stimulation to aggregate demand. We described this idea, developed by Robert Barro,[8] in Chapter 13.

Time-Inconsistent Policies   The rational-expectations analysis of the ineffectiveness of policies designed to control output have suggested a general problem with government policy actions. A policy that works in the short run may not work in the long run. The argument is that, if stated policy intentions are carried out, they are anticipated and, therefore, ineffective. If stated policy intentions are not carried out, they suffer from time-inconsistency and are ineffective because they lack credibility.[9]

time-inconsistent policies
Policies that, if pursued, realize their intended effects in the short run but have a reversed effect in the long run.

The problem of **time-inconsistent policies** is familiar to any manager. In the short run it is more efficient for the skilled manager to take any difficult task that comes along. He can do it better than any of his employees. In the long run, this means that no one else learns how to deal with the problems and the manager is overloaded. Efficiency in the long run requires sacrifices of efficiency in the short run.

Time-inconsistent policies are also familiar in industrial policy. In the 1960s, many patent-infringement cases were brought to court. One company had a patent and another company was producing a product that used the technology. Judges and juries would look at the situation and see a big profitable company that had developed a technology some years before and was now making a ton of money from it by charging consumers a high price for the product. The patent was being infringed by a small company that was cutting its price to sell in the big company's market. The courts very often ruled against the company that held the patent.

---

[8]   Robert Barro, "Are Government Bonds Net Wealth?" *Journal of Political Economy,* December 1974.
[9]   Finn Kydland and Edward Prescott, "Rules Rather Than Discretion: The Inconsistency of Optimal Plans," *Journal of Political Economy,* June 1977.

Over time, this trend in the courts created problems. Companies that were spending millions on R&D were having trouble getting a return from their ideas. If it is possible to wait and see what another company comes up with and then just imitate that product, why spend millions on R&D? R&D spending fell in the 1970s and there was concern that innovation would suffer. The courts were using a time-inconsistent policy.

Macroeconomic policies to stabilize the economy are time-inconsistent if they rely on surprises. In the equilibrium–business-cycle model, policies only affect output if they surprise people, so stabilization policy is a time-inconsistent policy within this model.

There is a problem of time-inconsistent policies even within the *IS–LM* trade-off model. We saw how expansionary policies in the 1960s resulted in large output gains in the short run but gradually created inflation problems in the longer run, which could only be cured by recession and high unemployment. The policies of that period were time-inconsistent.

We do not agree, however, that stabilization policies are always time-inconsistent. Indeed, the opposite may be true. If there are fundamental sources of stickiness and instability in the economy, then stabilization policy can work to improve stability in ways that do not rely purely on surprising people. In fact, as the economy became more stable in the postwar period, this actually reinforced stabilization policy, because private decisions become less volatile as people became more confident that the Great Depression would not return.

The Critique of Econometric-Policy Evaluation

The estimates of the parameters of economic relationships are made using the statistical analysis of economic data, a field called *econometrics*. Econometricians attempt to measure the direction and magnitude of economic relationships as well as assessing the probability that a relationship exists or has a particular value. Econometrics is used to verify or support the implications of economic models, and it is often used to evaluate the impact of economic policies. For example, policymakers facing a rise in inflation will not only want to know if raising taxes and reducing the growth of the money supply will bring down inflation, they also will want to know how much of a decrease in aggregate demand is required to generate a targeted drop in the inflation rate and how much of a drop in income and unemployment will accompany that policy action. Econometric studies conducted in the 1960s found a correlation between the accelerating inflation and the high level of output. That analysis supported the notion that the trade-off between inflation and output was relevant for policy.

One of the first arguments that Robert Lucas made when introducing rational expectations into the debate over macroeconomics is that much of the econometric work that had been done in the past to test either the effectiveness of policy or the nature of the output–inflation trade-off was invalid. The **Lucas critique** focused on the estimates of the parameters of the output–inflation trade-off. Lucas argued that the econometric evidence was misleading and that no such trade-off existed. Rather, the Fed in the 1960s had abandoned its commitment to price stability and allowed the money supply to grow rapidly and inflation to accelerate. This development was not

Lucas critique
When policy changes, this may change the relationship among economic variables.

expected by workers and firms, so the price level was consistently higher than anticipated and output was above potential output.

Inevitably this situation had to change, argued Lucas. Policymakers could not go on indefinitely fooling people in the same direction—by accelerating inflation. Econometric estimates made from data covering primarily the 1960s would not provide a guide to the output–inflation trade-off in other periods.

In a related argument, Lucas also critiqued the policy analysis by both Keynesian and Monetarist economists, which estimated the impact of monetary-policy and fiscal-policy changes on output. Relating output changes to monetary-policy changes is again a misspecification, says Lucas, because it does not distinguish between anticipated and unanticipated policy. In historical data there will be a correlation between changes in money and changes in output. But this correlation is being driven by the effect on output of the unanticipated part of the change in the money supply. As was shown in the policy-ineffectiveness theorem, this relation cannot be used as the basis for systematic stabilization policy.

In summary, Lucas argued that, if econometric estimates had been made over a period when the public correctly anticipated the course of monetary policy, the results would have been different. The estimates of the impact of monetary policy covered a period when much of the movement in the money supply was unanticipated.

REAL–BUSINESS-CYCLE MODELS

technology shock
Any increase or decrease in productivity separate from changes in the quantity of inputs.

real–business-cycle models
Neo-classical models that argue that all economic fluctuations are the result of technology shocks or labor-supply shocks.

Because of concerns about the ability of the equilibrium–business-cycle model to explain actual economic fluctuations, a new approach has been developed by rational-expectations economists that accepts many of the features of the equilibrium business cycle, but that posits an alternative source of cyclical fluctuations. The new models replace the conclusion of the equilibrium–business-cycle models that fluctuations result from policy surprises, with the hypothesis that fluctuations are the results of shifts in aggregate supply that are the result of **technology shocks** (productivity shifts) or labor-supply shocks (shifts in workers' willingness to work). Shifts in the money market will not change real output; only changes in the real economy can bring about changes in real income—hence these models are called **real–business-cycle models**.[10] The new models (like the equilibrium–business-cycle models) argue that markets are always in equilibrium and they reject the business-cycle analysis of the Keynesian models. The sources of fluctuations in output and employment are traced to shifts in supply or demand, or both, in the labor market, when the labor market is modeled in much the same way as in the classical model.

---

[10] Finn Kydland and Edward Prescott, "Time to Build and Aggregate Fluctuations," *Econometrica* 50 (November 1982), pp. 1345–70; and Robert G. King and Charles I. Plosser, "Money, Credit and Prices in a Real Business Cycle," *American Economic Review* 74 (June 1984), pp. 363–80.

FIGURE 15–4 Changes in Preferences and Changes in Technology Shift Employment and Hence Output

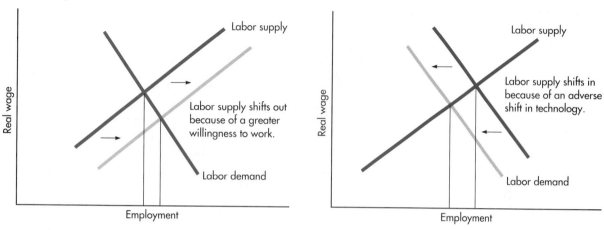

Figure 15–4 illustrates the way in which output variations occur in the real–business-cycle model. In the left panel, an increase in output is shown to have occurred, because of an increase in the number of people who want to work at a given wage. There has been a shift in people's preference for work. The right panel shows the case of a decline in the demand for labor, because of an adverse change in technology. Real–business-cycle theorists regard both shifts in workers' preferences and technology shocks as explanations of cyclical fluctuations in output. But technology shocks have been the focus of most of the attention in these models.

Technology Shocks

Within economic models, the term *changes in technology* has a broad meaning. It refers to changes in the way in which production is undertaken—any increase or decrease in output, separate from changes in the quantity of inputs. A positive or negative shift in technology—broadly defined—is a technology shock. Most technology shocks are thought to be positive, resulting from innovations in the design and engineering of production technologies and improvements in management practices. But conditions for production can deteriorate as well as improve. The adverse shift in technology shown in the lower panel of Figure 15–4 describes a drop in output due to a reduction of the marginal product of labor and labor productivity has fallen, because production conditions have worsened. This adverse shift may have resulted, for example, from changes in the environment or failures of management.

The measure of productivity that fits best with this broad meaning of change in technology is a concept called *multifactor productivity.* Multifactor productivity measures productivity net of changes in the amount of labor and capital used in production, thereby providing an indication of how technology is changing.

FIGURE 15–5
Multifactor-
Productivity
Growth and Output
Growth, 1949–1992

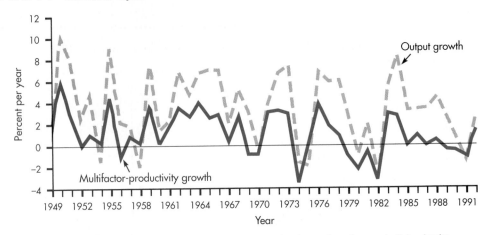

Output growth and multifactor-productivity growth tend to move closely together. Are productivity shocks leading to changes in output? Or are output changes leading to changes in productivity?

In support of their model of economic fluctuations, the advocates of real–business-cycle theory point to the close positive relation between changes in multifactor productivity and output. When output is unusually large, then productivity is unusually high; when output is low, productivity is also low. Figure 15–5 shows the year-to-year changes in multifactor productivity and in output, with the two series showing a strong positive association.[11] This positive correlation between output and productivity is not what one would expect from a standard analysis of production within the mainstream model. If fluctuations in output are driven by fluctuations in demand, as is assumed in both the mainstream model and in the equilibrium–business-cycle model, and if firms hire more workers and produce more output in booms, because of this high demand, then we would expect to see low productivity in booms, because of diminishing returns to labor. The advocates of real–business-cycle theory conclude that the year-to-year variations in productivity that are positively correlated with output indicate there are large technology shocks—shocks to *supply*—that cause changes in output.

It is important to be clear about where the difference of opinion is here. All economists recognize that technology and productivity changes are responsible for most of the long-run changes in output. However, the real–business-cycle models argue that short-run changes in productivity determine changes in output over the business cycle. In some years, the conditions for production are unusually good. Firms go out and bid for workers, driving up the real wage and increasing employment and output. Such periods are then called *booms*. In some years, the conditions are unusually bad, as the technology of production lowers the marginal productivity of

11 N. Gregory Mankiw, ''Real Business Cycles: A New Keynesian Perspective,'' *Journal of Economic Perspectives* 3 (Summer 1989), p. 84. Mankiw discusses real–business-cycle models in this paper, but he himself is not an advocate of them. We have updated his figure.

workers and firms lay off workers, drive down the real wage, and reduce output. These periods are *recessions.*

ASSESSING EQUILIBRIUM–BUSINESS-CYCLE AND REAL–BUSINESS-CYCLE MODELS

There are two key elements in the equilibrium–business-cycle model. (1) People have rational expectations but there is incomplete information, so there are fluctuations in aggregate demand. (2) Wages and prices are not only flexible but they also move toward equilibrium values. The real–business-cycle model essentially carries over these same elements, but it argues that incomplete information does not provide an adequate model of the business cycle. Instead, fluctuations in output and employment are driven by aggregate-supply shocks, primarily technology shocks.

In assessing these models, we look first at the issue of whether people have rational expectations. Proponents of rational expectations point to individual markets for goods and services that appear to work efficiently, with buyers and sellers making good use of information and forming expectations of future market conditions. They argue that the economy, which is the collection of all market activity, should also behave as if driven by rational expectations about the behavior of efficient markets. The case for or against rational expectations depends on the issues of just how efficient individual markets are and how well rational-expectations models describe the workings of many markets together.

Support from Efficient Markets and Arbitrage

arbitrage
Taking advantage of the profit opportunities of either price differences for the same asset in different markets or of price changes over time.

Proponents of the rational-expectations models argue that the assumption that expectations are formed by a rational assessment of future economic conditions does not require that all market participants individually have rational expectations and be wonderfully adept at economic decision making. Many people may not bother to inform themselves about the economy. Many others may be foolish or misunderstand the system. However, because of a phenomenon called **arbitrage,** as long as there are enough buyers and sellers who form rational expectations in any particular market, this may be all that is necessary for the market to behave as if all the people held rational expectations. Arbitrage involves people buying assets to sell them later for a profit. The opportunity to profit from arbitrage occurs when market participants hold different expectations about future asset values. Arbitrageurs who expect asset prices to rise will bid for assets from those who do not expect this. If those who hold rational expectations have a demand for assets that is sufficiently large, then arbitrage will drive prices to the same levels that would have prevailed if everyone had rational expectations.

Arbitrage also plays an important role in the rationale for the equilibrium–business-cycle model. The advocates of this model argue that the explanation of the business cycle that they propose is the only one consistent with markets that work efficiently. In the *IS–LM* model, a recession is a time when there are workers who want to work but who cannot find jobs at the going wage. There are firms who want to make profits, and consumers who want to buy more, but somehow the economy fails to coordinate these activities and exploit this opportunity. Rational-expectations economists argue this

Smart Money and Noise Traders

Is modern economics of any use in understanding the ups and downs of stock markets?

Market practitioners and academic economists seem further apart than ever in their explanations for the volatility of financial markets, especially stock markets. Most traders find the idea that markets are "optimally forecasting the future flow of real dividends" laughable. Most academic economists regard this notion as so obviously true that they take it as an axiom in their research, not as a claim to be investigated.

If communication is to improve, it will be thanks to those few academics who are both interested in the mechanics of real markets and want a scientific account of the forces that drive them. A leader of this band is Mr. Robert Shiller, a young professor of economics at Yale University. A volume of his papers has just been published. Here is an economics book about financial markets that thoughtful practitioners will find interesting.

To understand why academics and practitioners cannot agree, it is necessary to understand why the academics cling to their view of financial markets. They say that stock prices reflect the most informed possible view of future streams of dividends (a theory also known as the efficient-market hypothesis or random-walk theory, because a price that already reflects all that is known will be knocked either way by the next unknown). That may seem at odds with reality. But once you understand the idea, it is both plausible and resistant to counterargument.

A key point is this: If the idea were not true, it would mean that the market was failing to take account of information that was relevant for predicting future prices. Hence the forecast would not be optimal. In that case, (*a*) the discovery of such information would yield enormous profits to the discoverer and (*b*) in collecting those profits by trading in the market the discoverer would incorporate the information in market prices.

So a mechanism exists to make the efficient-market hypothesis true. What about evidence? Well, it is evidence of a sort that share prices are not forecastable. If they were, then the forecasting model would itself be a piece of unexploited information. Over longish periods (a year or more, say) share prices are, in fact, somewhat forecastable. One of Mr. Shiller's papers shows that in years when Wall Street began with a higher-than-average dividend yield (i.e., when prices were low in relation to dividends), prices rose by more than average. The correlation is not strong, but it is there, and it goes against the grain of the optimal-forecast theory.

Over shorter periods, however, many studies have shown that share prices do indeed follow a random walk. Prices are as likely to rise as to fall in the future, regardless of information about prices in earlier periods, or even (in stricter versions of the theory) of all currently available information. Overall, then, the evidence favors the optimal-forecast theory.

But consider another sort of evidence. The sheer volatility of stock markets seems to argue against the optimal-forecast idea. If share prices are a weighted

would mean there are profit opportunities in the economy that are not being exploited, and why should this be? After all, people do not leave $100 bills lying on the sidewalk. Efficient arbitrage should eliminate profit opportunities.

The same point is made in arguing against government policy as a way of improving the efficiency of the economy. How can the government through systematic policy expect to improve on the outcome of a market where arbitrageurs always stand ready to enter?

Doubts about Rational Expectations

When observing the behavior of actual markets to see whether they are consistent with the equilibrium–business-cycle model, we need to separate the assumption of price flexibility from the assumption of rational expectations. One market where prices are

average of discounted future dividends, they should iron out any fluctuations in dividends, and thus be less volatile than dividends. Actually, they are far more volatile. Mr. Shiller finds that, if uncertainty of future dividends can be measured by the past variability of dividends, stock-price volatility is between 5 and 13 times too great (depending on the period examined) to be consistent with optimal-forecast theory.

The theory can be rescued, mind. It might be incorrect to measure uncertainty about future dividends by looking at their past variability. Or you might assume that expected real interest rates vary a lot. This would account for big changes in share prices: it represents a change in the discount rate that the market is applying to the stream of future dividends. But Mr. Shiller works out how far expectations of real interest rates would have needed to move to account for the fluctuations in share prices. For 1928–79 the required variation (given certain other assumptions) was from minus-8 percent to plus-17 percent. It is hard to believe that expectations of real interest rates fluctuate within anything like such a wide range.

To reconcile all this conflicting evidence, Mr. Shiller favors a theory that divides stock and other financial markets into two sorts of participants: smart money and "ordinary investors," known unflatteringly in the jargon as noise traders. Broadly, smart money behaves like investors are supposed to behave in the optimal-forecast theory: it searches for all relevant information, incorporating this into prices quickly and smoothly.

Noise traders, who constitute most of the market, are influenced by fads and fashions. They are slow to under-

stand the significance of new information (including advice from smart-money experts). They are not stupid. They might often do better than smart money in the market, by being "wrong" at an auspicious moment. Smart money presumably fled the overvalued stock market in the first half of 1987; some lucky noise traders will have "incorrectly" stayed in, only leaving in the first week of October. Indeed, as Mr. Shiller and others have pointed out, the richest people in the market are unlikely to be smart money; they are more likely to be a tiny fraction of the noise traders who, in their time, have blundered into a fortune through recklessness or plain luck.

Analyzing this two-part market is difficult. Smart money and noise traders will interact in complicated ways—for instance, smart money will monitor not just the "fundamentals" but also the fashions (including the predictions of chartists) that drive noise traders. Working all this out is a matter not just of theory but of lots of close observation. Mr. Shiller is good at both.

This research is still at an early stage. However, it is already clear that the division of the market into smart money and noise traders can solve a big mystery. If smart money finds and exploits the profit opportunities contained in market information, then prices will be pretty unforecastable, as both the optimal-forecast model and the evidence suggest. At the same time, the combination of smart money and noise traders can account for the markets' puzzling volatility.

clearly flexible is the stock market, the market in corporate stocks and shares, so by looking at the stock market we can get a good sense of the validity of the rational-expectations assumptions.

Although the final verdict has not yet been given, some tests have indicated that share prices vary much more than would be predicted from the variability of the dividends and corporate earnings that give value to stocks.[12] The stock market is subject to bouts of speculative fever that drive individual stock prices or even market

---

[12] Robert J. Shiller, *Market Volatility* (Cambridge, Mass.: MIT Press, 1990).

averages way up and then way down—for example, the run-up of stock prices in 1987 that culminated in the October 1987 crash.

It seems that stock-market traders can be divided roughly into two groups: ordinary investors (noise traders) and smart money. The ordinary investors are influenced by fads and may drive stock prices up and down even when the fundamental determinants of stock values have changed very little. The smart-money investors understand the fundamentals and they should provide the arbitrage that results in a rational-expectations market. But it turns out that being able to read market psychology or being plain lucky is as good if not better a way of making money in the stock market as being an expert in the fundamentals of stock valuation. This means the smart investors do not necessarily come to dominate the stock market. And if this is the case, arbitrage does not ensure that the stock market behaves with rational expectations.

There is no general agreement concerning the question of whether the stock market behaves in a way consistent with rational expectations. Reasonable people can view the evidence and reach different conclusions. Once we look outside markets, such as the stock market, however, it is harder to make the case that arbitrage ensures rational expectations.

In such markets as the stock market or the bond market there are many arbitrageurs at work, but the situation is not the same in the markets for the goods and services that make up GDP, nor is it true for the labor market. Many of the people who buy and sell in these markets do not concern themselves with incorporating information about monetary policy or other macroeconomic variables into their decisions. And arbitrage may not be able to introduce rational expectations in this situation.[13]

If money wages are too high, causing unemployment, even a knowledgeable market participant who has rational expectations about future monetary policy cannot immediately profit from that superior knowledge. If autoworkers are laid off and they are overoptimistic about their chances of getting their old jobs back or they are overoptimistic about the alternative jobs they can obtain elsewhere, then the result will be persistent unemployment. Someone cannot come along and simply bet the unemployed workers that they are wrong. One could prove they are wrong by setting up a competing auto plant that pays lower wages, but it is not easy to start up a new auto plant to compete against an established company. Any such investment decision would have to be based on long-run considerations, not on errors in expectations.

The difficulties of making money when people have incorrect expectations also applies to many other situations. When the demand for single-family houses or for commercial real estate declines, we observe that houses stay on the market for many months and that commercial office buildings sit unrented. There is a phenomenon analogous to unemployment in the real estate market. Prices do not fall quickly to clear the market for single-family houses. Office rentals do not fall to clear the market for commercial space. One explanation for this is that people are overoptimistic about what price they can get for their house or how quickly they can rent their building. If

---

13 J. Haltiwanger and M. Waldman, "Rational Expectations and the Limits of Rationality," *American Economic Review,* June 1985, pp. 326–40.

this is indeed the case, there is no arbitrage mechanism by which someone with rational expectations can make a profit by using their superior information. Buying up overpriced houses or office buildings is a way to lose money, not make it.

To conclude on rational expectations: The rational-expectations revolution in economics has had a profound impact. Prior to the work of such economists as Robert Lucas and Thomas Sargent, naive macroeconomic models implied that people repeatedly expected inflation to be lower than it turned out to be. It was a mistake to assume such behavior. The analysis of financial markets, the trade-off, and the foreign-exchange market have all been affected by the idea of rational expectations and these impacts have been reflected in this book. In markets where similar events happen over and over, people will learn rational expectations by experience. In markets where arbitrage is possible, rational expectations will be important and may come to dominate the behavior of the market. These arguments can be taken too far, however. There are many markets where people do not incorporate all available information into their economic decisions. In many cases there are people who do not understand the implications of much of the information that is available to them. And it is unlikely that arbitrage can always lead to markets that act as if everyone had rational expectations.

Doubts about Price and Wage Flexibility

Equilibrium–business-cycle models assume perfect price flexibility as well as rational expectations. And many economists find this assumption to be harder to accept than rational expectations. An important reason for this skepticism is that the equilibrium–business-cycle model does not predict fluctuations in output that fit with the observed pattern of fluctuations in the economy. And the pattern of unemployment in these models does not fit with the kind of unemployment that we observe in recessions.

The Persistence Problem   An important discrepancy between the rational-expectations models and observation is these models imply that deviations from potential output should be short-lived. But the experience of the actual economy is that *output moves slowly and persistently above or below potential for periods of several years at a time.* This was pointed out by Robert Hall, who noted that the assumptions of complete price flexibility and rational expectations left no room for recessions that last a long time.[14] The assumption of rational expectations means that people overestimate the price level as often as they underestimate it. Price flexibility assumes there are not impediments to adjustment. Rational-expectations models predict that output next period is as likely to be above potential output as below potential output. This will be true regardless of whether the economy is in a boom or a recession in this period. The basic Lucas model, therefore, describes an economy that quickly bounces around full employment. The Great Depression stands out as a particularly difficult

---

[14]   Robert E. Hall, ''The Rigidity of Wages and the Persistence of Unemployment,'' *Brookings Papers on Economic Activity, 2:1975,* pp. 301–50.

period to reconcile with the Lucas model, because output remained greatly depressed below potential for about 10 years.

There have been attempts to incorporate adjustment costs into the analysis so as to develop an equilibrium model with a more realistic business-cycle pattern. Also a reconsideration of the role of inventories can be used to explain persistence.[15] However, to the extent that these modifications succeed, they make the equilibrium model look more like the mainstream models of fluctuations where the basis for fluctuation is due to miscoordination and stickiness, not random shocks (see box). In general, the business cycle is characterized by substantial changes in output and employment and by only a small cyclical response of prices. Equilibrium–business-cycle theorists try to explain this pattern with models where prices are flexible, but where output is costly to adjust. This is bound to be a tough task. The persistence problem remains as a serious objection to the rational-expectations, equilibrium–business-cycle model.

Voluntary or Involuntary Unemployment   In the equilibrium–business-cycle model, all unemployment is voluntary, because the labor market clears at a market wage. A generation of economists that grew up in the Depression years, as well as many contemporary economists, object forcefully to models implying that cyclical unemployment is in any way voluntary. They recall vividly the despair of the unemployed, the soup kitchens, and the overall hardship that accompanied the Depression. Even in later periods, hardship created by severe recessions in 1958, 1975, and 1982 was widespread.

Robert Lucas admits that it is hard to reconcile the 1930s with his model of the cycle. Wages do not appear to have adjusted to restore equilibrium. But advocates of the equilibrium–business-cycle model argue that anecdotes about hardship among the unemployed do not provide a suitable test of alternative macroeconomic models. Workers may indeed be very adversely affected by large, unexpected changes in monetary policy. Such changes mislead workers into believing that they can only remain employed if they accept a lower real wage. Faced with two poor alternatives, workers choose to become unemployed, rather than work at lower wages. In the rational-expectations view, it is the bad policy that has created the problem, not a sudden change in the willingness of workers to work.

In the Keynesian view, individual workers are not seen as having a choice between offering to work at a lower wage and taking time at home. Unemployed workers do not have the option of offering to displace an existing employee by taking a wage that is 50 cents an hour less. Labor-market institutions do not allow that kind of competition. This may reflect an implicit social contract or perhaps firms are reluctant to replace workers, because of the human capital imbedded in the experience of an in-

---

15   Thomas J. Sargent, "Estimation of Dynamic Labor Demand Schedules under Rational Expectations," *Journal of Political Economy* 86, no. 6 (1978). Alan S. Blinder and Stanley Fischer, "Inventories, Rational Expectations and the Business Cycle," *Journal of Monetary Economics* 6 (November 1981), pp. 277–304 (see box).

The Persistence of Recessions, Adjustment Costs, and Inventories

Thomas Sargent has argued that recessions are persistent because firms face costs of adjusting output and employment. The cycle, for Sargent, looks as follows. An unexpected decline in aggregate demand induces an unexpected decline in the price level. The real wage rises, and employment and output fall. Then output grows slowly because it is costly for firms to rehire workers and expand production quickly.

Sargent is correct that there are adjustment costs, but it is doubtful whether these costs are large enough to explain the observed persistence of recession. While there are certainly significant managerial costs associated with laying off or firing workers, these are seen to be much less acute for rehiring laid-off workers. Some companies make very large month-to-month adjustments to employment and output because of demand fluctuations specific to their particular industries, and some firms hoard labor rather than letting employees go when faced with a downturn in the business cycle. This suggests that the simple adjustment costs of hiring and firing are a small part of the story. Most firms cite continued inadequate demand as the reason for persistently low output, not an unwillingness to meet the demand because of adjustment costs.

Alan Blinder and Stanley Fischer have offered a different explanation of persistence that is consistent with mainstream models. Inventories accumulated during downturns have to be worked off during booms, thereby dampening the cycle. This creates a carryover effect from recession in one period to the next.

place work force. Sometimes the threat of violence is used by workers to prevent other workers from undercutting their wages. Regardless, labor markets do not appear to operate in the efficient mode necessary to validate a flexible-wage view of the economy.

Criticisms of the Real–Business-Cycle Model

The problems experienced by the equilibrium model in explaining the observed persistence of output fluctuations were instrumental in motivating the development of the real–business-cycle model. This model suggests that changes in aggregate supply caused by technology shocks have been the reason for cyclical output changes. If there are shifts in technology, it would be hardly surprising that these would lead to persistent output changes.

The new theory has been subject to criticisms, however. The first problem with the model is simple but serious. *If changes in output are the result of changes in aggregate supply, rather than changes in aggregate demand, then the price level should fall in booms and rise in recessions.* Now we have seen in our earlier discussion of output and inflation that indeed there have been periods when inflation has risen as output has fallen. These episodes of stagflation took place in the 1970s and we identified them as supply-shock inflations. But these episodes are more the exceptions than the rule. *The normal pattern in business cycles is for prices to rise with rising output.* To explain the normal pattern of prices over the cycle, real–business-cycle theorists have to suggest there is some induced change in the money supply when the economy expands or contracts. One cannot explain the normal cyclical pattern by means of supply changes alone.

The second problem with the model is that many economists are skeptical of the idea that declines in output have been caused by technology declines. And the third problem is that the real–business-cycle model does not make realistic predictions about cyclical fluctuations in employment. These two issues need further explanation.

Questions about Productivity   The relationship between multifactor productivity and output (Figure 15–5) is the most supportive evidence of real–business-cycle theories. It suggests, at first sight, that output must be fluctuating as a result of shocks to the technology. However, further analysis of this idea reveals some problems with it. In particular, it is hard to know what might be causing these technology shocks and why negative shocks—that reduced productivity—should occur frequently. It is likely that technological change comes about slowly as a result of advances in basic science and engineering, research and development programs, the adoption of improved production methods, and changes in the education and skills of the work force. These changes lead to gradual improvements in productivity, not sudden changes. There may be a sudden breakthrough in technology, but this is likely to affect only a single industry and not bring about a macroeconomic business cycle.

Declines in technology are even harder to explain. There may have been some deterioration in the skills of the work force in the past few years, but this is not a plausible reason for short-term fluctuations in productivity. The oil-price increases that took place in 1973 and 1979 are plausible candidates for negative productivity shocks, because there were declines in productivity after these episodes. But even if we were to accept the oil-price increases as legitimate technology shocks, however, the other recessions in the postwar period, plus the recessions of previous periods, have no comparable technology-shock explanations. This is particularly true for the Great Depression. Proponents of the real–business-cycle theory have not come up with enough sources of technology shocks, either positive or negative. Technology shocks that are big enough to increase or reduce output in the economy as a whole should be big enough to be directly observable.

Productivity and the Business Cycle: Cause and Effect   The apparent puzzle that productivity is low in recessions and high in booms can be explained by looking at labor markets from the perspective of the business manager. When companies face a reduction in demand, they reduce their output and employment, but employment falls by less than the fall in output. More workers are employed than are immediately needed, reducing productivity. One reason for this is that firms do not want to lay off certain valuable employees who have special skills and knowledge of the production methods in their firms. This phenomena is called **labor hoarding,** and companies report that indeed they hoard labor during downturns. For many firms, it would not be possible to cut back on employment in proportion to the cut in output, even if there were no workers with special skills. Their plants are designed to operate at a certain level of production. If production falls, it is not possible to reorganize the workplace in the short run. Even the reengineering and total quality management programs invoked to restructure corporate effectiveness take months or years to come into effect. Even though production may generally be subject to constant returns to scale in the long run

labor hoarding
Retaining employees in the face of a decline in demand.

(so permanent reductions in output bring about proportional reductions in employ-ment), in the short run, employment variations are less than proportional to output variations.

Real–business-cycle theorists see the strong correlation between output and pro-ductivity and conclude that technology shocks are causing output changes. The mainstream view is that variations in demand are causing the changes in output and then the changes in productivity. The causality is running from output to productivity and not the other way around.

The economists who have been developing the real–business-cycle models have had great difficulty showing how year-to-year variations in employment could have come about, given their view of the cycle. Figure 15–6 shows the actual growth rate of hours worked in the economy together with the prediction of hours worked from one version of the real–business-cycle model. As is shown, there are noticeable differ-ences between the actual series and the predicted series. The real–business-cycle theorists have not been able to make their models consistent with the ups and downs of employment that we see in actual recessions and booms.

The problems this theory has in explaining employment (or hours worked) are much greater even than this figure suggests. The model that was used to generate the prediction of hours worked shown in the figure assumes that labor supply is very

FIGURE 15–6
Annual Growth Rate of Hours Worked, 1955–1985

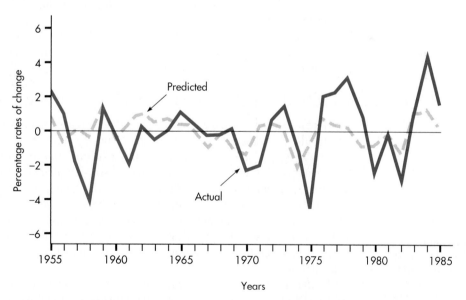

The actual fluctuations in hours worked over time are much greater than those predicted by the real–business-cycle model.

Source: Charles I. Plosser, "Understanding Real Business Cycles," *Journal of Economic Perspectives* 3, no. 3 (Summer 1989), p. 65.

responsive to changes in the real wage. The model assumes people want to increase their hours of work quite a bit when the wage rises, or lower their work effort when the wage falls. Empirical studies of labor supply do not find such responsiveness.

The real–business-cycle theorists have run into a serious problem in reconciling their model with actual experience, because they assume that the labor market is competitive with flexible wages and hence that employment varies only because workers respond to changes in the real wage. This same issue came up in the discussion of the Monetarist model, where we saw that the real wage does not vary much over the cycle. The only way to explain employment fluctuations in the real–business-cycle model is to assume that people want to increase the amount that they work a lot even though wages have gone up very little, if at all. This does not fit with the studies of how individuals respond to wages.

Conclusions on Equilibrium–Business-Cycle and Real–Business-Cycle Models

There are many ways in which the mainstream model of the macro economy has been influenced by the recent developments that have come out of the classical tradition. The assumption of rational expectations has become part of much mainstream analysis and the idea that cycles might be initiated by sudden bursts of technology is potentially an important one.

The advocates of the classical-based theories of the business cycle acknowledge there are problems with them. But they argue that the alternative mainstream model is fatally flawed, because it lacks a microeconomic foundation based on fully rational behavior. The economists that have tried to respond to this criticism are called "neo-Keynesians." This is an unfortunate name, because Keynes did not believe that such a framework was necessary or even desirable. But the name itself is not terribly important. More important is seeing how well these economists have done in providing explanations for wage and price stickiness.

NEO-KEYNESIAN ANALYSIS OF PRICE STICKINESS

A task that many neo-Keynesians have set themselves is to construct models in which individuals have rational expectations, make rational choices in which they maximize their own utility and companies maximize profit, but nevertheless the resulting decisions made by firms and workers involve slow adjustment of wages and prices. At the macroeconomic level, the sum of the individual decisions should lead to an economy where fluctuations in output result from changes in aggregate demand and there is involuntary unemployment during recessions. This task is an extremely difficult one. Indeed, it may be inherently impossible. But in the process of trying to complete it, much has been learned about price and wage setting and the reasons for price stickiness.

wage contracts
Union contracts set wages over periods of one to three years. There are also *implicit wage contracts*, based on an informal under-tanding between a firm and its workers.

We start by looking at the wage-setting process and the use of **wage contracts.** Then we turn to the price side and the adjustment (or nonadjustment) of markups. We conclude this discussion of **neo-Keynesian analysis** by looking at price flexibility or stickiness in the aggregate as well as the problem of coordinating price adjustments.

Wage Contracts

neo-Keynesian analysis
Models that accept the framework of rational choice and expectations and yet attempt to show how prices and wages may be sticky.

Wages in most companies are adjusted at intervals of six months, a year, or, in the case of many union wage contracts, every three years. Moreover, when the wages are adjusted, they are increased (or occasionally decreased) not primarily on the basis of the short-run conditions in the labor market but, rather, on the basis of the long-run trends of the economy. There is frequently some increase in the wage to adjust for the increase in the cost of living and then an additional amount that is linked to individual performance or to general productivity increases. Short-run market conditions have an impact, particularly if a firm is having trouble recruiting or retaining workers, when it may increase its wages. And if a firm is going broke, it may ask for wage concessions even if a union contract is not up for renegotiation. But the impact of short-run conditions is surprisingly small. Increases or decreases in the queue of unemployed workers have only small impacts on the wages being set for workers who have jobs. Even in recession when workers are losing their jobs, there is little change in the wages of the workers who keep their jobs. Wages depend on the overall economic climate, not on the current weather. Why is this?

The Wage in Long-Term Contracts   Young workers change jobs frequently and they may hold short-term jobs while in school. But as people get older, they usually settle into jobs that last a long time. Looking at data from the 1970s and taking men and women together, it has been found that *half of all work is done in jobs that last 15 years or more.* Among men, half of all work is done in jobs that last 25 years or more.[16] It is possible that job durations have shortened somewhat since then, but it is still the case today that this long-term relationship between workers and the companies they work for is extremely important to both sides. Firms count on having workers who know the ropes and will stay around to help train new hires. It is often necessary to give special training or retraining to employees; to make this worthwhile, companies have to know that their employees will remain on the job for some time after the training. From the employee's point of view, changing jobs is very costly. No one enjoys looking for jobs and being evaluated. Losing a job can create a stigma that makes it harder to find a new job.

Given that the employer–employee relationship is often a long-term one, it makes sense for firms to set up a wage policy that is geared not to short-term conditions but to the long term. Where there is a union, firms will negotiate a wage contract lasting one or more years that sets out the wages to be paid over the life of the contract. And union contracts usually have provisions governing work rules, hiring and firing, and grievances. When there is not a unionized work force (unions cover only about 15 percent of employment in the U.S. economy), employers will still be concerned about the long term and their reputations as employers. Employers will provide an *implicit contract.* This is an understanding between an employer and its employees about how wages will be adjusted, and it may also cover normal work rules.

---

[16]   Robert E. Hall, ''Employment Fluctuations and Wage Rigidity,'' *Brookings Papers on Economic Activity 1:1980,* pp. 91–124.

Since companies are in long-term relationships with many of their employees and use either implicit or explicit wage contracts, they will view the monthly or even the annual wage as being determined not by short-run supply and demand in the labor market but, rather, as one weekly or monthly payment on a long-term contract. Most people who take out loans to buy houses or cars arrange for stable repayment schedules. The monthly mortgage payment does not usually vary with short-run economic conditions. Similarly, the wage is like a partial payment on a long-term labor contract and it is not varied with short-run conditions.

Wage Stability versus Employment Stability   The analogy between the stable monthly wage and the stable monthly mortgage payment is not an exact one. There is an important difference between the two cases, because companies do not guarantee employment. When there is a short-run decline in product demand, workers are laid off. Why is it that implicit and explicit contracts specify that the wage does not respond to short-run market conditions while the level of employment does?

One answer is that firms are trying to reduce the risks faced by workers and *stabilizing wages helps to reduce worker risk, even when employment varies.*[17] Firms find it in their interests to reduce the income risks of workers, because it pays off as a long-run strategy. If workers knew that the wage they would receive would vary with short-run conditions, then they would demand a higher average wage or choose to work at a firm that offered more stability. Providing wage stability is something firms are willing to do as part of their competitive strategy in hiring and retaining workers. Since product demand varies widely over the business cycle, firms do not find that it pays to give employment guarantees, but they can provide some reduction in risk by avoiding variable wages.

A related reason is that workers consider that cutting wages in a downturn is unfair, whereas layoffs are not. Arthur Okun has described an economy with implicit contracts as operating with an invisible handshake, rather than with Adam Smith's invisible hand.[18] Firms have to treat their employees fairly to maintain morale, keep up productivity, and encourage workers to stay with the same employer. When the demand for autos or machine tools declines in a recession, workers see the drop in orders and understand that employment must fall. Cutting wages, on the other hand, is divisive. To workers it looks like getting more profit for the company at the expense of workers.

efficiency wage
Wages higher than are necessary to obtain enough labor. The extra wage motivates workers and boosts productivity.

This idea of setting a wage that is higher than the wage that would be required to retain the work force during recessions has recently been described as setting an **efficiency wage.** A firm sets an efficiency wage when it bases its wage decision not only on whether it can hire new workers but also because it believes there are benefits

---

[17] This was shown by Martin Neil Baily, "Wages and Employment under Uncertain Demand," *Review of Economic Studies* 41 (January 1974), pp. 37–50; and Costas Azariadis, "Implicit Contracts and Underemployment Equilibria," *Journal of Political Economy* 83 (December 1975), pp. 1183–1202.

[18] Arthur M. Okun, *Prices and Quantities, A Macroeconomic Analysis* (Washington, D.C.: Brookings Institution, 1981).

to productivity and morale from setting wages that are above the minimum required for hiring.

Finally, keeping wages stable while allowing employment to vary is a way of shifting the burden of the recession onto a fraction of the workers, typically those that have not been with the company very long. Layoffs are not made randomly. Workers with seniority or skills that the company judges are valuable are retained, while recent hires or workers that the company does not want are let go during recessions. This view of the labor market is called the *insider–outsider* model. Workers who already have jobs (insiders) have much more effect on wage setting than do workers queuing at the factory gate looking for jobs (outsiders).

Wage contracts provide an important reason why wages do not respond much to moderate variations in demand. But wage stickiness is not enough to provide a complete microeconomic foundation for Keynesian models. The neo-Keynesian analysis has also tried to explain price stickiness.

Price Stickiness

The classical model of competitive markets used simple supply and demand schedules. A decline in demand will lead to excess supply and then competition will force the price down. In most actual product markets, however, there is not perfect competition. Firms are choosing the price that they charge to maximize the amount of profit they will receive. Firms will usually make strategic decisions about prices. This means that they will take into account the responses of their principal competitors. In particular, a firm deciding to cut its price will know that other firms will probably match the price cut. The gain in profit from reducing price in recessions may be small or nonexistent.

This idea is illustrated in Figure 15–7, where the initial profit schedule for a firm is shown. This schedule indicates how the firm's profit varies with the price that it charges, and it implies that the firm will choose initially to be at point *A*. Its profits are maximized by setting the price P_0 and at this point it has reached the highest level of profit it can, *Profit$_A$*.

Suppose there is then a decline in the market demand for the product that is being produced by this firm. Following this decline, the firm's profit will be lower. It can no longer achieve the same level of profit. The figure indicates that the new profit-maximizing price is P_1. This says that it pays the firm to lower its price following the downturn. But the figure also illustrates that, if the firm does not lower its price, then the loss of profit will be very small. By lowering its price, it will receive the amount of profit shown at *Profit$_B$*. But by holding its price constant, it will receive the amount of profit *Profit$_C$*. The difference between the two is very small.

Menu Cost Models   Figure 15–7 is only an illustration, of course, but neo-Keynesian economists have worked with models of decision making by firms and concluded that the case shown in the figure is a plausible one. They suggest that the gains to firms from price adjustment may be very small. They then argue there are costs to adjusting prices, so in fact firms may even be better off to hold price constant, because any small gain in operating profit will be less than the cost of adjusting prices.

FIGURE 15–7
Effect of a Price Change on Profit

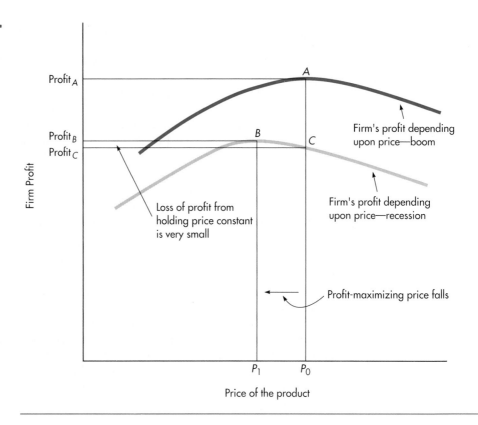

These models, with the unfortunate title **menu cost** models, point out that price lists (such as menus) will have to be altered when prices are adjusted.[19] More important than the cost of printing price lists are the costs of deciding price changes or the costs of renegotiating prices with suppliers or dealers.

Menu cost models are most applicable to cases where prices are set by contracts between buyers and sellers. Contractual arrangements are common throughout the economy as raw materials and intermediate goods are traded under contractual arrangements, and many producers also have long-term contracts with wholesalers and retailers. These contracts may be explicit and are often long, complicated, and costly to renegotiate.

The menu cost model is actually very applicable to the labor market, too. An important reason why union contracts are often two or three years in duration is that neither side wants to go through the bargaining process more frequently than that. In

menu cost
The cost of changing price lists or other costs of adjusting prices.

---

[19] Menu cost models have been stressed by N. Gregory Mankiw, ''Small Menu Costs and Large Business Cycles: A Macroeconomic Model of Monopoly,'' *Quarterly Journal of Economics* 100 (May 1985), pp. 529–37.

general, say neo-Keynesians, *firms are willing to give up some short-run profit when demand varies, because there are long-term gains from having stable prices and wages.*

The main emphasis of neo-Keynesian analysis has been on developing models of the behavior of individual firms or industries to see if rational behavior can be reconciled with wage and price stickiness. But there has also been another aspect to the theory. What happens when there are many different industries? What is the relation between individual price and wage adjustment and adjustments of the price level?

Coordination Failure and Real and Nominal Stickiness

The equilibrium–business-cycle model assumes complete price and wage flexibility and market efficiency. And the rationale for this is always given in terms of a single market, where arbitrage should eliminate any market inefficiency. But even if the assumption of price flexibility were accepted, there is a serious question about whether the whole economy with thousands of individual markets would converge to a single full-employment equilibrium. Advocates of the equilibrium model assume there would be aggregate equilibrium, but neo-Keynesians challenge that assumption. There may be a failure of coordination, so the economy could go to one of several underemployment equilibria. There are no realistic models of adjustment with many different markets that can show a smooth or rapid convergence of all wages and prices to a single full-employment equilibrium. The equilibrium–business-cycle theorists have assumed away a major problem in their analysis.

price-coordination problem
The difficulty of obtaining a coordinated decline in all prices and wages following a decline in nominal aggregate demand.

Real and Nominal Stickiness   The **price-coordination problem** is an important issue for the economists who assume price flexibility. But it becomes even more important in the neo-Keynesian models, where there is price and wage stickiness. There is a specific way in which a coordination failure may occur and make it difficult for the economy to achieve full employment. Coordination problems can mean that small costs of adjusting wages and prices for individual firms can become large costs for the economy as a whole.

The models of wage and price stickiness that we have just described are called models of **real stickiness.** This means they help us understand why the real wage does not fall during periods when unemployment is high or why firms do not lower the relative prices of their products when their demand curves shift down.[20] But critics of these models have pointed out that, if all prices and wages fell together in recessions, there would be no need for real wages or relative prices to change. For example, if the money supply fell by 10 percent, the chances are this would lead to a recession. But if all prices and wages fell by 10 percent, then there would be no change in the real money stock and hence no change in real aggregate demand. The fact this does not happen is called **nominal stickiness.** And some form of nominal wage and price

---

[20] The menu cost models that emphasize literally the cost of printing price lists provide a rationale for nominal stickiness, but such costs alone are not generally considered large enough to be important.

stickiness is essential to any model of the business cycle in which aggregate demand leads to changes in real output. Nominal stickiness means that any decline in the nominal value of output will lead to a decline in real output. How can it be explained?

Neo-Keynesians point out that, if all wages and prices were to decline by 10 percent when the money supply (or some other measure of aggregate demand) declined by 10 percent, this would involve an amazing act of coordination by everyone in the economy. How could this occur? Would the natural working of the economy lead to the development of such coordinated behavior? The answer is that it probably would not, and the discussion of real stickiness helps to understand why. Suppose the economy were divided into those who followed the Fed's policy changes and understood their implications and those who could care less about such matters. Would the people with rational expectations somehow impose coordination on the others, perhaps by lowering their own prices by more than 10 percent? The analysis of real stickiness suggests that the answer is no. If most firms do not change their wages and prices following a decline in the money supply, then a fall in nominal demand will lead to a decline in real aggregate demand. Moreover, with most prices unchanged, any reduction in wages or prices by the ''smart'' firms will be a decline in real wages or in relative prices. The models of real stickiness then suggest that profit-maximizing firms will decide that at most only small declines in real or relative wages are indicated. In other words, if some firms have nominal stickiness, this will tend to spread to all other firms. Unless coordinated adjustments of wages and prices were somehow the norm, it is hard to see how they would ever get started.

This discussion of a coordination failure has been rather abstract, given in terms of a thought experiment following a sudden fall in nominal demand. But the issue itself is far from abstract. If there were some way of encouraging firms to adjust their wages and prices to nominal aggregate demand, it would be possible to reduce the impact of fluctuations in nominal demand on real output and employment. And some small countries have had success in achieving coordination in practice, at least for a while. In Austria most wages are union wages that are all set at the same time in a kind of national wage-bargaining session. The Austrians have been able to cooperate in this bargaining and match wage and price increases to the growth in demand. As a result, they have been able to keep unemployment low. In other countries such attempts have failed, however. Achieving coordination in a large, individualistic economy is hard or impossible, while imposing coordination by government intervention in wage and price setting is likely to create more problems than it solves. In the last few years Austria too has succumbed to the problems of high unemployment.

Assessing the Neo-Keynesian Analysis

One criticism of neo-Keynesian analysis is that it is not all that new. The effort to explain why people behave in the way that is assumed in Keynesian or mainstream models has been an ongoing one for 40 years. But this is not a terribly serious criticism. There are important new ideas in this work and there has been a rigorous attempt to build a rational basis for Keynesian analysis.

The serious criticism of neo-Keynesian analysis is that it is trying to do the impossible. The neo-Keynesian models of price and wage stickiness may tell us a lot about why there is stickiness in practice, but these models are not watertight when judged strictly using the axioms of rational choice and rational expectations. Once the extreme equilibrium, rational expectations, framework has been accepted, it is probably impossible to construct a model of the business cycle that fits with what we observe. In a recession, we observe people being laid off. They are not making rational choices; they are losing their jobs involuntarily. When workers who have been laid off hold out desperately in the hope of getting their old jobs back, they are not using all available information rationally. They are hoping against hope. It is not that the neo-Keynesian analysis is wrong in modeling stickiness, it is that the attempt to reconcile stickiness with such a strict rationalist framework may be misguided. This framework may be ignoring much about the way people actually behave.

Good economic science is not based on models that assume people behave the way economists think they should. It is based on the way people are actually observed to behave. Long-term experience has demonstrated clearly that wages and prices do not adjust instantly, and that markets may take a long time before they adjust to equilibrium. The reasons for this stickiness are not necessarily irrational; they may reflect nonmarket considerations, which make perfectly good sense to managers and employees, but which are not reflected in models of pricing and wage-setting behavior. The fact that economists do not have a fully developed understanding of why there is stickiness is not a reason to assume the behavior away.

SUMMARY

- Equilibrium–business-cycle theorists and real–business-cycle theorists wish to explain fluctuations in output and employment within models that are based on rational individual choice and in which people have rational expectations.

- In the rational-expectations model of the economy, expectations are formed by using all available information efficiently.

- Rational expectations of future inflation are formed by looking forward, using the economic conditions that generate the future rate of inflation. Past inflation is only important to the extent that it forecasts future inflation.

- When expectations of inflation are formed on the basis of future forecasts, the public's understanding of which policy regime is in force is an important part of their rational expectations. The credibility of policymakers becomes a primary factor in determining the current rate of inflation.

- It is possible to assume rational expectations without price and wage flexibility, and vice versa. However, equilibrium–business-cycle models assume both price and wage flexibility as well as rational expectations. In

the view of the economists who combine rational expectations with price flexibility, markets are always in equilibrium.

- Business cycles occur in the equilibrium models but only because of unexpected shocks to aggregate demand.

- The Lucas supply schedule relates output to the ratio of the actual price level to the expected price level. The actual price level can differ from the expected price level because of a monetary surprise. An unexpected increase in the money supply leads to an increase in output. An unexpected decrease in the money supply leads to a decrease in output.

- Expectations can fail to be realized. Having rational expectations does not mean people know exactly what is going to happen. Rather, it means that people make the best use of the information available at the time.

- The policy-ineffectiveness theorem argues that stabilization policy is impotent, since only an unexpected shock can cause output to differ from potential, and, therefore, systematic policy is ineffective as a tool for raising or lowering output.

- The real–business-cycle model replaces the conclusion of the equilibrium–business-cycle models that fluctuations result from policy surprises. Instead, it is argued that all fluctuations are the results of technology or labor-supply shocks. Shifts in the money market will not change real output; only changes in the real economy can bring about changes in real income.

- Technology and productivity changes are responsible for most of the long-run changes in output. However, the real–business-cycle models also argue that short-run changes in productivity determine changes in output over the business cycle.

- The case for or against rational expectations depends on the issues of just how efficient individual markets are and how well rational-expectations models describe the workings of markets and macroeconomic events.

- An important discrepancy between the rational-expectations models and observation is the implication that deviations from potential output should be short-lived. The experience of the actual economy is that output moves slowly and persistently above or below potential for periods of several years at a time.

- Real–business-cycle models assume that output varies as a result of aggregate supply shifts. This should mean that prices fall in booms and rise in recessions. This is not the normal case. The models also are implausible in arguing that technology often declines.

- Neo-Keynesians start with the same framework of rational choice as the equilibrium models and then try to understand how wages and prices could be sticky even under these conditions. Models that look at wage contracts, efficiency wages, and menu costs help us understand how real stickiness occurs. The problem of coordinating price and wage adjustments helps us understand how nominal stickiness can occur.

- The neo-Keynesian models have given insight into stickiness, but it may be a mistake to try and explain actual business cycles using the extreme rational framework.

KEY TERMS AND CONCEPTS

adaptive expectations, p. 464

arbitrage, p. 483

choice-theoretic framework, p. 462

efficiency wage, p. 494

equilibrium–business-cycle model, p. 467

labor hoarding, p. 490

Lucas critique, p. 479

Lucas supply schedule, p. 470

menu cost, p. 496

monetary shock, p. 473

neo-Keynesian analysis, p. 493

nominal and real stickiness, p. 498

policy-ineffectiveness theorem, p. 477

price-coordination problem, p. 497

rational expectations, p. 462

real–business-cycle models, p. 480

technology shock, p. 480

time-inconsistent policies, p. 478

wage contracts, p. 492

DISCUSSION QUESTIONS AND PROBLEMS

1. Do rational expectations require perfect foresight?

2. How can an expectation of future reductions in the rate of inflation lower current inflation?

3. Why does the Lucas supply schedule depend on surprises to generate an increase in real output? Is such an increase in output a surprise that is likely to be permanent?

4. How does the Fed's establishment of its credibility in pursuing anti-inflationary policies contribute to the ineffectiveness of stabilization policies?

5. In the rationalist view, what might explain an increase in the unemployment rate? Is all unemployment voluntary?

6. In the rationalist view, an unexpected increase in aggregate demand will raise both output and prices. Does the less-than-complete allocation of the increase in demand to prices indicate price stickiness?

7. Contrast the sources of short-term fluctuations around potential output in an equilibrium–business-cycle model and a real–business cycle model.

8. What is the difference between implicit and explicit contracts? How are implicit contracts enforced? Why do wage contracts typically set wages that do not vary much over the business cycle?

9. What costs will firms face when they change their prices? If menu costs are important, does that mean that the government should subsidize the printing of price lists?

EMPLOYMENT CREATION, UNEMPLOYMENT, AND EARNINGS DISTRIBUTION

INTRODUCTION

The most important measure of economic well-being in a country is the per capita income of its residents. But a high per capita income on average does not mean that everybody in the economy earns a similar income nor does it mean that everyone is satisfied with the performance of the economy. Even though there may be enough income in the economy on average, there are many people whose income is very low. Many of these people are employed in low-wage jobs or they want to work and cannot. Even those who are working at adequate wage levels may fear for the loss of their jobs.

If a given per capita income is achieved with very high levels of unemployment, there is typically a high degree of dissatisfaction with the economic performance of the country, regardless of the level of per capita income.

Even if income levels are good and jobs are reasonably secure, there may still be problems in the economy if the income only comes about through extraordinary hours of work. A study of working professionals in the United States[1] suggests that, to be a successful lawyer or business executive, it is necessary to work very long hours. Many people might choose to work part-time, but they cannot do so without giving up their careers. We are not sure that many Americans are really forced to work more than they choose, but the study points to the fact that working long hours for extra income is only worthwhile if the sacrifice of leisure is worthwhile. Higher per

---

[1] Juliet Schor, *The Overworked American: The Unexpected Decline of Leisure* (New York: Basic Books, 1992).

capita income achieved through extra work is not as good as higher per capita income achieved through increased productivity.

As well as the level of per capita income, the distribution of income is also seen as important by some, although not by all people. Make up your own mind on this. Compare the economic well-being in an oil-rich kingdom, in which the king's family is fabulously wealthy while the rest of the population is poor, with the economic well-being in a different country having the same per capita income but where mostly everyone is comfortable and there is a much smaller range of income from rich to poor.

There is no absolute answer here about whether inequality is in itself a concern, but we offer our assessment. Provided wealthy people have earned their money fairly and honestly, then the accumulation of wealth and the enjoyment of very high incomes is justifiable and even desirable to provide incentives. We are concerned with the quality of economic performance when a large portion of the population does not have enough to live on with a tolerable level of comfort, judged by the prevailing standards of the society. As such, we want to look at the economic forces that generate high or low levels of employment—with lower unemployment generally preferred (though some unemployment turns out to be healthy and necessary to reallocate resources). We focus on the labor market and its relation to both the business cycle and long-term growth. We look at economic structures that produce short, rather than long, bouts of unemployment. We look at the reasons for differences in income across and among economies, and finally we discuss some policies designed to improve productivity and efficiency in the labor market.

EMPLOYMENT GROWTH PATTERNS

Since the early 1970s, the U.S. economy has created large numbers of jobs. In 1970, there were 78.7 million people employed in civilian jobs. By 1980, this had risen to 99.3 million, a 26 percent increase. By 1990, the total level of U.S. employment had risen to 117.9 million, an 18.7 percent increase over the 1980 figure. And there were an additional 1.4 million jobs added from 1990 to 1993, despite an intervening recession followed by a very slow recovery.

The fact that the U.S. economy has been so good at creating jobs comes as a surprise to many people, who are used to reading about layoffs, downsizing, and job losses. Were these new jobs created evenly across all sectors or was job creation concentrated in a few industries? Did the U.S. economy create good, permanent, high-paying real jobs or lousy, temporary, low-paying McJobs?

Employment by Sector   Figure 16–1 illustrates the sectors in which jobs have increased or decreased over the period 1980 to 1990. Overwhelmingly, the increase in

FIGURE 16-1
**Employment
Change by Sector,
1980-90**

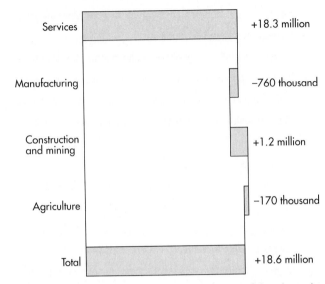

Services	+18.3 million
Manufacturing	-760 thousand
Construction and mining	+1.2 million
Agriculture	-170 thousand
Total	+18.6 million

The U.S. economy added nearly 19 million jobs in the 1980s, most of them in services.

Source: Bureau of Labor Statistics

jobs has come in the service sector, which increased its employment at an average rate of 2.5 percent a year, adding 18.3 million jobs. This is virtually equal to the total increase in employment of 18.6 million for the whole civilian economy. The other sector that increased employment over the decade was construction and mining, which added 1.2 million jobs. In contrast, both agriculture and manufacturing reduced employment over the decade, with manufacturing employment declining by about 750,000. As we describe in more detail later, this change in the pattern of employment toward a smaller proportion of workers in manufacturing and agriculture and a larger proportion in services is not a recent event—rather, it reflects a long-term trend for agriculture going back for well over a century and in manufacturing for nearly half a century.

Efficiencies in agriculture reduced the need for large numbers of family farms and farm workers; and then productivity in manufacturing generated more and more output, with larger inputs of capital and relatively smaller requirements for labor. Depending on what kind of service jobs are created, the trend toward a service-dominated labor market can reflect success in the economy as fewer and fewer people are needed to provide work energy to directly produce output and as more and more people contribute value-added in services.

We have seen that the bulk of new jobs have been created in services. Within this sector, the biggest job gains have come from business services (including advertising, computer and data processing services, and financial services), health services, and retail trade. Partly as a result of budgetary pressures, government has gotten relatively smaller. During the 1980s, employment in government services had grown slowly, by less than the rate of growth of the population. Within manufacturing, there were job losses in industrial machinery, consumer electronics, and miscellaneous manufacturing. There was growth in employment in transportation equipment, including both the auto industry and other transportation (air transportation and military aircraft and missiles). Employment also grew in industries producing computers and other office equipment and technical instruments.

Employment Turnover and Firm Size One of the surprising aspects of the U.S. labor market is its fluidity. Job duration is often very temporary. Companies add workers and then downsize. Some plants or service establishments rise and others fall. There is a very high level of turnover in the labor market.

Understanding the fluidity in the labor market is important in assessing another startling labor market characteristic—that most jobs are created by small companies. The high turnover in small firms points to an important corollary—*most jobs are also lost in small firms.* While it is certainly true that small firms create many new jobs, these jobs are typically much less stable than the jobs created in larger firms. Job creation and job destruction are both higher in small firms.

Figure 16–2 gives information about both the shares of employment by size class of firm and information on job turnover. The left panel of the figure shows that employment in firms with under 20 employees has risen from 17 percent of the total in 1980 to 25 percent in 1990. It appears that small firms have accounted for a growing fraction of employment.[2]

Employment growth is only part of the story. Contrast the left panel of Figure 16–2, which describes firms in all industries, with the right-hand panel, which concentrates on manufacturing. The manufacturing panel shows gross job creation and destruction and net job creation by firm size. This analysis is based on surveys and censuses of individual manufacturing plants and the firms are classified by size based on their average size over the entire period (or their entire life spans).[3]

The rate of gross job creation gives the average rate of employment increase for plants that increased the number of employees from one year to the next (expressed as a percent of total employment). Similarly, gross job creation measures the rate of job gain in plants that increased employment.

---

[2] These data should be interpreted with care, however. Firms can change their size classification. For example, a firm that has 30 employees and then lays off 11 of them will become a firm with 19 employees. This will add to the total amount of employment in firms with less than 20 employees. In some claims made from the data, this downsizing is considered ''job creation'' in small firms.

Another problem in interpretation is that many small firms are franchises. In a sense, your local McDonald's may indeed be a small firm, because it is owned and operated by one person or a small group. But obviously McDonald's is also a very large company that advertises nationally and controls the operations of its franchises carefully.

[3] The data from the censuses of manufacturers do not include employees in head offices and R&D facilities. The employment data in Figure 16–2 shows a larger decline than the total decline of 760 thousand in Figure 16–1.

FIGURE 16–2   Employment by Firm Size for All Industries and Rate of Job Creation and Destruction by Firm Size in Manufacturing

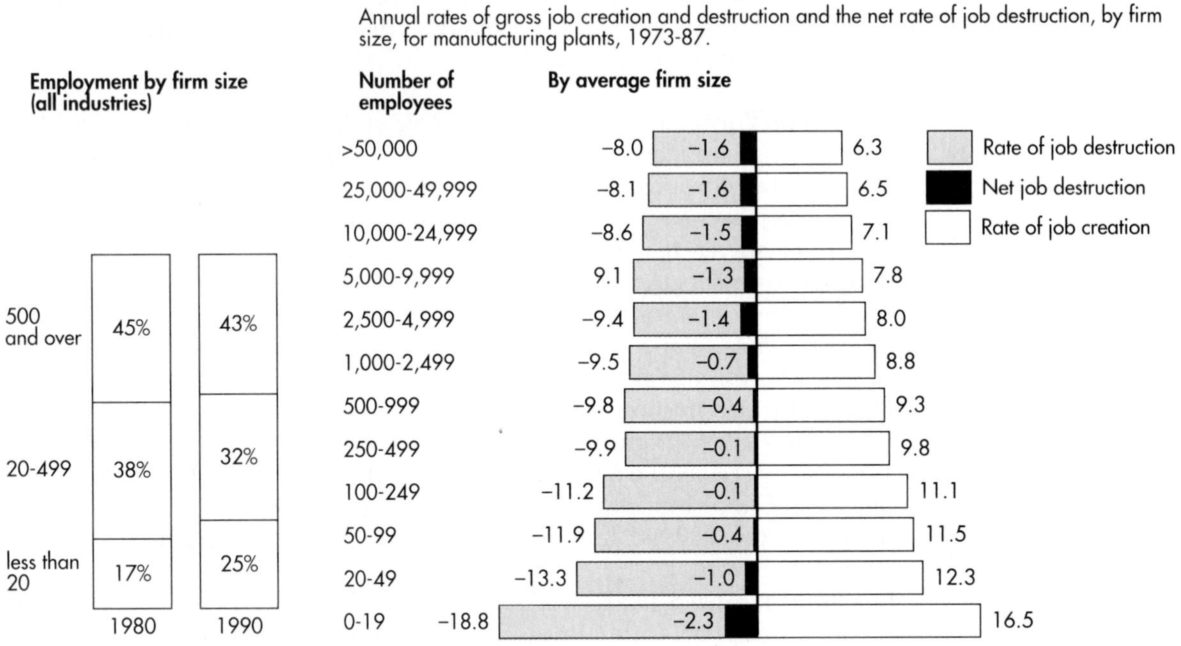

Annual rates of gross job creation and destruction and the net rate of job destruction, by firm size, for manufacturing plants, 1973-87.

Employment by firm size (all industries)			Number of employees	By average firm size				
	1980	**1990**						
500 and over	45%	43%	>50,000	−8.0	−1.6		6.3	■ Rate of job destruction
			25,000-49,999	−8.1	−1.6		6.5	■ Net job destruction
			10,000-24,999	−8.6	−1.5		7.1	□ Rate of job creation
			5,000-9,999	9.1	−1.3		7.8	
			2,500-4,999	−9.4	−1.4		8.0	
			1,000-2,499	−9.5	−0.7		8.8	
20-499	38%	32%	500-999	−9.8	−0.4		9.3	
			250-499	−9.9	−0.1		9.8	
			100-249	−11.2	−0.1		11.1	
			50-99	−11.9	−0.4		11.5	
less than 20	17%	25%	20-49	−13.3	−1.0		12.3	
			0-19	−18.8	−2.3		16.5	

Sources: The State of Small Business and Steven J. Davis, John Haltiwanger, Scott Schuh *Gross Job Flows in U.S. Manufacturing*, U.S. Department of Commerce, March 8, 1994.

The very large size of job turnover (the figures are annual averages) is striking. *The U.S. manufacturing sector (and indeed the whole labor market) is characterized by very large rates of turnover. Each year, in good times and bad, large numbers of jobs are created and large numbers are destroyed.*

Netting out the job destruction and creation shows there is some job destruction in all size classes.[4] Looking at the differences in net job destruction by size shows that small firms have job destruction rates commensurate with their higher job creation rates. Overall, netting job destruction from job creation, there is no tendency for jobs to be created differentially in small firms within U.S. manufacturing.

Jobs have been created in services and job turnover has been highest in small business, but what kind of jobs have been created?

---

[4] We know that manufacturing employment has been declining over time, although these data overstate that decline somewhat, because head offices and separate R&D facilities are excluded.

FIGURE 16–3   Years of Schooling Completed—1950, 1970, and 1992 (percent of persons 25 and over)

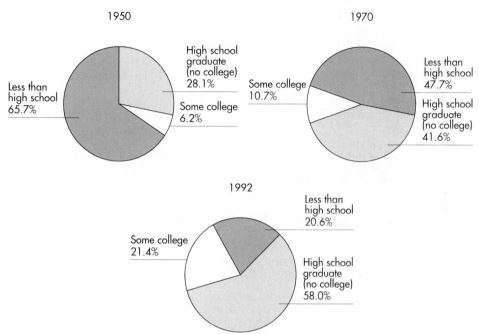

The U.S. population has greatly increased its educational level since 1950.

Source: Statistical Abstract of the United States, Washington, D.C., 1992.

Employment by Occupation and Education Level   The U.S. population has become much more educated over time. Figure 16–3 illustrates and shows that in 1950 nearly two-thirds of the U.S. population had not even completed high school and only 6.2 percent of the population had completed four years of college or more. By 1992, only about a fifth of the population had not completed high school and about the same fraction had completed four years of college or more.

As the U.S. population has become more educated, employers have adjusted their production methods to take advantage of the increased availability of better-educated workers. Figure 16–4 shows that the largest increases in employment from 1983 to 1992 have come in professional and technical jobs and in administrative and managerial positions. The commonly held belief that the only jobs created in the United States in recent years have been low-skilled jobs, such as working in a fast-food restaurant, is not correct. While this conclusion may be more true for some age groups and segments of the population than for others—during the decade, young people and minorities did not do as well in access to new high-quality jobs—overall most new jobs were of high quality. Women as a group did particularly well during this same period, making significant gains in moving into managerial and professional positions.

**FIGURE 16–4
Growth of
Employment by
Occupation,
1983–92**

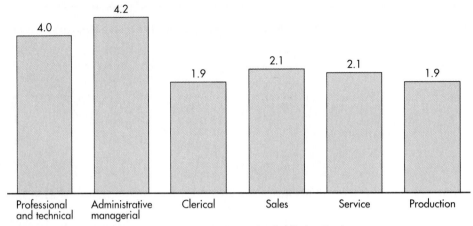

The U.S. economy has created more jobs in the educated and skilled professions.

Source: Statistical Abstract of the United States, Washington, D.C., 1993.

In 1983, 40.9 percent of these jobs were held by women and by 1992 this had risen to 47.3 percent.

International Employment Patterns   The U.S. pattern of rapid employment growth has not been replicated in all other industrial countries. Japan increased employment substantially along with the United States over the 1980s. But the European countries have created many fewer jobs. The weakness in employment performance in Europe is actually even worse, because there has been a lot of work sharing in Europe. In Germany, for example, fewer hours were worked in 1990 than in 1980, even before Germany went into recession. The European experience provides important policy implications, especially in contrast with the U.S. experience. As we will see later in this chapter, the differences between labor markets in the United States and Europe revolve around unemployment (high in Europe, low in the United States) and entry-level jobs (low wage in the United States and high wage in Europe).

**Explaining the
Patterns of
Employment
Growth**

Employment grows at different rates across sectors of the economy and among different kinds of jobs. Economic factors working over long time periods can help explain the changing patterns of employment growth.

Services Sector Growth   The decline in the shares of total employment in the manufacturing sector and in the agricultural sector and the corresponding rise in employment in services is part of the natural evolution of the economy. Since the middle of the 19th century in the United States, employment in agriculture has been declining. Manufacturing went through a period of employment growth through the first half of the 20th century, but the share of manufacturing employment has been declining since the 1950s. The U.S. economy has been ''deagriculturalizing'' and ''deindustrializing'' for a long time.

This pattern of economic evolution results from two forces. Productivity growth has been strong in both agriculture and manufacturing and the share of income that people spend on basic food and for manufactured goods has declined over time.[5] This means that fewer workers are needed to supply the amount demanded. The growth in service sector employment is just the flip side of the same coin. Consumers are devoting increasing fractions of their expenditure to services, and productivity growth has been slower in the service sector than in goods production. Consequently, the fraction of employment in services is rising.[6]

Turnover and Small Business Employment   The high degree of turnover in the labor market is the result of a multitude of shocks that hit firms, industries, and regions. Some of these are the result of new technologies, some from changing consumer tastes, some from the business cycle, some from international trade, and some from the normal competitive struggle as some companies increase market share and others lose share.

The increasing share of total employment in small firms may reflect changes in technology that give small firms advantages in speed of response or in their ability to be innovative. In part it may be actions by larger firms, which are outsourcing parts of their business to avoid high labor costs. Small firms typically offer lower wages and less in fringe benefits.

Employment Growth and Labor Market Flexibility   The fact that the total volume of employment has increased and that the share of managers and professionals has risen is mostly the result of increased labor supply in a flexible economy. There has been an increase in the number of women wanting to work. The baby boom generation has entered the work force. The United States absorbs a million immigrants a year. And the expansion of the education system has qualified many people able to work at managerial and professional jobs.

---

[5] It is actually a bit misleading to say that people spend less of their income on goods as their income increases. People continue to buy food and manufactured goods, but the service component of those purchases increases. People eat at restaurants or buy prepared foods at the supermarket. They do not buy more of the output of the farmer. People buy plenty of manufactured goods, too, but the value added in those goods is created increasingly in design, marketing, and distribution. The $15 compact disc purchased in the local mall probably had a manufacturing cost of only $0.50, with most of the price going to cover the costs of service providers, including the performing artists.

[6] Some people worry that eventually the demand for services will become saturated, that demand for services will stop rising, that employment growth will stop, and that unemployment will rise. There is little reason to worry about that any time soon for the United States. If people in general have enough income to supply all of their needs, they can save more or work less. More saving can be a short-run problem in creating a recession, as we have seen so far in this book. But in the long run an efficient capital market will channel saving into capital goods (items that are produced by workers). And if people decide to work less, that is not a long-term problem, either, since that would reflect a reduction in the labor supply, not in chronic unemployment. Just such a trend occurred in the United States between the 1920s and the 1970s as hours worked per week fell from over 60 hours to below 40 hours coupled with a massive growth in overall employment. Since the 1970s, this trend has reversed somewhat, with saving rates falling and the hours worked increasing. There is little evidence that consumers are becoming saturated with goods and services.

One feature of a flexible economy is that real wages rise and fall with supply and demand. If many low-skill workers are looking for jobs, this holds the wages down and encourages employers to hire them. If the globalization of the capital market creates the opportunity to sell interest-rate swaps or currency swaps, then the demand for financial wizardry increases and the people who can set up and price these swaps can earn large salaries.

This flexibility in the labor market is not good news for everybody, however. If technology or shifting demand reduces the demand for workers of a certain type, their wages will fall or grow very slowly. The forces of supply and demand in the labor market can lead to very large differences in earnings.

If supply and demand are not matched—which can occur for a variety of reasons—then the economy will experience excessive unemployment. The unemployment rate provides our link between the labor market and the policies and circumstances that characterize the macro economy.

UNEMPLOYMENT

If unemployment is rising and there are no artificial barriers being erected that prevent or discourage employment, then it is likely that the economy is failing to create enough new jobs. One obvious solution is to increase the aggregate demand for goods and services. As companies supply these goods and services, they will hire more workers and create more jobs. The constraint on doing this is the same as the constraint on any policy that simply stimulates aggregate demand: If output goes above potential output, then inflation begins to accelerate. The output–inflation trade-off limits the ability of macroeconomic policies to create additional employment and reduce unemployment.

We have seen in earlier chapters that, when output goes above potential output, it leads to an acceleration of inflation. The link from this constraint to unemployment and the labor market is provided by the concept of the nonaccelerating inflation rate of unemployment, or NAIRU.

Potential output is a benchmark for GDP, the point where inflation starts to accelerate. This also sets a benchmark for unemployment. The rate of unemployment that prevails in an economy when output equals potential output is called the NAIRU (or sometimes the natural rate of unemployment). It follows that, when aggregate demand growth pushes the unemployment rate below the NAIRU, this also triggers an acceleration of inflation.

A key issue for policymakers in the United States is why the NAIRU is as high as it is. And a key issue for policymakers in Europe is why the NAIRU there has been rising over time, much more so than it has in the United States.

The Phillips Curve

The analysis of the trade-off between output and price inflation in the goods market began with the work of A. W. Phillips on the labor market. In 1958, he described a negative relationship between the rate of change in wages and the unemployment rate.

This finding about the workings of labor markets is now called the **Phillips curve.**[7] It was based on observations of data for the British economy over many years. Lower rates of unemployment were associated with higher rates of increases in wages. Phillips' analysis of the British data indicated that the values of the trade-off between the two had remained very stable over time.

In Figure 16–5, we depict a Phillips curve. It shows wage increases varying with the unemployment rate in the economy. At point *A*, the unemployment rate is 6 percent and the rate of wage increase is 1 percent. If unemployment falls to 4 percent, the rate of wage increase rises to 2 percent (point *B*).

The curve that Phillips found was used by U.S. policymakers in the 1960s in their theories of the output–inflation trade-off. This was done by linking the labor market to the goods market in two key steps. The first step was to show the relation between output and unemployment (**Okun's law**) and the second was to link the rate of wage increase to the rate of price inflation.

Okun's law
The relationship between output and unemployment. If output exceeds potential output, then the unemployment rate will be below the NAIRU.

The NAIRU and Okun's Law

The link between output and unemployment is known as *Okun's law,* a relationship estimated by Arthur Okun in the early 1960s.[8] Calling this relationship a law is a rather old-fashioned terminology. Economists do not talk about laws much these days, but in this case the relation it expresses has withstood the test of time quite well and so the name has stuck. The ''law'' relates the unemployment rate at any point in time to the natural rate of unemployment and the output gap. In a modern version of Okun's law, each percentage-point rise in the output gap reduces the unemployment rate by about 0.4 of a percentage point. When the output gap is negative (current output is less than potential output), then the unemployment rate is above the NAIRU. When the output gap rises to zero (current output equals potential output), then unemployment equals the NAIRU. If the output gap were to go above zero (current output in excess of potential), the economy would be in a boom with unemployment dipping below the natural rate. Okun's law is shown as:

$$\text{Unemployment rate} = \text{NAIRU} - 0.4 \text{ (Output gap)} \qquad (16\text{--}1)$$

While there is no consensus about the size of the NAIRU in the U.S. economy, most estimates range between 5.5 and 6.5 percent. In the spring of 1994 the Fed tightened monetary policy when the unemployment rate was 6.4 percent. They were concerned that continued rapid growth of the economy would carry GDP above

---

[7] A. W. Phillips, ''The Relation between Unemployment and the Rate of Change of Money Wage Rates in the United Kingdom, 1861–1957,'' *Economica* 25 (November 1958). A precursor to the Phillips curve is attributed to Irving Fisher. In 1926, he wrote an article titled ''A Statistical Relation between Unemployment and Price Changes,'' which was reprinted in *Journal of Political Economy,* March/April 1973, pp. 496–502.

[8] Arthur M. Okun, ''Potential GNP: Its Measurement and Significance,'' reprinted in Okun's *The Political Economy of Prosperity* (Washington, D.C.: Brookings Institution, 1970), pp. 132–45.

FIGURE 16–5
The Phillips Curve

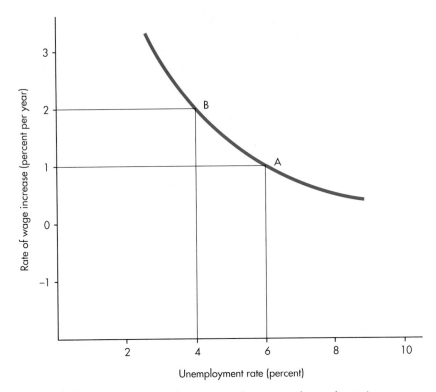

Phillips suggested there is a stable relation between wage increases and unemployment.

potential GDP and the unemployment rate below 6 percent—with inflationary consequences.

Recalling the definition of the output gap, this means that Okun's law can be given as:

$$\text{Unemployment rate} = 6 - 0.4[(Y/Y^P) - 100] \qquad (16\text{–}2)$$

Some alternative values for output and the unemployment rate from Equation 16–2 are then as follows:

Unemployment Rate	Output Ratio
4 percent	105 percent of Y^P
6 percent	100 percent of Y^P
8 percent	95 percent of Y^P

Using Okun's law to relate unemployment to output was one of the two steps required to go from the relationship between unemployment and wage increases to the output–inflation trade-off. The second step is to relate increases in wages to price inflation.

Relating Wage Increases and Productivity to Inflation The connection between wages and inflation works through costs. When there is an industrywide increase in the cost of production, the rise in cost is reflected in an upward shift in the supply schedule of that product. To the degree that demand is not perfectly elastic, the rise in costs will result in a rise in price.

For the economy as a whole, wage costs are the largest fraction of total cost even though for many companies, the largest fraction of their own costs comes from the parts and materials that they buy from other companies. Recall that GDP is equal to the total value added at each stage of production. What is important to overall inflation is the fraction of value added that is labor cost. For the U.S. economy, that fraction is about 70 percent. And the remainder reflects the markup over labor costs that then becomes the return to capital.

Productivity growth allows prices to grow more slowly than wages. For instance, producers may face higher wages each year, but their labor costs will rise more slowly than wages if output per hour of work increases; that is, if productivity increases. As long as there is productivity growth in the economy, firms can pay for wage increases without raising prices. Since 1979, productivity has increased by about 1 percent a year.[9]

The unemployment rate can be linked to the output ratio by recalling Okun's law. Lower output means higher unemployment. Wages are connected to prices because businesses would increase their prices by the amount of wage increases minus the increase in productivity. This means that higher rates of wage increase translate into higher rates of price inflation. Thus the Phillips curve, by connecting unemployment to inflation, was a precursor of the output–inflation trade-off.[10]

The relation between the original Phillips curve and the output–inflation trade-off that was developed in the 1960s has had to be revised since then. First, even though labor costs are the largest component of cost for the economy as a whole, prices and labor costs do not always move together. When demand is strong, businesses raise markups, so price inflation will be greater than cost increases at high levels of the output ratio. When the output ratio is low, markups are compressed and price inflation is less than cost increases. The output–inflation trade-off reflects this tendency for markups to rise and fall with variations in demand.

Second, prices can move very differently from labor costs when there are shocks to the supply of nonlabor inputs. When world energy prices and agricultural prices rose sharply, this led to increases in the U.S. prices of these commodities, increases that were not linked to wage increases.

As you recall form earlier chapters, the combination of rising inflationary expectations and supply shocks caused the output and inflation trade-off to shift. In the case of

---

[9] Productivity growth exceeded 3 percent per year from 1945 to 1973, but the rate of growth fell after 1973. See Chapters 2 and 17.

[10] We are referring to the Phillips curve as the relation between unemployment and the rate of increase of wages. This was Phillips' original formulation. Because of the close links between the Phillips curve and the output–inflation trade-off, many people will describe the output–inflation trade-off itself as a Phillips curve.

the Phillips curve, there is no direct impact of oil price increases on wage inflation. But inflationary expectations plus the increase in the cost of living pushed up wages and shifted the Phillips curve.

There is no need for us to revisit the supply shock story, since that was covered in Chapter 12. Here we are interested in understanding why the output–inflation trade-off and labor markets combine to require a sizable level of unemployment (around 6 percent recently in the United States) to prevent inflation from accelerating. Why is it that unemployment remains this high when aggregate demand policies have done all they can to reduce unemployment without accelerating inflation?

JOB SEARCH UNEMPLOYMENT

As we showed in Figure 16–3, there is a vast amount of turnover in the economy. Workers quit to find better jobs, employers lay off workers when there is not enough work for them to do. And some workers are fired because they cannot perform in a satisfactory way. Many of these labor market transitions take place without a spell of unemployment—the majority in fact. Someone decides to apply for another job and then quits if he or she is successful. Firms laying off workers may give them notice and help them find alternative jobs without being unemployed. Even persons entering the labor force after being at school are often able to line up employment without a spell of unemployment.

For many workers, however, losing a job means spending some time looking for work while unemployed. And for persons who are entering the labor force for the first time, or who are reentering after a period away form the labor force, there is very often a spell of unemployment. People are defined as unemployed if they are actively looking for work and are not currently employed. Workers on temporary layoff are also defined as unemployed.

The fact there is some unemployment does not indicate that a labor market is working inefficiently. While they are unemployed, people are searching for jobs, and the search process itself is a productive economic activity even though no formal employment or output is associated with the search.

Think about someone moving to a new city and finding an apartment. She looks in the paper or goes to an agency or asks friends and puts together a list of the apartments for rent. She drives around checking them and trying to decide which one is just right. She may decide not to rent any currently available but, instead, to wait for a better apartment to go on the market. This search for an apartment does not show on any survey or measurement in the same way that work at a job shows; but the search was certainly a "productive" activity in the economic sense—resources were expended to generate a useful output—in this case information about the rental market.

The search analogy applies to the labor market: Finding the right job is usually at least as important as finding the right apartment. It is appropriate to spend some time looking and waiting for the right opportunity, and the ways of searching for information are similar to those for apartments. The decision to accept a job reflects a weighing of the possibility in getting a better offer by searching more and of the lost earnings from remaining unemployed longer. If the main criterion is the wage on the

reservation wage

The lowest wage a person is willing to accept in a new job. It is set by balancing the chances of a better offer against the loss of earnings from waiting.

frictional unemployment

Results from normal job search as people enter and reenter the work force or change jobs.

job, then the search will proceed until the person finds a job that pays at least the amount that is called the **reservation wage.**[11]

One view of the unemployment that exists when the economy is at the NAIRU, therefore, is that it is a normal and productive use of people's time associated with the large volume of labor market transitions. Unemployment of this kind is called **frictional unemployment.** It reflects the "friction" associated with the normal changes taking place in the economy.

The average duration of a spell of unemployment in the United States is only a few months. This relatively short average duration tells us that the typical person becoming unemployed in the United States could expect to leave unemployment rather quickly—job search is fairly short on average. The average duration of unemployment is a bit misleading as a measure of the importance of lengthy episodes of joblessness, however. Some people who are unemployed stop looking for a while (and hence are no longer counted as unemployed) and then reenter the labor force and experience another spell of unemployment before finding a job.

Unemployment Insurance Benefits   When they decide whether to accept a job, people weigh the costs and benefits of that decision. At a personal level the money received as unemployment insurance benefits while searching will lower the cost of waiting longer for a better job. The availability of benefits will encourage people to hold out longer for better jobs. It raises people's reservation wages and increases the duration of job search.

For the taxpayers who have to pay for the unemployment benefits, this extension of job search is a cost. Most forms of insurance suffer from a problem called "moral hazard," where behavior is affected by the insurance payouts. For example, if the government provides disaster insurance, people may build houses on flood plains. If I buy an extended warranty on my car, I may be less careful in making regular oil changes. In the case of unemployment insurance, increasing the generosity or extending the duration of job search induces a change in behavior that will increase the NAIRU. Unemployment insurance is one reason that the NAIRU is as high as it is.

This conclusion does not mean the insurance is a bad idea. It lowers people's risks in working, improves job matching, and helps stabilize the economy. The price of the program consists of the taxes paid to finance it and the increased unemployment that it causes.[12] The impact of unemployment insurance on the NAIRU is not terribly large, however, perhaps 0.50 to 0.75 percentage points.

---

[11] A reservation price at an auction is something set by a seller: The lowest price the seller is willing to receive, although obviously he or she would like to get a higher price.

[12] There is another way in which unemployment insurance may change behavior: It may encourage companies to put workers on temporary layoff, rather than producing for inventory or putting them on other work activities during temporary dips in demand. Since this increases the number of short unemployment spells, unemployment insurance does not necessarily increase the average duration of unemployment spells.

STRUCTURAL UNEMPLOYMENT

structural unemployment Longer-term unemployment that results from imperfections in labor and product markets and barriers to job transitions.

A substantial fraction of unemployment during normal times consists of frictional unemployment, but not all of it. There is also **structural unemployment.** There is no clean dividing line between frictional and structural unemployment. We cannot label each unemployed person. But the concepts are useful as we seek to understand the sources of unemployment. Whereas frictional unemployment reflects the normal job search process, structural unemployment is often longer term and results because of imperfections in the market and barriers to job transitions.

We look now at one important reason for structural unemployment, namely, the problems of teenagers and minorities.

Teenagers and Minorities   The overall unemployment rate reached a low of 5.3 percent in 1989. In that same year, the unemployment rate of all 16–19 year olds was 15.0 percent and the rate for 20–24 year olds was 8.6 percent. Among blacks in 1989, the unemployment rate was 11.4 percent and among black youth the rates were 32.4 percent for the 16–19 years olds and 18.0 for the 20–24 year olds. These high rates of unemployment do not look like normal job turnover; they look like a symptom of labor market problems.

First, the problem of teenage unemployment should be put into perspective. Many teens seeking jobs are in school and they want to find part-time employment for the evenings or weekends. Even among those who are out of school, there is naturally a high turnover of jobs as teenagers try out various different types of occupation to see if they fit. And teenagers are not always the most stable of employees. They quit to take a vacation or because they are tired of a job. They take short-term jobs that end after the summer or after the Christmas rush.

There is no way to completely explain the high teenage unemployment rates, however, especially those for minorities. Research has suggested a number of problems that contribute to excessive unemployment in this group.

- The school-to-work transition is poor. Teachers do not have much contact with employers and neither school grades nor teacher recommendations are widely used for students not going to college.
- Given the lack of connection between school and work, many teenagers see little reason to work hard or acquire skills that would be useful to them in the labor market.
- Given the very high turnover among teenagers, employers do not have an incentive to train them.
- Drugs and other illegal activities provide a source of income for many teenagers and reduce work effectiveness.
- Many employers are unwilling to hire young people, especially minorities, prejudging them as being poor workers.

For many years, unemployment rates among blacks were about double those for whites. In recent years, this unemployment differential has actually widened. The rate

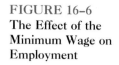

FIGURE 16-6
The Effect of the
Minimum Wage on
Employment

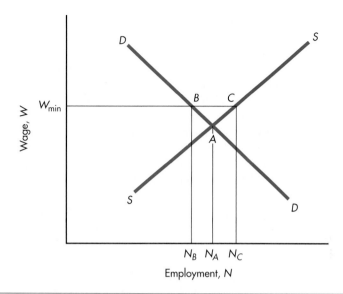

for Hispanics is between the black and the white rate. There are a variety of reasons for these differentials, including discrimination.

One reason that teenagers or other low-skill workers may find it difficult to find jobs is that wages are not set freely by the market, but are sometimes rigid and some of that rigidity can come from government policies.

Wage Rigidities In the U.S. economy, there is a legal minimum wage. There is controversy over whether this minimum wage actually reduces the employment of teenagers (or of low-skill workers more generally). A simple supply and demand framework suggests any minimum that is binding (i.e., one that actually increases the wages paid) will reduce employment. Figure 16–6 illustrates this effect. The market supply of low-skill labor is *SS* and the demand is *DD*. Without any restrictions, supply and demand intersect at point *A* and employment is N_A. At this point, we can expect there to be frictional unemployment, but nothing above this level. If a minimum wage W_{min} is imposed, this results in a reduction of employment to N_B. At this wage the number of people wanting to work is N_C and there is structural unemployment equal to the segment *BC*.

Not everyone accepts this description of the market for low-skill workers. Some economists argue that the high teenage unemployment rates are because of excessive quits. Teens are not willing to do menial jobs for low wages, so they work for a while; then they quit and stay unemployed for a while; then they work some more; and so on. In this view, raising the minimum wage actually increases the attachment teenagers have to their jobs and reduces unemployment.

Evidence is mixed on this point, but most economists think that minimum wages somewhat raise the unemployment rate of teenagers and other low-skill workers. It may discourage companies from offering jobs that have low wages but offer train-ing.[13]

Wage rigidities come not only from legal minimum wages. Unions usually set wages that are well above free market levels for lower-skilled workers. This makes for a more equal distribution of wages among workers within a given plant; but it may discourage employers from hiring lower-skilled workers, because they have to pay them close to the amount that they pay higher-skilled workers. This makes the lower-skilled workers very vulnerable to income loss in the event that they are laid off.

And, perhaps most important of all, when wages are not set in competitive markets, this tends to insulate the wage-setting process from the excess supply of labor that is reflected in high unemployment. Wages that are not market determined are not just rigid, in that they do not fall, they also tend to rise even in the presence of slack in the labor market. This shows up as a high NAIRU.

There have been many problems of structural unemployment in the U.S. labor market, but these pale in comparison to the problems of the European labor market.

Rising Unemployment in Europe   In the 1950s and 60s, the unemployment rates in Europe were generally lower than those in the United States. Many articles were written about the labor market programs, such as apprenticeship programs, that reduced the school-to-work transition in Europe and avoided the teenage unemploy-ment problem. Unfortunately for the European economies, these programs failed to prevent a continuing rise in unemployment after the 1960s. The first source of this job market deterioration in Europe has been an exceedingly slow rate of growth in the creation of new jobs.

There are two main reasons for the slow growth of employment in Europe. The first is simply that their populations have not grown as rapidly and they have not had as much immigration. There was not the need to create as many jobs. The second and more critical reason is that the European economies are much less flexible than the U.S. economy. Even though fewer jobs were needed, the number created was inade-quate.

In part, the difference between the United States and Europe reflects different social choices. Europeans view the U.S. economic system as being very harsh. They provide generous income support for those not working. They insulate firms and workers from competition, and so wages are not determined by supply and demand. When European governments attempt to end this insulation, political pressures pre-vent them from doing so.

The political constraints are especially tight in the areas of unemployment compen-sation, wage rigidities, and minimum wages. As we discussed earlier, a high minimum wage may well work to keep teenage labor market entrants out of entry-level jobs— just the very jobs that are necessary for skill development on the job. In March 1994, the French government, recognizing that the minimum wage was too high to bring about even nearly full employment of teenagers, decided to lower the minimum wage

---

[13]   There is a training wage below the minimum that can be paid for a period.

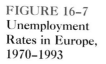

FIGURE 16–7
Unemployment
Rates in Europe,
1970–1993

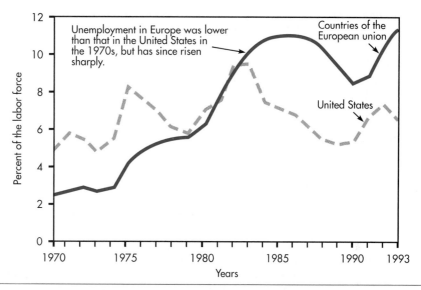

Source: Organization for Economic Cooperation and Development.

for young people by 20 percent, thereby encouraging more employment and getting teenage labor demand closer to labor supply. After three weeks of rioting in Paris, the government backed off and rescinded the lower minimum wage law. The attempt by the French government to bring together labor supply and demand failed.

A key question for Europe is whether the forces of supply and demand can be held at bay indefinitely and still have those economies participate effectively in global competition. In Europe, the real wages of production workers have risen steadily in Europe despite the fact that employment has fallen and unemployment has steadily increased. The consequences of attempting to use policy to insulate the European economy from supply and demand pressures has been an all too high rate of unemployment.

In Figure 16–7, we show how unemployment in Europe has evolved compared to that in the United States in recent years. Whereas the unemployment rate in the United States has fluctuated up and down around a fairly stable level since 1970, the unemployment rate in Europe has shown a markedly increasing trend. The rising trend in Europe, combined with the lengthy recession of the early 1990s, has created an unemployment crisis in Europe.

There are a number of reasons why unemployment has risen in Europe.

- The social safety net is much more generous in Europe, allowing unemployed workers to live at a level comparable to what they would achieve working at low-wage jobs.
- The duration of unemployment benefits is much greater in Europe, with benefits being available almost indefinitely in some countries. Figure 16–8 shows the correlation between unemployment benefits duration and the percentage of

FIGURE 16–8
Maximum Duration of Benefit,
1985, and Percentage of Unemployed
out of Work for
over a Year,
1983–1988

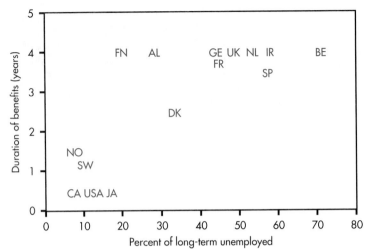

Generally, the countries that give unemployment benefits for several years have a large fraction of long-term unemployed. Countries with indefinite benefits are graphed as having a 4-year duration. AL: Australia; BE: Belgium; CA: Canada; DK: Denmark; FN: Finland; FR: France; GE: Germany; IR: Ireland; JA: Japan; NL: Netherlands; NO: Norway; SP: Spain; SW: Sweden; UK: United Kingdom; USA: United States.

Source: Richard Layand, Stephen Nickell, and Richard Jackman *Unemployment* (Oxford University Press, 1991), by permission of Oxford University Press.

unemployment that is long term. Some people in Europe may be remaining on unemployment insurance even though they are not really searching for jobs.

- In several European countries, a relatively small fraction of wage rates is set by supply and demand in the market. Instead, there are high minimum wages, state-owned companies, strong unions, and legal requirements that a union wage be paid to all workers in that industry regardless of whether it is unionized.

- There are many restrictions in the product market that affect the labor market. For example, zoning laws restrict residential housing construction and make it difficult for shopping malls to be created, inhibiting the growth of employment in small specialty stores that need to group together to attract customers. It is difficult to build new plants in many areas, particularly if the new plant will compete with existing plants.

- The education and training system is geared to preparing young people for industrial jobs that are no longer available. In Germany in 1990, over 40 percent of the unemployed had an apprenticeship training.

As we noted earlier, to many Europeans, the U.S. labor market seems harsh. People are forced to work if they want an adequate income or any income at all. But it is not clear at this point that the European system is sustainable in the long run. It may be possible to provide a stronger social safety net than currently provided for in the United States, one having transportable benefits that encourages job flexibility and one encouraging redevelopment and retraining as job requirements change and still maintain incentives for people to work. But designing and implementing such a support system is an enormous task that has yet to be accomplished successfully in any large industrial economy.

FIGURE 16–9
Average Annual
Growth of Mean
Family Income by
Income Quintile

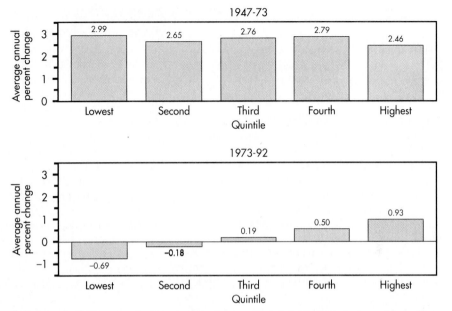

Family incomes in all income groups grew more or less evenly, but slightly faster for lower income groups, before 1973.

Sources: Department of Commerce; Economic Report of the President, 1994.

Because the labor market places very different values on the work of different employees and because of sectoral variations in employment and unemployment experiences, market-based economies generate sizable differences in earnings across the population. Most of the per capita income is generated through earnings, and earnings are unevenly distributed. We turn next to a description and explanation of the distribution of earnings.

HOW EARNINGS ARE DISTRIBUTED

Figure 16–9 shows how family incomes have changed over the periods of 1947–73 and 1973–92. Two patterns are evident. First, the growth of family income after adjusting for inflation was much slower after 1973. And second, the families in the top quintiles of income have done much better than the ones in the bottom quintiles during the latter period.

There are several reasons for these two patterns. In part, the changes are the result of changes in family structure. There are fewer families with married couples and many more single-parent families. But beyond this, the main source of change has come from changes in the labor market. The overall growth of wages has been much slower since 1973, because of the slow growth of productivity that we described in Chapter 2 and that we talk about again in Chapter 17. And the distribution of earnings has widened. The wage or earnings gap between the upper-income groups and the lower-income groups has widened.

Unlike Rest of Europe, Britain Is Creating Jobs, but They Pay Poorly

Glasgow, Scotland—Something unusual is popping up in this long-depressed industrial city lately. Jobs.

The Kvaener Govan Ltd. shipyard, on the verge of closing a few years ago, has added 300 employees. Claremont Garments Ltd. has hired 100 new workers and may take on 200 more. TSB Homeloans has added 100. There is work to be found at a new hospital, the Sainsbury supermarkets and the foreign-owned electronics plants in nearby "Silicon Glen."

Isn't this Europe, the land of nearly 20 million unemployed and few new jobs? Yes, but Britain has gone its own way. While the Continent has largely resisted change, 15 years of Conservative Party rule have helped make Britain's once-rigid work force more flexible. Unions and workers' rights have been weakened, minimum wages struck down, jobless benefits cut and some wages squeezed. Productivity has risen an average of 4.5% annually since 1979.

Tough on Workers

This, the government and its laissez-faire supporters believe, has led to increased investment, new business, and more jobs. The strategy has come at a high cost: It has left Britain with a low-paid, low-skill work force.

Whether Britain can—or should—be a model for the rest of Europe stirs intense debate. Many in the European Union, intent on creating high-skill, high-wage jobs, want no part of Britain's strategy.

Union Group's Argument

The Trade Union Advisory Committee to the Organization for Economic Cooperation and Development argues that the solution does not lie in forcing the unemployed to become the 'working poor' through a negative interpretation of labor-market 'flexibility.' " It says such a strategy "will entail a downward spiral of competition based on low quality standards, continued stagnation of markets, growing inequality and increased social conflict, which will also undermine economic growth."

Instead, many EU people talk about creating 15 million new jobs by the year 2000 by training workers and spending vast sums on public-works projects.

Of course, Europe has been trying that strategy for a decade, to little avail. As a result, many experts predict that eventually the Continent will come to terms—as the U.S. did and Britain is doing—with the notions that the world has changed and that it must change to compete on the world's terms. "They don't have any option, really," says Patrick Minford of Liverpool University.

Britain is not an economic miracle. Over the past decade, restructuring has wiped out hundreds of thousands of jobs in its coal, steel, auto and banking industries. The work force is undertrained compared with that of some European countries, says the National Institute of Social and Economic Research in London.

As in America, large companies in Britain are still cutting costs by laying off workers, and the U.K. unemployment rate remains uncomfortably high at 9.8% (9.3% in Scotland). But the rate is declining and is well below Germany's 11.5%, France's 12%, Italy's 10.4% and Spain's more than 20%. Economists say Britain is adding an average of about 100,000 jobs every three months, compared with quarterly losses of about 50,000

Causes of Increased Earnings Inequality

Inequality of earnings is not always bad. The doctor who has piled up $150,000 worth of medical school bills expects to receive a fair return on that investment. And similarly for many professionals. The fact that Bill Gates can make several billion dollars provides an incentive for others to innovate and to try and hit the jackpot. Even the criticism that the United States has any low-wage jobs has to be considered carefully. If there are many low-skill workers, perhaps many low-wage jobs are needed.

Inequality of earnings provides a signal to workers about the things they must do to increase their productivity and market value.

jobs at this stage in previous recoveries. Within several years, Prof. Minford predicts, British unemployment could fall to a 3% of 4% rate while the Continent remains stuck at about 10%. . . .

A Host of Government Moves

The Conservative government gave workers little choice but to change their tune. It made it easier to hire and fire. it diluted union power by banning secondary strikes and closed shops; the 187 strikes last year were the fewest since the tally began in 1891. It delayed workers' eligibility for employment rights—protection against unfair dismissal and payments to people laid off—until they had been on the job for two years. It abolished "wage councils," which had set minimum wages. And it cut unemployment and related benefits to make the dole less attractive while increasing job-hunt requirements for the unemployed.

As a result, British wages have risen more slowly since 1980 than the EU and OECD averages. Hourly compensation costs of U.K. production workers, according to the U.S. Bureau of Labor Statistics' latest figures, average $14.69, compared with $25.94 for Germany, $19.41 for Italy, $16.88 for France and $16.17 for the U.S. And that stirs controversy.

Trying Out Workers

The government's policies have won over many companies. In downtown Glasgow, TSB Homeloans has added 340 "full-time equivalents" since the division of TSB Group PLC opened three years ago. Many of these replaced jobs in small offices that were closed, but the company has added 100 new jobs in the past year.

TSB uses the new labor flexibility to the fullest; that is crucial in a business in which wages constitute 70% of costs. Some 10% to 15% of its workers are on three-month tryouts; it then hires the temporaries it likes. The division has five different business areas for processing mortgages, and each morning it assigns workers to a function depending on the day's mail. It has no union, no job "demarcations" and almost no overtime.

Despite adding employees, the company hasn't increased its overall labor costs. It has eliminated some managers in favor of lower-wage clerical workers. "If I've got a manager earning £30,000 [$44,925] a year, that's equivalent to four or five clerical people," says Alan Power, general manager. "If I shed five managers, I'm into 25 more people."

Mr. Power terms the low pay a necessary, temporary, strategy. "If we're cheaper and more efficient, we get more business and deliver more jobs," he says, noting a 25% increase in assets last year. He figures that British companies can build a high-wage economy after they gain a greater share of world markets. Until then, "we've got to sacrifice, accepting that it's a very difficult marketplace we're in—marketplace Earth." Workers find that argument difficult to counter.

Yet in spite of the reasonable explanations about why earnings inequality may be both a necessary and effective characteristic of labor markets, the recent experience in the United States of inequality is puzzling and troubling. The rise in inequality may mean that increasing numbers of families are ending up as working poor, with limited options and dismal prospects for the future. We need to look at the causes of the increased inequality to assess the permanent or transitory nature of this trend.

Education   The first reason for increased inequality is described in *The Economic Report of the President.* The return to education has increased.

Between 1974 and 1992, the wage premium paid to college graduates versus high school graduates increased by over 100 percent for workers aged 25–34, while increasing 20 percent for all workers 18 and over. In addition, among workers without college degrees, the average wages of older workers increased relative to those of younger workers. Since the relative supply of educated workers has increased at the same time that wage disparities have grown, the demand for educated workers must have increased faster than their supply.[14]

Technical Change   In many manufacturing plants around the country, innovative new production processes have been introduced that have sharply reduced the number of production workers needed to produce a given level of output. At the same time, the number of people doing design, marketing, and other tasks requiring higher education has increased. The past decade has seen a rising demand for "knowledge workers"— employees who bring education and conceptual/creative skills to bear on work assignments. In many service industries, business systems have been redesigned to reduce the number of low-skill workers that are needed. Telephone companies have released thousands of operators. Computer systems have made clerks much more productive, so fewer are needed.

These and many other innovations in technology and organizations have been described as "skill-biased technical change." This shift in technology has reduced the relative demand for lower-skilled workers and put downward pressure on their wages and increased the relative demand for higher-skilled workers. In the last 10 years, it appears that technical change has been a reason for increased earnings inequality.

International Trade and Competition   It is often said the main reason that wages are falling for low-skilled workers is because they are now competing directly against workers in South East Asia or in Latin America who are ready to work for only a fraction of the wage of U.S. workers.

There is a grain of truth to this argument, but not much more than that. Only a fraction of the U.S. economy is directly exposed to international trade. And our biggest trading partners, such as Canada, Japan, and Europe, have wage rates that are close to or even above ours.

On the other hand, the internationalization of the economy has had a larger impact on earnings inequality than is suggested by the flows of imports and exports. Many of the innovations in manufacturing that lead to production worker layoffs were made first in Japan and were introduced into the United States as a result of intense international competition. That said, however, almost all of the service-sector innovations originated in the United States and are now being exported to other countries.

One of the groups hard hit by international competition and deregulation has been unionized workers. Union workers with modest skill levels find their next best job after they have been laid off pays only a fraction of the job they left.

---

[14] *Economic Report of the President*, 1994, pp. 116–17.

Immigration   The flow of immigrants into the United States has also contributed to the widening of the earnings distribution. Again, however, the effect seems to have been small. A study of the impact of immigration on the wage differential between college-educated and high-school–educated workers found that only about 1 percent of the increase in this differential from 1980 and 1988. The flows of immigration increased in the late 1980s, and so the effect could have been increasing. But there is a long way to go before immigration can become important, starting at 1 percent.[15]

In conclusion, it appears that the nature of technical change has been the main reason for the increased inequality of earnings. This is bad news for those stuck at the bottom. But it gives a clear signal to all workers about the importance of increasing their human capital.

POLICIES TO FOSTER FLEXIBILITY AND PRODUCTIVITY IN THE LABOR MARKET

The forces of technical change, the impact of international competition, the changes taking place in people's tastes, the population shifts from one part of the country to another—all of these factors and more contribute to the constant pace of structural change in the economy. Productivity growth will reduce employment in mature industries, but it will increase demand and create jobs in others. Innovation will make some jobs obsolete, but it will create others. Labor market policies should be directed toward facilitating change, not toward inhibiting it.

Eliminating Barriers   Despite the fact that the U.S. economy is relatively unregulated in comparison to other countries, there remain a variety of barriers to the free movement of resources into new lines of business even in the United States. Many workers have been unable to transfer their pension rights from one company to another. Some workers feel locked to a company because of a medical condition that they cannot transfer into another company's health plan.

Many trade associations and licensing groups prevent workers from joining certain professions. For example, it is quite difficult for foreign-trained doctors to enter the United States and practice medicine, because of barriers created by the American Medical Association. Partly as a result, U.S. doctors are paid three times what European doctors are paid, and many small towns in the United States have trouble recruiting a doctor. Licensing laws may be necessary for some professions; but when the requirements for receiving a license are controled by the members of that profession, it is like putting the fox to guard the chickens. Many professional and trade groups end up reducing the supply of skilled workers.

Despite the move toward deregulation, many regulations are still in place. These are often justified on the grounds they are needed to protect jobs or provide stability. We believe instead that generally the most effective way to create jobs is by freeing markets.

---

[15] See *Economic Report of the President,* 1994, pp. 120–21.

Investing in People, Part I

Governments in rich and poor countries alike have come to realize that human capital—the skills embodied in the workforce—matter as much for economic success as physical capital such as roads or machines. What role, if any, should government play in fostering investment of this kind?

Typically the argument goes as follows. When a firm pays for workers to be trained, the trainees become more productive not only in their present employment but also in any number of different jobs, with different employers. If a trained worker should be poached by another firm, the employer that paid for the training has merely subsidised a competitor. The fact that the firm cannot capture the benefits of its spending is a kind of market failure—and firm will spend less on training than they otherwise would. Hence, there is a case for public subsidy.

The argument has an impressive pedigree: as far back as 1920, A.C. Pigou, one of this century's most brilliant economic theorists, said that training was a classic case of "externality". But the argument is wrong.

True, employers cannot directly capture the benefits of their spending on training—but the workers who receive the training can. Once equipped with new skills, they will be paid more than untrained workers, either by their present employer or by some other. So the benefits of training do accrue chiefly to one of the parties in the transaction; they are not sprayed over the economy at large.

As far as the decision to invest is concerned, it does not matter whether this capturing of benefits is done by employers or by workers. If the benefits are captured by workers, then Mr. Becker of the University of Chicago has shown that the market succeeds.

The market's answer is simple: workers undergoing an expensive training will be paid less, for the time being,

than the value of their work to the firm. This came as a surprise to economists, but will strike trainee lawyers, accountants, architects—and anybody else receiving an education in highly marketable skills—as terribly obvious.

All such people gain skills that are not firm-specific; skills, in other words, that will be as valuable to other employers as they are to the firm that pays for the training. That being so, the market-failure argument suggests that little on-the-job training should take place. But lawyers, at least, are hardly in short supply. The reason is that workers, not employers, meet the cost—by accepting low wages during the period of training.

Less than perfect

The standard market-failure argument for subsidising investment in human capital may be wrong, but this does not mean that market forces get everything right. Markets may fail in other, subtler ways. If they do, this will just as surely upset the calculations that society makes about how much to invest in training and education.

In principle, an economy should invest in human capital (as in any other kind of capital) up to the point where the rate of return yielded by the last bit of investment is just equal to the rate of return yielded by the best alternative use of the resources. It should invest, that is, up to the point where the marginal benefit equals the marginal cost. Please note: the idea that you can never have enough investment in human (or any other sort of) capital is nonsense. Investment is not free. You can have too much as well as too little.

To the private investor, weighing costs and benefits means investing so long as the rate of return exceeds the private discount rate (the cost of borrowing, plus an allowance for risk). For the economy as a whole, it means investing so long as the social return (which includes broader benefits to society, net of all costs) is greater than the social discount rate (which is the preference that society as a whole has for spending now rather than spending in the future). Plainly, these criteria are not the same.

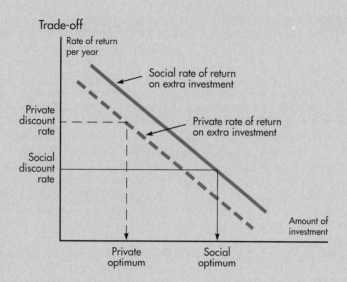

Trade-off

The chart plots private and social rates of return against the amount of investment undertaken.* Both rates of return fall as investment increases (ie, the two lines slope downwards). This reflects the law of diminishing returns—a truth that economists take to be self-evident. Also, at every level of investment, the chart says that the social return is higher than the private return. There are five reasons why this might be true. In each case, the cause is indeed a sort of market failure—though not always an obvious one.

- A big **stock of skilled labour** may deliver economy-wide benefits over and above the private ones that spring from the fact that skilled labour is therefore cheaper to buy.
- Perhaps, for lack of information, would-be trainees **underestimate** the return to investing in skills.
- **Income taxes,** especially "progressive" ones, reduce the private (post-tax) return to training, relative to the social return.
- If unskilled workers are more likely to be **unem-ployed** than skilled ones (as they are), then it follows that the social return to training will exceed the private return.
- If firms have a degree of **monopoly power** as buyers in the market for labour (and many do), it will be profitable for them to meet some of the cost of their workers' training—but not as much as makes sense from society's point of view.

What is the net effect? If, as in the chart, (a) the private return to investing in human capital is lower than the social return and (b) the private discount rate is higher than the social discount rate, then there will be too little investment. The investment that is actually undertaken (the "private optimum") will be lower than makes sense for the whole economy (the "social optimum").

Source: © 1994 The Economist Newspaper Group, Inc. Reprinted with permission.
* The chart and the explanation that follows are drawn from a forthcoming study, "Britain's Training Deficit", edited by R. Layard, K. Mayhew and G. Owen for the Centre for Economic Performance at the London School of Economics.

Investing in People, Part II

Most empirical studies of investment in human capital have looked at education rather than on-the-job training. Quantitative research on in-firm training is difficult to do (spending on "training" is much harder to define than spending on "education"); comparative studies are few and far between and, by necessity, anecdotal.

However, the education studies are interesting in their own right, and shed some light on the broader issues. The figure on page 529 comes from a survey of the literature by George Psacharopoulos, an economist at the World Bank.* His findings appear to confirm (thank heaven) the law of diminishing returns: the social returns to education fall, by and large, as national income (and aggregate spending on education) rises.

Judging by their education policies, most governments would be surprised by another of the study's findings: the returns to primary education are significantly higher than the returns to secondary education, which are themselves higher than the returns to higher education.

An important reason for this is expense: university education costs far more per student than secondary or primary education. Governments everywhere, but especially in the poorest developing countries (where the social return on primary education is 23%, against 11% for higher education) would be well-advised to shift their education budgets away from universities and towards primary schools.

Composition aside, the figure suggests that further spending on all forms of education may be warranted. To take the worst case—higher education in the rich OECD countries—the social return, at more than 8%, is probably higher than the social discount rate appropriate for those countries. Admittedly, that number is itself a matter of controversy—but many rich-country governments already use explicit or implicit discount rates of less than 8% to evaluate public-sector projects.

Another of Mr. Psacharopoulos's findings may strike you as surprising. Studies that compared "academic or general" secondary education to "technical or vocational" secondary education found, on average, that returns to the first were higher—16% compared with 11%. Again, cost is the crucial thing: vocational education is far more expensive to provide than the academic sort.

Within the context of the macroeconomic framework of the Phillips curve trade-off, this is also the right strategy to follow for job creation. Deregulation and increased competition make it much harder to raise wages and prices, when there are long queues of unemployed workers looking for jobs. This helps to reduce the NAIRU. Innovation that creates jobs in new lines of business provides new supply and increases price competition on substitute products. Again, this should help the inflation unemployment trade-off. Overall, a competitive economy is likely to have a lower NAIRU than a regulated economy with low competitive intensity.

Sponsoring Training Programs   With a few exceptions, government-run training programs for the unemployed have not had a good record of success. The most successful training programs are run by companies, because the workers are motivated and the companies know what skills they will need.

There is a potential market failure in this area, because firms that do not train their own workers can recruit trained workers from firms that do train them and thus "free ride" on the training programs. In some countries this has been used to justify a

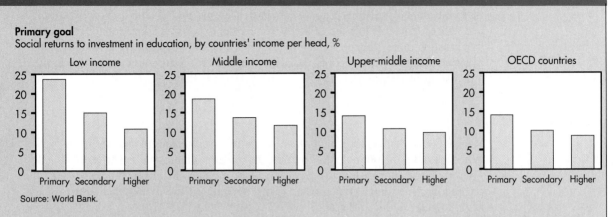

Primary goal
Social returns to investment in education, by countries' income per head, %

Source: World Bank.

Mr. Psacharopoulos's figures, and the theoretical arguments discussed above, suggest that popular demands for a lot more public money to be spent on training may be overdone. The conviction that firms have no incentive to provide training (except training that is highly specific to the firm) is economically unfounded and, for good measure, refuted by the facts. Firms do train their workers—largely at the workers' expense (which, since the trainees later reap the rewards, is as it should be).

Economic theory does point to a variety of subtler reasons why firms may provide less than the socially optimal amount of training. Therefore, some subsidy may be called for; training the unemployed makes especially good sense, on social as well as economic grounds. However, within limited public budgets for investment in human capital, extra spending on primary education seems likely to offer the best value for money.

*"Returns to Investment in Education." Policy Research Working Paper 1067, January 1993.
Source: © 1994 The Economist Newspaper Group, Inc. Reprinted with permission.

training tax levy that is rebated back to those companies that train. In practice, we would not recommend a new payroll tax in the United States, even for a worthy cause such as this, given the heavy weight of payroll taxes already in place. We do think that, when setting a level playing field for small and large firms, it is worthwhile to keep in mind that most of the formal training is done in large firms. (See box entitled, "Investing in People, Part I.")

Supporting General Education   In a changing economy perhaps the best investment to be made in human capital and heightened future earnings potential is to give students a quality general education from preschool through high school. We do not know what specific skills will be needed 5, 10, or 50 years from now, and so it is important to make sure that general, literacy, math, and reasoning skills are taught. This is also the area of investment where government has a larger role, because the social benefits of improved schooling exceed the private benefits—a general, basic, universal education is a public good. (This does not mean that all primary and secondary education should be provided by public agencies.)

In the United States, the current system of public schools is facing severe problems. Inner city schools, and even many suburban schools, are not able to motivate students and hence are unable to educate them. We are not experts on education, but we suspect that creating more competition among schools and more experimentation and privatization would give better results than the ones we are getting now. (See box entitled, "Investing in People, Part II.")

CONCLUSIONS

We have seen there is a strong link between the macro economy and the labor market. When output is below potential output, the unemployment rate is above the NAIRU. There are not enough jobs to go around, and policies to increase demand can also create jobs. The limit to this process is that pushing unemployment below the NAIRU leads to accelerating inflation.

The United States has created millions of new jobs, and the biggest increases have been in skilled jobs. Despite the increased supply of educated workers, the demand for skills has been even greater, raising the returns to education. The slow growth of productivity after 1973 has slowed earnings growth for most workers. In addition, the wages of low-skill workers have grown little or have even declined in some cases, after adjusting for inflation. Many jobs have been lost in manufacturing among unionized workers who have found that their alternative employment options pay much lower wages.

Europe has had much weaker employment growth than has the United States. The distribution of earnings has not widened in Europe, however, as it has in the United States. Rigidities in wages and restrictions in product markets probably have contributed to the slow growth of European employment. Unemployment benefits that continue for long periods have probably exacerbated long-term unemployment there.

Policies to improve the labor market should aim to facilitate the changes that any market economy must make and should not impede those changes. Improving skills, especially in general education and in company training programs, can help both employment and earnings.

We conclude this book in the next chapter by returning to a theme we discussed at the beginning of this book: When the short-run variations in aggregate demand and employment are observed over long periods, they become relatively unimportant in determining the level of economic performance—rather, the growth trends in aggregate supply become the critical concerns. We turn to an examination of long-term economic growth.

SUMMARY

- There is a direct link between output growth and unemployment, captured in Okun's law.
- The Phillips curve related wage increases to unemployment. This relation underpins the output–inflation trade-off after taking productivity increases into account.

- Increasing aggregate demand can create jobs, but inflation starts to accelerate once the unemployment rate goes below the NAIRU.
- The United States has created millions of new jobs, more of them skilled jobs than unskilled.

- Unskilled workers have seen their wages grow very slowly or even fall. The distribution of earnings in the United States has become more unequal in the 1980s.
- Spells of unemployment and changes in labor market demand result in interruptions in earnings. In market economies, such turnover is necessary to maintain efficiency and productivity.
- Small firms create many new jobs, but they also destroy many jobs.
- High unemployment is a particularly troublesome event, and most economies employ policies designed to combat unemployment.

- Some of the policies have the dangerous potential of separating supply and demand in labor markets, thereby exacerbating the very problem they were designed to mitigate. Europe has too much rigidity in wages and in product markets and has seen its NAIRU increase.
- Over the long run, employment, earnings, job creation, and job growth are all enhanced by a policy environment that encourages flexibility and investment in skills and education.

KEY TERMS AND CONCEPTS

frictional unemployment, p. 515

Okun's law, p. 511

reservation wage, p. 515

NAIRU, p. 510

structural unemployment, p. 516

DISCUSSION QUESTIONS AND PROBLEMS

1. Suppose a policy had the effect of raising the incomes of the poorest 10 percent of the population, but it also lowered average income. How would you decide whether the policy should be used?

2. What are the key patterns of employment growth in the United States and Europe? What explains these patterns?

3. Suppose there is a Phillips curve as follows:

$$\text{Current } \Delta W/W = 0.1(6 - U) + Exp(\Delta W/W)$$

Where the rate of wage increase (in percent) is equal to one tenth of the difference between the unemployment rate (in percent) and 6, plus the expected rate of wage increase.

Suppose that Okun's law is as follows:

$$U = 6 - 0.4(Y/Y^P - 100)$$

Where the unemployment rate is equal to 6 percent minus 0.4 times the output gap (in percent).

Suppose that the relation between wages and prices is as follows:

$$\text{Current } \Delta P/P = \text{Current } \Delta W/W - 1$$

Where the rate of price inflation is equal to the rate of wage increase minus 1 percent (for the effect of productivity increase).

What is the output–inflation trade-off for this economy? What are you assuming about expected price inflation?

4. Which of the following would you call frictional unemployment and which structural?

   a. After having a child, a woman seeks to return to employment.

   b. After completing a college degree, a student looks for a summer job before going to graduate school.

   c. A manufacturing plant in a small town closes.

   d. A teenager drops out of school, looks for work some weeks and not others, and cannot find a job.

5. Are there ways in which the unemployed can be given income support without seriously reducing the incentive to find new jobs?

6. What are the main reasons for the rising inequality in U.S. earnings?

AGGREGATE SUPPLY, LONG-TERM GROWTH, AND PRODUCTIVITY

INTRODUCTION

The controversies over the business cycle and stabilization policies focus on aggregate demand, short-run fluctuations, and the effectiveness of policies aimed at changing aggregate demand. In the realm of stabilization, the application of modern macroeconomic theory and policy has been a success—there has been no return to mass unemployment and deficient demand. Despite continued problems of recession and bouts of inflation, the economy has become less prone to the worst of business-cycle fluctuations.

The greater challenge for modern economies involves aggregate supply and long-term growth. The aggregate supply of the economy reflects the capacity of the economy to supply goods and services to the market. And as we pointed out in Chapter 2, long-term improvements in the standard of living require growth in aggregate supply and improvements in output per capita. By and large, policies that enhance the growth of aggregate supply involve avoiding restrictions that inhibit productivity or avoiding chronic budget deficits that reduce national saving. In this chapter we look at how improvements in aggregate supply, long-term growth, productivity, and job creation respond to particular patterns of saving and investment—in both physical and human capital.

We examine first the theory of economic growth and the development of the Solow growth model. A principal finding from this theory is that most of the increase in productivity over time comes from changes in technology. So in the remainder of the chapter we talk about what is in the "black box" of technological change. We look at the accumulation of knowledge capital and the incentives to apply what is already known. We will use a very different approach in the last part of the chapter, making use of recent studies by economists and business consultants of productivity in different countries. These studies use the knowledge of industry experts to examine why some companies are more productive than others.

In Chapter 2 we introduced the concept of the aggregate production function, but it is worthwhile starting with a brief review of the properties of the production function as we develop the theory of economic growth.

A REVIEW OF THE AGGREGATE PRODUCTION FUNCTION

The amount of output that can be produced depends on how much capital and labor are employed in production, the state of technology.

The aggregate-production function describes the economywide relationship between potential output (Y^P) and capital (K) and labor (N) inputs, using a particular technology (T_{ECH}). This is shown in Equation 17–1:

$$Y^P = F(K,N,T_{ECH}) \tag{17–1}$$

Increases in the inputs (capital or labor, or both) will raise potential output even if there is no change in technology. Improvements in technology will increase potential output using the same amount of inputs. Technological change combined with increases in the amount of capital or labor, or both, will increase potential output by more than the increase in technology or inputs alone.

Average Labor Productivity

average labor productivity
The ratio of output to labor input.

Average labor productivity is the ratio of output to labor input:

$$\text{Average labor productivity} = \text{Output per unit of labor input} = \frac{Y^P}{N}$$

Average labor productivity will generally rise when potential output rises, but this is not always the case. It will move in the opposite direction from total output when there is a change in labor input (a change in the denominator N), with no change in capital or technology. If employment increases, with a given technology and given capital, this will raise total output—more labor generates more output—but, because of diminishing returns, each additional worker adds less to output than the previously hired workers. The average level of labor productivity will fall. Hiring more workers or using more hours per worker to produce more output will depress average labor productivity unless the amount of capital rises by enough to offset the diminishing returns. An important question for growth theory is: How much capital is needed to prevent running into diminishing returns as the labor force grows?

Constant Returns to Scale Labor is not very productive without capital—factories, machinery, offices, computers, and so on. When new workers are hired to produce more output with a given technology, they need the same capital equipment to work with that existing workers have; otherwise, labor productivity will fall.

constant returns to scale
A characteristic of production where a given percentage increase in all inputs leads to an equal percent increase in output.

The need to equip new workers with much the same level of capital as old workers to keep productivity from falling is captured in the presumption that production takes place with **constant returns to scale.** For example, if two identical operations (factories or offices) are constructed and set into operation with the same complement of machines, materials, and employees, production under constant returns to scale implies that the two sites will produce twice the output of one operation alone. The idea of constant returns to scale describes production as a process where proportional increases in the scale (amount or size) of capital and labor employed result in output going up proportionally, holding technology constant. A 10 percent increase or decrease in both capital and labor will result in a 10 percent increase or decrease in output.

Returns to scale are assessed by considering the impact of increases in capital and labor with technology taken as given. Of course, in any practical situation, technology will change as the amount of capital and labor change, so statistical methods have to be used to decide whether there are constant returns to scale.[1] Since the assumption of constant returns to scale greatly simplifies the analysis of productivity with very little loss of realism, we will assume constant returns now and talk about other possibilities later in the chapter.

When production is described by constant returns to scale and there is an increase in the work force, capital has to be added to the economy so as to prevent a reduction in average labor productivity. Average labor productivity will remain the same if capital is increased in the same proportion as the increase in the labor force.

Capital per Worker and Economic Growth

capital intensity
The ratio of capital to labor. On average, the amount of capital available for use by each worker.

intensive production function
A production function in which labor productivity depends on capital intensity—how much capital is available for use by each worker.

Proportional increases of capital and labor only keep average labor productivity constant. If there are to be increases in the standard of living, average labor productivity must rise over time. One way to secure higher levels of average labor productivity is to increase capital by more than any increases in labor. In such a case there is an increase in the amount of capital available for each worker and this increases the **capital intensity** of the economy.

The Intensive Production Function The greater is the capital intensity (capital per worker, K/N) of the economy, the greater is output per worker and the greater is the standard of living obtained in the economy. The **intensive production function** (Equation 17–2) is the production function rewritten so labor productivity depends on capital intensity and technology:

$$\frac{Y^P}{N} = f\left(\frac{K}{N}, T_{ECH}\right) \tag{17–2}$$

With a given technology, the capital intensity of the economy, rather than the separate amounts of capital and labor, determines labor productivity and the standard of living provided there are constant returns to scale.[2] The intensive production function is

---

[1] Zvi Griliches and V. Ringstad, *Economics of Scale and the Form of the Production Function* (Amsterdam: North-Holland, 1971).

[2] We are ignoring the effect of land or natural resources in this analysis (or grouping them with capital). In addition, for individual industries, labor productivity also depends on intermediate goods and services purchased from other industries.

FIGURE 17–1   The Intensive Production
Function: Diminishing Returns

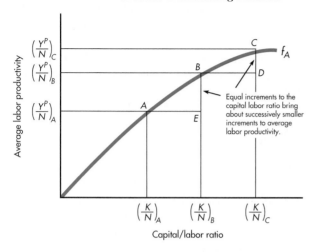

As the capital/labor ratio increases, there are diminishing returns.

FIGURE 17–2   The Intensive Production Function: Shifts in Technology

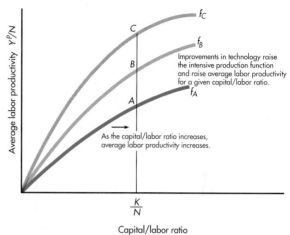

Average labor productivity depends upon the capital/labor ratio
and technology.

illustrated in Figure 17–1. Along a particular production function (f_A), successive increases in capital intensity $[(K/N)_A$ to $(K/N)_B$ to $(K/N)_C]$ bring about increases in average labor productivity. However, raising productivity by raising capital intensity will run into **diminishing returns** to *capital*—average labor productivity rises, but at a declining rate. (*CD* is less than *BE*.) Movements along the intensive production function do not represent increases in the scale of operations where all increases are proportional and productivity is unchanged. Rather, they reflect increases in output per worker obtained when capital is increased more than labor—*output increases less than proportionally to the increase in capital.*

The constraints of diminishing returns to capital can be avoided if there is an improvement in technology. In Figure 17–2 we describe several intensive production functions $(f_A, f_B,$ and $f_C)$ where average labor productivity rises because of improvements in technology. Even with no change in capital intensity [points *A* to *B* to *C* line up along the constant capital/labor ratio (K/N)], improvements in the state of technology raise productivity.

diminishing returns
There are *diminishing returns to labor* if the labor input increases but all other inputs remain constant. Output increases by less than the increase in labor. There are *diminishing returns to capital* if the capital input increases but all other inputs remain constant. Output increases by less than the increase in capital.

Labor-Force Growth and Capital Adequacy   In economies with growing populations there will usually be growth in the work force. With a given technology, this growth in the work force requires an equal growth in the stock of capital, just to keep standards of living constant, let alone allow for any improvements. If the work force is growing, and there is not enough new capital added to match the growth of the work force, capital growth will be inadequate and the economy will suffer from a falling standard of living. In this case of inadequate capital growth, there will be a decline in the capital/labor ratio, leading to successively larger and larger declines in average labor productivity. Increases in capital become essential to avoid diminishing returns to labor.

The intensive production function shown in Equation 17–3 describes how average labor productivity depends on the capital/labor ratio (K/N). And the capital/labor ratio depends on the relative rates of growth of capital and labor. The capital/labor ratio rises when the rate of growth of capital exceeds the rate of growth of the labor input, it falls when the rate of growth of capital is less than that of the labor input, and it stays the same when the two growth rates are equal. This connection between capital intensity and the growth of inputs is set out in Equation 17–3:

K/N is rising when $\Delta K/K > \Delta N/N$
K/N is constant when $\Delta K/K = \Delta N/N$ \hfill (17–3)
K/N is falling when $\Delta K/K < \Delta N/N$

Economies with constant technology that are increasing their stocks of capital at a rate that is just adequate for their rates of labor-input growth will be just maintaining their average labor productivity. In some countries of the world, however, population and labor-force growth have exceeded the ability of the economies to save and increase their capital. These countries have falling standards of living. In Figure 17–1 an economy that starts out (point C) with a high level of average labor productivity [$(Y^P/N)_C$] will slip back to a lower level of average labor productivity [$(Y^P/N)_B$] when the labor input grows by more than the capital stock. (K/N falls as labor grows relative to capital.) And if this process continues (point B to point A), the declines of living standards will get even worse. (BE exceeds CD.)

With a given technology and labor-force growth, the amount of capital growth that is adequate for maintaining living standards is known—it is a growth rate of capital equal to the growth of the work force. But that adequate rate of capital formation may or may not be obtainable. The capacity of an economy to maintain or improve its standard of living is related to the adequacy of its rate of capital formation. *Whether an economy is capable of sustaining an adequate level of capital growth depends on the amount of saving.*

To see just how saving rates affect productivity growth, we now look at the requirements for capital adequacy within a model of economic growth that abstracts from technological change. Changes in technology will be reintroduced later in the chapter. Omitting technology at this point has the advantage of allowing us to focus in a simple fashion on the contribution of capital accumulation to growth and the question of whether economies save too much or too little. When we reintroduce technological change, we will find that much of the analysis we undertook with a fixed technology is easily transferable to economies experiencing both capital accumulation and technological change.

THE SOLOW LONG-TERM GROWTH MODEL

A major modern contribution to the understanding of long-term growth was the development by Robert M. Solow of a growth model using the production-function framework combined with saving behavior.[3] The Solow model focused on the way in which saving frees resources that can then be used for capital accumulation. Capital accumulation might then lead to more economic growth and rising living standards.

Saving's contribution to capital accumulation and growth starts with the relationship between saving and income. Since we are analyzing long-term growth, we assume that consumption and hence saving are fixed proportions of income. Using a simple proportional function to describe saving is appropriate in a model of growth, since the distinctions between current income and permanent income are issues of concern for explaining fluctuations in income and consumption, not long-term trends during which transitory elements in income will disappear. This assumption corresponds roughly to Milton Friedman's description of consumption as a constant fraction of permanent income. The proportional relationship between saving and potential output is shown in Equation 17–4 where s is the proportion of income saved.[4]

$$S = s \times Y^P \qquad\qquad (17\text{–}4)$$

Saving is also equal to investment in this model and investment is also equal to the change in the capital stock (ΔK). Again, since this is a long-term model we can safely ignore short-run investment-demand fluctuations. Since saving equals investment, changes in the capital stock are proportional to income:

$$S = I = \Delta K = s \times Y^P \qquad\qquad (17\text{–}5)$$

Our analysis is motivated by an interest in living standards and average labor productivity. We want to know how much saving is available per worker, because that will translate into how much new capital is available per worker. The amount of new capital per worker will tell us if labor productivity is rising or falling. To see if capital is growing more or less proportionally with labor, in Equation 17–6 we divide output and saving by the size of the labor input, N:

$$\frac{S}{N} = \frac{\Delta K}{N} = \frac{s \times Y^P}{N} \qquad\qquad (17\text{–}6)$$

Here, we see that the ratio of saving to employment is equal to the amount of new capital per worker ($\Delta K/N$), and it depends on output per worker (Y^P/N). Since the propensity to save (s) is set, a fixed proportion of output per worker will be saved.

---

[3] Robert M. Solow, "A Contribution to the Theory of Economic Growth," *Quarterly Journal of Economics* 70 (February 1956), pp. 65–94; "Investment and Technical Progress," in *Mathematical Methods in the Social Sciences,* ed. K. J. Arrow, S. Karbin, and P. Suppes (Stanford, Calif.: Stanford University Press, 1959), pp. 89–104, and "Technical Change and the Aggregate Production Function," *Review of Economics and Statistics* 39 (1957), pp. 312–20.

Other economists also contributed important work to the early development of growth theory, especially James Tobin and T. W. Swan.

[4] We are defining both saving and investment *net* of depreciation for simplicity. The growth model can easily be modified to include depreciation explicitly.

Combining Equation 17–6 with Equation 17–2 gives:

Ratio of saving to employment		New capital per worker		Saving rate × Output per worker		Saving rate × Intensive production function		(17–7)
S/N	$=$	$\Delta K/N$	$=$	$s \times (Y^P/N)$	$=$	$s \times f(K/N)$.		

Equation 17–7 indicates that the amount of new capital added per worker ($\Delta K/N$) depends on the existing capital/labor ratio [$f(K/N)$]. The existing capital/labor ratio determines output per worker and a fraction of that output per hour is saved. Total saving divided by employment is the source of investment—new capital per worker. Notice that, if there were a rise in the existing capital/labor ratio, current productivity would rise along with future productivity as more output generates more saving, which leads to more new capital.

Having laid out the connection between saving and capital per worker, we are ready to answer the important question about how much capital accumulation is required for growth.

Capital Adequacy in the Growth Model

capital adequacy
The increase in capital required to keep the capital/labor ratio constant.

How do we define **capital adequacy** in a growing economy? Capital adequacy is the increase in capital per worker ($\Delta K/N$) necessary to keep the capital/labor ratio constant, thereby keeping labor productivity constant. It turns out that, in the face of a growing labor force, quite a lot of new capital is needed to simply prevent the capital/labor ratio from declining. Even more is needed to raise it. This is because the new entrants to the labor force require a full set of new machines, office space, and so on just to stay even with the existing workers. If the full allocation of new capital is not provided, the growth of the work force will end up diluting the available stock of capital per worker.

We saw in Equation 17–3 that the capital/labor ratio remains constant when the rate of growth of the capital stock is equal to the rate of growth of the labor input ($\Delta K/K = \Delta N/N$). A simple manipulation of this gives us the capital-adequacy condition we need, namely one related to the increase in capital per worker ($\Delta K/N$):

Capital-adequacy condition

The capital/labor ratio remains constant when

$$\Delta K/K = \Delta N/N. \qquad (17–8)$$

Multiplying both sides by the capital/labor ratio, K/N, gives

$$\Delta K/N = \Delta N/N \times K/N$$

This is the capital-adequacy condition.

In general, when the labor force grows, capital growth is adequate if the amount of capital added per existing worker is equal to the amount of capital per worker (K/N) multiplied by the rate of growth of the labor force.

As we showed in Equation 17–1, the amount of new capital added per worker is related to saving and the existing capital/labor ratio. That relationship allows us to describe the connections between saving per worker and capital adequacy:

When Saving per Worker Exceeds Capital Adequacy

$$s \times f\left(\frac{K}{N}\right) = \frac{\Delta K}{N} > \frac{\Delta N}{N} \times \frac{K}{N}$$

Productivity (Y^P/N) and the capital/labor ratio are rising.

When Saving per Worker Equals Capital Adequacy

$$s \times f\left(\frac{K}{N}\right) = \frac{\Delta K}{N} = \frac{\Delta N}{N} \times \frac{K}{N} \qquad (17\text{--}9)$$

Productivity and the capital/labor ratio are constant.

When Savings per Worker Is Less Than Capital Adequacy

$$s \times f\left(\frac{K}{N}\right) = \frac{\Delta K}{N} < \frac{\Delta N}{N} \times \frac{K}{N}$$

Productivity and the capital/labor ratio are falling.

capital deepening
Capital investment taking place at a rate that increases capital intensity and hence raises labor productivity.

The amount of saving per worker in the economy determines the extent to which new capital can be provided to new entrants to the work force at the same level of capital as is provided to the ones that are already there. If saving per worker is large, then there is more than enough capital investment being made to equip the new entrants, and the rest of the investment can then be used to raise the capital/labor ratio for everyone, a process called **capital deepening.** This is the situation in a successful developing country, such as South Korea, that is saving enough to spread capital-intensive production methods more widely among its growing work force.

If saving per worker is lower than capital adequacy, then the capital/labor ratio in the economy will be falling. The capital stock is growing more slowly than the labor input, so there is not enough extra capital to go around and the capital intensity of the economy is declining and so is output per worker. This is the situation in some struggling developing countries where the labor force, fueled by a population explosion, is growing too fast for its ability to provide new capital. These economies may even have relatively high savings rates; but, because their saving per worker cannot maintain their capital/labor ratio in the face of rapid increases in population, their economies are suffering an ongoing decline in productivity and living standards, slipping further and further behind the developed world.

The capital-adequacy conditions under which labor productivity and the capital/labor ratio will rise or fall are illustrated in Figures 17–3 and 17–4. In Figure 17–3, the curve labeled $f(K/N)$ is a particular intensive production function and the curve below it, labeled $s \times f(K/N)$, shows how saving per worker varies with the capital/labor ratio. Total output per worker (at point A, measured by AA'' from the top of the production function to the horizontal axis) is divided up into consumption per worker (the distance all the way from A, on the intensive production, as far as A', on the saving function). Saving per worker is $(A'A'')$.

FIGURE 17–3   Capital Adequacy and the Capital/ Labor Ratio: Falling Ratio

FIGURE 17–4   Capital Adequacy and the Capital/ Labor Ratio: Rising Ratio

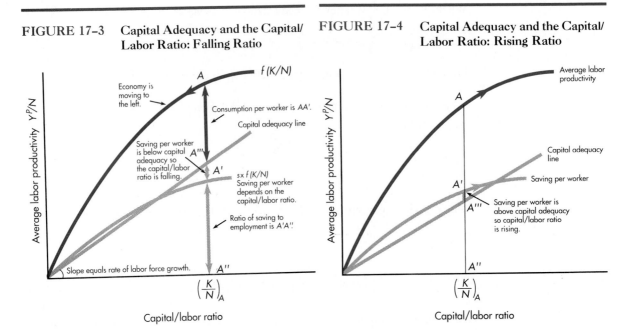

If the capital/labor ratio is $(K/N)_A$, then the capital labor ratio is falling.

If the capital/labor ratio is $(K/N)_A$, then the capital labor ratio is rising.

The straight line in the figure is the capital-adequacy line $[(\Delta N/N) \times (K/N)]$. The line is straight, because the adequate level of capital investment per worker is a constant fraction of the capital/ labor ratio. The fraction is equal to an assumed constant rate of growth $(\Delta N/N)$ of the labor force. Even if the rate of growth of the labor input is kept constant, the adequate level of capital rises in proportion with increases in the capital/labor ratio. As the labor force grows, it takes more new capital to stay even if everyone has a higher level of capital to begin with. This is quite reasonable—compare an advanced economy where all employees have a large stock of sophisticated machinery at their disposal with an economy where workers produce without very much machinery or equipment at all. While the former is certainly preferable (average productivity and living standards are higher), it is much more expensive to equip new workers in the former economy than in the latter. The problem of capital deepening holds for businesses as well. Giving every employee a personal computer may contribute to productivity, but it will also raise the cost of hiring new employees, since each new employee has to be allocated a personal computer to keep even.

Figure 17–3 is so drawn that the economy has an inadequate saving rate. Saving per worker (point A' on the saving function) is below capital adequacy (point A''' on the capital-adequacy line). Saving per worker is insufficient to maintain the capital/labor ratio. Since its capital intensity is falling, productivity in this economy is declining. To prevent this decline, there would have to be either more saving, less growth of the labor force, or a combination of the two.

The opposite case, where the capital/labor ratio is rising and average labor productivity is also rising, is shown in Figure 17–4. In this case, higher saving and/or a lower rate of labor-input growth has the economy at a point where saving (point A' on the saving function) exceeds capital adequacy (point A''' on the capital-adequacy line). This means there is more than enough saving to supply the new entrants to the labor force with the same amount of capital per hour as the existing workers. The capital/labor ratio is rising, so there is capital deepening taking place. Increases in the capital/labor ratio will work to increase productivity.

Worked Example 17–1   We illustrate the condition that ensures rising capital per worker. With a lower rate of saving and/or a faster rate of labor-force growth, this condition will not be satisfied.

Steady-State Growth

It is apparent from Figures 17–3 and 17–4 that an economy's capital/labor ratio can rise or fall, depending on where saving per worker is in relation to capital adequacy. We take the growth rate of the labor force as given. Just to stay even, an economy that has a very high capital/labor ratio requires much greater increases in capital for new workers than does an economy with the same labor-force growth and a low capital/labor ratio. The economy with a high capital/labor ratio is more likely to experience a declining capital/labor ratio. (As shown in Figure 17–3, $A''' > A'$.) The economy with a low capital/labor ratio is more likely to be experiencing a rising capital/labor ratio. (As shown in Figure 17–4, $A''' < A'$.) *There is a tendency, therefore, for growing economies to move toward the point where the amount of saving and new capital is just equal to the amount of capital adequacy.* Economies move toward a position where capital adequacy is just obtained and growth is constant: At this point, the economy is in **steady-state growth.** The steady state is illustrated in Figure 17–5. Where the economy has a low capital/labor ratio $[(K/N)_A]$, productivity is low (point A) and the saving rate per worker (point A') exceeds capital adequacy. The capital/labor ratio and average labor productivity are both rising. Notice that saving per worker is also rising, but at a declining rate. The economy is heading toward the point where saving per worker is just equal to capital adequacy. This condition is shown at point B', where the saving curve intersects the capital-adequacy line. Since capital adequacy means that just enough new capital is being provided new workers so as to keep the existing capital/labor ratio constant, at points B and B', the capital/labor ratio $[(K/N)_B]$ remains constant.

The situation of an economy with a high capital/labor ratio $[(K/N_C]$ is depicted at point C' where the saving curve is below the capital-adequacy line. Here, the capital/labor ratio and average labor productivity are both falling. Since capital adequacy is proportional to capital intensity, this situation will also drive the economy to the point where saving per worker is just equal to capital adequacy. Once more, the saving curve intersects the capital-adequacy line at the same point (point B') this time from above, rather than below. Again, the capital/labor ratio will remain constant.

steady-state growth
A sustained constant rate of growth. Steady state is reached when the amount of saving and new capital is just adequate to maintain capital intensity.

FIGURE 17–5
Capital Adequacy and the Capital/Labor Ratio: Steady State

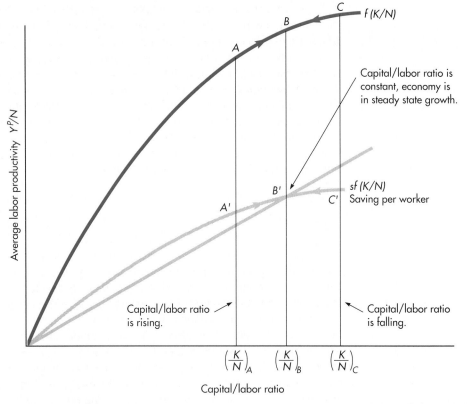

With no technological change, economics will move toward a point where the capital/ labor ratio is constant and there is steady-state growth.

Regardless of its initial capital/labor ratio, therefore, a growing economy will converge to a point where the capital/labor ratio remains constant.[5] At that point (point *B* on the production function, point *B'* on the saving curve and the capital-adequacy line) the economy is experiencing steady-state growth. In this discussion, where we have excluded technical change, steady-state growth occurs where the rate of growth of output is equal to the rate of growth of the capital stock and both are equal to the rate of labor-input growth. This means that, in steady-state growth, the capital/labor ratio and average labor productivity will both remain constant.

Steady-state growth is important because we have just shown that, regardless of the initial level of productivity and the initial level of the capital/labor ratio, the economy will move over time toward the point of steady-state growth. Steady-state growth is

---

[5] This statement has some technical qualifications. It is possible that the saving curve and the capital-adequacy line will not intersect except at the origin or at infinity. These possibilities are not terribly relevant for advanced economies, but it is possible for low-income, high–labor-force–growth economies to get trapped in a downward spiral with no steady state.

something we would expect to see in mature economies. If we want to see how saving affects growth, we can look first at how it affects steady-state growth, and then we can see how an economy might change from one steady-state growth path to another.

Does Thrift Lead to More Rapid Growth?   Prior to the development of the neo-classical theory of growth, many people believed that increasing the fraction of income saved and devoting this increased saving to increased capital accumulation would *indefinitely* generate a higher rate of economic growth. Still today, we hear frequently that the Japanese and the European economies are growing faster than the U.S. economy and they will continue to do so because of their higher rates of saving, compared to spendthrift Americans' rate. *What we will see now is that, while more saving increases the levels of productivity and standard of living, steady-state growth rates are not affected by thrift.* It still pays to save, since an economy with double the standard of living of its neighbor, both having the same growth rate, will continue to have a standard of living double that of its neighbor. The two economies will not grow further apart, but they will not grow closer together, either.

Comparing Two Steady States   In the steady state, how does the sacrifice of more saving and less consumption in the short term pay off with a higher living standard in the long term? We take a look at this question of the benefits and limitations of saving for economic growth by comparing two economies with the same technologies and different saving rates. Two such economies are described in Figure 17–6. They have the same production technology, shown as a single production function [$f(K/N)$], and two different saving curves corresponding to an economy that has a low saving rate [$s_A \times f(K/N)$] and an economy that has a high saving rate [$s_B \times f(K/N)$]. Both economies are assumed to be in steady-state growth.

The level of average labor productivity will be higher in the high-saving economy. *Comparing economies that are in steady-state growth, a higher saving propensity means more capital per worker and a higher level of productivity.* The higher level of productivity will generally mean higher consumption in the high-saving economy. Consumption per worker is probably higher in the high-saving economy (point B to point B') than in the low-saving economy (point A to point A'). But this result is not certain. While output per worker is higher in economy B, saving propensities are higher in economy B. In economy B a smaller fraction of output is devoted to consumption, so the consumption standard of living is not higher by the full amount of the difference in productivity between the two economies.[6] *The high-saving economy has to devote a larger share of its higher income to capital accumulation than does the*

---

[6] Consumption per worker refers to total consumption divided by the total number of workers. Total consumption includes the consumption made by the owners of capital.
   It is possible that consumption per worker in economy B is actually lower than in economy A. In this case, economy B is said to be *dynamically inefficient.* The people in economy B could cut their saving, raise their consumption, and be able to consume more in the future as well as in the present. There is no evidence that the U.S. economy is even close to being dynamically inefficient. Japan may find itself moving close to such a situation, although foreign investment, which is not included in this discussion, would solve the inefficiency problem.

FIGURE 17–6
The Effect of
Different
Propensities to
Save

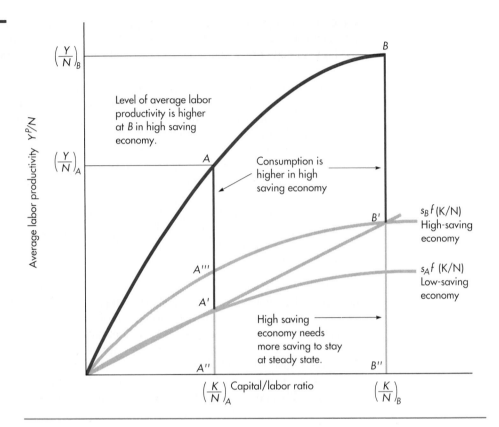

low-saving economy to keep its capital/labor ratio constant. As shown in the figure, at the constant steady-state capital/labor ratio in economy B $[(K/N)_B]$, the segment B' to B'' (saving per worker) is larger than the segment A' to A'' at the steady-state capital/labor ratio $[(K/N)_A]$ in economy A. In economies where there is growth in the labor force, like Alice in Wonderland, the economy has to keep running to keep its capital/labor ratio constant. In the high-saving economy, the steady-state capital/labor ratio is higher, so the growing labor force requires more new capital, and the economy has to run even harder to stay still.

We have seen that differences in saving propensities will result in differences in productivity levels and living standards. But the two economies shown operating at points A and B are both in steady-state growth and will, therefore, have the same rates of output growth. *Once an economy has converged to its steady-state growth path, it will keep the same rate of growth regardless of its propensity to save and accumulate capital.* Having a high propensity to save affords a higher standard of living but not as much higher as the differences in saving among low- and high-saving economies. Moreover, it does not allow an economy to have a higher rate of growth forever.

An important reason why saving and capital accumulation have limited effects is that we have assumed diminishing returns to capital, so successive increments to capital per worker result in smaller and smaller increments to productivity. The effect of diminishing returns is reflected in the shape of the intensive production function curving over and intersecting the capital-adequacy line.

Changing from One Steady State to Another   We have seen how changes in the propensity to save affect steady-state growth. But what about an economy that is growing along a steady-state growth path and then decides to increase its saving propensity? What happens then? We can find the answer by using Figure 17–6, not to compare two economies, but to look at a single economy whose members first have a low saving propensity (s_A at point A') and then change consumption behavior such that there is an increase in the saving rate (s_B at point B'). When the saving rate increases, there will be an immediate sacrifice in the consumption standard of living. Consumption per worker will fall (from AA' to AA'''). Over time, however, the higher saving rate, now that it is greater than capital adequacy, will raise the capital/labor ratio [$(K/N)_A$ to $(K/N)_B$]. Average productivity and the standard of living will increase, as shown by the movement around the intensive production function (point A to point B). During this period of transition, it will have a growth rate of output that exceeds the growth of its labor input, so productivity will be growing. At some point in the transition, it will find that its consumption and living standards have become higher than they were in the previous steady state. And once it has converged to the new steady-state growth path, the economy will have higher living standards forever.

Summarizing the Effect of Thrift   Growth theory tells us the following about the role played by saving in economic growth:

1. The long-run (steady-state) growth rate of an economy does not depend on the propensity to save and accumulate capital.

2. For an economy in steady-state growth, the level of output and productivity will be higher, the higher is the level of the propensity to save in the economy.

3. For an economy in steady-state growth, the level of consumption will generally be higher, the higher is the propensity to save. Some part of output has to be used to maintain the ratio of capital to labor. This has the effect of reducing the benefit to consumers of having a higher capital/labor ratio and higher productivity.

4. An economy that decides to raise its saving propensity will make an immediate sacrifice in reduced consumption and living standards. Productivity and living standards will then rise more rapidly for some period, eventually overtaking the former level. They will then be higher for the indefinite future. This process is an important part of economic development. Countries that have stagnated at a low level of income can try to raise their rates of saving and investment and move up toward the developed countries.

5. An economy that decides to lower its saving propensity will gain an immediate benefit in increased consumption and living standards. Productivity and living standards will then fall for some period, eventually falling below the former level. They will then be lower for the indefinite future.

The immediate gains and longer-term losses that result from a reduction in national saving are relevant to the U.S. economy in the 1990s. Americans have been consuming a very high fraction of their income since the 1980s and there is concern that this will erode future living standards. An important difference between the U.S. situation and the model of growth is that foreign saving has provided some alternative to low U.S. saving, allowing capital formation to exceed the supply of domestic saving.

Worked Example 17–2   In Worked Example 17–2 we show that it becomes harder to satisfy the condition for *rising* capital per worker as the level of capital per worker rises.

LONG-TERM GROWTH WITH TECHNOLOGICAL CHANGE

Over the long-term history of the U.S. economy, output has grown more rapidly than has the labor force—productivity has risen very dramatically. How can that growth experience be reconciled with the conclusions of our growth model—that the economy moves toward steady state and, in steady state, the capital/labor ratio is constant, and output grows only at the rate of growth of the labor force? In the model, moving from one steady state to another was accomplished through the accumulation of physical capital. Allocating more resources to capital as a way to raise productivity and living standards is limited by diminishing returns. These limits to growth were derived from models in which technology was assumed constant.

Technological change increases the steady-state growth rate, and in practice has been the main source of increases in productivity and living standards.

The Contribution of Technology to Productivity Growth

What portion of the increase that has taken place in average labor productivity in the business sector of the U.S. economy can be attributed to increases in the capital/labor ratio (movements around the intensive production function) and what part to technological change (shifts in the intensive production function)? This question was addressed by Solow when he developed his growth model. Figure 17–7 illustrates his findings. Solow found that, over time, the intensive production function had moved up from f_A to f_B and the economy had moved around the function from point *A* to point *B*. Solow estimated that the increase in average labor productivity (the segment *BD*) had come 87 percent from technological change (the upward shift in the function, point *B* to point *C*) and only 13 percent from the increase in capital per worker at the same level of technology (the movement along the function, point *D* to point *C*). Other researchers using different methods came up with somewhat different results,[7] but *there was a general and surprising consensus that technological change, rather than the accumulation of capital, was the primary factor in the long-term growth of productivity and hence living standards.* This meant that technological change had to be accounted for in any realistic model of economic growth.

---

[7]   Edward F. Denison, *Trends in American Economic Growth, 1929–82* (Washington, D.C.: Brookings Institution, 1985); J. W. Kendrick, *Productivity Trends in the United States* (Princeton, N.J.: Princeton University Press, 1961); and Dale Jorgenson, Frank M. Gollop, and Barbara M. Faumeni, *Productivity and U.S. Economic Growth* (Cambridge, Mass: Harvard University Press, 1987).

FIGURE 17–7
The Contributions of Capital and Technology to Productivity Growth

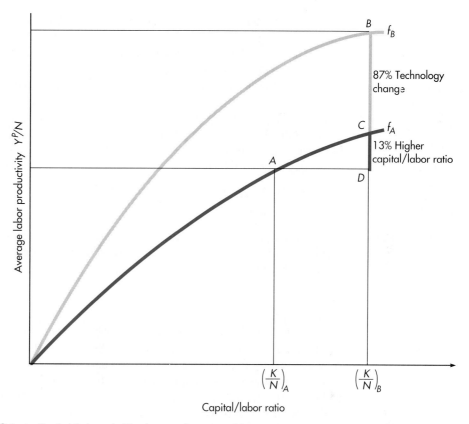

Solow estimated that most of the increase in average labor productivity came from an upward shift in the production function.

The Solow Long-Term Growth Model Where Technology Augments Labor

The production function and the intensive production function (Equations 17–1 and 17–2) contained the assumption that output and labor productivity depend on the state of technology, T_{ECH}. We made no assumption about the way in which technology might affect the contributions of capital and labor to output.

In incorporating the effects of technological change in the Solow model of growth now, we will make an important additional assumption. *We will assume that technological change has the effect of augmenting the labor input to production.* We assume that, when technology improves, it augments the productive capacity of labor—it makes each worker or hour of labor more productive. This assumption is a very useful one, in that it focuses on the notion that technological change is meant to be a broad technical and managerial term, including all sorts of productivity enhancements that, when combined, have the effect of increasing the productivity of workers. This assumption also allows us to make use of the tools we have already developed for analyzing long-term growth.

augmented labor
The labor force adjusted by the state of technology. As technology grows, the augmented labor force grows faster than the actual labor force, because a unit of augmented labor is equivalent to more than a unit of actual labor.

As the growth of technology augments labor, each hour of work with new technology is equivalent to more than an hour of work with old technology. We now have two ways in which the labor input can grow: more employment or hours worked and more productive workers. We combine these two types of labor growth into a concept called **augmented labor,** N^*. In some initial base year the amount of augmented labor is simply equal to the amount of actual labor, N (set $T_{ECH} = 1$ in the base year). As technology improves over time (T_{ECH} increases), augmented labor grows faster than actual labor. With this assumption, we rewrite the original production function given in Equation 17–1 by combining the labor input, N, and the technology term, T, into the single augmented-labor term, N^*. This is shown in Equation 17–10:

$$Y^P = F(K,N,T_{ECH})$$
$$ = F(K,N^*) \tag{17–10}$$

The assumption of constant returns to scale is retained, so a new intensive production function can be used, in which output per augmented worker depends on capital per augmented worker:

$$\frac{Y^P}{N^*} = f\left(\frac{K}{N^*}\right) \tag{17–11}$$

Why would technological change augment labor? One reason is that technical advance can be used to increase the skill and knowledge of each worker. But that is not the only possibility. If technology augments labor, this does not necessarily mean that capital is unaffected. Although it may not be easy to see the intuitive reason for it, technological change that augments labor could come about simply because workers have more efficient machines to work with.

One reason why we assume technology is labor augmenting is that it fits with an important fact about economic growth observed in several market economies. *Real wages generally increase along with increases in average labor productivity.* Most of the increase in productivity comes from technological change and, since labor markets allocate much of those gains to workers, this suggests that technology is augmenting the labor input.

Steady-State Growth with Labor-Augmenting Technology   Earlier, we assumed that the labor input grows at a constant rate, and we will carry this over and assume that augmented labor grows over time at a constant rate, a rate that is equal to the rate of growth of the labor force plus the rate of technological change:

$$\text{Growth rate of augmented labor} = \frac{\Delta N^*}{N^*}$$
$$= \text{Growth rate of labor force}$$
$$+ \text{Rate of labor-augmenting}$$
$$\text{technological change}$$

Growth in augmented labor is a combination of growth in the actual labor input (the number of workers) and growth in labor-augmenting technology. Looking back at Figure 17–7, there the effect of technological change was to shift the intensive

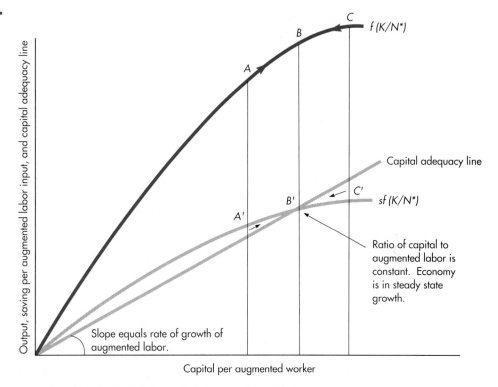

FIGURE 17–8
The Growth Model with Technical Change

Economies with technological change that augments labor will move toward steady-state growth, with a higher growth rate than in economies with no technological change.

production function upward. By defining the concept of augmented labor, we can now describe a new intensive production function (Figure 17–8) that incorporates changes in technology. The new intensive production function shows how output per augmented worker varies with the amount of capital per augmented worker and the saving curve shows the ratio of saving to the augmented labor input. The capital-adequacy line also involves augmented labor, rather than actual labor; and this leads to a difference between Figure 17–8 and the earlier figures. The rate of growth of augmented labor is greater than the rate of growth of actual labor, with the difference being the rate of technological change.

In the previous examples, the intersection of the capital-adequacy line and the saving curve (point B') is where the capital/labor ratio is constant at steady-state growth. This is true in Figure 17–8, also, except that it is the ratio of capital to augmented labor that is constant at the steady-state point. If the economy is not in steady-state growth (e.g., at points A and A' or at points C and C'), then the ratio of capital to augmented labor will be changing. An economy with technological change that augments labor will move toward the point where steady-state growth occurs. In the steady state, the ratio of capital to augmented labor remains constant at B. And at point B' on the intensive production function, the ratio of output to augmented labor remains constant. The capital-adequacy line is steeper in this case than in previous examples without technological change. It takes more saving per worker to keep the ratio of capital to augmented labor constant than the amount necessary to keep the ratio of capital to actual labor constant. There is a flip side to this, however. With technological change, it is possible to achieve a much higher rate of investment without running into diminishing returns to capital. An economy that experiences labor-augmenting technological change is not free of the need to improve its level of investment to maintain its growth rate. However, the steady-state growth rate and standard of living it can obtain are higher because of technological change.

Technological change confers a double productivity benefit for the economy. Improvements in technology generate growth in output and, since saving is a constant proportion of output, this will mean in turn that there will also be a faster rate of growth of the stock of capital. *In an economy with technological change, average labor productivity is growing directly because of the contribution of technology as a factor of production, but it is also growing as an indirect consequence of the technological change because faster output growth leads to faster capital growth.* Success (faster output growth) breeds more success (faster capital accumulation). With technological change, the ratio of capital to actual labor is growing even when there is steady-state growth.

Let's summarize what we have found out from our model of growth in an economy with technological change.

1. The long-run (steady-state) growth rate of output is constant at a rate equal to the rate of labor-augmenting technological change plus the rate of actual labor-input growth (growth of the work force).

2. In steady-state growth, average labor productivity grows at a rate equal to the rate of labor-augmenting technological change.

3. In steady-state growth, the capital stock grows at the same rate as output and the capital/labor ratio grows at a rate equal to the rate of labor-augmenting technological change.

4. For a developing economy that is accumulating capital at a rate that exceeds the rate of growth of augmented labor, the rate of productivity growth will exceed the steady-state rate of growth.

5. For an economy that is "declining," the rate of productivity growth will be below the steady-state rate of growth. Because of technological change, however, the rate of productivity growth will generally still be positive. *Technological change provides an alternative source of productivity growth for an economy where the rate of capital accumulation is low.*

In our discussion of growth so far, we have been concerned mostly with putting together a model or framework for growth analysis. Using this framework, we have been able to say something about how changes in the propensity to save will affect the growth rates of output and productivity, and how wages and profits will be affected by a slowdown in the rate of technological change. And we have used the Solow growth model to interpret some aspects of the actual experience of growth in the U.S. economy.

At this point, however, it is time to look beyond the growth model. Models can be a straitjacket as well as a guide and we are going to take a more detailed look at the sources of growth in the U.S. economy. Of course, we will not forget the analytical framework, which will continue to inform the discussion.

As we look further at U.S. growth, we want to know more about the concept of technological change. What is it? Where does it come from? Although we have used the word *technological,* in fact it is not just developments related to science and engineering that are driving ''technological change.'' Improvements in management techniques, increases in the amount of training and skill of the work force, and many other possibilities may be causing the upward shifts in the production function.

THE ACCUMULATION OF KNOWLEDGE TO IMPROVE TECHNOLOGY

Technological advance must come about through the accumulation of knowledge and its use in the production of goods and services. Companies and workers use expanded knowledge to increase the productivity with which they use capital, the materials and services they buy from other companies, and their own labor. The accumulation of knowledge can occur in three ways.

First, the education and skill level of the work force can increase over time, allowing workers to perform their jobs more productively. This is described as the accumulation of human capital, and, as we discussed in Chapter 2, there is some concern today that skills in the U.S. work force are growing more slowly or are even declining.

Second, companies can perform R&D themselves and make use of the scientific and engineering advances that result from the basic research carried out in universities and research labs. This R&D then increases the stock of technical knowledge that can be applied to the production process.

Third, companies can accumulate knowledge about the best practices and techniques in production and management. The organization learns how to increase productivity.

The Congressional Budget Office (CBO), an advisory agency to the Congress, has prepared estimates of the national capital stock, taking into account not only physical capital but also two of the types of knowledge capital that we have just described, coming from education and from R&D. Here knowledge capital is measured by cumulating the level of expenditure allocated in past years to education and R&D, rather than by trying to measure the contribution that those expenditures make to future productivity. The amounts invested each year in education and research and development can be measured more easily than the output of those investments.[8] Table 17–1 shows their findings.

The CBO reports that in 1960 the United States had $17 billion of U.S.-based capital assets. Of this total, the share of physical assets was 61.2 percent, with 16.5

---

[8] There is an attempt to account roughly for the depreciation of educational capital, just as the depreciation of physical capital is accounted for.

TABLE 17–1
Capital Assets in
the U.S. Economy
(trillions of 1987
dollars)

	1960	1970	1980	1990	1991	1992	1993
Publicly owned physical assets	$ 2.8	$ 3.4	$ 5.0	$ 4.8	$ 4.7	$ 4.7	$ 4.6
Privately owned physical assets	7.6	10.4	17.5	19.9	19.3	18.8	18.6
Education capital	6.3	10.7	14.9	22.7	23.7	24.9	26.3
Research and development capital	0.3	0.7	1.0	1.5	1.5	1.6	1.6
Total assets	$17.0	$25.3	$38.5	$48.9	$49.3	$50.0	$51.2

Source: Congressional Budget Office.

percent made up of physical assets held by all levels of government and the remaining 44.7 percent being privately held physical assets. Measured knowledge capital was 38.9 percent of the $17 billion of assets, including education capital at 37.1 percent and R&D capital at 1.8 percent.

By 1993, physical assets, public and private, accounted for a smaller fraction of total assets (45.4 percent combined), while education capital and R&D capital accounted for the remaining 54.6 percent. In fact, physical capital actually declined from a peak in 1990 (because of the effect of the recession on investment in equipment and structures).

A good deal of the value of knowledge accumulation and adoption is not measurable even when the measurement is restricted to inputs. How would we discern which portion of a firm's expenditure or which portion of an employee's time goes into the informal learning that leads to productivity enhancement? In fact, this aspect of organizational learning is not counted in the CBO calculation. It comes as a result of innovations and changes that are made as part of the normal work of companies. If workers and managers are motivated to improve productivity, they will constantly evaluate the way they are doing business and look for improvements. In the service sector it is assumed that no R&D is carried out, even though innovations are taking place.

Even though it is not measured, examples of the process of organizational learning are found in many industries. Toyota has collected suggestions from its workers over many years. The resulting changes in the production process have contributed to Toyota's uniquely high level of productivity.

Another example is provided by the computerization of business operations. Expenditure on hardware is counted as part of investment and adds to the physical capital stock; but software, system development, and the time allocated to employee learning is, for the most part, not counted as part of asset accumulation. The software and training costs now make up a much larger share of computer system costs than does hardware.

Organizational learning involves more than creating new knowledge; it extends to implementing the new methods that result from innovation. Within a single economy, this process of dissemination of knowledge increases the average level of the technology in use in the economy. Best-practice methods are first used in one company and then gradually spread more widely. In addition, the transfer of technology can also occur among countries. Best-practice methods developed in one country are used in another.

This discussion, together with the CBO data on capital assets, provides some indication of the ways in which technological change takes place. But it does not provide any direct estimates of the relative importance of the different sources of change. There are three ways of making such estimates. The first is the growth accounting approach, the second is the use of econometric estimates, and the third is to use direct knowledge of companies.

Growth
Accounting and
Econometric
Estimates

We said earlier that Solow had developed a method of estimating the contribution of capital accumulation to productivity increase and the contribution of technological change. This method was based on his growth model and has since been further developed to try and unravel the technological change part and to assess the likely contribution of education and other factors. Dale Jorgenson of Harvard and the late Edward Denison of Brookings have carried out the most careful work of this type, and their studies indicate that education has indeed been an important source of improved productivity increase.[9]

Denison estimates that increases in the amount of education per worker accounted for about 30 percent of the increase in labor productivity in the business sector of the U.S. economy over the period 1929–1982. By including more types of physical capital, Dale Jorgenson has suggested that capital accumulation has played a larger role in productivity growth than was indicated in Solow's estimate in the 1950s.

Many studies over the years have found that education contributes to the earnings of individuals. And in a market economy, this is indirect evidence that it adds to productivity.[10]

Recent econometric work has looked for direct evidence on the role of education on growth, using data on a number of countries. And as part of this work, the studies have also considered the contribution of physical capital to growth. In comparing the productivity growth rates of different countries around the world, is it the case that the countries that have rapidly accumulated educational capital or physical capital have achieved higher rates of growth? As well as its interest for us in understanding U.S. growth, this is obviously an important question for poor countries that are trying to increase their living standards. Unfortunately, the evidence is pretty mixed.

For education, several studies have found that the fraction of students in a country who were enrolled in school in 1960 seems to be correlated with growth from 1960 to 1985.[11] However, there is little evidence the countries that invested more than average

---

[9] Edward F. Denison, *Trends in American Economic Growth, 1929–82* (Washington D.C.: Brookings Institution, 1985); and Dale Jorgenson, Frank Gollop, and Barbara Fraumeni, *Productivity and U.S. Economic Growth,* (Cambridge, Mass.: Harvard University Press, 1987).

[10] If wages reflect the marginal productivities of the workers, then a worker with a higher wage will have a higher productivity.

[11] Robert J. Barro, "Economic Growth in a Cross-Section of Countries," *Quarterly Journal of Economics,* May 1991. Paul M. Romer, "Human Capital and Growth: Theory and Evidence," *NBER Working Paper, No. 3173,* 1989. N. G. Mankiw, D. Romer, and D. Weil, "A Contribution to the Empirics of Economic Growth," *Quarterly Journal of Economics,* May 1992.

in education over the same time have been able to grow more rapidly.[12] This is true for the industrial countries and the developing countries. The data do not speak clearly on the role of education in growth across countries.

For physical capital, there is stronger evidence that physical capital adds to growth than does educational capital, but the extent of that contribution is hard to determine with any certainty. Generally, the studies find that physical capital contributes to productivity growth about as much as the Solow model suggested. Some studies have suggested it contributes more than this.

A variety of econometric evidence and case study evidence suggests that R&D contributes to productivity growth.[13] And there is even some fragile evidence connecting basic research to productivity increase. But the data from the CBO that we looked at earlier showed the amount of R&D capital in the economy is very small. Even though R&D has a big effect on productivity per dollar of expenditure, it is not a large enough factor to have a big effect on productivity growth overall.

Using Business Knowledge to Explain Productivity Differences

Models, aggregate data, and econometric estimation could only go so far in unraveling the mysteries about the sources of productivity growth. Since organizational learning and best-business practices are candidates for sources of productivity enhancement, analysis has to be conducted at the level of the individual company. Starting in 1991, a group of economists, including Robert Solow, who had done work on growth accounting and econometric estimation, participated in a project to look at the sources of productivity by making a detailed study of business practices. The project was initiated and conducted by the McKinsey Global Institute, part of the business consulting firm of McKinsey and Company. The team of academic economists and business consultants measured the extent of productivity differences in companies and industries across countries and then worked to understand the reasons for the differences that they found.[14]

Two studies were completed in 1992 and 1993, with the first looking at five service sector industries and the second at nine manufacturing industries. They compared productivities in the United States, Europe, and Japan in 1989 or 1990. The framework for measurement and analysis was based on the production function and the growth model and was then extended as new causal factors were uncovered. Analysis of how productivity differences occur was based on the specialized knowledge of industry experts from McKinsey, interviews with corporate personnel, and benchmarking studies that compared similar operations in different plants or companies.

---

[12] Jess Benhabib and Mark M. Spiegel, "The Role of Capital and Political Instability in Economic Development," *Economic Research Report RR# 92–24,* New York University, May 1992.

[13] For a summary of the evidence, see Zvi Griliches, "Econometric Estimates of R&D Returns," paper presented at the OECD–TEP Conference on Technology and Investment, January 21–24, 1990. See also Edwin Mansfield, "How Economists See R&D," *Research Management* 27 (1982), pp. 23–29.

[14] McKinsey Global Institute, *Service Sector Productivity,* McKinsey and Company, October 1992, and *Manufacturing Productivity,* McKinsey and Company, 1993. The studies were directed by William Lewis of McKinsey and the economists were Martin Baily, Francis Bator, and Robert Solow.

FIGURE 17–9
International
Comparisons of
Service Industry
Productivity

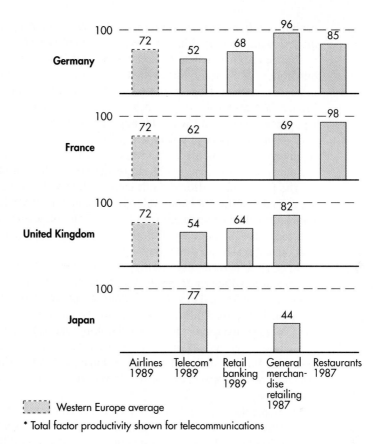

Source: McKinsey, 1992.

Looking at a cross-section of industries across countries in a single year is obviously different from looking at productivity growth. Nevertheless, there is a relation between the level of productivity reached and the growth to achieve that level. If we can understand international productivity differences, this should give us some insight into how or why productivity growth occurs.

Figure 17–9 shows the results of the study of five service industries. It shows that, in the telecommunications industry, in the airline industry, in the retailing industry (excluding food and drug stores and car dealers), and in the banking industry, the United States had substantially higher productivity in most cases than these industries in Europe and Japan. There was little difference measured in productivities in the restaurant industry.

What were the companies doing that was different in the U.S. industries? The answers varied by industry. In telecommunications, the industries in Germany and the United Kingdom were backward technologically. They had been state-owned (telecom still is in Germany) and had not invested in modern electronic switches or other equipment. Germany still has no high-speed data transmission lines and businesses cannot install voice-mail equipment. The U.K. industry had never invested much in modern equipment and had many excess employees.[15]

France also had a state-owned system and Japan's was state-owned until recently; but policy in these countries had pushed investment in modern equipment. Both industries suffered from a lack of market incentives, however, and had excess labor. France had also paid a very high price for its modern system, having bought its equipment from state-owned monopoly suppliers.

In banking, Germany and the U.K. had industries with very low competitive intensity, a gentlemen's club in the U.K. and also in Germany for the large banks. Germany also has many small protected cooperative or state-run banks.

The U.S. banks suffered the lingering effects of years of regulation and there were some small inefficient banks still operating here in 1990. Nevertheless, the pressure of competition had encouraged U.S. banks to automate and computerize their operations and to reduce the number of employees needed to operate the check clearing system and other back-office functions.

In general merchandise retailing, it was found that productivity depends heavily on the extent to which more productive retail formats have taken over the market. Such stores as Wal-Mart, Toys R Us, Home Depot, and Circuit City have driven out large numbers of the small stores that used to sell this type of merchandise. By operating at greater scale, using information technology, integrating their operations to eliminate the wholesalers and other innovations, these stores have greatly increased productivity. In Europe, and particularly in Japan, regulations and restrictions designed to protect small shopkeepers have slowed the evolution of retailing and held back productivity.

The operations of an airline were broken down into different functions, and it was found that productivity was higher in all of the functions in the United States than in Europe, particularly in aircraft maintenance. After controlling for a variety of possible reasons for this, it was concluded that the most important reason was that the European airlines lacked flexibility in the deployment of their work forces and, in several cases, they simply had more employees than they needed. Most of the larger European airlines are state-owned and they face political constraints and strong unions that make it difficult for them to change work rules or to lay off excess workers. The U.S. airlines have been battered by competition since deregulation and have been forced to cut costs.

There were no significant differences in the restaurant industry, one that is competitive with relatively easy entry of new competitors in all of the countries.

Figure 17–10 shows the results for the nine manufacturing industries, where the comparisons were made for Germany, Japan, and the United States. For Japan and the United States, the figure shows a very mixed picture. In several internationally traded industries, such as autos, auto parts, steel, consumer electronics, and metalworking,

---

[15] Japan and the U.K. have privatized and deregulated their telecom industries and there is rapid change taking place.

FIGURE 17-10
International
Comparisons of
Manufacturing
Productivity

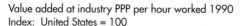

Value added at industry PPP per hour worked 1990
Index: United States = 100

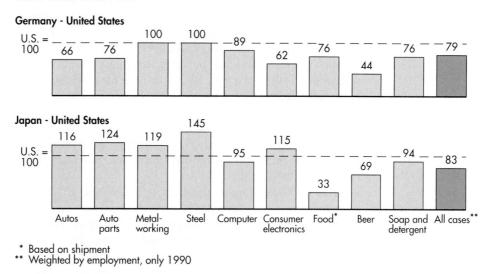

Germany - United States

U.S. = 100

66 | 76 | 100 | 100 | 89 | 62 | 76 | 44 | 76 | 79

Japan - United States

U.S. = 100

116 | 124 | 119 | 145 | 95 | 115 | 33 | 69 | 94 | 83

Autos | Auto parts | Metal-working | Steel | Computer | Consumer electronics | Food* | Beer | Soap and detergent | All cases**

* Based on shipment
** Weighted by employment, only 1990

Source: McKinsey, 1993.

the Japanese companies have achieved higher (in the case of steel, much higher) levels of productivity than the U.S. companies. The computer industry has similar productivities in the two countries. And the United States has higher or much higher productivity in processed food than does Japan. Since the food processing industry in Japan has many more employees than any of the other industries (more than autos, auto parts, steel, metalworking, and consumer electronics combined) the average of the case studies showed Japan with 83 percent of the U.S. level.

The comparison between the United States and Germany has a different pattern. There is no equivalent of the Japanese processed food industry in Germany, but most of the industries are below the productivity level of the United States. And this means that some of the German industries are way below best-practice Japanese productivity. The average for the case studies for Germany was 79 percent of the U.S. level.

What explains these differences? The McKinsey study found three main causes: the organization of the workplace, the design of the products, and the combined effect of scale, capital, and technology used. Together these elements point to the validity of both lessons learned from the models of growth theory—capital and technological change matter—as well as the lessons learned from looking inside the technological black box—how organizations learn and how knowledge is accumulated and applied affect productivity growth.

Organization of the Workplace   Starting in Japanese companies in the auto and electronics industries, incremental innovations have been made in process design over the last 20 years or more. These innovations are not large or dramatic taken one by one. They reflect the placement of machines and people, making sure the parts arrive in the right place at the right time, specifying in detail the exact movements by the worker that will be most efficient, and the training and motivation of the work force. Despite the fact that these innovations are not dramatic, they have raised productivity substantially when taken as whole.

One reason for the lower productivity in the United States and Germany, compared to the Japanese industries in autos, auto parts, metalworking, steel, and consumer electronics is that these process innovations have not been adopted to the same degree, especially in the case of Germany.

Design for Manufacturability At the same time the Japanese companies were making process innovations, they were also redesigning their products, so they used fewer parts and were easier to manufacture. Autos, for example, were designed to almost snap together.

This innovation has also been applied more extensively in Japan than in the United States and Europe, although the U.S. auto industry is catching up.

By combining a lean organization of the workplace with design for manufacturability, the most productive manufacturing plants, including now some in the United States, have made huge increases in productivity. Toyota had about a 40 percent productivity advantage *over other Japanese companies* in 1987.[16] The Ford Taurus plant in Atlanta had about the same advantage over the average U.S. auto assembly plant in the late 1980s.

Scale, Capital, and Technology Very large productivity increases can be achieved as industries evolve from small local craft producers to large-scale industrial producers. This transition happened early in the United States in the processed food and beer industries and has either not happened much at all (beer in Germany) or has happened to a much more limited extent elsewhere (food processing in Japan). This transition involves a consolidation of the industry to achieve optimal scale of plants, and it requires substantial capital investment. When it first happens, it requires innovation to create the new technology.

In the steel industry, the evolution of the capital and technology has been important, also. Integrated steel mills are an early example of modern industrial-scale plants, and many of the U.S. plants were built in the 1920s. Germany has more modern and productive integrated mills than the United States, and Japan has more modern and more productive integrated mills than Germany. However, starting in the United States, innovative minimills that use scrap, rather than iron ore, have entered the industry. The U.S. minimills are about twice as productive as the U.S. integrated mills. Japan had about the same share of minimills as the United States in 1990 and its productivity is similar. Germany has very few minimills because of regulation.

The productivity advantage of the Japanese steel industry over the U.S. industry is the result of its more productive integrated mills.[17] The parity between the United

---

[16] This is for its manufacturing plants, excluding head office and R&D facilities.

[17] This is one case where productivity is not a good guide to success. There is too much steel capacity in the world and the minimills are gaining market share. Japan has some very productive dinosaurs.

States and Germany is the result of an offset between higher productivity integrated mills but the absence of minimills in Germany.[18]

Lessons for Productivity Analysis from the Studies   There is always a danger in drawing lessons from a relatively small set of industry case studies, but nevertheless some clear messages seem to emerge from the results.

Process Innovation   Innovation is sometimes divided into "hard" and "soft." Hard innovations involve R&D and science or engineering. Soft innovations involve changing the business system or reorganizing the workplace. The case studies of both services and manufacturing suggest soft innovations that improve the production process can result in very large increases in productivity. Such innovations appear to have contributed heavily to productivity growth over time in these industries (e.g., organization of the workplace and design for manufacturability).

Hard Technology and Information Technology   There was surprisingly little evidence that international productivity differences occurred because of differential access to proprietary technology. By the time a new product or service becomes a large part of the market, the technology to provide it using best practice is available worldwide as a result of imitation or of licensing. Examples include minimills, the technology to make mainframe computers, and the computer reservations and flight scheduling programs used by the airlines. The advanced machinery needed for best-practice production is generally available worldwide.[19]

As well as airlines, information technology played an important role in achieving high productivity in banking (automated check clearing, networking branches with terminals, automatic teller machines), retailing (scanning, inventory control), and telecommunications (electronic switching) and contributed to productivity in the manufacturing industries (computer-controlled machines, computer-aided design, inventory management).

Despite the result about proprietary technology, R&D-driven innovations are obviously still important, however, to success in high-tech industries. And the continued development of such hard technology innovations is surely vital to the worldwide advance of productivity over the long run. Someone has to make the initial innovations before others can copy or license it.

Scale   There were numerous examples where achieving optimal scale in operations had allowed substantial productivity improvements. These include airlines (schedul-

---

[18] Another example is metalworking, where the Japanese producers were able to so redesign standard machine tools that they could be manufactured on a production line, rather than with a series of stand-alone machines and operators. This led to a dramatic productivity improvement. Japanese transplants are bringing this technology to the United States.

[19] The soap and detergent industry is also one where there has been a shift to modern industrial technology. This has proceeded to a greater extent in the United States than in Germany and Japan. A second reason for the lower productivity in the soap and detergent industry in Germany is that it has more of its output in powdered, rather than liquid, detergent.

The German beer industry uses an older craft technology that was largely phased out in the United States and Japan many years ago. The machinery used in breweries in the United States and Japan is made in Germany.

ing and maintenance), banks (back-office operations), retailing (larger stores and integration with wholesalers), food processing, soap and detergents, and beer (industrial scale operations), autos and metalworking (production line operations require large volumes). However, these benefits of scale occur through an appropriate industry structure, one that often requires the consolidation of companies.[20] Having a large economy or a big industry is not necessary.

Capital   There were examples where shifting to modern industrial operations requires substantial new investment (food processing, beer). But adding more capital to an existing business system was not always the means to higher productivity. For example, the push to much higher levels of automation in several U.S. plants in the auto industry did not pay off, whereas product and process redesign in Japan did pay off. The metalworking industry in Germany is about as capital intensive as the Japanese industry, but in Germany the capital consists of stand-alone machines that are less productive than the Japanese production lines.

Basic Labor Skills and Training   There was no evidence that differences in basic labor skills were an important reason for productivity differences.[21] Transplants in all three countries or regions are able to operate with best-practice productivities using local labor forces. The Ford plant in Atlanta used its existing union work force and, through product and process innovation, it raised its productivity and achieved best practice. Training and motivating workers, however, was vital to successful operations.

Competitive Pressure   There were many examples where companies had excess labor compared to best practice. In most of these cases, the ways in which productivity could be increased were widely known or could be discovered by modest efforts. Why were the improvements not made? There is a resistance to change in companies, coming both from managers and workers. Change is risky and involves costs. Unless there is competitive pressure to improve, managers may choose not to innovate.[22]

The lessons that we have just described are about the reasons for the productivity differences that are at the production process level. Many of them are related to the usual elements in the production function. But there is also a lesson that can be drawn at a higher level. Why is it that some companies use more productive methods than others? In part this is random, reflecting the nature of innovation. But more important is the role of competitive intensity and regulation.

---

[20] Outsourcing of operations can be a substitute for having large firms. For example, small U.S. banks outsource their check clearing and other back-office functions.

[21] This conclusion was qualified by two things. First, turnover is greater among U.S. workers than in the other countries. This necessitates the use of more resources for training. Second, German workers have higher rates of absenteeism than workers in other countries. This cuts productivity. For these reasons there is a productivity penalty of about 5 percent in both the United States and Germany compared to Japan.

[22] See Chapter 11 and Figure 11–9, which shows how exposure to competition with best-practice companies helps to increase productivity.

One of the reasons that companies fail to adopt best practice is that they are prevented or discouraged from doing so by regulations or work rules. For example, minimills were discouraged in Germany by European Community rules that allocated steel production quotas to companies. Another regulation slowing productivity increase comes from the fact that very high levels of compensations have to be paid to laid-off workers in Germany. In some industries, regulations prevent the evolution of an industry to more productive formats. Retailing in Japan, for example, has been greatly affected by laws that protect small stores.

A lack of competitive intensity was also found to be important. Many of the European and Japanese telecommunications companies and airlines are state-owned and are protected from full competition. In such situations, companies are reluctant to lay off unnecessary workers (including unnecessary managers) or to change their methods to be more productive.

Conclusions on Growth and Productivity in Theory and Practice

In a broad sense, the empirical studies of actual productivity growth and the comparisons of industries across countries have confirmed some important conclusions of the growth model.

Capital plays an important role in growth: It is a necessary element in implementing innovations; and countries that grow more rapidly than average generally have above-average rates of capital accumulation.

The empirical analysis also confirms that, while capital is important, the greater part of productivity growth does not come from physical capital accumulation. It comes from something that one can describe as technological change.

The international comparisons suggest, however, there are changes to be made in the way we should think about growth and productivity. These comparisons strongly indicate there is no mechanical link between productivity, on the one hand, and inputs of capital, R&D, and education, on the other. The underlying driver of productivity growth is innovative ideas (from individuals, or management teams, or workers on the production line) that are adopted in one company and then spread to others. Many of these are soft and not hard innovations. The inputs of capital, R&D, and skills are needed to develop and implement these innovations so that the factor inputs have to be available. But they do not drive the process of productivity change.

It is hard to know why innovations occur in one place and time, rather than in another, but a highly competitive environment seems to be a necessary stimulus. Certainly, such competitive pressure is important in determining how rapidly new methods are spread. And regulations and other barriers to change can greatly impede the changes needed for best-practice production.

One of the great controversies that societies grapple with is the extent to which governments should intervene in markets. With the end of the Soviet system and the changes taking place in China, there is no major country today that believes in rigid control of the economy from the top. The superiority of the market system in providing economic well-being is now largely unchallenged. Nevertheless, there are quite different perspectives around the world on the extent to which government policies should try to affect market outcomes. European countries generally follow more interventionist policies than does the United States.

Our goal in this book is to present the main ideas, and the evidence to support those ideas, about the determinants of aggregate supply and aggregate demand. We certainly want you to evaluate those ideas yourselves and see if they lead you to support specific policies. To the extent that our own thinking has evolved as a result of assessing these ideas, it is that government policies can be used to mitigate instability in the economy in aggregate demand. Even there, we find that government should do less, rather than more; but we find that there is a case for policies to avoid deep recessions or runaway inflations.

When it comes to aggregate supply, we conclude that government policies in practice have had an adverse effect on performance.[23] Structural budget deficits have eroded national saving; regulations have inhibited innovation and the natural evolution of industries, particularly in Europe and Japan. Trade restrictions have reduced competitive pressure.

WORKED EXAMPLES

Worked Example 17–1

Saving, Capital Accumulation, and Labor Force Growth
The following conditions hold in an economy at a given time.

$$Y^P = 4{,}000 \text{ Output}$$

K = 12,000 Capital input
s = 6 percent Saving propensity
N = 120 million Labor force
ΔN = 1.8 million Increase in the labor force
$\Delta K = S = sY^P$

Questions

a. What is the level of saving and the rate of labor-force growth in this economy?

b. Will the ratio of capital to labor rise or fall?

c. How does your answer change if the saving propensity were 4 percent and the rate of labor-force growth were 2 percent.

---

[23] We want to acknowledge that some policies are helpful to aggregate supply—maintaining property rights, for example, and encouraging competition through antitrust policy. And there are policies that we have not looked at here, such as policies to affect the environment or health and safety, which may be needed despite their adverse effects on productivity.

Answers

a. Saving is 6 percent of output and output is 4,000, so saving is 240. The rate of increase of the labor force is 1.5 percent (1.8 million is 1.5 percent of 120 million).

b. Saving is equal to the increase in capital, so the rate of increase of the capital input is 2 percent (240 is a percent of 12,000). Then, since the growth of the work force is only 1.5 percent, it follows that the ratio of capital to labor is rising.

c. If the saving propensity were only 4 percent, then saving would be only 160 and this is only 1.33 percent of capital. Since the rate of labor force growth is 2 percent, the ratio of capital to labor is falling.

Worked Example 17–2

The Amount of New Capital to Equip New Workers

Consider the economy described in Worked Example 17–1. Initially there were 120 million workers and the capital stock was 12,000 ($12 trillion). This meant there was $100,000 of capital for each worker.

Questions

a. With 1.8 million new workers arriving in a year, how much new capital would be needed to give these new workers the same capital per worker as the old ones—$100,000?

b. What fraction of total investment is used simply to prevent the capital per worker from declining?

c. Suppose this economy had been different. There is now an initial capital of 24,000 ($200,000 of capital per worker), twice as much as before. But the work force is the same and output is only 25 percent higher, $Y^P = 5000$. With the same saving propensity (6 percent), what is the new level of saving? With the same number of new workers arriving in a year (1.8 million), will there be enough new capital to keep the capital per worker from falling?

Answers

a. 1.8 million workers times $100,000 per worker means that $180 billion is needed just to keep capital per worker constant.

b. Since there was in fact saving and capital accumulation of $240 billion, the amount needed represents 75 percent of the total (180 is 75 percent of 240). This result shows that 25 percent of the total saving is available to increase capital per worker.

c. The new level of saving is 6 percent of 5,000, or $300 billion. The amount of capital needed to provide $200,000 to each of 1.8 million new workers is $360 billion. This means there is not enough saving and capital accumulation. Capital per worker is actually declining in this economy.

SUMMARY

• Long-term improvements in the standard of living require growth in aggregate supply and potential output per capita.

• The economy's productive capacity (potential output) depends on how much capital, labor, and technology are available for production.

- With a given technology, increasing only the labor input will depress average labor productivity and living standards.

- A decline in labor productivity can be avoided if either the amount of capital rises or the application of technology improves by enough to prevent the effects of diminishing returns from lowering labor productivity.

- In an economy where production is subject to constant returns to scale, average labor productivity does not depend on the size of the economy. Rather, it depends on the capital/labor ratio—the capital intensity of the economy.

- An increase in capital intensity is a disproportional increase of capital relative to labor. More capital per worker raises the level of average labor productivity, but there are diminishing returns to capital as capital intensity increases.

- Capital adequacy is the amount of new capital added per worker that is just necessary to maintain the level of capital intensity, thereby keeping labor productivity constant.

- Regardless of whether an economy is saving at a rate above or below capital adequacy, it tends to move toward steady-state growth, where the amount of sav-ing and new capital is just equal to the amount of capital adequacy.

- Among modern industrial economies, technological change, rather than capital accumulation, has been the main source of increased productivity and living standards.

- In an economy with technological change, average labor productivity is growing directly, because of the contribution of technology as a factor of production; but it is also growing as an indirect consequence of the technological change, because faster output growth leads to faster capital growth.

- The actual process of technological change involves the accumulation of knowledge and its use in the production of goods and services.

- The accumulation of knowledge occurs via increases in the education and skill level of the work force, investments in R&D, and through organizational learning about the best practices and techniques in production and management.

- Studies of the differences in productivity across companies, industries, and countries confirm the roles of capital, technology, knowledge accumulation, and implementation in generating growth.

KEY TERMS AND CONCEPTS

augmented labor, p. 548

average labor productivity, p. 533

capital adequacy, p. 538

capital deepening, p. 539

capital intensity, p. 534

constant returns to scale, p. 534

diminishing returns, p. 535

intensive production function, p. 534

steady-state growth, p. 541

DISCUSSION QUESTIONS AND PROBLEMS

1. How are living standards tied to productivity? Can't wages rise over time even though output levels are constant? What has to happen to the return on capital and the labor force to raise wages in this scenario?

2. Is capital adequacy a target level of saving that an economy should shoot for, is it a minimum acceptable level, or is it a rate of saving that is inevitable in the steady state?

3. Consider aspects or conditions in the economy that would make labor more productive. Can any of the sources of productivity enhancement be described as an improvement in technology that augments labor? If so, explain.

4. A higher rate of saving frees more resources for capital accumulation than a lower rate of saving. Since a more capital-intensive economy generates a

higher level of productivity, saving more should lead to a higher rate of growth. Is this the finding of the growth models? If not, why not? Does saving more buy any improvement in the economy?

5. The U.S. economy has been operating for over 200 years. Aren't we already in the steady state? If so, what would be required to move to another steady state with higher growth? If not, which steady state are we headed for?

6. Consider the following production function:

$$Y^P = (T_{ECH})K^{0.4}N^{0.6}$$

where (T_{ECH}) is an index of technology, K is capital, and N is labor.

a. Show that this production function has constant returns to scale.

b. Suppose T_{ECH} increases by 3 percent each year while K increases by 5 percent each year and N by 1 percent a year. By how much will average labor productivity increase each year?

7. Consider an alternative production function:

$$Y^P = (T_{ECH})KN^{0.6}$$

a. Show that this production function has increasing returns to scale.

b. Suppose T_{ECH} remains constant over time, while K increases by 5 percent a year and N increases by 1 percent a year. By how much will average labor productivity increase each year?

c. Comment on your answers to questions 6 and 7.

8. Japan has higher productivity than the United States in some industries and lower productivity in others. Why is this?

9. Rich countries have populations that are well-educated. Does this necessarily imply that education contributes to economic growth?

10. How could the production function be modified to take account of some of the sources of productivity differences that were identified by the business consultants?

NAME INDEX

A

Ando, Albert, 269 n
Arrow, Kenneth J., 537 n
Azariades, Costas, 494 n

B

Baily, Martin Neil, 54 n, 62 n, 282 n, 321 n, 351 n, 356 n, 393 n, 494 n, 554 n
Balke, Nathan S., 430 n
Banks, Jeffrey S., 55 n
Barro, Robert J., 427, 478 n, 553 n
Bartelsman, Eric, 356 n
Bator, Francis, 554 n
Baumol, William, 40–41
Becker, Gary, 526
Benhabib, Jess, 554 n
Bernanke, Ben, 316 n, 324, 327 n
Blair, Margaret, 321 n
Blanchard, Oliver J., 133 n, 249 n, 478 n
Blinder, Alan S., 65 n, 273, 280 n, 377 n, 488 n, 489
Bosworth, Barry, 270 n, 376 n
Brunner, Karl, 446, 468 n
Bryant, Ralph, 205 n
Burns, Arthur, 405
Bush, George, 2, 213, 249, 290, 344, 373, 418

C

Cadette, Walter, 9
Cagan, Phillip, 446, 454
Campbell, John Y., 205 n, 273, 324
Carroll, Christopher D., 273 N
Carter, Jimmy, 2, 373
Clarida, Richard, 205 n
Clark, Peter K., 275 n
Clinton, Bill, 2, 124, 220, 344, 416
Cohen, Linda R., 55–56
Collor de Mello, Fernando, 456
Cutler, David M., 365 n

D

Deal, Angus S., 273
Deaton, Angus S., 273
DeLong, J. Bradford, 53 n
Denison, Edward F., 546 n, 553 n
Dornbusch, Rudiger, 8, 205 n, 339 n
Duesenberry, James S., 266, 272–73

E

Eaton, Bob, 50
Eckstein, Otto, 408, 410
Edelman, Susan A., 55 n
Eggert, Robert J., 405 n
Eris, Ibrahim, 456

F

Faumeni, Barbara M., 546 n, 553 n
Feldstein, Martin S., 271, 365 n
Fischer, Stanley, 8–9, 488 n, 489
Fisher, Irving, 511 n
Flamm, Kenneth, 56, 353 n, 355
Fleming, Marcus, 205 n
Flood, Robert, 366 n
Ford, Gerald, 2, 373
Frankel, Jeffrey, 365 n
Friedman, Benjamin, 412
Friedman, Milton, 104, 161, 166–69, 271, 272, 314 n, 317, 365 n, 370 n, 433 n, 446, 447, 450–53, 459, 478, 537
Friedman, Philip, 348
Frisch, Ragnar, 408

G

Garber, Peter, 366 n
Gates, Bill, 522
Gertler, Mark, 316 n
Gollop, Frank M., 546 n, 553 n
Gordon, Robert J., 13 n, 60 n, 65 n, 315 n, 393 n, 430 n
Gramlich, Edward M., 133 n
Grauwe, Paul de, 205 n
Greenspan, Alan, 143, 220, 422
Griliches, Zvi, 534 n, 554 n
Gurley, J. G., 445 n
Guttentag, Jack M., 310 n

H

Hall, Robert E., 54 n, 153 n, 249 n, 272–73, 487 n, 493 n
Hall, Ted, 351 n
Haltiwanger, John, 356 n, 486 n
Heller, Walter, 104
Hicks, John R., 104, 145 n
Holtz–Eakin, Douglas, 65 n
Hussein, Saddam, 249, 288

J

Jensen, Michael C., 321 n
Johnson, Lyndon B., 104
Jorgenson, Dale T., 54 n, 284, 546 n, 553 n
Judd, John P., 128 n

K

Karbin, S., 537 n
Kendrick, J. W., 546 n
Kennedy, John F., 104, 416, 418
Keynes, John Maynard, 80–81, 104, 123–24, 128, 145, 275, 434, 457
Kindelberger, Charles, 365 n
King, Robert G., 480 n
Klein, Lawrence, 408
Knox, A. D., 275 n
Kotlikoff, Lawrence, 427
Krugman, Paul, 46, 339 n, 345 n, 349 n, 364 n
Kurihara, K. K., 269 n
Kydland, Finn, 480 n

L

Lawrence, Robert Z., 321 n, 322 n, 376 n
Layard, R., 527
Lewis, Bill, 50
Lewis, William, 554 n
Lipsey, Richard G., 150 n
Litan, Robert E., 321 n, 322 n
Loftness, Robert L., 377 n
Lown, C., 327 n
Lucas, Robert E., Jr., 465, 467–68, 472, 479–80, 487, 488

M

Mankiw, N. Gregory, 273, 482 n, 496 n, 553 n
Mansfield, Edwin, 554 n
Marris, Stephen, 358 n
Mayhew, K., 527
McCallum, Bennet, 446
Meese, Richard, 192 n, 365 n
Meltzer, Allan H., 446, 46 8 n
Minford, Patrick, 522–23
Mishkin, Frederic S., 270 n
Mitchell, Wesley C., 405
Modigliani, Franco, 269–72, 408, 445 n

Moore, Geoffrey, 405 n
Mundell, Robert, 205 n
Munnell, Alicia H., 271
Muth, John F., 465

N
Nelson, Richard R., 56 n
Netto, Antonio Delfim, 456
Nixon, Richard M., 104, 362, 378, 418
Noll, Roger, 55–56

O
Obstfeld, Maurice, 345 n, 349 n, 363 n, 364 n
Okun, Arthur M., 13, 494 n, 511
Owen, G., 527
Owen, Henry, 430 n

P
Pegman, William M., 55 n
Perlman, Mark, 56 n
Perry, George L., 62 n, 430 n
Phelps, Edmund S., 161, 468 n
Phillips, A. W., 156 n, 511
Pigou, A. C., 526
Plosser, Charles I., 462–63, 480 n, 491 n

Poole, William, 446
Poterba, Martin, 365 n
Power, Alan, 523
Prescott, Edward, 478 n, 480 n
Psacharopoulos, George, 528–29

R
Reagan, Ronald W., 359, 373, 418, 466
Ricardo, David, 345, 427
Ringstad, V., 534 n
Romer, Christina, 429–30
Romer, D., 553 n
Romer, Paul, 41
Romer, Paul J., 553 n
Roosevelt, Franklin D., 362

S
Sachs, Jeffrey D., 339 n
Sahlman, Bill, 51
Samuelson, Paul A., 33, 104, 156 n, 278–79, 293
Sargent, Thomas J., 476, 487, 488 n, 489
Scadding, J. L., 128 n
Scherer, F. M., 56 n
Schor, Juliet, 502 n
Schultze, Charles L., 322 n, 430
Schwartz, Anna J., 104, 317, 433 n, 446

Shaw, E. S., 445 n
Shiller, Robert J., 484–85
Sinai, Allen, 249 n
Smith, Adam, 494
Solow, Robert M., 37–39, 41–42, 156 n, 351 n, 536–37, 546, 553, 554
Spiegel, Mark M., 554 n
Stock, James, 411–13
Summers, Lawrence, 53 n, 365 n
Suppes, P., 537 n
Swan, T. W., 537 n

T
Tinbergen, Jan, 408
Tobin, James, 104, 171, 408, 537 n
Tyson, Laura, 349 n

V–Z
Van Ark, Bart, 48
Volcker, Paul, 143, 243
Waldman, J., 486 n
Wallace, Neil, 476 n
Watson, Mark, 411–13
Weil, D., 553 n
Weir, David, 430 n
Wolff, Edward, 40–41
Zarnowitz, Victor, 315 n

SUBJECT INDEX

A

Absolute advantage, 345
Accelerator
  definition, 275
  and interest rates, 284–85
Accelerator model of investment, 71 n
Accelerator model of investment demand,
  275–85
Accelerator-multiplier interaction, 278–80
Adaptive expectations, 159, 464
Adjustment costs, 489
Adverse supply shocks
  definition, 374
  food prices, 377–79
  oil prices, 376–77, 396–97
  productivity decline, 379
Aggregate demand
  and capital investment, 274
  cause of inflation, 148
  and changes in money and goods mar-
    kets, 106–7
  definition, 61
  and goods-market equilibrium, 72–76
  impact of fiscal expansion, 207–8
  and inflation of 1970s, 374
  and interest rates, 77–78
  in international economy, 198–202
  and investment demand, 68–71
  monetarism and inflation, 44–46
  monetary basis, 473–74
  and price levels, 148–50
  and quantity adjustment, 64–71
  during supply shock, 376
Aggregate demand for labor, 437
Aggregate demand schedule, and short–run
  output changes, 62–63
Aggregate production, exclusion from,
  27–28
Aggregate production function, 34–36
  classical model, 435
  review of, 533–36
Aggregate supply
  definition, 61
  policies to enhance, 532
  and price levels, 148–50
  and quantity adjustment, 64–71
Aggregate supply and demand in classical
  model, 443–44
Aggregate supply schedule, 61–62
  Lucas schedule, 470–73
  vertical, 64
Agricultural sector, 380

American Medical Association, 525
APC; see Average propensity to consume
Arbitrage, 483–84
Assets; see also Financial assets
AT&T, 51
Augmented labor, 548
Automatic stabilizers, 134, 417, 430
Automobile industry, 50
  improvements in, 352–53
Autonomous consumption, and investment
  demand, 76
Autonomous-expenditure multiplier
  definition, 122
  and government spending, 122–23
Autonomous expenditures, 72–73
  effects on money market, 106–7
  and trade, 83
Availability of funds, 229
Average labor productivity, 6, 533
  and technological change, 550
Average propensity to consume, 68

B

Balance of payments; see also External
  balance
  in capital account, 186
  in current account, 185–89
  current account deficit, 187–89
Balance of trade, 48–49
  definition, 82, 185
  and equilibrium income, 84
  and exchange rates, 183–85
  and import demand, 81–82
  and income changes, 342–43
  and J-curve, 339–41
Bank failures and panics, 20–21, 317–19
Banking system
  deposit insurance, 318
  deregulation, 301
  fractional reserve system, 301–3
  money creation, 299–308
  types of institutions, 300–301
Bankruptcy, during recovery of 1980s, 325
Banks; see also Central banks and Commercial banks
  borrowed reserves, 312–13
  credit crunch, 319–20
  credit rationing, 228–29
  decline in lending, 327–28
  default rate, 320
  discount rate, 313

Banks—Cont.
  disintermediation, 319–20
  excess and required reserves, 306
  fractional reserve system, 100
  reserve ratio, 302–3
  reserves and reserve account, 302
Base year, 4, 47 n
Basic labor skills, 560
Bell Atlantic, 50
Blue Chip Economic Indicators, 405,
  406–7
Boeing Corporation, 180
Bond rating, and risk premium, 246–48
Bonds, 93–94
  consols, 234
  financing investment by, 222
  long- and short-term interest rates,
    232–35
  and real rate of interest, 226–27
  short-term, 230
Borrowed reserves, 312–13
Borrowing, by government, 130–31
Brazil, attack on inflation, 456
Bretton Woods system, 333
  operation of, 362–63
Bubble, 364
Budget balance, 130
  effect on saving, 131–32
Budget deficit, 21–22, 53, 129–30
  assessing, 322
  attempts to decrease, 344
  and automatic stabilizers, 134
  and borrowing, 130–31
  over business cycle, 132–33
  cyclical, 133–34
  and recession of 1990–91, 213
  short-term versus chronic, 132
  structural, 133–35
  and taxation, 478
  and trade deficit, 211–13
  trade deficit and crowding out, 209
Budget surplus, 129–30
Built-in rate of inflation, 159
Bureau of Labor Statistics, 19–20
Business confidence, 316–17
Business cycles; see also Real-business-
  cycle models
  and budget deficit, 132–33
  consistent factors, 263
  definition, 12–13
  forecasting, 402–3
  international context, 23

Business cycles—*Cont.*
  inventory variability, 280–81
  investment fluctuations, 286–91
  and long-term growth, 14–15, 57–58
  multiplier and accelerator model, 278–80
  policy effectiveness theorem, 476–78
  and productivity, 490–92
  real wages over, 457–58
  and recession, 11–15
  reduced in severity, 21
Business investment demand; *see* Investment demand
Business Week, 404

C
Capacity utilization, 288–89
Capital
  and productivity, 560
  scale and technology, 558–59
Capital account, 186
Capital accumulation, 41
  and labor force growth, 37–39
Capital adequacy
  and labor force growth, 535–36
  and Solow growth model, 538–41
  and technology-augmented labor, 549–50
Capital assets, total in United States, 551–52
Capital consumption allowance, 31, 276
Capital deepening, 539
Capital flows
  and changes in expectations, 191–92
  and exchange rates, 195–98
  and expansionary monetary policy, 205–7
  and fiscal policy, 207–9
  and interest rate changes, 191
  interest-rate differential, 195–97
  international, 191–92
Capital input, 34
Capital intensity, 37–38, 534
Capital investment, 53–54, 221–29; *see also* Investment
  and economic fluctuations, 274–85
  and flexible accelerator, 277–78
  in inventories, 280–81
  multiplier-accelerator interaction, 278–80
  variability of total, 274–75
Capital/labor ratio, 538–45
Capital markets, expectation revisions, 422
Capital per worker, 44
Capital stock, 30
  depreciation, 52 n
  depreciation estimate, 276
  durability, 275
  expectations and IS–LM equilibrium, 285–91

Cartels
  OPEC, 375–77
  trade associations, 525
Cash management, 97
  in international economy, 200–202
Caterpillar Corporation, 51
Central banks, 99–100
  foreign exchange open market operations, 186
  monetarist view, 445
  sterilized intervention, 370
Certificate of deposit, 97 n
Chaos theory, 410–11
Choice-theoretic framework, 462–63
Chronic deficits, 132
Chronic inflation, 388–89
Chrysler Corporation, 50, 352
Circuit City, 556
Classical model
  of aggregate supply and demand, 443–44
  demand for labor, 435–38
  of economy, 434–35
  equilibrium output and labor market, 439–40
  of quantity equation, 441–42
  supply of labor, 438–39
  of unemployment, 440
Clinch River Breeder reactor, 55–56
Coincident indicators, 405
Commercial banks; *see also* Banks
  definition, 300
  financial intermediaries, 301
Comparative advantage, 345–46
Competition, 32
  and deregulation, 54
  and earnings inequality, 524
Competitive markets, 54
  output-inflation tradeoff, 150–53
  and price stickiness, 153–54
Competitiveness
  of American manufacturing, 46–51
  definition, 9
  and increased exports, 346–47
  international, 6–9
  and long-term growth, 3–9, 32–58
  new United States edge, 50–51
  policies for, 51–58
  and trade, 23
Competitiveness puzzle, 49–50
Competitive pressure, 560–61
Computerization of business operations, 552
Computer memory chips, 353–55
Computer technology, 56
Congressional Budget Office, 551–53
Consols, 234
Constant-money-supply-growth rule, 451–52, 478
Constant returns to scale, 35–36, 533–34

Consumer price index, 19
  food price increases, 379
  growth in, 383
  volatility of, 167–68
Consumer Research Center, 404
Consumption
  in National Income and Product Accounts, 29, 265
  permanent or transitory, 267
  recent studies, 272–73
Consumption-demand schedules, 74–75
Consumption expenditures, and disposable income, 120
Consumption function, 67–68
Consumption smoothing, 264–66
  constraints, 272–74
  Friedman's explanation, 268–69
  saving and borrowing for, 266
Consumption standard of living; *see also* Standard of living
  constraints on consumption smoothing, 272–74
  consumption smoothing, 264–66
  definition, 264
  life-cycle hypothesis, 269–71
  permanent-income hypothesis, 266–69
Continental Illinois Bank, 320
Contraction, *see* Recessions
Contractionary monetary policy, 164–65, 170–71
  and expected inflation, 240–41
  and interest rate gap, 238–40
  and interest rates in 1979–83, 242–48
  recession trigger, 413
Contract theory, 153
Convergence, 40–41
Corporate debt, 321–22
Cost of capital, 386 n
Cost of funds, 222
  and credit rationing, 228–29
  discounted cash flow view of, 224–26
  and inflation, 227–28
  inflation and real interest rate, 225–26
  and interest rate gap, 236–37
  and risk premium, 228
  summary, 229
Cost of living
  and supply shocks, 382–86
  and wage increases, 383–85
Costs of holding money, 97 n
CPC International, 51
CPI, *see* Consumer price index
Creating the Computer (Flamm), 56
Credibility effect, 394
Credibility issues, 466
Credit conditions and monetary supply, 144–45
Credit cards, 94
Credit crunch, 319–20, 395

Credit crunch—*Cont.*
  of early 1990s, 327–28
Credit rationing, 228–29
Crisis of confidence, 336
Crowding out effect
  budget and trade deficits, 209
  of fiscal policy, 128–29
Currency, 94; *see also* Dollar; Money; *and*
      Exchange rates
  exchange rates for, 180–85
Currency speculation, 360–62, 362–65
Current account, balance of payments,
      185–89
Current account deficit, 187–89, 332 n,
      334
  changes in, 342–43
Cyclically adjusted budget, 133
Cyclical deficit, 133–34

D

Data Resources, Inc., 408
Decision lag, 414
Default rate, 320
Defense Advanced Research Projects
      Agency, 56
Deficit financing, 130–31
  during recession, 132
Deflation, 19
Demand; *see also* Aggregate demand *and*
      Investment demand
  for labor, 435–38
  for money, 95–99
  for services, 509 n
Demand deposit, 300
Demand deposits, 92
Demographics, of employment, 507–8
Department of Commerce, 31, 188, 276,
      354
  index of leading indicators, 412
  National Income and Products Accounts,
      26, 28–31
Department of Defense, 56
Department of Labor, Bureau of Labor Sta-
      tistics, 19–20
Deposit insurance, 318
Deposits, reserves and loans, 302
Depreciation, 30–31, 52 n
Depreciation estimate, 276
Depressions, 11; *see also* Great Depression
      and Recessions
Deregulation, 54
  of banking system, 301
Derivatives market, 337 n
Design for manufacturability, 558
Desired capital-output ratio, 275–77
Desired capital stocks, 275–85
Diminishing returns, 35, 535
Direct foreign investment, 186
Discounted cash flow view of cost of
      funds, 224–26

Discounted future dividends, 485
Discount rate, 224, 313
Discretionary policies, 417
Disintermediation, 319
Disposable income, 120
Dollar
  exchange rate index, 182–83
  exchange-rate overshooting, 359–60
  and exchange rates, 180–85
  and exchange rate swings, 358
  in fixed exchange rate system, 365
  foreign demand for, 212
  potential collapse in value, 336
  supply and demand, 192–98
  and yen, 182
Dow Jones Industrial Average, 50, 220
Dumping, computer chips, 354
Durability of capital stock, 275
Durable goods, 29, 221 n

E

Earnings distribution, 521–25
Earnings inequality, 522–25
Eckstein model, 408, 410
Econometic analysis, 67 n
Econometric models, 408–11, 553–54
  Lucas critique, 411, 479–80
Economic fluctuations, 274–75; *see also*
      Business cycles
Economic growth; *see also* Long-term
      growth *and* Solow long-term growth
      model
  convergence issue, 40–41
  models, 34–39
  new growth theory, 36, 41
  policies for, 51–58
  postwar, 42
  productivity slowdown, 43–46
  worldwide, 40–41
Economic model, 60
Economic performance
  fluctuations and trends, 9–10
  GDP measures, 3–6
  output ratio, 13–14
Economic reform, 2
Economic Report of the President, 523–25
Economics
  contract theory, 153
  Friedman's influence, 104
  game theory, 153
  Keynes' influence, 104
Economic stability, 426–30
  policy regime for, 418–26
Economist magazine, 50–51
Economy
  aggregate supply and demand, 61–71
  automatic stabilizers, 134
  classical model, 434–35
  comparative strength, 8–9

Economy—*Cont.*
  competitiveness and long–term growth,
      32–58
  and election of 1992, 2
  in equilibrium, 65
  equilibrium-business–cycle model,
      467–76
  equilibrium models, 462–64
  fine-tuning, 415
  foreign sector, 81–84
  goods-market equilibrium, 66–67, 72–76
  government versus market initiatives,
      55–57
  growth slowdown, 6
  impact of short–term interest rates,
      220–21
  incomplete information, 468
  long-term growth, 3–6
  long-term trends and short–run fluctua-
      tions, 10–11
  policy effectiveness theorem, 476–78
  rational expectations model, 462
  real-business–cycle models, 480–83
  in recession, 11–15
  Solow growth model, 536–36
  stabilization policies, 413–18
  stagflation, 156
  underground, 28
Education
  and earnings inequality, 523–24
  investment in human capital, 528–29
  and productivity, 553–54
  support of, 529–30
Efficiency wage, 494–95
Efficient market hypothesis, 484
Efficient markets, 483–84
Electronic Data Services, 51
Employment
  and economic policy, 14–15
  growth patterns, 503–10
  international patterns, 508
  by occupation and education, 507–8
  by sector, 503–5
  turnover and firm size, 505–6
Employment Act of 1946, 426
Employment stability, versus wage stabil-
      ity, 494–95
Equilibrium-business cycle theory, 153
Equilibrium; *see also* Goods–market equi-
      librium
  adjustment to, 73–74
  in foreign exchange market, 192–93
  with given interest rate, 72–73
  interest rates and expectations, 197–98
  monetary basis, 473–74
  of output, 152–53
  output in labor market, 439–40
  and quantity adjustment, 65
Equilibrium-business–cycle model, 467–76
  assessment, 483–92

Equilibrium income
  and balance of trade, 84
  and change in investment demand,
    75–76
  changes and multiplier, 75
  and changes in government purchases,
    123–24
  and interest rate gap, 235–42
  and interest rates, 72–75
  IS schedule and, 78–79
  multiplier effect/interest rate effect,
    106–7
  with unchanged interest rate, 121–24
Equilibrium models, 462–64
Equity finance, cost of, 222–23
ERISA (Employee Income Retirement
    Security Act), 271
Eurodollars, 94
Europe
  breakdown of Exchange Rate
    Mechanism, 369
  employment, 508
  job creation, 522–23
  long-term unemployment, 55
  productivity comparisons, 554–61
  rising unemployment, 518–21
European Airbus, 180
Excess-reserve ratio, 306
Excess reserves, 306
Exchange rate index, 181–82
Exchange Rate Mechanism, 369
Exchange-rate overshooting, 359–60
Exchange rate risk
  elimination of, 366
  and foreign assets, 193
  hedging, 361–62
Exchange rates
  and balance of trade, 183–85
  and capital flows, 195–98
  changes and trade flow, 180–81
  changes in, 196
  definition, 180
  driven by market forces, 358
  and expansionary monetary policy,
    205–7
  expectations and, 196–97
  failure to adjust external balance,
    337–44
  and fiscal expansion, 208–9
  fixed, 362–63
  fixed versus flexible, 365–71
  fluctuation problem, 336–37
  income and changes in, 194–95, 343
  and inflation, 183 n
  interest-rate differential, 195–96
  and international financial assets, 189–92
  real, 182–83
  short-term swings and speculation,
    360–62
  sterilized intervention in, 370

Exchange rates—*Cont.*
  and supply and demand, 192–98
  sustained swings, 358–60
  trade-weighted, 181–83
  volatility since 1973, 333
  yen versus dollars, 182
Expansion, 12
Expansionary monetary policy, 164–65
  and capital flows, 205–7
  and fixed exchange rate, 367–68
  and interest rate gap, 241–42
Expectations
  adaptive, 159
  capital flows and changes in, 191–92
  in capital markets, 422
  capital stock and IS–LM equilibrium,
    295–91
  credibility effect, 394
  and exchange rates, 196–97
  in exchange rates, 362–64
  of financial crunch, 320
  and forecasting models, 411
  of inflation in 1979–83, 248
  and interest rate gap, 237
  interest rates and investment demand,
    282
  international interest rates, 190
  sales and inventories, 280
  slope of yield curve, 235
  of supply-shock inflation, 389–90
  variability in investment demand,
    282–84
Expected-future interest rates, 232–33
Expenditures, planned and unplanned,
    65–67; *see also* Autonomous expendi-
    tures *and* Government expenditures
Exports
  and competitiveness, 346–47
  increased demand, 202–3
  in National Income and Products
    Accounts, 30
External balance, 332; *see also* Balance of
    trade
  definition, 334
  and exchange rates, 337–44
  iron law of, 344
  job loss, 334–35
  and loss of wealth, 335–36
  trade policies to achieve, 345–58

F
Farm policy, 379
Favorable supply shocks
  definition, 374–75
  example, 395–96
Federal Deposit Insurance Corporation,
    318, 320, 325
Federal funds market, 306
Federal funds rate, 220

Federal income tax, 18
Federal Open Market Committee, 309–10
  open-market operations, 310–12
Federal Reserve
  controlling inflation, 394–97
  discount rate, 313
  and failure of Bretton Woods, 363
  and financial crunches, 315–28
  inflation-fighting and, 162
  inside/outside lags, 414–15
  lender of last resort, 312
  monetary policy, 143, 220–21
  monetary policy in 1979–83, 243
  monetary policy in 1990–93, 249–50
  and money creation, 299–308
  and money supply, 99–100, 200
  open-market operations, 310–12
  operation of, 309–15
  policy credibility, 394
  powers of, 298–99
  response to supply shock, 391
  sustained policy change, 321–23
  targeting money supply and interest
    rates, 314–15
  temporary policy change, 319–21
Federal Reserve banks, 309, 310
Federal Reserve Board, 78, 104
Federal Savings and Loan Insurance Cor-
    poration, 325
Financial assets, 91
  foreign, 187
  international, 189–92
  money and 93–95
  types of holdings, 96–97
Financial crunch
  banking panics, 317–19
  bank sector credit, 327–28
  and corporate debt, 321–22
  credit crunches, 319–20
  definition, 315–16
  excessive indebtedness, 322–27
  fears of, 320
  loss of business confidence, 316–17
Financial intermediaries, commercial banks,
    310
Financial markets
  interest-rate differential, 197
  volatility, 484–85
Fine tuning, 415
Firms
  corporate debt, 321–22
  credit during recession of 1982, 246–48
  efficiency wage, 494–95
  employment turnover, 505–6
  equilibrium-business–cycle model,
    467–76
  investment demand, 221–22
  investment financing, 222–23
  labor hoarding, 490
  menu cost models, 495–97

Firms—*Cont.*
  timing of investments, 283
  wage contracts, 493–94
First Pennsylvania Bank, 319
Fiscal policy; *see also* Stabilization poli-
    cies, 478
  and capital flows, 207–9
  coordinated with monetary policy,
    142–43
  crowding out effect, 128–29
  definition, 114
  effectiveness and money demand,
    127–28
  finance and budget balance, 129–35
  with fixed exchange rates, 367–68
  gross and net tax revenues, 118
  ineffectiveness, 478
  interest rate effects, 125–27
  monetarist criticism, 459–60
  and money market conditions, 125–29
  permanent and temporary, 425–26
  taxes and income, 119
  transfer payments, 119
Fixed-exchange-rate system, 362–63
  characteristics, 366–68
  definition, 365
Flexible accelerator model of investment
    demand, 277–78
Flexible-exchange-rate system
  definition, 365
  policy intervention, 368–70
Flow of services
  in consumption standard of living,
    264–65
  in National Income and Product
    Accounts, 265
Food price increases, 377–79
Ford Motor Company, 50, 352
Forecasting
  and chaos theory, 410–11
  econometric models, 408–11
  leading indicators, 405–8
  lessons for stabilization policies, 413
  prediction failures, 409
  statistical analysis of leading indicators,
    411–13
  surveys of managers and consumers,
    404–8
  uses, 403–4
Foreign assets
  and exchange-rate risk, 193
  income earned in, 187
Foreign currency speculation, 360–62,
    362–65
Foreign exchange forward contracts,
    361–62
Foreign exchange market
  capital flows through, 191
  and demand for imports, 208
  economic policies toward, 358–71

Foreign exchange market—*Cont.*
  equilibrium in, 192–93
  exchange rates, 180–85
  in international trade, 179–85
  intervention in, 186
  sterilized intervention, 370
  supply and demand in, 192–93
  volatility since 1973, 333
Foreign interest rates, rise in, 203–4
Foreign investment
  to finance structural deficit, 212
  in United States, 186
Forward contracts, in foreign exchange,
    361–62
Fractional reserve system, 100, 301–3
Franklin National Bank, 319
Frictional unemployment, 515
Full employment, 17, 154

G

Game theory, 153
GDP; *see* Gross domestic product
GDP deflator, 167–68, 382 n
General Agreement on Tariffs and Trade,
    2, 357
General Electric, 51
General equilibrium analysis, 152
General Motors, 50, 352
*General Theory of Employment, Interest,
    and Money* (Keynes), 104, 434, 457
Germany
  hyperinflation, 455
  productivity, 47
  productivity comparisons, 554–61
  unemployment rate, 8
GNP; *see* Gross national product
Gold prices, 362–63
Goods—market equilibrium, 66–67, 72–76
  with fiscal policy, 120–25
  with foreign sector, 199
  with foreign trade, 82–83
  interest rates and, 76–79
  inventory investment, 280–81
  investment and saving, 79–81
  and money market equilibrium, 105–7
  and national saving, 131
  savings and investment condition, 79–81
Government; *see also* Budget deficit
  borrowing by, 130–31
  deregulation of industries, 54
  finance and budget balance, 129–35
  versus market initiatives, 55–57
  nonmarket contributions to GDP, 27–28
  policy ineffectiveness theorem, 476–78
  support for research and development,
    56
  time-inconsistent policies, 478–79
Government expenditures
  and autonomous–expenditure multiplier,
    122–23

Government expenditures—*Cont.*
  crowding out effect, 128–29
  definition, 115
  and goods-market equilibrium, 120–25
  transfer payments, 119
Government purchases of goods and ser-
    vices
  changes in, 123–24
  definition, 115
  in National Income and Product
    Accounts, 30
  reasons for, 116–18
Government regulation, and productivity
    decline, 45
Gramm-Rudman–Hollings Act, 135
Great Britain, job creation, 522–23
Great Depression, 11, 104, 263; *see also*
    Recessions
  bank failures, 317–19
  import restrictions, 348
  interest rate gap, 316
  Lucas critique and, 487–88
  monetary policy and, 145
  unemployment rate, 16
Gross domestic product
  American manufacturing, 46
  and budget deficit, 21–22
  determination, 64–65
  exclusions from aggregate production,
    287–28
  function, 3–6
  and GNP, 26–27
  and government expenditures, 115
  and government purchases, 115
  measurement, 25
  and national income, 30–31
  and national income accounting, 25–31
  in National Income and Product
    Accounts, 28–31
  nominal, 4
  and output ratio, 13–14
  as percent of world output, 178
  potential, 13
  and price level, 18
  real, 4–5
  real and nominal, 227
  in recession of 1990–91, 249–50
Gross investment, 276
Gross national product, 3, 26–27
  mining and agricultural sectors, 380
  and stabilization policies, 426, 429
Gross tax revenues, 118, 119
Growth accounting, 553–54
Growth slowdown, 6
Growth theory, and savings/thrift, 545–46
Gulf War, 396

H

Hard technology, 559
Hedging, exchange rate risk, 361–6

Home Depot, 556
Honda Motor Company, 50
Hourly compensation, 379 n
Hours of work, 502–3
Households
  constraints on consumption smoothing, 272–74
  consumption function, 67
  consumption standard of living, 264–74
  and income reductions, 283
  indicators of financial crisis, 323–24
  life-cycle hypothesis, 269–71
  mortgage financing, 223
  permanent-income hypothesis, 266–69
  savings by, 52
Housing investment, 70
Housing stock, depreciation estimate, 276
Human capital
  and education, 528–29
  worker training, 526–27
Hungary, hyperinflation, 455
Hyperinflation, 453–55

I

Identity equation, 65
Immigration, 525
Implicit price deflator for GDP, 19
Implicit wage contract, 493–94
Import demand, 81–82
Imports
  decreased by trade policies, 347
  and income accounting, 212
  in National Income and Products Accounts, 30
Income
  and consumption standard of living, 264–74
  disposable, 120
  earned in foreign assets and transfers, 187
  and exchange rates, 194–95
  generation of, 52
  impact of government purchases, 123–24
  and import demand, 81–82
  interest rates in money market, 102–5
  per capita, 32–33
  sustaining during recession, 210–11
  and taxes, 119
  transitory reduction in, 267
  used for saving or consumption, 80
Income changes
  and exchange rate change, 343
  and trade balance, 342–43
Income distribution, 503
  of earnings, 521–25
Income levels, and hours of work, 502–3
Income redistribution, 117
  transfer payments, 119
Incomplete information, 468

Increasing returns to scale, 35
Indebtedness, 322–27
Index of leading economic indicators, 405–8
Indirect taxes, 31
Inequality; *see* Earnings inequality
Inflation, 141; *see also* Hyperinflation *and* Output-inflation tradeoff
  adaptive expectations, 158–59, 464
  and aggregate demand, 374
  in Brazil, 456
  built-in rate of, 159
  caused by supply shocks, 374–86
  changes in expectations in 1979–83, 248
  chronic, 388–89
  comparative, 21
  and contractionary monetary policy, 240–41
  under control in 1980s, 249
  controlling, 394–96, 418
  and cost of funds, 227–28
  current and expected rates, 163–64
  definition, 18–19
  determining current rate, 157
  effect of monetary shocks, 474–76
  effect on Treasury bills and money, 230–31
  expectations and rational forecasts, 162
  measures of, 18–20
  monetarism and aggregate demand, 444–60
  and monetary policy, 162–71
  monetary policy to fight, 167–71
  and output, 1
  popular expectations, 157–58
  and real money supply, 163
  real rate of interest and cost of funds, 225–26
  reduction to pre-shock level, 393–94
  related to wage increases and productivity, 513–14
  sacrifice ratio, 393–94
  short-run output fluctuations, 22
  and stagflation, 156–57
  and uncertainty, 17–18
  and unemployment, 373
Inflation-accommodating money supply, 164–65
Inflationary price shocks, 148
Inflation–output tradeoff; *see* Output–inflation tradeoff
Information, incomplete, 468
Information technology, 559
Infrastructure, 44
Inside lag, 415
Insider-outsider model of labor market, 495
Institute for Social Research, 404
Insurance, moral hazard, 515
Intensive production function, 35–36, 534–35, 536

Intensive production function—*Cont.*
  neo-classical growth model, 37–38
  and technology–augmented labor, 547–49
Interactive–television, 50
Interest-rate differential
  and capital flows, 195–97
  and exchange rates, 192–93
  and expansionary monetary policy, 205–7
  and foreign interest rates, 201–2
  widening, 197
Interest-rate effect, 106
Interest-rate gap
  and equilibrium income, 235–42
  and expansionary monetary policy, 241–42
  in Great Depression, 316
  and monetary contraction, 238–40
Interest rate parity, 190–92
Interest-rate risk, 233–34
Interest rates
  and accelerator, 284–85
  and aggregate demand, 77–78
  changes and capital flows, 191
  and contractionary monetary policy of 1979–83, 242–48
  cost of funds, 222
  and crowding out effect, 128–29
  and equilibrium income, 105, 121–24
  and exchange-rate overshooting, 359–60
  and exchange rates, 195–96
  expectations and market equilibrium, 197–98
  expected in future, 232–33
  Federal Reserve targeting, 314–15
  fiscal policy effect, 125–27
  and foreign investments, 212
  foreign rise in, 203–4
  and goods-market equilibrium, 72–73
  international, 190
  international transmission of, 203–4
  and investment demand, 69–71
  and investment demand over business cycles, 290
  IS schedule, 78–79
  and LM schedule, 102–5
  and money supply, 102
  negative, 230
  opportunity cost of funds, 223
  and recovery of 1991–93, 250–51
  responsiveness and investment, 144–45
  responsiveness of money demand, 146–47
  risk premium, 228
  short-term increase, 220
  term structure of, 232–35
  and Treasury bill prices, 307–8
  volatility, 20–21
International capital flows, 191–92

International competitiveness, 6–9
International economy, 178–79
  aggregate demand in, 198–202
  financial assets and exchange rate,
    189–92
International monetary policy, Bretton
  Woods system, 362–63
International monetary structure, 333
International trade; *see* Trade
International transfer payments, 187
Intertemporal elasticity of substitution in
  consumption, 273
Inventories
  in recessions, 489
  unwanted accumulation, 73–74
Inventory cycle, 280–81
Inventory investment, 65, 280–81
Inverted yield curve, 235
  and tight monetary policy, 244–45
Investment; *see also* Capital investment
  and Foreign investment
  accelerator model, 71 n
  capital adequacy condition, 538–41
  and credit crunches, 320
  credit rationing, 228–29
  discounted cash flow view of cost of
    funds, 224–26
  financing alternatives, 222–23
  fluctuations and business cycle, 286–91
  foreign assets and transfers, 187
  inflation and cost of funds, 227–28
  interest rate parity, 190–92
  international interest rates and expecta-
    tions, 190
  in National Income and Product
    Accounts, 29, 265
  need to increase, 53–54
  net and gross, 276
  in open economy, 210
  opportunity cost of funds, 223
  planned, 65–67, 69
  and real rate of interest, 226–27
  response to economic conditions, 283–84
  responsiveness to interest rates and credit
    conditions, 144–45
  saving and, 790–81
  time horizon, 225
  unplanned, 65–67
  variability, 71
Investment demand, 68–71
  accelerator model, 275–85
  changes and multiplier, 75–76
  components, 276
  crowding out effect, 129
  definition, 221–22
  and interest rates, 77–78
  and interest rates over business cycle,
    290
  and real rate of interest, 228
  during recession of 1990–91, 288

Investment-demand schedule, 74–75
Investment function, 69
  and interest rates, 70–71
  shift in, 77–78
Investment tax credit, 54
Invisible handshake, 494
Iraq, 396
Iron law of external imbalance, 344
IS-LM framework, 105–7
  aggregate supply and demand model,
    443
  capital stock and expenditures, 285–91
  combined with tradeoff, 165–67
  and inflation, 162–71
  interest-rate gap, 235–42
  in international economy, 202–3
  output-inflation tradeoff, 391–92
  prices and money, 448–49
  real and nominal GDP, 227
  and recession, 290
  and taxes and government spending,
    120–25
  time-inconsistent policies, 479
IS schedule
  definition, 78–79
  and fiscal policy interest rate effect, 125
  goods-market equilibrium, 80
  and monetary policy, 142–43
  and money demand, 127–28
  and trade, 347
  in trade, 199

J
Japan
  automakers, 352–53
  employment, 508
  productivity comparisons, 554–61
  productivity level, 47, 49
  recession in, 8–9
  semiconductor pact, 354–55
J-curve
  and balance of trade, 339–41
  and demand for foreign exchange,
    364–65
Job creation policies, 525–30
Job duration, 493
Job loss, 334–35
  small business, 505
Job protection, 355–57
Junk bond market, 51
Junk bonds, 321
Just-in-time inventory, 281

K
Keynes, John Maynard, 434
Keynesian analysis, 104
  income-expenditure model, 445
  monetarist criticism, 459–60
  responses to, 462–63

Klein model, 408
Knowledge capital, 39, 41
Knowledge workers, 524
Kuwait, 396

L
Labor
  augmented by technology, 547–51
  demand for, 535–38
Labor force, 16
  growth and capital accumulation, 37–39
  growth and capital adequacy, 535–36
  input, 34
  input growth rate, 42
  output per worker, 44
  quality and skill, 44
  training, 55
Labor hoarding, 490
Labor market
  equilibrium output, 439–40
  insider-outsider model, 495
Labor market flexibility, 509–10
  policies to foster, 52–30
Labor productivity, slowdown, 379
Labor skills, 560
  education, 528–29
  and education levels, 528–29
  job training, 526–27
Labor supply, 438–39
Lagging indicators, 405
Leading indicators, 405–8
  statistical analysis of, 411–13
Learning curve, 349
  and trade restrictions, 353–55
Lender of last resort, 312
Leveraged buyouts, 321
Licensing laws, 525
Life-cycle hypothesis, 269–71
  critics of, 272–73
Liquid assets, 225
Liquidity, 234
Liquidity trap, 124 n
LM schedule; *see also* IS–LM framework
  definition, 103
  and interest-rate effect, 125
  international money market, 201–2
  and monetary policy, 142–47
  monetary policy alternatives, 165
  and money market, 102–5, 128
  money market equilibrium, 230
Loans
  and credit crunch of 1990s, 327–28
  and money creation, 301–2
  reserves and deposits, 302
Long-run trends, 9–10
Long-term growth; *see also* Solow long-
  term growth model
  aggregate production function, 34–37
  and business cycle, 14–15, 57–58
  and competitiveness, 32–58

Long-term growth—*Cont.*
neo-classical model predictions, 38–39
policies for, 51–58
and productivity, 23
productivity and competitiveness, 3–9
Long-term interest rates, 232–35
relevance to investments, 225
Lucas critique, 411
of econometrics, 479–80
Lucas supply schedule, 470–73
and variability of prices, 472

M
M1 money supply, 94, 99, 299, 314
M2 money supply, 94, 99, 299–300, 314
M3 money supply, 94, 300, 314
Macroeconomic policies
domestic, 205–9
fiscal policy and trade deficit, 207
international comparisons, 209
on trade, 198–204
Macroeconomics
critical issues, 22–23
employment and unemployment, 15–17
focus on trends and fluctuations, 9–10
Friedman's role, 104
issues of, 2–3
Keynes' role, 104
key questions, 1
scoreboard, 21
Management problems, 45–46
Manufacturing
competitiveness, 46–51
and foreign competition, 8–9
in international economy, 48–49
large turnover rates, 506
reason for trade problems, 49–50
Marginal productivity of labor, and real
wage, 439–40
Marginal product of labor, 436–37
Marginal propensity to consume, 67–68
Marginal propensity to import, 82
and multiplier, 83
Marginal propensity to invest, 69
Marginal propensity to tax, 119–20,
125–26
Market clearing, 467–76
Market failure training programs, 526, 528
Markets, perfectly competitive, 62
McCaw Cellular Communications, 51
McDonald's Corporation, 51
McDonnell Douglas, 50
McGraw-Hill, Inc., 404, 408
McKinsey Global Institute, 554, 557
Measurement error, 44–45
Medium of exchange, 92
Menu cost models, 495–97
Mercedes-Benz, 352

Merit goods, 118
Micron, Inc., 354
Minimum wage, 440
and wage rigidities, 517–18
Mining sector, 380
Minorities, structural unemployment,
516–17
Misery index, 156
Modigliani model, 408
Monetarism, 104
aggregate demand and inflation, 444–60
assessment of, 455–59
basic framework, 445–51
classical roots, 434–42
critique of Keynesian model, 459–60
definition, 433
link of money to prices, 448–49
monetary policy, 451–55
on money and prices, 457
origins of, 434
and short-term output variations, 447–48
Monetarists
criticism of Keynes, 128
and rational expectations model, 476
Monetary aggregates, 458–59
Monetary base, 307
open-market operations, 310–12
Monetary-growth equation, 446–47
Monetary History of the United States,
(Friedman), 104
Monetary policy, 298–99; *see also* Stabilization policies
case study of 1979–83
closed versus open economy, 205
conclusions on, 171
coordinated with fiscal policy, 142–43
expansionary, 205–7
Federal Reserve alternatives, 164–65
fighting inflation with, 167–71
and financial crunch, 315–28
and fiscal policy, 125
with fixed exchange rates, 366–67
history of 1990–93, 249–51
independent, 143
ineffectiveness, 476–78
inflation and aggregate equilibrium,
162–71
investment responsiveness, 144–45
of monetarists, 451–55
and money demand, 146–47
and money market, 222
during 1970s, 378
output-inflation tradeoff, 147–57
and output-inflation tradeoff, 167
and recession, 141
sterilized intervention, 370
and supply-shock inflation, 391–94
variations in 1979–82
Monetary revolution, 446
Monetary shocks, 473–76

Monetary surprise, 473–74
Monetary union, 369
Money
cost of holding, 97 n
exchange rates, 180–85
Federal Reserve definitions, 299–300
and financial assets, 93–95
impact of inflation, 230–31
nature of, 92
and prices, 448–49
and prices in monetarism, 457
problem of defining, 94–95
short-term interest rates and demand for,
231–32
unit of account, 93
use of, 91
velocity of, 99
Money creation
by banks, 299–308
loans and reserves, 301–2
Money demand, 95–99
and crowding out effect, 129
and fiscal policy effectiveness, 127–28
interest-rate responsiveness, 146–47
international money market, 200
Money demand function, 97–98
Money demand schedule, 98
Money market, 91
crowding out effect, 129
and decline in money supply, 243–44
effect of changes in autonomous expenditures, 106–7
equilibrium income and interest rates,
105
and fiscal policy, 125–29
LM schedule, 102–5
and monetary policy, 222
and money demand, 95–99
short-term, 220–21
and short-term nominal rate of interest,
230–32
supply of money, 99–100
Money-market equilibrium, 100–102, 165
with foreign sector, 200–202
and goods-market equilibrium, 105–7
Money-market mutual funds, 94
Money supply, 99–100
and amount of reserves, 304–6
and banking panics, 317–19
and bank reserves, 302
changes after deregulation, 301
Federal Reserve target, 314–15
international money market, 200–202
monetarist view, 104
and monetary base, 307
monetary policy, 142–47
money-market equilibrium, 100–102
usefulness of concept, 314
Monopoly power, 527
Moody's Investors Service, 246

Moral hazard, 515
Mortgage financing, 223
Mrs. Thatcher effect, 47
Multifactor productivity, 481–82, 481–82, 490
Multiplier
    autonomous-expenditure, 122–23
    and changes in equilibrium income, 73–75
    and changes in investment demand, 75–76
    and marginal propensity to import, 83
Multiplier-accelerator interaction, 278–80
Multiplier effect, 106

N

NAIRU; *see* Nonaccelerating inflation rate of unemployment
National Aeronautics and Space Administration, 55
National Bureau of Economic Research, 405
National income, and GDP, 30–31
National income accounting, and GDP, 25–31
National Income and Product Accounts, 26
    balance of payments on current account, 185
    components, 28–31
    consumption, investment, and flow of services, 265
    and disposable income, 120 n
    for econometric forecasting, 408
National investment, 53–54
National saving, 53–54, 131–32
Natural rate of unemployment, 154
Neo-classical growth model, 37–38, 40–41
Neo-Keynesian analysis
    assessment of, 498–99
    of price stickiness, 492–98
Net domestic product, 31
Net investment, 276
Net national product, 276
Net saving, 52 n
Net tax revenues, 119
New growth theory, 36–37, 41
Noise traders, 485, 486
Nominal GDP, 4, 227
Nominal rate of interest
    and investment decisions, 226–27
    short-term, 230–32
Nominal values, 227
Nominal wage, 439
Nonaccelerating inflation rate of unemployment, 17, 390, 510, 528
    Okun's law, 511–12
    and potential output, 154
    and unemployment insurance, 515

Nonmarket production, 27–28
Normal price stickiness, 479–98
Normal yield curve, 235
North American Free Trade Agreement, 2

O

Ohio savings and loans, 320
Oil price increases, 375, 376–77, 378
    future, 396–97
Okun's law, 511–12
Open-market operations, 243 n, 310–12
Opportunity cost of funds, 223
Oracle, 50
Organizational learning, 552
Organization of Petroleum Exporting Countries, 148
    price increases, 375–77, 380
Output
    actual versus potential, 13–14
    and aggregate demand schedule, 62–63
    in business cycles, 12–14
    capital-output ratio, 275–77
    and GDP per capita, 4–5
    impact of monetary shocks, 474–76
    and inflation, 1, 22
    inflation and expectations, 157–62
    and multifactor productivity, 490
    per full-time worker, 33
    postwar growth, 42
    and production function, 34–37
    productivity decline, 43–46
    in real-business–cycle models, 480–83
    short-run variations, 447–48
Output equilibrium, 152–53
Output gap, 14
Output-inflation tradeoff, 147–47, 147–57
    combined with IS-LM framework, 165–67
    with competitive markets, 150–53
    definition, 150
    Lucas policy critique, 579–80
    and market clearing, 467–76
    and monetary policy, 167
    during nineteen seventies, 373
    Okun's law, 511–12
    and past inflation, 159
    Phillips curve, 510–14
    shifts of, 156–57
    short-run, 155–56
    with sticking prices, 153–54
    and supply shocks, 387–90
    and unemployment, 154
    vertical long–run, 159–62
Output ratio, 13–14, 155–56
Outside lag, 415
Outsourcing, 560 n
Overnight repurchase agreements, 94
Ownership of assets, 26

P

Patent-infringement cases, 478–79
Pay-as-you-go pension plans, 271
Peak of business activity, 12
Penn Central Railroad, 319
Pension plans, 271
Per capita income, 32–33, 502
Perfectly competitive markets, 62
Permanent consumption, 267
Permanent income, 267
Permanent-income consumption function, 267–69
Permanent-income hypothesis, 266–69
    critics of, 272–73
Perpetuities, 234
Phelps-Friedman hypothesis, 161–62
Phillips curve, 156 n, 444, 510–14
Planned expenditures, 65–67
Planned investment
    definition, 69
    and excess of saving, 80–81
Policy change
    sustained, 421–23
    temporary, 419–21
Policy credibility, 394
Policy-ineffectiveness theorem, 476–78
Policy regime, for economic stability, 418–26
Pork barrel politics, 57, 118
Portfolio, 96
Portfolio argument, 321
Portfolio choice, 96
Potential GDP, 13
Potential output
    compared to actual output, 13–14
    definition, 13
    and full employment, 17
    growth over time, 165
    and inflation, 152–53
    labor and capital inputs, 34–35
    and nonaccelerating inflation rate of unemployment, 154
    and supply shocks, 390
    targeting return to, 391–93
    and technology, 34–35
    and unemployment, 510
    and vertical long–term tradeoff, 160–61
Precommercial research and development, 56
Present value, 224
Price-coordination problem, 497–98
Price flexibility, 487–89
Price indexes, 19–20
Price level
    and aggregate demand, 443–44
    and aggregate demand and supply, 148–50
    and aggregate demand schedule, 62–63
    and aggregate supply schedule, 61–62

Price level—*Cont.*
  and GDP, 18
  and incomplete information, 468–70
  and inflation, 1181–19
  Lucas supply schedule, 470–73
  monetary shocks, 473–76
  and money demand, 96
  output-inflation tradeoff, 150
  and supply shocks, 379–82
Price of money, 449
Prices
  economic theories, 153
  inflation and, 147–50
  and money, 448–49
  and money in monetarism, 457
Price stickiness, 62
  definition, 154
  neo-Keynesian analysis, 492–99
  normal and real, 497–98
  and output-inflation tradeoff, 153–54
Price-wage spiral, 385–86
Private saving, 131
Process innovation, 559
Procter and Gamble, 51
Production
  constant returns to scale, 534
  and inventory accumulation, 73–74
  nonmarket, 27–28
  rearranged by trade, 345
Production function, 34
Productivity
  accumulation of knowledge, 551–61
  aggregate production function, 533–36
  aggregate supply schedule, 61–62
  American manufacturing, 47
  and business cycle, 490–92
  capital adequacy condition, 538–41
  comparative international, 21
  contribution of technology, 546
  decline in competitiveness, 6–9
  explaining national differences, 554–61
  growth related to savings, 536
  improved by trade, 350–53
  in Japan, 47, 49
  and knowledge capital, 39
  lessons from studies on, 559–61
  and long-term growth, 3–9, 23
  long-term trends and short–term fluctua-
    tions, 9–10
  measurement error, 44–45
  measures, 6
  multifactor, 481–82, 481–82, 490
  policies to enhance, 525–30
  reasons for slowdown, 43–46
  related to wage increases and inflation,
    513–14
  scale, capital, and technology, 558–59
  Solow long-term growth model, 536–46
  steady-state growth, 541–46

Productivity—*Cont.*
  and technological change, 38–39
  workplace organization, 557–59
Protectionism, 347
Public goods, 116–17

Q

Quantity adjustment, 64–71
Quantity equation, 441–42, 445
Quotas, 348–49; **see also** Trade restrictions
  on auto imports, 353

R

Random walk, 272
Random-walk theory, 484
Rate of adjustment, 277
Rate of inflation, 18–19
Rational expectations model
  assessment, 483–92
  critique of econometrics, 479–80
  critique of stabilization policies, 476–80
  definition, 462
  with market clearing, 467–76
  output-inflation tradeoff with, 465–66
  real-business-cycle models, 480–83
Rational-forecast model of inflation, 162
Reagan administration, 116
Real-business-cycle models, 464, 480–83
  assessment, 483–92
Real exchange rate, 182–83
Real exchange rate index, 182–83
  and balance of trade, 184–85
Real GDP, 4, 227
  and potential output, 13
Real GDP per capita, 4–5, 32–33
  hypothetical trends, 9–10
Real income, growth of, 165
Real money supply, inflation and, 163
Real price stickiness, 497–98
Real rate of interest
  adjusting for inflation, 226–27
  inflation and cost of funds, 225–26
  and investment demand, 228
Real stock of money, 78
Real values, 227
Real wages, 439
  over business cycle, 457–58
  and demand for labor, 437–38
Recessions
  and business cycle, 11–15
  and deficit spending, 132
  fiscal policy and, 124
  and monetary policy, 141
  of 1982, 246–48
  of 1990–91, 213, 249–50, 286–89
  persistence of, 489
  savings-investment coordination, 80–81
  sustaining income in, 210–11

Recessions—*Cont.*
  triggered by monetary policy, 413
  and worsening deficits, 132–33
Recognition lag, 414
Recovery, 12
  of 1991–93, 289–91
Replacement capital, 276
Repurchase agreements, 94
Required reserve ratio, 306
  changes in, 313–14
Required reserves, 306
Research and development, 550–51, 554
  and patent infringement, 479
  precommercial, 56
Reservation wage, 515
Reserve accounts, 302
Reserve ratio, 302–3
Reserves
  borrowed, 312–13
  definition, 302
  deposits and loans, 302
  excess and required, 306
  and money creation, 301–2
  money supply and amount of, 304–6
Retailing, 556
Retirement, pensions and Social Security,
  271
Returns to scale, 35; *see also* Constant
  returns to scale
Rex; *see* Real exchange rate index
Risk, and term to maturity, 234
Risk premium
  and cost of funds, 228
  and credit availability, 246–47

S

Sacrifice ratio, 393–94
Sales expectations and inventories, 280
Saving
  and capital adequacy, 539
  and economic growth, 536
  effect of budget balance, 131–32
  and investment, 53–54
  need to increase, 53–54
  old versus young attitudes, 272–73
  in open economy, 210
  and permanent income hypothesis,
    266–69
  relation to investment, 79–81
  in Solow growth model, 537–38
  and steady-state growth, 541–46
Saving-investment coordination, 80–81
Savings and loan banks, 301
Savings deposits, 94
Says' law, 443–44
Scale, optimal, 559–60
Scientific management, 46
Self-fulfilling prophecy, 362–64

Semiconductor industry, 51
Semiconductor Trade Agreement, 354–55
Service industry
    employment growth, 508–9
    in National Income and Product
        Accounts, 265
    reregulation of, 54
    trade in, 187
Short-run output–inflation tradeoff, 155–56
Short-term bonds, 230
Short-term deficits, 132
Short-term exchange rate swings, 360–62
Short-term fluctuations, 9–10
Short-term interest rates, 220, 232–35
    and Treasury bill prices, 307–8
Short-term money markets, 220–21
Short-term nominal rate of interest, 230–32
Skill-biased technological change, 524
Small business, financing for, 223
Small business job turnover, 509
Smart money traders, 485, 486
Social returns on education, 528–29
Social Security, 269, 271
    increase in revenues, 130
Solow long-term growth model, 37–42,
        532, 536–46; *see also* Long-term
        growth
    with technological change, 546–51
Space shuttle, 56, 57 n
Speculation bubble, 364
SST project, 55
Stabilization policies; *see also* Fiscal policy
        and Monetary policy
    automatic stabilizers, 417, 430
    credibility issues, 466
    definition, 413–14
    goals and instruments, 417–18
    monetarist criticism, 458–60
    rationalist critique, 476–80
    success of, 426–30
    timing lags, 414–15
    timing problems, 415–17
Stagflation, 156, 159, 162, 378
Standard and Poor's, 246
Standard of living, 5, 264
    and long-term growth, 57–58
    real GDP per capita, 32–33
State and local governments, provision of
        goods and services, 116
Statistical discrepancy, 186
Steady-state growth, 541–46
    technology-augmenting labor, 548–51
Steel industry minimills, 558–59
Sterilized intervention, 370
Stock markets
    fluctuations, 484–85
    and rational expectations, 485–87
Stock of skilled labor, 527
Stocks, 93; *see also* Bonds
    financing investment by, 223

Structural deficit, 133–35
    and trade deficit, 211–13
Structural unemployment, 516–21
Supply; *see* Aggregate supply
Supply and demand
    cause of inflation, 148–50
    classical model, 434–35
    in foreign exchange market, 192–98
    market responses to, 62
    and output-inflation tradeoff, 150–53
    Says' law, 443–44
Supply-shock inflation, and economic pol-
        icy, 391–99 .
Supply shocks, 148
    adverse or favorable, 374–75
    cause of inflation, 374–86
    and cost of living, 382–86
    definition, 374
    and forecasting, 410
    and output-inflation tradeoff, 387–90
    and potential output, 390
    price level, 379–82
Survey of Current Business, 405
Supply of labor, 438–39
Surveys of forecasts, 404–5
Synfuels project, 56

T
Tariffs
    costs and benefits, 347–48
    definition, 347
Taxation
    and budget deficit, 478
    and goods-market equilibrium, 120–25
    gross and net revenues, 118
    and income, 119
Tax cuts
    thought to be sustained, 425–26
    thought to be temporary, 425–26
Tax function, 119–20
Tax leakages, 122–23
Tax-rate multiplier, 124–25
Tax receipts, 417
Tax Reform Act of 1986, 213
Technological change
    and earnings inequality, 524
    key to growth, 38–39, 41
    and Solow growth model, 546–51
Technological depletion, 45
Technology
    accumulation of knowledge, 551–61
    hard, 559
    information, 559
    input, 34
    labor augmented by, 547–51
    precommerical research and develop-
        ment, 56
    scale and capital, 558–59
Technology policy, 55–57

Technology Pork Barrel (Cohen and Noll),
        55
Technology shocks, 480–82, 490
Teenagers, structural unemployment,
        516–17
Telecommunications industry, 555–56
Term structure of interest rates, 232
    and yield curve, 235
Three M Corporation, 51
Thrift, and steady–state growth, 543–46
Time deposits, 94
Time horizon of investment decisions, 225
Time-inconsistent policies, 478–79
Timing, of stabilization policies, 415–17
Total employment, 15
Toyota Motor Company, 558
Toys ''R'' Us, 556
Trade; *see also* Balance of trade *and* Exter-
        nal balance
    and Bretton Woods system, 362–63
    comparative advantage, 345–46
    comparative performance, 21
    and competitiveness, 23
    and earnings inequality, 524
    effect on multiplier, 83
    and equilibrium income, 84
    and fixed exchange rates, 366
    and foreign exchange market, 179–85
    and goods-market equilibrium, 82–83,
        199
    increased export demand, 202–3
    macroeconomic policies, 198–204
    and manufacturing, 48–49
    money market equilibrium, 200–202
    policies to achieve external balance,
        345–58
    and productivity improvement, 350–53
    and rise in foreign interest rates, 203–4
    in services, 187
    supply and demand in foreign exchange
        market, 192–98
    worldwide imbalances, 332
Trade adjustment lag, 340
Trade associations, 525
Trade deficit, 23, 48–49, 184–85, 332,
        338–39
    budget deficit and crowding out, 209
    from fiscal policy, 207–8
    increasing, 7
    and structural delict, 211–13
Trade restrictions
    arguments for and against, 349–50
    and job protection, 355–57
    and learning curve, 353–55
    protectionism, 347
    tariffs, 347–48
    voluntary restraint agreements, 348–49
Trade Union Advisory Committee of
        OECD, 522
Trade-weighted real exchange rate, 181–83

Training programs, 55, 526–27, 560
    sponsoring, 528–29
Transactions
    definition, 92
    and money demand, 95–96
Transfer payments, 27, 30, 119, 417
    automatic stabilizers, 134
    international, 187
Transitory consumption, 267
Travelers' checks, 94
Treasury bills, 91, 130
    impact of inflation, 230–31
    interest rate risk, 234
    open-market operations, 310–12
    prices and short-term interest rates,
       307–8
    rate and yield curve in 1979–83, 243–46
    in recovery of 1991–93, 250
    term structure of interest rates, 235
Treasury Department
    financing of expenditures, 115
    source of government borrowing, 130
Trough, 12
TSB Homeloans, 523

U

Underground economy, 28
Unemployment; *see also* Nonaccelerating
    inflation rate of unemployment
    classical model, 440
    comparative, 21
    and economic policy, 15–17
    increase in Europe, 518–20
    and inflation, 373
    job-search, 514–15
    and output-inflation tradeoff, 154
    Phillips curve, 510–14
    rate of, 16
    in recession of 1990–91, 249–50
    and retraining, 55
    structural, 516–21
    voluntary or involuntary, 488–89
Unemployment compensation, 417

Unemployment insurance, 55, 515
Unions
    in Great Britain, 523
    and wage rigidities, 518
United Kingdom, productivity, 47
United States
    auto industry, 352–53
    cost of living change, 382–83
    crisis of confidence, 336
    current account deficit, 335
    employment growth patterns, 503–5
    farm policy, 379
    foreign private investment in, 186
    GDP percentage of world output, 178
    inflation and unemployment in 1970s,
       373
    job losses, 334–35
    loss of wealth, 335–36
    manufacturing competitiveness, 46–50
    national productivity comparisons,
       554–61
    new competitive edge, 50–51
    petroleum use, 377
    postwar growth, 42
    semiconductor pact, 354–55
    strength of economy, 8–9
    trade deficit, 48–49, 332
    value of capital assets, 551–52
    wage competition, 356
United States International Trade Commis-
    sion, 357
Unit labor cost, 379
Unit of account, 93
Unplanned expenditures, 65–67
Used goods, 27

V

Values, real and nominal, 227
Vault cash, 302
Velocity of money, 99, 441–42
    Friedman's view, 451–53
    in monetary-growth equation, 446
    stability versus unpredictability, 449–51

Vertical aggregate supply schedule, 64
Vertical long-run tradeoff, 159–62
Volkswagen, 352
Voluntary restraint agreements, 348–49
    auto imports, 353

W

Wage and price controls, 378, 418
Wage-and-price guidelines, 418
Wage competition, 356
Wage contracts, 492–94
    inflationary, 157
Wage flexibility, 487–89
Wage-price spiral, 385–86
Wage rigidities, 517–18
Wages
    and cost of living, 383–85
    in equilibrium business cycle model,
       467–76
    increases related to productivity and
       inflation, 513–14
    and supply shocks, 382–86
Wage stability, versus employment stabil-
    ity, 494–95
Wall Street Journal, 404
Wal-Mart, 556
Wealth, 93–94
    total net value, 96
Wealth loss, 335–36
Weighted average of price rate increases,
    20
Wharton forecasting model, 408
Wholesale price index, 467
Worker training; *see* Training programs
Workplace organization, 557–58
World Trade Organization, 357

Y–Z

Yield curve, 235
    and term structure of interest rates, 235
Zero coupon bonds, 234 n
Zero sum game, 52

Symbol	Definition
NNP	Net national product
NX	Net exports
Y^P/Y	The output ratio
P	The price level
P_f	The foreign price level
PIM	Nominal value of imports
PV	Present value
PX	Nominal value of exports
PY	Nominal income or output
R	Bank reserves
RR	Required bank reserves
Rr	The ratio of bank reserves to demand deposits R/DD
RRr	The ratio of required bank reserves to demand deposits RR/DD
r	The rate of interest
rex	Index of the real (inflation adjusted) exchange rate. If the value of the inflation adjusted dollar increases in foreign currency markets (on average) then rex is higher.
$rex_{\$/yen}$	A particular real exchange rate. As shown here, the real exchange rate between the dollar and the yen. If the inflation adjusted value of the dollar relative to the inflation adjusted value of the yen increases in foreign currency markets then $rex_{\$/yen}$ is higher.
r_{gap}	The interest-rate gap, equal to the long-term real rate of interest minus the short-term nominal rate of interest. Also equal to the maturity premium minus the expected rate of inflation.